W9-BQL-414

A HISTORY OF
MODERN NORWAY
1814–1972

A HISTORY OF
Modern Norway
1814 -1972

T. K. DERRY

CLARENDON PRESS · OXFORD

1973

Oxford University Press, Ely House, London W. 1

GLASGOW NEW YORK TORONTO MELBOURNE WELLINGTON
CAPE TOWN IBADAN NAIROBI DAR ES SALAAM LUSAKA ADDIS ABABA
DELHI BOMBAY CALCUTTA MADRAS KARACHI LAHORE DACCA
KUALA LUMPUR SINGAPORE HONG KONG TOKYO

*Printed in Great Britain
by W & J Mackay Limited, Chatham*

Uxori Carissimae Norvegiensi

Preface

This book presents the history of Norway since its separation from Denmark as a study in the growth of a small nation with aspirations towards political democracy, egalitarian social forms, economic advances, and cultural achievements. In spite of setbacks and disappointments, the record of progress made in all these respects during the past one and a half centuries seems to deserve more attention than has usually been given to it outside Scandinavia.

While basing his text very largely upon Norwegian sources, the author has had in mind readers to whom the country and still more its languages are likely to be unfamiliar. Norwegian place-names are therefore given their present-day spelling throughout (Oslo, not Christiania or Kristiania; Trondheim, not Trondhjem; Halden, not Fredrikshald), and the Norwegian letter ø has been replaced by its more familiar equivalent, ö. Except for persons of special interest, whose careers in many cases are described in a footnote, names of individual Norwegians have been mentioned rather sparingly, and notes that concern mainly the student have been placed with the source references at the end of the book. It is hoped, however, that the survey of works available in English will prove serviceable to every type of reader who would like to know more about some aspect of modern Norwegian history.

This account could not have been written without the generous co-operation of Norwegian institutions and historians. Encouragement and advice were received at the outset from Lagdommer Helge Refsum, Bergen, and from Professors Sverre Steen and Magne Skodvin of the University of Oslo. The author is of course solely responsible for all remaining errors, but the text has benefited greatly from the help of Professor Ragnhild Hatton of the University of London, who brought her extensive experience as teacher and writer to bear upon the entire project, and from the reading of the draft by two senior lecturers in history at Oslo University, Dr. Per Fuglum and Dr. Per Sveaas Andersen, as well as from the advice of other scholars who have been consulted upon particular questions. The library staffs of the Royal Norwegian Ministry of Foreign Affairs, of the Nobel Institute in Oslo, and of Oslo University Library have rendered indefatigable assistance to an often importunate inquirer; the last-named institution provided the bulk of all the materials that have been used, with a helpfulness that did much to make work a pleasure. Permission for the reproduction of copyright illustrations has been kindly given by the authorities of the Storting, the Norwegian National Gallery, and the Edvard Munch and Gustav Vigeland Museums. Finally, the author wishes to express his grateful appreciation to the Norwegian Research Council for Science and the Humanities for the two grants that launched his work, and to the British–Norwegian North Sea Foundation for the grant that ensured its completion.

Oslo, January 1973   T. K. DERRY

Contents

List of Plates and Maps

1. Introductory: Norway in 1814

As a small and scattered people, occupying a large, mostly barren expanse of territory on the northern rim of Europe, the Norwegians have owed their living above all to the sea. The warm Atlantic currents mitigate the climate all the way up the long west coast; its teeming fish, and the sheltered waters of the Leads and fiords, encouraged settlement. Ottar sailing south for a month of days with the coast of 'the Northmen's land' for ever on his left, to bring the first authentic reports of life in the farthest north to the court of King Alfred; the Vikings creating their Atlantic empire of conquest and colonization; and Hanseatic Bergen busily exporting the dried cod from Lofoten to feed hungry mouths in many parts of Europe—these are among the most representative scenes of earlier Norwegian history. Almost equally important, though perhaps less vividly remembered, is the service that the sea rendered in the carriage of corn to Norway from lowlands farther south, without which the growth of population would have been held in check, especially in the far north, and a medieval urban civilization (such as Sigrid Undset has pictured for us) could scarcely have existed.

A long period of national decline began in the century of the Black Death and culminated at the Reformation, when Norway for a time was little more than a Danish province. But again the sea helped recovery, as a multitude of waterside sawmills sprang up, from which the timber of Norwegian forests was shipped to raise Amsterdam on its piles or to rebuild London after the Great Fire. In the eighteenth century the prosperity, not only of the timber and fish trades but also of shipping and metal exports, recreated a modestly thriving society. With the establishment of absolutism in 1661, Denmark–Norway had become the 'Twin Kingdoms', in which every citizen was an equal subject of the nominally all-powerful sovereign, though Copenhagen remained the capital of both his realms: the institutions of government and the university were centred there, and its culture permeated the established residents in the towns of Norway as well as the members of the bureaucracy, sprung largely from families of Danish origin, which ruled in the Norwegian countryside. The peasant freeholders, indeed, never ceased to cherish their independent status and vernacular speech, both of which they derived from the more glorious, pre-Danish era, and the upper classes were increasingly disposed to voice high-flown national sentiments, especially on festive occasions. Yet Norway was one of the few European states where the French Revolution of 1789 excited no widespread demands for new liberties: in a decade of European convulsions the biggest movement of opinion among the masses in Norway was a religious revival (see p. 30).

From 1792 onwards the Revolutionary Wars enabled the Norwegians to enjoy enhanced profits from the sale of their exports and the services of their shipping to belligerents on both sides, albeit Nelson's attack on the Danish–Norwegian fleet in the roadsteads of Copenhagen in April 1801 compelled the Twin Kingdoms to modify their assertion of neutral rights on the high seas. The nineteenth century opened propitiously with seven fat years, in which the towns sold Britain about three-fifths of a record output of timber, exported with additional profit in Norwegian vessels. Then events outside their control suddenly placed in jeopardy the whole way of life of a people which, as we have seen, depended on free access to the seaways for its very existence.

THE UNION WITH DENMARK DISSOLVED

In the summer of 1807, the completion of Napoleon's triumphs over the armies of the Third Coalition and his negotiations with Tsar Alexander at Tilsit left him the undisputed master of the western half of the European mainland, whereas Trafalgar had confirmed Britain in the mastery of the surrounding seas. The crown prince regent of Denmark–Norway (who next year became king as Frederick VI) was therefore confronted with an unenviable choice between the land power and the sea power, which Canning virtually decided for him by sending a second British expedition to Copenhagen in anticipation of a French attempt to seize Frederick's remaining fleet. Outraged by this gross breach of neutrality, he became the firm ally of Napoleon, against whom he was in any case powerless after every ship of the line except one had been towed away to England.

As Britain's enemy, however, Frederick was automatically cut off from his Norwegian kingdom by a naval blockade, which also inflicted serious economic hardship upon his subjects there, who could only export by special licence—issued when the British were in acute need of timber—and could no longer import their corn supply from Denmark or even from Archangel. In many districts the population declined during these 'Hunger Years', which reached a climax in 1812, when the harvest failed and bark bread was often the only substitute. But some political compensation was offered for this period of isolation—a temporary Commission of Government in Oslo and some new developments of a more permanent character, including a nation-wide Welfare Society (*Selskapet for Norges Vel*), a university, and as a sequel to the virtual bankruptcy declared for both kingdoms in January 1813, plans for a long-desired national bank. Finally, Frederick sent his cousin and heir-presumptive, Prince Christian Frederick, in May 1813 to hold office as stattholder, with instructions to foster the mutual affection between king and people, 'without which no state can subsist'.[1]

So far, the only direct threat to the paternalist monarchy in far-off Copenhagen had come from a minority movement in south-west Norway, headed by the youthful Count Wedel Jarlsberg,* who had been a very active member of the Commission of Government. Although Norway had been briefly at war with Sweden as recently as 1808–10, he advocated a union with that power on terms of equality as offering the best prospect of restoring the timber trade with England, on which his part of the country was specially dependent. But stronger forces outside Norway were already planning such a union on terms of inequality. In Sweden the loss of Finland to Napoleon's temporary ally, Tsar Alexander, in the war of 1808–9

---

* 1779–1840. He was brought up from 1790 to 1798 in England, where his father was Danish-Norwegian minister; commanded a free corps against the Swedes in 1808, but in 1809–10 plotted a union of the Swedish and Norwegian crowns; and inherited the countship of Jarlsberg in south-west Norway, 1811. Minister of finance, November 1814–October 1822; stattholder, 1836–40.

had precipitated a revolution, which gave the Swedish people a new constitution, a new king (Charles XIII, the childless uncle of the monarch whom the revolutionaries had deposed), and finally a new crown prince. This was the French marshal, Jean-Baptiste Berna-dotte, who played for high stakes by siding with Alexander against his former master, which meant that he must look to the opposite side of the Scandinavian peninsula to compensate his future subjects for Finland. Russia promised Norway to him at the treaty of Åbo in April 1812; Britain made him a similar promise at the treaty of Stockholm in the following March; and after playing his part against Napoleon on the field of Leipzig, Prince Charles John (as he was now called) led his Swedish army into Holstein to claim his reward. The king of Denmark–Norway, who had been too honest to desert Napoleon when his fortunes turned, was now too uncertain of his own position to risk a major battle: defeat, followed by an invasion of Denmark proper, might well have proved fatal to the dynasty.

The new year therefore opened with the negotiation of the treaty of Kiel (14 January 1814), by which King Frederick agreed to cede Norway to the king of Sweden, under whom it was to 'constitute a kingdom, united with the kingdom of Sweden'.[2] While niceties of style probably account for the fact that the cession was made to the king rather than to the kingdom of Sweden, which some have found significant, Charles John showed a deliberately conciliatory attitude when he preferred 'union' to 'integration' or 'incorporation',[3] the two latter being the terms used to define Norway's future relation-ship with Sweden in the treaties of Åbo and Stockholm. Denmark successfully avoided any reference in the treaty to the former Nor-wegian colonies of Greenland, Iceland, and the Faeroes: the Swedish negotiator was apparently unaware of their original connection with Norway, but their possession was in any case irrelevant to Sweden's strategic interests—the aspect with which Charles John chiefly con-cerned himself. The Danish representative also secured that a due proportion of the public debt of the Twin Kingdoms should be taken over by Norway's new sovereign. King Frederick, who by the same treaty also made peace with Britain (at the cost of Heligoland) and undertook to join the alliance against Napoleon, was to be com-pensated in part for the loss of his Norwegian kingdom by the acquisition of Swedish Pomerania and the island of Rügen; these were to pass into his possession as soon as the four fortresses of south-east Norway—at Fredrikstad, Halden, Kongsvinger, and Oslo—were handed over peacefully to Swedish garrisons.

INDEPENDENCE CLAIMED

When news of the treaty reached Norway, many factors contributed to its indignant repudiation by the more vocal elements in the population. Six years of isolation from Denmark had strengthened nationalist feelings and confidence in their ability to manage their own affairs. The educated argued that the doctrine of popular sovereignty, so often asserted by other nations since the Declaration of Independence in 1776 and the formulation of the Rights of Man in 1789, justified a refusal to be transferred like dumb cattle to a new owner. In the eyes of the peasantry, too, a transfer to the Swedish crown was likely to be obnoxious, on account of the privileged position of noble landowners in Sweden and the more rigorous system of military service, both of which might be introduced to Norway. Moreover, the situation in Europe encouraged the thought of resistance: Napoleon might recover strength as the fighting approached the borders of France, so that the coalition of the four great powers collapsed—and with it the fortunes of Charles John; alternatively, if they won, the former French marshal might transfer his ambitions from Scandinavia to France. Lastly, there was a very widespread belief that the British people, who had figured as the champions of liberty against Napoleonic despotism in Spain and elsewhere, would support them if they rose against the imposition of an alien master who had served Napoleon.

How large the nucleus of more or less determined resisters was at the outset is quite unknown, but two personal factors stimulated its rapid growth. As long as Charles John was absent on the Continent the almost senile king of Sweden was indisposed to push his troops across the frontier, where Norwegian forces had been placed on guard during the Swedish operations in Holstein; and the statt-holder, Prince Christian Frederick, a romantic adventurer who had formed a warm attachment to Norway and its people, was ready to take full advantage of the power vacuum thus created. He was at first disposed to claim that his position as heir to the throne of the Twin Kingdoms gave him a legal right to that portion of his eventual inheritance of which King Frederick was seeking to dispose. Frederick was very quickly obliged to repudiate any action on his cousin's part to nullify the effects of the treaty of Kiel, though he may privately have continued to wish for that cousin's success. But in any case a brief visit by the prince to Trondheim to sound opinion was followed in mid-February by a meeting with twenty-one leading citizens (*Notabelmötet*) at Eidsvoll, the home of his principal Norwegian mentor, Carsten Anker. He accepted their advice to assume authority as regent rather than as heir, and it was in this capacity that he announced the will of the Norwegian people 'to exist as an independent nation and to give itself a free constitution'[4] both to that people and to the principal foreign powers, including the United States of America. As regent, too, he summoned a constituent assembly, which he was assured by the meeting of notables would offer him the throne on the indefeasible basis of the sovereignty of the people.

Accordingly, he called upon the congregation in every parish to take an oath to defend the independence of their country in face of the treaty of Kiel. At the same time the congregation was to choose two electors from the official, property-owning, or farmer class, of whom at least one must be a peasant; these electors would meet subsequently to appoint members of the same classes to represent their county or large town* at a national assembly, to be held at Eidsvoll in April. In the meanwhile the regent formed a cabinet, and sent Carsten Anker to plead Norway's cause in London, where he worked indefatigably upon the Whig Opposition leaders, the more liberal newspapers, and the trading community at large.† Sympathy with the Norwegian claim to self-determination was widespread in those quarters; but the prime minister, Lord Liverpool, told Anker

---

* In each of the smaller towns, consisting of one parish, the congregation chose one representative by direct election.

† He was authorized to make an offer 'at an opportune moment'[5] of a depot for British trade at Kristiansand, on the same terms as had been conceded by the Swedes at Gothenburg.

plainly that Britain would fulfil her treaty obligations to Sweden, though she would help a submissive Norway to obtain favourable conditions. An opposition motion in support of the Norwegian cause was eventually defeated by a 3:1 majority in both houses of parliament. But as none of Anker's voluminous despatches from London reached Norway until mid-June, the regent continued to judge the international situation with invincible optimism in the light of such reports as reached him from the Continent via Denmark. Thus when it became known in April that the Allied leaders had entered Paris and Napoleon was in exile, he argued that they would have no further need to conciliate Charles John; in actual fact the latter was with them in Paris, where he secured the firm support of Tsar Alexander for his request to the British government to renew the blockade of Norwegian ports. Since he acted as his own foreign minister, Norway's regent was able to maintain an optimistic state of opinion regarding future prospects while the making of the constitution gave what the world called disparagingly 'the Norwegian rising' the semblance of an established state.

Except for the absence of any representatives from the two northernmost counties, which could not complete their arrangements in time, and the over-weighting of the towns, the 112 delegates who met at Eidsvoll on 10 April fairly represented the property-holding sections of the community: fifty-nine members held office in the civil administration. the armed forces, or the church; thirty-seven belonged to the landholding peasantry (including thirteen from the rank and file of the forces); and eighteen were merchants or estate-owners. Their deliberations were helped to some extent by the fact that a dozen constitutional drafts had been prepared during the preceding weeks, including one by two of their own members, J. G. Adler* and C. M. Falsen,† which was used as a basis. Even so,

---

* 1784–1852. He was the principal of a school in Halden; his expert knowledge of French later gained him a post as confidential secretary to Christian Frederick, whom he accompanied back to Denmark, his country of birth, and served again in 1839–48.

† 1782–1830. Member of a leading judicial family, 'the father of the constitution', and the most ardent champion of Norwegian independence. Bitterly disappointed by the Convention of Moss (p. 13), he became a county

the members had no practical experience on which to build, since major representative institutions had not existed in Norway for many centuries, which makes their businesslike approach to their problems very impressive. They appointed a constitutional committee, made up of fourteen officials and one leading merchant, which took only eight working days to prepare a draft constitution, and the full Assembly required only seven more to finalize a document which has stood the test of time. Viewed in retrospect, this was the cardinal achievement of the Norwegian people in 1814, but before examining its terms we must record what other progress was made with Norway's claim to full independence.

The existence of a constitution might prove a desirable safeguard in the event of a forced union with Sweden, a consideration which the regent in one of his less optimistic moods had mentioned in his private correspondence with the king of Denmark. Count Wedel and a minority of about one-quarter, known pejoratively as the 'Swedish party', took this line in the Assembly, where they opposed the inclusion in the constitution of any explicit provision for a separate Norwegian monarchy; they also demanded that the regent should disclose the position of the country *vis-à-vis* foreign powers, a disclosure which would have added weight to Wedel's arguments. He was defeated by Falsen on both issues, the only non-constitutional business undertaken by the Assembly being an issue of paper money under their guarantee to cover the first year's expenditure of the independent state of Norway. Although the minority still feared that they were building their throne on sand, the ever memorable Seventeenth of May brought unanimous approval not only of a constitution but also of a monarchy under Christian Frederick. Two days later an address to the throne (voted by a 94:8 majority), which invited the new king to announce the decisions of the National Assembly to the powers, referred to the oath taken in February and described the Norwegian people as 'determined to prefer death to slavery'.[6]

Its determination was soon to be put to the test. News was now reaching Christian Frederick of the renewal of the British blockade, and a week later he learnt of Charles John's return to Sweden. Moreover, a British emissary, J. P. Morier,* was on his way to Norway, with instructions which would help to make independence a dream but the constitution a lasting reality.

THE CONSTITUTION ESTABLISHED

Since their venture came at the close of an era of constitution-making, which had been inaugurated on the other side of the Atlantic in 1787, the men of Eidsvoll could derive plentiful inspiration from foreign models. Besides the work done at Philadelphia and that which had set up limited monarchy in France under the ill-starred Louis XVI—this 'constitution of 1791' had the unique honour of being translated into Norwegian for the occasion—reference was made to various evanescent creations, such as that which the French gave to the Batavian Republic in 1798 and that which the Spanish insurgents established under British influence in 1812. In addition, Count Wedel and some of the merchants in the Eidsvoll Assembly were more or less familiar with English parliamentary institutions, and something was known of the changes introduced in Sweden in 1809. Nevertheless, the constitution would not so quickly have become sacrosanct in Norwegian eyes if it had not been shaped in close accordance with the national temperament: one such characteristic feature was the succinctness which in a later age has made it readily adaptable to changing circumstances.

The 110 clauses, more than half of them expressed in a single short sentence, are divided into five sections, the first of which defined the kingdom of Norway as 'a free, independent and indivisible realm',[7] with a limited and hereditary monarchy as its form of government and with the Evangelical Lutheran religion continuing to be that of the state. Then follow three sections based on the

---

* 1776–1853. The son of a naturalized Swiss of Huguenot origins, he was a professional diplomat, who had been posted to Washington in 1810, and was now sent direct to Norway as a private secretary of Lord Castlereagh. He later became acting under-secretary of state for foreign affairs, August 1815, and minister to Saxony, 1815–25.

separation of powers, familiar from the writings of Montesquieu, which may be briefly summarized.

The executive power is entrusted to a king, whose direct male heirs have the right of succession; failing such heirs, he may propose a successor for approval by the legislature. 'The king himself chooses a council of Norwegian citizens' (the cabinet or *Statsråd*), whose members are responsible for the advice tendered to him; this is to be recorded in official protocols, but they cannot refuse to countersign the royal decisions. The king commands the armed forces, controls foreign policy, and exercises authority over the church; he also appoints all officials, but except in the case of cabinet ministers and other very senior appointments. they are to be irremovable except by legal process. Ordinances may be issued by the crown in matters of trade and police, but they are subject to existing law and valid only until the meeting of the legislature.

'The rights of citizenship and the legislative power' are significantly grouped together, no fewer than eleven clauses being devoted to the elaboration of the electoral system; this treats only the propertied classes as fit to exercise the franchise, even as primary electors, and distributes a variable total of seats between town and country in a manner which was intended to maintain a rural majority of two to one. For law-making the Storting or 'grand assize'—a deliberate archaism—is to divide itself after each election into two sub-chambers, every bill being introduced into the *Odelsting* and submitted later to the *Lagting*, whose members are one-fourth of the whole. In the event of disagreement between the two sub-chambers, a bill can only be enacted by a two thirds majority in a plenary meeting of the Storting, where the financial and other day-to-day business is in any case transacted. Besides matters of legislation and public finance, the Storting examines the protocols of cabinet meetings and controls the naturalization of foreigners. Its activities are restricted to a single session of three months following each triennial election, unless the king either prolongs the session or recalls the members to a further session, known as a Special Storting: but if the same bill is passed by three regular Stortings in succession, it becomes law in spite of the imposition of a veto which is vested in the crown.

The section on the judicial power is much the briefest of the three. It provides for the institution of a Supreme Court, under a chief justice (*justitiarius*), and of a Court of the Realm (*Riksrett*), to be composed of members of the Lagting and the Supreme Court; here the Odelsting may impeach ministers, judges, or members of the Storting for offences allegedly committed in the discharge of their official duties.

The final section defines certain public liberties, including the right to fair trial under known laws, the freedom of the press, and freedom of trade except for restrictions already in existence. Two significant clauses forbid the creation of new countships, baronies, or the like, but preserve the udal law and limited rights of primogeniture* for the benefit of the landowning peasant farmer. The last clause of all provides for the amendment of the document which had been drawn up so speedily. This is to require a proposal published during one regular Storting and carried with a two-thirds majority by its successor, that is to say, after the electorate has had a chance to show its wishes. Even so, 'An alteration must . . . only concern modifications in detail, which do not affect the spirit of this constitution.'

A UNION WITH SWEDEN ACCEPTED

Only three weeks after his accession, King Christian Frederick was convinced by Morier—who had hoped to find the National Assembly still sitting—that British policy contemplated full self-government but not an independent monarchy for Norway. He therefore decided, after consultation with his ministers, to put in hand preparations for a Special Storting, whose decisions he promised Morier he would accept, it being presumed that the result would be his own withdrawal to Denmark. But he also ordered a general mobilization (9 June) to meet the threat of a Swedish invasion, and hoped against

---

* *Odelsrett*, entitling a family to repurchase within five years of sale any freehold land that had been held by one of its members for not less than ten years, and *Åsetesrett*, entitling an eldest son to buy out his coheirs on favourable terms when a freehold farm passed by inheritance, were ancient rights, much treasured by the peasantry but already modified by legislation.

hope that the general situation in Europe might still change to his advantage. Morier before his departure made the British attitude clear to such Norwegians as he could contact, but when commissioners of the four powers reached Oslo at the end of the month, they were impressed by the leadership of 'the prince'—whom they did not of course recognize as king—and by the determination of the people to resist Swedish claims. They had satisfied themselves in Copenhagen that the king of Denmark had not instigated 'the Norwegian rising', were antagonized to some extent by the failure of Charles John to meet them for consultation before they crossed the Norwegian border, and were disposed to negotiate generous terms for the Norwegians, provided they would accept Swedish sovereignty coupled with self-government. An armistice and the suspension of the naval blockade were therefore offered, pending the meeting of the Special Storting, which the prince must undertake to influence in favour of union with Sweden before his own agreed return to Denmark.

Three main factors underlay the negotiations which followed. Both Russia and Britain preferred to keep Sweden weak; the former viewed her as a suspect neighbour to be kept under control, the latter as the ally of a potential rival and therefore not to be encouraged, while all four powers deprecated the outbreak of a new war at this juncture, because it might lead to complications elsewhere in Europe. Charles John, who had now mustered a second Swedish army to add to the one that had long been waiting on the southern frontier of Norway, was not eager to run the risks inseparable from hostilities, if they could be avoided; on the other hand, he was alive to the loss of prestige that might result from his receiving Norway at the hands of the Allied commissioners. As for the Norwegian people, an excited public opinion was influenced less by Christian Frederick, who regarded war as an unmitigated disaster, than by the patriotic fervour which had culminated at Eidsvoll, the encouragement of a good harvest, and recollections of successes in their last short war against the Swedes—when the latter were also facing eastwards against the Russians. In this very uncertain situation the final breach came on the refusal of the Norwegians to admit Swedish garrisons to the fortresses at Halden and Fredrikstad in return for an armistice which would cover the rest of the short campaigning season.

If the ensuing struggle had been prolonged, the Norwegians might have given a good account of themselves as the enemy advanced into the heart of their country, where the mountains favoured the defence: but neither Christian Frederick, who was no soldier, nor Charles John, a soldier who needed no fresh laurels, was disposed to put this to the test. The fighting lasted less than a fortnight and was confined to the south-east frontier districts, with the Norwegians winning three small engagements on the inland flank, near Kongsvinger, but failing back steadily along the coast, where the Swedes had naval support. Fredrikstad surrendered before the garrison had incurred a single casualty, and although the strongly placed fortress at Halden still held out, the Norwegian military authorities advised their government that they could not hold Oslo and had supplies for only one more week—a statement which was next day corrected to three weeks.

The sequel was the Convention of Moss, signed on 14 August together with an armistice, under which the Norwegians had to surrender Halden and demobilize the bulk of their forces, while the Swedes retained sufficient men on Norwegian soil to prevent any renewal of the conflict. The convention provided for the meeting of the Special Storting, which was to establish the terms of union with commissioners to be appointed by the king of Sweden, who now undertook to accept the Eidsvoll constitution as a general basis. Provision was also made secretly for Christian Frederick to relinquish the executive power immediately to his ministers, who were to issue their orders 'on behalf of the supreme authority';[8] and he undertook to leave Norway as soon as he had tendered his formal abdication to the Storting, even if he were asked to remain.

At Moss, as previously at Kiel, Charles John sought to achieve a limited objective quickly: he had forced the Norwegians to accept union as inevitable and had eliminated Christian Frederick, who was a dangerous opponent because of his dynastic claims. But three special reasons may be adduced for his decision to approve the Eidsvoll constitution, which was to prove a stumbling-block for him and his successors. In the first place, no Frenchman who remembered all the changes of regime in his own country since 1789 could doubt the possibility of altering an instrument of government to meet new circumstances. In the second place, his personal leanings towards liberalism, which earlier in the year had caused him to be considered as a possible ruler for France, were still encouraged by influential friends, such as Madame de Staël, who had written to advise him 'that enlightened people believe that it would be wise for you to accept the constitution which the Norwegians recently gave themselves'.[9] And finally, there is the interesting suggestion, made after his death by one of his Swedish confidants, Carl Löwenhielm (see p. 71), that as an upstart crown prince of Sweden Charles John thought it politic by all means to conciliate his future subjects in Norway, 'in case his Swedish throne should totter'.[10]

When the Special Storting met at Oslo in early October, Christian Frederick departed to Denmark, sick and discredited, yet toying with chimerical plans for a marriage with Princess Charlotte, the second heir to the British throne, which might secure English support for Denmark 'and perhaps for Norway'.[11] He passed into obscurity until King Frederick's death in 1839 (see p. 78), and later generations have raised no memorial to the first independent sovereign of modern Norway. Its fate now rested with a gathering of seventy-nine of its own citizens, which comprised fifty officials, twenty-one of the peasant class, and eight merchants. Bergen, which bound its four members to persist in the claim for independence, was typical of the more bellicose attitude in constituencies remote from the Swedish army. Count Wedel, on the other hand, headed a group of about twenty members who positively favoured union, while the majority were disillusioned patriots reluctantly facing the need for compromise; fewer than one-quarter had been present at Eidsvoll six months before. Great importance therefore attached to the adroit management of the Special Storting by its president, W. F. K. Christie,* who had acted as secretary in the proceedings at Eidsvoll.

* 1778–1849. A strongly nationalist magistrate, who represented Bergen in 1814 and in the Stortings of 1815 and 1818, where he continued to play a leading part. He then retired from politics, partly for reasons of ill health and partly because his popularity with Charles John aroused unjust suspicions; later generations have recognized his statesmanlike qualities.

For Norway's bargaining position was obviously weak, except for the fact that Charles John, guiding the Swedish commissioners from his headquarters at Halden, was determined to get its affairs finally settled before the newly assembled Congress of Vienna should be tempted to interfere.

Although the Storting began by authorizing the cabinet to exercise in its name the powers which had been exercised since August on behalf of an unspecified 'supreme authority', Christie dissuaded it from any immediate formal recognition of Christian Frederick's abdication; in this way revision of the constitution would precede any acknowledgement of a new sovereign. The Swedish commissioners, whose instructions required the reverse procedure to be followed, were fobbed off with a formula devised by Christie, which promised that, after the constitution had been revised, the Storting would 'solemnly elect and acknowledge the king of Sweden, His Majesty Charles XIII, as constitutional king of Norway'.[12] Since the acknowledgement might be taken to imply recognition of his rights under the treaty of Kiel, which the Norwegians did not explicitly repudiate, a temporary harmony was achieved which sowed the seeds for a later disharmony.

Acting on another proposal from Christie, the Special Storting, although it was in fact a second constituent assembly, restricted its attention to such changes as were necessary for the Union and must therefore be negotiated with the commissioners. On the one hand, it was agreed that the king might appoint the crown prince as viceroy in Norway, and provision was also made for a stattholder, who might be of Swedish nationality. On the other hand, Norway sought to safeguard its position by setting up its own bank and currency, by limiting its future financial responsibilities to a National Debt separately incurred, and by claiming the right to a trade flag. Although this and other national symbols were to cause friction later on, serious difficulty arose immediately over only two issues—the degree of control by the crown over the armed forces, and its claim to share in the Storting's power of naturalization. In the former case, the right to employ the forces outside the frontiers of Norway was restricted to troops of the line (see p. 86), and the risk of involvement in an aggressive Swedish foreign policy was further reduced by restricting the king's power of declaring war, for which he must first obtain the advice of his Norwegian as well as his Swedish ministers.★ In the latter case the Storting, which had already rejected an offer to make civil and military appointments in both kingdoms available to both nationalities on equal terms, persisted in retaining its existing monopoly. This meant that the king would be unable to intrude Swedish subjects into office in Norway—or even to extrude Danes, of whose possible infiltration Charles John was seriously afraid.

On 4 November 1814 Charles XIII of Sweden was 'unanimously elected and acknowledged as king of Norway', but the wording used by Wedel in announcing the event to Charles John at Halden glossed over the fact that forty-eight members of the Storting had declared him to be elected, as against thirty-one who declared him to be acknowledged.[13] The Storting likewise implied that he was not their sovereign until the moment of election by placing no signature but those of its own members upon the revised constitution, to which the Swedish commissioners appended a certificate to state that it had been 'negotiated and agreed' with King Charles XIII.[14] Time would show which were the shrewder tactics—the forbearance of the crown prince of Sweden, who cared much less about the definition of rights that he had won in January or August than about the prospect of a gradual amalgamation of the two kingdoms, which would make such definition superfluous; or the legalistic methods employed by the Storting, in the belief that the precise wording of an agreement could and should be used to protect the interests of the weaker party.

One of the most eventful years in Scandinavian history closed with the arrival in Stockholm of a deputation from Norway, on whose behalf Christie addressed the monarch in his crown as his 'elected and acknowledged sovereign', and then turned to the glittering assembly of Swedish dignitaries: 'You offer us the hand of a brother; we grasp it with an honest handshake, and we shall never withdraw our hand'.[15] 'Never' is a big word.

★ Their rights were secured by the Swedish constitution of 1809.

2. Government by an Élite, 1815–1884

TWO DECADES AFTER THE CROWDED EVENTS OF 1814 had reached their conclusion, a reflective Scottish visitor described the Norwegians as a 'handful of free and happy people living under a liberal constitution, flourishing under their own legislation, and making no demands, asking no favours, from the other governments of Europe'.[1] The framework was, indeed, superior to that then to be found under most of those other governments: but it was only a framework. In domestic politics this was the age of small things: in seventy years the only substantial changes were the setting up of local self-government (1837) and the introduction of annual sessions in the Storting (1869). The age of effective political organization, with ministries representing clearly defined popular parties, did not come until after the major upheaval in the system of government which makes 1884 a cardinal date in Norwegian history. That upheaval depended in large measure upon two parallel developments: the build-up of nationalist sentiment, which entered by degrees into almost every political question and was to dislodge the Bernadottes from the Norwegian throne in 1905; and the accelerating economic advance of the country, which made a wider democracy possible. These matters will be left for consideration in two following chapters. The 'government by an élite' must first be examined as a system, working through king, cabinet, Storting, and electorate, and firmly based on two strong classes, namely the bureaucracy and the landholding peasantry. Its operations were marked, as we shall see, by some important social developments and agitations, but from 1872 onwards a political deadlock supervened, from which an alliance between peasants and urban radicals eventually emerged triumphant.

THE BERNADOTTE KINGS AND THEIR MINISTERS

In the summer of 1815 the first regular Storting unanimously endorsed the settlement with the Swedish monarchy by making a formal Act of Union, which was passed in identical terms by the

Swedish Riksdag. The act expressly stated that the Union had been established 'not by force of arms, but by free conviction',[2] which left the exact means of its establishment in a politic obscurity. But the elaborate provisions for filling a vacancy on the throne and for the regency during a sovereign's minority are a reminder that the Norwegian constitution had placed the executive power firmly in the hands of whoever wore the crown: these were now the strong hands of the Frenchman, Charles John, as the duly appointed heir to Charles XIII, king of Sweden and Norway.

Three generations of Bernadottes headed the government of Norway, and in no case was the headship purely nominal. At the outset this attitude was encouraged by the tradition of a paternal monarchy, which lingered on from the era of Danish rule, and by their own awareness that they were a dynasty of parvenus, who could not rely on traditional sentiment in either of their realms to protect them from the consequences of an inept choice of ministers and measures. Moreover, the Swedish constitution of 1809 allowed a rather high degree of political leadership on the king's part, which would naturally extend to all his dominions: even after the conversion of the Swedish Riksdag from an assembly of four estates to a bicameral parliament in 1867, the monarch in Sweden played a bigger part in the choice of men and measures than he did, say, in Victorian Britain. And the kings must in any case pay special attention to Norway, since it was often viewed by Swedish eyes as their national compensation for the loss of Finland, while in fact organically linked with Sweden through the monarchy alone. To sum up, although the Bernadotte sovereigns seldom resided in Norway for more than a few weeks at a time, they all took a continuous interest in its affairs, for the sake of Norway itself as well as for their impact on the double monarchy as a whole and on the well-being of the larger of their two realms.

In Norway at least, the first Bernadotte king left the largest mark. For practical purposes the reign of Charles John spans the first thirty years of the Union, since in 1814–18 he was virtually regent. As the Frenchman spoke neither Swedish nor Norwegian, he was in a sense equidistant from both his peoples, though Norwegian historians have drawn attention chiefly to his persistent demands for their politically more advanced constitution to be assimilated in various ways to the Swedish—in particular by making the king's suspensory veto on legislation absolute. In June 1821, as we shall observe in another context (see p. 66), he went so far as to address a Circular Note to the powers on this subject, but he felt less sure than he pretended to be of any heartfelt sympathy from the legitimist monarchs. In Sweden he never lost his fear of the Gustavian dynasty, deposed and exiled since 1809. In Norway the most striking feature of his long reign, when viewed in retrospect, is that he never actually pushed matters to extremes or made any overt move towards the dreaded amalgamation with Sweden, albeit the reign of the ex-marshal of France coincided with the period when Norway was at its weakest. It seems likely that the king's intention all along was to temper assertion of royal claims with politic compromises: his revolutionary past gave him at least a qualified sympathy with the idea and practice of self-government. At all events on his later visits in 1832 and in 1838–9 (when he spent five months in Norway), the popularity of Charles John among his Norwegian subjects was unquestionable.

Oscar I, who reigned from 1844 to 1859, was the only son of Charles John and his bourgeois French queen, Désirée, so his marriage in 1823 to a Bavarian princess, who was also a grand-daughter of the Empress Josephine, had marked a 'break-through' for the Bernadotte family. He inherited little of his father's capacity for adroit compromises. On the other hand, he took his profession seriously, was the author (while crown prince) of a work on penal reform, and until shocked by the republican revolution in his native France in 1848, had a generally liberal outlook, from which Norway derived due benefit. On his accession he was prompt to conciliate its people in minor matters, but his later years were devoted mainly to an active foreign policy which did not rouse their enthusiasm. In the later years, also, they had to deal less than hitherto with the king in person and more with his aristocratic and conservative Swedish advisers.

Two of Oscar I's sons followed him upon the throne. Charles XV achieved a romantic popularity in both his kingdoms, and devoted much of his attention to the common defence which had been one of the main objects of the Union. In foreign affairs, however, he failed to carry either of his peoples with him. He died young, in 1872, feeling that his reign had been a failure and leaving only a daughter by the Dutch princess to whom he had been married. Oscar II differed from his elder brother in many ways: he was more serious and less flamboyant, a little self-righteous, and decidedly well informed—the only one of his line who spoke and wrote Norwegian without effort. His German consort, Sophia, was a strong character who did much to make the royal family respected, but Oscar himself at bottom resembled his predecessor in combining an impressive exterior with a vacillating will. The loss of Norway after he had been king for a third of a century casts a rather unfair shadow of failure over the entire reign. In his earlier years Oscar II seemed to his Norwegian subjects to be the embodiment for better and worse of kingly authority and self-confidence, though the *Memoirs*[3] published long after the author's death show that even then his capacity was for writing and speech-making more than for action.

The organization of the ministry through which the royal powers were exercised in Norway was complicated by the location of the court in Stockholm. Until 1891 the king's eldest son might deputize as viceroy in Oslo, which happened for several short periods; otherwise the constitution as modified in November 1814 had provided for a *stattholder* ('lieutenant') to preside over the king's ministers in Norway; he also deputized for the king as commander-in-chief. At the outset the post was held by a succession of four Swedish noblemen. From 1829 to 1836 it was left vacant, after which Charles John appointed two Norwegians of aristocratic birth, Herman Wedel Jarlsberg in 1836 and Severin Lövenskiold* in 1840. After the death of the latter at the age of seventy-nine the post fell into abeyance: but it was characteristic of the formal difficulties that often beset the double monarchy that its actual abolition later raised a hurricane of controversy.

---

* 1777–1856. A member of a German family ennobled in Norway in 1739; studied mining and forestry in Germany as a boy, in preparation for the administration of his large properties. Strongly opposed to popular government, but ready to assert his views against those of the king, e.g. in objecting to the November treaty of 1855 (see. p. 84).

From a practical point of view the weight of the administration normally centred in Oslo. Wedel Jarlsberg was a dominant national figure, both while he served as minister of finance during the difficult early years of the new regime and when he presided as stattholder. His successor in the former office, Jonas Collett,* likewise had the advantage that the Norwegian people regarded him as being in some sense their own leader. This was not the case, however, with Lövenskiold, who described his politics as 'conservative monarchist' and just before he was made stattholder had been impeached on a charge of disregarding the rights of the Storting (see p. 71). But a great deal of authority was exercised by J. H. Vogt,† an administrator of very long experience, who remained as the senior minister in Oslo until 1858, when Prince Charles planned a new ministerial system to be accompanied by the formal abolition of the office of stattholder.

In theory and in social status the senior member of the whole body of Norwegian ministers was the minister-resident in Stockholm, who was assisted by two other ministers freed from departmental duties in Oslo in annual rotation. He held the title of *statsminister* ('minister of state'), whereas the lower title of 'first minister' was given on the basis of seniority to one of his colleagues in Oslo, who presided over the meetings of the cabinet there but was not necessarily its effective political leader. It was not until 1873 that the leading minister in Oslo became a second 'minister of state', enjoying the same salary as the minister-resident in Stockholm and also receiving substantially larger allowances in recognition of his position as prime minister.

---

* Great-grandson of a London timber-merchant who established himself in Norway, he managed the national finances skilfully and also helped to establish local self-government. In 1836 Charles John compelled him to resign office, because he had warned the Storting of its impending sudden dissolution by the king; this made him a popular hero, whom Wergeland honoured with a poem and the Storting with a unanimous grant of his full salary by way of pension.

† 1784–1862. Entered government service at seventeen and the cabinet at forty-one; a minister in six departments over a period of thirty-three years, except for 1829–36, when he was seconded to the criminal law commission. Regarded as a typical bureaucrat; but he also helped to equip Oslo with its first savings and business banks and was one of the founders of the temperance movement.

These distinctions were closely related to the fact that there were three levels of cabinet meeting. Matters of common concern to both kingdoms were settled at the rather infrequent 'joint cabinet meetings' (*sammensatte statsråd*), at which the king presided over the Swedish cabinet ministers reinforced by the three Norwegian ministers in Stockholm; on very rare occasions three Swedish ministers accompanied the king, in order that he might hold a joint cabinet meeting with his Norwegian cabinet ministers in Oslo. Purely Norwegian business, however, was transacted by the king at formal meetings with the three Norwegian ministers in Stockholm—or with his ministers in Oslo if he were in residence there. The latter group also held their own meetings in the absence of the king, at which they dealt with the day-to-day Norwegian business of all kinds and drew up their proposals on more important matters, for submission by their three colleagues at their meetings with the king in Stockholm. In addition, the conduct of foreign policy, which was regarded initially as a prerogative function of the crown, eventually occasioned yet a fourth type of cabinet meeting, at which the king was advised by two Swedish and one Norwegian minister on external affairs directly concerning Norway.

So cumbrous a system of cabinet government involved frequent misunderstandings and minor crises, but broadly speaking it served Norway's main interests fairly well for nearly half a century. During that time the general political trend was conservative, and in any case many—perhaps most—of the tasks of government did not involve political choices. Since the constitution envisaged a rather strict separation of powers, the king as head of the executive acted to some extent as his own prime minister, the individual ministers being nominated by him to run the departments of government and to give him advice. If the advice was unacceptable to the monarch, their duty was sufficiently discharged by registering their dissent in the council record: resignations were seldom offered and were not necessarily accepted. In 1835, however, the ministry acquired the rather muffled voice in matters of foreign policy to which allusion has been made, and in the 1840s they gained the right for their leading members at least to be consulted confidentially by the king when any new minister was to be appointed. Thus the Norwegian cabinet

came to have the character of a self-renewing corporation: down to
1884 there was no occasion on which a ministry resigned or was dismissed from office.

THE STORTING AND THE ELECTORATE

The purely legislative activities of the Storting developed slowly.
Its attitude in the first generation or so was one of jealous watchful-
ness in order to preserve the existing balance of the constitution. It
is significant that the first measure in which three successive Stortings persisted, so as to override the suspensive veto of the crown,
was a bill for abolishing titles and privileges of nobility. Although
only three baronies and thirty-three very minor dignities were involved, Charles John's intense personal indignation could secure no
concession beyond some compensation payments to the holders.
Since the constitution already forbade any new creations, the matter
was a small one in which to flout the customs of the Europe of that
era, but it was deemed important to demonstrate that the royal veto
could be overridden. On the positive side some projects left over
from the constitution-making were continued, such as a military
service law and the reshaping of the legal code, though the latter
project was abandoned to the hands of the government after the
experience of fifteen years had shown that the task was too complex
for a lay committee. With rare exceptions, the Storting for a long
time left the initiative in major legislation to the government, which
could prepare the way by appointing a Royal Commission, on which
members of the Storting sometimes figured alongside officials and
other experts. The situation changed, however, as soon as the Storting began to hold annual sessions. In the 1870s an average of 80
legislative proposals a year originated with the government, 144
with the members of the legislature; in the 1880s the respective
figures were 86 and 247.

The Storting used its wide powers of control over the public income and expenditure primarily to keep down the cost of government. Most representatives were directly concerned to spare the
pockets of their constituents, and a policy of rigid economy had the
further merit of curbing many activities of the executive which the

legislature could not otherwise bring under its control. But occasional use was made of a right not to be found, for example, at Westminster, when the Storting would vote money for which the government had not asked, in order to mark its special approval of some person or institution. Finally, we may notice the vigour of the Storting committees, to one or more of which each member was appointed, in the regular examination of constitutional, military, and many other categories of public business. Here too, however, a handicap was imposed by the generally accepted doctrine that committees had no power to act when the Storting itself was not in session.

Until the constitution was changed in 1869, the preponderance of the ministry rested securely upon the fact that the Storting had no legal claim to sit for a longer period than three months in every third year. Until about mid-century ministers made use of their right, when it was not sitting, to issue their own ordinances in matters of trade and police; and even during its brief sessions the Storting was handicapped by a widespread belief that party groupings were unnecessary and probably harmful in a legislative body whose members should be united by a high-minded devotion to the common good. In 1836 only eleven members would support a proposal to formulate a policy by voting an address in reply to the speech from the throne at the start of the session, since it was observed with regret that in other constitutional monarchies, notably Britain and France, this device was linked with a system of parties. In these circumstances it is easy to understand the alacrity with which the crown veto was applied to every bill which was disliked by king or ministers—an average of one measure in every six.

Nevertheless, the Storting had at least two ways of controlling ministers. One instrument was the Protocol Committee of the Storting, which had been set up as early as August 1815, when fears of Swedish encroachments on the constitution were particularly rife. It was entitled to examine the official records of cabinet meetings, so that each separate minister could be publicly criticized for his recorded attitude to any particular decision. Even so, it was not until 1868 that the Storting succeeded in driving any minister from office, so long as he retained the confidence of the sovereign. The other instrument was the rather clumsy device of an impeachment, to be conducted by the Odelsting (on the initiative of the Protocol Committee) before a tribunal composed of the judges of the Supreme Court and the members of the Lagting; the defence could reduce its numbers to the extent of one-third by challenging individuals. In the first thirty years six such trials were held, and proposals for four others were rejected by vote of the Odelsting. Only two cases resulted in a conviction. In 1821 the minister of marine was sentenced to repay his salary as a naval officer, which he had continued to draw with the king's express approval in addition to his ministerial emoluments. In 1836 Lövenskiold, then minister-resident in Stockholm, was fined 1,000 specie dollars (*Spesiedaler*, see p. 104) because he had not protested against Charles John's sudden decision to dismiss the Storting (see p. 71). As for the unsuccessful cases, they concerned chiefly matters of finance—including the unauthorized purchase by a minister of two paddle steamers which were urgently needed for the public service—where the main object was the demarcation of authority between rival powers. It was only when the entire ministry was impeached in 1883–4 (see p. 56) that any decisive political result was achieved: in 1836 Lövenskiold had tendered the resignation of his office, but the king refused to accept it and subsequently promoted him, as we have seen, to be stattholder.

This partial subordination of the legislative to the executive power was closely related to the smallness of the electorate and the limited interest it showed in politics. Throughout the period now under consideration the constitution and the detailed election regulations made in 1828—which even prescribed penalties for voting in favour of oneself—provided for the franchise to be exercised by the following (male) groups: higher government officials of all kinds, including those in retirement; the actual owners or five-year leaseholders of tax-registered rural land; duly enrolled burgesses of towns, both traders and artisans; and other persons who owned a town house or land worth at least 300 dollars. These primary electors voted for secondary electors, the voters each putting forward a list of names which must not exceed one-fiftieth of their own numbers. In two instances (Oslo, 1817, and Bergen, 1838) the workings of this elaborate process have been fully examined:[4] the electoral colleges were found to contain roughly twice as high a proportion of officials and merchants as did the bodies of primary electors. Finally, the electoral colleges chose representatives (and their deputies) from candidates who must be qualified locally as electors. The number of these representatives or *Stortingsmenn* was intended to vary within limits of 75 and 100 in accordance with the number of qualified voters (weighted differently for urban and rural constituencies), the intention being that there should be no Norwegian counterpart to the English 'rotten borough'. However, in 1816–30 the towns were given a special advantage by a law which restricted rural representatives to a maximum of three per county,[5] and for this and other reasons it was not until 1859 that the proportion of two-thirds for the country and one-third for the towns was fixed in accordance with what the constitution intended. Even then the towns were over-represented in relation to their share of total population. All this gave the Storting in its first sixty years a class structure which may be tabulated as follows:

TABLE I[6]

Rural representation (per cent)		Urban representation (per cent)	
farmers etc.	62	officials	51
officials	29	traders and artisans	36
lawyers (other than officials)	4	lawyers (other than officials)	7
other occupations	5	other occupations	6

Thus urban voters preferred members of the official class—about one-half of whom resided in the towns—to any other group in their community. What is more remarkable, in the widely scattered rural constituencies peasant farmers elected one official for every two representatives they elected from their own class.

As these results tend to suggest, a wide spectrum of the newly-formed Norwegian electorate did not feel closely engaged in political life. Indeed, for the eighteen elections held between 1829 and 1879 the average turnout was less than one-half of the duly registered voters.[7] Moreover, in the last two decades of this period, for which the records are more detailed, it has been ascertained that one-third of those entitled to vote did not trouble to take the necessary oath to the constitution and get themselves placed upon the register. This is all the more striking in view of the fact that by the 1870s Norway, with an enfranchised population of only 7 or 8 per cent, restricted the right to vote to a very much smaller section of the community than did Disraelian Britain or many nations of the Continent.

TWO DOMINANT SOCIAL CLASSES

Both the dominant classes in Norway were governed chiefly by conservative instincts, even if their interests compelled them to accept occasional innovations: the bureaucracy enjoyed the exercise of power, to which it had long been accustomed; the landholding peasantry enjoyed a stable way of life, based on largely self-sufficient exploitation of the land and the water. Neither term is a satisfactory description for the English reader, for the *embedsmann* or higher civil servant belonging to the Norwegian bureaucracy was in some respects more like the 'civilian' who administered British India in the days before Gandhi, and the Norwegian *bonde* or 'peasant' more like the French *paysan* after the Revolution had got rid of landlord authority and feudal dues. These two classes were all the more inclined towards social conservatism because of their absolute predominance in a community where the urban population at mid-century was only 12·2 per cent—a little higher than in the vast spaces of the United States, but a bare quarter of the proportion of townspeople in England.

In 1815 Norway had a total of approximately 2,000 higher officials, distributed among civil, military, and ecclesiastical posts, all of which were held under warrant from the crown. About 130 of them had been born in Denmark, and all (except some of the soldiers) had qualified for office by studies undertaken at the university of Copenhagen. The substitution of the new university founded by Frederick VI in Oslo, which had opened its doors in 1813, while severing the Danish connection, intensified the corporate feeling. Although it fostered its greatest genius, the mathematician H. H. Abel, in these early years the university remained small, with an attendance after two decades of fewer than 700 students, who were chiefly sons of officials seeking to follow in their fathers' footsteps. In 1835, for example, law and theology were the largest faculties, with medicine a poor third, and a remnant of only ten students taking final courses in philology and four in mining. Once an academic qualification had been acquired, the young official might aspire to climb slowly upwards: he might perhaps start as an assistant to a magistrate in a remote valley; he might end as a minister of the crown. But one consideration which helped to mould him to a pattern was that promotion at every stage depended upon earning—or at all events gaining—the good opinion of his official superiors.

The financial position of the official class was relatively strong, especially after the Norwegian dollar, the depreciation of which was already a serious problem in 1814, regained its full value in silver in 1842. While the Storting did its best to depress salaries and pensions for officials, security of tenure was almost absolute and there was no fixed age of retirement. Efficiency and zeal brought extra profit, since more than half the emoluments might come from fees for signing and registering documents, valuing land and other property, and similar activities. Moreover, the occupants of rural posts usually resided on state-owned farms which they were entitled to run for their own benefit.

In Oslo officials staffed the six government departments: ecclesiastical affairs and education; justice and police; finance, customs, and trade; war; the navy; and audit. This organization, completed by 1822, underwent only one major change in the next two generations, namely the institution of a Department of the Interior in 1845 (see p. 111). At its summit the official class included the justices of the new Supreme Court, whose chief received a salary almost equal to that of a minister, and by 1822 the ministers themselves were all of them officials by training and professional experience. Indeed, the description fits all save five of the seventy members of Norwegian cabinets down to 1884. In the social life of the capital and other towns this class had few rivals. The old urban patriciate, whose wealth was in timber and shipping, had largely been ruined by the post-war collapse of trade. A new bourgeoisie gradually took their place among the 'people of condition', recognizable as such by their education, manners, dress, and above all by their speech. But for a long time these few families tended to defer to the cocked hat and gold-braided uniform of the official class—into which their daughters often married.

This exalted status was most evident, however, in the life of the countryside. Since there was no class of country gentry and (until 1837) no regular form of rural self-government, the resident officials were not much hampered by local opinion in their interpretation of laws and regulations. The quinquennial reports of the county governors show that they exercised a paternal oversight of economic and social life in every aspect. This local administration was often denounced as burdensome in much the same terms as had been heard throughout the period of Danish rule, and the farmers lent a ready ear to accusations of peculation and extortion. Though less closely supervised than before 1814, the administrative work—from record-keeping to road-making, from the mustering of recruits for the army to the distribution of paupers among the farms required to feed them, and from the preparation of confirmation candidates to the tracking down of criminals—must nevertheless be judged to have been both cheap and efficient, especially when allowance is made for the dearth of communications in Norway. In matters of culture, too, the parsonages and other spacious, though spartan, homes of official families were the centres from which fashions in furniture and clothing, health improvements, some agricultural novelties, and even some new political concepts spread slowly outwards into the tradition-bound world of the peasant. Cultural diffusion was helped by the fact that officials were constantly on the move, both on business arising within their districts and on change of post; some had direct experience of conditions in every main part of the national territory.

The landholding peasantry are less easily defined and described because, unlike the ubiquitous official, their way of life varied in accordance with the character of the particular district in which the individual was born and, almost invariably (until the tide of migration and emigration began to flow in the 1860s), lived out his days. Broadly speaking, in eastern Norway the members of this class were comparatively affluent, and they often employed much labour on a considerable acreage of arable and profitable woodland. In most parts of west Norway, on the other hand, and along much of the south coast the typical farm was small and poor, and near the sea the holder was likely to eke out his living as a seasonal fisherman. North of the great mountain plateau the Tröndelag resembled eastern Norway, but beyond this lay the thinly peopled counties which depended almost entirely upon the harvest of the sea—extremely poor, debt-ridden, and carrying very little weight in national affairs. Yet for the present purpose the peasant stands out from the rest of the rural population as the owner or leaseholder of a duly registered farm, who could not be ousted from his holding and who, as we have seen, possessed the franchise.

What were the political objectives of the peasantry? In 1815 this was by no means clear, since in their case—unlike that of most newly enfranchised groups in other countries—no great grievance had stimulated a demand for representation. The events of the preceding year had, indeed, brought to the surface in many communities the feelings of national pride which traditions of Norway's past greatness had fostered, and there seems to have been a fairly widespread fear lest the union with Sweden might deliver them and their land into the power of the Swedish nobility. In some western and southern districts a second common sentiment was devotion to the puritan or fundamentalist religion which had been preached at the turn of the century by a lay evangelist of genius, Hans Nielsen Hauge;* this clashed violently with the rationalist outlook still common among the clergy. But for the most part the peasant attitude was negative—suspicious of any encroachment by the official class in church or state; resentful of taxation, as imposing unreasonable burdens upon their class, whose wealth consisted in goods produced for their own consumption rather than in crops marketed for cash; and much more interested in local than in national affairs.

Since the towns depended at least as much upon their ships and

---

* 1771–1824. His conversion in 1796 was followed by preaching tours into all parts of the country and the organizing of converts in local groups, which combined religious edification with important trade activities. In 1804–11 Hauge was imprisoned for illegal preaching under conditions that broke his health, but by the time of his death Haugeanism had become a laymen's movement with lasting influence inside the Norwegian church. A Haugean revivalist meeting *c.* 1850 is shown in Plate 4.

overseas commerce as upon trade with the hinterland, their population on the whole had wider views—and the urban franchise (as we have seen) was available to craftsmen as well as to the merchant class. Accordingly, from the 1830s onwards the revival of overseas commerce, and then the sporadic growth of machine industry, increased the number of urban voters; they were organized and led by new middle-class elements, such as struggling solicitors and ill-paid government clerks. Rural Norway on the other hand had a large but voteless population of cottars, holding a house and usually some land on more or less precarious conditions as dependants of farmers. Both country and town also contained a mass of labourers and servants, oppressed by the scarcity of land and living accommodation. These classes were politically unrepresented and largely neglected.

THE POLITICAL DÉBUT OF THE LANDHOLDING PEASANTRY

In view of the suddenness of the transition from enlightened despotism to representative government, the political immaturity of the Norwegian peasant farmer in 1815 is less surprising than the degree of maturity he had reached by 1884. Peasants had indeed participated in the constitution-making at Eidsvoll and in the shaping of the union with Sweden; and among the delegates who accompanied Christie to present the formal address in recognition of the latter event at the palace in Stockholm, the Danish minister remarked on 'the two peasants in their grey garb conversing unembarrassed with the highest dignitaries in their uniforms and orders'.[8] But the history of the following years showed that their class still lacked any coherent programme or effective leadership.

The Storting of 1815–16 did something to remove long-standing grievances. The right of the farmers to set up sawmills on their own property was approved after long discussion, though the government delayed action until 1818 (see p. 108). The more dangerous privilege of distilling brandy from their own crops was conceded*

---

* Twenty years later a Scottish traveller noticed that even farm servants had brandy twice daily with their meals. At that date a barrel containing four bushels of potatoes, valued at one dollar, provided the farmer with the basic raw material for 18 quarts of brandy.[9]

and some alleviation was made in the irksome obligation to provide *skyss*—the post-horses, boats, and oarsmen without which inland travel would have been impossible: henceforth officials were to pay for these services like other travellers, and the duty of providing them could be restricted to fixed posting stations in each neighbourhood. In the matter of military service the Storting refused to honour the principle of equality of obligation laid down in the constitution; for the upper classes and townspeople continued to provide only the officers. The rural burden was, however, reduced in practice by halving the number of recruits required and allowing married farmers to purchase substitutes.

The landholding peasantry remained dissatisfied. In the Storting of 1818 they agitated against the 'silver tax' (see p. 104), and some hundreds of them made a rather half-hearted march on the capital. This was halted *en route* by a force of soldiers and its leaders were imprisoned; what was significant was that some at least of the demonstrators aimed at a return to royal autocracy, on the ground that the Storting involved the country in unnecessary expense. When Charles John visited Trondheim for his coronation in the following autumn, he gave a discouraging answer to a peasant deputation which denounced the Storting to him as their oppressor. But this did not altogether allay the fears of the ruling class, since the king's policy was liable to change quickly and his huge private fortune maintained both secret agents and pensioners in Norway: the latter eventually included the principal agitator against the Storting. One consequence was that in 1821 C. M. Falsen, the main author of the constitution, proposed amendments which would have turned the Lagting into an Upper Chamber from which the peasants were totally excluded and would have restricted their numbers in the Odelsting to one per county; he also wished to increase the influence of ministers by entitling them to take part in the Storting debates.

However, in the decade then opening, the Storting as a whole stood firm in defence of the constitution as it was, both against Falsen and against the king himself, whose proposed amendments would have given him an absolute veto on legislation and the right to institute a new hereditary nobility. These proposals were widely believed to portend some form of amalgamation with Sweden (see p. 60), and peasant members therefore rallied to the support of the constitution. They also welcomed ancillary measures to stop the building of a royal palace in Oslo, to refuse an appanage for the king's first grandson, to reduce the salaries of the stattholder and the minister-resident in Stockholm, and to restrict the Norwegian contribution to the diplomatic expenditure of the United Kingdoms— items which embittered relations between crown and legislature in 1827.

The Storting that met in March 1830 contained a record proportion of more than one-half of its members drawn from the official class. On the advice of its constitutional committee, which found that the distribution of seats between town and country was now heavily disturbed,[10] to the detriment of the latter, it passed the law (already mentioned) that allowed the representation of rural constituencies—which *might* choose officials—to increase. However, this was the year in which both the July Revolution in France and the military revolt in Russian Poland made a stir in Norway, and this no doubt added to the effect of a venture by a peasant politician, John Neergaard: having agitated in the previous Storting for the measure passed in 1830, he now began to distribute an elementary political tract in country districts under cover of peddling other wares. Popularly known as *Olaboka*[11] from the name of one of its rustic characters, his 32-page booklet taught in dialogue and dialect the simple 'lesson' that the official class sought election to the Storting in order to raise its salaries and that, if the peasants did not wish to see all the land in Norway pass into its clutches. they must support their own class at the polls. At about the same time the youthful genius, Henrik Wergeland (see p. 73), was embarking upon the work of popular enlightenment as pamphleteer, newspaper editor, and organizer of rural libraries and schools, which reinforced the intense national appeal of his poetry.

In consequence of all this, the Storting of 1833 included forty-five peasant members (out of ninety-six), as compared with an average of twenty-three at the six previous elections. Later, however, the proportion of peasant members declined again, and they did not secure any share of the presidential positions in the Storting and its two subdivisions, whose holders guided the proceedings: indeed, it was not until 1851 that so much as a committee chairmanship was given to a peasant. But from this time they began to press even minor measures in which they were interested through three successive Stortings, so as to override the royal veto, and began slowly to accustom themselves to following a political leader. For a third of a century the leadership lay with O. G. Ueland,* who was born on a poor western farm and became a peripatetic rural school-teacher at the age of eighteen. He acquired a farm by marriage, and sat in every Storting from 1833 to 1869, the year before his death. Although his policies were not always consistent, he was a strong, fearless character and a resourceful debater. A devout follower of Hauge and a worshipper of the constitution, he espoused the cause of democratic development within the framework of the Union and the monarchy. It is noteworthy that he served for fourteen years as the first chairman of the local council in his home district.

The introduction of rural self-government was the big political change in this period. It had been proposed as early at 1821, and was in principle desired by the ministers as a replacement for an untidy system of loose collaboration between the officials and the peasant landholders, who had to be consulted informally—often outside the church after Sunday service—about any intended innovations. But it was not until 1833 that the peasants themselves began to claim full control of their own affairs; and then it took time to work out a compromise between the autonomous communities they had in mind and the nurseries of self-government, well supervised from above, which the authorities thought more suitable. Finally, in 1837 two laws gave the same institutions to town and country alike. The impact on life in the towns was at first relatively slight, since they already possessed the rudiments of self-rule through their 'elect men' and occasional town meetings. Rural Norway, on the other hand, had to go back to the long obsolete assemblies of freemen in

---

* 1799–1870. He demanded ruthless economies at the expense of the official class, but his general outlook was profoundly conservative: 'The people of Norway treasures two things as the apple of its eye, religion and the Constitution.' He was parish clerk as well as schoolmaster from 1827 to 1852, when he became a rural bailiff (*lensmann*).

the regional *ting* for a genuine tradition of self-government: the committees set up under the School Ordinance of 1739 had provided little but the spectacle of rural parsimony preventing progress.

Except for the ineligibility of local magistrates, the local councils were to be elected by and from the same categories of persons as the Storting. One-half of the seats were to be filled biennially, both in the executive committee (*formannskap*), to which the main powers were entrusted, and in the representative body (*representantskap*); this was four times as large as the executive—whose members were included—and was required to endorse major financial and some other proposals. The elected chairmen of the executive committees were also to meet annually under the county governor to handle business common to the districts of each county. Government approval was needed for sales of communal property and for the imposition of any special local charge for a longer period than five years, while the local clergymen still presided over poor relief and school management business, which now came before an expanded executive committee. Essentially, however, each town and rural district was set free to manage its own affairs.

Looking back after two generations, the ardently nationalist historian, J. E. Sars, hailed this legislation for cogent reasons as

so great an advance in relation to the political development of the people that on that account it can almost be placed alongside the Constitution. By it the free constitution was given a broad basis to rest upon and be nourished from, and became related to the daily life and activity of the people in such a way that its principles could penetrate everywhere and be most effectively acquired. . . . There was at that time scarcely any European state where local self-government was so well organized and so widely ramified as it became in Norway by the legislation of 1837.[12]

But all this was of rather slow growth. In 1837 the main interest of those who possessed the local franchise was to keep public expenditure to the minimum. They were still not confident of their own abilities: after the first election to rural councils, where nine-tenths of the constituents were landholding peasants, only two council chairmen in five emerged from the peasantry, and as late as 1862 only three in four. Given the stultifying isolation of most of the rural communities, it was bound to require many other influences to mould an effectively self-governing people.

One such possibility was the introduction of a jury system, which could be regarded as a revival of the ancient *ting*, where every free man had been a judge, and was therefore envisaged as constituting a 'people's court' (*folkedomstol*). Ueland proposed this in 1845, but after two experts had reported on their inquiries into the subject (which took them as far afield as Canada) in three thick volumes, the government's delays provoked the Storting into appointing a preparatory commission of its own. The government regarding this as an encroachment upon its prerogatives put petty obstacles in its way,* vetoed the resulting bill, which was based on the English and American jury system, and appointed a new Royal Commission. This produced an alternative scheme, which found that jury decisions by a three-quarters majority accorded better with Norwegian views of law than the system requiring verdicts to be unanimous, but this was not ready until 1863—by which time the mood of the farmers had changed (see p. 49). Little progress could be made without the backing of a better-informed and livelier public opinion. Six years after Wergeland's death in 1845 specific tasks of enlightenment were entrusted to a new society,† sponsored by the education authorities, while the growth of voluntary organizations for many different purposes—from foreign missions to cattle shows—began to exercise a slow, imponderable, but cumulatively decisive influence upon the once self-contained world of the Norwegian countryside.

DEVELOPMENTS IN PUBLIC MORALS AND RELIGION

The middle decades of the century were remarkable for a whole series of movements which in the long run reshaped the life and out-

---

* Ueland, for instance, had to resign his post as rural bailiff because the county governor was instructed to refuse leave of absence for the work of the commission.

† 'The Society for the Promotion of Popular Enlightenment' (*Selskapet til folkeoplysningens fremme*) whose periodical, *The People's Friend* (*Folkevennen*), was edited for nine years by Eilert Sundt (see p. 43) and continued until the end of the century.

look of the rural population. Since two of the leaders are of special interest to the foreigner, their activities are treated separately below. But it may be remarked at once that the leadership in general came from outside the ranks of the peasantry—either from the ruling élite or from a handful of urban liberals who made their voices heard in the Storting.

The temperance movement met at first with stubborn opposition from farmer legislators, who shut their eyes to the grave increase in habitual drunkenness sooner than sacrifice their recently won privilege of distilling their own fiery potato brandy. Following the American and Swedish example, temperance societies were introduced in Norway in 1836 by K. N. G. Andresen, whose tracts remained in print for half a century; but they first gathered momentum in 1844, when they secured government patronage. By the end of the following year 14,000 persons had been brought together in 118 local groups, with a central organization which had a cabinet minister as chairman and A. M. Schweigaard (see note, p. 107) as vice-chairman. The result was the passage of two laws, one of which prohibited the use of small stills, such as formed part of the regular equipment of farms (including those of the official class); the other required distillers to retail their wares through authorized innkeepers, unless dealing directly with the consumer. Excesses which recall the 'Gin Lane' of Hogarth a century earlier now dwindled, though brandy remained the poor man's obvious remedy against the bitter northern winter. Consumption of brandy per head of population was reduced by about 60 per cent between 1833 and 1851; at the latter date the brandy, wine, and beer consumed was equivalent to 3·55 litres of pure alcohol, which remained almost exactly the average for the next three decades. The number of distilleries had sunk by mid-century from 1,387 to forty; breweries increased, but import figures showed that coffee now rivalled beer as a national beverage.

In 1842 the government substituted a new criminal code for the Law of Christian V (1687): this was more liberal than the laws in force in Sweden*—which was one reason for a delay in bringing it

* The government had been prompted by the Storting to submit a translation to four German jurists, who declared that the Norwegian code 'would take a leading place in European penal legislation'.[13]

forward: even for murder, capital punishment fell into disuse in Norway as early as 1876. A start was also made with the reform of the system of penal servitude, under which long-term prisoners were incarcerated in fortresses and brought out to work in public in heavy chains on the erection of the palace and other buildings. For the first time an attempt was made to reform the convicts—or at least prevent the spread of depravity—by isolating them in single cells, according to the Philadelphia system introduced by the Quakers in Pennsylvania. The new prison built in Oslo in 1851 was remarkable as one of the first of its type to be opened in Europe; but in spite of a one-third reduction in the length of sentence, complete isolation was found to have grave drawbacks.

A more clear-sighted humanitarianism could be seen in three other measures. In 1845, when poor relief was brought fully into the system of local self-government, all districts were obliged to reach at least a minimum standard. There was also a gradual rise in the expenditure on public health; in 1836 the number of district medical officers had been increased from forty-one to sixty-three, in addition to municipal officers in the four principal towns. And in the treatment of the insane Norway gave a lead to other states by its enlightened legislation of 1848, which was the almost single-handed achievement of Herman Major, the son of a refugee from the Irish troubles of half a century before. He introduced the principles of strict legal control over asylums and over the admission of their patients, supervision by a resident physician, and provision 'for the patients to lead a sociable life and have regular occupation.'[14] The first asylum to meet these requirements was completed in 1853 and is still in use; unfortunately, its founder had quarrelled with the authorities and was drowned next year, when his ship sank on the way to America.

Religious developments, however, had the most pervasive influence. In the first place, there was a movement towards toleration. By an unexplained oversight, the constitution had been passed without an intended declaration of freedom for all Christian religious bodies except the Jesuits and other Catholic Orders. In 1836 Ueland and other followers of Hauge's teachings proposed to let religious follow political freedom to the extent of abolishing the

Conventicle Ordinance of 1741, under which the clergy could in-
hibit the work of the Haugean lay evangelists; a successful opposition was headed by all the bishops except one and by the entire
theological faculty of the university. But lay evangelists had been
increasingly active since 1814, with the Bible Society helping them
to bring the Word into the remotest homes, and after six years the
peasants forced the abolition through the Storting. Ueland and two-
thirds of his followers were, however, hostile towards a subsequent
measure for freeing the Christian sects outside the state church,
which was carried by more liberal influence in 1845. It allowed their
members 'to practise their religion within limits of law and de-
cency',[15] with rights of civil marriage and exemption from religious
instruction for their children in attendance at state schools. Ueland
and his followers were again ranged among the anti-liberals in the
opening stages of a third religious controversy, when Wergeland in
1842 urged that the constitution should be modified so as to admit
Jews to the country. This did not achieve the necessary two-thirds
majority in the Storting until 1851, by which time sufficient peasant landholders had changed their minds to outweigh increasing
opposition from the trading community as well as many of the clergy.

In general, the middle decades of the century were remarkable
for the triumph of religious orthodoxy. This was achieved partly by
lay influences. For a time the broader views of the church and its
teachings, which Grundtvig had popularized in Denmark, enjoyed
a vogue among some clerics and in the new teachers' training colleges. But the more puritanical element among the laity organized
a successful nine-year campaign against a decree of 1843, which had
ordered the adoption of a revised version of Pontoppidan's hallowed
exposition of Luther's Catechism;[16] the revision followed Grundtvig's belief in the 'living word' as opposed to an exclusive reliance
upon the text of Scripture, and even presumed to omit the eight-
eenth-century bishop's universal condemnation of 'novels, dancing,
and the theatre'. The Haugean or (as they often called themselves)
the 'awakened' or converted laity were also the dominant force
in the Norwegian Missionary Society, which had been founded at
Stavanger in 1842, the year of the repeal of the Conventicle
Ordinance.

The biggest personal influence, however, was exerted by Gisle Johnson, who joined the theology faculty of the university in 1849 and inspired many generations of ordinands by his adaptation of the ideas of the great Danish philosopher, Kierkegaard, so as to provide 'a Lutheran orthodoxy in completely modern dress'.[17] Johnson was likewise the driving force behind a powerful Home Mission, based on a German model, which mustered the devout laity in local branches to preach the gospel and serve the poor. It did valuable social work among the neglected denizens of the slums in Oslo and other towns, but its most conspicuous mark was the 'prayer houses' (*bedehus*) for Bible classes and devotional meetings, which it built all over the country to provide for activities which were still legally banned from official church premises.

Since the employment of lay preachers did not altogether square with the Lutheran orthodoxy of which Johnson was a dedicated champion, he argued that it was legitimized by an 'emergency principle',[18] thus offending the most zealous devotees of ecclesiastical democracy as well as their conservative opponents, who claimed that the Augsburg Confession restricted the preaching ministry to the person who was *rite vocatus*. Politically, in fact, the church was deeply divided. A High Church party, in which the clergy themselves predominated, resented the intrusion of democracy into a sphere in which they had long ruled alone. To some extent they also objected to the power exercised by lay officials in the Department of Church Affairs, with whom they nevertheless joined in preserving the *status quo*. But the Low Church party drew much more extensive support from the traditional puritanism of the countryside, especially in west Norway; it nurtured a new class of peasant clergy, and men like Ueland demanded a system of congregational councils to provide the lay control appropriate to a 'people's church'. As regards religious belief, however, Norway more than almost any other state remained fully under the sway of orthodox Lutheran theology. As late as 1874—fifteen years after the publication of the *Origin of Species*—the author of an annual survey could still claim that 'The streams of unbelief which have passed over other countries have really not yet reached into our fiords and valleys.'[19]

TWO SOCIAL PIONEERS

Though lying on the periphery of Europe, Norway had inevitably felt some effects from the revolutionary ideas that spread from Paris and other centres during the disturbances of 1848. On the surface at least, the results were slighter than elsewhere, but they were in two respects remarkable. Norway experienced the only considerable labour agitation that was not based on industrial changes; and the leader, Marcus Thrane,* though fated to spend all his later years in complete obscurity, was among the most original and forceful figures in the history of pre-Marxian socialism.

He was born the son of a director of the Bank of Norway, who was dismissed for malversation of funds. Brought up in penury, Marcus made a poor living as a schoolmaster and in the eventful summer of 1848 was glad to accept a post as editor of a small news-paper in the timber port of Drammen, near Oslo. He used its columns to expound socialist ideas with which he had become acquainted ten years before on a visit to Germany and France, when he spent two months in Paris.[20] In Drammen, too, he started his first 'workers' union' for bringing together the unenfranchised labouring class on the Chartist model. Dismissed from his editorship at the end of the year, he moved to Oslo, and founded a propaganda paper on behalf of his unions, written with the homely argumentation of a Cobbett and embellished with cartoons which still amuse. He also toured many of the neighbouring counties, and even extended his activities to some extent to Sweden. The result was that by the summer of 1850 he had 273 unions with more than 20,000 members.[21] widely spread through eastern Norway and the Tröndelag; con-sidered in relation to total population, this was as significant a move-ment as any of those that had recently risen and fallen in other European states. The area through which the movement spread is also significant, for this was where the acute pressure of population

---

* 1817–90. After emigrating in 1863 he revisited Norway only once, to find that he had been forgotten. In America his socialist propaganda was persis-tent but aroused little interest, one of his last ventures being a play based on the anarchist trials after the Haymarket bomb explosion in Chicago in 1886. His remains were reinterred in the Grove of Honour at Oslo in 1949.

had compelled cottars to accept the worst conditions.* They paid for their *husmannsplass*—a tiny cottage, a scrap of land, and closely restricted grazing and wood-cutting rights—by an unlimited obligation to work for their farmer landlord at a fixed low rate of payment, which in some cases extended to obligatory work by a man's wife and children. Since the holding could be forfeited as soon as the cottar was past work, he often died a pauper, as outside earnings were usually confined to casual employment in forestry.

Thrane's theoretical teachings were based chiefly on Proudhon, though his emphasis upon the exploitation of the worker often recalls the early English socialists with their doctrine of the right to the whole produce of labour. His immediate programme was expressed in a petition to the crown, which was supported by an assembly in Oslo of more than 100 delegates. This called for manhood suffrage; the reduction of the cottar's obligatory work to a maximum of four eleven-hour days a week; facilities for the landless to obtain holdings; free trade in corn; and various other measures to alleviate distress.

After the government had rejected the petition, the movement tried to influence the Storting. The unions included an element of artisans who possessed the vote, and they helped to return a few urban radicals at the 1850 election. When the Storting met next year, the anti-government members expressed great indignation over the expulsion from Norway in May 1850 of a foreign ally of Thrane, a kind of lesser Mazzini from Schleswig named Harro Harring.† But there was no welcome for a delegation from a second, rather smaller, assembly of the unions, in which four groups—small farmers, cottars, artisans, and other employed persons—were about

* Out of the 65,600 *husmenn med jord* ('cottars with land') reported by the census of 1855, two-thirds were in east Norway or the Tröndelag; elsewhere they were to be found mainly on small farms, whose owners had little need for their work, so these cottars lived chiefly by fishing or other more or less independent activities. In addition, the census recorded 22,000 cottars without land, who may be defined as cottage-holding labourers.[22]

† 1798–1870. He went on to London, and wrote to Thrane offering to represent the Norwegian workers' unions at an international labour congress there in May 1851. Apart from his contacts with Sweden, this is the only known link at this time between Thrane and the international labour movement.

equally represented. The assembly went home disappointed, but the only overt action that followed was the so-called 'Hatter's War',[23] in which a militant tradesman was re-arrested after his rural supporters and quondam rescuers had run at first sight of soldiers sent from Oslo. But the king, the official class, the large farmers, and other property owners believed that they had narrowly escaped a socialist revolution. Every unguarded utterance from the assembly was therefore rigidly scrutinized without paying any heed to its lack of practical effect, and although a public subscription engaged the best advocate of the day for the defence, no fewer than 117 prison sentences were eventually confirmed by the Supreme Court. Thrane himself served a four-year term, including two years in the new-model prison which impaired his health; he emerged to find his followers cowed into submission, and soon afterwards emigrated to the freedom of the United States.

The only direct positive result of the movement was a government measure to better the condition of the cottars by providing for contracts in writing, for compensation to be made for improvements when they had to leave their holdings, and for the more general adoption of contracts for life. Some rural despots observed the law 'not more than they found practicable',[24] but the cottar system was in any case doomed to collapse as soon as the New World offered its victims an alternative to what was widely regarded as degradation. The example of this early struggle for the rights of man and a more egalitarian society also prepared the way for later developments in the fields of the modern co-operative and labour movements; sometimes surviving followers of Thrane took the lead. Lastly, we may note that the anxiety concerning the state of the poor, which was not entirely stifled by the silencing of Thrane, helped to engage support for the work of a second social pioneer, who commanded wider attention, at any rate among the ruling class.

Eilert Sundt,* who belonged to that class by aspiration but not by

---

* 1817–75. From the start of his observation of gipsies, by which he first made a name, Sundt interested himself in German, English, and French writing in the fields he explored. The fact that this pioneer sociologist had little impact in his own day outside Scandinavia may be attributed to the language

birth, was a provincial tradesman's son whose mother cherished ambitions for him to make a career in the church. He did well in his theological studies, but was inspired to his life work by an encounter with a gipsy in his Sunday-school class at the Oslo House of Correction, to which the unfortunate man had been consigned as the regular punishment for the evasion of Confirmation preparation. Sundt examined the existing literature of the subject, including the writings of George Borrow, and obtained a small government grant to study Norway's 1,145 gipsy and other vagrants in their nomadic activities. The result was a book published in 1850, which attracted some attention as far away as France and a salary from the Storting to enable him to undertake further studies of the life of the poor. By the end of the decade he had produced five more pioneer works, examining the death rate, marriage conditions, sexual morals, and inebriety in the country as a whole, and analysing in detail the poverty of one Oslo slum area.

Sundt's methods were remarkably modern in their scope. He read widely, undertook a historical analysis of census reports and other official materials, issued searching questionnaires of as many as 109 clauses to his clerical brethren, travelled assiduously to record experiences in all classes of society and in every region of Norway—and he never failed to present his results in a readable form. His observation was sharp, and he seldom allowed it to be blunted by religious predilections: demographers still recognize as Sundt's Law his discovery that the age groups in a population rise and fall like the tide, because any group that is unusually large or small tends to reproduce its relative dimensions after a period of between twenty-five and thirty years.[25] Moreover, his wide humanity and lack of class prejudice led him to formulate and publish some disagreeable though factual conclusions. If one birth in every eleven was illegitimate, the fault (he explained) lay partly with the poor accommodation on many farms, where servants of both sexes had to sleep in outbuildings which their employers did not supervise, and partly with the long delay before a young man

---

barrier, but the society he examined may also have been regarded as too small and untypical to deserve serious scrutiny.

could acquire a holding so as to set up a home. When his inquiries regarding 177,000 married men and widowers, which he made through the rural school teachers, revealed 3·8 per cent of unequivocal 'drunkards' and no fewer than 33·5 per cent who were 'unreliable',* he was prompt to point out that property holders contained the same proportion of drunkards as the workers and only 4 per cent less of the 'unreliable'. His study of Oslo slum conditions likewise served to demonstrate that the proportion of paupers in the capital, which was one-half larger than the national average (14·9 : 10·4 per cent), reflected the extreme poverty of the rural hinterland from which these unfortunates were in the main fairly recent immigrants.

In the 1860s Sundt's writings, published partly in *The People's Friend*, dealt on the whole with brighter themes—a historical exposition of Norwegian building traditions; an examination of fishing boats and ancillary equipment, demonstrating that the fisherman was just as skilled a craftsman as the agriculturist; a study of home handicrafts as a source of supplementary income; and an elaborate description of traditional housekeeping methods. Unfortunately, his assertion that these methods were on the whole hygienic made him unpopular with the medical profession, which feared that he would encourage conservative resistance to changes instigated by the new local health commissions (see p. 47). Other ill-informed attacks were launched against his work by farmers in the Storting, who misunderstood his methods and grudged the expense; they were supported by Johan Sverdrup (see note, p. 46) for opportunist reasons, and Sundt ended his days as a disappointed country clergyman.

He had once been a member of Thrane's workers' union in Oslo, and in 1864 he founded the 'association for workers' (*arbeidersamfunn*) there, a long-lived artisans' welfare institution which kept his memory green. In recent times, too, he has received international recognition as one of the more important precursors of the modern social scientist.[27] But Sundt made his biggest impact upon the

---

* The 'unreliable' category is defined as follows: 'When opportunity offers, at a celebration or on a trip to town, it happens only too often that he gets drunk.'[26]

Norwegian intelligentsia, the small but significant group of which he was himself an ornament. By narrowing the gap between town and country and helping to replace a vague romanticism by a more balanced appreciation of the social and economic conditions of rural life, he prepared the way for effective co-operation between the urban liberal and the peasant.

ORIGINS OF THE PEASANT-RADICAL ALLIANCE

In 1859, thirty of the forty farmer members of the Storting, who were still under the leadership of Ueland, linked themselves with a group of seven urban radicals in the Reform Union. The driving force was Johan Sverdrup,* whose first election in 1850 had been helped by the Thranite movement: he was a provincial solicitor, who had been in contact with peasant problems and grievances from an early age, as his father, Jacob Sverdrup, had been an estate manager and founder of the first private agricultural school in Norway. One reform that the union helped to carry reasserted the constitutional requirement that two-thirds of the *Stortingsmenn* must represent rural constituencies: this had been abandoned for the second time in 1842, when the Storting had been allowed to grow beyond the limit of 100 members to accommodate the growing numbers of qualified voters in the towns. The Storting was now fixed at 111 members, of whom the rural areas were to elect 74, and except for a readjustment to 114 and 76, made in 1876, these figures were left unchanged until the following century and the proportions until 1952. Thus the farmers were potentially the dominant force in the Storting, as Sverdrup fully realized. The Reform Union, however, is chiefly of interest as setting a precedent, for the feeling against parties was still so strong that it broke up within twelve months, when Sverdrup tried to insist that its members should vote according to the decision of the majority.

---

* 1816–92. Nephew of a classics professor who led the *Notabelmötet* (p. 6). His great skill as a parliamentarian has caused him to be described as 'Norway's Gladstone', but his inspiration came above all from the ideas of the French Revolution. A man of many followers and few friends, who was intensely ambitious and not always fastidious in his choice of means.

But co-operation between radical and peasant in the Storting furthered social progress in the countryside. In 1860 Health Commissions were introduced, which gave wide powers to the local authority, acting under the guidance of the district medical officer, in all matters of public health; decentralization has been a feature of Norwegian health organization ever since. A new Poor Law made the local community more clearly responsible than before for the welfare of orphans and the sick and aged; in 1873, ten years after its enactment, it began to be interpreted in favour also of the unemployed. But the biggest political consequences sprang from improvements to rural education, championed especially by Sverdrup's foremost ally, Johannes Steen,* who for a whole generation combined a grammar-school headmastership with a career in national politics.

Since 1848 the towns had been required to provide public elementary schools and properly paid teachers; these schools gave instruction to all children, except such as were educated privately, from the age of seven until they were confirmed. But Ueland and other peasant leaders had considered it too expensive to make the same provision for rural districts, where one-half of the children still depended upon peripatetic teachers, who imparted the rudiments to as many members of near-by families as could be spared from other work during their short stay in a particular farmer's household. In 1860, however, after examination of the Scottish system a new law was passed, requiring the building of a school wherever a minimum of thirty children could be assembled. Within twenty years the proportion of children dependent upon the travelling schools had dropped to one in twelve. The reading material in the primary curriculum was at the same time extended to include 'geographical descriptions, a knowledge of Nature, and history'.[28] A projected system of rural continuation schools unfortunately received little public support, so the 'peasant student', whose numbers had now risen to 11 per cent of the university enrolment, still suffered the handicap of a double migration—to a typical town

* 1827–1906. First elected to the Storting in 1859; gave up his school post on becoming prime minister in 1891. For many years Sverdrup's second-in-command, but personal relations were never close and eventually very hostile.

school, or a crammer's, in order to matriculate, and thence to over-crowded Oslo lodgings. But secondary education while remaining an urban monopoly was at least modernized by a measure in 1869, which introduced an intermediate school (*middelskole*) to fill the gap between elementary education and the final preparation for matriculation at the *gymnasium*—both name and pattern were German—and also allowed more scope for non-classical subjects.[29]

Two other educational developments influenced politics even more directly. One was the changing status of the rural school-master. The training colleges, which had been established in 1827 as diocesan seminaries for parish clerks as well as for the teachers in permanent elementary schools, had gradually given him a wider culture, which was accompanied by the growth of teachers' organizations and average earnings. Thus the teacher rose from one of the humblest to one of the most influential positions in rural society: but as he did not qualify for the franchise, he tended to become the natural leader for radical propaganda in his neighbourhood. The other, to some extent connected, change was the introduction of the Folk High School from Denmark. The three pioneers of the movement in Norway were a wealthy timber merchant's son, a Grundtvigian cleric who had fought for Denmark in the war of 1864,* and a farmer whose mother was a daughter of the parsonage*—a striking illustration of the extent to which the rural population still depended upon outside leadership. The Folk High Schools offered mainly residential courses of a few months' duration, designed to nourish the slow-moving peasant mind with what Gruntvig had called 'the living word', as expressed in lectures, free discussion, poetry reading, and song. Twenty were started in the first ten years (1864–74), but the difficulty of financing voluntary institutions even on a very small scale cut short the careers of many of them. They were not designed as a substitute for the stricter academic disciplines of the university, but were an almost ideal means of binding together the different elements in rural society, imparting to sons of cottars and labourers as well as substantial farmers a sense of individual worth, and inculcating the wider interests that made for a liberal

---

* Christopher Bruun (1839–1920), an unflinching idealist and champion of a 'people's church', provided a model for Ibsen's 'Brand'.

attitude in politics. The Establishment saw the danger and set up a rival system of county continuation schools, financed and governed by the state. But in 1877 these came under the county authorities, with the result that their general tone became almost as liberal as that of the institutions they had been designed to replace.

Political activity among the peasantry was greatly stimulated by the improvements in transport and communications, which gathered momentum about the middle of the century (see p. 112). Newspapers, for instance, penetrated to many of the remoter settlements, and a larger proportion of the population could attend the meetings of religious and social organizations. The 1860s accordingly witnessed an increased participation by rural voters at elections, but their attitude seems to have been dominated by the agricultural depression (see p. 122), which made the cry for economy in public affairs more popular than ever. Thus Sverdrup in 1863 found that most of the farmers in the Storting were no longer prepared to back his jury bill: an institution of an obviously democratic character, which would have increased the power of the peasants at the expense of the officials who sat on the bench, lost much of its appeal to the former because it would involve some extra public expenditure.

However, it was this cry for economy that two years later led to the foundation of the first nationwide organization of electors, styled 'the Friends of the Peasantry' after a movement that had prepared the way for the Danish constitutional reforms in 1849. Its leader, Sören Jaabæk,* was a self-educated farmer's son who, like Ueland, had become a teacher and married into property. He sat in every Storting from 1845 to 1891, but his influence reached its climax by 1871, at which date his organization comprised about 300 local groups and the paper that he edited had some 20,000 subscribers. His programme declared war on every form of alleged extravagance, from the cost of a salary for a prime minister in Oslo

---

* 1814–94. As a rationalist, he supported expenditure on popular enlightenment and on the university but incurred the relentless hostility of the clergy. His movement (*Bondevennerne*) was based on the little southern port of Mandal, which was in his constituency; his paper (*Folketidende*, the *People's Times*) was written mainly by himself, and showed a keen interest in Britain as well as in the United States.

to that of a modest travel award for Henrik Ibsen. But if Jaabæk was unreasonably hard on elderly officials and their widows—the cost of pensions had in fact fallen in forty years from 6·7 to 1·9 per cent of the budget—he and his followers also reduced the number of the agricultural schools, needed by their own class, from eighteen to six. Moreover, the programme included other liberal policies besides retrenchment, such as extension of the franchise, free trade, and freedom for private economic enterprise in general, with an exception in respect of a strict control of interest rates on behalf of the hard-pressed rural mortgagees.

Though Jaabæk's authority among the peasant members of the Storting was never unchallenged, he was the obvious successor to Ueland on his retirement in 1869. His impressive lack of personal ambition then paved the way for an alliance with the intensely ambitious Sverdrup. The latter had been exerting his influence chiefly through a small group of urban radicals—the *collegium politicum*, known also as the Attorney Party or even as Young Norway—who helped him to carry a Franchise Reform Bill through the Storting. Support came both from the towns and from enlightened elements in the countryside: the diocese of Trondheim, for example, sent in a petition bearing 1,028 signatures, of which 269 were those of teachers.[30] But the wealthier farmers of eastern Norway, always strongly represented in the Storting, were very loath to unchain the forces once released by Thrane. The bill therefore proposed an income qualification for voters of 100 dollars (£20) in country districts and twice as much in the towns, and was to apply in the first instance to local government elections alone. Even so, it was vetoed by the ministry and the changes adumbrated in 1869 had to wait until 1885.

In the same year, however, Sverdrup enjoyed his first big political success, when a bill for annual sessions passed the Storting by an 81 : 30 majority. This was the first important change since 1814 in the position of the legislature, and had been proposed twelve years earlier. It was now acceptable to ministers, partly because an annual budget was seen to be administratively convenient and obviated the need for special sessions, but chiefly because it appeared desirable for Norway to have a counterpart to the annual sessions of the newly reformed Swedish Riksdag. No one was quite sure what would be the consequences: Jaabæk, formerly an opponent of the measure, now thought that yearly meetings would facilitate a closer watch on public expenditure and more than recoup the extra expense, whereas the Conservative leader, Schweigaard, formerly a supporter, had turned against the idea as likely to render the parliamentary opposition increasingly formidable. Few, even among Sverdrup's radical followers, foresaw the rapidity with which the change would advance the cause of parliamentarism. As for 'the little general'[31] himself, his strategy and tactics were very adaptable: for him, this was merely the opening phase in a struggle for power between rival political forces, such as he knew had accompanied the development of self-governing institutions in France and other lands.

THE SUPREMACY OF PARLIAMENT ESTABLISHED, 1872–1884

The position of the executive in Norway was still very strong, for the ministers stood at the head of a paternalist system under which great economic advances had been made by their country and its status within the Union on the whole effectively protected. After 1869 the proportion of officials in the legislature—on whose support the government could normally rely—remained stable for a quarter of a century at one-fourth, while peasant members constituted one-half. In any case, ministers could reasonably claim that their position set them above party politics of any kind, as they were precluded by the separation of powers from any obligation to traffic with their enemies, or even with their friends, in the Storting. They were also set apart by their position as royal nominees in a community where other claims to social pre-eminence were very few. This, however, had not prevented them from developing much of the strength of a close corporation, whose will could prevail even against that of their royal master.

The strength they had acquired *vis-à-vis* the crown was clearly shown when Charles XV died in September 1872, five months after their first major clash with the Storting (described below). Oscar II was able to inaugurate his reign with the formal abolition of the post of stattholder, a concession which had been held up since 1859 through Swedish opposition (see p. 87); and he further conciliated the Storting by abandoning the recently reasserted right of the crown to terminate its sessions at any time after the statutory three months. But when the new king tried to get rid of Frederik Stang,* formerly minister of the interior, who had been head of the government since 1861 and had long been at loggerheads with the Storting, his colleagues stood by their chief. To change the entire ministry would have been a formidable task for which there was no precedent. Stang therefore became the first titular prime minister in Oslo, and did not retire until the autumn of 1880, when his health and spirits failed him after eight years of conflict in which king and ministers perforce stood together against the representatives of the people. A highly gifted administrator, who embodied in his person most of the virtues associated with the rule of an élite, Stang relished power; the obstinacy of old age further disinclined him to yield ground, even on such a disputable question as *statsrådsaken*— whether ministers should attend parliament—which provided the occasion for the forthcoming trial of strength. A good case could indeed be made for following the practice of other constitutional monarchies in linking the ministers more closely with the work of the legislature. The view that they should be entitled to take part in its debates but not to vote—which we may for convenience call the 'Inclusion Policy'—had been championed by Falsen in 1821 and had been discussed in every Storting since then. Stang himself in his university lectures on law had favoured the change, and in 1839 had ventilated the subject in the first number of the Scandinavian periodical, *Brage og Idun*. Sverdrup, on the other hand, was originally against the change, which was consistently opposed by Ueland. But in the new era of annual Stortings it became clear that the prime effect of Inclusion would be to increase the influence of the Storting on the ministers and not vice versa, whereupon Sverdrup became

* 1808–84. Reader in Law in Oslo University at twenty-one, government attorney at twenty-nine, and minister of the interior at thirty-seven; a dignified and conscientious head of 'a doomed regime', against whom the Storting demonstrated on his retirement by halving his special pension.

the foremost champion of the policy and Stang its committed opponent—unless, indeed, the Storting would agree to strengthen the executive in other ways.

It is tempting to imagine that the many Norwegian admirers of Gladstonian Liberalism wished to imitate the practices of Westminster: the word 'parliamentarism' figured in Vinje's *Dölen* (see p. 77) in the same year (1870) in which it made its début in the English press. But since both Sweden and Denmark at this time had seated their ministers in the legislature without the direct responsibility of ministers to parliament being established as in Britain, the aim of the Inclusion Policy should be envisaged as something very much vaguer. In an address to the crown on 15 May 1872, the Storting defined it as 'effective and lively co-operation between the powers of the state'.[32] This may be expanded to mean that in times of emergency—such as the recent bitter conflict with Sweden about the stattholdership (see p. 88)—the two powers should act together, and that at all times the contact between executive and legislative authorities should be closer than hitherto.

In 1872, when Ueland was dead and Jaabæk a convert to his own view of the matter, Sverdrup put an Inclusion Bill in the forefront of his programme and carried it by 80 votes to 29; this provided the two-thirds majority requisite for a constitutional change. Charles XV then interposed the veto, as desired by Stang on a temporary basis until additional measures had been devised so as to preserve the balance of the constitution. The more intransigent conservatives, headed by a professor of jurisprudence, T. H. Aschehoug,* wanted an Upper House, but in the absence of any aristocracy this could only have been based upon a special property franchise. Instead, Stang put forward a number of relatively modest changes— the crown to be entitled to dissolve the Storting and hold elections at any time; sessions to be restricted to four months; the crown to

---

* 1822–1909. A member of the Storting from 1869 to 1882 and Schweigaard's successor as the intellectual leader of the conservative element: 'The separation of powers is essential to human liberty.'[33] His handbook on the constitutional law of the Scandinavian states was translated into German in 1887, and he completed a standard four-volume work on economics at the age of eighty-six.

be entitled to give its decision on bills when the Storting was no longer sitting; allowances to members of the Storting to be kept below, and those to pensioned ministers above, a certain level. In the eyes of many conservatives these proposals seemed too weak, but they were in any case unacceptable to Sverdrup and his followers, for whom the whole bill and nothing but the bill had now become a matter of prestige and a test of the ultimate supremacy of the Storting. In 1872 he had already organized the presidents and deputy presidents of the Storting and its two subdivisions into a kind of collective leadership, designed to champion the legislature against the executive.

It is, however, easy to read into the situation an 'either-or' character which it did not at this stage possess. Although the 1872 election was the first at which the names 'Left' (*Venstre*) and 'Right' (*Höire*) came into fairly widespread use, and although the press was increasingly partisan, the number of peasant voters going to the poll continued to fall throughout the decade, in spite of the fact that the Storting connived at the enfranchisement of faggot-voters (*myrmenn*), who acquired minute parcels of registered land in order to qualify.[34] Moreover, each of the two groups in conflict in the Storting contained an element of moderates, amounting to one-quarter of the total membership in 1877 and one-fifth in 1880, who would gladly have co-operated with a ministry chosen from the Centre. A suitable leader was, indeed, available in the person of O. J. Broch,* a mathematician and economist of international reputation, who had been a popular member of the Storting before he became minister of marine in 1868, and who had eventually resigned office (with two of his colleagues) in protest against the vetoing of the Inclusion Bill in 1872. But officialdom had acquired a blinkered outlook. Stang let the opportunity for compromise pass, and the quarrel was soon exacerbated by the application of the veto to other measures which had passed the Storting, by a failure to come to terms over the long-overdue reform of the franchise, and

* 1818–89. Professor of pure mathematics at Oslo, 1856; member of the Storting, 1862–9. From 1879 until his death he was head of the International Bureau of Weights and Measures at Sèvres, whence he was summoned to attempt to form a government in June 1884.

by a series of collisions regarding matters of administration, where the Storting deliberately set itself up as a rival centre of authority.

In 1877 the Inclusion Bill was passed for a third time, but as the institution of a *statsminister i Oslo* had necessitated a slight rewording, it was not until 1880, when the majority had risen to 73 (93:20), that the suspensory veto ceased to be applicable. Stang, who in his law lectures had held the veto power to be in all cases merely suspensory, now declared that in constitutional matters it was absolute. But at this stage Sverdrup was able to rally the support of a considerable fraction of the more radical peasant members, popularly known as the Thirty Tyrants, who had been alienated for a time by his cautious attitude on the franchise. It is also likely that other, less politically minded rural representatives were becoming more closely interested in his plans for subordinating the executive to the legislative power, because they were very much alive to matters of economic planning (such as railway projects) which would have to be decided by a central authority. Be that as it may, on 9 June 1880 Sverdrup secured a solid majority of supporters for a resolution which directly challenged the legality of the veto by demanding that the ministers should now promulgate the Inclusion measure as a lawful constitutional enactment.

In doing so, Sverdrup raised the fundamental question of the character of the Norwegian constitution. Was it a contract between the executive and legislative powers, the terms of which could not properly be changed except by the consent of both parties? Or was it based directly upon the sovereignty of the people, which was also sovereign over the contract, so that the constitution could lawfully be changed in any of its parts in accordance with the popular will as expressed by the electorate and the elected? While expounding the latter proposition as a principle Sverdrup, who was a politician to his finger-tips, had other, more practical considerations in view.

He could inflame opinion by making this a national issue, since the veto was nominally, and to an undefined extent in practice also, the prerogative of a 'foreign' king, who was concerned above all to preserve his powers as constituting the chief link between his two kingdoms. Furthermore, it was an issue in which he could count on the support of youth against age—always an attractive rallying cry.

And whatever his argument might be, he could count on the support of the writers and other cultural leaders of the rising generation. The conservatives, indeed, mustered all the bishops, six professors, seventy-seven clergy (headed by Gisle Johnson), and 160 other notables as signatories of *An Appeal to the Friends of Christianity in our Land*, which was sent out as an apologia for their cause at New Year, 1883. The professor of philosophy at the university, the venerable Hegelian M. J. Monrad, even wrote an anonymous newspaper article, in which he recommended the authorities to get their way by means of a *coup d'état*. But these influences were very small in comparison with that wielded by the new school of 'realist' writers; most of them had radical political sympathies and all of them helped to create a climate of opinion which favoured sweeping changes (see pp. 251–259). Ibsen, for instance, surveyed Norwegian political life with detachment and from a distance: yet within five years of the publication of *A Doll's House*, women were being admitted to the 'private Liberal Club' in the tradition-bound city of Oslo. In the early 1880s both Jonas Lie and Kielland were writing brilliant novels which undermined the old order of society. As for Björnson, for better and worse his art was always at the service of his intensely felt political convictions of the moment. At this time he lived for the Left. In 1879 he broke with Christianity; in 1882 he broke with the monarchy; and in the same autumn he framed the battle cry which reverberated through the election: 'In Norway the Norwegian people shall be master, they and no one else, now and for ever'.[35]

The final trial of strength took the form of an impeachment of the ministers for misuse of the royal veto. The law professors of the university, led by Aschehoug, gave a unanimous opinion that there was no valid case against them. But the real trial took place beforehand at the bar of public opinion, since only an overwhelming electoral victory would enable the Left to pack the court with enough of its own supporters from the Lagting to outvote the professional judges; the attitude of the latter could be deduced from many past decisions, including two recent convictions of republicans on charges of *lèse-majesté*. The fateful electoral campaign of 1882 ran all in favour of the Left, which in February (1883) established a formal party organization in the Storting and twelve months later made it nationwide. The Right, which had begun to take shape in 1880 with an association of large farmers and local 'constitutional associations', now lagged behind: it did not set up a managing committee in the Storting until May 1884 or a regular party organization until August—when the game was lost. Stang's successor, Christian Selmer,* a little-known official who had been minister of justice since 1874, was a further handicap for the Right; even the king who chose him admits that he lacked 'extraordinary abilities'.[36] The partisan support that Oscar II gave to his ministers, both in a speech from the throne before the dissolution of the Storting and later on the occasion of the opening of a new railway, may also have made matters worse for them.

At all events, the Centre dwindled to six, and the twenty-six members of the Right were confronted in the new Storting by eighty-three supporters of the Left, made up of all the rural representatives and one-third of those sent by the towns. The result of the long trial that followed was therefore a foregone conclusion. All those ministers who had approved the use of the veto against the Inclusion Bill were sentenced to deprivation of office, while one minister who had opposed its use in 1880 and two others appointed later, who had only approved its use in lesser matters concerning financial appropriations and parts of a bill, were let off with a fine.

It may be accounted to the credit of the constitution, which is still revered by every Norwegian, that its lack of precision made it possible to effect the momentous transition to full parliamentary government without any formal breach. The situation had been very tense, since the king was widely expected to engineer a *coup* in his ministers' favour with help from the officers of the Norwegian army, who were overwhelmingly conservative, or even by marching in troops from Sweden. As a possible counterweight, in 1881 a school teacher had started a local association of volunteer

---

* 1816–89. A lawyer and magistrate from Drammen, which he represented in the Storting (1871–4) as a zealous supporter of the government. In 1884 he advised the king to retain the ministry in defiance of the impeachment, but he does not appear to have planned any clear course of action and was opposed by his colleagues.

rifle clubs (*folkevæpningssamlag*); the movement soon reached such dimensions that the royal veto was invoked to prevent a grant for their benefit from being included in the Budget. However, at the culmination of the trial the Norwegian army authorities went no further than to remove the bolts from stored rifles, put cartridge stocks out of harm's way, and load some of the cannons of the Oslo fortress. The judgement was followed, not by any attempt at a *coup* but by the retirement from office of each of the deprived ministers and a search for a solution under legal forms.

The indignant king first appointed a new cabinet under C. H. Schweigaard,* the son of the economist, who had entered the ministry in December 1880 and therefore had no responsibility for the vetoing of the Inclusion Bill. The Storting in reply showed its determination to remain master of the situation by calling the minister of war to account for the military precautions taken by his predecessor, whom it now planned to impeach. A cabinet of moderates was next projected under Broch. This solution was held up for a time, because the king impetuously declared that he would abdicate sooner than accept the condition that the cabinet must include supporters of the key resolution of 9 June 1880. This difficulty was smoothed over by balancing Right against Left in Broch's choice of prospective colleagues; but this promising venture failed almost fortuitously in the end, because no High Churchman would consent to serve in this ministry of reconciliation.[37] Thus King Oscar was eventually brought round to the acceptance of a ministry headed by Sverdrup and containing other 'men of June 9th', who clearly represented the new principle of ministerial responsibility to the Storting. Nevertheless, the legal issue of the king's right to veto constitutional changes was left discreetly in abeyance, while the continuance of his right to choose his ministers within broad limits was acknowledged by allowing him to exclude from office one of his most eminent—and most outspoken—opponents. This was Johannes Steen, whom the king with some apparent justification believed to have perjured himself as a witness during the impeach-

---

* 1838–99. Appointed prime minister on 3 April, tendered his resignation on 31 May. Later deputized for Emil Stang as Conservative Party leader in the Storting.

ment.* Seven years later, however, he was admitted as the second prime minister of the Left.

* Steen denied an allegation that on an occasion in 1880 he had expressed support for the absolute veto: only one out of three witnesses of the occurrence testified in his favour.[38]

3. Nationalism, Unionism, and Scandinavianism

THE UNION OF THE NORWEGIAN WITH THE SWEDISH crown has so far been considered chiefly as a factor that greatly affected the strength and influence of the executive power in Norway. But it also established a special relationship between the two peoples, whom the outside world often regarded as already one: they were clearly presented with an opportunity to develop the common monarchy into some closer form of association—if they wished. The failure to do so was due primarily to the acutely sensitive nationalism of many Norwegians: at first they feared an outright amalgamation that would swallow them up, and although their self-confidence soon increased, they never lost the fear that any closer form of union would involve some disparagement of the smaller nation.

Because the stronger power never seriously attempted to carry out an amalgamation, it is easy for historians to regard the fears of the Norwegians as unwarranted. In this connection it is important to notice that they had little direct contact with Sweden. Except among the farming population of the border districts and in the vicinity of seasonal trade fairs, the two nations had intermingled very little since the termination of the long series of wars between them in 1720. In the early years of the Union the evidence of diaries and letters shows that those Norwegians whose official duties took them to Stockholm seldom found the more elaborate society of the Swedish capital congenial. And at no time were the economic links that resulted from the Union close enough to give the smaller partner such benefits, for instance, as made the English connection appear worth while to so many Scotsmen. Accordingly, Norwegian assessments of the Swedish attitude to Union affairs tended to be determined by the crucial importance that the partnership had for their own development. For them, it was the framework within which their painful struggle to exercise their rights as a free nation was set—a predicament which they could never for a moment ignore. For the Swedes, the Union served primarily as the frame for their foreign and defence policy, its failure to fulfil larger hopes being seldom referred to. At the present day, Swedish accounts of the relationship with Norway take the line, 'Least said, soonest mended'—a homely philosophy which the Norwegians never shared.

THE SWEDISH 'PRESENCE' IN NORWAY

These Norwegian fears arose partly out of the immediate situation. The centuries-old association with Denmark had ended in a year of catastrophe, shock, and improvisation. Although the establishment of complete independence had quickly proved a chimera, only a minority followed Count Wedel in welcoming the new association with Sweden, the traditional enemy, whose troops stayed on Norwegian soil until late in the spring of 1815. The new Norway was very poor, and had still to build up nearly all its public institutions; in these circumstances Charles John's wealth bought him an influence which rumour exaggerated. As for his Swedish subjects, they would have been more than human if they had not at the back of their minds thought of Norway as a national compensation for the loss of Finland, awarded to them by the treaty of Kiel and secured, in practice if not in theory, by the convention of Moss. Prudence dictated silence about their future expectations, but the Norwegian public knew that the secretary of the Swedish committee that prepared the Act of Union had concluded a historical survey of the events of 1814 by looking forward to 'the time when Swedes and Norwegians stretch out their arms in brotherly feeling to become amalgamated into one people'.[1]

The feeling might be brotherly perhaps, but the Norwegians were acutely sensitive to the fact that it would be amalgamation with 'Big Brother'. In 1815 the Swedes were nearly three times as numerous as themselves (2,300,000 : 885,000). They had a much larger agricultural area, far greater mineral resources, and a rather more advanced industry. Their civil and military administration inherited strong traditions from the days when they had been a great power, and although the Riksdag with its cumbrous system of four estates still left the nobles in a strong position, its financial and legislative authority had been much increased by the constitution of 1809. Socially nevertheless, there was an implied threat to Norwegian peasant landownership in the influence, wealth, and supposed ambition of the Swedish nobility, who held great properties. Even in the cultural sphere, the difference of language was not large enough to obviate the possibility of eventual absorption by a nation that had made notable advances in the arts and sciences during the Gustavian era and whose poetry was just entering upon its golden age.

The constitution and the Act of Union together provided the Norwegians with strong barriers against any encroachment on their liberties, and it is significant that they asked and obtained the consent of the Swedish Riksdag to the insertion of a special precautionary clause in the act, which required any alteration to be carried in Norway (though not in Sweden) by the same elaborate procedure as a constitutional amendment. Since they had steadfastly resisted Swedish proposals for introducing a common citizenship or even facilitating naturalization, the Swedish 'presence' in Norway was reduced from the outset to the single supreme office of Stattholder; this post was not specified in the Act of Union, but the constitution expressly provided that Swedes were eligible for it. Given the aristocratic structure of contemporary European society, a wealthy Swedish nobleman might well appear to be the fitting representative of the common monarchy in its smaller, poorer, and more democratic component: yet it took the Norwegians only fifteen years to extrude the foreign body from their midst.

The four successive occupants of the makeshift 'palace' in Oslo— a single-storied mansion originally built for a timber merchant— were very different in character and outlook, but they had a similar disappointing experience. General Count von Essen, who had been designated as military governor of Norway a month after the signature of the treaty of Kiel, played little active part in Norwegian politics or society, accepting no more than the duty to reside as long as was required of him among 'this dark, wild people',[2] upon whom he reported faithfully week by week to his prince. After less than two years he was replaced by a second elderly nobleman of ancient lineage, Count Mörner, whose lavish hospitality brought him many friends but little political influence. His resignation was accepted only two years later because he had failed to foresee the peasant disturbances, but he had also incurred the disfavour of Charles John by unmasking his secret agent* who had perhaps encouraged them.

The third stattholder, Count Sandels, was an active politician—a member of a recently ennobled family, a hero of the Finnish War of 1808–9, an experienced administrator, and a confidant of Charles John. He held office for nine years, assisted materially with the settlement of the Danish debt (see p. 64), and gave his colleagues in the cabinet the benefit of his long experience of affairs—which Wedel rewarded by nicknaming His Excellence 'His Pestilence'.[3] Like his predecessor, he spent freely on political entertainment and he experimented with a club for Storting members on palace premises, but this did not prevent the Storting from persisting with a reduction in his salary. In the end he lost the confidence of his royal master, who feared that he was too much in sympathy with the Norwegians: in 1827 he even believed that he had brought the king round to his own view that there was nothing disloyal intended in their celebrations of May 17th as the anniversary of their constitution, which merely happened to coincide with the long-forgotten accession of King Christian Frederick. Accordingly, Sandels was replaced in January 1828 by Count von Platen, who had planned the union of Norway and Sweden with Wedel as far back as 1810, the year in which he also started his life work on the Göta Canal. His instructions stressed the undesirability of any further celebrations of May 17th, and in March he urged the king to use force if there was no other way of overcoming the general opposition in the Storting, 'which apparently aims at attacking the king's rights . . . with a view to placing the people under the most frightful of all yokes, the yoke of an aristocracy of lawyers in office'.[4]

That year Charles John intervened in Oslo in person, as we shall see in another context (p. 69), but in 1829 a further ebullience of

* C. H. Röslein, whom Mörner deported from Norway in March 1817, was a subordinate Swedish civil servant, employed by Charles John to sound out opinion among the peasants. Another such agent was reported to be in Bergen the following summer, and it is believed that Charles John used the private reports obtained in this way as a check on his higher officials, in accordance with French practice.[5]

nationalist feelings on May 17th resulted in the complete discomfiture of the stattholder. A private celebration of the anniversary by about thirty students was frowned upon by the authorities, but it helped to create an atmosphere of excitement among the crowd which had gathered for its usual Sunday evening entertainment of watching the arrival of the paddle steamer *Constitution* (see p. 112). Von Platen himself was on the quay, not in uniform but wearing the star of his order, and the people made way for him with customary respectfulness. Since the streets were still thronged at the unusual hour of 10 o'clock, a legal proclamation requiring people to go home was read in the market place, which was subsequently cleared by troops, and soon after midnight the little town was quiet. The military were under the command of Wedel's brother, but the stattholder had given his approval for the action, on which he reported to the king next day: not one casualty had been brought to hospital and not even a window had been broken. Nevertheless an official public inquiry, in which more than 300 witnesses were called, served to build up the 'Battle of the Marketplace' as a kind of Peterloo. Von Platen, who died before the end of the year, was made a scapegoat for all the authorities concerned. From that time no Swedish stattholder was ever appointed: modern Norwegian historians attribute to the enthroned French marshal the belief that 'To place a Swede in the post would represent a challenge to Norwegian opinion which might be dangerous'.[6] Be that as it may, the office was given to a Norwegian in 1836, and twenty years later it was allowed to fall into disuse. Thus for five sixths of the total duration of the Union, there was not even an outpost of Swedish influence in Norway.

A VIGILANT NATIONALISM

In other matters besides the Swedish 'presence' in their country, the attitude of the Norwegians during the early decades of the Union were characterized by a nationalism which was always vigilant but sometimes impolitic. The latter feature is well illustrated by the history of the debt settlement with Denmark. The treaty of Kiel had provided for the national debt incurred by Denmark–Norway to be divided between the two, but the Norwegians claimed that they were not bound by the treaty, since the king had no right to cede their country without the consent of its inhabitants. This legal argument was reinforced by counter-claims for the return of the ancient Norse Atlantic colonies of the Faeroes, Iceland, and Greenland, which had not been specifically included in the cession, and of Norwegian archives and other state property accumulated over the centuries in Copenhagen. But considerations of equity favoured the Danish case, and the refusal to recognize the Kiel treaty might mean that Norway was still in the eyes of international law united with Denmark. Their desperate poverty therefore prompted the Norwegians to fall back upon the argument that, as the Kiel negotiations were conducted on behalf of the Swedish state, financial responsibility rested with the Swedes.

A good many Swedes would have welcomed this solution as a means of securing an increased influence on the affairs of Norway, but Charles John—who found the Swedish nobility powerful enough already—saved the Norwegians from a remedy that might well have been against their own long-term interests. The discussions were therefore allowed to drag on until the powers began to press for a settlement. In July 1818 a meeting summoned by Lord Castlereagh in London hinted at a retransfer of Norway to the Danish crown as the ultimate resort, but the matter was referred to the forthcoming congress at Aix-la-Chapelle, where the five powers agreed to address letters of remonstrance to Charles John. He then forestalled further trouble by asking for British mediation, and in September 1819 an agreement was negotiated in Stockholm under the auspices of the British minister there, with the Danish minister, the Swedish foreign minister, and a Norwegian official participating. Charles John agreed on behalf of his Norwegian subjects to pay the sum of 3,000,000 dollars in ten years with interest at 4 per cent: the total debt before apportionment between the two states was 25,000,000 dollars.

The Storting of 1821 expressed much ill will towards Denmark, resentment against the pressure exerted by the powers, and to some extent a wish for Sweden to share the burden. One opposition spokesman even declared that he 'would much rather see Norway more closely united with Sweden or even, as they call it, amalgamated with Sweden, than have to listen to threats every minute of . . . war and other possible disasters for the country'.[7] Although a statesmanlike speech from the veteran C. M. Falsen carried the day and, after an ineffectual request for an extra twenty years in which to pay, the payment was made at last, two other events of the same year show that the 'amalgamation' which sprang so readily to the lips of the more impulsive members of the Storting was still one of the alternatives that their king had in mind for them.

On 1 June 1821, while the decision about the debt was still in doubt, Charles John had addressed a Circular Note to the powers, indicating that, if the Storting remained obdurate, he might be obliged to impose certain modifications of the Norwegian constitution by unilateral action. The terms of the Note were not generally known until many years later (though the Stattholder was given a copy to use at his discretion), but the steps taken by the Holy Alliance to suppress constitutionalism in southern Europe at this time suggest that they might have supported even an upstart northern king, if he had taken a strongly reactionary line with his contumacious subjects. Later in the same summer, the king held joint manoeuvres with Swedish and Norwegian troops and a Swedish naval squadron in the vicinity of Oslo. Although they had been planned as early as April and may have been designed in part to discourage intervention by the powers so long as the royal authority was not directly challenged, he indicated in a letter to his son Oscar that picked reinforcements had been stationed on the Swedish border ready to cross. Furthermore, the Norwegian troops mustered for the manoeuvres contained a body of officers whom the king had actually to restrain from demonstrating in his support.

Nevertheless, Charles John had recently shown some sympathy with Norwegian nationalist aspirations by authorizing the use of a purely Norwegian flag on the shorter trade voyages—those where it was not necessary to prove the connection with Sweden in order to benefit from the heavy payments made for immunity from the Barbary pirates. He showed the same conciliatory tendency when he quickly abandoned the proposal of a press censorship to damp down expression of anti-Swedish sentiments. On the other hand, he alarmed the Norwegians by his many proposals for amending their constitution, especially the two in which he persisted longest, namely that he should have an absolute veto on legislation and the right to create a new hereditary nobility. Both these changes would have assimilated Norwegian to Swedish institutions, especially as the new nobles might have been used to recruit a Second Chamber, which would bring the Storting more nearly into line with the four estates of the Riksdag.

Justifiably or not, the Storting continued to fear amalgamation and adopted a policy of strict constitutional conservatism as its only sure defence, even when the king's proposals included expedients which might have proved valuable, such as a power to hold additional elections or modifications in the court for trying impeachments. Treating the constitution as a palladium of national rights and liberties, the Storting of 1824 rejected each amendment unanimously. In 1827 the king withdrew them from consideration pending a more favourable opportunity; but no progress was made with them in the Stortings of 1830 and 1833, and in 1836 the subject was shelved without much discussion in a manner that (as we shall see) aroused the king's intense indignation. From 1830 onwards the Liberal opposition was a factor of importance in Sweden, but the extent to which his Swedish subjects as a whole would have backed him against the Norwegians in earlier years remains uncertain. 'The scope of Swedish amalgamation plans in the decade after 1814 has never been satisfactorily examined', says a recent official history of the Storting; 'That such plans were considered at the top level in Sweden is however indubitable.'[8]

In 1827 the Storting marked its adoption of a more self-assertive attitude by staking out a claim for Norwegian participation in the foreign policy of the United Kingdoms. In this field the constitution offered no guidance, since in May 1814 it had seemed best to leave King Christian Frederick a free hand in dealing with the tangled international situation. The Act of Union was likewise silent, perhaps because the Norwegians in 1815 shrank from involving themselves in more than the bare minimum of joint organizations. At all events, Charles John's practice of conducting his own foreign policy, with such assistance from the Swedish foreign minister as suited his convenience, had been tacitly accepted by his Norwegian subjects.

But the Storting now seized its chance when the king laid before it a series of trade treaties and an important agreement signed with Russia in 1826, by which Norway secured one-third of three border districts in the far north previously held in common. Instead of expressing appreciation, as expected, the Storting set up a special committee to examine the treaties—and called attention to a long-standing grievance concerning the 'Bodö Case'.

The establishment of Bodö in 1816 as a new trade port for North Norway had attracted a British export firm, on which the Norwegian authorities were prompt to pounce with well-justified charges of large-scale smuggling. After using violence to effect their escape from what they called 'a remote and inhospitable quarter of the globe',[9] the British presented inflated counterclaims through diplomatic channels, and were eventually (June 1821) granted an indemnity of £2,500 in cash and £15,500 in customs exemptions. Although the matter had been discussed in the joint cabinet, the British minister in Stockholm conducted his negotiations exclusively with the Swedish foreign minister; indeed when the king offered the excuse that he had difficulties with his Norwegian ministers, 'mais qu'il leur ferait entendre raison', the British rejoinder was 'that we recognized no separate government of Norway'.[10]

It was natural that the Norwegians should believe that a settlement that was manifestly unjust must be due to Swedish neglect of Norwegian interests. The Swedish authorities had indeed sympathized with the British view of North Norway as a kind of no-man's-land, where the rights of foreigners could not safely be left for determination by the native law courts. But the effrontery of the British claimants made the truth very hard to disentangle, and the Swedish negotiators were handicapped by consideration for interests which were of as much concern to Norway as to their own country. For Britain openly threatened them with special reprisals against the timber trade of both kingdoms, and they also risked forfeiting her implied political support as a counterweight to the Holy Alliance. Some share in the blame probably attaches to the inexperienced Norwegian cabinet, which was very dilatory in collecting information and in laying it before the king. Certainly, it failed to take any effective action in 1833, when one of the British merchants involved brought to light the fact that the demands for compensation had been based on forged documents, obtained by a certain F. G. Denovan—in 1833 police inspector of Glasgow—through collusion with a minor Norwegian official in Oslo. But it was as an anti-Swedish theme that the Bodö Case lived on for generations, while its immediate effect was to cause the Storting of 1827 to refuse an increased contribution to the foreign-affairs expenditure of the United Kingdoms pending an increase in Norwegian influence on policy. The king replied by a sharp reminder of 'Norway's smaller capacity for contributing to the expenses of a war',[11] which must logically restrict that influence.

A more significant clash followed over what might seem to be a mere symbol. In 1824, a decade after the event, Norwegians had begun to celebrate the anniversary of the adoption of the constitution on May 17th, and in 1827 (as we have already seen) Stattholder Sandels had rashly given his tacit approval. This excited Charles John's displeasure to such an extent that in 1828 he informed the leaders of the Storting that its decision to join in these celebrations in the previous year ranked, together with his entry into war against his native France and his setting foot on Norwegian soil 'sword in hand',[12] as one of the three most painful experiences in his life. Why so much pother about a mere anniversary? To some extent the answer probably lies in events abroad, especially in Germany, which made it politic for Charles John to indicate support for Metternich's view of popular national celebrations as a threat to the conservative cause in Europe. Certainly, too, there was an element of direct personal resentment of Norwegian ingratitude for what he had done to establish their liberties. But the desire to celebrate May 17th rather than November 4th, when the Union was inaugurated, also signified a more general obstacle to the king's hopes for his kingdoms: nationalism was proving to be a plant of much more vigorous growth than unionism.

When he summoned the Storting to an extra session in the spring of 1828, Charles John apparently contemplated meeting defiance by a *coup* to put through his constitutional amendments. A Swedish frontier regiment was placed under marching orders, and preparations were made for throwing a pontoon bridge across Svinesund, the narrow fiord at the border. But the Storting gave way. After the harangue referred to above, it resolved unanimously to ignore May 17th; it also augmented its foreign affairs contribution by 40 per cent. Next year, however, when the king had already shot his bolt in the struggle, national feeling reasserted itself almost fortuitously in the challenge to von Platen's authority at the 'Battle of the Marketplace'. The mock-heroic episode, which has been described already, secured tacit acceptance of the Norwegian people's claim to celebrate May 17th—and the lesson in the dynamics of nationalist propaganda was not lost upon them.

In 1830, and again in 1833, a lawyer with a strongly nationalist outlook, J. A. Hielm, raised in the Storting a demand for equal rights in the control of the foreign policy of the United Kingdoms. In 1830 a new regulation conceded some influence on consular business, but matters did not come to a head until 1834, by which time the effects of the July Revolution in France had driven Charles John so completely into the conservative camp that Norwegians feared he might side with Russia in the event of an Anglo–Russian war over the fate of the Ottoman Empire. In that year the ministry addressed formal demands to the king, first regarding consular transactions and later regarding diplomatic affairs in general. Next March the king accepted the request that a Norwegian minister should be admitted to meetings of the Ministerial Council, at which he had hitherto discussed the foreign policy of the United Kingdoms with the foreign and one other Swedish minister. The position was still unequal, not only in number of representatives but because the Norwegian minister was entitled to be summoned only when the business directly concerned the foreign policy of Norway. Nevertheless, this arrangement, which was left undisturbed until 1905, was the greatest organic advance achieved by Norway within the union. Early in the following year provision was also made for consuls to be appointed by the joint cabinet and sworn in as officials of both kingdoms.

The immediate sequel, however, was the third and last of the periodic crises in which Charles John registered his accumulated dissatisfaction with Norwegian obstinacy and ingratitude. Whilst its constitutional committee continued to press for further alleviations of inequality in Union matters, the Storting on this occasion

dismissed the royal amendments for the constitution without allowing two of them the customary courtesy of formal reference to the
committee. In early July 1836 the king suddenly dissolved the
Storting, which before dispersing laid an impeachment against
Lövenskiold, who as minister-resident in Stockholm had approved
his decision. Charles John was supported by his Swedish advisers,
and although no European power is known to have given its approval,
the unsettled condition of Europe at this juncture would perhaps
have made a firm demonstration of authority in the north not unwelcome. Carl Löwenhielm, a Swedish noble of long political experience, who advised that 15,000 troops would suffice to enforce
the king's wishes regarding the Norwegian constitution, favoured
prompt action on the ground that, before the next Storting met, the
assassination of Louis Philippe might set Europe ablaze. However,
when the Norwegian court fined Lövenskiold for backing up the
king, the latter did not resort to the *coup* that many people feared.
Instead, he recalled the Storting in October to listen to a speech
from the throne extolling the Union, which 'gave Norway a permanent position among the independent states of Europe, provides
the surest guarantee for the political freedom of the nation, and is the
lever which powerfully and effectively influences the growth of its
wealth and prosperity'.[13]

The legislators were not wholly convinced; they continued to list
the signs of inequality in flags and other symbols of sovereignty and
to press their criticisms of the new diplomatic arrangements. Wergeland, with the insight and irresponsibility of a true poet, had gone
further, urging in a propaganda leaflet that, as companions for Norway in a union, the Swedes were too strong and at the same time
too much hampered by their aristocratic form of society: 'Separation? That was a thought!'[14] Yet, inasmuch as the monarchy never
again attempted to amend the institutions enshrined in the constitution of Norway, it was plausible to suppose that a process of
trial and error was creating a satisfactory basis for a stable relationship between king and people.

THE UNION STABILIZED IN AN AGE OF CULTURAL GROWTH

From 1837 onwards the Union enjoyed its period of greatest stability. In the 1840s liberal influences were modifying the character of Swedish society, so that in such matters as local government, education, the criminal code, and craft regulations it became more like the Norwegian. Oscar I's liberal tendencies led him to inaugurate his reign in 1844 by making concessions to Norwegian sensibilities over the royal title, which was to be 'King of Norway and Sweden' in all Norwegian references, and over the claim to a half-share in the union coat of arms. The use of the Norwegian trade flag, authorized for all waters in 1838, was now extended to warships, though satisfaction was damped by its being redesigned so as to yield one-eighth of its space to a union symbol. And in 1847 the Order of St. Olav was introduced, which made it unnecessary for successful Norwegian officials to be honoured with Swedish insignia.

Several of these minor matters were the subject of recommendations from the (first) Union Committee of five members from each kingdom, which Charles John, after long hesitation, had appointed in 1839, on the proposal of his Norwegian ministers and in response to further complaints from the Storting about inequality. Its powers were widened in 1843 to cover the Union as a whole, and next year it produced a 150-paragraph draft for a new Act of Union, from which only one member (a Swede) dissented. The first paragraph describes the two kingdoms as 'indissolubly united under one king, with mutual equality and co-ordinated position, as defined more closely in this Act of Union'.[15] The foreign minister might be either Swedish or Norwegian at the king's discretion, but he would have a deputy from the other nation and would be answerable to a jury nominated equally by each legislature. Three types of joint cabinet were proposed, each based on equal representation but controlling different aspects of union business. Even the common expenditure, whose burden was to be shared in proportion to population, was to be controlled by a congress in which the two legislatures held the same number of seats. Thus the principle of equality was worked out in painstaking detail, which makes it at first sight surprising that the report got no further than the respective governments.

Norwegian ministers took two and a half years to favour their Swedish colleagues with their comments, by which time the latter had lost interest.

The Swedes, busy with their own internal problems, had no particular incentive to give the smaller partner additional weight in common affairs and risk a quasi-federal experiment. It is more interesting to notice that Norwegian opinion was already dividing along lines that persisted until 1905. One section was prepared to accept a closer union, implying a more closely integrated foreign and defence policy, as the price to be paid for achieving a status of full equality in the law and practice of the Union. The other section, which gained strength as Norwegian society became more democratic, shrank from any measure, however equitable, that tended to make the Union closer: its arguments were often factitious, but its appeals to sentiment unfailing. Nevertheless, the balance of opinion in both countries was now friendly towards the Union in its existing form. Norwegians felt more confidence in an institution that had survived the turmoils of a generation, while the Swedes were making fewer references to their rights under the treaty of Kiel: perhaps it was significant that in 1836–7 an optimistic survey of Union affairs by the editor of the Swedish liberal periodical *Argus* had reached two editions. Moreover, the detail of common business was often handled more smoothly, as the sovereign in both kingdoms became more dependent upon his ministers, who got to know their opposite numbers better and in some cases developed a personal intimacy which augured well for the future.

Meanwhile, many Norwegians were acquiring a greater confidence in their own cultural inheritance, so that they became less apprehensive of losing the national identity through submergence in a larger unit. This was above all the achievement of Henrik Wergeland, who wished to be judged as a 'poet and nothing else'[16] but whose life had a wider impact than his poetry. This included a rather chaotic epic, *Creation, Man, and Messiah* (first published in 1830, when he was only twenty-two), a number of plays and farces, and many lyrics; but although the debt to Shakespeare, Byron, and other foreign models is very evident, very little of it has been translated and even in Norway 'only a few of his poems have become a national possession'.[17] The range of Wergeland's prose work deserves emphasis: he wrote a series of books of popular instruction (*For the Common People*, 1830–9), edited two radical periodicals, produced six annuals (*For the Working Class*, 1839–45), and traced the history of the Norwegian constitution. As for his life, this had many facets. Wergeland was a bohemian: the son of a well-known cleric, he studied theology, but his propensity for riotous living made him unacceptable in the church; he married happily but outside his class, and his only child was an illegitimate son, born in his father's parish. He was a strident opponent of Danish influences in language and literature, who repaid with interest each critical onslaught on his own less disciplined style of writing made by his university contemporary and poetic rival, Welhaven (see note, p. 78). He was a radical politician and an instinctive democrat, who employed all his talents as writer, speaker, and agitator to rouse the slumbering masses, but who could also forfeit his popularity for a time by accepting both a pension and a post as archivist from the hands of the king. He was also a citizen of the world, who admired the liberty he saw behind 'the white cliffs of Dover'* and still more that of revolutionary France, and who agitated for many years to secure the admission of the Jews to Norway. He was a sensitive observer, too, of the world of Nature, who wrote his finest lyrics from an untimely death-bed, sighing for the flowers of the summer he would not live to see. But every other aspect of his personality contributed to the impact he made as a Norwegian patriot, who believed with the intensity of genius in a great future for his small country. Half a century after he had been laid in his grave in 1845, Björnson wrote of him: 'His dreams are those of our own young freedom. All that is promising for its future was first given form by him, or was prophesied by him, or was blessed by him.'[18] †

The national romanticism, which swept over Europe in Wergeland's lifetime, inspired certain other manifestations in Norway,

---

* English south-coast scenery figures prominently in his 4,000-line narrative poem *The English Pilot*, which ends however with a rapturous landfall in 'divinely beautiful Hardanger'.

† The impression that Wergeland made on later generations is also conveyed by Vigeland's statue (Plate 14).[19]

whose effects on the outside world will be examined in a later chapter
(see p. 238). Here we may only notice that in the 1830s Norway's
first great painter, J. C. Dahl, and the violinist, Ole Bull, revealed
the deep-hidden beauties of their native country to a wider public,
and that their efforts were continued by a whole school of landscape
artists, by Norway's first romantic composer, Halfdan Kjerulf, and
by the collectors of folk melodies. In the 1840s, too, Asbjörnsen and
Moe began their epoch-making publication of fairy tales, and in the
1850s both Ibsen and Björnson employed their dramatic talents to
recreate for the national imagination the greatness of medieval
Norway.

The concern for history as a direct stimulus to national feeling
had been strikingly exemplified by Christie (see p. 14), who from
1825 onwards devoted himself for nearly a quarter of a century to
the task of assembling Norwegian antiquities for the museum that
he founded in Bergen. A growing interest in historical research led to
the establishment in 1832 of 'The Society for the Language and
History of the Norwegian People' (*Samfunnet for det norske Folks Sprog
og Historie*); its 550 members were drawn mainly from the official
class, but more than one-third of them resided in rural areas where
their influence would be widely diffused. 'The Association for the
Preservation of Ancient Monuments' (*Foreningen til norske fortidsmin-
nesmerkers bevaring*) followed in 1844, and provision was made soon
afterwards for commencing the publication of medieval laws and
other documents.

The task of the historian was unfortunately rendered more difficult by the dispersal of Norwegian records among Danish and other
foreign archives as well as by the circumstance that interest was
naturally concentrated upon the remoter periods of history, in
which Norway had figured most prominently. The first product of
such studies was J. R. Keyser's work, *The Origin and Racial Affinities
of the Norwegians* (1839), which by an unlucky chance propounded
the theory that Norway had been first populated by immigrants
entering from the far north, so that its people were more purely
'nordic' than the Swedes or Danes. This view was taken up by a
more eminent successor, P. A. Munch, who persisted with it long
after the archaeological and other new evidence had made informed

opinion sceptical. But both Keyser and Munch ministered more
effectively to patriotic feeling by emphasizing the fact that the rich
saga literature of medieval Iceland was an Old Norse, not an Old
Scandinavian, inheritance. Munch was a tireless researcher, with a
talent for unearthing fresh sources and exploiting them to the full;
his 8-volume *History of the Norwegian People*, published in 1851–63,
became the main authority for their history down to the Union of
Kalmar in 1397, and he further vindicated his country's importance
as a historical force in thirty-six minor works and a wide correspondence.

Language reform was another cultural interest that developed in
Norway at this time—and has never lost its grip. The separation
from Denmark led many patriots to look askance at the dependence
of educated speech and writing upon what could be regarded now as
a foreign language, though Danish was pronounced in a distinctive
Norwegian way and was diversified by some characteristic Norwegian words and expressions. One remedy was to increase the
native element by a gradual introduction of rural phraseology,
wherever it suited the subject matter. Wergeland was eager for this,
and it was a widely appreciated feature in the writings of Asbjörnsen
and Moe. The more drastic alternative was to build up a new
language out of the Norwegian of the middle ages, surviving in rural
dialects which had been little affected by the long Danish ascendancy. Munch, indeed, suggested at one time that such a language
might be modelled directly upon Old Norse literature; but the lead
was taken by an autodidact of genius, who based his work upon
living dialects, especially those of his native west Norway, and
employed Old Norse chiefly as a standard by which to judge the
purity of words and forms still in use.

Ivar Aasen was a cottar's son, born in 1813 in a fiord district south
of Ålesund. He became a rural school master, learnt five foreign
languages, and in 1836 began to plan 'an independent and national
language' for Norway. After extensive field studies in western districts and a few of the eastern valleys, he published a grammar, a
dictionary, and a third volume containing samples, which by 1853
had effectively launched his concept of *landsmål* or neo-Norwegian,
known since 1929 as *nynorsk*. Though he was a poet of some distinc-

tion, Aasen was primarily a philologist, who continued to influence his fellow scholars while living as a recluse in Oslo for many years before his death in 1896. The language conflict was made much more acute by another cottar's son turned teacher, A. O. Vinje,* who in 1858–70 employed the new language in *Dölen* (the *Dalesman*), a periodical which he wrote single-handed and published at irregular intervals. Vinje's life was embittered by poverty and failure, but his lyrics and his descriptions of the countryside, in which he loved to roam, showed the aesthetic potentialities of *landsmål*. Its development was to become increasingly involved with the social claims of the peasantry, which resented polite urban speech not merely for its foreign origins but also as a mark of class distinctions; yet there can be no doubt that the language movement did much to foster national feeling and one of its constituent elements, the pride of locality.

SCANDINAVIANISM AND THE CRISIS OF 1848–1849

The Norwegians of that time did not only look inwards; many of them believed that both their cultural and political development depended also on their reaction to outside influences, especially from Denmark, with which their country had been so long associated. The nature of the association had indeed changed, but ties still existed which were to help the growth of Scandinavian sentiment.

Political relations had been clouded after 1841, not only by the debt question but also by Charles John's suspicion that, in spite of its evident weakness and poverty, Denmark aimed secretly at the recovery of Norway. It was to prevent Danish infiltration into official posts that he demanded a veto on naturalizations; he even delayed the charter of Oslo University because it was styled *Universitas Regia Fredericiana* in commemoration of its Danish founder. Traditions of grasping Danish officials lived long in the Norwegian countryside, and in 1816 Nicolai Wergeland, father of the poet and one of the constitution-makers at Eidsvoll, published *The Political Crimes of Denmark against Norway*, which carried the general allegations of

* 1818–70. He wrote a highly critical account in English of a journey from London to Edinburgh, which he made mainly on foot (*A Norseman's View of Britain and the British* (Edinburgh, 1863)).

oppressive conduct as far back as the year 955. On the other hand
an influential publicist belonging to the older generation, many of
whom had spent impressionable years of their youth as students in
Copenhagen, could write in 1833 of strong ties which had nothing to
do with politics past or present but were 'a consequence of remembered joys and heartfelt gratitude for benefits and friendship,
of which no Norwegian need be ashamed.'[20] Politically, too, the
picture of Denmark began to be modified the following year, when
the introduction of the Consultative Estates marked the beginning
of the trend away from autocracy; still more, when Norway's
quondam king ascended the throne in 1839 as Christian VIII and
aroused great expectations among Danish liberals because of his past
achievement in 'granting a beloved brother country the constitution
which has called forth its slumbering energies'.[21]

Meanwhile, in the world of the arts Norway's need for continued
study of Danish literary models was stoutly championed by Wergeland's rival, Johan Sebastian Welhaven,* whose assiduously polished
verses at their best showed no lack of true poetic feeling. In the early
1830s his attitude to Wergeland and his more or less disorderly
associates was shared by a group of fellow students, the so-called
'Intelligence Party', headed by Christian Birch-Reichenwald (see
note, p. 87), Schweigaard, and Frederik Stang, whose opponents
denounced them as 'danomanes'. Soon after they had passed on to
become leading figures in public life, Welhaven himself was appointed
lecturer and (in 1846) professor of philosophy, a position which he
used for popular courses in literary history which enhanced his influence with successive generations of students. Outside the university, lending library records suggest that the public preferred
Danish books, while the clergy, whose general influence on culture
was obviously formidable, subscribed to Danish theological periodicals. Finally, it must be borne in mind that the Norwegian news-

---

* 1807–73. The son of a Bergen clergyman, and related on his mother's side to
the leading Danish poet and critic, J. L. Heiberg, he expounded his views of
Norway's cultural poverty and needs in a sonnet sequence, *The Dawn of
Norway*, 1834; the best of his later poems were influenced by his attachment to
Wergeland's sister Camilla (Collett,) and more lastingly to the composer
Kjerulf's sister, who died shortly after their betrothal.

papers struggled into existence without the benefit of regular correspondents abroad, much less any press agency of their own: Copenhagen was consequently the centre through which much of their foreign news was filtered.

The liberal Danes were the principal champions of Scandinavianism, for its most obvious practical importance lay in the ideological support that it provided for Denmark on its southern frontier, where since the 1830s a tug-of-war had developed between Danish and German nationalist claims in the duchies of Schleswig–Holstein. Yet this never clearly defined nineteenth-century Scandinavian movement derived early inspiration from German sources, which generated pride in a single 'Nordic culture' as an ancient folk inheritance to which Germans too owed an incalculable debt. As a sentiment it found its first expression at Lund in 1829, when the Swedish poet laureate Tegnèr crowned the Danish poet Oehlenschläger 'Scandinavian King of Song'. The scene was much to the taste of the Swedish and Danish students who had met to fraternize at the Swedish university, and periodic student gatherings of this kind continued for nearly four decades to provide the best-known manifestations of the Scandinavian spirit. In 1839–42 Scandinavianism had its own periodical, *Brage og Idun*—the names are those of nordic gods. Hans Christian Andersen, too, wrote a poem which won fame in all three countries, with the refrain:

> In hills and woods and on the night-blue oceàn
> I shout for joy—I am a Scandinavian![22]

There was also a series of Scandinavian scientific congresses, to one of which no less a figure than the world-famous Danish physicist, H. C. Örsted, addressed the argument that 'A misconceived national pride has divided us and brought foreigners to consider our achievements of little significance. . . . Let six million Scandinavians place their entire weight in one scale, and surely it shall not be found too light.'[23]

The Norwegian students first joined in in 1845, though they had urged the other countries to observe as a Scandinavian occasion the annual 'Feast of Our Forefathers', at which the rising generation—inspired originally by Wergeland—was wont to recall in suitably riotous fashion the good old days of their pagan Viking ancestors. More than 800 Danes were the hosts at Copenhagen to nearly 400 Swedes from Uppsala and Lund and 144 unofficial representatives of the university of Oslo. For many it was primarily a summer excursion by paddle steamer, and Scandinavianism a sentiment evoking the misty past rather than a principle that might affect future action. Yet the students of those days were a highly select body, whose influence upon the political and cultural developments of later years was bound to be great. Therefore it was not without significance that Orla Lehmann, the leader of the Danish liberals, an orator of mature years and considerable talent, induced the assembled Norwegian and Swedish students to make a sacred 'promise' of loyalty to 'our great common fatherland'.[24]

In 1848 the Year of Revolutions confronted Scandinavian sentiment with a practical challenge, for it brought into power in Denmark the National Liberals, such as Lehmann: as Liberals, they secured a parliamentary constitution; as Nationalists, they proposed to halt German encroachments at the river Eider, the boundary between the two duchies. Thus Holstein, which was already a member of the Germanic Confederation, might eventually be sacrificed to Germany, but Schleswig, which had long been guaranteed to the king of Denmark by the powers,* must remain Danish, notwithstanding the predominance of the German language and culture in its southern parts. On 9 April the Danes defeated a pro-German rebellion in the duchies, but the Prussians intervened in the name of the German parliament, then sitting at Frankfort, and drove the Danish army back into Jutland, which they invaded. The result was a complex international crisis, which presented King Oscar with an opening for a Scandinavian dynastic policy. Frederick VII, who had succeeded his father on the Danish throne in

---

* For the general bearings of the long-drawn-out international disputes regarding Holstein and especially Schleswig (in the Scandinavian languages 'Slesvig'), which do not directly concern the history of Norway, the reader may be referred to two recent studies: by W. E. Mosse in *The European Powers and the German Question 1848–71* (Cambridge, 1956) and by Ragnhild Hatton, with special reference to 'Scandinavian Union', in her contribution to *Studies in International History*, edited by K. Bourne and D. C. Watt (London, 1967).

January, had no direct heir: if Sweden–Norway helped to save his possessions from dismemberment, the fourteenth-century union of the north might be restored on his death under the House of Bernadotte. On 11 May King Oscar signed a convention, which promised the support of 15,000 troops and a naval squadron within a month.

Public opinion among the Norwegians, as among the Swedes, was broadly sympathetic with their fellow-Scandinavians as victims of German aggression. P. A. Munch, for example, in spite of his many disagreements with Danish historians, convened a mass meeting on May Day at the Oslo Exchange, and wrote in the leading newspaper *Morgenbladet* under the title, 'We Must Help Denmark'; he anticipated brilliant exploits from the armies of the United Kingdoms, which 'burn with eagerness to join the fray'.[25] The paper published a reply, however, by 'A Voice from the Country', which demanded a plebiscite to decide how much of Schleswig was genuinely Danish and expressed doubts about the eagerness of 'the poor and simple' to fight in, or pay for, a war. The voice was that of Marcus Thrane, whose first point was forcefully argued in the cabinet by Vogt, while the second perhaps finds corroboration in the fact that no more than 111 Norwegians and 243 Swedes served as volunteers in the Danish forces. In endorsing the royal policy which had resulted in the Convention, the Norwegian cabinet recorded that a minority of three members would have preferred the defence obligations of the United Kingdoms to be confined to their own peninsula, leaving it to the great powers to protect Denmark. The Storting likewise supported the king's action, though it also approved a report from a committee, noting with satisfaction the absence of 'any evidence that a more permanent approach to Denmark was contemplated'.[26]

No Swedish or Norwegian sword was actually drawn in the conflict on the southern borders of Scandinavia. But during the summer of 1848 4,000 Swedes were stationed as a precaution in Fünen, a reserve force of Swedes and Norwegians was assembled in Scania, and the presence of a Swedish-Norwegian squadron emphasized Danish control of the sea. On 26 August King Oscar with Russian support negotiated the Armistice of Malmö, though the

Danes ignored his wishes by renewing the war in 1849. After a second armistice in July of that year, the king arranged for Swedish and Norwegian troops to garrison northern Schleswig pending a settlement in 1850, by which the great powers helped to restore the *status quo* in the duchies. Here we may leave the issue for the time being, noting only that the troops of the United Kingdoms showed a doubtless reprehensible tendency to fraternize as readily with the Prussians as with their Danish brethren.

THE UNION FACES EAST

In 1851 Swedish and Danish students were fêted in Oslo. A song for the occasion, extolling the military feats of the Danes in the recent war, was composed by Ibsen, and an English friend of Munch contributed a speech which urged Nordic students to 'take the road of practical life'.[27] But such an exhortation was not very meaningful at a time when the foreign policy of all three countries was entering upon a new stage which involved partly divergent interests. The dynastic ambitions of the Bernadottes were indeed, checked by the Protocol of London (1852), which declared it to be a European interest that all the possessions of the Danish crown should pass undivided on Frederick's death to Prince Christian of Glücksburg, notwithstanding his ineligibility under the Salic law which prevailed in the duchies. New problems, however, arose almost immediately through the outbreak of the Crimean War, which was also to a limited extent a Baltic war.

The frontier settlement in the far north in 1826, which Norway had welcomed, was viewed in Russian opinion as unduly favourable to Norwegian interests. John Rice Crowe,* a British viceconsul who had the ear of Palmerston, adduced this ostensible

---

* 1795(?)–1877. He was the nephew of an English admiral in Russian service, and had spent six years in the Russian navy and two in the Russian embassy in London before he became a trade and mining entrepreneur on behalf of British interests in North Norway. He was made British vice-consul at Hammerfest, 1823–43 (suspended in 1836, until cleared of complicity in the Bodö smuggling case); consul-general at Oslo, 1843–75; C.B., 1859; knighted, 1874. He died in Oslo.

generosity as corroboration of his own view that the Russian authorities had designed the settlement as a screen behind which to work for the eventual cession of a site for an ice-free harbour. He drew up elaborate reports on the subject in 1836 and 1840, in apparent ignorance of the fact that the Murman coast, already in its possession, would have served Russia's hypothetical purposes. But his reports fitted in well with the anti-Russian policy of Lord Palmerston, who tried in vain to persuade Charles John of his danger. The latter relied on Russian friendship and the strength of the natural frontiers that he had secured for the peninsular kingdoms, and contented himself with assuring the British minister in Stockholm that no cession of Norwegian territory was contemplated.

In September 1851 Oscar I gave a similar assurance. At that time, however, negotiations were going on in Stockholm about alleged depredations by Norwegian Lapps while pasturing their reindeer in Russia's Grand Duchy of Finland, and the Russians then claimed that a section of the Norwegian coastline should be set aside to meet the fishing and hunting requirements of the border Finns. When this was refused, they closed the Norwego-Finnish frontier, an action which directly inconvenienced no one except the nomadic Lapps, but lent credence to the idea that the Russians had in mind a naval station. Accordingly, when the Crimean War broke out, the Storting discussed the propriety of requesting the ministry to see that territorial rights in Finnmark were safeguarded in the eventual peace negotiations, but no action was taken for fear of complicating relations with the great powers. The part that Russia played in suppressing the European revolutions of 1848–9 had also fed Norwegian anxieties, and although the press in general was cautious like the Storting, at the turn of the year 1854–5 *Morgenbladet* informed its readers that 'it was not only England and France which were at war with Russia, but European civilization'.[28]

Since Denmark was fully aware that Russia had been its most consistent supporter among the great powers in the dispute over the Duchies, the policy adopted was only to a limited extent Scandinavian in character. At the outbreak of hostilities, indeed, the three states joined in a declaration of neutrality which admitted belligerent warships to all but seven Scandinavian harbours, an arrangement which directly benefited Britain and France, since they had no bases of their own in the Baltic. But when the western powers angled for direct support, they could do nothing with Denmark, though they hoped that she might eventually follow a lead from the other two. King Oscar, on the other hand, nourished vague but ambitious schemes for the recovery of Finland, in which the Swedish nobility might be expected to participate enthusiastically, and conducted a secret press campaign. Some of the material was fed to Crowe, now more influentially placed as consul-general in Oslo, who duly included it in a further review of the situation in Finnmark; he now feared that most of its population were ready to transfer their allegiance to Russia. But when the French made the first serious bid for help from the United Kingdoms, Oscar's conditions proved to be too onerous—full belligerence on the part of Austria, big subsidies, and unspecified guarantees.

However, when Palmerston became prime minister in Britain in February 1855, he returned to his earlier concern regarding Finnmark. In June he got France to agree to the offer of a guarantee for the territorial integrity of Norway, which King Oscar and the Swedish foreign minister induced him to extend to Sweden as well. When the treaty was signed in November, the king expected the war to continue in spite of the fall of Sebastopol; he had already entered into discussions with the French General Canrobert about operations to be undertaken with Swedish and Norwegian support. But peace came quickly, with the result that the servitude imposed on Russia in the disarmament of the Åland Islands was his only concrete gain. The November treaty nevertheless endured for half a century, giving security against the threat of Russian naval expansion in northern waters (which at first seemed more likely because of the reverse in the Black Sea)—and imposing an effective barrier against any political rapprochement with the Tsardom. Moreover, although the negotiations had not been forwarded by Norway, where King Oscar on a visit in August 1855 had found 'great political indifference',[29] common action in face of a supposed threat to the integrity of the smaller partner did help to draw the peninsular kingdoms closer together.

SCANDINAVIANISM AND THE CRISIS OF 1863–1864

When the Scandinavian student meetings were resumed at Uppsala in 1856, the organizing committee in Oslo was headed by Welhaven, and Björnson accompanied the students on the voyage. The key speaker from Denmark drew the conclusion from recent events that in isolation both parts of Scandinavia faced grave dangers: 'Russia looks as greedily towards the harbours of Finnmark as does Germany towards those of Schleswig.'[30] On their way home the students were received by King Oscar in the presence of the Danish minister and members of the Swedish and Norwegian cabinets. Describing himself significantly as the king of Denmark's 'faithful ally', he proposed a toast to 'King Frederick, not only the first but also the best Dane in his kingdom'.[31] Under the influence of dynastic ambition, the movement for a Great Scandinavia was approaching its climax. Britain and France doubted both the wisdom and the finality of the settlement which had been made in 1850–2, and by the autumn of 1856 both governments might be described as holding a watching brief for Scandinavianism. Napoleon III's cousin, Prince Jerome, visited the northern capitals, including Oslo; and J. R. Crowe was encouraged to produce one of his voluminous reports on the situation as seen from there. It was received by the foreign secretary with considerable interest, but Crowe and the other British representatives in the Scandinavian countries were subsequently instructed to avoid any partisanship in the matter.

In the early months of 1857, indeed, King Oscar's offer of a military alliance foundered on the demand of the Danish foreign minister, who ardently supported a conservative *helstat* ('wholestate') policy, that it should cover the defence of Holstein as well as Schleswig. But his son Charles, who became regent in June of that year, was young, impulsive, and greatly interested in military affairs: only time would show that he lacked the determination and other qualities that had enabled his grandfather to rise so high as a man of action. Charles's aims had the same general character in both his realms: to give more personal direction to the government; to build up the defence forces; and to pursue a foreign policy of expansion, for which Scandinavianism might be the watchword. In

Sweden he received credit for a reforming policy which was actually imposed on him by his ministers. In Norway, as we shall see, he achieved the opposite of his intentions. And as regards a Great Scandinavia, he failed to carry his peoples wholeheartedly with him, which mattered less because his efforts were in any case outmatched by the external forces opposing his ambitions.

As viceroy in Norway in 1856, Charles found the Storting obdurate in three matters affecting the Union. Proposals for modifying the mutual tariff arrangements of 1827 (see p. 103) and for giving equal legal validity to court decisions in both kingdoms could be left for reconsideration at a later opportunity; but the third proposal concerned the state of the defences, a question of obvious urgency in the unsettled conditions that followed the Crimean War.

In 1815 it had been supposed that the unification of the peninsula left Norway with no reason to spend money on protecting her land frontiers, while the disasters suffered at Copenhagen in 1801 and 1807 meant that there was virtually no Norwegian navy. The Storting having refused to legislate for universal military service, provision was made in 1816 for a first-line army of 12,000 men, including 2,000 regulars (*hvervede*). The conscripts, who were picked by lot, did five years service in the line, after which they were liable for a further period of five years in the militia (*landvern*), but this was not organized in any form until 1837. In 1854, indeed, a much larger supply of manpower was made available by the inclusion of the towns, but the first-line force was not increased: all those upon whom the lot did not fall—or who purchased substitutes when they were allotted to the line—constituted the reserve, which received only a short recruit-training and could not be required to serve outside the kingdom. As for the navy, its reconstruction was approved in principle in 1836, but fifteen years later it comprised—apart from tiny gunboats for use inside the skerries—no more than seven vessels, of which the largest were two frigates. The Storting's insistence on rigid economy, which had produced this situation, extended also to the coastal forts, several of which had fallen into disuse, while the only new construction was Oscarsborg on the Oslofiord, first manned in 1853. Prince Charles accordingly presided over a committee of soldiers and civilians from both kingdoms with a view to co-ordinating their defence. One equitable proposal was to base manpower for the services upon an agreed figure of $2\frac{1}{2}$ per cent of population, but the Storting treated every approach to a common system as an insidious advance towards political amalgamation. It rejected even a request that it should take the same precaution as the Swedes of providing specific 'credits',[32] upon which the crown would be entitled to draw without Budgetary authority in the event of an emergency, and justified its economies by Sverdrup's parochial argument that Union defence measures benefited chiefly 'the most powerful and most exposed state'.[33]

Defence needs largely motivated the scheme for changing the personnel of the Norwegian cabinet, which Charles took in hand (together with similar changes in Sweden) as regent and completed as king. Christian Birch-Reichenwald,* a county governor who had won his confidence, knew Sweden well and shared the royal view that Norway ought to contribute more effectively to the armies of the union; his friend, Georg Sibbern,† had been secretary to Charles as viceroy after diplomatic service in London and Washington, which gave him a broad outlook upon the needs of the two kingdoms. In December 1858 Birch-Reichenwald was appointed minister of justice and Sibbern minister-resident in Stockholm. Their intention was to work through the Storting, where they hoped to establish 'a reliable majority to go hand in hand with an enlightened, strong government',[34] by which the union would benefit. Their ability to do so depended primarily upon the king's design of propitiating his Norwegian subjects by an accession gift that would soothe many susceptibilities.

This was the abolition of the office of stattholder, which had been in abeyance since 1856 but still impeded the creation of a premiership in Oslo and assumed great symbolic importance as a badge of Norway's subordinate position in the Union. Since it was not named

---

* 1814–91. The son of a senior army officer, he received his first schooling there; who was posted to Stockholm, entered the university of Oslo at sixteen, and was a county governor at thirty-three.

† 1816–1901. In 1878–84 he served as Norwegian and Swedish minister in Paris; in 1880 Oscar II twice contemplated his appointment as prime minister.

in the Act of Union, Norway could claim the right to abolish it by unilateral action, and a bill for the purpose had been passed by the Storting in 1857, though without the two-thirds majority required for a constitutional change. In 1859, however, the measure had the support of the new king, who believed that there would be no objection from the three most influential members of his Swedish cabinet, a belief that was shared by the Norwegian ministers in Stockholm; the minority in the Storting therefore lost its fears of an unfavourable Swedish reaction. The bill was passed by a vote of 110 to 2, and Björnson announced in a precipitate newspaper article: 'The decision has been promised sanction in advance by His Majesty the king. This unanimity between king and Storting means that consideration for Sweden has been taken into proper account.'[35] But a veteran oppositionist in the Swedish House of Nobles, C. H. Anckarsvärd, had expressed the view that, since King Oscar's accession gift had not made his Norwegian subjects more amenable, it would be better to settle the stattholder question in the context of a general revision of the terms of union. Since many politically active Swedes, including some liberals, held much the same view, it is not surprising that all four Estates now declared that revision must have priority over acceptance of the Norwegian proposal. What is perhaps surprising is that only one Swedish minister, Count Hamilton, resigned on account of his previous commitment to the king's wishes, when the cabinet threatened to leave office unless the bill was vetoed.

Charles showed the weakness that lay behind his bold exterior by breaking his promise to assent to the Norwegian bill, and made matters worse in Norwegian eyes by allowing the records of the Swedish cabinet to show that his veto, recorded at a Norwegian cabinet meeting, had been imposed in accordance with Swedish wishes. Once a major clash had developed, Charles was virtually bound to act in support of the *status quo* as less damaging to the union than any positive move would be. But his younger brother, the future Oscar II, judged in retrospect that, 'if he had ventured to take a bold decision' by sanctioning the bill as soon as it had passed the Storting, Swedish resentment would quickly have subsided.[36] The consequences were in any case disastrous. Birch-Reichenwald, who showed his resentment at the king's defection, left office for ever; he was replaced by Frederik Stang, under whom the more diplomatic Sibbern continued to serve as minister-resident in Stockholm, but the prospect of a royal *and* parliamentary government had vanished. The sensibilities of Norwegians were outraged by what they regarded as a direct challenge to their traditional right to control every particle of their own constitution. Worst of all, the union as a slowly growing bond of sentiment had suffered the severest possible setback, while its material embodiment in a complex of rules and conventions which urgently needed to be amended and expanded was left unchanged and for the time being unchangeable. On 23 April 1860 the Storting resolved unanimously 'That no Norwegian citizen who has a due regard for the rights of his country and his own honour will take part in a revision. . . . until a truer conception of the relationship between the two countries prevails in Sweden'.[37]

Scandinavianism, however, retained much of its impetus, for the enhanced Norwegian distrust of the Swedes gave additional weight to the argument that, if a tripartite union could be established, Norway and Denmark together would counterwork any attempt at Swedish domination. This view was entertained, for example, by the British consul Crowe, whose experience in Oslo led him to stress the affinity between the Norwegians and the liberal element among the Danes and their common antipathy to Swedish conservatism. In 1856 he had reported to London: 'Norway appears to be the state specially suited. . . . to be the means of uniting the three kingdoms into one compact harmonious unity.'[38] Moreover, the rebuff that the king had experienced in a matter of internal policy made him all the more eager for a brilliant external policy: might not Norwegians as well as Swedes prove zealous defenders of a Great Scandinavia, if once the dream became reality?

In the summer of 1861 King Charles paid official visits to the French and British courts, which did not discourage his hopes of eventual support. In January 1863, when the Polish revolt attracted the sympathy of liberals throughout Europe, he was temporarily distracted by the thought of recovering Finland, through a crusade against Russia to be headed by Napoleon III. However, in the

same month Count Hamilton, who was now his minister in Copenhagen, lent an attentive ear to an unofficial Danish suggestion that
it might be possible to placate the Prussians with Holstein and
embody the rest of the Danish possessions in a federative state of the
north, with Charles as its destined sovereign. In July Charles duly
visited the ailing Frederick VII at Skodsborg Castle, when he promised the support of 20,000 Swedes and Norwegians for the defence
of Schleswig to its southern border: the National Liberals, who had
regained power in Denmark, now intended to defy German opinion
by uniting the entire duchy with the kingdom in a new constitution from which Holstein would be excluded. But in September
Charles was advised by his leading Swedish ministers and Georg
Sibbern that the lack of any commitment from a great power made
the risk unacceptable—and was compelled for a second time to
break his promise. Only two months later the death of Frederick
was followed by the uncontested succession of Christian, 'the protocol prince', to the Danish throne. This finally removed the dynastic
incentive to any action in anticipation of German aggression in the
duchies.

When the Germans moved forward in January 1864, many organs
of the Norwegian press and the leading poets espoused the Danish
cause as that of all Scandinavia. Enthusiastic resolutions were passed
by the academic community in Oslo and by a meeting of citizens
in general, whose address was presented to the ministry by Broch.
As regards military resources, although many of the proposals of
the Union Defence Committee had been rejected, a law passed in
March 1863 extended the period of service in the line from five to
seven years,[39] so that 18,000 men could now be mustered, which was
only one-sixth below the total that had been proposed by the crown.
The navy too had been strengthened by two steam-frigates, its
most important acquisition in half a century. But when the Storting met in March 1864 to consider the royal demands for men and
money in case of eventual hostilities, the German advance had
already swept through the duchies and secured possession of most of
Jutland. In these circumstances, it was not surprising that both
grants were made subject to the express condition that at least one
great power should first commit itself to active support of the hard-

pressed Danes. What was more serious as a blow to sentiment, which might have survived a military discomfiture, was a resolution which Sverdrup carried by a majority of three—including only six votes from urban representatives in a total of fifty-seven: this recorded 'That the great majority of the Norwegian people do not desire any closer political connection between the United Kingdoms and Denmark'.[40] In the ministry, both Stang as its head and Sibbern opposed intervention, the latter fearing to encourage an adventurous spirit among their Swedish colleagues. However, at this juncture public opinion in Sweden was even less warlike than in Norway, so the king was left with no scope for further bold initiatives.

Thus the sixteen-year period in which Sweden–Norway was at least intermittently active in European affairs ended in failure. Ibsen, who passed through Denmark in its hour of defeat on his way to live abroad, and Björnson, who for a time thought of joining the few Norwegian volunteers with the Danish army, put on permanent record their bitter feeling that Norway failed conspicuously to rise to a great opportunity. The military strength of Sweden–Norway, however, was much smaller than they liked to suppose. If an opportunity was lost, it was in the sphere of diplomacy, for the great powers might have been induced to save the Danish possessions from dismemberment. Behind lurks the larger question, to which it would be rash to attempt an answer. If Scandinavia had found in Charles XV a ruler with the gifts of a Cavour or a Bismarck, would its unity have been established in the era when the great powers by their action and inaction enabled Italy and Germany to unite?

THE UNION DURING THE LAST DECADES OF ÉLITE RULE

Neither Scandinavianism nor the cultural fellowship with Denmark died any sudden death in 1864. On the contrary, that year saw the foundation of a Scandinavian Society which for nearly a decade led a flourishing existence in all three capitals; and there was no interruption of what a present-day Norwegian historian calls 'the strange phenomenon that the whole succession of our leading authors in the second half of the nineteenth century had their books published in

Denmark'.[41] But far greater practical importance attached now to the possibility of improving the Swedish–Norwegian union. De Geer, the powerful prime minister of the larger partner, had worked with Sibbern in 1861–2 on framing new terms, though both the king and the joint cabinet then judged the moment to be unpropitious for any action. However, in June 1863, when the international situation emphasized the value of the union for the defence of both kingdoms, the Storting formally withdrew its opposition to a revision, while still insisting upon 'the equal rights of the two kingdoms and the sole jurisdiction of each in all matters not designated as of union concern'.[42] Next year the jubilee of the Union was celebrated with enthusiasm by the many Norwegians who welcomed the approaching institution of a more democratic, bicameral legislature in the neighbouring country. Accordingly, in 1865 both ministries were prepared to launch a new venture: in the cautious phrase employed by Sibbern, the moment seemed ripe for an 'inoffensive revision'.[43]

The seven Norwegian members of the second Union Committee ranged from Professor Aschehoug to the veteran peasant leader, Ueland, but the official element predominated, as it did among the Swedes. A little more than two years were spent in drafting seventy-one paragraphs for a new Act of Union: the principle of equality was fully acknowledged, and care taken to provide for all matters of mutual concern which required bilateral treatment if friction was to be avoided. The central institution proposed was a Union cabinet, composed of an equal number of ministers from each kingdom, whose far-reaching powers included the right to take cognizance of all major questions of foreign policy; this reduced the importance of the fact that the foreign minister would continue to be a Swede and answerable to Swedish authorities. Defence was to be organized as a common concern, with armies proportionate to the respective populations. Although the Norwegian members insisted on the rejection of the Union parliament desired by De Geer and the Swedish members of the committee, the new framework proposed might have stimulated the growth of a real union, capable of conferring internal benefits on both countries sufficient at least to counterbalance their recent loss of external prestige.

The Swedish and Norwegian ministries approved the report, which the joint cabinet recommended as a basis for legislation. The Riksdag was willing, but for Norway it was too late: since 1863 the tide of opinion had been turning fast. The report would have had some enemies in any case: Birch-Reichenwald and his friends still nursed their resentment against the king; Sverdrup, who had declined nomination to the committee, thought that this might be his chance to overthrow the ministry; and whereas Ueland's death in 1870 deprived the report of an influential champion, Jaabæk was content to follow Sverdrup's lead. But the main factor was the rapid growth of active nationalist sentiments among the rural voters, which became evident at the elections of 1868 and 1871. The rising historian, Ernest Sars,* in alliance with the poet Vinje—who was dismissed from a government clerkship on account of his outspoken opposition to official policy—provided formidable backing for the oratory of Björnson. Björnson had given the report a favourable first reception, but was then completely converted by the arguments of a lawyer.† These denounced the retention or introduction of innumerable badges of Norway's inferior status in the union, many of which—the placing of the monarchy in Stockholm, for example—were in fact unavoidable concomitants of its smaller population and resources. In many peasant homes whatever Björnson said was gospel. In vain did Aschehoug, who had been anti-unionist in his youth, expound the merits of the revision from a wider standpoint. There was now a strong underlying fear that the land of their fathers might lose its character as a peasant community by strengthening its ties with an alien society and a king whose authority could be invoked by his Norwegian ministers to bolster up their own position. Thus it became an easy ruse for

---

* 1835–1917. The son of a distinguished zoologist, he modelled his schematic presentation of history on the French school; author of a four-volume *Survey of Norwegian History* (1873–91) and a *Historical Introduction to the Constitution* (1882), which traced the evolution from the distant past of an independent Norwegian nation of peasant democrats. He was in bad odour with the university authorities as a liberal and a positivist, so in 1874 an extraordinary professorship of history was created for him by the Storting.
† Bernhard Dunker (1809–70), whose two-volume work opposing any revision of the Union (which he had formerly championed) was published in 1866–8.

Sverdrup in 1871 to rally votes by a rhetorical denunciation of the
Swedes: 'When it dares to invite the Storting of Norway to traffic
in the nation's first and most precious possessions, the nation that
does this thing must for the time being be so blinded that one cannot possibly negotiate with it.'[44]

The bill embodying the proposals of the second Union Committee was accordingly defeated by a crushing majority —92 : 17—with
not one farmer voting in its favour. Sibbern resigned office, as he
had said he would do if 'an innocent revision' were rejected. The
accession of Oscar II in the following year (1872) was marked by
the removal of one bone of contention between the two nations,
namely the stattholdership. This was achieved through a legalistic
compromise, by which the bill for its abolition received the royal
assent in a meeting of the Norwegian cabinet after the joint cabinet
had duly placed on record the Swedish ministers' contention that the
latter was the proper location for the taking of that decision. Such
formalism did not augur well for the future, but during the next
few years (as we saw in the last chapter) the attention of Norwegian
politicians was concentrated very largely upon the primarily domestic issue of the Inclusion Bill.

Certain factors outside politics did something to hold the two
countries together. Sverdrup, indeed, used his power in the Storting to restrict defence expenditure to national objectives: the fleet,
which had acquired four monitors and its first torpedo boat, was
specifically assigned in 1877 to the defence of its own coasts, and
when the choice of men for the first line of the army was improved
at about the same time by the abolition of the right to substitution,
he tried hard to increase the reserve for home defence at the expense
of the line. However, the government succeeded in retaining the
period of seven years for line service, which might benefit the United
Kingdoms, and the two armies continued to collaborate fairly closely
at Staff level; the king's Norwegian Guard Company, which formed
part of the small and shrinking element of Regulars, provided a
military link with Stockholm for some of the rank and file. In
1874 a revised interstate treaty substantially increased the flow of
trade between the kingdoms, and in the next year Norway adhered to the Scandinavian currency union (see p. 129). Some Nor-

wegian entrepreneurs found favourable opportunities in the richer country: one of Sverdrup's future cabinet ministers, for example, began his career selling Swedish timber in Spain and returned home eventually with a capital of £250,000 accumulated in Sweden.[45] At the other end of the scale, Swedish navvies helped to build the Norwegian railways; when the government decided in 1880 to reduce construction, more than one-third of the 5,000 workers paid off were Swedes.

But as the constitutional struggle in Norway became more acute, the relationship with Sweden was once more brought into the foreground. When Björnson made his famous appeal to the electorate in 1882 for the people to assert itself as master (see p. 56), he was invoking nationalist sentiment against three supposed usurpers of its authority—the ministers, the king who stood behind them, and the Swedes who were presumed to stand behind him. Unlike his two predecessors, Oscar II had never been viceroy in Norway, and after his accession his visits were short and usually overshadowed by political conflict. Was he not to be regarded as a Swedish functionary, whose veto might be employed at any time to protect Swedish as well as his personal interests? This view was encouraged by the consideration that the Swedish constitution accorded him the veto on constitutional changes which his Norwegian subjects disputed, and by the fact that his position as head of the army in both countries might facilitate a move to 'restore order' in the smaller one. In February 1882 an unsigned article in a Stockholm newspaper[46] warned the Norwegians that the king must be accorded the same veto powers in Norway as in Sweden for the sake of the union: its author was King Oscar. A series of pamphlets, published by a provocative Stockholm journalist[47] under a pseudonym, followed up with the suggestion that the Swedish people would support strong action, such as the arrest and prosecution of Sverdrup.

The Swedish ministers, however, and the nation as a whole were more cautious and conciliatory than their sovereign. In 1880, although the Swedish cabinet could not of course give the king any direct advice on a domestic Norwegian issue, its members would have favoured his sanctioning the Inclusion bill. In 1883–4— when Sweden for the first time had a non-noble premier—they did indeed give a formal opinion that an absolute veto on legislation plus the royal command over the armed forces was needed in both kingdoms for the sake of the union, but added a private corollary to the effect that the king should accept the result of the impeachment. Moreover, in the final stages of the crisis in Norwegian affairs the Swedish government's point of view, and the popular support that it enjoyed, had some practical importance, for King Oscar was informed that German diplomatic assistance would only be available if 'a different state of opinion in Sweden'[48] called for intervention in Norway. Swedish opinion also helped to undermine the king's attempt in April 1884 to impose a new Norwegian ministry under C. H. Schweigaard: the Agrarians organized a dinner in Stockholm to pay significant homage to a visiting Norwegian Folk High School leader, Christopher Bruun, and next day a motion criticizing the king's policy was passed by the Second Chamber. Finally, both the prime minister and the foreign minister of Sweden used their influence in support of the terms which Broch sought to impose on the king as prerequisites for the establishment of an alternative government.

To sum up, the triumph of Sverdrup and his cause in June 1884 did not in itself involve any serious impairment of Norwegian–Swedish relations. Reactionary circles associated with the court had, indeed, suffered a reverse, but they received no sympathy from the more democratic elements in the Second Chamber of the Riksdag, upon whose support the ministry in Sweden was increasingly dependent.

4. The Economy Under Élite Government

As WE HAVE SEEN, THE PREDOMINANCE OF THE OFFI-
cial class during the first seventy years of self-government in Norway tended in many respects to delay the advance of democracy,
and in some respects that of nationalism as well. But at the same time
it ministered to an economic growth which eventually stimulated
those two developments. For by 1884 a greatly increased population enjoyed a slightly higher standard of life—and had on an average a correspondingly better opportunity of cultivating political
interests.

The population, of which fairly reliable records had been kept
since 1735, grew after the Napoleonic Wars with an unprecedented
rapidity. For two generations the rate of increase was no less than
1·30 per cent per annum. Since Norwegian women married rather
late, the birth rate was never outstandingly high, even when due
allowance is made for illegitimacy, but there was a sustained fall
in the death rate. One contributory cause was the fact that by the
1850s eight infants in ten were vaccinated, as against three during
the second decade of the century, while in 1835 Schweigaard
calculated that more than one-fifth of the population could be fed
from one comparatively new crop, the potato. A modern economist,
after surveying the statistics for the entire century, concludes: 'The
decline in the general death rate was due first and foremost to the
advance in public and private health measures and the enlightening
of the people regarding the importance of cleanliness for their health.
People got to know that many diseases were infectious, and gradually learnt to avoid infection.'[1]

The population figures may be allowed to speak for themselves:

TABLE II[2]

| Year | population in thousands | percentage | | in more densely populated rural areas |
		urban	rural	
1815	885	9·8	90·2	
1825	1,051	10·9	89·1	
1835	1,194	10·8	89·2	

TABLE II (continued)

Year	population in thousands	percentage urban	rural	in more densely populated rural areas
1845	1,328	12·2	87·8	3·4
1855	1,490	13·3	86·7	3·6
1865	1,701	15·6	84·4	4·0
1875	1,806	18·1	81·9	6·3
1890	2,000	23·7	76·3	7·6

The rate of growth is almost identical with that of Britain, where the new machines could occupy so many hands and feed so many mouths. But in Norway the absence of coal and the scarcity of capital were only two of the many factors that delayed the onset of the 'industrial revolution': at mid-century the towns supported one-eighth of the Norwegian people, as compared with the British proportion of one-half.* Yet the Norwegian standard of living slowly rose. In the early years the successful exploitation of rather meagre natural resources depended mainly on unremitting toil, for large-scale emigration did not then provide substantial relief for excess of population. Later on, progress was helped by a skilful adaptation to the principles of economic liberalism at home and, still more, abroad; in particular, Norway found a special and very profitable role in the world's maritime carrying trade. After the establishment of a Central Statistical Office (*Statistisk Sentralbyrå*) in 1865, economic growth can be measured with some degree of precision. In 1865–84 the gross national product increased by 30 per cent, in spite of three years (1877, 1881, and 1882) of actual decline; the former head of the office has estimated that the average growth rate from 1842 was of the same order.[3] The activities of countless individuals—at work in farm or forest, in small industrial complexes, or on the high seas—provided the main driving force: but progress was assisted, as we shall see, by a competent and conscientious administration.

* The percentage of population living in denser rural areas, where small-scale industry created some employment, would be at least counterbalanced by the percentage of agriculturists of a rural type in the smaller Norwegian towns.

INITIAL HANDICAPS SLOWLY OVERCOME

In 1815 many districts in western and northern Norway still resembled the underdeveloped countries of today. A Norwegian writer justifies such a comparison by naming, as characteristic of his country then, 'a low standard of living, lack of capital, a system of production based on self-sufficiency, old and mainly primitive techniques, low yields, and undeveloped natural resources'.[4] Tillage was handicapped by a growing-season so short that it was sometimes necessary to spread ashes on the snow in order to get ploughing done in time, a terrain so uneven in summer and icy in winter that only a minority of farms possessed wheeled equipment of any kind, and arable soil that was insufficient in quantity and inadequately enriched with animal manure. Rotation of crops was still an unusual practice in Norway, the same crop being sown year after year until the land was exhausted and had to be left fallow to recuperate. Two-thirds of the ground was under oats, one-fourth under barley, and very little under rye or wheat; the sowing of turnips, sugar beet, or flax was quite exceptional. Scarcity of capital inhibited change, as did the intermingling of plots, which a repartition law of 1821 did little to remedy, one reason being the want of trained surveyors. In the west and south the dividing up of the original farm properties had produced holdings which might consist of as many as 100 patches of arable only a few yards long, while it was still usual for untilled land and woods to be exploited communally—which meant conservatively. The total yield from animal husbandry was believed to be greater than that from tillage, but it was based upon the practice of keeping the maximum of cattle alive on the minimum of food through the long, cold winter, when they were confined in dark, overcrowded, and undrained byres. Ploughland being so scarce, there were virtually no meadows cultivated for hay. About one-third of the farms had a *seter* in the mountains for summer grazing, where on an average about a ton of fodder was also reaped for conveyance down to the valley every autumn. The rest of the winter feed was obtained by scouring the farm area for a natural harvest of grasses, foliage, bracken, and young bark.

Nevertheless, at the end of the first two post-war decades such statistical material as is available suggests that, if all crops are evaluated by a single unit of measurement, those of 1835 were more than double those that had been normal before the war. An official estimate of that date, which was based on returns by farmers (who would think it to their advantage to understate rather than over-state their resources), put the corn at 166,000 tons, supplemented by no less than 261,000 tons of potatoes.[5] The fact that the potato crop had increased tenfold in 1809–29 confirms the impression of its special importance in coping with the growth of population, though potatoes provided most of the 50,000 tons of potential foodstuffs which were diverted to the brandy stills. If nothing had been diverted, Norway could have been nine-tenths self-sufficient in bread or meal.

The explanation of this remarkable result lies partly in the exis-tence of a reserve army of labour: because no other employment was available for them, the additional work force was deployed on the land. New farms were registered, many new cottar holdings (which did not require registration) were carved out on existing farms, and much marginal land was brought under cultivation. Totals of 25,000 acres for the area added in the 1820s and 40,000 acres for the 1830s are almost certainly too low, since they are based on estimates, not on measurement. The advance fortunately permits other forms of measurement, comparing 1835 with normal years before 1809: sowings had increased by one-sixth per farm unit and one-fifth per member of the farming population, and the harvest in each case by about two-thirds.

The back-breaking toil of men, women, and children, who won new land by clearing trees and undergrowth and piling up the ubiquitous stones and boulders, was of course a task dictated mainly by poverty: in some districts the need was so great that the clear-ances had stone heaps which were more extensive than the new patches of arable soil. But credit must also be given to the spread of technical improvements. The new devices were often extremely primitive by the standards of other West European countries: the cultivation of potatoes, for instance, bringing a very simple wooden plough (*ard*) to fields hitherto worked entirely by the spade. Small's and other iron ploughs of foreign origin, harrows in lieu of rakes, and wheeled equipment—especially carts—spread to the great eastern valleys and some other districts from the most advanced agricultural area round Oslo; by the 1830s hand-made threshing machines were in fairly common use. But diffusion was very slow. Jacob Sverdrup based the instruction at his pioneer agricultural school on the hypothesis that his pupils would have to make the improved equipment for themselves; this is particularly significant because they were sons of moneyed people rather than ordinary farmers. Finally, progress was undoubtedly stimulated by non-technical factors, including the sale from 1821 onwards of church lands (about one-tenth of the whole), which turned many tenants into owners, and the long depression in the timber trade, which encouraged forest-owning peasants to concentrate upon agriculture proper. May we not add to these a half-conscious desire in many breasts to enrich the 'free Norway' which patriots were so busily extolling?

The fisheries, which provided a part-time activity for many small farmers and cottars along and near the coast, likewise showed some technical advance, the gill-net for cod and the seine for herring being used increasingly, wherever larger boats were available. A growing proportion of the cod which was caught in the north was processed into 'klipfish': that is to say, it was cleaned, split, and salted before drying, a practice previously brought into use farther down the west coast. Whereas the wind-drying of the traditional stock-fish, for which Lofoten offered ideal conditions, was undertaken by the fishermen themselves, the new process passed into the hands of owners of shore rights, who let out space to fishermen during their short sojourn, and of local merchants all along the coast. The latter class now became the main creditors of the fishermen, from whom they bought their catch for processing and eventual resale to the export firms in Bergen. Still farther north, where there was virtually no agriculture, a summer cod-fishery flourished off the coast of Finnmark, but its importance lay in direct barter sale to the Russians for corn. The big new factor in the fisheries, however, was the return of the fickle 'spring herring' to the Norwegian west coast in 1808, after a quarter of a century's absence. This enabled cottars and others to earn money in the bleak early months of the year from a catch which they conveyed to Bergen and some smaller coastal centres; it was then gutted, salted, and barrelled for export to Sweden and the Russian Baltic ports. Between 1815 and 1830 the trade in both cod and herring approximately doubled.

The other main primary product of the country, namely its timber, suffered a depression which affected mainly the south but was so dramatic and severe that it tended to colour the whole picture of the period. This trade lost its chief market as a result of the big preference that the British post-war tariff gave to Canadian timber: imperial sentiment no doubt played some part, but the result was a profitable freight for British shipping and a profitable outlet for British capital in Canadian sawmills. The situation was all the more difficult for Norwegian exporters because the forests of Russia, Prussia, and Sweden, where felling for export had begun more recently, paid no higher duty on their longer timber than Norway did on shorter lengths.

The major firms held out for a time, helped by the depreciation of the currency, which lowered the export prices, and buoyed up by hopes of a renewal of war in Europe which might turn to their advantage. But from 1817 onwards bankruptcy wrought havoc among the old urban patriciate of southern Norway. Their creditors were their trading partners in England and the Hamburg bankers to whom they had resorted for loans, but most of the business passed eventually either to immigrants from the south, especially from Germany and the Baltic lands, or to Norwegians of peasant origin who had husbanded their resources throughout the crisis. The trade picked up again more rapidly in volume than in profit. France, where there was said to be a novel demand for floor boards among peasant families, was now the growing market: in 1829, for example, it took rather more timber than Britain, but these two markets together absorbed only two-thirds of what Britain alone had taken in 1805. The declining profits of the merchant meant reduced earnings for the forest-owning farmer and for the woodcutter and the haulier. Moreover, since the timber trade had been the mainstay of Norwegian shipping, this too experienced a decade of decline, during which tonnage fell by more than one-fourth, while the size and quality of new ships also suffered.

As for metals, iron mining did not reach the pre-war level until the 1840s. This was due in the first instance to the termination of the union with Denmark, which imposed on its former partner a tariff 50 per cent above that for the most-favoured nations, thus putting an end to the long-established interchange of Norwegian iron goods for Danish corn. The position was made worse by the Interstate treaty (*mellomriksloven*) with Sweden in 1827,* which gave free entry to Norway for overland imports of Swedish iron manufactures; these were as good as the native products and cost less, since wages were higher in Norway and charcoal dearer as a result of the abolition in 1816 of compulsory deliveries from all farms within a given radius of the works. English coke-made iron was also a competitor because of its cheapness. But the domestic market for iron goods gradually recovered; iron increasingly replaced wood in agricultural implements; and in the 1840s Norwegian bar-iron gained a new market in North America, only to be ousted by cheap steel after a couple of decades.

The ancient copper-mining industry at Röros likewise passed through a difficult period. In 1818 anxiety for its well-being led to the passing of the last full-scale mercantilist legislation, which prescribed the mode of operation for each separate shaft and fixed wages, hours, and pensions for the workers. But the works continued to stagnate until the coming of the railway in the 1870s. Few of the smaller metal deposits had attracted attention, but the absence of artificial dyes gave value to the state-owned cobalt mine; in 1821, however, it had only fifty-nine workers, whereupon it was sold to a private owner—under whom it enjoyed two decades of prosperity. The government for a time contemplated disposing of the Kongsberg silver mine, which was reopened in 1815 and ran at a loss for fifteen years before a new era of prosperity.

So large a part of the Norwegian population still lived mainly on their own produce, or bartered their goods or services for payments in kind, that the financial troubles that beset the new state cast a

---

* This extended to other commodities an arrangement made in 1815 for food-stuffs, namely free trade by land and half-duty if seaborne; Norway shipped about one-third of its export herring to Sweden, but trade by land was mainly in the opposite direction.

smaller shadow than they would in a more modern society. A poor harvest by land or sea, such as the one that reduced many districts to a diet of bark bread in 1830, had wider repercussions among the masses than problems of public finance; yet these were serious enough. They began with a repudiation by the first regular Storting of the 'Eidsvoll Guarantee', which had promised redemption at a fixed proportion of their face value for bank-notes previously in circulation as well as for the new issue made in May 1814. Strictly speaking, indeed, the breach of faith was the work of the Lagting alone, but the Storting as a whole failed to raise the necessary two-thirds majority to overrule it; the result in any case was a sweeping reduction of 60 per cent.[6] The sequel was acute difficulty in raising a fund for the new Bank of Norway, set up by the Storting in February 1816, which had been authorized to issue notes to twice the value of its capital; for capitalists not unnaturally preferred to place their money in Hamburg and other relatively safe foreign centres rather than call it home to run obvious risks. A regulation against making contracts in foreign currencies had little or no effect, and the fear that the country was doomed to go bankrupt for a third time was made more alarming by the supposition that the result would be the amalgamation of Norway's finances with those of Sweden. It was therefore decided to take the drastic step of allotting shares in the bank compulsorily; they were to be assigned locally in proportion to capital—in Oslo, one-twentieth was demanded—and the sum was to be paid entirely in silver. Even the finance minister, Count Wedel, had to melt down part of the family plate to provide the last quarter of his share, while persons with less sense of duty held out grimly against paying. In east Norway, which felt the collapse of trade most acutely, one-half was still owing six months after the date for final settlement.

An agreement to make bank-notes redeemable in silver on New Year's Day 1819 had to be abandoned, and three years later a strikingly modern proposal by Wedel to make redemption available in bars of silver bullion but not in coin was likewise rejected. The result was that there were big fluctuations in the value of the Norwegian paper dollar,* which became a favourite subject for specula-

* The silver dollar or *spesiedaler* had been coined throughout Scandinavia since

tion on the exchanges abroad, thus adding to the difficulty of negotiating loans. In 1820 the government was only able to raise the equivalent of £100,000 in Berlin by pledging the customs as security and agreeing to an effective interest rate of $8\frac{1}{2}$ per cent. The reluctantly accepted obligation to refund a share of the pre-1814 national debt to Denmark created further trouble, which was met in 1823 by obtaining a larger loan from abroad at 7·9 per cent, so as to make a lump-sum payment to the Danes. This helped to restore Norway's credit in the money market, but two more decades passed before the Bank of Norway outgrew its fear that a fixed rate of exchange would drain away its silver.

The public finances were further complicated by the fact that the self-sufficient element in the population, which lacked ready money even for the most necessary purchases, had a special interest in keeping down the cost of government; we have already seen how the peasant members of the Storting concentrated upon so doing from the very outset. Moreover, they wished such costs as were unavoidable to be covered by indirect rather than by direct taxation, and therefore voiced a persistent demand for the abolition of the land tax, which rested solely on registered farm properties, and of the tax in municipalities, levied on property and trading activities. These were reduced on several occasions, and in 1837 were completely swept away.

In 1824-7 customs duties already provided almost two-thirds of the sums raised for the Budget. Since they were levied on the export trades more than on imports, they did little or nothing to stimulate home production. Nor could it be claimed that duties were needed in order to discourage luxurious living: in 1828—the first year for which we have adequate records—Norwegian imports amounted to 110 pounds of bread-corn (chiefly rye and barley) per inhabitant, rather more than two pounds of sugar, a pound and a half of coffee, and very small quantities of tobacco, syrup, meat, and bacon.[7] But to meet the deficiency in direct taxation, the

---

the sixteenth century; its value was approximately that of the United States dollar or four English shillings. The paper dollar or *riksbankdaler*, issued by the Bank of Norway, was convertible at 2·005 in 1822, 1·115 in 1825, 1·39 in 1832, and 1·12 in 1836.[8]

indirect taxes were raised further, even when the increased resilience of the economy offered a prospect that lower rates plus more effective measures to discourage smuggling might yield a larger revenue. The inflated tariff was therefore one of the problems left over for the new era, whose coming was foreshadowed by a successful conversion loan in 1834. Eight years later Norway went back on to the silver standard—and by that time the average consumption of sugar and coffee mentioned above had been respectively doubled and trebled.

THE TRANSITION TO FREEDOM OF TRADE

Although the industrial revolution had scarcely touched Norway, which imported its very first stationary steam engine as late as 1831, there were now many indications of increasing economic vigour. The timber trade had satisfactory markets in France and the Netherlands, and Norwegian shipping was helped to revive by admission to the conveyance of Swedish timber to Britain; so that in 1838 its total tonnage was greater than before the Napoleonic Wars. When the 1840s began, the export and import trade of the country, treated as a single whole, was at least twice as great both in quantity and value as it had been in 1814.⁹ Moreover, in the course of that decade Norway derived new impulses from the big changes of economic policy on the other side of the North Sea. The repeal of the British restrictions on the export of machinery in 1843 encouraged industrial experiment. The halving of the British timber duties, though delayed until 1851, gave Norway a share in a rapidly expanding market, where five years earlier she had been selling only 50 per cent of the quantities of 1805. Above all, the repeal of the Navigation Laws, which opened even the coastal trade of the British Isles to foreign shipping, enabled the Norwegian mercantile marine to find a special role in the world economy, which successive skilful adaptations to new conditions enabled it to keep (see pp. 116 and 188).

Meanwhile, Norway reshaped its own trade policy on the same lines as Britain. The teachings of liberal economists had been current since the days of Adam Smith, and the lowest tariff system in

Europe had been introduced for the Twin Kingdoms in 1797, a decade before the great upheaval that led to their separation. The new Norway was therefore ripe for conversion to a liberal regime as soon as an economically more influential neighbour led the way. Tariff reductions were indeed opposed by the peasants. They feared that the result would be a burden of direct taxation falling upon their own shoulders; deprecated the influence of foreign luxuries, which the Haugeans regarded as a temptation to worldliness; and wished to keep up the prices of home products—though the last of these arguments exposed a conflict of interest between the dairy farmers, who predominated in many western districts, and the big corn-producers of the east. But the government triumphed over this opposition with the help of a free-trade champion inside the Storting, A. M. Schweigaard,* a professor of jurisprudence, political economy, and statistics, who throughout a long career preferred to exercise his very considerable talents as a legislator rather than as a minister. Like Cobden, whom he resembled in many ways, he gained added respect as a largely self-made man.

Schweigaard's reshaping of the Norwegian tariff in 1842 coincided with the first free-trade Budget of Sir Robert Peel. But his work had begun earlier, with a series of newspaper articles published in 1836 and his membership of a tariff commission, which made its recommendations to the Norwegian government in October 1841. Raw materials were freed entirely or given a maximum duty of 10 per cent on importation, while the so-called 'natural trades' in timber, fish, and ores were encouraged by a great reduction in export charges: as late as 1830 timber had paid an export duty of about 16 per cent of value. Household necessities were now subjected to a light tax or none at all, while the duty on wines and certain other luxuries was increased. Thus home production was encouraged without 'feather bedding', shipping was helped, and tariff rates were brought down to the minimum consistent with the

* 1808–70. The orphaned son of a small-town tradesman, he had been to sea as a cabin boy at thirteen, but his performance in the law examinations was one of the three best in a hundred years; professor, 1814–70; Storting representative for Oslo, 1842–69. His advanced views on free trade were combined with a strongly conservative attitude on constitutional questions.

avoidance of a revolutionary change in general taxation. This cautious start was followed by the halving of the duties on the different bread-corns and on potatoes in 1851–7, while further reductions on foodstuffs resulted from the decision of a tariff commission in 1860 that duties should in principle be retained for revenue only. Five years later an agreement with France on the lines of Britain's Cobden–Chevalier treaty gave mutual shipping privileges, customs reductions, and a most-favoured-nation clause. Finally, a further interstate treaty with Sweden in 1874 extended the reciprocal trade arrangements made in 1827 by allowing free entry to many categories of goods (including textiles) when carried by sea, provided that the shipping employed was Norwegian or Swedish.

The general success of the free-trade policy in Norway is attested by its retention until the very last years of the century, by which time Britain was its sole remaining prop. As regards the shorter period, it may be sufficient to notice that the revenue proved to be elastic enough to avoid the resort to heavy direct taxation which was the bugbear of the farmer. To some extent this was the result of the pressure he exercised through his representatives in the Storting to secure rigid economy in expenditure; but the Budget was approximately doubled between 1822 and 1842, and again between 1842 and 1865.[10]

In the contest over the mercantilist restrictions on internal economic activities, the peasants sided naturally with the liberals. In 1818 the first inroads were made into the privileges affecting sawmills. Henceforth any person was allowed to set up a mill on his own property for sawing his own trees, and might sell the product as he liked; he might also saw other people's timber for domestic purposes. But the strength of the opposition by wealthy entrepreneurs to freedom of trade in this connection is shown by the fact that ministers had invoked the crown veto against the measure in 1816 and would have done so again if the king had not intervened personally on the other side; even so, it was claimed in the Storting in 1851 that the system of saw licences still left export in the hands of less than a score of big capitalists. Three years later a further law was passed, abolishing privilege at a cost of 150,000 dollars in compensation to existing holders, who eventually secured a respite until 1860. At that date Norway contained 3,325 sawmills, of which the majority served only local purposes, while the export industry remained in part under the control of combinations originally formed to organize the flotation of logs along the principal rivers.

The urban monopoly of commerce had been redefined as late as 1818 by a law distinguishing between small-scale retail trade, which was available to any duly registered burgess of a town, and the business of a merchant, for which a four-year training and familiarity with a foreign language and book-keeping were prescribed. In 1842, however, the trade in goods of one's own production, in some foodstuffs, and indeed, in food for the mind (books, artistic objects, and instruments) was thrown open to everyone, and burgesses of towns were relieved of the restrictions imposed in 1818. At the same time Schweigaard's influence secured big concessions for rural traders. Although it was still deemed important to avoid 'distracting the mind of the countryman from his natural pursuits to trade and barter',[11] he could now be assigned a royal trading licence without paying for the status of burgess in the nearest town, and might deal in food and other agreed necessities of country life without any form of licence. In 1857 all groceries were included among the said necessities, in 1866 the towns lost the monopoly of importation, and in 1882 their export monopoly was lost as well. Though the system of urban privilege was thus brought to an end, the towns remained the natural centres of wholesale trade, sending out commercial travellers to offer supplies to rural shopkeepers. Facilities were also improved by a steady increase in the number of town charters, which lovers of monopoly in the existing towns opposed in vain. The nineteen towns which sent representatives to Eidsvoll in 1814 had become twenty-eight by 1842 and thirty-five by 1884.

In the smaller handicrafts the countryside had long enjoyed a large degree of independence. The variety of crafts was naturally smaller than in the towns, and the standard of execution often declined as new techniques spread slowly outwards from urban centres, though there were some rural workmen of the highest repute.

The general position at the beginning of the nineteenth century was that rural craftsmen were twice as numerous as those of the towns, but they had as a rule no regular journeymen or apprentices, were commonly self-taught, and might be dependent upon such tools and equipment as they could carry with them from farm to farm in their search for employment. The attention of free traders was accordingly directed chiefly to the effects of urban gilds, which had been introduced for the most part as late as the seventeenth century and were purely local.

Any 'new and perpetual restrictions on freedom of trade' infringed the constitution, but it was not until 1839 that legislation was passed to replace gild regulations by a uniform code, prevent the formation of new gilds, and limit those already in being to the lifetime of the existing master craftsmen and their widows. The number of gilds had then shrunk to thirty-seven, scattered among half a dozen of the older towns, and their membership averaged only about thirty-six apiece.[12] Tests of skill, however, could still be demanded from both masters and journeymen. These were very intermittently enforced by prosecution, and in 1869 it was laid down that a master needed no qualifications except registration as a burgess; the testing of journeymen was abolished soon afterwards. But the very small-scale handicrafts which were still characteristic of the Norwegian towns tended to keep the spirit of regulation alive. In 1865 Oslo, which was by far the largest of them, had only a handful of workers, including apprentices, to each master, and the apprentices for the most part still resided in the master's home.[13] In such circumstances it is no surprise to find that a majority of journeymen had received formal training, to which the law gave fresh encouragement in 1881–2 by enacting new apprenticeship regulations and re-establishing a test of skill for journeymen. At that period handicrafts (including those practised independently in rural areas) still occupied several times as many hands as were employed in factories.[14]

The principle of freedom of trade was slowly extended to women. In 1839 women over forty years of age were authorized to practise a craft, if it was necessary for their support, and three years later women without husbands were allowed to engage in trade; by the 1860s these rights were extended to all their sex, as was the control of their own affairs in general. An important law of 1854 granted equal rights of inheritance, except that the *odelsrett* system (see note, p. 11) gave priority to sons and the property of married women remained for a further quarter of a century under the husband's control. Other forms of economic opportunity were soon opened to every woman. Nursing was recognized as a feminine vocation in 1870, in 1879 the first evening courses were organized to equip women for office work, and in 1882 the admission of the first woman student to the university—an event of sufficient importance to occupy half a page in the *Graphic*—prepared the way for their conquest of the professions. But liberalism in this context meant much more than the concession of facilities for earning a living. The key event in Norway was the publication in 1854 of Camilla Collett's *Amtmandens Döttre (The County Governor's Daughters)*—its earliest realistic novel and an enduring protest against the conventional acceptance of marriage as the all-sufficient goal of woman's existence.

THE 'NORWEGIAN SYSTEM' ESTABLISHED

The practice of economic liberalism in Norway was always combined with constructive activities on the part of the state. These derived their first momentum from the work of Frederik Stang, the brilliant lawyer who was picked at thirty-eight to become head of a ministry of the interior, newly carved out of the finance department. It was becoming generally recognized that the national product— to use modern terms—could not be expanded as it should without the provision of more adequate communications and additional credit facilities. In Britain such needs might safely be left for private enterprise to fill, but Norway was too poor for anything substantial to be attempted in these fields unless the State participated. On the other hand the Storting, for political reasons, would have liked to keep government intervention to a minimum, and jealously guarded the taxpayer's interest in a low level of public expenditure—an interest which ministers on the whole respected. Hence the development of a hybrid device which Schweigaard called 'the

Norwegian system' in 1868, when he was contrasting the Norwegian mortgage bank under government auspices with the private mortgage associations which had proved a less satisfactory alternative in Sweden.[15] Under this system new public institutions or facilities were not expected to originate in any national plan but in a proposal from a regional or group interest, supported by private capital which would cover some such proportion as one-fifth of the cost. The central authorities would then use their superior credit-rating to obtain the rest of the capital, much of it from abroad, and would supply technical supervision and general oversight for the project. Wherever possible, the resulting institution remained in form a private company: down to 1884 the Norwegian state never budgeted for more than 7 per cent of the gross national product.

As regards communications, Norway was—and to some extent still is—handicapped by its hard climate, rugged terrain, and scattered population. Even in the impoverished 1820s the state had given a high priority to the provision of two paddlewheel steamers, *The Constitution* and *Prince Charles*, to provide better connections round the west coast to Bergen and southward to Gothenburg and Copenhagen. By 1850, at which date privately owned Norwegian steamships were still a rarity along the coast, government steamers under the charge of naval officers were conveying passengers, mail, and some cargo as far north as Hammerfest and also maintained links with Germany and England. The provision of lighthouses and light-buoys followed—in the far north it was only beginning in the 1880s—and much of the coast still had to be charted.

A very few new main roads had been constructed by military engineers in the 1820s and 1830s, but they had unfortunately accepted gradients of 1:5, as compared with a maximum of 1:8 in other European countries, including Switzerland. When Stang took office, there was a general demand for a network of roads suitable for vehicles, which must often follow a different line from the old tracks running from farm to farm along the valley. Local labour was easily obtained, and there was no great difficulty about finance: down to 1851 only roads that linked the two kingdoms required the approval of the Storting, while after that date the money was voted, not unwillingly on the whole, either by the Storting or by the elected authorities of the county concerned. The technical difficulties, however, proved a grave handicap, even after a strong directorate of roads was set up in 1864. Neither the gravel surfacing, which was usually employed, nor the full macadam system, which provided the first *chaussée* leading out of the capital in 1850, escaped serious disturbance at the annual thaw; and until the 1880s maintenance was entrusted to the unpaid efforts of the locality. The erection of iron suspension or other substantial bridges was needed wherever wheeled traffic must be brought across a deep river or a precipitous gorge. Most important of all, the high mountain passes had somehow to be surmounted by easier gradients than in the past; but the solution adopted was a corkscrew design of road, executed with a very narrow width in order to save money and producing whole series of hazardous hairpin bends, which survived into the motor age. In the first ten years—at the end of which Stang left office temporarily on account of his health—only 100 km. of new main roads were constructed, but 600 in the next decade and 800 in the third. At the close of the century the total network was about 29,000 km. (18,000 miles), but it was discontinuous, as tourists often found to their surprise, particularly in the western fiord districts.

Although Norway never experienced a 'Canal Age', its first railway took the place of a canal, which had been proposed for conveying timber from the foot of Mjösa, the largest lake, to the wharves at Oslo—a distance of about 50 miles. In 1848 the Storting accepted the government's view that the construction of the railway justified raising a foreign loan, but it was originally intended that the work should be done under government auspices or, as a subsidiary alternative, by a private company receiving government support. At one stage scarcity of money caused a Swedish engineer to be brought in, who would have reverted to the idea of a canal combined with a railroad for horsedrawn traffic. However, Robert Stephenson, who had been called over from England by Consul-general Crowe to survey the intended route in 1846, devised the plan finally approved; he was to build the line, while both the cost of construction and the subsequent profit were to be divided equally between a body of British shareholders and the Norwegian state.

Engineers, key workers, and a good deal of material were brought from England. The work was completed in three years (1851–4), with results that exceeded expectation: in the first twelve months the railway carried 83,000 tons of goods and 128,000 passengers, and freightage costs for timber fell by two-thirds.[16] The financial basis unfortunately proved less satisfactory, as Stephenson himself was the agreed arbitrator over construction costs, which were twice as high as those of their next railway, which the Norwegians built for themselves; they also resented the fact that the shares stood too high for the British interests to be bought out. Those ardent nationalists, such as Sverdrup and Jaabæk, who had opposed the concession in the Storting, probably went too far when they asserted that Stang and Schweigaard had been 'led by the nose by tough English business-men';[17] what is certain is that the railway building of the next decade was based exclusively on private Norwegian companies handling the proceeds of State loans raised abroad.

Meanwhile, the first electric telegraph had been erected between Oslo and Eidsvoll, as the railway contract provided. But as a result of inquiries made in Sweden, a commission which included Broch soon recommended the construction of a general telegraph network to meet the needs of foreign trade, the fisheries, and military contingencies; three links with Sweden were proposed, as well as lines round the coast and between the principal towns. This work was duly authorized by the Storting in April 1854 as a necessary adjunct to the postal service. This too was now reaching the general European standard, with the rather belated introduction of a uniform cheap rate of postage, prepaid by stamps, which quadrupled the number of letters in the first two years. By the end of the 1860s the mail steamers ran right round to the Russian frontier, and the laying of the first submarine cable (to Peterhead in Scotland) had given Norwegian trade and shipping almost instantaneous contact with the outside world.

Of all the modern improvements to communication, the canal alone, though long established in Sweden, has proved permanently unadaptable to the Norwegian terrain. After half a century of intermittent discussion, Norway's first canal was authorized in 1862. It connected Skien, one of the very few river ports, with its hinterland

and even after it had been extended a generation later did not exceed a length of 80 miles, including several lakes. Its main use was for the transportation of timber; the same purpose was served by a second, very short canal, constructed in the 1870s above the port of Halden near the Swedish frontier.

The expansion of communications was accompanied by the establishment of new credit institutions. In the early years of its history the Bank of Norway employed its capital chiefly for land mortgages, a need which it met only inadequately, and did very little to supply the needs of industry. Savings banks, indeed, made their first appearance in 1822; by 1840 there were twenty-six, widely distributed over the country, having a capital equivalent to £330,000; an din the next decade their number was more than trebled and the capital more than doubled. But since their primary object was to meet the small saver's need for safe employment of his money, they did not help general requirements for credit, which down to 1848 had little to fall back on except the cash balances which were beginning to accumulate in the possession of the finance ministry. Shipping ventures, for example, were commonly financed by subdivision into very small parts, but between 1820 and 1839 money was so scarce that no insurance was available in Norway for either ships or cargoes.

The period of the later 1840s, when the state began to face the need to use its own credit for raising capital abroad in support of railway building and other productive objects, was therefore marked in addition by the authorization of the first commercial banks. These were designed originally as acceptance houses for bills, but found it necessary to seek deposits in order to have the wherewithal to lend. Surviving the first crisis of confidence in the autumn of 1857 (see p. 129), they soon became strong enough to borrow considerable sums in London and other financial centres to meet the increasing needs of Norwegian industry and commerce. The earliest regular insurance companies likewise date from the end of the 1840s, when for instance Broch helped to provide Norway with the first private life-insurance organization in Scandinavia.

In contemporary eyes, however, the most significant new foundation was the Mortgage Bank (*Hypotekbanken*), whose hybrid structure was specially representative of the 'Norwegian system'. The farmers had clamoured for help of this kind as early as 1817, but the government delayed its consent until 1851: by then their needs could no longer be ignored with impunity, and the alternative under discussion was the hazardous step of increasing the note circulation through one or more additional banks of issue. The Mortgage Bank satisfied the demand for long-term agricultural credits by raising funds abroad: the money was fairly readily obtainable because the initial capital had been supplied by the state and the bank's affairs were controlled by three directors, of whom the ministry appointed one and the Storting the others. At first the main sources of supply were Hamburg and Copenhagen, but after the first decade an increasing proportion of the bonds was marketed at home. In 1857 the nominal rate of interest on the mortgages was raised to 5 per cent, which the poorer mortgagees vainly agitated to bring back to the older rate of four.

SHIPPING AND THE CARRYING TRADE

Although the 'Norwegian system' provided many of the prerequisites, the modernization of economic life from mid-century onwards owed a special debt to the concomitant expansion of the mercantile marine. By 1840 its tonnage had already passed that of the palmiest days before 1807: it comprised 2,900 vessels in all and, although the average crew was only half a dozen, the number of larger ships, designed for something more than coastal traffic, had also increased. What was more significant, their voyages were beginning to reach beyond north European and Mediterranean waters into the oceans, where to a greater extent than in markets nearer home their employment must be in the carrying trade of other, larger nations. But Swedish timber and Russian corn were the only foreign freights readily available until the repeal of the British Navigation Laws took effect on New Year's Day, 1850. This gave Norway its great opportunity: a load of timber from Quebec reached London docks on 5 January in the first of forty-four Norwegian ships which sailed that year from the St. Lawrence, to cite only one of the many long hauls now open to them. Moreover, the British example was quickly followed by the Dutch with their empire, and other countries more gradually abolished differential charges against foreign carriers.

In the early 1850s the carrying trade already employed rather more than one-third of Norway's mercantile marine, and new opportunities continued to arise. In 1854–5 the Allied governments spent large sums to secure the rapid conveyance of munitions and supplies of all kinds to the Crimea. The conference at Paris which ended the conflict set up rules to protect neutral shipping in time of war. A year later the abolition of the Danish Sound tolls eased every nation's dealings with the Baltic trades and, although the Crimean War was followed by a short trade recession, the emigrant traffic from Europe to North America was by then helping Norwegian shipping to find its way into American markets. The tea and rice trades of the Far East were also opening up at this juncture, while the introduction of Norwegian klipfish to South America established the first contacts with the carrying trade of yet another continent. In the course of the decade the Norwegian mercantile marine grew from 305,552 to 587,727 net registered tons,[18] a rate of growth which exceeded that of world shipping as a whole.

Success was attributable to various causes. As a nation of seafarers since Viking times, trained in the fisheries and the traffic of the fiords, the Norwegians never lacked competent seamen, albeit the 35,000 men required for the crews of 1860 amounted to nearly twice the percentage of population that mans the machine-driven vessels of the present day. Equally important was the unfailing supply of competent skippers, men who were capable both of commanding a ship and of arranging the most profitable charters as it worked its way from port to port across the world. Moreover, the ships they sailed were cheap. Most of them had been built and rigged in the small harbours between Lindesnes and the Swedish frontier, where local craftsmen worked with local timber, and the costs were closely watched by local people of all classes who were taking small shares in the venture. Others were bought second-hand in Britain and other countries, where the price of wooden sailing ships had already depreciated in competition with steam and iron; moreover, the prices paid by Norwegians were often below market level because their long experience of the timber trade, where the cargo could be trusted to keep an old tub afloat, accustomed them to accept low standards of seaworthiness. Lastly, it must be recognized that the ships were run on the cheap, with poor victualling and accommodation for the crew, low wages, and rough-and-ready management. In 1839 200 Scandinavian ships were alleged to possess only five sextants and two chronometers among them: this was one year before Norway introduced its first qualifying examination for mates and captains and five years before its first local school of navigation was established in Oslo. Even after these modest beginnings had been made, a new Norwegian code of maritime law, which *inter alia* offered the seaman a modicum of protection against ill usage, was held up from 1851 to 1859 because the ministry was reluctant for elected local authorities to share in the appointment of lay judges for maritime courts.

Between 1860 and 1880 the fleet grew to 1,519,000 tons, which made it the third largest in the world. It was an immense achievement for so small and poor a country to have become the owner of 7 per cent of global shipping resources; to give a single example, it meant that Norwegian vessels were conveying nearly half the trade of their Swedish neighbours, whose fleet as recently as the 1840s had been growing equally fast. Yet the position was still extremely vulnerable. In 1870 five-sixths of the freights were still made up of timber (including much Swedish timber) and the rest mainly tramp cargoes, which were easily picked up at a period when other shipping nations were busy starting regular lines. Even more perilous was the continued reliance upon sailing ships. In 1878—nine years after the opening of the Suez Canal—the sailing tonnage under Norwegian ownership was still mounting: in the entire decade only 6 per cent of the additions to the fleet were steamers.

This dangerous conservatism depended primarily upon relative costs. Wooden sailing ships and no others could be built cheaply all along the south coast; their obsolescence also meant that they could be bought very cheaply in foreign ports, from which one-half of all acquisitions in 1860–79 were obtained. The fact that they needed three times as much crew as steamers required for the same amount of trade was offset partly by low wage rates and partly by the consideration that sailing vessels were cheap to lay up, when the Baltic ports were closed by ice or cargoes were for other reasons unobtainable. Admittedly, voyages under sail were slow, the proportion of wrecks often serious, and dates of arrival always unpredictable, but it was still possible to supplement the traditional bulk cargoes of timber, corn, wool, cotton, and coal with newer requirements—rails, Chilean saltpetre, or petroleum—for which the speed and regularity of steamship freightage were not essential. As early as 1877, some Norwegian sailing ships were partitioned with bulkheads for service as tankers, to obviate the risk of conveying petroleum or naphtha in barrels.

The west coast port of Bergen, however, took a different view from those of the south coast. Its staple export of fish had never suffered such a depression as had ruined the timber exporters after the Napoleonic Wars, so capital was comparatively plentiful in the hands of Bergen merchant families of long experience. Moreover, since they exported a perishable commodity at almost all seasons of the year, they were always interested in speed of transportation: they had been relatively successful, for instance, in copying the American and English tea clippers. As for steamers, Bergen was prompt to employ them on the coastal routes which the State had pioneered, and added its own connections south to Hamburg and west to Newcastle. It competed with Spanish steamships for the trade between Norway and the Peninsula, and in the early 1870s, when emigrants still commonly faced an eight-weeks sail passage to Quebec, Bergen tried to organize its own steamship route to North America, to convey emigrants in summer and cargo in winter. This venture did not survive a temporary decline in emigration in 1874, but the expanding Black Sea corn trade offered better prospects. In 1880 one-half of a total Norwegian steam tonnage of 54,000 was concentrated in Bergen, including 123 vessels (out of a total of 324) which plied outside Norwegian waters.

The main transition to steam belongs to a later chapter. Here we may pause to sum up the economic facts which justified Björnson's 'Song of the Norwegian Seaman', written in 1868:

> Our glory and our might
> Are borne on sail-wings white.

The huge growth of the mercantile marine helped exports, since freight costs were usually lower for conveyance in Norwegian ships.

It also stimulated imports. English coal, for example, was often carried to avoid making a voyage home in ballast, while the new transoceanic contacts increased both the demand for, and the availability of, sugar and other 'colonial' commodities: between 1851–5 and 1871–5 the annual value of such imports trebled. But the carrying trade in particular had a special importance as a source of capital, for a second-hand sailing ship, bought without too much regard to its seaworthiness, could be expected—if it escaped disaster—to cover its initial cost in the first twelve months. Representative statistics for the years 1867–9 show that, after allowing 33·4 per cent for provisions and wages—but only 4·5 per cent for depreciation—the net profit on freights carried averaged 16·2 per cent.[19] The distribution of that profit cannot readily be traced in detail, but it represented an important addition to the capital without which the economy could not at that time have been modernized.

MODERNIZATION OF THE ECONOMY

In the third quarter of the century Norway began to adopt the technical improvements that were already transforming industry and to a less extent agriculture in many parts of western Europe. The state led the way by its importation of the first paddle steamers, the railway, and the electric telegraph; indeed, the ex-naval officer, P. Steenstrup,* who had negotiated the purchase of the steamers in England was also the originator in 1842 of the first engineering workshop. By 1850 there were a dozen small workshops and foundries, which repaired existing machinery, manufactured iron tools and equipment, and could make small steam engines, such as had begun to reach Norway from abroad. Some Danish spinning machinery had been set up as early as 1815 for a small cotton mill in Halden;† but the impact of a modern textile industry dates from

---

* 1807–63. Akers Mekaniske Verksted, Oslo, which he soon developed into a flourishing ship-and engine-building concern at the harbour, was started at a site on the River Aker, where water power was available. A good deal of the iron, and nearly all the textile, industry of Oslo grew up on the river bank.
† So small that in the first seventeen months it used only five bales of cotton; in 1823 it stood idle because there was no demand for yarn.[20]

1845, when the first two Oslo pioneers encountered each other in Manchester on rival tours of investigation, from which they returned with knowledge of the business, the machinery, and some skilled workers.* By 1860 thirty-four textile factories had been established for spinning or weaving of cotton, wool, or linen, with an average of 74 workers, and the corresponding figures for engineering workshops and foundries were 39 and 37.

In both cases the smallness of the units is attributable in large measure to the absence of coal, the basic raw material of the nineteenth-century 'industrial revolution'. The textile and many other mills employed chiefly the waterwheel, as Britain had done before the days of Watt. As for the new iron foundries, their growth was restricted by their dependence upon coke-made iron, which they imported as their raw material from England. The big traditional ironmasters, who owned mines and forests, lost interest in the industry: when their charcoal-made iron was no longer saleable in America after the invention of the Bessemer process in 1856, they transferred their capital to the timber trade. But while industry lingered in this intermediate stage of development, so that as late as 1875 it employed only one-third as many Norwegians as did agriculture, fishing, and forestry, modernization was also affecting these primary occupations, which will therefore be examined first.

At the census of 1855 the category of independent peasant farmers numbered about 113,000; cottars had reached their recorded maximum of 65,600; and the bigger farms disposed of a very large labour force, much of it recruited from cottars' children who were unable to get a holding of their own. But, for the farmer at least, times were good: after 1850 corn prices rose by one-half, which produced a corresponding rise in land values, and in 1855 the corn harvest reached an all-time record in relation to the size of population. Farmers borrowed readily from the new Mortgage Bank either to finance improvements or to convert leasehold into freehold, with the

---

* Including a foreman with the promising name of Hargreaves Jameson. The iron industry likewise imported artisans as well as machinery; what is still the biggest nail-making concern, for example, founded its fortunes upon the Coates machine, bought in 1854, and brought over an English foreman to work it at the high annual wage of 700 dollars.[21]

result that by 1880 only one-twenty-fourth part of their land was leased, as compared with one-third in 1830. In 1857 the intermingled plots still amounted to 50 per cent or more all along the west coast, and about 20 per cent even in the big eastern valleys; but in that year a new law provided the services of expert surveyors and other encouragements for laying out land in severalty. The adoption of improved techniques[22] was stimulated by the district agricultural schools, established in the course of the 1840s; in 1849 the Norway Welfare Society organized the first National Agricultural Meeting, which had many local counterparts; and in 1854 a Higher Agricultural School was set up for instruction in theory. The Great Exhibition of 1851 had aroused interest in imports such as the movable steam-powered thresher and the mower, both of which came to Norway in the 1850s. But greater importance attaches to the increased use of native equipment which was better suited to Norwegian needs. Some of this was manufactured in the ironworks, but mostly it was still made by local craftsmen; for novel designs they used sets of models, many of them produced in the prison at Oslo.

The general trend can be shown from the lists of chattels recorded in typical farm probates. A comparison between the situation in 1801–10 and 1850–60 shows that in the later period the average number of ploughs per farm had risen from one and two-thirds to two and one-third, of harrows from less than one to nearly one and one-half, and of carts and other wheeled equipment from three-quarters to two and one-quarter items per farm. The values given also show that these chattels were superior to, or at any rate more complex than, what the farms had owned before. As for the efficiency of the work done, there is good evidence that the normal depth of ploughing increased from four inches in 1800 to between six and eight inches in 1850; and in its roller-harrow, manufactured as early as 1823, Norway possessed at least one tool which found a market in England, Germany, and Sweden. The bigger farms in the eastern valleys now enjoyed a recognizable period of 'high farming'.

However, the reopening of the Russian and other European corn trades after the Crimean War caused a fall in corn prices, accompanied by a greater fall in land prices, which in the best arable districts of Norway went down by as much as 30 per cent. One consequence was that the farmers clamoured for the reduction of public expenditure; at the local level they cut the appropriations for agricultural schools and advisers. But the most hopeful remedy for the situation was an adaptation to dairy farming—involving the study of new methods—which gradually prevailed. Lighter and less cramped byres were erected; attention was given to the quality, and not merely the quantity, of the stock that could be kept alive through the long winter; more trouble was taken over the fodder supply; and some of the biggest farms even imported Swiss workers to show how an all-year-round milk production should be organized. A market for milk sprang up among the growing population of the towns, as it became less usual for the burgesses to keep their own cows on patches of meadow outside the built-up area, while the railway in some districts made it feasible to bring milk from a distance. Most of it, however, had still to be processed into butter or cheese. The introduction of the ice-cooler and the cream separator (a Swedish invention of 1877) made the work easier; but after the first margarine factory in northern Europe had been established in Oslo in 1876, the price of butter fell by one-third in ten years, and a new condensed milk manufacture, using 40 per cent of sugar, failed to absorb the surplus. Co-operative dairies could only mitigate the disadvantages of a very restricted market: the first in Scandinavia was set up in one of the east Norway valleys in 1856; by 1870 Norway had ten, and by 1881 they were organized in a National Dairy Association.

It was fortunate that the harvest of cod and herring, which employed large numbers of farmer fishermen, commanded an expanding market overseas. Technical changes came very slowly, but the state encouraged production, firstly by abolishing tithe and export duties on fish, and secondly by legislating, in 1851 and 1857 respectively, for both the herring and the cod fisheries to be supervised by public officials. Their function was to regulate times, places, and conditions for fishing, and to protect those taking part from unreasonable exactions by shore owners. In Lofoten the traditional handline fishing began to disappear, and most of the cod was now exported more profitably as 'klipfish'. In the case of the spring herring, the processing was unchanged but passed into new hands, as fishermen and other peasants in localities close to the fisheries took over the salting and barrelling and traded direct with markets in east Norway and Sweden, leaving only the more distant export trade to the Bergen wholesalers.

In the first two decades after the Lofoten cod harvesting was brought under official supervision, the number of participants doubled.[23] Farther south the summer of 1863 saw the first attempts to follow up a Swedish intiative by launching larger, decked boats to fish the banks out in the North Sea; this created a new export trade in haddock and halibut. Industry also helped, as a Norwegian invention of 1853[24] made it possible to prepare by a steam process an improved and consequently more saleable cod-liver oil for medicinal purposes, while in the 1870s a further fillip was given by the commencement of a canning industry in Stavanger; this turned the tiny, neglected brisling into a commodity that undercut the market for the Mediterranean sardine.

Still bigger results were to accrue eventually from the enterprise of Svend Foyn,* who in the 1840s introduced a purpose-built vessel for seal hunting, enabling large profits to be earned on the edge of the polar ice west of Jan Mayen Island. He later turned his attention to the whale fishery, long practised against the smaller kinds off the Norwegian coast. He used a specially designed steamboat to approach the quarry, and in 1868 invented a harpoon gun for firing a missile which exploded inside the whale. This deadly device which was the first known Norwegian invention of world importance made the big finback whales more vulnerable, and by 1883 twenty-three boats were at work along the coast of Finnmark, killing and hauling the carcasses ashore for processing.

Exports of fish were rivalled by those of timber products,† which had for centuries provided Norway with its chief machine industry. When the trade revived in the 1830s, the circular saw and multiple

---

* 1809–94. A seaman from the age of eleven; in 1864 his first steam whaler, *Spes et Fides*, caught only one whale, in 1868, with the new gun, thirty-two; from 1872 onwards a ten-year monopoly of the gun earned him a large fortune, which he devoted almost entirely to mission work at home and overseas.

† In 1866–84 the respective percentages of total exports varied as follows: fish and products, 48·76–34·59; timber and products, 45·84–31·90.[25]

blades were introduced to increase the cut, and when industrial establishments were counted for the first time at the end of that decade, sawmills were nearly nine times as numerous as the corn-mills, which were their closest rivals*. In the early 1870s, when the trade reached its zenith with an annual export of $2\frac{1}{3}$ million cubic metres, some part of its success might be attributed to better care of the trees. The state forests had been put under the charge of official foresters, of whom the first completed their training in Germany in 1857; communal woodlands were regulated by local committees; and expert advice was made available to private owners, though their felling rights were still left uncontrolled. But the most significant change was the sanctioning of the use of steam saws and the importation of the steam-powered planing machine from England; county governors' reports from three widely separated areas suggest that in the early 1880s about one-ninth of the sawmills were steam driven,[26] and it is safe to conclude that these would be among the largest units. Moreover, by that time the modernization of the industry had been carried a stage further by converting the wood into products of higher value. Pulp was first exported in 1868, the first cellulose factory built in 1874, and by 1881 there were thirty-seven pulp mills and eight paper mills. In terms of employment, sawing and planing mills provided the largest industrial occupation throughout the period, but at the 1885 census their work force of 10,300 had an important adjunct in the 2,343 engaged in production of pulp and paper.

Although half the capital invested in Norwegian mines by 1870 was foreign, the 'natural trade' in ores made little progress. Nickel enjoyed a boom in the 1870s, when a single Norwegian works with 300 employees was responsible for one-seventh of the world output, but in the next decade the discoveries in New Caledonia gave the Norwegian industry a severe setback. Röros copper could be smelted with coke after the coming of the railway in the late 1870s, which also made export easier; some of the smaller copper mines, however, fell into disuse. Iron mining almost ceased after the discontinuation of charcoal smelting, and the only considerable new development was the export of pyrites (mainly for its sulphur content),[27]

* 3,543:407. There were 1,387 distilleries, but they used little machinery.[28]

which was begun in 1861 from a source near Trondheim and spread rapidly to half a dozen other centres. Scattered British interests included the exploitation of titanium (from rutile), begun in the 1860s, and even a short-lived venture in gold mining, in which the workers had an annual output worth £3 a head. Two other natural resources may be mentioned which at this period did better than most of the mines. The quarries of eastern Norway exported much granite; and clear, firm ice in accessible positions formed the basis of a flourishing trade, particularly to England, where the demand from breweries, fish and meat packers, and the homes of the wealthy was almost inexhaustible. The first load had been sent abroad in 1822, and at mid-century the total was less than 20,000 tons, but it then rose by stages to a climax of 554,000 tons in 1898.

During the period 1850–85, the numbers employed in mining scarcely rose above the average for the first quinquennium, which was 1,890. This stands in marked contrast with the growth in manufacturing industry, as shown in a selective Table.

TABLE III[29]

Industrial Employment

	1850	1860	1865	1870	1875	1879	1885
Total	12,279	17,281	24,431	31,358	45,657	41,593	45,313
saw and planing mills	4,090	6,026	6,997	10,020	12,048	10,217	10,300
iron foundries, machine shops, iron shipbuilding	1,057	1,251	4,594	6,701	9,853	7,011	7,110
textiles	1,481	2,982	3,359	3,898	5,128	4,901	6,037
breweries, food manufacture	1,879	1,794	2,425	2,668	4,031	4,010	4,691
brick and tile works	1,539	2,079	2,100	2,366	3,013	3,540	2,354
pulp and paper	192	144	202	353	1,191	1,363	2,343
corn mills	913	1,151	1,647	1,515	1,979	2,039	1,787
match factories	30	95	153	436	1,293	1,208	1,578

Nevertheless, these eight types of industry that predominated at the end of the period were not for the most part fully modernized. The iron works, though dependent on two imported raw materials, had developed an export trade in small hardware, such as nails, horseshoes, and fish hooks, built some iron ships, and supplied most of Norway's own requirements in steam engines. Except for ship's engines, those requirements continued however to be rather modest. In 1870 the enterprises that used water power for their prime mover were at least seven times as numerous as those using steam. By 1885 the disparity had indeed been reduced to a proportion of 2:1, but the 490 steam engines of which particulars were collected in that year developed an average of only 21 h.p. In spite of the importation of much coke in ballast, the Norwegian industrialist found water power to be more economical: some of the steel turbines with which the water mills were now equipped provided as much as 350 h.p. The textile manufactures flourished, partly because the many advantages of cotton over woollen materials created an eager home market, and partly because both cottons and woollens could be exported cheaply to Sweden: in the mid-1880s one of the biggest Oslo textile firms* sold nearly half of an annual production worth kr. 2 million to its Swedish customers, who were almost twice as numerous as the Norwegians. Otherwise, the Table shows only one modern-type industry, apart from the wood products already mentioned. The match factories achieved a considerable export because they had cheap native supplies of sulphur (from pyrites) as well as match sticks: in 1879 they numbered fourteen, but falling prices and competition from Swedish safety matches soon reduced their profitability, though not their output.

The remaining industries in the Table concentrated their attention upon the tastes and needs of the home market, as did the glassworks (which revived about 1850), the single porcelain factory, and many other small units. That market expanded largely as a result of the continued improvement of communications, which helped to increase town populations and—what in Norway was much more important—brought the fashions and labour-saving products of the towns to tempt rural housewives. Imperfect as the roads still were,

---

* Hjula Væveri, founded with capital from a brewery and, in 1849, the earliest user of steam power in the textile industry; in 1854, however, it migrated to the Aker river. Its manufacture of woollen clothing started when supplies of raw cotton were interrupted during the American Civil War.

it made a difference to trade every time a wheeled vehicle was enabled to pass along a former bridle-path, while by 1880 waterborne communications included what Murray's *Handbook for Norway* called 'a singular service of steam-packet omnibuses, following the convolutions of the coast'.[30] Moreover, the government had borrowed large sums abroad in order to finance more railway construction. During the 1860s the lines had reached out from Oslo to the Swedish frontier and to five of the principal lakes,[31] where they could be linked up with steamboat traffic—six stumps with a total length of 225 miles. But in the course of the next ten years the original Eidsvoll railway was extended to provide a through route to Trondheim; the total distance was almost 400 miles and involved a passage through the mountains surrounding Röros. Two additional links with Sweden were completed by 1880, increasing the total network to more than 1,100 miles. As the natural obstacles to railway building in Norway were supplemented by political impediments due to intense local rivalries, construction was then virtually suspended for a time. Later generations inherited, too, one extra problem resulting from the heavy cost of the permanent way: more than half the track was narrow gauge.

Tourism may be mentioned here, as an industry of growing importance which could not have come into existence apart from the improvements in communications. Norway had been known to the salmon fisher since shortly after the Napoleonic Wars; he had soon been followed by individuals in search of an adventurous holiday— and perhaps the subject matter for a popular book—which could be readily found posting through Norway in a carriole, walking the mountains with a knapsack, or climbing on the rock faces. In the 1850s direct steamer services became available to Britain as well as to the Continent, and travel agencies, guidebooks, and modern hotels began to make their appearance. In 1873 Oscar II used the occasion of his coronation at Trondheim to pay a visit to the North Cape, which then came to rank as a special tourist attraction. By 1886, when 13,529 foreigners were recorded entering Norway, twofifths of them by train, Norway was beginning to cater extensively for middle-class tourists from many lands. Though the industry was still confined to the short summer months, it brought much-needed extra earnings to many districts, especially in the western fiords—a favourite holiday resort of the German emperor, Wilhelm II—whose barren mountains had never yielded a profit before. One by-product was that Norway and its people became a little better known in the outside world, even if the tourist was disposed to view their social conditions through romantic, rose-coloured spectacles.

SOCIAL REACTIONS TO ECONOMIC CHANGE

Although Norway delighted the Victorian tourist by its quaint remoteness almost as much as by its natural grandeurs, closer examination would quickly have shown that it was only to a diminishing extent dependent upon any hand-to-mouth primeval exploitation of land and water. In 1815 the autarkic peasant farm, covering nearly all its wants by household production or local barter, had predominated; two generations later this was a phenomenon confined to the remotest settlements. For better and worse, Norwegian society was now exposed more directly than ever before to the effects of world changes. This was shown in 1857, when the collapse of international trade after the boom years of the Crimean War brought discount rates in London to 12 per cent and the firm that negotiated most of the Norwegian business there went bankrupt,* as did more than half of the fourteen concerns in Hamburg that traded with Bergen. The government had to raise a state loan in London and send silver to support its credit in Hamburg, while Schweigaard and Broch with backing from the Bank of Norway organized mutual support among the Norwegian banks and firms chiefly affected.[32] Though the crisis was quickly surmounted, the decline in agricultural prices (already noticed) continued for a whole decade. Norway likewise felt some repercussions from the sudden collapse of confidence in German and Austrian business circles in 1873, and two years later she was tied more closely to the international economy through her entry into a Scandinavian currency union. This had first been proposed at a conference of economists in 1863 and—like

---

* Sewell & Nock: 'Among the broken merchants, very many were described as in the German or North European trades' (J. H. Clapham, *Economic History of Modern Britain*, ii. 370).

the metric system of measures, which was also adopted in 1875—it was originally intended to have a French orientation; but after the Franco–Prussian War, a wholly separate Scandinavian monetary unit was found preferable. The *krone* or crown, minted independently in each country but legal tender in all of them, was given a fixed value in gold, slightly above that of the English Victorian shilling;[33] the change from silver to a gold standard meant that Norway had no possible cushion against the full effects of the fall in the international level of prices, which continued from the mid-seventies to the mid-nineties.

The attitude of the government to economic changes imposed by outside forces was still mainly passive, as was shown for example in the report from a tariff commission appointed in 1874:

Experience has shown that those branches of industry which are rooted in the natural conditions of the country can thrive and flourish without the support of protective duties, while the Commission is disposed to believe that the internal development of a country will be best promoted when its forces can be securely concentrated upon those trades which its own resources promote.[34]

The advance of industry was checked at this time for about a decade, while agriculture, which was still the way of life of most Norwegians, suffered a more serious and prolonged setback. Although Norwegian corn prices did not fall as far as the British, the statistical curve from the 1870s onwards follows closely the general price pattern of the period long known in Britain as the 'Great Depression'.[35] Some of the cheap wheat from the American Middle West which was pouring into Europe entered Norway from 1874 onwards, but the quantities were insignificant; its influence was felt indirectly, through its effect on the price level in the other European markets from which Norwegian ships brought imports. It has even been suggested that the strong rural interest in the election of 1879 was inspired by protectionism rather than the political radicalism inculcated by Sverdrup. When stock-keeping with close attention to quality offered the only hope, it was discouraging to be confronted by tariff reductions which even brought in some foreign meat. Although the cultivated area did not begin to diminish until about

1890, the load of debt for improvements hopefully undertaken with borrowed money in better times, together with the mortgages commonly raised in order to buy out coheirs, had long made the situation very harassing for much of the rural population. One attempted solution was to subdivide farm properties into smaller parcels, but these often proved unviable. The only lasting remedy was a large-scale uprooting of the people from the soil. The cottars went first, their numbers being halved by the end of the century. Next the smaller independent farmers began to diminish, and finally, rising labour costs drove even a proportion of big farmers from the land. Their immediate destination was often the towns, whose share of the population rose from 12·2 per cent in 1845 to 18·3 in 1875 and 28 in 1900. But for very many rural migrants the towns served only as staging posts on their journey to the New World.

The voyage itself was a disincentive. In the earlier period, when emigrants were placed on sailing ships in lieu of cargo, they were crammed between decks and usually had to find their own food for a period of uncertain duration: in 1862 one party of 300 lost a quarter of its members on the passage to Quebec, where a further 10 per cent died in quarantine. Even in later days, when it became more usual to cross by emigrant steamer from Liverpool, the double voyage was an alarming prospect for a family from an isolated valley. What they hoped to gain by the venture was, however, overwhelming—an abundance of fertile soil at a negligible price, and a place in a society where even the cottar and the labourer were assured of equal status and opportunity. Their fortunes will be traced in a later chapter (see p. 206), but the figures speak for themselves. In 1836–65 the annual average of Norwegian emigrants was about 2,500; in 1866–73 it rose to nearly 14,000, and after falling below 5,000 in 1874–9— partly on account of alarming reports of the grasshopper plague, sent home by settlers in the Middle West—in 1880–93 it rose again to nearly 20,000. In the peak year 1882, when 29,000 persons left Norway, and in three other years during the same decade, the population actually declined; moreover, the majority of these later emigrants were men in the prime of life.

The exodus from the farms, while directed especially to the emigrant ships, also left its mark upon the towns, which (as already noticed) received many migrants who eventually went on farther, and upon the denser rural areas, which were increasingly likely to have some form of industry. In a quarter of a century (1865–90) the proportion of inhabitants occupying the scattered rural areas fell by nearly 12 per cent, of which the rise in town populations accounted for rather more than two-thirds (see Table II, p. 97). Some of the newcomers made their way into handicrafts, of which they might have some previous experience: by 1890 83 per cent of craftsmen in the eight principal trades of Oslo had been born elsewhere.[36] But many looked for employment to the new factories and workshops, which expanded very rapidly in 1860–75. The work was largely unskilled; wages and hours compared favourably with those which the small handicraft employers imposed on their journeymen; and many jobs were available for women and even for children.

During the long price fall from the middle of the 1870s onwards, the real value of wages tended to rise—but so did the incidence of unemployment. In 1875–9 the total of industrial workers declined by 10 per cent, and in 1885 it had not quite reached the level of ten years before. In denser rural areas they might have a small-holding to fall back upon, but for the great majority unemployment meant dependence on very meagre poor relief. Norwegian winter conditions rendered the life of the out-of-work especially hard, as Knut Hamsun found during his stay in Oslo in 1879,* and migrant workers experienced a chronic shortage of housing. When Eilert Sundt in 1858 investigated the accommodation for 294 families in a working-class quarter of Oslo, he found an average of four persons per room and three families to every kitchen;[37] in the next quarter of a century, during which the town doubled its inhabitants, such new housing as was put up by private enterprise for the workers was normally occupied at the rate of a family to each room.[38] Less easily measured but at least equally depressing was the sense of absolute dependence upon the employer, whose services to the economy were not hampered by social regulations, even in the case of child labour.

Children had always been required to make themselves useful on the farm: as soon as they could walk and wield a stick, it was common for them to spend long hours herding cattle or goats in solitude

---

* *Hunger*, though not published until 1890, is largely autobiographical.

upon the hillside. Nevertheless, it tells something of parental poverty that an official inquiry in 1875 recorded the employment of relatively large numbers under the more stringent conditions of factory work. At that date 2,565 boys and 561 girls, all of them under fifteen and some under ten, provided 8 per cent of the labour force for all Norway's nascent factory industries, with special concentrations of 18 per cent among glass-workers, 33 per cent in match-making, and 43 per cent in tobacco. It is also noteworthy that an inquiry, which grew out of the laudable desire to make sure that children were not employed 'in a manner hurtful to their health and obstructive to a profitable attendance at school',[39] took seventeen years to produce any legislative result. Ministers and legislators alike were too engrossed in party politics to deal with the exploitation of child labour —or even with the fencing of dangerous machinery, though both of them were matters in which precedents were readily available in the legislation of leading industrial states.

In these circumstances, it was natural that the people tried to organize different forms of self-help. The need for producers' co-operatives had been voiced by Thrane, as early as November 1849, but the co-operative dairies (see p. 123) consisted for a long time of small units which easily disintegrated when times were hard. Out of a total of 247 in 1870, only sixty-six survived to be included among the 276 which were in operation after a period of revival during the 1880s. Consumers' co-operation likewise had a chequered early history. It is possible that the first co-operative shops—at least four existed in the 1850s—owed something to the example of the Rochdale Pioneers, of whom Thrane may well have heard and spoken; certainly Eilert Sundt lectured on the Rochdale Movement to the Association for Workers in Oslo. Generally speaking, these associations provided the nucleus of supporters in the towns, as did the Friends of the Peasantry for such support as the movement received in country districts, though with the exception of Jaabæk himself the leaders came chiefly from other classes. But after the shops had achieved a membership of 32,000 and had established their own wholesale society, numbers fell off in the hard times of the later 1870s and the wholesale society eventually collapsed—a decline which is at least partly attributable to abandonment of the Rochdale principle of dealing only for cash. In spite of the fact that other Rochdale principles, such as allowing one man one vote in the management of any co-operative concern and the distribution of profits in proportion to participation, are shown by later history to have a very strong appeal to the Norwegian temperament, we mut look elsewhere for the most significant reactions to the new economic pressures.

For nearly two decades after the arrest and imprisonment of Marcus Thrane, no militant organization of workers was practicable. The Associations for Workers which existed in Oslo and some other towns were largely under the control of philanthropists drawn from other classes: at most, they served to ventilate the question of extending the franchise. Whatever groups representing journeymen's interests survived the dissolution of the gilds avoided dangerously provocative actions such as strikes. But in 1870 the formation of trade unions was discussed at a meeting of Scandinavian workers in Stockholm, where Norway was represented; developments on the Continent were also known through the press and from the reports of Norwegian craftsmen, who often had a *Wanderjahr* abroad to gain experience. Accordingly, when the trade boom in 1872 enabled the Oslo harbour workers to strike successfully for a 20-per-cent rise in wages and their example was followed by a number of skilled trades, the upshot was the formation of the first modern trade unions. The lead was taken by 112 Oslo printers, inspired by memories of a previous journeymen's organization and by the example of their fellow workers in Copenhagen. At least half a dozen other Oslo trades followed, and in 1876 Bergen printers set up the first union outside the capital. But the movement barely survived the ensuing collapse of trade, which made it easier for employers to refuse recognition and dismiss union organizers as agitators. When trade revived again in the early 1880s, the number of local unions was swollen by shortlived philanthropic associations which were concerned with education and welfare rather than wages; but there was a nucleus of militant unions, including one formed in the Oslo engineering workshops and several in the traditional handicrafts. In 1882 the first nationwide union emerged in book printing, through the efforts of Holtermann Knudsen,* a Bergen typographer who had moved to

* 1845–1929. A key figure throughout the early history of the Labour Party,

Oslo, and in 1883 a Central Committee or trades council for Oslo was formed by thirteen of its unions under his chairmanship.

A workers' political organization also began slowly to take shape. This was for a time completely overshadowed by the efforts made by politicians of the Left Party to enlist the support of the workers for their campaign against the government. Björnson and others used the Associations for Workers for this purpose, and after an initial meeting at Trondheim in 1882 they succeeded in establishing the United Associations for Workers in the critical year 1884; manhood suffrage was the main rallying point in its programme, which attracted many of the unions. A small group of workers, however, had cherished an independent political outlook since 1873, when an immigrant saddler, Marius Jantzen, who had been a member of the Danish section in the First International, set up a social democratic organization. In addition to dissatisfied artisans and labourers, this found support among peasant students who felt themselves to be outcasts in Oslo society; its first meeting attracted an uproarious attendance of more than 500 persons, but interest quickly ebbed and Jantzen went on to America. In 1878 the small surviving group was strengthened by the arrival, again from Denmark, of Carl Jeppesen.* He was only twenty, but had worked in Hamburg, where he came into contact with the German social democratic movement. By 1882 Knudsen, too, declared himself a socialist: in that year the first abortive attempt to organize the factory workers, in whom the craftsmen's unions had hitherto shown little interest, prepared the way for the establishment of a socialist Labour Party, which Knudsen proposed at a meeting organized by the Oslo trades council in January 1885.

---

of which he was chairman in 1889, 1900–2, and 1912–18; member of the Storting, 1906–15; a sound organizer, who became 'the symbol of continuity in the Norwegian labour movement'.[40]

* 1858–1930. A cigar-maker and, when he came to Norway, a brush-binder by trade; editor of *Social-Demokraten*, 1887–92 and 1906–12; represented Norwegian Labour Party at foundation of Second International, 1889, and promoted Labour policies on Oslo city council, 1889–1925.

5. The Separation from Sweden, 1884–1905

NO SOONER HAD PARLIAMENTARISM BEEN ESTABLISHED in Norway in 1884 than its parliament became the forum of a bitter and eventually successful struggle to throw off the yoke of the union with Sweden. In 1895 the Norwegian aspirations were humiliatingly checked: all the more glorious was their triumph ten years later, when the work begun at Eidsvoll in 1814 was completed by the re-establishment of a separate Norwegian monarchy, such as had flourished in oft-recalled medieval centuries. The story is usually regarded as that of a victory of right over wrong, of progressive over reactionary forces, of a historic movement that admitted of no compromise—a justification of Parnell's dictum that it is impossible to set limits to the onward march of a nation. But now that the future seems to lie with the association rather than the dissociation of nations, we may perhaps look at the story a little more critically. For Norway had much to lose as well as to gain by separation from her larger, stronger, and wealthier neighbour in the eastern half of the peninsula, so that those who strove to preserve the union—Oscar II and Crown Prince Gustaf, most of the Swedish political leaders, and some of the Norwegian—were not necessarily more selfish and short-sighted than their opponents.

For better and worse, the national issue was kept in the forefront of the stage. The voting at elections, however, suggests that in reality it was only one of many competing interests, even among the enfranchised classes: this chapter will therefore take account of other political issues arising in this period. Norway's modern industrial development also had its starting-point at this time, but this will be left to the following chapter, since its full impact was not felt until after the political climacteric of 1905.

SVERDRUP AND THE REFORM PROGRAMME

The admission of Johan Sverdrup to the office of prime minister in June 1884 was itself the fulfilment of a programme. He was the undisputed leader of the majority party in the Storting, whose claim

to dominate the administration of the country had been so long contested by king and cabinet during the struggle over the Inclusion
Bill and over the definition of the royal veto. The labour of political
agitation, which he had sustained for more than thirty years with
tremendous spirit and resource, had likewise made him the undisputed leader of the Left Party in the electorate, which in the autumn
of 1885 confirmed his ministry in office with an 84:30 majority. The
election cry of 'Show your confidence in Sverdrup!'[1] referred, however, not only to the programme he had already carried through, but
also to a further programme of reforms, long demanded by his supporters and long postponed by the exigencies of the constitutional
struggle. Some of the most pressing items, such as a new franchise
law, reached the statute book shortly before the 1885 election, but
it will be convenient to treat as a single whole all the legislation of
Sverdrup's premiership, which lasted until 1889.

A widening of the franchise having been proposed by the Left
majority of the Storting in 1881, its acceptance by the crown followed almost automatically when Sverdrup came into power three
years later. Judged by contemporary European standards, it was not
a big move that Norway took in the direction of political democracy,
for the new qualification, which was sponsored by Sverdrup himself,
was the possession of an income equivalent to £44 in towns and £24
in rural areas. Calculations based on the year 1877 (after which falling prices had some negative influence) indicated a rise of 49 per cent
in urban, and 27·5 per cent in the much larger category of rural,
voters.[2] The richer farmers of eastern Norway would have offered
bitter opposition to any more extensive change, and their attitude
was not challenged by any vociferous demand among the unenfranchised. But the introduction of an income qualification at least
left the door ajar, so that further changes could follow more easily.

It is significant that, in the absence of any system of direct state
taxation, the decision regarding individual suffrage qualifications
would now rest in practice with the local authorities as the tax-
levying instance. This was in keeping with the habit of mind which
attached maximum importance to everything connected with local
self-rule. This showed itself in two other enactments for which the
politically active element in the countryside had been struggling

for forty years. The jury system was introduced in criminal cases to bring in some degree of local lay control over the activities of the professional magistrates, and the elected representatives of the peasantry likewise acquired a share in the appointment of the executive rural police officials, the *lensmenn* or bailiffs.

In cultural matters, too, local self-rule made further advances. A Public School Law of 1889 deprived the bishops and parish clergy of their long-established powers of control over the elementary schools, whose internal management (including the appointment of teachers) passed entirely to local representatives. At the same time the influence of Folk High School enthusiasts and other educational reformers brought about modifications in the curriculum, so that the public elementary school or *folkeskole*[3] rapidly became a school for all classes of the population, effectively linked up with the institutions for secondary education—a measure of integration which gave Norway some advantages in comparison, for instance, with the English school system. But the same democratic sentiment which rendered local self-government such a vigorous force might also have a disintegrating influence. Thus in May 1885 Johannes Steen, himself a classically educated headmaster, strengthened his position in the Storting by advocating a kind of charter of liberty for 'the Norwegian people's language',[4] a vague concept which attracted a majority of seventy-eight votes. Only forty-one of these came from outright supporters of *landsmål*, but the result was to enable devotees of neo-Norwegian to make it the language of instruction in the schools of some western districts and to claim equality of status for it in the transaction of public business. In its literature Vinje's death was quickly followed by the emergence of another gifted writer, Arne Garborg (see p. 259), and in the 1890s the movement was to gather fresh strength through the rapid growth of the rural Youth Societies, where *landsmål* was fostered as part of a national heritage of culture; in 1896 these societies were linked together in a federation (*Noregs ungdomslag*), which gave important support to the Radical Left.

Another project, illustrating the desire of local democracy to assert itself in the cultural sphere, was the demand for congregational church councils, voiced long before by Ueland. But times had changed. A scheme which envisaged the introduction of popular control over the clergy, and in particular over their appointment to parishes, was now suspect in the eyes of many radicals as involving also the introduction of control by church councils over the morals of parishioners. The premier's nephew, Jakob Sverdrup,* who had entered the cabinet in 1884 and soon became minister for ecclesiastical affairs, accordingly omitted all reference to church discipline from the measure that was put before the Storting. This did not stop the radical or Broad Church section of the Left from arguing that it was implicit in the proposed exclusion from the right to vote in church affairs of any parishioner who 'has openly broken with the beliefs of the Church or notoriously leads a profligate life'.[5] The same section of opinion also demanded that the churches should be more readily available for devotional and cultural activities within the parish; this offended the High Churchmen. The resulting defeat of the measure was a serious blow to the administration, whose unity had already been broken on another cultural issue, the restriction of literary freedom, to be discussed later (p. 144). As for the church, its advance towards self-government was postponed for more than a generation, though Jakob Sverdrup made ingenious use of the ecclesiastical powers of the crown to throw open the doors of the churches to lay speakers and to home and foreign mission meetings sponsored by laymen.

Finally, there was the question of the army, which some elements of the Left Party, intoxicated by the success of the volunteer rifle clubs, proposed to transform into an 'arming of the people'. Sverdrup, who had long been interested in military affairs, sought in 1885 to achieve something of the same democratic result by a reorganization. This divided the available man-power into thirteen year-groups, of which only five were assigned to the line, leaving four for the militia and four for the *landstorm* or territorial reserve; the last regulars were now disbanded. Not more than 18,000 line troops could be called up

* 1845–99. A Low Church clergymen and former Folk High School principal, whom his uncle intended as his political heir; minister for ecclesiastical affairs, 1885–6, 1888–9, and 1895–8; the Church Councils Bill was inspired by him, though he held another cabinet post during the final discussions. More ambitious than devout, he was often denounced as an intriguer, but died as bishop of Bergen.

in the event of war without the prior consent of the Storting, and their training period was reduced from 162 to 90 days.[6] Sverdrup was alive to the fact that some of his peasant supporters would have welcomed a further reduction to seventy days: if perpetual peace proved to be only a dream, they professed to believe that it would be early enough for the resourceful Norseman to prepare for war when the threat became actual. The minister responsible for the army, who was more concerned with efficiency than political advantage, resigned office. What was more significant was the effect on Swedish opinion. King Oscar supposed at first that the reduction in the line regiments would be compensated by the amendment of Section 25 in the Norwegian constitution, which restricted the rest of the army to the defence of Norwegian territory. When this was not brought about, he recorded his view that 'Nothing had done so much to make the union unpopular in Sweden as the unamended S.25, together with the reduced period of service and diminished strength of the troops of the line.'[7]

SVERDRUP AND THE RELATIONSHIP WITH SWEDEN

Like many other unions between nations, the Swedish-Norwegian operated most harmoniously when its machinery was least in evidence. But the movement towards parliamentarism in Norway had helped to direct the attention of the Swedish Riksdag to the fact that the Ministerial Council, which had handled foreign affairs for so long, had been set up by their constitution of 1809 as a mere instrument of the royal will. A constitutional amendment had therefore been proposed in 1883 and adopted in 1885, which made the foreign minister directly responsible for foreign policy and enlarged the representation of the Swedish cabinet in the ministerial council, so that it comprised the premier, the foreign minister, and one other. Although the change formally involved the constitution of Sweden alone, common sense indicated that the Norwegians must be compensated with a second seat in the ministerial council, and the Swedish government in fact offered a third as well, on condition that the nationality of the foreign minister, who acted on behalf of both countries, should be expressly defined as Swedish.

Although the effect would be to confirm an existing practice, the addition of any such clause to the Act of Union was too humiliating to be contemplated. Instead, a visit by Sverdrup to Stockholm was directly followed by the adoption of a formula, which was finally agreed between Ole Richter,* the Norwegian minister-resident, and his Norwegian and Swedish colleagues; it was then recorded by the Joint Cabinet (15 May 1885). This envisaged the addition of a new section to the Act of Union, 'by which it is prescribed that ministerial business shall be laid before the king by the minister for foreign affairs in the presence of two other members of the Swedish, and three members of the Norwegian, cabinet'.[8] The definition of the foreign minister's nationality was indirect but unmistakable: yet Sverdrup tried to convince the Storting that the question was still open. He then cast about in vain to find some alternative formula which might satisfy Swedish opinion without committing the Norwegians too far; in March of the following year the Joint Cabinet resolved to let the matter drop.

However, Norway's claim to equality of status was an issue which no minister of the Left Party could afford to ignore, so Sverdrup revived a proposal which had found favour with the former Union Committees. Might not unity be preserved without any sacrifice of national equality, if the foreign minister were made responsible to a delegation composed of an equal number of members from both parliaments? As a common minister, he might then be chosen by the sovereign from either nation without one legislature by itself wielding any direct powers of control. But when he commended this logical solution to the Storting with all his customary eloquence, a newly elected member of the Left burst out in a calculated aside, 'You have lost your hold on Norway now, Johan Sverdrup!'[9] For the Left Party, which claimed to speak for Norway, was now instinctively opposed to any growth in the institutions of the Union, which it believed—or at least hoped—to be moribund. The Storting then passed the first of a number of Orders of the Day in which

* 1829–88. A political moderate, who in 1878–84 left the Storting to become consul-general for Norway and Sweden in London. In 1884 King Oscar regarded him as a possible choice for prime minister, but he reluctantly agreed to serve under Sverdrup.

it embodied its views on Union matters: this demanded that share in the control of foreign affairs which was due to Norway's position as 'an independent state having an equal status with Sweden in the Union'.[10]

For Sverdrup, so long the unwearying champion of popular causes, the sands were now running out fast. His seventieth birth-day fell in this year (1886), and the financial worries of a whole-time politician who had no private means had helped to make him old for his age. The future of the army and the fate of the Congrega-tional Councils Bill were only two among a series of issues over which his party was divided. By 1888 the fissure had become a complete split, so that after the elections Sverdrup's followers, known as the Moderate Left, were the smallest of the three parties in the new Storting. Their leader's reputation had suffered a serious blow a few months before through the suicide of Richter; he had been forced to resign his post as minister-resident in Stockholm by an indiscreet newspaper article, in which Björnson gave publicity to the minister's privately expressed resentment of Sverdrup's failure to take any share of responsibility for the protocol of 15 May 1885. It was easier to forgive Björnson's blunder than the premier's disloyalty, or at best his cold indifference, to a colleague.[11]

Sverdrup still clung to office, in the belief that he could rely on the backing of King Oscar, with whom he had sought to ingratiate himself by a deferential approach which appealed to that monarch's love of ceremony. The King however, had long been in correspon-dence with the Conservative leader, Emil Stang,* behind his prime minister's back. In July 1889, when Sverdrup was still trying to save himself by some further reconstruction of his cabinet, Stang was ready to take over, and the most remarkable career in modern Nor-wegian politics was brought abruptly to an end. Because he held office as a minister, Sverdrup could not be elected as a representative

---

* 1834–1912. A prominent barrister before he entered the Storting in 1883; in August 1884 he was elected chairman of the newly formed Conservative Party organization. As the son of Frederik Stang, he was regarded as a kind of pater-familias (*husfader*) by his party in the Storting; he avoided any close personal relations with the king.

at the Storting elections of 1885 and 1888.* He was one of only fourteen of the Moderate Left who won seats in 1891, but death intervened before the Storting met in the following February. Thus the parties were left free to adopt new attitudes to old questions, such as the relationship with Sweden.

PARTY DEVELOPMENTS

The political parties were of too recent origin and growth for them to command a loyalty based on tradition, and with the waning of Sverdrup's star they ceased to have any leaders whose personality commanded very wide support. Moreover, they operated within a rather small electorate, which was drawn from a people who set the greatest store by individualism and the right of private judgement. Although the Storting was now the acknowledged power centre of the country, no government could maintain a majority there—as even Sverdrup had found to his cost—unless its policies made a sufficient appeal to retain the sympathy of the voters from one three-year electoral period to another.

The Right had made a remarkable recovery after the débâcle of 1884. Under the astute leadership of Emil Stang, it had ceased to be a party of bureaucrats. The cabinet that he formed after the fall of Sverdrup included no member from the abortive Schweigaard administration of April–May 1884, which contained eight officials, and their number in the Storting was allowed to fall from thirty-three in 1888 to twenty in 1903.[12] The party accepted without further demur the new principle that the cabinet was responsible to parliament, together with the corollary that its relations with the monarchy, though closer and more cordial than would be possible for ministers of the Left, must be free from any appearance of courtier-like dependence upon the royal favour. Its strength lay chiefly in the capital and the other larger towns and in support from the owners of substantial property—real estate, forest enterprises, and industrial undertakings—wherever they were to be found.

* This constitutional rule—which did not affect *ex*-ministers—was continued in spite of its inconvenience until 1913, partly with a view to keeping down the number of professional politicians in the legislature.[13]

As regards policy, the Right had a strong natural interest in economic development: railway building, for instance, was resumed under Stang after a ten-year intermission. In 1892 Stang made the first move towards much-needed factory legislation, as proposed by a Labour Commission which had been set up at the king's suggestion in 1885 (see p. 133). In Union affairs the Right was more aware than its opponents of the economic and military advantages of the association with Sweden, where its leaders mingled more easily with the governing class. But the party could not hope to achieve much in the way of concrete results unless it could attract enough support from rural voters to build up a majority in the Storting.

Hence the importance of the Moderate Left, defined by Sverdrup in one of his last letters as 'the representative of a prudent, enlightened, and moderate democracy, which corresponds to our conception of our people's mode of thought'.[14] Such a group had begun to take shape as early as 1885, when the Left Party at the height of its success proved unable to achieve a working compromise among its members over cultural issues, where fanaticism so easily clouds judgement. The first storm arose over a proposal, strongly back by Björnson, for the stipend or *diktergasje* enjoyed by other leading authors to be given to the novelist, Alexander Kielland (see p. 258). The distinction of his work could hardly be disputed, but the object of his most polished satire was the puritanical church milieu in his native Stavanger. His claims were indeed prejudiced to some extent in the Storting by the fact that some of his younger supporters also supported 'literary freedom' in the very different case of a disreputable novel by Hans Jæger (see. p. 259); their rejection was, however, due mainly to the fierce hostility of the West Norway religious organizations, headed by a clerical member of the Storting, Lars Oftedal.* Resentment of what they regarded as the hypocrisy of the Moderates in this affair influenced the radical element of the Left Party against the Congregational

---

* 1838–1900. A revivalist preacher and ardent social worker, who shortly before his ordination in 1870 had charge of the Norwegian seamen's mission in Cardiff. He and his followers, 'the rabbits', were attacked in 1887 in Kielland's novel, *Sankt Hans Fest*.

Councils Bill, over which the Moderates (as we have seen) suffered a direct reverse.

That Kielland's satirical attacks had some factual basis was shown only a few years later when Oftedal, whose parish was in Stavanger, made public confession of an adulterous association with a parishioner. But the Moderates had other, weightier leaders, such as Jakob Sverdrup, the intimate of his uncle, and the latter's finance minister, B. M. Haugland, a shopkeeper from one of the west-coast islands, who had been acclaimed in 1884 as 'the first peasant ever summoned to the council table of the king'.[15] Although the group was powerful only in the Low Church strongholds of the west and south, and shrank from twenty-five to fourteen in the Storting as a sequel to Sverdrup's loss of office, in 1895 it was allotted two places out of ten in a national coalition government (see p. 152) and it retained ten seats at the ensuing election. Except on religious and ethical issues the Moderate Left had no very clear-cut programme, but it served as an adaptable instrument for transferring part of the rural vote from its rivals inside the Left to its allies of the Right.

Nevertheless, the party of the Pure or Radical Left (*Rene Venstre*) contrived to win an over-all majority at four successive elections, which reached a maximum of forty-four seats in 1897; although its preponderance in votes was much smaller—even in 1897 it was less than 7 per cent—the party showed a remarkable ability to retain the sympathy of the electorate. This was not primarily due to magnetic leadership. While it is true that Steen in August 1891 was the first head of any Norwegian government to set out his party's programme at an election meeting, the imbroglio regarding the consular question prevented him from carrying much of it into effect. As for his second term of office from 1897 to 1902, his age then reduced him more and more to a mere figurehead, derided by opponents as 'the leader who did not lead.' The Radical Left possessed, indeed, a compelling spokesman in Björnson, but his contribution was to stir up emotion and to crystallize the sentiments of the hour in telling phrases, not the long-term pursuit of any consistent policy.

The Radical Left certainly stood for a thoroughgoing adherence to the principle of parliamentarism, as established by the impeachments of 1884. Thus it held up Johan Sverdrup to reproach as a traitor to his own principles, when the rejection of the Congregational Councils Bill did not result in the resignation of his nephew Jakob, the minister whose policy had been defeated. Still greater indignation was aroused by the devious manoeuvres in which Sverdrup indulged in trying to retain office with support from the Right, when he no longer had a Storting majority behind him. And in 1893, when the Right (as we shall shortly see) formed a minority government as the only way out of a crisis over relations with Sweden, the Radical Left contemplated impeaching the ministry —provided the next election gave them enough votes to be sure of success.

But the cry for parliamentarism was chiefly an echo of old conflicts. After 1884 it was no longer sufficient for a party to have its representatives at the king's council table: the basis for their activities there was to be derived from a party programme, approved by local delegates at the party congress and watched over by a central executive. It was not until 1909 that any prime minister was allowed to become chairman of his party, and even then the principal organs of the press retained their independence. Prime ministers had to pay close attention to party opinion: in Steen's case this meant finding a policy that would command the support of every element in the Radical Left, while isolating the Moderates and embarrassing the Right in its attacks.

The demand for manhood suffrage had been raised by the Radical Left as early as 1886, but although it figured in the party programme of 1891 Steen did not press it, because what would delight the urban radicals would alienate his following among the larger farmers. Another obvious reform was to initiate State intervention in working conditions in industry, but so long as the workers were shut out from political life such a reform would attract few votes: seven years after a Labour Party had been formed in 1887, it was supported by only 4 per cent of the voters in Oslo, the chief industrial centre;[16] factory legislation (as we have noticed) was first introduced belatedly by Stang. Yet a third problem of the day was provided by the incidence of taxation, which affected both voters and non-voters. Although some important interest groups would have welcomed a general reversal of the free-trade policy, the Radical Left did not risk bold changes. Instead, it conciliated the poorer farmers, and with them the workers, by reducing the revenue duties on coffee, sugar, and paraffin, from which one-fifth of the government's income was derived. The necessary corollary to this was the introduction of income tax, to be levied on a percentage basis, which favoured the farmers, and with an exemption for small incomes, which benefited the poorest category of electors. In 1895 the tax was made progressive, but at the close of the century this so-called 'rich man's tax' still covered no more than 7 per cent of a revenue which had risen from kr. 13 million in 1850 to kr. 83 million in 1900.[17]

Even so summary a review of other possible fields of political conflict suggests some of the reasons why the Radical Left was eager to seize upon the issue presented by the Right, when it launched a new attempt to settle the vexed question of the forms under which foreign-policy decisions ought to be made. Thus the way for Steen's victory at the polls in 1891 was prepared by a party congress which resolved that Norway must enjoy constitutional responsibility for its foreign policy. The resolution was widely interpreted to imply the creation of separate Norwegian institutions for the purpose— the solution which appealed most strongly to nationalist sentiment.

THE UNSUCCESSFUL CLASH WITH SWEDEN, 1891–1895

At the beginning of 1891 the minority government of the Right under Emil Stang agreed with the Swedes upon a compromise arrangement; this was designed to secure full equality in the transaction of the foreign and diplomatic concerns of the two countries, while leaving the nationality of their minister for foreign affairs undefined. In order to avoid controversy the Norwegian government ignored the assumption on the part of their Swedish colleagues, duly recorded by the Joint Cabinet, that the responsible minister would continue to be a Swede. The Storting majority thereupon proclaimed 'Norway's right to safeguard its foreign affairs in a constitutionally adequate manner'.[18] Since Stang chose to treat this resolution as a vote of no confidence, the king was obliged to invite

Steen to form a new government of the Radical Left. In August one of his colleagues, Wollert Konow (H.),* raised public expectations by a speech at Skarnes in his constituency, in which he said: 'We can set up our own foreign minister and our own envoys any day, on a decision in the Norwegian government.'[19] During the ensuing election campaign Björnson spoke on fifty occasions, and the result was a majority of sixteen seats for the party which had whipped up feeling in favour of a transformation in the control of foreign policy.

Steen's tactics, however, were to direct attention to a less drastic change, namely the institution of a wholly separate Norwegian consular service. This procedure had two general advantages, namely that it offered a less direct challenge to the stronger power and that it was in principle supported by the Moderates and the Right. As a practical reform, too, it could be justified on many grounds: the worldwide activities of the Norwegian mercantile marine; the handicap suffered by seamen, applying for help in some emergency to officials who spoke an unfamiliar language; and the availability of a consular and trade division, established in the ministry of the interior in 1858, on which to found the new institution. Finally, in the eyes of the Radical Left there were two further gains in prospect: a separate consular service would prepare the way for other forms of separation, and it would appeal directly to national pride because this first important change could be made—according to their interpretation of the legal relationship—without calling for any co-operation by Swedish authorities to bring it into effect.

The Storting of 1814 had voted against having consuls separate from those of Sweden, and since 1836 these officials had been appointed by the Joint Cabinet and sworn in as servants of both countries. For Norway to claim in these circumstances that she was entitled to set up an independent service, before she consulted her partner over the closing down of a system which had served them

---

* 1847–1932. A landowner who represented Hedmark in the Storting from 1885 to 1924; in national issues his views were extremely radical, but his conservative views on economic questions carried him eventually into the group of Moderate Liberals. The initial of his constituency was used to distinguish him from a cousin of the same names (see p. 174).

both for nearly eighty years, involved relying upon strained legalistic arguments. Here the Right parted company from the Left, not because its leaders lacked national feeling but because they favoured an expeditious, common-sense settlement of the matter, such as might be achieved through agreement with the Swedes. Broadly speaking, the king held the same view; in any case, he knew that his Swedish cabinet would resign, if he were to abet the scheme of his Norwegian cabinet by authorizing a grant to cover arrangements for a separate consular service.

When King Oscar accordingly refused his sanction, Steen and his fellow ministers withheld the official countersignature to the royal decision and resigned in protest, thereby inaugurating a three-year political crisis (June 1892–June 1895). For a time Steen and his colleagues continued in office at the express request of their supporters in the Storting, whose proposal that they should serve for the time being under a parliamentary mandate was formulated by an able newcomer to its deliberations, named Christian Michelsen.* Early in 1893 the Swedish foreign minister offered them 'the hand of a brother',[20] in the shape of a formal commitment to the principle that his post should be open to men of both nationalities, if the Norwegians as a *quid pro quo* would concede that a change in the consular arrangements was a common concern, to be negotiated under the terms of the Act of Union. The fraternal gesture was rejected by the Radical Left, although Björnson was among a minority of its leaders who would have preferred instead to abandon their own gesture, which he not ineptly termed 'the policy of the clenched fist'.[21] At this juncture Steen won applause in the Storting by announcing that he would employ 'lawful means as far as they would go, and after that—' a pregnant aposiopesis in which (as he explained later on in the debate) he anticipated the collapse of the Union.[22] In April 1893 he renewed the demand for the prepara-

---

* 1857–1925. A Bergen solicitor, who founded one of the biggest shipping businesses and became first chairman of the Norwegian Association of Shipowners (1910); member of the Storting, 1892–4 and 1903, and of the government, 1903–7. As prime minister, he ended the Union in 1905; as an elder statesman, he was active behind the scenes in politics down to the year of his death.

tory grant, which the king again rejected—this time with the prior approval of the Swedish Riksdag—and when his Norwegian government once more tended its resignation, a threatening situation was met by the formation of a second minority ministry of the Right under Steen's rival, Emil Stang (2 May 1893).

For more than two years parliamentarism was effectively in abeyance. The Storting had no means of establishing the separate consulates, about which it continued to pass resolutions, but demonstrated its ill will in many other ways. Approval of the diplomatic Budget was made conditional upon the abolition of the legation at Vienna, so the Swedes covered Norway's share of the expenditure there pending a settlement. A bill was passed, but vetoed by the crown, for removing the Union emblem from the flag worn by the ubiquitous Norwegian mercantile marine. To the intense indignation of King Oscar, who claimed that he spent more money in Norway than he received from there, his appanage and that of the crown prince were substantially reduced. The cardinal event of the period, however, was the election due in the autumn of 1894, for which the Radical Left made its advance preparations at the Party Congress.

By a fortunate chance the notes made by a young historian, Halvdan Koht, who was present as a journalistic sympathizer, take us behind the scenes. When the projected demand for separate control of foreign affairs, which lay behind the consular claim, was subjected to some criticism among the delegates, 'Steen had a definite impression that this was a project on which we could unite and get a big majority.' His view was endorsed by three other speakers, who added: 'It would be a shame if we could not defend ourselves as they did in 1814'; 'We accept war rather than surrender a scrap of our independence'; and—most significant—'It is the question of the foreign minister that makes the biggest impression at public meetings.'[23] Accordingly, at the congress the critics of a bold policy found themselves reduced to a minority of one. But when the election came, the party won by only four seats, which represented a majority of less than 3 per cent at the polls.[24] The ministry of the Right accepted the constitutional obligation to resign office as a result of the election, but continued to function in a caretaker capacity while the king vainly addressed himself to their opponents. For they would admit no corresponding obligation to form a new ministry of the Left, unless and until the consular claim was settled in accordance with their demands. But so long as the Swedes maintained their opposition to the proposed innovation, the king's duty to the Union compelled him to support the *status quo*, a consideration which lent some justification to the view commonly held in Sweden that the Norwegian intransigence involved treating the sovereign with contumely.

At least three other factors helped to render the Norwegian position in the long run untenable. A strange mixture of idealism and fanaticism had induced the Radical Left to reduce the appropriations for defence, which in 1892 had been raised temporarily from their previous modest level: its members preferred to pin their faith to international arbitration or alternatively to the volunteer rifle clubs. But their position was made more dangerous by a complete absence of international support. Gladstone, who liked to regard the Union as a serviceable precedent for Irish Home Rule, had presented a Norwegian inquirer with the practical objection, 'I cannot cope with the problem of a double Foreign Office', and added that he favoured 'whatever keeps or draws together' the small states of north-west Europe.[25] The German emperor, who represented a very different approach to European problems, visited Stockholm at the height of the crisis in the summer of 1895; he advised King Oscar to take strong measures in Norway without consulting the powers, since otherwise Russia and Britain would seize Norwegian territory and Germany might be obliged to do the same.[26]

The third ominous factor in the situation was a propaganda drive in Sweden, which linked together tariff demands, defence projects— especially a call for lengthening the period of military service— and a strident nationalism; some influential supporters were hoping thereby to divert attention from the campaign for a more democratic suffrage. An Uppsala professor, Oscar Alin, founder of the Association for the Rights of Sweden, directed much of this propaganda against the Norwegians, who were said to want equal rights without equal duties. One result was a decision to give notice for terminating the interstate treaty of 1874: when this became effective in 1897, Norwegian industrialists would forfeit many advantages. But for Swedish public opinion in general, the main criterion was the contribution to the common defence needs: in the light of the recent military changes, it was easy to show that the Norwegians evinced little readiness to help to defend the peninsula, in case Sweden was attacked.

Accordingly, in February 1895 Norway's consular demands were rejected in the First Chamber of the Riksdag almost unanimously, and in the more representative Second Chamber by a majority of four to one. The Secret Committee,[27] last summoned at the time of the Crimean War, deliberated under the king's chairmanship; supplies were voted for unspecified military purposes; and it is now known that the Swedish General Staff had detailed plans in readiness for movements against Norway, which had been first considered in 1893. At the beginning of June a direct threat seemed to be implicit in the appointment of a new foreign minister, Count Douglas: he was a second cousin of the German-born crown princess and a firm supporter of her husband, Prince Gustaf, who was believed to have talked lightly of 'a military parade' to take possession of the Norwegian capital. The rumours were alarming, and although the Swedes would doubtless have been reluctant to proceed to extremes, they had at least made it clear that they expected the Norwegians to find a way out of the dangerous impasse. On 7 June the Storting agreed by 90 votes to 24 to take the initiative in reopening negotiations. In October the burden of humiliation that the surrender inevitably created was shouldered by a national coalition government. This consisted of four members of the Right, four of the Radical Left, and two Moderates; its head was George Francis Hagerup,★ a professor of jurisprudence since 1887 and minister of justice under Emil Stang, by whom his name was submitted to a triumphant sovereign.

★ 1853–1921. Writer on Norwegian law; as premier he continued to be head of the department of justice. A cautious 'academic' attitude to the problems of 1905 ended his political career, but he was prominent as a delegate to the Hague Conference of 1907, and in 1920 led Norway's first delegation to the League Assembly.

DÉTENTE AND DISTRACTION

The coalition government had the approval of the Storting for repaying the money that Sweden had advanced for common diplomatic expenditure, with the interesting exception of a small sum for secret service activities; the royal appanages were eventually restored to their former amounts; and other matters in dispute were left for examination in a wider context by the third Union Committee, whose formation the Swedes had requested six months before. In foreign policy the Storting now put forward a unanimous resolution in favour of compulsory arbitration, to be put on a treaty basis and administered through an international court. But greater significance might perhaps be attached to a sudden volte-face over defence. A loan was raised to build Norway's two first ironclads and to construct additional forts for coastal protection. In 1897, too, military service was extended to the northernmost counties, hitherto exempted on account of their very poor and widely scattered population. In domestic policy a coalition could not be expected to accomplish much. The extension of the local government franchise to all tax-paying male citizens over twenty-five showed the direction in which events were moving, as did the Education Act of 1896. This cleared a wide path from the public primary school via the intermediate school to the *gymnas* and the university, and it set an example to most of western Europe by dethroning Latin from its place as a class symbol in higher education.[28]

When the autumn of 1897 came, the election campaign directed attention mainly to Union issues, and the Radical Left won its largest majority. Steen thereupon formed his second government, which enjoyed a rather less resounding success at the next election and continued in office after his retirement in 1902 in favour of the minister-resident in Stockholm, Otto Blehr.* The latter had been one of the Radical representatives on the third Union Committee, whose report, published just after the 1897 election, showed only

---

* 1847–1927. A lawyer, who had been one of the three prosecutors in charge of the impeachments of 1883–4; he held the same post in Stockholm during Steen's first administration. Prime minister, April 1902–October 1903 and June 1921–March 1923.

the wide divergence of opinion. Four different sets of proposals, two Swedish and two Norwegian, offered no common ground on which to reconstruct the Act of Union, so Steen contented himself with such nationalist moves as the Swedes could not readily counter.

One of these was the Flag Law, to restore to the mercantile marine the flag which had been authorized for all voyages in 1838–44 (see p. 72); the bill passed the Storting for the third time in 1898, so the royal veto could no longer prevent the fleet from hoisting the flag it flies today. But since the Union emblem which was to be removed was not a Swedish emblem and was equally in use by the shipping of both kingdoms, Norway's action in this instance was plainly directed against the Union itself rather than at any inequality in its mode of operation. Count Douglas therefore commanded much sympathy in Sweden for his action in blocking notification of the change through diplomatic channels until he was replaced in 1899 by Lagerheim, a minister of more conciliatory temperament. Steen followed up this success by placing an ambitious new arrival on the political scene, Henrik Ibsen's only child, Sigurd,★ at the head of an enlarged division of the ministry of internal affairs for commercial, shipping, and foreign business. There he employed his considerable administrative talents in drawing up a report on the proper relations between a hypothetical Norwegian consular organization and the common institutions for diplomacy and the conduct of foreign affairs. But before this report was ready in 1901, the murmurings of the Radical Left against what it regarded as the inertia of the government over the prosecution of the national claims had led to a reconstruction of the cabinet, which brought a new man to the ministry of defence. Georg Stang was a senior officer in

★ 1859–1930. Educated in Germany and Italy, where he took a doctorate in law; served as a Swedish–Norwegian diplomat, 1885–9; and married Björnson's daughter Bergliot. He wrote extensively on the union and other subjects, but was refused a professorship of sociology by Oslo University, 1897. His political career ended abruptly in 1905, when his views on appropriate action were thought to be weak and his subsequent publication of them offended Norwegian opinion. He was appointed to the Hague Court in 1906, and lived the last years of his life abroad.

the coastal artillery with strong technical interests,* who had recently been an observer of the siege of Santiago in the Spanish–American War;[29] he persuaded the Storting to follow up a decision to build two more ironclads by purchasing new field artillery and constructing a line of forts along the Swedish frontier.

Nevertheless, the climate of opinion had become less favourable to an uncompromising nationalism. Manhood suffrage, which had long featured in the Radical programme, was enacted in 1898 for the elections to the Storting, and three years later it was extended to local elections; in the latter instance only, women were enfranchised, subject to the possession by themselves or their husbands of a small income qualification (equivalent to £22 in towns and £17 in rural areas). It had been confidently expected that manhood suffrage would add weight to the national demands. But on the first occasion (1900) an expansion of the electorate by 125 per cent added only 40 per cent to the numbers who actually went to the poll.[30] Moreover, at this election the Right regained control of the representation of the capital, whose loss in 1894 had been considered a good indication of a swing of opinion against the ties with Sweden, since both their good and bad effects were more immediately felt in Oslo than elsewhere.

One reason for the swing in opinion was certainly the sudden collapse of a trade boom, which in the winter of 1899–1900 hit Oslo very hard. The increased expenditure of the Left on armaments began to appear burdensome to many people, and its management of the finances was subject to direct attack by the advocates of tariff reform. If agrarian and industrial protectionists still weakened their case by disagreeing over what duties they should demand, the workers could make a clear case against the government over its social policy. Since the first belated Factory Act in 1892, which closed the factories to children under twelve and forbade them to employ young persons at night, the sum total of additions had been a ban on night work in bakeries, the introduction of an eight-hour day in the military workshops, and a system of accident insurance for factory employees. Otherwise, the main advance had been on the temperance front. Town councils had been empowered in 1871 to

* He invented a range-finder, which was still in use in Norway in 1940.

adopt the 'Gothenburg' licensing system, under which fifty-one towns set up spirit monopolies of this kind, eliminating private profit. In 1894 the total abstainers' association secured a Local Option Law, based on a poll in which women might vote. By the end of the century twenty-four of the fifty-one spirit monopolies had been closed:[31] what proportion of the urban proletariat welcomed this is hard to determine.

Meanwhile, efforts at self-help grew rather slowly. Consumers' co-operatives, for example, had to make a new start with the foundation of the existing Oslo society in 1894; this was the achievement of a Radical lawyer, Ole Dehli, who brought back the strict 'Rochdale' principles from a visit to England. Trade unionism asserted itself in 1889 by two serious strikes in Oslo; one was among the relatively well-organized printers, the other among the female employees of the match industry, who commanded public sympathy both for their miserably low earnings and for the inroads of phosphorus necrosis upon their health. Both strikes collapsed after a bitter struggle, but the increase of industrial employment encouraged the formation of more substantial unions, such as the Iron and Metal Workers' (1890) and the General Workers' Union. In 1899 Norway, acting upon a resolution from a Scandinavian workers' congress, formed a trade union federation (*Landsorganisasjonen*); 16,000 trade unionists were represented at the constituent congress, but only two unions with one-tenth of that membership were than prepared to join 'L. O.', which would involve some sacrifice of funds and independence. The same congress rejected a proposal that the unions should associate themselves with the Social Democratic Party, as their fellows in Sweden had already done.

From 1885 onwards the party had been struggling into existence under Holtermann Knudsen's leadership, with a newspaper, *Social-Demokraten* (which he printed through a firm set up for the purpose at the cost of his life savings), a policy copied from the German Gotha Programme, and a few hundred members, drawn mainly from the trade unions.* By 1894 it had won over the Associa-

---

* In 1887 the Social Democratic Union joined with the Democratic Labour Union of Bergen to form the United Norwegian Labour Party, which adopted a socialist programme at its annual conference in 1891.

tion for Workers (see p. 135) in Oslo and in at least one rural county, where its energetic chairman was Christopher Hornsrud.* But the Radical Left worked hard to retain control over the associations, which by 1894 were nationwide, and their annual congress was induced to vote for the exclusion of any workers' organization that adhered to Knudsen's party. In 1900, indeed, one group of rural Associations for Workers was skilfully organized by an ambitious Radical politician with advanced views on social questions to return him to the Storting as a kind of one-man party: this was Johan Castberg,† Norway's closest counterpart to Lloyd George. Otherwise, the associations were by then losing ground, but their membership of about 10,000 still compared favourably with the total of 7,000 votes, which was all that Holtermann Knudsen's party was able to muster at the first election with manhood suffrage.

In retrospect it seems clear that the workers were not yet politically aroused, while Castberg in the Storting was a general without an army. But in a small country, where the apparition of Thrane had once arisen almost overnight, it did not take much to give the upper bourgeoisie a feeling of disquiet. Would it not be better to face the collapse of trade and the accompanying budgetary problems rather than spend so much time and energy on barren controversy with the Swedes? Again, if trade were to recover (as it soon did), was there not an alternative risk that good opportunities of development would be missed for the same reason? The arguments were not so bluntly stated, but among the politically active compromise was certainly in the air. By July 1902 the shipowner, Christian Michelsen (see p. 149), had formed a breakaway group in Bergen among 'liberals' of the Radical Left. Their programme was to get the consular issue settled, not as a preliminary to further attacks on the Union but with a view to closing discussion of an

* 1859–1960. A small farmer, who was chairman of the Party in 1903–6, its leader in the Storting from 1921, and the first Labour prime minister, 1928; his views were always moderate and conciliatory.

† 1862–1926. Practised as a lawyer in Oppland, a county with many big farms, where he made the Associations for Workers the basis of a party. A great social reformer who was also anti-Swedish, anti-monarchist, anti-protectionist, and anti-German. His failure to become prime minister may be attributable to a rather aggressive personality, which is revealed in his diaries.

unprofitable subject. It was a programme that might bridge the gap between Left and Right, and it soon received the influential support of Björnson.

At this juncture developments outside Norway made a *rapprochement* with Sweden look more feasible. In the first place, neither country could ignore the object lesson that the Russian repression of Finnish liberties gave as to their own exposed position in the north. The Swedes showed their readiness to run a common risk by building the railway from their Arctic ironfield to the frontier, where it was linked up by Norwegian enterprise with the purpose-built harbour of Narvik.* In the second place, the Swedes had begun to doubt whether in a given situation they would receive enough support from the mercurial German emperor to outweigh whatever backing the Norwegians might obtain from Britain. This might even prove a more important factor than the additional money they were spending on their armed forces with a view to preserving their ratio of superiority over the Norwegians. In the third place the attitude of the new Swedish foreign minister, Lagerheim, who had previously represented the two kingdoms in Berlin, was conciliatory: by 1902, three years after his appointment, Norwegian-born consuls outnumbered Swedish.[32]

Accordingly, the publication of Sigurd Ibsen's report, in which he demonstrated that it was technically possible to combine the proposed separate Norwegian consular service with 'the common diplomacy and the common control of foreign affairs',[33] led Lagerheim to suggest an inquiry to see if such a scheme was feasible. This was the first time that the Swedes had formally entertained the idea of separate institutions. It took only six months for a small committee, appointed on the authority of the Joint Cabinet (and sometimes known as the fourth Union Committee), to endorse the general lines of the report already made by Ibsen—who was one of the members—and agree that the general control of the foreign minister over Norwegian consuls should be transferred to a Nor-

* The Swedish and Norwegian Railway Company had linked the mines in 1883–9 with the Swedish Baltic port of Luleå, but lacked capital for constructing the link with the Atlantic outlet at what was then called Victoriahavn. The financial difficulty was partly due to protectionist influences in Sweden.[34]

wegian authority, though the nature of the relationship with the foreign minister required special agreements. Their character was then discussed at length between the two governments, which in March 1903 issued a communiqué, declaring that regulation must be by means of 'identical laws, incapable of unilateral modification'.[35] Georg Stang and a second passionate nationalist, Wollert Konow (H.), claimed that Norway's liberty of action would be restricted, and eventually resigned from the cabinet.

The sequel was an election, in which the rump of Blehr's government was defeated by the United Party (*Samlings partiet*), an informal coalition for electioneering purposes between the Right and a large section of 'liberals' from the former Radical Left; its members rallied round a reassuring slogan of 'negotiations and nothing else'[36] as a means of clearing the Union issue out of the way to make room for economic and social problems. The urgency of these was underlined by the fact that the majority of sixty-three faced an opposition in which the forty-nine remaining members of the Left were supported by a new element in the Storting—a group of five Socialists.[37] Hagerup again presided over the coalition, with Michelsen as minister of finance and Sigurd Ibsen as minister-resident in Stockholm, where he was well regarded in court circles. Since the Right had now included the establishment of a separate consular service in its party programme, it looked as though the new government might be able to settle this issue in a manner which would receive inter-party support.

But it was not to be. A combination of skill, patience, good faith, and good leadership was needed on both sides of the frontier if the Norwegian concept of a separate consular service, as demonstrating a status of independence and equality within the Union, was to be reconciled with the Swedish concept of an organically undivided foreign policy, apart from which the Union in their view was virtually meaningless. By April 1904 Michelsen was warning the Swedes against allowing the existing negotiations to fail on the easy assumption that they could be resumed at some later time: yet it was natural for them to suppose that a ministry that had been elected for 'negotiations and nothing else' would show exemplary patience. In fact, what the Norwegians proposed for the 'identical laws' was that consuls should be required to consult the foreign ministry or its representative in critical situations only, and even then should not be bound to follow its recommendations. In other words, the consul who acted on behalf of one of the kingdoms would be free to counter-work the head of legation who acted on behalf of both. This pro-posal was inacceptable to Lagerheim, but he favoured some form of compromise, which was still under discussion in the Swedish cabi-net when he resigned on domestic issues. The matter therefore fell to be decided by the prime minister, E. G. Boström, who, like many other members of the First Chamber of the Riksdag, saw the relationship with Norway chiefly in terms of its value for defence.

In November 1904 Boström produced his counter-proposals. These gave the foreign minister powers of control over a consul, and entitled the head of a legation in certain cases to suspend him. In the following month the Swedish cabinet offered to make some slight modifications—in which case Boström would have resigned the premiership—but the Norwegian governemnt refused to discuss conditions that had been denounced by the voice of an outraged public opinion as 'dependency clauses' involving a direct breach of faith on the part of Boström.[38] On 7 February 1905 the Joint Cabinet recognized the failure of the negotiations; the Norwegian coalition government, which had been elected to negotiate, then rapidly broke up.

1905: THE BREACH OF RELATIONS

Hagerup would have preferred to avoid a crisis and the possibility of hostilities with Sweden by starting a new round of negotiations, whereas Michelsen now intended to provoke a crisis by presenting a direct demand that the setting up of separate consuls should re-ceive the royal sanction. While never losing sight of his ultimate objectives in domestic policy, he was well aware that a quick solu-tion to the immediate problem presented by Swedish obduracy would yield him the maximum support. The presence of the national hero, Fridtjof Nansen (see p. 231), on the same political platform as the activist, Georg Stang, showed the trend of opinion; a demon-stration against the offices of the cautious conservative newspaper,

Aftenposten, was a straw in the same wind. In mid-March Michelsen emerged as the head of a new Cabinet, which combined the representatives of the United Party with men of the Radical Left, including a fellow shipowner, Gunnar Knudsen, as finance minister, and an ardent nationalist, Jörgen Lövland,★ as minister-resident in Stockholm. Nansen, whose withdrawal from the State Church rendered him ineligible for the Cabinet, was sent to conduct propaganda for the Norwegian cause in London, where Michelsen raised a loan for purposes of defence.

The crown prince, who was acting as regent for his ailing father and therefore came to Oslo to appoint the new ministry, was informed by Michelsen of his intended method of procedure, which must result either in the acceptance of an act establishing Norwegian consuls, drawn up without reference to Swedish wishes, or in a confrontation between the two countries. Prince Gustaf, who in 1895 had favoured strong measures against Norwegian recalcitrance, was now conciliatory. Convinced by the soundings he had taken in Oslo that there was no longer any pro-Swedish party to fall back on, he was half reconciled to the loss of a kingdom whose politics might infect Sweden as well with the germs of a rampant democracy; and he feared possible complications with the great powers. In March he warned the Secret Committee of the Riksdag that Michelsen's intentions were serious, and apparently canvassed the introduction of a system under which there might be separate foreign ministers but 'common affairs should be dealt with by a Union Chancellor, responsible to the representatives of both countries'. †Failing this, the crown prince preferred that Sweden should safeguard its prestige by being the first to propose the termination of the Union. The Riksdag, however, would go no further than to offer fresh negotiations, to be based on separation of the consular services and an acknowledgement that the common foreign

★ 1848–1922. A teacher of peasant stock, who first made his mark as an opponent of Sverdrup in 1886 (see p. 141). After the termination of the Union, he conducted a pacific foreign policy from 1905 to 1908 (prime minister, 1907–8) and did much to promote neo-Norwegian, both as president of the Storting, 1913–15, and as minister for church and education, 1915–20.

† *The North American Review*, 1906, p. 292 (an article by the Swedish Liberal, Karl Staaff, outlining Swedish policy in the crisis).[39]

minister might be of either nationality, in which the Norwegian government refused to participate.

Instead, their strategy was to keep public opinion at fever heat by a feast of patriotic oratory, which reached its natural climax on May 17th; by the publication of suitable material in the newspapers; and even by half-concealed military precautions—all to ensure that the bill for setting up a Norwegian consular service might be seen to represent the will of a united people. When the measure came before the Storting, Hagerup pleaded in vain for postponement until after the next election, and it was then passed unanimously. This gave the Norwegian ministers in Stockholm full justification for pressing King Oscar (who had resumed the exercise of the royal functions) to sanction a measure that his subjects in Norway so evidently desired. But his mind was made up to support the interest of the Union as he saw it, so he pronounced the fateful veto. When the three ministers refused to countersign his decision and one of them declared that any Norwegian who did so would find himself without a fatherland, the king protested, 'I am just as good a Norwegian as you are.' So far as intentions are concerned the verdict of history would probably confirm this, but King Oscar's action now, as on some previous occasions, failed to achieve the results intended. By pre-arrangement the ministers tendered the resignation of the entire Norwegian cabinet, and this the king refused to accept, on the expressly stated ground that 'no other government can now be formed'.[40]

Their refusal to countersign a royal decision with which they disagreed had a precedent in June 1892, but the right to refuse had never been conceded by the crown. The closest parallel to the situation now arising had been in 1895, when a tense and alarming period of 'caretaker government' had elapsed between Stang's formal offer of resignation and his replacement by Hagerup and the national coalition. But in the intervening ten years the Norwegian people had become much better prepared psychologically to stand a strain, as the money spent on defence strengthened the self-confidence slowly accumulated over a long period of economic and cultural advance. Furthermore, in Michelsen they had a leader whose successful career in shipping had taught him to make the most of an opportunity, whatever the risk. The veto was pronounced on 27 May; one week later the premier's mind was made up in favour of a *coup*.

The king's state of health rendered it improbable that he would hurry to Oslo to negotiate for a new cabinet, and the rather colourless ministry of administrators which had succeeded the Boström regime in April was unlikely to precipitate any other move on the part of the Swedish authorities. But some step towards breaking the deadlock might very well be taken by the crown prince who, after an unavoidable attendance at his eldest son's wedding in London, might reach Oslo by 10 June. Michelsen accordingly arranged with the president of the Storting, the veteran Radical Carl Berner, for a secret meeting to be called on the evening of the 6th to consider a plan, for which he had prepared the ground by numerous discussions with individuals. In this way he was able to ensure its speedy adoption in open session on the following morning.

In response to his formal announcement on the 7th that the members of the cabinet now ceased to discharge their official duties, the president of the Storting moved a carefully worded resolution for filling the power vacuum which Michelsen's action had created.

Whereas all the members of the Cabinet have laid down their offices, Whereas his Majesty the King has declared himself unable to provide the country with a new government, and Whereas the constitutional monarchy has thus ceased to operate,
The Storting authorizes the members of the Cabinet which has this day retired to exercise provisionally as the Government of Norway the authority assigned to the King in conformity with the constitution of the Kingdom of Norway and existing laws—with those changes which are necessary inasmuch as the union with Sweden under one king is dissolved in consequence of the King having ceased to function as Norwegian king.

The Storting gave its approval unanimously, and Michelsen on behalf of the cabinet immediately resumed office, with the royal powers now placed without restriction at their disposal.

This was undoubtedly a revolutionary measure, since it treated the monarchy as a purely functional institution, a point of view which is not defensible in terms of the 1814 constitution, and in any case it ignored the important limiting word 'now' in the king's declaration which was cited to justify the claim that the monarchy had ceased to operate.[41] It also passed over in silence the Act of Union of 1815, by which the common institutions including the monarchy were made unalterable except by consent of the Swedish as well as the Norwegian legislature. Nevertheless, Michelsen showed a politic desire to render the revolution tolerable to Swedish and world opinion by adding an address to King Oscar. This was passed at the same short meeting of the Storting, against the votes of the five Socialists and with what an eyewitness of the scene describes as 'much less elated feelings'.[42]

The address excused Norway's action as being the result of 'a process of evolution, which has been more powerful than the desires and will of the individual'. It assured the world of the Norwegian people's wish to live at peace and harmony with the Swedish and every other people 'and with that dynasty, under whose rule our land despite much bitter controversy over the Union has made such important spiritual and material growth'.[43] Then, as a practical evidence of goodwill, which had the further merit of placing 'revolutionary' Norway firmly on the side of the established order in the European comity of nations, King Oscar was formally invited to allow a prince of his house to renounce his dynastic claim in Sweden and accept election as king of Norway.

1905: THE CONFRONTATION

'Confrontation' is perhaps too strong a term to describe the manoeuvring for position, in which the monarchy, the cabinets, and the parliaments of the two kingdoms were engaged throughout the summer months. King Oscar, indeed, had sent his personal assurances immediately before the breach, to the effect that no mobilization was then contemplated on the Swedish side, and at least one section of Swedish opinion, namely that of Hjalmar Branting and the Social Democrats, expressed immediate sympathy with what the Norwegians had done. In retrospect, too, it seems likely that the great powers would have brought strong pressure to bear if they had regarded war in the north as really imminent: they had trouble enough that year over their own rivalries in Morocco and the repercussions of the Russo–Japanese War. But a later generation also knows from experience how easily the logical course of events is upset by miscalculation or mere chance.

Apart from the obvious disparity in physical resources, Norway's chief disadvantage lay in the fact that her government had no international status. Although Michelsen had succeeded in borrowing rather more than £2 million abroad shortly before the breach, indefinite delay in obtaining foreign recognition could still produce overwhelming difficulties. Unofficial emissaries were therefore set to work to publicize Norway's case. Nansen, who had a book already in the press,[44] sent a copy to the British prime minister (Balfour) on 19 June, accompanied by a letter which reveals the sort of appeal that was deemed necessary at this juncture.

By the extreme attitude of the Crown (only considering Swedish interests) the step taken became inevitable . . . I believe that the best solution would be that Sweden allowed us to get one of the Princes of the Bernadotte House as king. We do not wish to become a republic, but it might be that it will otherwise be difficult to find a king, as we cannot easily get one from you or any other Great Power, as is easily understood.

The greatest misfortune would however be, if Sweden should go so far as to attack us; that would naturally be nearly suicide for both nations. Sweden is not so much stronger that she should conquer us easily, and even if she could, she cannot keep us.

I remember well that you laughed at the idea of a war between Sweden and Norway as an 'absurd folly'. But that folly is in this moment not quite so impossible as I wish it were. There is in this moment a very strong feeling in Sweden in favour of an attack on Norway. I hope, however, that the cooler heads will be able to prevent the 'folly', and we also hope that the Great Powers will not encourage this.[45]

On the day that Nansen wrote his letter, the Storting adopted with some modifications a conciliatory address to the Riksdag, which a leading Conservative, Benjamin Vogt*, had drafted with Lagerheim and other well-disposed political leaders in Stockholm.

* 1863–1947. A son of one of the ministers who had been impeached with Selmer in 1883–4, and a member of Hagerup's cabinet, 1903–5; he went to

But when the Riksdag met in emergency session, its members were not willing to accept the proposals of the Swedish cabinet for recognizing the separation and negotiating the details of a settlement afterwards. Instead, they appointed a special committee, which met in private to consider no fewer than forty possible demands, which ranged as far as a cession of territory in North Norway. The committee also received a report on the state of Sweden's defences and discussed a war grant, which was eventually fixed at £5 million and placed at the disposal of the Riksdag.

Four main recommendations were adopted by the Riksdag on 25 July, and were then made public. They gained additional force from the fact that these happenings had caused the replacement of the existing cabinet by the first fully parliamentary government in Swedish history; the new prime minister, Lundeberg, who was Conservative leader in the First Chamber and its spokesman in defence questions, had been chairman of the special committee. Two of the recommendations from the Riksdag named prerequisites for a separation: to assuage the injured pride of the Swedes, the Norwegians must agree to bilateral negotiations conducted without any reference to the unilateral action of June 7th; and they must prove that their demands were clearly based on the will of the people, either through a new Storting election or through a plebiscite. The third recommendation was that an inter-governmental conference should be held to arrange a final settlement, while the fourth —which was to prove the most troublesome—added to the various adjustments necessary for the separation the demand that the Norwegians should demolish their new fortifications on the frontier, where a neutral zone might be established if they wished.

Michelsen, knowing what was in the wind, arranged a plebiscite before it was demanded. On 13 August, when 85 per cent of the electorate went to the polls amid scenes of wild enthusiasm, only one person in 2,000 recorded a desire that the Union should continue, though one of the 182 negative votes was cast by a former prime minister, Emil Stang. The resounding success of the plebis-

Sweden as a private intermediary for Michelsen on 14 June. He became the first representative of an independent Norway in Stockholm, 1906–10, and was minister in London, 1910–34.

cite was duly followed by an agreement to negotiate, which the Storting approved by a large majority. So far, so good: but in spite of two months of strenuous effort, on the last day of August Norway had to enter upon the agreed negotiations at Karlstad without any very strong cards in her hand.

When Nansen wrote his letter to Balfour on 19 June, Norway's most experienced diplomat, Fritz Wedel Jarlsberg,* having resigned his post as Swedish and Norwegian minister to Spain, was already busy with the idea that Prince Charles of Denmark, a grandson of the reigning king, should be invited to occupy the vacant throne as soon as it had been formally rejected by King Oscar for his family. Since Prince Charles was the son-in-law of Edward VII, his candidature was bound to attract popular support in Britain for Norway's cause, which already appealed to liberal sympathies. The German emperor and the Russian Tsar, who met at Björkö in July, would have preferred the choice of Prince Waldemar—the king of Denmark's youngest son, who was the Tsar's uncle; but they were too much engrossed in matters nearer home to press the case when Michelsen objected to the fact that Waldemar's wife was a Catholic and their children too old to become fully Norwegian.[46] The Swedes, however, used the offer made to them on June 7th so as to block the way. In private, their king spurned it with an indignation that was not purely histrionic, but in public he kept it open pending the settlement of all other matters at issue. Michelsen hoped that Prince Charles would accept the Norwegian overtures notwithstanding, and thus enable him and his colleagues to proceed to the conference table as the accredited ministers of a new sovereign, whose presence on Norwegian soil had rescued their country from its isolation. The prince was for a time inclined to listen to the promptings of his father-in-law, who wished him to be ready to move to Norway in immediate response to any request; but on 18 August he bowed to the decision of the Danish king and cabinet that the need to preserve good relations with Sweden made any such action impossible.

* 1855–1942. A great-nephew of the Stattholder Wedel; he had been Swedish–Norwegian *chargé d'affaires* in London, *c.* 1890, and minister in Madrid, 1891–7 and 1902–5; his private residence at this time was in Denmark.

In addition to the respective prime and foreign ministers, the Norwegian representatives at Karlstad were Vogt and Berner, the Swedish Hjalmar Hammarskjöld and the future Liberal premier, Karl Staaff. The proceedings lasted a little over three weeks, including a critical adjournment from 7 to 13 September, after an impasse had been reached over frontier fortifications at Kongsvinger and Halden which the Norwegians refused to demolish. The Storting then held a secret session, at which the defence minister expressed grave doubts both about defence prospects in general and about the effectiveness of the new forts, intended as a screen to cover the mobilization of the main forces. Norway had 22,500 men under arms at this juncture and the fleet was ready for action, but the Swedes had called up twice as many men, nominally for manoeuvres, and had a naval squadron of superior strength poised for an attack on the Oslofiord.[47] While Castberg and Konow (H.) advocated resistance to the Swedish demands, whatever the cost, a large majority of members favoured a compromise if possible over a problem which was rendered intractable by historical as well as military considerations, since for practical reasons Georg Stang had sited new works on ground that held proud memories from past wars.

On reassembling at Karlstad, the two sides were described by Michelsen as standing 'like one rock against another',[48] but a sensible compromise emerged eventually. Kongsvinger was left intact, but its fortifications must never be further developed; Halden was disarmed but not demolished; and the other new fortifications directed against Sweden were removed. In return, the Swedes agreed to an arbitration treaty and an extension of the neutral zone beyond its intended terminus at Kongsvinger. Staaff did much to produce a peaceful result, as did the Russian and French ministers in Stockholm, who emphasized the sympathy of their governments with the natural desire of the Norwegian people to have their historic memorials respected. But in the last analysis, conciliation succeeded because the leaders of public opinion in the two countries directly concerned had not lost all sense of proportion and because no great power was interested in fomenting their conflict. The results of the conference were ratified by the Riksdag unanimously and by the Storting against the votes of sixteen activists—two socialists, three members of the United Party, and eleven of the Left. Castberg and Konow (H.) again headed the opposition, which they tried to extend to Radical circles outside the Storting with the help of the social democratic leader, Eriksen (see note, p. 201), and a young republican enthusiast, Johan Scharffenberg.

1905: THE SETTLEMENT

Three of the Karlstad conventions dealt with matters of practical convenience: the preservation of the right of the nomadic Lapps to cross the Swedish–Norwegian frontier in the seasonal search for pasture for their reindeer; the continuance of existing facilities for transit traffic through the frontier districts of either state; and corresponding arrangements for the common use of lakes and watercourses. The settlement regarding the Norwegian frontier forts formed part of the provision for a neutral zone 12 miles wide, stretching from the coast to the 61st parallel. The Swedes had proposed that it should merely be denuded of defences, but deferred to the Norwegian wish that it 'shall enjoy the benefits of a perpetual neutrality'.[49] No troops might be stationed there except to keep order—or in the event of war against a third party, such as befell the Norwegians in 1940. But the convention by which the Norwegians set most store was the agreement to submit all future disputes between the two powers to the arbitration of the Hague Court. An exception was, indeed, made for disputes 'affecting the independence, integrity, or vital interests of either Kingdom', but this was almost the first such treaty to leave it for arbitrators to decide whether a given dispute came within the category of 'vital interests'.[50]

On 26 October, the day that the conventions were signed in Stockholm, Oscar II formally renounced the Norwegian throne which, he declared, had brought him 'so many bitter sorrows'.[51] Not many of his Swedish subjects can have experienced the same personal regret, as the integration of the two peoples had never been very close, but they certainly felt that the aged monarch had been badly treated. As for their own position, the more far-sighted deplored the weakening of the defence of the peninsula at a time of increasing international tension, but the Union had caused so much friction that some were glad at heart to hoist the 'pure' Swedish flag.

For Norwegians, however, the settlement was still incomplete, since their sovereign independent state had no acknowledged head. In Europe at large, the predilections of that distant pre-1914 era ran strongly in favour of a monarchical form of government, which was supposed to connote respectability and stability. We have already seen how Michelsen made use of this outlook, first to soften the blow on June 7th, and later in the hope of strengthening Norway's position in negotiation. Although he had failed in his immediate object, he still intended to promote Prince Charles's candidature for the throne as part of the campaign against radical tendencies which had originally brought him back to politics. Albeit Björnson now professed himself a royalist, a more or less open republicanism had long been characteristic of many leaders of public opinion on the Left, and was accepted doctrine among the socialists.

The republicans claimed that the events of June 7th had put the constitution out of operation. They therefore proposed that, a settlement having been reached with the Swedes, a constituent assembly should be summoned, as in 1814; alternatively, the people should be left free to indicate what form of government they preferred by their votes at the next regular Storting election. Michelsen and Lövland, who had acted as foreign minister since mid-June, claimed on the other hand that the cabinet was morally bound by the negotiations with Prince Charles, for which Wedel Jarlsberg had been the secret intermediary. On the legal plane too, they argued that the constitution was not inoperative, since it provided for the choice of a new sovereign to be made by the Storting, a right which that body was disposed to exercise forthwith. But there was no constitutional objection to a third alternative, namely a plebiscite, and it is significant of his character that Prince Charles's first independent action in Norwegian affairs was to press for this solution. The government thereupon formulated the course to be taken in harmony with its own views: a plebiscite to be held, but the negotiations with the prince to be authorized to continue in the meantime, and the decision by plebiscite, if favourable, to be followed by his election in constitutional form by the Storting.

Soon after June 7th, a leading Danish newspaper had estimated that about two-thirds of the Storting were republicans at heart; though this was certainly a journalistic exaggeration, the prospect of bringing in a scion of some foreign house and establishing a royal court in Oslo was not in itself widely attractive and very many Norwegian families had learnt to admire republican America. However, since June Castberg, Konow (H.), and other republican enthusiasts had lost ground through their attitude during the crisis at Karlstad, which in retrospect seemed rash and provocative, while support for monarchy was considerably strengthened by the sense of a great debt owing to Michelsen and his colleagues: the men who had extricated the country from such a perilous situation might be credited with good reasons for committing themselves to Prince Charles. The Storting adopted the government's proposal by a vote of 87 to 29, and the second plebiscite of the year was held at a fortnight's notice. One minister, Gunnar Knudsen, resigned office so as to campaign for a republic; otherwise, the efforts of the socialist and labour organizations were supported mainly by a few radical spokesmen of an older generation, including Blehr and Georg Stang. The size of the poll was 10 per cent smaller than in August and the 4:1 majority in Prince Charles's favour was likewise smaller, but it was amply sufficient.

The Storting endorsed the decision of the electorate by a unanimous vote, and the prince on accepting the invitation to the throne adopted the Norwegian style of Haakon VII—a choice which is said to have been inspired by his reading of Wergeland—and the name of Olav for the two-year-old crown prince. The Danish king, his English consort, and the heir who might grow into the hundred-per-cent Norwegian of the people's hopes arrived in Oslo on 25 November. When Haakon had taken the oath to the constitution in the presence of the Storting, the ship of state was safely launched upon a wholly independent course for the first time since the decline and fall of medieval Norway.

6. Climax of a Century of Growth

THE NINE YEARS PRECEDING THE OUTBREAK OF THE
First World War marked the start of a new era for the Norwegian
people, who felt themselves to be at long last in unfettered control
of their own political destinies. Did not the establishment of the new
monarchy set the seal upon the whole course of their development
under the liberal institutions that their forefathers had established
in the face of such difficulties at Eidsvoll in 1814? The coronation of
Haakon VII at Trondheim cathedral in 1906, which was attended
by many foreign dignitaries (but no representative of the House of
Bernadotte), ministered to national pride, while the democratic
bearing of the new king and his strict obedience to the principles of
the constitution caused republican sentiment to dwindle: a resolution passed in 1913,[1] which specifically denied him the right of veto
in constitutional matters, seemed to lock the stable door when the
horse was already doped. Moreover, by a felicitous coincidence a
united people now faced a technological revolution which opened
up new vistas for Norway as a land of advanced industry; for these
were the very years when hydro-electricity began to rival the
steam engine as a source of power for manufacturing processes.
This had a cumulative effect upon an economy which was already
making a good deal of progress, with the result that the biggest
political issue of the day concerned the claims of capital, challenged
by Concession Laws, and the growing demands of labour. But these
matters must be placed first in their general setting—the course of
party politics, which the crisis of 1905 had interrupted, and the
growth of Norway's new international relationships which it had
made necessary.

PARTIES AND PROGRAMMES, 1905–1914

Two new factors influenced the politics of this period. One was the
adoption in 1906 of a system of single-member constituencies, with
provision for a second election among the best-supported candidates
whenever no one had the support of a majority at the first election.

By attaching the Storting representative more closely to his constituents, this gave increased play to local interests and enabled pressure groups to win seats on temperance, language reform, and church policies. The other new factor was the extension of the franchise to women, a reform which was helped on by the action of the women's suffrage organization in 1905, when it collected a quarter of a million female signatures to back up the August plebiscite. In 1907 women were given the vote in parliamentary elections on the income qualification which already entitled them to vote at local elections. In 1910 universal suffrage, with an important exception for persons in receipt of poor relief, was introduced for local elections, and in 1913 for those to the Storting. Although most official posts were opened to women in 1912, membership of the cabinet being added four years later, their influence was felt rather through the rising general concern for social reform than through any conspicuous leadership in the field of politics.

The party system was dominated at the outset by Michelsen, who hoped to preserve the bourgeois coalition, based on the United Party which he had begun to establish in 1903. But the election of 1906 produced a very confused result, since the long-standing party organization of the Left had a clear majority, but many of its nominal members had nevertheless been returned as avowed supporters of the United Party programme. Michelsen soon quitted politics for the less frustrating activities of his shipping business in Bergen, leaving the succession to Lövland, who brought the coalition government finally to an end early in 1908, when its supporters were faced in the Storting by a 'negative majority' made up of two mutually conflicting elements[2]—the Consolidated Left under Gunnar Knudsen and the ten socialists.

The erstwhile republican Knudsen★ was a strong leader, who had consolidated the Left by excluding right-wingers who were not receptive to party discipline. While at the head of a minority government, he contrived to settle the vexed question of the Concession Laws (see p. 196) for controlling the new industrial developments,

★ 1848–1928. A shipowner and industrialist with strong interests in social reform; first entered the Storting in 1891, the cabinet in 1901; prime minister, 1908–10 and 1913–20.

measures which his opponents denounced at the 1909 election
—but did not afterwards reverse. The odium incurred among
property owners was, however, sufficient to secure his defeat at the
polls by a combination between the Right and a body of moderates,
who styled themselves the Liberal Left (*Frisinnede Venstre*)* in contrast to the main body from which they had been excluded. The
new prime minister, Wollert Konow (S.B.)† was an estate owner
from the vicinity of Bergen and a friend of Michelsen, but he picked
his cabinet too largely from among his fellow members of the Liberal
Left to please the Right, who held nearly twice as many seats in the
Storting. Early in 1912 the Right welcomed a chance to get rid of
him on the ever-controversial language question, when Konow informed a gathering of rural youth societies that the language movement, meaning the advance of *landsmål*, was 'what had done most to
carry the Norwegian people forward in the last half-century'.[3] Konow
was replaced by J. K. M. Bratlie,‡ a conservative army officer with
long political experience and a special interest in defence, which was
again becoming a live topic. However, the forthcoming election
proved to be a decisive victory for the Consolidated Left. 'We have
the power now,' declared Gunnar Knudsen, 'and it is going to be
used.'[4]

His second ministry, strongly based on the middle classes in
general and the solid mass of farmers in particular, lasted from 1913
to 1920. It was the longest Norway had experienced under the
parliamentary regime—a marked contrast to the period of weak
ministries with little power over the Storting or the electorate, by
which it had been preceded. Leaving the Concession Laws and the

---

* Never a numerous or highly organized body, but the presence of well-known
leaders enabled it to figure in elections, usually as an enlightened wing of the
Conservatives, as late as 1936.

† 1845–1924. A grandson of the Danish poet Oehlenschläger and a supporter
of the proposed grant to Kielland (see p. 144), which caused him to lose his
seat as a member of the Storting for Söndre Bergenhus; except for 1898–1900,
he did not return to parliamentary life until 1909, by which time he had lost
his radical sympathies.

‡ 1856–1939. Held many posts in connection with defence, including that of
head of Services Enrolment (*Generalkrigskommissær*), from 1898 to 1929; Conservative Party chairman, 1911–19.

growth of the Labour movement, which returned twenty-three socialists at the 1912 election, to be considered in an economic context, we may now outline the reform policies of 1905–14. Their character was no doubt influenced by a natural reaction in favour of issues less dramatic but more diversified than those to which the nation's attention had been riveted during the critical months of the separation from Sweden.

As regards the language question, indeed, it was argued with renewed vigour by one side that deliverance from the political union with Sweden should have as its natural sequel deliverance from the linguistic union with Denmark. *Landsmål* or neo-Norwegian, whose growth was fostered by the rural youth movement (see p. 138), made a many-sided appeal to poetic, patriotic, provincial, or proletarian sympathies—according to the social class or cultural bent of the individual. Until the turn of the century, it had struggled for minority rights; but in the next decade, when the university, which had so long been the citadel of the bureaucracy, had come to contain 16 per cent of students from peasant homes,[5] enthusiasts cherished higher hopes. In 1906 a nationwide organization was founded (*Noregs Mållag*), and in 1907 a new measure of equality was achieved at the expense, one might say, of both liberty and fraternity by requiring all matriculation candidates to pass a serious test in whichever form of the Norwegian language they preferred *not* to use. A few years later the veteran Lövland delighted the supporters of *landsmål* in the Storting—who belonged almost entirely to the Consolidated Left—by his use of it from the dignity of the presidential chair. But in 1907 a rival society was started, with a much larger membership, to defend standard Norwegian or *riksmål*,* which was made less Danish in that year by the first of several statutory reforms of spelling, designed to bring it into conformity with 'cultivated' everyday speech, which had a very different pronunciation from the softer and more guttural diction of the Danes. Thus language questions became an issue not only at every election but even at the family breakfast table, since children in Norway are taught to spell more 'correctly' than their parents.

* 'language of the realm', a name first popularized by Björnson in 1899.

The foreigner perhaps finds it easier to sympathize with the motivation of two other cultural struggles which were characteristic of the period. One arose out of the crisis in church affairs, which every Protestant country experienced through the growth of modern science. In the Norwegian church laymen's activities of a more or less fundamentalist and also anti-clerical complexion had been notably strengthened by the establishment in 1898 of a separate Home Mission organization for western Norway and by the work of Ludvig Hope, an ardent lay preacher and devotee of the China Inland Mission (see p. 227), who demanded that the law should recognize the right of the laity to celebrate Holy Communion. The university, on the other hand, which had formerly wished to reject the historian Sars because he was alleged to be a positivist, was now so liberal in its outlook that, when a candidate for the chair of dogmatic theology (Dr. Johannes Ording) combined the best academic qualifications among the competitors with the drawback of unorthodox views on the sacraments, its authorities demanded in the name of academic freedom that the government should appoint him. This was done by a decision which shook Michelsen's cabinet in 1906, the consequence being that within two years opponents of liberalism in the many puritan congregations had raised funds to set up a Congregational Faculty for training clergy along strict and narrow lines. In 1913 this voluntary body was given the same rights as the existing university faculty in the examination of candidates for ordination; lay Communion was authorized in the same year, and demands for disestablishment of the church died away.

The temperance cause, which drew much of its strength from the same quarters, attempted to win new ground when the chairman of its Storting group, L. K. Abrahamsen, was minister of trade in the first Knudsen government. But a proposal to impose restrictions on the sale of wine resulted in a threat from France to deny access for Norway to further supplies of capital, and although this was at the moment when the Concession Laws were being established, the government was—perhaps too easily—intimidated. The French authorities agreed to reopen the Paris stock exchange to Norwegian funds, in return for a reduction of duties and a promise to refrain from any legislation 'to the detriment of the trade in French wines and spirits'.[6] Nine of the twelve votes cast against this accommodation to French capitalist interests were cast by the socialist group in the Storting. The advance towards Prohibition was plainly evident in 1913, however, when votes under the system of local option established in 1894 reduced the number of towns where spirits were still on sale from twenty-seven to thirteen.[7]

Social reform in general began to make rapid progress in Norway contemporaneously with, and to some extent under the unfluence of, the Britain of Asquith and Lloyd George. Michelsen had been sympathetic towards such alleviations of social conditions as might diminish the appeal of socialism to the workers without imprudent risk to the public finances. Gunnar Knudsen's attitude was much less reserved: he had been a member of the Labour Commission of 1885, and it was a matter of conscience with him to ameliorate hardships with which he was personally conversant from his experience as an employer. Furthermore, he had an importunate ally in Castberg, who had made himself an expert in the social policies of Germany and other European countries. Although his base in the electorate was only the little regional party of Labour Democrats, (see p. 157), he exercised a great influence upon their allies of the Consolidated Left. In 1913 Gunnar Knudsen made him head of a new combined department for social affairs and trade, from which he resigned in April of the following year after many clashes with the premier, who disliked (among much else) his free-trade principles and advocacy of the taxation of land values. But Castberg remained a great driving force in social legislation.

In 1906 the first public grants were made for unemployment funds. In 1908 and 1911 respectively, the accident insurance system was extended to fishermen numbering about 90,000 and to seamen; in the former case the state shared the cost with the individuals, in the latter the shipowner was made responsible. The introduction of sickness insurance had long been delayed, in spite of such ominous facts as the heavy incidence of tuberculosis, which reached its peak as late as 1900, while the death rate in 1910 was still grievously high for the age groups from fifteen to twenty-nine.[8] Its adoption in 1909 for the poorer wage-earners was therefore an important innovation, modest as it was in comparison with the socialist proposals for a national health scheme, to be financed from taxation. In the same year a new Factory Act extended protective regulations to all workshops equipped with engines of more than 1 h.p. or employing more than five persons in handicrafts; this law also gave a five-hour day to child workers of 12–14 years of age,[9] and restricted work at night and on Sundays and holidays. In 1915 this was followed up by the introduction of a ten-hour day and fifty-four-hour week for all industrial workers. All these measures embodied to a large extent the views of Castberg, but his most radical social achievement was his Children's Acts (1915), which were in a sense a sequel to an easier code for divorce and separation of spouses approved six years before. They safeguarded the interests of illegitimate children by giving them a right to the father's name and to an equal share in any inheritance; they also entitled necessitous mothers, whether married or unmarried, to support from the local authority for a period of six weeks before, and up to six months after, confinement. Many respectable matrons campaigned angrily against a policy which might loosen the ties of marriage, but Castberg had the support of feminist leaders in an action which helped to build up a position for Norway as a pioneer of humanitarian reforms.

INITIATING A FOREIGN POLICY

'The foreign policy of Norway should be to have no foreign policy':[10] this was a saying of Björnson's in the mid-1890s which still reverberated after 1905. Idealists held that international relations could be reduced to rule of thumb by arbitration agreements and recourse to the services of the Hague Tribunal; realists deprecated the extravagance of representation at foreign courts; and both bodies of opinion wished to avoid entanglement in the rivalries of the greater powers. A passive attitude was further encouraged by the inevitable scarcity of experienced personnel, even to staff the half-dozen legations that were judged to be the indispensable minimum. Wedel Jarlsberg, who had hoped to be foreign minister, was sent instead to Paris, where he cut a considerable figure. Nansen went to the Court of St. James's, but stipulated that he should return to Oslo after a couple of years to his professorship of oceanography.

Otherwise the only available Norwegian with suitable international connections was Sigurd Ibsen, but he was completely estranged from the new rulers of Norway.

Lövland, the first foreign minister, became involved in negotiations which won him little credit, especially as he offended the Storting by practising what its members regarded as an unwarrantable secretiveness. The starting-point was the need to replace the November treaty of 1855, made when Norway was not a separate sovereign power. Crown Prince Gustaf had raised the subject with the British foreign office shortly before the union was broken, his desire being that the powers should sign an integrity treaty to cover Sweden as well as Norway; but after Norway had for some time awaited a further lead in the matter, it appeared that Swedish opinion was unfavourable.[11] The discussions on which Lövland therefore embarked with the representatives of the great powers soon extended to the further possibility that Norway might secure a status of permanent neutrality; this had been urged in a unanimous Storting resolution of 1902. Lövland also had a third object in view, which for obvious reasons was not explicitly stated: in breaking away from the anti-Russian framework of the November treaty, Norway must avoid any commitment to either of the two camps into which Europe was being redivided.

In November 1907 Norway signed a new treaty with Britain, France, Germany, and Russia. The first two articles bound Norway to cede no territory to any power 'either for occupation or for any disposition whatever', in return for which the other four signatories agreed to recognize and respect her integrity. Although Norway had rejected the humiliating suggestion that Sweden should also sign, the wording was widely held to imply a second-class status. What was much worse, the support for her integrity that Norway might solicit was to be given 'by those means which might appear most suitable'[12]—an escape clause to be invoked at will by any or all of the powers concerned. Thirdly, though the preamble mentioned the neutral zone set up in 1905, no reference was made to the project for a permanently neutral status; the British in particular had private objections, so long at least as Sweden and Denmark were not neutralized. In the event of war against Germany, the British navy might for instance need a base in southern Norway to counterwork a German challenge elsewhere in southern Scandinavia.

The mention of the Conventions of Karlstad was plainly obnoxious to the Swedes, who were inclined to regard Norway's new treaty as a measure directed against them by Norwegians who suspected that they were planning a war of revenge. This view was strengthened by Lövland's clumsy failure to keep the Swedes informed of the course of the negotiations, which he carried to such lengths that the diplomatic corps at Oslo expressed its formal sympathy with the Swedish minister, when the latter accused Lövland of a breach of good faith. However, a totally unexpected result of Lövland's original initiative brought a double compensation to the Swedes, for two new treaties of April 1908 were linked with the agreement they had been induced to give to the abrogation of the November treaty of 1855. The first of these *status quo* treaties protected them against the remilitarization of the Åland Islands, a change which would have presented them with a far more serious defence problem than anything that alleged Norwegian machinations could lead to. The second treaty, for preserving the *status quo* along the shores of the North Sea, was inherently of less importance to the Swedes, but they would have been less than human if they had not observed with some complacency the meagre results that the Norwegians achieved in the diplomatic field, where they had been so prone to belittle the work done by Swedes on their behalf. For this treaty, which concerned Norwegian interests very closely, excluded Norway from its signatories, along with Belgium, as a 'guaranteed state' which the Germans held incapable of entering into such an agreement on an equal footing with the rest. Wedel Jarlsberg urged that the point should be contested by the French and British, who expressed their willingness to do so, but Lövland preferred not to risk further complications.[13]

In general, however, the Swedes showed a sensible readiness to bury the past, and after the death of Oscar II in December 1907 they looked forward in their Scandinavian relationships and never harped upon the power they had lost. Thus the details of the 1905 settlement were carried out without friction. Within twelve months three impartial outside observers certified that the new fortifications in south-east Norway had been duly razed, after which the neutral zone occasioned no further controversy. There was successful arbitration regarding some territorial waters, important to the lobster fisheries of both countries, whose ownership had been a matter of uncertainty since 1661; and the Storting acceded to a Swedish proposal to amend the arrangements for the annual migration of the Lapps and their herds across the frontier. An active 'Scandinavian' policy, indeed, was less practicable now than it had been during the last period of acute great-power rivalries in the 1860s. Swedish fears of Russia were so intense that an alliance with Germany was contemplated, while Danish fears of Germany led to a secret policy of appeasement in relation to her mighty neighbour. Norwegians, on the other hand, believed that they had nothing to fear, so long as their coastline remained under the surveillance of the British Grand Fleet: the possibility that Britain might covet one of their ports for an advanced base against Germany, though mentioned in 1905 and again (by Admiral Fisher to Nansen) in 1907,[14] was not taken very seriously. These cleavages made it all the more important that the three Scandinavian states should still support one another in such measures as lay within the compass of small powers for reducing international friction, helping to preserve peace, and in the last resort safeguarding the rights of neutrality.

As regards the work of the world peace movement, Norway had held a special position since the turn of the century. In 1899 the Inter-Parliamentary Union, founded for its promotion by W. R. Cremer, held one of its early conferences in Oslo, with the result that a Norwegian, Christian Lange,* eventually became its secretary and driving force. Then in 1901 the Peace Prize was awarded for the first time by the committee whose selection Nobel had entrusted to the Storting. Whether he intended to pay tribute to the Norwegian people as peace lovers or to the Storting for its advocacy of arbitration or to Björnson as a sonorous preacher of internationalism, is uncertain: but the result was to give Norway a unique annual opportunity to direct world attention to activities by which peace

---

* 1869–1938. As secretary of the Inter-Parliamentary Union, 1909–33, he promoted its work in many parliamentary states, kept it alive from Oslo during the First World War, and in 1920 arranged the transfer of its headquarters to Geneva. In 1921 he shared the Nobel Peace Prize with Branting.

was being promoted. One-half of the first award, for instance, went to Dunant, the founder of the Red Cross; in 1903 the choice fell on Cremer; and in 1908 the joint recipients were leaders of the peace movement in Sweden and Denmark. At the same time the Danes followed up their conciliatory actions during the Swedish-Norwegian crisis of 1905 by proposing that the Inter-Parliamentary Union should develop a special Scandinavian section. In 1910 the holding of the first full congress of this new organization in Oslo marked the completion of a satisfactory *rapprochement* between Swedes and Norwegians in the work for world peace, a sphere in which the Norwegians already enjoyed considerable prestige.

Common Scandinavian interests in social and economic matters continued to be fostered by common organs, ranging from associations of bankers and other businessmen to the formal congresses of social democratic parties and of trade unions, which had been held in the different capitals from time to time since the 1890s. There were also common cultural interests, on which political changes had little effect. But in the years now under consideration the most important practical advance was in the negotiation of neutrality rules, which had to be redrawn as the result of the Hague Conference of 1907, where all the Scandinavian states were vigorous participants. During the international crisis of 1908–9 Hammarskjöld drafted common rules for Sweden and Denmark, but Norway was excluded on account of her integrity treaty. However, when the First Balkan War broke out in 1912, Norway joined the other two in a common declaration of neutrality, and it was agreed that any change in neutrality rules must have the approval of all three.[15]

Most of the above-mentioned activities lay on the periphery of foreign policy as understood by larger powers. The Storting preferred inactivity as less expensive and the government found optimism a good reason for avoiding action which might prove rash. In the critical month of July 1911 the belief that Norway could keep clear of international complications was shaken by the unexpected and unwelcome arrival of the German High Seas Fleet for manoeuvres near the west coast, but the trouble over Agadir passed off in the autumn without Norway's ability to assert its neutral status being put to the test. In February 1914, at a time when King Gustaf V of

Sweden sided openly with demonstrators who wished to force the Liberal majority in the Riksdag to increase expenditure on defence, the Liberal prime minister of Norway showed a politic optimism. 'From the point of view of international relations,' declared Gunnar Knudsen, 'the sky is cloudless to an extent that has not existed for many years.' As late as July, he struck the same note when Wedel Jarlsberg reported to him on a visit home from his post in Paris, so soon to be in peril.[16]

The policy of economy at first dominated thinking about defence, too, under the new conditions of complete independence. The danger from Sweden having been at last eliminated, it was tempting to fall back upon romantic ideas of a 'people's army', to be based on the volunteer rifle clubs. But in 1909 Bratlie, as chairman of the military committee of the Storting, carried through an army reorganization which made a different appeal to democratic principles, since it tightened up the arrangements for imposing military service upon all alike. It also increased the period of liability for service in the line to twelve years, followed by eight in the *landvern* or militia, and the *landstorm* had a further call on all able-bodied men to the age of fifty-five. The traditional basis in regiments, which had been abolished in 1818, was restored, but the biggest change was the apportionment of the national territory among six brigades combining all arms, each with its recruitment area and mobilization centres; this made the short periods of training* more effective and would facilitate the transfer to a war footing if occasion ever arose.[17] The defence Budget remained meagre, but in the years immediately preceding the outbreak of war in Europe defence associations were set up to conduct propaganda for preparedness, one result of which was that the duration of the periodical regimental exercises was extended from twenty-four to thirty days.

The navy likewise made some progress. Although the reduced sense of urgency just after 1905 caused delays to two new ironclads, with the result that the British commandeered them from the shipyards where they still lay in 1914, a £1,000,000 building programme

---

* Recruit training and regimental exercises for infantry totalled 144 days, as compared with the period of 180 days generally considered requisite by continental armies.

was adopted in 1912 for smaller vessels. Moreover service in the navy, for which Norway never lacked suitable personnel, was extended early in 1914 from six to twelve months. The opposition of the Socialist Party, which besides proclaiming its faith in internationalism asserted that defence forces were used primarily to bolster up the capitalist system, remained a factor of some weight on the other side. During Bratlie's term of office as premier, however, he felt sure enough of Service morale to use ships and men of the navy in order to break a strike among the engine-room staff employed on the coastal steamers. In the judgement of a Conservative historian, 'The years preceding the World War were excellent from the point of view of defence.'[18]

THE ECONOMY IN GENERAL

Norway in 1900 still had a rapidly growing population: this was, indeed, one reason why strikes were soon to present a serious problem. Its inhabitants then totalled 2,240,000 or about two and a half times as many as in 1815. In spite of emigration they increased by 150,000 in the next decade and by 250,000 in the decade after that, when the outward flow to America was checked by the First World War. Although a district medical officer from North Norway informed the Storting in 1891 that preventives had been 'for a long time extremely well known and practised on Norwegian soil',[19] the birth rate at the turn of the century was higher than that of the United Kingdom or of some more obviously comparable countries, such as Sweden and Switzerland. The number of births reached its peak in 1901, but ten years later the net reproduction rate was still as high as it had been two decades earlier: thus the statisticians forecast continuing pressure of population on the means of subsistence, if the rates of birth and death could be assumed to remain the same. The growth of towns had accelerated in the last decades of the nineteenth century, and in 1900 their birth rate was 5·6 per thousand above that of the countryside. Nevertheless, at that date only 28 per cent were town dwellers and the proportion did not change appreciably down to 1914, so that Norway still depended primarily upon a rural economy.[20]

Agriculture went through a period of consolidation. Between 1875 and 1900 the acreage under corn had been reduced by 15 per cent, which meant that two-thirds of the bread requirements had to be covered by imports. But by 1912 better tillage, and especially the use of improved seed corn from Sweden, was producing harvests almost equal to those of the 1870s. The most striking innovation, however, was the spread of meadowland, to which two-thirds of the cultivated area was devoted: with the help of the horse-rake and mower, it could be worked with less labour than the arable, which made it possible to concentrate upon dairy farming. By 1907 milk production was twice what it had been half a century before, and the effects of a better fodder supply showed in a 50-per-cent addition to the milk yield per cow plus a 20-per-cent improvement in slaughter weight. The stock of sheep and goats was allowed to decline, because its profitability depended upon a plentiful supply of cheap labour, but in suitable areas the cultivation of fruit and vegetables was proving worth while. The first tractor was brought to Norway in 1908.

As for the organization of agriculture, this was the period when the co-operative dairies came into their own: by 1914 they numbered 620 and three-quarters of the milk passed through them. Their success stimulated the growth of other types of farmers' co-operatives. The state also began to play a more active part. In 1893 the Storting adopted a proposal from a Folk High School leader pledging it to bear three-quarters of the cost of the local agricultural schools, which were replanned to suit the needs of the farmer rather than the farm hand, with increased emphasis on theory and accounting. A Department of Agriculture was set up in 1900, and next year the Agricultural High School, based on the existing 'higher school', was launched as an institution for both instruction and research, under a director who had urged the need 'to think big for once, even when it is the peasant who is under consideration'.[21] His views were not lost upon one of its first graduates, who gave a new impetus to the Farmers' Federation (*Landmandsforbundet*). Fourteen years after its foundation it had only 10,000 members, but in 1910–14 it grew to 50,000, constituting a formidable pressure group on social and cultural issues, where its standpoint was ardently nationalist, as well as for its economic demands—cheap transport, cheap credit, and tariff benefits.

A parallel body, dating from 1913, marked a still more significant trend, for the Smallholders' Association (*Småbrukarlaget*) owed its existence to the fact that the cottar class, which by 1920 shrank to 14,000, was being replaced by a new category of owners. Castberg helped to organize them as potential supporters for the Labour Democrats, and in 1903 had been instrumental in setting up a 'bank for workers' holdings and homesteads' (*Arbeiderbruk-og Bolig-banken*) which financed many of the land purchases. But the versatile Norwegian countryman took advantage eagerly of the opportunities offered him by the diffusion of industry, so that the majority of small holders were part-time farmers, with one foot on the land and the other in the workshop or rural trade or the fisheries. In 1907 there were nearly 125,000 smallholdings, containing 1–12 acres of cultivated land: more than one-half ranked as the secondary occupation of the owner, and less than one-quarter provided his sole occupation.

The fact that nearly one in three of the larger farmers as well had other economic interests helps to explain the ineffectiveness of the pressure exercised by the agrarians as a whole in favour of protection. In 1905 a tariff was imposed on some animal products, but it required a further agitation to secure the inclusion of pig meat, of which the domestic production was on the increase. As for helping the native corn-grower, by 1914 the argument that some degree of self-sufficiency ought to be encouraged because of the risk of war in Europe had led to nothing more practical than the canvassing of various schemes for accumulating reserve stocks of wheat and rye.

The trend away from free trade showed itself more clearly in industry. In 1897 those textile and other manufactures, which lost their chief market abroad when Sweden cancelled the interestate treaty, had been awarded some protection in the home market as a kind of national compensation. But it was not until 1905 that Gunnar Knudsen, whose wide business experience had made him an ardent protectionist, saw his chance. As finance minister under Michelsen in that critical summer, he induced many members of the Storting to accept an industrial tariff for the sake of national unity. In the circumstances the duties were bound to be small, even if

Norway's dependence for her livelihood upon the export trades and shipping freights had not in any case counselled restraint. How far industry benefited from the change of course at this time is hard to determine; growth during the next decade was most rapid in branches that received no direct assistance.

Without her merchant fleet, Norway would still have been quite unable to pay for her imports, of which nearly one-half were consumer goods that maintained the standard of living. Between 1851 and 1913 imports multiplied thirteen times over, exports only nine times, yielding an unfavourable balance of trade which was always substantially reduced and in one decade (1878–88) completely cancelled by freight earnings.[22] Yet the basic resources of the fisheries, the forests, and the mines were being exploited with increasing vigour. In 1908 the first herring-oil factories were set up along the coast, to supply fishmeal to the farmers and add to the stock of hardened fats for manufacture. A year or two later the petrol engine became available for small fishing craft—just in time to prevent this arduous, traditional small man's occupation from being completely eclipsed by the employment of steam-driven fishing vessels of large size, often equipped with the purse-net. In 1898 a Forestry Association had been formed to safeguard the future supply of raw material for the woodworking industries, which was increasingly valuable as one-half of what was sent to the mills was now destined for sale as pulp or cellulose. In the first sixteen years of the new century these two industries doubled their workers and trebled their output. As for ore exports, pyrites began to be exploited in two new areas in the 1890s, and iron mining, which had been reduced to a single location, was developed early in the new century at two sites in the far north, one of which grew into the arctic town of Kirkenes.

Important transport developments stimulated the growth of the home market. In 1894 the entire coastline north of Trondheim was linked up by a government-subsidized service of express steamers (*Hurtigruten*), and in the same year Michelsen negotiated a compromise among the conflicting railway projects put forward by different districts to the Storting. This enabled work to be begun on the Bergen–Oslo route, joining the two coasts and the two principal towns of Norway across a roadless and almost uninhabited district of precipitous mountains and perpetual snow. Although it took fifteen years to complete, the decision in 1898 to make this a standard-gauge railway showed great faith in the future.

Nevertheless, economic progress was very patchy. Employment in industry rose by one-quarter in the last five years of the century, but railway building based on foreign loans produced a speculative boom and then, in the summer of 1899, a sudden collapse. For about four years unemployment was rife in Oslo and to some extent in other towns, and recent arrivals tended to drift back to the country. It was indeed fortunate that Norway had other dependable resources—on the oceans, where her sons continued to show their adaptability to new opportunities; and in the 'white coal' from her waterfalls, soon to remove her chief industrial handicap.

SHIPPING AND WHALING

As was remarked in an earlier chapter, the changeover from sail to steam-driven vessels was more difficult for Norway than for countries which were well supplied with coal and iron. This transition was prolonged by the availability of cheap sailing ships in the second-hand market, to which the Norwegians were accustomed to go for many of the additions to their fleet. Thus it came about that by 1906 Norway owned more sailing ships of iron or steel than of wood, and although numbers had fallen by two-thirds before 1914, in that year she still deployed a sailing fleet of 275 vessels with a tonnage of 158,812.[23] Steam tonnage, however, had grown fairly steadily since the 1880s: that was the decade in which Michelsen began to figure among the well-established steamship owners of Bergen and Gunnar Knudsen became the first steamship-owner in eastern Norway. In 1905–14 a more rapid growth carried the total from 800,000 to more than 1,300,000 tons, Bergen remaining in the lead.

The fleet still operated to a great extent by offering itself for tramp service from one foreign port to another, but did not specialize in oil cargoes: believing that purpose-built tankers would be run by the big oil companies on their own behalf, the Norwegians in 1914 had only half a dozen. The main advance was in the development of liner services, which would convey package goods for any consignor to points along a given route, with fixed days of arrival. Since the Norwegian lines were all home based, it was a remarkable achievement to get one-tenth of the entire fleet transferred to this more profitable activity in the course of less than two decades. The pioneer was the Mediterranean Line,[24] established under a trade treaty of 1892, in which Spain—which was Norway's fourth-best customer—required the establishment of a subsidized shipping service by the Norwegians, so as to encourage Spanish exports in return for the continued admittance of klipfish at low duty. The line also served Portugal and Italy, and in 1906 it was extended to the Canary Islands, taking out wooden crates from Norway and bringing back bananas to London. A Mexico and Gulf Line was started in the next year, after which five other transoceanic routes were opened up in quick succession, culminating in a passenger and cargo service to North America. This last was the Norwegian America Line, the institution of which was strongly contested by the Danish-owned line which had for many years picked up Norwegian emigrants at Oslo and Kristiansand. The Danes proposed that the new line should be owned by all three Scandinavian countries but placed under Danish management, and they enlisted the support of Gunnar Knudsen. But in spite of this surprising ally, they were eventually defeated by a combination of Norwegian national feeling with financial backing from Norwegian–Americans; the Swedes also joined in against the Scandinavian plan.

One consequence of these transatlantic activities was that by 1911 about 10,000 Norwegian seamen were serving under the American flag, tempted by the wages, which at the turn of the century had been two and a half times as high as Norwegian rates. But the growth of seamen's organizations was beginning at last to deprive Norwegian shipowners of their traditional advantage of a cheap supply of labour. The example of the skippers and ship's engineers, whose unions dated from 1889 and 1902 respectively, was followed by the seamen in 1910. The shipowners had started their own association one year before, but wages could no longer be held at something under 10*s.* a week, which was below the amounts given in any other of the leading maritime nations.

This was also a time of new developments in whaling, a subject to which public attention had been drawn by the complaints of North Norway fishermen, who attributed poor catches to the extirpation of the whales, which were believed to drive the shoals of fish towards the coast. After they had wrecked one of the shore stations in protest, the Storting agreed to the government's proposal for a ten-year ban on whaling operations in the territorial waters and shore stations of North Norway. The ban did not prevent the hunting of whales farther out in the Norwegian Sea by ships based on foreign stations, and in the year after the enactment of 1904 the number of whales taken increased considerably.[25] However, the price of whale oil had fallen so low that Norwegian whaling firms were easily deterred from participating.

Instead, accumulated tradition and experience stimulated interest in a new venture. The notion of a profitable whale fishery in Antarctic waters had been entertained by the Scots and others since the middle of the nineteenth century, and it was one reason for a mounting interest in the exploration of Antarctica. The Norwegian pioneer, Carl Anton Larsen, first became convinced that finback whales existed there in quantities which must prove remunerative, when he was engaged to transport a Swedish scientific expedition to the far south in 1901–3. He then founded an Argentinian company, with himself as station manager and crews and equipment from Norway, which shot its first whale off South Georgia in December 1904. A Norwegian company was established a year later, when Christen Christensen, an enterprising shipowner in the little port of Sandefiord at the mouth of the Oslofiord, diverted his pioneer factory ship from Spitsbergen to the Antarctic. In 1907 a second Norwegian company received British permission to build a shore station in South Georgia.

Meanwhile, the demand for whale oil was reviving, after a period in which the substitution of mineral oils both for lighting and greasing had left it with little value except for soap makers. By 1908 new methods were under development for solidifying fatty oils, so that the oil from rorquals, such as the finback and the still larger blue whale of Antarctic waters, could be used in new ways, especially as an ingredient in margarine. Between 1908 and 1911 output was quadrupled, four Norwegian stations being established in South

Georgia and others in the South Shetlands and South Orkneys. The British authorities then decided to restrict the granting of further concessions, so the Norwegians operated partly in the seas off South Africa and Australia, where whaling reached its peak in 1912–13. In the last pre-war season Norwegian profits amounted to £2 million, which was twelve times what they had been only seven years before. Sandefiord was becoming the whaling capital of the world.

Indeed, the gain to the Norwegian economy was even larger than the figure suggests, for the whaling expeditions of foreign companies employed mainly Norwegian crews, who brought high earnings home with them at the end of each season in the Antarctic. Much equipment, too, was sold to foreign users. Indeed, the history of the whaling enterprises was altogether most encouraging, because it showed that, where the physical conditions were on their side, a people of the barren north could rival the industrial inventiveness of their more fortunately placed neighbours. Modern whaling had begun with Svend Foyn's harpoon, mounted by him in a steam-driven whale-catcher. Christensen's factory ship, a 2,400-ton cargo boat which he converted into a 'floating boiler', was the device that made it possible to conduct whaling operations on reasonable economic terms in the antipodes, the vessel being anchored off shore or moored in a harbour for the catchers to tow in their kill. In 1912–13, when a Norwegian factory ship could not make harbour in the South Orkneys because of the ice, its manager contrived to process the whales at sea instead. This was the start of pelagic whaling, and one of the gunners already had the idea of using a slipway to haul carcases on deck for flensing in any weather—the technique which was to be adopted in the inter-war period by every whaling nation.

THE IMPACT OF HYDRO-ELECTRICITY

Between 1906 and 1916 the gross national product of Norway increased by 5 per cent per annum, which was five times the rate of growth during the first five years of the century. After making due allowance for the wearing off of the urban trade depression of 1900 (already mentioned) and for the effects of transport improvements and other general developments, we should still expect to find some special factor stimulating such a sudden break-through in a country that had hitherto derived little direct impulse from the industrialization of western Europe. That factor was the harnessing of waterfalls to generate electric power, which equipped Norway at large for the first time with a more effective prime mover than the watermill.

The profusion of steeply falling water in Norway made it certain that its people would sooner or later exert themselves to copy the hydro-electric installations which had been successfully set up in the 1890s at Niagara, at the Schaffhausen Falls of the Rhine, and at some less well-known sites in both France and Italy. Although Norway had to import nearly all its heavy electrical equipment from Sweden or Germany,[26] at least three circumstances encouraged its introduction at an early date. The steam-driven industrial plant in Norway was comparatively small, because it depended upon an imported coal supply, so a changeover would not involve discouragingly heavy losses in fixed capital. In Norway, too, the use of electricity for lighting, which normally preceded its adaptation for industry, had been specially stimulated by the fact that it usually replaced paraffin lamps rather than the comparatively convenient gas lamp: coal for coking was too expensive and the long distances, together with the deep penetration of frost into the soil, made mains distribution of gas in many districts both difficult and risky. Above all, when it came to the location of industry with reference to the new power source, the proximity of many high falls to the western seaboard besides facilitating exports made it easy to import bulky raw materials, for processing by new methods which called for plenty of cheap electric power.

The first two arc-lights were installed as early as 1877, and in 1885 a small works was set up on the initiative of Gunnar Knudsen (who had been trained as an engineer), which supplied some outside subscribers as well as 120 lamps on the premises of the factory to which it was attached. In 1890 Hammerfest in the far north, having a conveniently situated waterfall, introduced a service of electric street lamps to penetrate the polar darkness, and in 1894—only ten years after the electric tram had been pioneered by Siemens in Germany—Oslo's horse-drawn tramway was in process of conversion. Electric railways, too, were already being discussed at least by

Knudsen, who had commended the idea to the Storting in 1892 with the assurance that, in the coming age of hydro-electricity, Norway had 'conditions for development in every department of economic life requiring mechanical labour, such as are possessed by no other country in Europe'.[27] In 1896–1900, accordingly, eleven sizeable hydro-electric plants were constructed, together with three steam generators and two in connection with gasworks. By the latter date industry was employing three times as much horsepower from electricity as from steam engines. The biggest power station, situated at Sarpsborg on the lower course of Norway's principal river, the Glomma, had six units of 1,200 h.p., which were being used experimentally for a wholly new venture—the production of carbides in a high-temperature furnace.

This was an outstanding example of a site already owned and occupied by concerns that had required water power for timber processing and similar purposes. The great majority of the falls, however, belonged to farms in their vicinity, for which they had little direct value, and much ill will was caused by the activities of speculators, who bought the rights from farmers for derisory sums and resold them to industrialists after a few years at profits which ranged up to kr. 200,000 on an outlay of kr. 50,000. At first, interest centred upon low falls carrying much water: at Sarpsborg, for instance, the river was 116 feet wide and flowed from the huge lake Mjösa, but the drop was only 74 feet, which by Norwegian standards is very little. In such a situation it was relatively easy to construct the necessary dams, channels, and sluices and to install the turbines. But soon after 1900 the improvement of transformers made it possible to transmit at high voltages over long distances without serious loss of current. At this second stage the huge falls on the edge of the central mountain plateau came under consideration, including such famous tourist attractions as the stupendous descent of 800 feet at Rjukan. Vast magazines were constructed at a high level to keep the flow steady throughout the year, pipes channelled the water down the mountainside, and halls were hewn out for turbine stations in the solid rock. In this way almost unlimited power was made available for use, either in a new industrial complex at the foot of the fall, like Rjukan, or wherever the pylons carried it throughout the region. In 1911 the first Rjukan power station was the largest in the world; its output of 140,000 h.p. was nearly as much as the whole of Norwegian industry had used in 1897.[28] During approximately the same period the amount of power per industrial worker had doubled, and the figure of 5·1 h.p., which was reached in 1912, bore comparison with that of the most industrialized nations.

The most important use to which the new power was put was for the production of electrochemicals, for which cheap power was the chief requisite. The Sarpsborg project, for example, began with calcium carbide, of which Norway by 1909 made one-fifth of the world output. In 1907 the manufacture of aluminium was tentatively introduced, from raw materials shipped across the Atlantic. But the most remarkable early success was the manufacture of nitrates from the atmosphere, established through one man's farsightedness and financial expertise, for Sam Eyde* possessed the happy combination of an engineer's training, early experience in the management of big building schemes (such as main railway stations), and contacts with moneyed men in Sweden and other foreign countries.

By 1903 Eyde had bought up rights in a number of waterfalls, and was exploring the possibilities for the manufacture of artificial nitrates from atmospheric nitrogen as a way of exploiting hydro-electric power on the very large scale which would be most profitable. He then came into contact with a leading scientist among his compatriots, Kristian Birkeland,† whose experiments for the invention of an electric cannon suggested a type of electric arc that would give the necessary heat, namely a disk of flame with a temperature of about 3,000°, derived from a 500-volt current. The method was patented in 1904, shortly after Eyde (whose first wife was a Swedish baroness) had interested a group of Swedish financiers in forming a company for the general development of electrochemicals in Norway.

---

* 1866–1940. Trained at Charlottenburg, he did his first work as a constructional engineer in Germany; in addition to his establishment of Norsk Hydro, he developed two other big Norwegian power projects, one of which served carbide and cyanamide manufactures, the other aluminium and corundum, the firms concerned being British, French, and German.

† 1867–1917. Known also for his solution of the Maxwellian equations (1895) and pioneer studies of the Aurora Borealis.

Next year it was clear that the manufacture of nitrates alone would need more capital than Swedish and Norwegian resources together could make available. Thus it came about that, in the very months when the political union was being dissolved, a union of Swedish and Norwegian capitalists under Eyde's adroit management was busy securing the support of a French bank, so that most of the capital for a separate nitrates company, 'Norsk Hydro', was finally raised in Paris. Both companies were directed by Eyde, who in 1907–10 was also chairman of the Norwegian side of a short-lived combine with the German 'Badische' firm, which was developing a different nitrates process. Furthermore, he led the team of young engineers who tackled the formidable problems of constructing plant of a size and complexity hitherto unknown in Norway—and constructing it, too, on very remote sites, where they had also to provide communications and living quarters for the workers. To sum up, by the time of his withdrawal from these multifarious interests in 1916–17, he had made the kind of impact on the Norwegian economy that one associates more readily with the career of an American tycoon.

By 1913 the export of 'Norway saltpetre', as the new nitrate fertilizer was called, had risen to nearly 100,000 tons, and the total for electrochemicals was 180,000 tons. The value of kr. 33 million was equal to that of the entire traditional export of timber.

The electro-metallurgical industries made a slower start: in 1909 they employed only 282 workers, as compared with 1,767 in electrochemicals,[29] where the *per capita* output would be about as high. But whereas the Birkeland–Eyde process became obsolete after the First World War, so that Norsk Hydro had to change its method and diversify its products, such an activity as the electrolytic smelting of aluminium from imported bauxite was capable of almost indefinite expansion. Thermic zinc, too, began to be produced in Norway in 1904–5, and nickel from native ores in 1910. The revival of the iron and steel industry after a long period of depression was likewise stimulated by experiments in the production of electric iron and steel, which were begun in the last years before the war.

As Lenin was later to proclaim, electrification was the key to social progress. By 1914 Norway had laid the foundations for a modern type of industry, in which a small number of technicians operate a very costly automatic plant for the continuous production of basic materials or actual consumer goods. Once such a plant had been built, it offered employment that was clean, hygienic, and physically less exhausting than the strain that hand processes had imposed on human muscles. In Norway there were other social advantages resulting from the rapid spread of electricity through the countryside. Small-scale machine industry could be established where surplus labour—much of it seasonal or part-time—was readily available in semi-rural communities. In addition, the convenience of electric lighting in the long, dark winter, as well as the usefulness of refrigeration and other labour-saving possibilities, was appreciated at once on the farms, even in the most isolated districts. In 1914 the state provided help for planning local installations on a 'do-it-yourself' basis; each county set up an advisory office; and by 1920 Norwegian power stations had a capacity of about 500 watts per head of population—the most lavish provision in the world. What was perhaps more remarkable, a country which had always been handicapped by the wide dispersion of its dwellings also led the world in the proportion—two out of every three—that were now lit by electricity.

But there was another side to the picture. Great power projects required great accumulations of capital, as was illustrated by the history of Norsk Hydro. Was Norway to give free play to capital interests, including foreign interests, regardless of the political and social consequences? Or were the rights of the nation and the local community to come first, even if the result was to delay and impair the long-term development of economic resources? These questions produced the acute political controversy over the Concession Laws, which lasted for a whole decade and affected the growth of the economy for at least two decades to follow.

THE CONCESSION LAWS

Although a law of 1888 required all foreigners except Swedes to secure crown permission for the ownership of real property in Norway, the restrictions were not enforced in practice, for the exploitation of the mines and forests depended in large measure upon foreign initiative and resources. Up-to-date mining equipment was expensive and the profit uncertain; out of the three biggest pyrite mines two were Swedish and one British, and other ore enterprises at different times attracted German, French, and even Belgian capital.[30] Wood pulp was of even greater interest to the British, because fully owned subsidiaries abroad kept down the cost of independent foreign supplies: accordingly, in the 1890s Kellner–Partington and Edward Lloyd Ltd. were the two main operators in Norway. Some waterfalls were obtained direct from the riparian owners for use in such undertakings, as in the case of Kellner–Partington, which had bought one-half of the Sarpsborg fall to turn its grinding mills. Others, as already mentioned, were bought up cheap by Norwegian speculators for resale to the highest bidder, who might well be foreign. Yet a third type of situation was that in which development was attempted by Norwegian interests, but failed for lack of capital. At one very advantageous site on the Glomma within 30 miles of Oslo,[31] financial weakness compelled the native would-be developers to sell out to a German concern, which in 1904 was absorbed in Siemens. The entire plant was then offered as a going concern to the Oslo municipality at three-quarters of its cost price: but although the local demand for current already far exceeded the supply, the city fathers either would not or could not find money for the purchase.

It is against this background that we must view the excitement that arose in the early months of 1906. Three-quarters of all hydro-electric installations yielding more than 3,000 h.p. were already owned by foreigners: Eyde's recently completed negotiations in Stockholm and Paris indicated that this was merely a beginning. The value of Norwegian power sources to world industry was thought at this juncture to be virtually unlimited, so it was easy to suppose that the country might find itself suddenly transformed into an industrial dependency of foreign states. Far-sighted individuals also foresaw the irreparable damage that might be done to the natural beauty which was an important part of the national heritage, while representatives of the farmers were incensed by the way in which some of their fellows had been bamboozled into parting with valuable property rights: had not one-half of Rjukan been sold in the 1890s for kr. 600? But the predominant feeling was an outraged nationalism, which resented the idea that foreign capitalism should be enthroned in place of a foreign king.

In April 1906, after an outcry by Castberg and private debate in the Storting, the Michelsen government carried the so-called Panic Law, to which there were only six dissentients. This imposed a temporary ban on the purchase of waterfalls by foreign citizens or by limited companies, which might conceal foreign interests; if the crown chose in any instance to waive the ban, it would be entitled to make conditions. Two months later, the prohibition was continued by a second temporary law, which added (by a much less decisive majority) an extension to cover forest and mining properties and the requirement that any company receiving a concession must have its seat of management in Norway. Next year the hiring out of hydro-electric power was likewise brought under public control; otherwise the system was left unchanged until 1909.

The dispute over reversionary rights then brought into prominence the issue of state socialism. From 1894 onwards a few waterfalls had been bought by the state with a view to railway electrification plans; a good many of the smaller electricity plants, too, were financed by local authorities for local purposes. Under the temporary Concession Laws Michelsen had gone much further in the same direction, announcing the intention to insert in any concession the proviso that all rights and installations should revert to the state without compensation after seventy-five years in the case of a foreign company, or with full compensation after ninety-nine years in the case of a Norwegian company employing any foreign capital. Lövland as his successor in office brought forward a bill which maintained the same principle, namely that these penalties were to be regarded primarily as deterrents against the intrusion of foreigners. But Lövland fell from power before he could carry his bill, so that a definitive concession law was the work of Knudsen's first government in the Storting session of 1909.

Supported by the radical Castberg as minister of justice, Knudsen brought forward a measure to extend the reversionary rights of the state to cover all companies receiving a concession, including those whose capital was exclusively Norwegian; it was even implied that an exception made for electricity developments promoted by individual Norwegian citizens might be merely temporary. The case was upheld by ingenious arguments: one raised a fine dialectical distinction between property in a site and property in the water passing through that site; another urged the desirability of conciliating foreign opinion by treating all capital with equal severity regardless of its place of origin. But the underlying motive was plainly hostility to the whole class of big entrepreneurs and the investors they served, at home and abroad. Uncompensated confiscation by the state would take place after 'a fixed period of at least 60 and at most 80 years . . . from the announcement of the concession'.[32] The same legislation gave the government authority to control the price of electric power; and while mines and forests were not rendered liable to reversion, the former—whose capital was 80·3-per-cent foreign—were subjected to a production tax and the latter to a preferential right of purchase for local authorities.

After discussions of almost unprecedented length, the Storting passed these measures. The ensuing election showed that the electorate was in much doubt about their desirability, especially as the peasants became alarmed by concurrent suggestions for the taxation of land values according to the ideas of Henry George. But as we have already seen, the Konow and Bratlie governments of 1909–12 lacked internal unity, and although both prime ministers were strongly opposed to the principle of reversionary rights accruing to the state, they failed to take any effective counteraction. After that it was too late to do so. In alliance with Castberg, who expressly disclaimed any allegiance to the ideas of George, Gunnar Knudsen secured a majority in the Storting which kept him in office for seven years. When the First World War began, the opponents of the Concession Laws were trying as a last resort to have them set aside as contravening the guarantee given to private property in the constitution. In December 1913, after a delay of three years, the Oslo town court decided that the laws were not unconstitutional, a decision which was upheld by the Supreme Court in April 1918— after a still more inexplicable and clearly prejudicial delay—by a majority of four judges against three.

In 1909 more than one-third of the total capital investment in all Norwegian industrial corporations was foreign, thirty-two wholly foreign corporations operated in Norway, and 13·6 per cent of industrial workers were employed by foreigners.[33] But next year the big Swedish banking interests began to withdraw their support, and until the war intervened to give Norway a sudden increase of bargaining strength, the Concession Laws indisputably hindered development. Whatever might be the long-term effects on the economy of this check to foreign enterprise, it is obvious that in 1905–14 nationalist sentiments were not to be denied. The hostility shown to large-scale capitalism of native origin is, however, at first sight more surprising. To some extent it may be attributable to that decline in the old liberal principles which was a common European phenomenon at this period. But Norway cherished in addition a special romantic sympathy with the 'little man' as representing the true native culture. *Aftenposten*, a Conservative paper which took the opposite side in the controversy, admitted grudgingly: 'It may perhaps sound attractive to go in for the view that waterfalls and natural resources should remain in the hands of the local folk.'[34] Michelson went even further, employing the socialist argument that large-scale industry leads to the formation of a large proletariat to justify the conclusion 'that our country in the long run will be better served by maintaining a population of two million or thereabouts, whose circumstances allow them all to be about equally well off'.[35]

The high level of emigration, much of it from barren regions to which hydro-electric installations and new industrial development might have brought new prospects, is a reminder that there was another side to the argument about the interest of the 'little man'. Yet Michelsen was right in thinking that the new trends—which Concession Laws might check but could never wholly reverse— were liable to introduce a new element to the population. By 1914 a militant proletariat was on the march, and socialism, on which Michelsen had long ago declared war, was becoming for the first time a factor of importance in national politics.

ADVANCE OF THE LABOUR MOVEMENT

Nineteenth-century Norway owed the beginnings of a Labour movement very largely to the example of its Scandinavian neighbours
with their more advanced industrial development: as late as 1905
the membership of the trade union federation was only 15,000. But
special circumstances had created a united body of Labour opinion
in the far north, where the riot against the whaling companies in the
summer of 1903 gave expression to a much wider sense of grievance
among the fishing population, who attributed their extreme poverty
above all to the local traders to whom they were bound by their
chronic need of credit. Later in the year that region returned the
first group of four socialists to the Storting by a vote which exceeded
that of the other parties combined, and a fifth *Stortingsmann* from the
same region soon joined their ranks. They had an able leader in a
clergyman journalist, Alfred Eriksen,* who eloquently denounced
the system under which 'the fisherman has to pay tribute to capitalism four or five times over on every single fish'.[36] In 1905 he helped
to win the sympathy of the Swedish socialists for the Norwegian
cause, and was one of the strongest and most consistent advocates of
a republican form of government.

At the election of 1906 Holtermann Knudsen (see p. 134) was
returned for the first time and the membership of the group in the
Storting rose to ten. This became eleven in 1909 and twenty-three
in 1912, when the vote in its favour rose to 26·52 per cent.[37] Its
continued growth under an electoral system that notoriously
favoured the larger parties showed that socialism was potentially
formidable; this was realized by the Conservatives, who in 1912
devoted more of their electoral propaganda to the 'socialist menace'
than to their opponents of the Consolidated Left, who ousted them
from office. Nevertheless, as a parliamentary force the socialists
achieved little. Their support for the Concession Laws was luke-
warm, while their campaign against compulsory military service
(which replaced an earlier enthusiasm for 'the people in arms')

* 1864–1934. He had taken a Ph.D. in psychology, and championed co-
operative production rather than systematic socialism; a devotee of individual
liberty and in his last years a Conservative.

served chiefly to infuriate the Conservatives. Eriksen became side-tracked by his chairmanship of the *riksmål* society, and Holtermann Knudsen as his successor in the leadership proved ineffective in debate. Their position in the Storting was in any case complicated by the presence of Castberg's rival group of Labour Democrats, whose leader schemed to use them as the nucleus for a larger Labour Party under his control, embracing the socialists as well as the more radical elements in the Left Party. Both in and out of office, Castberg for many years promoted a policy of advanced social reform, which obliged the socialists to play second fiddle to him, though they steadfastly resisted any merger.

The first years of the new monarchy coincided with new growth in the trade unions, whose membership in the autumn of 1907 was approaching 36,000. One landmark in that year was the negotiation of the first full wage-scale agreement on a national basis by the well-organized association of iron and metal workers. Their example was followed by the paper industry workers, who struck to get an agreement. The employers replied by a lock-out which forced the workers to accept mediation, but the eventual award was much in favour of the latter. In the same summer Castberg launched the idea of compulsory arbitration of labour disputes, which was unanimously approved by the Storting. In 1912 Gunnar Knudsen included in his election programme 'compulsory conciliation procedure and, for labour disputes of a comprehensive nature, compulsory arbitration,'[38] so when he was returned with a secure majority and Castberg at his side, the way seemed clear for a bill such as had actually been drafted before his party left office three years before. The reaction from the labour movement was rather surprising. While the employers' organization denounced the bill in the belief that compulsory arbitration might lead to a general regulation of wages by the state, the trade unions denounced it as a direct threat to the right to strike. The socialists thereupon opposed the measure in the Storting, and were supported by Castberg, who was quite willing to sacrifice consistency in the hope of enlarging the party that followed him. There was still a parliamentary majority for passing the bill, but the government gave way to the threat of a general strike, which the trade unions made known on 2 April 1914.

Thus by the outbreak of the First World War new impulses were beginning to reshape the Norwegian Labour movement, with the result that it was ready to take full advantage of the situation when the collapse of the capitalist system across the Russian border lessened its prestige in Norway as well. Among the Social Democratic youth groups a new impulse can, indeed, be traced back to 1900, with anti-militarism as one of the main action points. In 1905 they denounced Eriksen as a warmonger when he opposed the Karlstad Conventions, and later on, when they had adopted the 'broken rifle' as a popular symbol of the movement, the youth groups, many of whose members were below voting age, made heroes of those who preferred imprisonment to military service. Their attitude to politics in general was anti-parliamentary and tended towards syndicalism, in accordance with teachings which spread to them from the Young Socialists of Sweden. Meanwhile, syndicalism was making a more direct impact upon the trade unions.

A rapid increase in the average size of work place facilitated the organizing of the employees. In 1900 Norway contained only two that had more than 1,000 workers, twenty-six with more than 300; by 1909 the first category had increased to three (including Kellner Partington with 2,000 workers) and the second to thirty-six.[39] Moreover, special opportunities were presented by the big concentrations of navvies, many of whom had drifted across the border from Sweden, for the heavy manual labour required to build the hydro-electric installations. These workers were herded together in very remote areas, where they lived rough, ran big risks, and earned good temporary wages—only to be moved on again when the costly new equipment was ready to earn the shareholders their profits. Yet two dramatic events seemed to teach the lesson that trade unions organized along the conventional lines produced little result. In 1909 the Swedish workers suffered a resounding defeat when their funds were exhausted in a long-drawn-out 'big strike', in which one in twenty-five of the entire population had taken part. Two years later, the Norwegian miners, who with the allied trades formed one of the largest organized groups of workers in the country, came off worst in their own opinion after a strike had led to a big lock-out and the lock-out to an arbitrated settlement arranged by the prime minister.

This gave revolutionary agitation a chance to win a hearing. It was being preached by an eloquent and ascetic house-painter from Trondheim, Martin Tranmæl,⋆ who had returned from America in 1905 with syndicalist ideas; he had imbibed them in those radical circles that in that year organized the Industrial Workers of the World. He opposed long-term wage agreements as a soporific; proclaimed the usefulness of such weapons as boycotting, obstruction, and sabotage; and gave direct, if not specific incitements to violence. In November 1911 Tranmæl's opposition programme was adopted by a conference of trade unionists at Trondheim, where he was then active as a journalist, and next January he made a famous speech in Oslo, which included the following:

Is it not ridiculous to leave a well-polished machine when one enters upon a conflict? Is it not stupid to make working conditions safe for strike-breakers in the mining industry? Or suppose that there were a few shots of dynamite left in the holes, which only the strikers knew about, don't you think strike-breakers would think twice about taking up the work?[40]

Tranmæl's methods were denounced as unethical by the established leaders in the trade union movement and in the Norwegian Labour Party, both of which were weakened by the resulting dissension. But he succeeded in forming an organized 'trade union opposition', and on the political side he found an able ally in a middle-class Oslo socialist, Kyrre Grepp.† The successful threat of a general strike against compulsory arbitration, which has been mentioned in another context, was in line with their teachings. The approach of the centenary celebrations of the constitution in

⋆ 1879–1967. Journeyman painter in U.S.A., 1900–2 and 1903–5. Secretary of the Norwegian Labour Party, 1918, and editor of its principal newspaper, 1921–49; led illegal strikes and was imprisoned, 1924–5. An agitator of great powers, who led the Labour Party into, and out of, a close association with the Third International, but wished for no public office. In 1940–5 he served the national cause in Stockholm.

† 1879–1922. A socialist before he left school for the university, where tuberculosis prevented the completion of his studies; a member of Oslo City Council from 1913, but chiefly active behind the scenes in the management of the Labour Party, of which he became chairman in 1918.

the spring and summer of 1914, which had made the government particularly anxious to avoid the strike, also enabled them to black-mail the government into promising that the festivities would be shorn of any royal or military pomp which might offend the suscep-tibilities of the extremists. However, from May 17th until the world catastrophe struck, as it seemed, from cloudless skies in early August, the attention of most Norwegians was happily concentrated upon the past, not the future, as they reviewed a century's achievement in terms of political, social, and economic benefits felt in every home —and in the Norwegian contribution to the development of North America and to the progress of civilization in the world at large.

7. Norwegians Abroad

THE NORWEGIAN SENSE OF ACHIEVEMENT, SO STRONGLY felt and expressed in 1914, was not concerned only with the development of the 'seamed and weather-beaten land' of Björnson's Anthem. While the inhabitants of the neighbouring island had been busy extending and developing the dominions of the British crown, the Norwegians too, though incurring neither the glorious responsibilities nor the bitter disappointments of empire, had crossed the seas to set their mark upon distant quarters of the globe. Their polar explorers have won lasting fame. The contribution of their Lutheran missions to the cause of humanity in Africa and Asia deserves to be better known than it is: in proportion to its population Norway supported more missionaries than any other Christian country. But this chapter must consider first and foremost the Norwegians who settled abroad and made parts of North America the second homeland of their race.

THE MOVEMENT ACROSS THE ATLANTIC

As is the case with other groups of 'hyphenated Americans', the Norwegians who made a place for themselves and their descendants under the Stars and Stripes do not present the historian with an easily distinguishable subject of study. Their movement into and across the new country continued for a century at varying speeds; it had little formal leadership, no central organization, and nothing in the way of general records beyond bare statistics. Even these last leave much to be desired, since it was not until 1869 that the American immigration authorities classified Norwegians separately from Swedes, and those who entered the United States overland from the St. Lawrence valley (which was at one time the cheapest route) were usually not counted at all.[1] As for contemporary examination of the phenomenon, Norwegians of the more educated classes at first played very little part in the movement, which they commonly denounced as unpatriotic and at variance with the true interests of the nation. Among the major political figures, Björnson was almost the only one to entertain a serious interest in the motives that sent so many of the masses overseas or in their situation on the other side. The emigrants themselves, on the other hand, had their attention absorbed in winning a livelihood, and when an intellectual élite developed among them, its first interest was in theological disputation. It was not until the 1890s that the specific Norwegian contribution to the making of America began to be seriously examined, as forming part of the westward movement of the frontier of settlement which was already entering on its final stages. Even then it was difficult for the history of so small a people to win recognition in so large a country, where values that those of Norwegian stock hold dear were often obscured by an impatient use of the omnibus term 'Scandinavian'.

Nevertheless, the migration from Norway was not merely very large in relation to the size of the population from which it was drawn—this we have already noticed—but also a considerable contribution to the population to which it was added.

TABLE IV[2]

Period	Approximate total of Norwegian immigrants	Annual average
1836–40	1,200	240
1841–50	17,000	1,700
1851–60	36,000	3,600
1861–5	23,000	4,750
1866–73	110,000	13,750
1874–9	33,000	5,500
1880–93	255,000	18,200
1894–1900	35,000	5,000
1901–10	190,000	19,000
1911–20	66,000	6,600
1921–30	68,000	6,800
1931–40	4,000	400

From 1870 onwards the contribution shown above admits of a rough comparative measurement, because the American censuses record country of birth. Admittedly, the system was somewhat haphazard: Scotland and Wales, for example, are treated as separate countries throughout, whereas Finna and Czechs first receive separate enumeration in 1900 and 1920 respectively. All the same, it is remarkable that in the censuses of 1870, 1880, and 1890 the Norwegians ranked seventh, fifth, and again seventh among the foreignborn. In 1900 their position had fallen to eleventh, and by 1940 to fifteenth.

When the first emigrant ship sailed from Stavanger in 1825, the entire population of Norway was a little over one million: yet within three generations it was to send altogether three-quarters of a million on the same voyage over the Atlantic. There must have been compelling reasons for an exodus which, viewed as a proportion of population, was exceeded only by that of the Irish. The Irish—and many other European peoples—were pushed out of their homelands by extremes of political and economic pressure which were not so characteristic of Norway; but it is possible to see that there were special inducements pulling the Norwegians into the New World. The availability of cultivable land for all comers had an almost mesmeric effect on a people for whom the *odelsbonde* (see note, p. 11) was the archetype of the free man and for whom the extreme scarcity of tillable soil had always been the chief limiting factor in the national development. The freedom of American life was of course its second outstanding feature in the eyes of all newcomers. But here again, the full attractions of the American constitution—in particular, the democratic franchise, the opportunities for local self-government, and the absence of a state church and other authoritarian institutions—would be most avidly seized upon by a people like the Norwegians, whose constitution of 1814 had already carried them part of the way along the road to a genuinely free society.

The very fact that Norwegians were readily mobile* and comparatively literate made the pull of the New World more effective. Occasionally, even in the earliest days, someone returned from America to recount his experiences: one who did so in 1838 recalled many years later how 'the rumour of my homecoming passed like a flame through the country. Many travelled 168 English miles

* See Plate III for the setting out of a party of emigrants, as seen by Tidemand in 1843.

in order to talk with me about my trip.'[3] But a much greater and more regular influence was exercised by letters home: soon after 1840 those written by 'an intelligent and liberal peasant from Hardanger', describing a dozen years, experience of conditions on the other side, were said to be circulating in hundreds of copies.[4] After the American Civil War, when emigrants were more numerous and postal services cheaper and more efficient, the flow of what were familarly called the 'America Letters' took on much greater dimensions, penetrating to every corner of Norway and forming part of the staple diet of local newspapers. They even achieved a national circulation through publication in Jaabæk's *Folketidende*, which presented America in a very favourable light.

The argument was not all on one side. *A Word of Admonition to Peasants in the Diocese of Bergen Desiring to Emigrate*, a pastoral letter from their bishop in 1837, ran to at least three printings.[5] Wergeland denounced the 'emigration frenzy' in his paper for the workers, and satirized it in a play written on his death-bed in 1845.[6] More than one gloomy pamphlet recorded the disillusionment of an unsuccessful emigrant who contrived to return, which in the early days was by no means easy. But the weight of the argument seemed to be on the other side. In 1837–8 the leader of a recently arrived party wrote a *True Account of America*,[7] which gave encouragement and advice to those who might be inclined to follow them; its sincerity made a big impact on the Norwegian public, in spite of the fact that the author died soon afterwards as the result of the hardships of a wrongly located settlement. This was followed in 1844 by a more complete *Pathfinder for Norwegian Emigrants*. While acknowledging that immigrants without capital would have to work for at least two years to earn the money to set up as farmers on their own, the writer declared on the basis of a wide experience that 'All those who have been in America for a few years, with a few individual exceptions, are in a contented and independent position. . . . They do not suffer want. Taxes and rent encumber no one.'[8] This was confirmed in a collective letter, signed by eighty settlers, which was published in full in *Morgenbladet* in 1845, and a few years later a group of Norwegians in Chicago formed a Correspondence Society to counter unfavourable reports.

One or two mid-western states began to employ emigration agents in the middle of the century, and when it seemed likely that the Civil War would retard immigration, an enterprising American consul of Swedish extraction issued a stream of circulars in Bergen, including one that gave a full Norwegian translation of the Homestead Law of 1862.[9] But it was during the Reconstruction Era that the America Letters came to be effectively supplemented by the organized propaganda of federal and state authorities in search of suitable immigrant types and railway and steamship companies in pursuit of traffic. Moreover, as a large number of immigrants rapidly made good in the new country, there was an increased flow of money to connections at home: this was in itself a silent advertisement for American life, and some of it was earmarked for transatlantic tickets, about 30 per cent of crossings being financed in this way.[10] In 1905 a newspaper investigation estimated Norwegian-American gifts to the Norwegians at home at a total of kr. 20 million a year.[11] In addition, American life received a free advertisement from the many artisans who went over temporarily to gain experience and from others, whose object in going was to accumulate a modest capital for buying a farm in Norway: by 1914 they were a noticeable element in the population of some southern coastal counties. What Norway saw most frequently, however, was the summer visitor to the scenes of his or her youth; they might be derided by caricaturists and behind their backs by envious former neighbours, but their prosperity was usually very much in evidence.

A Society for the Limitation of Emigration[12] was set up in 1908, with support from all the interests which felt themselves threatened by a depleted labour force in agriculture, industry, and shipping. But although the evasion of military service by young men who emigrated at the age of call-up caused special recriminations, the right to emigrate was never directly challenged, and the record of the years since 1825 suggested that the magnet of a higher standard of living might long continue to draw Norwegians across the Atlantic. In 1914 times were good in Norway, so emigrants were fewer: this was as in previous boom periods. But then came the war, the introduction by stages of the quota system, the Wall Street crash of

1929, and the depression years—events altogether outside the control of the Norwegian people, which brought to an end their greatest movement into the outer world since the age of the Vikings.

THE 'LAND-TAKING' IN NORTH AMERICA

The settlement of Iceland, recorded with 400 names of the Norse participants in the thirteenth-century *Landnámabók* or 'book of the land-taking', was, indeed, an event to which the 'land-taking' in North America by a far more numerous body of nineteenth-century Norsemen bore a kind of resemblance. The settlers themselves liked to recall their Viking ancestry, and although they shared the credit of opening up America's wide spaces with much larger peoples, their achievement still had something of an epic quality, because the Norwegians clung with such determination to the primary task of winning and exploiting new soil. This motive runs right through the story.

The first fifty-three immigrants, known as the 'sloopers' because they voyaged from Stavanger to New York in the over-crowded sloop *Restaurationen*, resembled the Pilgrim Fathers in being a group of religious dissidents who prepared the way for a mass immigration which had mainly secular motives. Their leader was a professed Quaker and about one-third sympathized with Quakerism;[13] the rest were likewise at variance with the Norwegian state church, probably on account of their Haugean practices. Cleng Peerson,★ their footloose and enterprising compatriot who met them at the quay, had obtained land for them in upper New York State by arrangement with the Quaker interest, and there was again a Quaker element in the first reinforcement of the original party, which arrived almost eleven years later, in the summer of 1836. By that time, however, the agricultural opportunities of America had become the main attraction.

The original allotments in New York State were not sensationally

★ 1782–1865. Born near Stavanger; he had travelled to England, Germany, and France before he went to America in 1821 via Gothenburg on behalf of Stavanger's persecuted Quakers. He paid brief visits to Norway in 1824 and later, and regarded himself justly as 'the father of Norwegian emigration'.

cheap at 5 dollars an acre payable in instalments, and they proved difficult to clear. But by 1834 Peerson had prospected for a second settlement in Illinois, where land could be had at a quarter of the price and values were expected to rise through canal construction. Accordingly, some of the settlers of 1825 and the bulk of those who came in 1836 and the following years made their way to 'Ellenaais' where, after surviving the hazards of the freezing winter cold on the open prairie or of malaria in the lower ground, the great majority lived to see their first hastily erected shacks grow into substantial farmsteads. At mid-century Illinois had 2,500 Norwegians in a population of 81,000 and in the next two decades their numbers were multiplied by five.

But Norwegians were not content to stay put. New arrivals from home commonly used the existing settlements as a starting-point from which to move to other, possibly more desirable, areas which were just being opened up; and there was nearly always an adventurous element in the existing settlements which preferred to join them. The indefatigable Peerson, for example, led one of the first parties of Norwegians into Iowa and tried with less success to organize a movement south-west into Missouri and as far as Texas, where he himself died after fifteen years' residence in a small community of his fellow countrymen. Most immigrants were deterred by reports of the climate farther south and of the slave society they must encounter there. A second, much more resounding failure was 'Oleana'. Ole Bull, the famous violinist, arrived in America early in 1852 and planned to provide Norwegians with a home from home in Pennsylvania, where he made an initial purchase of 120,000 acres. But the land proved unfertile, communications were lacking, and there was a flaw in the title-deeds. By the end of the following year Ole Bull had lost at least 40,000 dollars, and nothing was left of his settlement but a song which laughed at his Utopia.[14]

The great trek at this time was directed along trails which crossed the Mississippi in a north-westerly direction into Minnesota. The Swedish authoress, Fredrika Bremer, having visited the first governor of the newly organized territory in October 1850 published a glowing rhapsody about the prospects there, which was not lost upon her many Scandinavian readers.

What a glorious new Scandinavia might not Minnesota become! Here would the Swede find again his clear, romantic lakes, the plains of Scania rich in corn, and the valleys of Norrland; here would the Norwegian find his rapid rivers, his lofty mountains, for I include the Rocky Mountains and Oregon in the new kingdom; and both nations their hunting fields and their fisheries.[15]

Miss Bremer was pardonably vague about the limits of this Promised Land, but in 1854 more than 300 wagonloads of Norwegians could be counted moving west from Wisconsin and heading mainly for Minnesota. In 1860 12,000 resided there, in 1870 50,000, and after another sixty years Minnesota still had the largest Norwegian population of any state and its industrial centre, Minneapolis, the largest proportion of Norwegians to be found in any major city of the Union.

In 1863 the flow of immigrants from Norway was temporarily checked by reports of the Sioux outbreak, in which some of those who had settled in north-central Minnesota were barbarously murdered and many more had to abandon their homes and possessions. Otherwise, the Civil War years did not prevent some increase in numbers,[16] which after 1865 rose rapidly, more Norwegians arriving in the next eight years than in the previous forty. These larger numbers were made up to a decreasing extent of whole families migrating *en bloc*: from 1866 onwards two-thirds emigrated at 15–35 years of age.[17] The proportion of wage-earners increased among both men and women, but in the 1870s the former began to include a sprinkling of persons with professional qualifications, which gradually became significant.

The Red River Valley on the western border of Minnesota was examined and written up in 1869 by P. H. Hansen, a gifted Norwegian journalist employed by the State Board of Immigration.[18] In the same year the completion of the first transcontinental railway ushered in the era when steam power conveyed new settlers to a railhead, from which the journey to the final destination by ox-drawn 'prairie schooners', such as Hansen had used, was comparatively short. In addition, the making of the railroads provided wages for many of the young men, while they got together the minimum of settler's equipment; for young women there was always the chance of domestic service. A succession of drought-free seasons and the introduction of hard spring wheat completed the picture. As early as 1880 the Dakota Territory contained more than 20,000 people of Norwegian stock, who had come direct from the transatlantic steamers or from existing settlements where life had become unadventurous and land expensive. When it was divided into states in 1889, Norwegians of the first or second generation totalled nearly 50,000 in North Dakota and nearly 35,000 in South Dakota.

The census of 1910 reproduced the same pattern of development. The Norwegian stock was most numerous in Minnesota and Wisconsin, regions where it had settled successfully at an early date. North Dakota ranked third, while Illinois, Iowa, and South Dakota (in that order) each had just about half as many Norwegians of the first or second generation as North Dakota's total of 123,000. They were present in significant numbers in only two other states, one being New York and the other, more surprisingly, the west-coast state of Washington.

In the Far West the 'land-taking' had more complex causes than elsewhere. In 1849 Norwegians were among the gold-seekers in California; some made their way across the continent, but the great majority voyaged round Cape Horn either direct from Europe or from New York, including a good many sailors who jumped ship on arrival. A smaller group figured among the Scandinavian settlers in Utah; a few of these were early converts who joined in the great Mormon trek from Iowa, the rest were brought to America by the Mormon mission which was set up in Norway in the 1850s. The mining of lead, copper, and precious metals also attracted immigrants, especially such as had been mine-workers in Norway, to several of the Rocky Mountain states. But Washington—and, to a less extent, the other States of the Pacific coast—made a special appeal. On the one hand, the land-taking there represented the final stage in the progression westwards. It was facilitated by the new railways and was in any case attractive to a considerable element in the older Norwegian settlements, which was dissatisfied by the low wheat prices of the 1890s and yet by selling up could realize enough capital for a hopeful start elsewhere. On the other hand, there were many coastal districts like Puget Sound—of which they wrote de-

lightedly, 'This is just like Old Norway'[19]—where the monotonous single-crop tillage of the prairies could be replaced by some
combination of small-scale farming with work in the fisheries or
lumber camps.

The pioneers found their last outpost in United States territory
in Alaska, where the gold finds of 1896, followed by the development of the fisheries, and even the introduction of reindeer from
Siberia, provided new chances for a people whose homeland had
familiarized them with arctic conditions. However, neither the
motives which brought fresh immigrants from Norway nor those
which impelled settler families to move westward on to new land
took much account of political frontiers. Even a summary outline
must therefore mention the land-taking in western Canada.

Although the availability of timber cargoes from the St. Lawrence valley had made Quebec in the 1850s and 1860s the main port
of arrival for the cheap emigrant traffic to North America, only one
in a hundred Norwegians chose then to remain in Canada. In 1853
an attempt was made to recruit Norwegians under five-year contracts to serve the Hudson's Bay Company as watermen and hunters, but the men who answered the advertisement were found by
the Administrator to be mutinous and otherwise unsuitable.[20] A
few years later a Norwegian-born lumber agent was helped by the
Canadian minister of agriculture to establish a Norwegian settlement on the Gaspé peninsula at the mouth of the St. Lawrence, but
the climate, the thick forest, and the lack of sea frontage for fishing
disappointed the settlers, who (in the words of the minister) 'be-
took themselves elsewhere . . . breathing curses.'[21] By 1890,
however, Canada offered a very different prospect through the
opening up by the railway of southern Manitoba, which was quickly
followed by that of Saskatchewan and Alberta. In the first three
five-year periods of the new century the percentage of emigrants
from Norway who selected Canada as their destination was 5,
6·81, and 10·81. The total of about 16,000 persons was approximately
matched by the number of Norwegian-Americans who crossed the
frontier in search of new land. In 1894, for example, the first well-
known Norwegian settlement in British Columbia was made by
eight-four Minnesotans, who were suffering from the depression in

grain prices and agreed to move together to the wooded valley of Bella Coola for a new start.[22]

By 1921 Canadians of Norwegian stock numbered nearly 70,000, of whom four-fifths lived on, and presumably by, the land. Thirty years later, they amounted to 0·9 per cent of population and were the largest Scandinavian element in Canada. Their chief distinctive institution was the Lutheran church, through which they were affiliated with the much larger Norwegian-American community across the frontier. In 1903–16 this 'new province of emigrant Norway'[23] took shape in 224 congregations in Saskatchewan, 150 in Alberta, 29 in Manitoba, and 20 in British Columbia;[24] but under twentieth-century conditions Norwegian-Canadians as a whole quickly became absorbed in the general life of the Dominion.

THE CONTRIBUTION TO AMERICAN SOCIETY

At the time of the 1910 census the United States was the home of 403,858 persons born in Norway and of 410,951 persons with two Norway-born parents. Since this pure Norwegian stock, whose members were at most only one generation away from the society of which their ancestors had formed part—in most cases from time immemorial—was more than one-third as numerous as the Norwegians remaining in the kingdom on the other side of the ocean, the historian of the emigration is fully entitled to conclude that 'It made Norway bigger.'[25] Yet this Norwegian stock was numerically one of the smaller elements in American society: since the end of the Civil War it had even been replaced by the Swedes as the largest of its Scandinavian components. In claiming nevertheless that, down at least to 1914, the projection of Norway into American life made a significant contribution to society, one may point to three characteristic features of the Norwegian settlers. They had an absorbing interest in land, as we have already seen; they were reported to 'show a greater tendency towards concentration than any other nationality';[26] and these two factors encouraged some persistent efforts to transplant their culture from the Old World to the New.

The Norwegian economic contribution to the making of America was of course most evident in agriculture. Inured to hardship and extremely self-reliant, the Norwegians made excellent pioneers: in the early days it was not unusual for them to break new ground three times over in their working lives, leaving a final result which encouraged the next generation to stay on the land. In 1900 almost exactly one-half of first-generation Norwegians and nearly two-thirds of the second generation were classified by the census as farmers, which suggests that the immigrant wage earner usually had the ownership of land as his ultimate goal. Two decades later, they still made their homes predominantly in the north-western states, the great grain-bearing region where land had twice the average value—and in that region the average farm-holding of a Norwegian was one-third larger than those of his neighbours of other races. The achievement is all the more remarkable in view of the fact that the Norwegian agriculturist had come originally from a country where mixed farming predominated.

Fishermen, ex-sailors, and wood-workers were types of immigrant that often graduated from wage earning to farm owning. But others among them made a distinctive economic contribution through the skills they brought with them. They fished off the Pacific coast and in Alaska; Norwegian skippers, sailors, and shipbuilders figured largely in the traffic on the Great Lakes; and on both coasts the mercantile marine was all the more eager to recruit Norwegians because relatively few native Americans chose to follow the sea. In 1893 the total of Norwegian-born sailors serving on American ships was estimated at 23,000, but an unknown proportion of these were domiciled in Norway: for the whole period 1881–1915 Norwegian records show that 39,200 seamen emigrated officially and a further 32,500 deserted ship—chiefly on the far side of the Atlantic.[27] At all events, from the 1870s onwards the Brooklyn district of New York contained a recognizable element of Norwegian seafarers and their families. As for the wood-workers, they found their place naturally in sawmills and shipyards, in the construction of frame houses, and in many other building crafts required by the rapid growth of American cities. A few, indeed, went further, like the Montana lumber king, A. M. Holter, who by 1900 was registered as a founder of forty-six companies and president of

sixteen: he had entered America nearly fifty years before as a
carpenter.[28]

Chicago, Minneapolis, and New York each in succession became
the home of a bourgeois urban element of Norwegian extraction, to
which professionally qualified immigrants made a notable addition.
In 1870–1915 more than a quarter of the graduates of the Trondheim College went across the Atlantic, and some big reputations
were made—for example, in sunken-tube tunnelling.[29] Norway,
however, produced able supporters of great enterprises rather than
the titanic figures to initiate them—a generalization which may be
applied to politics as well as business.

From the very outset settlers in pioneer communities had to
learn to work the institutions of local self-government: in the words
of an immigrant journalist of wide experience, 'The ballot was as
much of a necessary tool in their life as the ax, the spade, the hoe,
the plow and the harrow.'[30] But it was the Civil War that first
engaged them seriously in politics at the national level. Hating
slavery, they joined the Union armies with alacrity, serving with
particular distinction in the 15th Wisconsin Regiment, which had a
Norwegian colonel, chaplain, and surgeon, and a predominantly
Norwegian rank-and-file membership*.[31] One-third of its strength
of about 9,000 men lost their lives, but the regiment ended its three
years in the field 'marching through Georgia'. Veterans of the Grand
Army of the Republic were prominent among the Norwegians who
began to make their appearance, first in state legislatures and
finally in Congress. Knute Nelson, an illegitimate child whose
mother had brought him from west Norway at the age of six,
became the first Norwegian-born governor in 1892 and represented
Minnesota in the Senate for thirty years. By 1914 the cumulative
total was four governors, four senators, and thirteen Congressmen.

In state politics it would be difficult to pick out any specifically
Norwegian proposals, apart from unsuccessful attempts to introduce
conciliation courts on the Norwegian pattern,[32] first in Wisconsin
and later in North Dakota. Still less are they in evidence on the

* The companies gave themselves such unofficial titles as 'The Wergeland
Guards' and 'The Norway Bear Hunters'; 128 soldiers had the Christian name
'Ole'.

national scene—though Congressman Andrew Volstead, the second-generation Norwegian from Minnesota who carried the Prohibition Enforcement Law of 1919, represented a view that many of his compatriots had campaigned for. What was significant, however, was the adhesion of the mass of Norwegian-American voters to conservative Republicanism. When wheat prices were low, there might be defections to Populism and other radical causes, but in general the politics of the Norwegian were the politics of content-ment. He belonged to the have's rather than the have-not's of American society: 'Americanization comes to him as a matter of course.'[33]

Part of that contentment resulted, indeed, from the fact that so many characteristic features of Norwegian society had accompanied the emigrants to America, where they were left free to maintain, adapt, or abandon them in accordance with what they judged to be their own interest as members of a much larger community. A Norwegian-American historian describes the culture they brought across the Atlantic as 'a realm that took visible form in immigrant institutions but existed largely in the hearts of men—in both cases isolated by a curtain of language'.[34] Settlers who lived in small rural townships, many of them knowing little English, treasured the way of life that they had known in Norway because it was the only way they knew, and sought to pass it on to their children as the *lares et penates* which had accompanied their exodus. At a slightly later stage the church and the language press took over, as institutions ministering to specifically Norwegian needs. Finally, there were visionaries like the novelist O. E. Rölvaag, who cherished Norwegian literature old and new and proclaimed the 'duty to protect and augment all the high and noble cultural values which our race has shared down through the ages'.[35]

The church grew up under difficulties. Haugean lay preachers were among the original 'sloopers', but it was not until 1843 that the first two clergymen were ordained in America by German Lutherans, while those sent out by the church in Norway, of whom the first arrived in the following year, were never very numerous.*

---

* In 1825-60 the church at home provided seventeen out of thirty-eight pastors; in 1915 it was calculated that 454 Norwegian-born clergy had served

In an atmosphere of complete religious freedom discussion of points of doctrine and ecclesiastical order flourished to excess. Some Norwegians found the Baptist, Methodist, or Mormon faith more attractive than that of their forebears, while the great majority, who remained loyal to Lutheranism, split up into half a dozen rival synods which were not substantially reunited until 1917. There were also great geographical difficulties in meeting the spiritual needs of a multitude of scattered agricultural settlements. One cannot but admire the religious zeal of countless pioneers and their devout women folk, who from their very slender resources raised the first churches and found stipends for pastors.

Clergy and laity were not always in agreement. At the time of the Civil War clergymen trained under the influence of the German Missouri Synod caused scandal by denying the absolute sinfulness of slavery. Many clergy also attempted to swim against the tide of Americanization by the generally impracticable proposal that children should be sent exclusively to their own parochial schools at least until the age of confirmation, so that the Word of God might make its full impact upon the young in the language of their ancestors: English, they suggested, could be learnt at the common schools later on. In these instances the laity turned a deaf ear, but they responded with remarkable generosity to the call to provide for higher education, so that each of the rival synods of the church should be able to train its own clergy. Luther College erected its buildings at Decorah, Iowa, during the Civil War; the Augsburg Seminary and St. Olaf College in Minnesota followed soon afterwards. Altogether, the immigrants set up thirty colleges and secondary schools—the two were sometimes combined—by 1890, to which they added thirty-eight more after that date.[36] From the outset, they served the needs of others besides prospective ordinands, and although many of these institutions were small and short lived, they cherished Norwegian cultural values and gave them status in the eyes of the younger generation, while also teaching the subjects and syllabuses required to meet American needs.

The Norwegian-language press achieved something of the same

in America, but only ninety-two of these received their theological training in Norway before emigrating.[37]

working compromise. In 1847 the very first issue of such a news-paper[38] included a translation of parts of the Declaration of Independence; in a later generation the political expositions published by the leading organs, such as *Skandinaven* of Chicago, *Decorah-posten*, and *Minneapolis tidende*, kept many Norwegians within the Republican Party. But they also spread news of Norway, news of the settlements, and church news; reflected the Norwegian way of life in matters great and small; and printed a great deal of pains-taking verse and prose written by Norwegian-Americans in the old language. In the course of three-quarters of a century about 500 more or less ephemeral newspapers and periodicals were founded, reaching across the continent from Brooklyn to the Pacific coast.

Since the Norwegian-Americans constituted a small community within a much larger whole, it was perhaps inevitable that their institutions should decline, even if the tide of emigration had con-tinued to flow freely. In 1890 14 per cent of the Norwegian stock already married outside their own group,[39] a proportion which would obviously increase rapidly with the growth of social oppor-tunity in a prosperous society. The church was in a sense the cita-del of Norwegianism, but in 1905–20 the percentage of sermons preached in English rose from 5 to 34 and the percentage of Sunday School children taught in English from 17 to 75.[40] In 1917 America's entry into the First World War gave the signal for a brief but ugly outbreak of feeling against 'hyphenated Americans' and their lan-guages: the newly formed union of Norwegian Lutheran churches even found it prudent to omit 'Norwegian' from its official title,[41] though the decision was rescinded in quieter times. The 1950 census reported that about 750,000 American citizens still spoke some Norwegian, but by then the Norwegian Lutheran church held 97 per cent of its services in English, and even so a sociologist claimed that its ministrations no longer appealed to more than a minority of persons of Norwegian descent.[42]

What remains? A century after the voyage of the sloop *Restaura-tionen* the founders of the Norwegian-American Historical Associa-tion claimed for their forebears that, 'Conscious of their backgrounds and origins, they desired to give to the new nation the best ele-ments in their nature and their cultural experience.'[43] Something of

Norway has become embedded in American society, ranging from its literature and language, which occupy a less inadequate position in the universities of America than anywhere else outside Scandinavia, to the sport of skiing, which had its folk hero in 'Snowshoe Thompson', who more than a century ago skied with the mail across the winter-bound Sierra Nevada. Some striking personalities owed the effectiveness of their impact upon American life, in part at least, to a Norwegian background. H. H. Boyesen made his name with novels and short stories which often had the Norway of his boyhood as their setting. Thorstein Veblen, whose *Theory of the Leisure Class* created a ferment in many minds, though American born, could not escape the influence of his parentage: he was the sixth of the twelve children of Norwegian immigrants who had arrived in Wisconsin in 1847 with 3 dollars in their possession. Andrew Furuseth, who won the American seamen their Magna Carta in 1915, had first experienced the hardships of the sea at the age of sixteen in the vessels of his native Norway. Rölvaag, a professor at St. Olaf College, achieved the astonishing feat of producing great literary work in his native Norwegian, which lost almost nothing of its quality when translated into English under his own supervision. His *Giants in the Earth*, published in the 1920s, is still accepted as one of the two or three classic accounts of the nineteenth-century pioneers from many nations who lived and died to tame the American prairies. Rölvaag's genius makes the Dakota of the 1870s live again, and in so doing he illuminates what was after all the main contribution of the nameless multitude.

As late as 1914 an outside observer recorded admiringly 'the continual repetition of the experiences of the early Norwegian immigrants. . . . At the present time, in remoter parts . . . the same story is being retold in the same terms of patience, hardship, thrift, and final success.'[44]

OTHER EMIGRATION MOVEMENTS

Although North America proved supremely attractive to the Norwegian emigrant, a people whose ships frequented every coast was bound to play some part as lands in other quarters of the world were opened up to European settlers. In the 1850s a few Norwegians went to the gold diggings in Australia, and in the 1870s a larger number took advantage of the virtually free passages advertised through agents in Norway to 'country people, ordinary workers, and servant girls', who were wanted in Queensland and also in New Zealand. Sailors who went ashore found ready employment, too, in the coastal trade of the Australian colonies. Yet at the end of the century about half of the Norwegians dying in Australia had to be buried at the public expense, and in 1911 the Norwegian-born population of Australia totalled only 3,450 and that of New Zealand about 1,350.[45] The proportion of women was very small, confirming the general impression of a community that never took root. The fact that the journey was so much longer and—for those who travelled independently of government schemes—so much more expensive than the well-trodden path to North America is no doubt the main explanation. The newcomers were also irked by a rather aggressive Britishness and handicapped in some cases by the exclusiveness of the Australian trade unions.

In 1880 a bold attempt was made to establish a party of Norwegians in Hawaii, on the basis of free passages arranged by a Norwegian plantation owner in return for work under contract for three years on the sugar plantations. Nearly 600 persons, including families with children, were readily recruited in eastern Norway, but once arrived in the South Sea paradise they sent home bitter complaints regarding the climate, food, accommodation, and above all the wages, which were about one-third of those paid for non-contract labour. The Left made a political issue of the matter, so the Norwegian government had to send out an official, who ascertained that illegalities were mostly on the part of his fellow countrymen, many of whom had absconded in defiance of their obligations. The upshot was that the great majority removed themselves by degrees to America, though as late as 1945 the islands contained a small but flourishing Norwegian community, of which the contract labourers had supplied the nucleus.[46] The episode illustrates the dislike of the individualist Norwegian for organized colonial ventures: this had been shown previously over Gaspé, and even earlier, when a clergyman[47] visited Brazil, wrote a book, and planned a colony there—

but attracted no support. It also illustrates the magnetic appeal of
America, though this did not apply to the American empire: in
1907 a scheme for a Norwegian settlement on Cuba had to be abandoned, although the island was still under United States administration.

Mention must, however, be made of a partly planned emigration
to South Africa. This was carried out by two shiploads of pioneers
from the west of Norway, who financed their own ventures after a
ship's captain had opened up a trade with Madagascar and learnt
that a settlement might be feasible a little farther north, on the
Aldabra Islands. The first shipload became discouraged about prospects in the islands, so they sailed on to Durban instead. In 1880
they formed a Lutheran church there, and two years later a second
ship brought a party of 233 to a river mouth a little farther south, in
the vicinity of the future Port Shepstone, where the authorities
offered land and hard work brought some success.[48] Thus two
groups became established in Natal under the British flag. In the
following decade gold attracted a rather different type of Norwegian to join the Uitlanders under the Boer flag on the Rand: some
of them later helped to form the Scandinavian free corps, which received the special thanks of General Cronje for its contribution to
his victory over British arms at Magersfontein. Nevertheless, when
the Union of South Africa was set up in 1910, its Norwegian-born
population in all its four huge provinces was 1,600—only a few
hundred more than in New Zealand.[49]

LUTHERAN MISSIONS IN AFRICA AND ASIA

It was no mere chance that the first settlers came to South Africa
via Madagascar and came there from the Norwegian west coast: for
the interest in the Dark Continent had originated, so far as Norway
was concerned, in a missionary enterprise which had its headquarters and chief support in the west. Unlike the missionary ventures of
some larger powers, those of the Norwegians led neither to territorial annexations nor to economic exploitation of the areas concerned. But culture in the deepest sense was transplanted by the
evangelical fervour that caused Norway to send so high a proportion

of its sons and daughters into the mission field. In total numbers, of course, the British, German, and American Protestants, with whom they often co-operated closely, built up more important missionary churches. But in three regions at least, the Norwegians have had an enduring influence, and their smaller undertakings included several vigorous societies in China and more sporadic work elsewhere.

Although Norwegian Lutheran missions claim Hans Egede as their founder, his work in Greenland in 1721–36 was an official enterprise of the Danish-Norwegian monarchy. No popular basis for such missions existed before 1826, when an English Congregationalist evangelist on a visit to Stavanger united the Haugeans and other pietists in a society, which sent a single young Norwegian for training at a mission school in Germany. After ten years there were four of these little societies, but then a certain John Haugvaldstad, Haugean lay preacher and leading Stavanger industrialist, resolved to form a nationwide network of local branches on the German model. In 1842 sixty-five of these met at Stavanger to form the Norwegian Missionary Society, which is still the principal driving force in missionary work. In 1843 a High Church group in eastern Norway attached one ordained clergyman, H. P. S. Schreuder, in rather loose association to the Society, which in the same year opened its own school for training missionaries; this was likewise located in Stavanger, and two decades elapsed before the stricter ecclesiastics entrenched in Oslo University accepted its trainees for ordination.

Thus the starting-point was a movement among the laity, which was powerfully reinforced a few years later by the influence of a Swedish lay revivalist, C. O. Rosenius. A second feature was the part played by women: although they were given no vote in the direction of mission affairs until 1904, from the earliest years their parochial organizations did much to keep interest alive. A third feature, which was in some respects a source of weakness, was the multiplication of independent missionary efforts within the same small country. By 1900 at least seven missionary societies had been sponsored by the state church and several others by Protestant sects. But it is at least possible that, as in the English rivalry between church and chapel, the existence of several institutions serving similar purposes created competition among their supporters. The divisions were in any case congenial to the Norwegian passion for uncompromising independence, and they bred leaders of a strongly individualist stamp.[50]

Although the first suggestion for Norwegian work among the Zulus came from the Scottish Congregationalist missionary pioneer, Robert Moffat, it was the High Churchman, Schreuder, who heard the call. Political and other hindrances kept him waiting eight years for admission to the then independent kingdom of Zululand, and sixteen years for his first native convert. But the mission school at Stavanger sent its first three students to reinforce his efforts; he compiled the earliest Zulu grammar and translation of the gospels; and when the work began to spread, he was consecrated in 1866 as bishop over 'the mission field of the Church of Norway'. His elevation was, however, unacceptable to the Haugeans and other Low Churchmen: the result was one of the many splits referred to already and Schreuder's return home. But the seed had been sown. When the 'Apostle of the Zulus'[51] died in 1882, only about 350 converts had been made and the mission continuing under his name was very small: half a century later it was taken over as a going concern by the Norwegian-Americans, and Zulu Lutherans eventually numbered about 300,000.

Schreuder's diocese had included Madagascar, to which he sent across two missionaries in 1867. But the dominant Norwegian figure there was Lars Dahle, the son of a farmer who had been a personal friend of Hauge. He received his first training at Stavanger, but had also studied at the university of Oslo and abroad before he landed on the island in 1870. During the next eighteen years he gave the mission a thorough organization, set up schools for 10,000 pupils, collaborated with an English missionary, W. E. Cousins, in an exemplary translation of the Bible from the original languages into fluent Malagasi,[52] and showed his wide sympathies in his classic *Specimens of Malagasy Folk-lore* (1877). Dahle devoted all the later part of a long life to work at home as general secretary of the Missionary Society; but after the establishment of the French protectorate in Madagascar the Norwegian Lutherans were an important counterweight to the Jesuit influence, and at the turn of the century a native revivalist movement had its starting-point in their midst.

When Dahle revisited the island in 1903, he farsightedly encouraged the growth of self-help and independence in the native church. Wherever the paramount power was Christian, missionaries were placed under an insidious temptation to claim secular support: it was Dahle who exhorted the World Missionary Conference at Edinburgh in 1910, 'Let the Bible be our consul'.[53]

He had concentrated Norwegian attention upon these two geographically related fields, but in 1889 a visit from the English pioneer, Hudson Taylor,* aroused interest in the China Inland Mission, which Ludvig Hope spread far and wide, so that within a few years Norway was supporting the interdenominational work as well as several Lutheran ventures in China. And there remains the remarkable story of the mission to an aboriginal tribe in the northeast of British India, where Norwegian participation resulted from one man's initiative—and he had been formally rejected as unsuitable for missionary work. This was Lars Skrefsrud, a poor cottar's son, whose conversion to a faith like Hauge's while serving a four-year sentence for theft was deemed by the church authorities to be insufficient atonement for the past. Undeterred, in 1867 he began work among the neglected Santals in association with an English Baptist missionary, became himself for a short time a Baptist, and when his work prospered was accorded the Norwegian ordination which had been denied him in his youth. Although a Danish colleague at his side gave a Scandinavian character to the enterprise, he remained its somewhat autocratic head until his death in 1910, and its civilizing activities in what is now Bangladesh are supported mainly by Norwegians.

Skrefsrud was a man of wide abilities. His literary achievements included a version of the Gospels, original hymns, and a standard work on native traditions, all in the Santal language. His gifts as a preacher are evidenced, not only by the 16,000 converts he made in India, but also by his successful appeals on missionary tours in Britain and America as well as nearer home: in Sweden the future archbishop Nathan Söderblom was one of the students upon whom he left a deep impression. His determined efforts to secure justice

* His book on *China's Spiritual Needs and Claims* had been translated into Norwegian two years before.

for a depressed social group—in their relation to the Hindu land-owners the position of the Santals was in some ways comparable to that of the *husmann* class into which Skrefsrud himself was born—won him the Kaisar-i-Hind medal in gold from the viceroy. He introduced irrigation schemes, co-operatives, and a credit bank, and he organized the migration of a part of the Santal people to Assam. In 1889 they started their own tea plantation there, which by 1945 had become the largest single support of the mission's finances.[54]

The driving impulse in all these missions was evangelical, but their social impact has also been of incalculable significance. Day schools have already been mentioned in connection with Mada-gascar—where the native authorities were willing to make attend-ance compulsory, if the Christian missions could provide a place for every child. The Norwegians sent their first medical missionary to the island in 1869; hospitals followed; and among both the Malagasi and the Santals a special work was done for lepers. In Skrefsrud we see an anticipation of several present-day methods of helping the under-developed countries. Finally, against the sombre background of recent South African history it is interesting to observe that the Norwegians, having no imperialist and few racial prejudices, were reorganizing their Zulu mission field as early as 1903 with a view to self-government based on self-sufficiency.

INTEREST IN POLAR EXPLORATION

Strictly speaking, the Arctic regions are those lands and seas where the temperature in the warmest month is below 48°F. and the annual mean lies under freezing point: no part of Norway is in this sense 'arctic'. But so much of North Norway lies within the Polar Circle that throughout history a section of the population has lived and worked on the very threshold of those strictly Arctic regions; and since southern Norway too has its areas of severe winter con-ditions, the nation as a whole has always had some special interest in the hazards of exploration under conditions of perpetual ice and snow. Greenland, it will be remembered, was the site of a medieval Norse colony, and as late as 1619 a Dano–Norwegian expedition sailed from Norway to take part in the search for the North-West

Passage. Accordingly, when the return of peace to Europe after the Napoleonic Wars enabled the British and Russians to resume the work of northern exploration by sea and land, representatives of the new Norway were eager to join in, so far as very meagre financial resources might permit.

In 1827 Norway's pioneer geologist, B. M. Keilhau, went to Spitsbergen and Bear Island to study the mountain formations, and in the following year one of his colleagues at the newly established Oslo university, Christopher Hansteen, who had been a disciple of the Danish physicist, Örsted, began an extensive journey through northern Siberia as part of his studies of the magnetic pole. His theory of terrestrial magnetism was subsequently discarded, but the account of his travels, published in German and French, aroused considerable interest. In 1876–8, when public funds had become available on a rather ampler scale, two other notable scientists, the zoologist G. O. Sars and an early authority on meteorology, Henrik Mohn,[*] collected seven volumes of information from the Norwegian Sea, which they examined over a large area south of Spitsbergen and the coast of Greenland. This had a sequel in August 1882, when Norway was one of ten states which set up a station for synchronous observations during the first International Polar Year. But the Norwegians were most actively concerned with the trade prospects of the far north. Such were the prime interest, for example, of E. Carlsen, who circumnavigated Spitsbergen in 1863; of N. F. Rönnbeck, who two years later made the first definite sighting of Franz Josef Land; of E. H. Johannessen, who sailed round Novaya Zemlya (1870); and of Sivert Kristian Tobiesen, who successfully ventured on a northerly route from Novaya Zemlya to Spitsbergen but perished on one of the smaller Russian islands in 1873, when his ship was frozen into the ice. All of these were skippers of arctic hunting vessels, penetrating into unknown regions to exploit fresh stocks of seal, walrus, and bear.

In the case of the far-off Antarctic an economic motive was still more obviously needed before Norway could be involved. The testing of the long-lived hypothesis that a great Southern Continent

[*] 1835–1916. Joint author with C. M. Guldberg of the pioneer theoretical work, *Études sur les mouvements de l'atmosphère* (1876–80).

awaited discovery, and even the first more realistic efforts to explore what lay in fact within the circuit of the pack-ice, were left to the government-sponsored expeditions of wealthier powers. But when the sixth International Geographical Congress in 1895 formally directed attention to Antarctica as the last great field still awaiting exploration, Norwegian trade interests were already active there. The first expedition from Norway had been sent out in search of right or whalebone whales in 1892–3—the same season as the British went out for the same purpose from Dundee—and the Norwegians tried twice more in successive years before it was agreed that this was no hunting ground for right whales. In this way it came about that C. A. Larsen was the finder on Seymour Island of the fossilized evidence that Antarctica had once had a temperate climate, and another Norwegian, H. J. Bull, with financial support from Svend Foyn, made the earliest landing on the mainland at Cape Adare (24 January 1895).[55] Larsen, who is now remembered chiefly for his later contributions to the hunting of the great rorquals of the far south, also discovered—but did not claim for Norway—several of the present British possessions: his were the first Antarctic discoveries since James Clark Ross's voyage half a century before and the most important down to Scott's first expedition in 1901–4.

Norwegians in many cases played a distinguished part in expeditions under foreign flags. Thus the Carlsen who sailed round Spitsbergen also acted as pilot for the Austro-Hungarian expedition which gave Franz Josef Land its name, as did another skipper for the Duke of Abruzzi, when the Italians attempted a sledge journey towards the North Pole from the same area. A Belgian expedition, which in 1898–9 was the first to winter in the pack-ice of Antarctic waters, employed a Norwegian vessel and a first mate named Roald Amundsen, who proved an apt apprentice to polar exploration. A few years later a Swedish expedition under N. O. G. Nordenskjöld (a nephew of the Baron, see p. 231), whose ship was crushed by ice in the same waters, escaped worse disaster through the resourcefulness of its captain, the highly experienced C. A. Larsen. A still more remarkable example is that of C. E. Borchgrevink, a Norwegian residing in Australia who had taken part in the first landing at Cape Adare. Although he was a scientist as well as a veteran and enthusiastic explorer, he found that his only means of sailing south again was to depend upon the generosity of the London newspaper magnate, George Newnes. His ship, his crew, and all but a couple of his team of explorers were Norwegian, but it was under the British flag that the *Southern Cross* expedition wintered and conducted its scientific observations on the Antarctic mainland; reached the Great Ice Barrier; and travelled across it with skis and sledges to the farthest south yet reached by man (February 1900).

Many Norwegians made contributions to polar discovery which for various reasons gained little prestige for their country. Against this background it appears all the more impressive that, in a period of less than two decades (June 1893–December 1911), Norway was able to launch the series of famous expeditions which put her sons indisputably in the fore of an international contest comparable *mutatis mutandis* with our own generation's ventures into space. The Norwegians as a people have long admired and cultivated a rugged individual resourcefulness and power of endurance: this was the epic quality of the Vikings. By a fortunate chance their country produced three outstanding specimens of this type at the very time when their efforts could be borne along on a wave of nationalist enthusiasm.

MAJOR ACHIEVEMENTS IN THE FAR NORTH AND THE FAR SOUTH

Fridtjof Nansen,* the undisputed national hero of modern Norway, was a born leader of men; a sportsman, athlete, and artist; and a dedicated scientist. At twenty-one he visited Arctic waters for the sake of his zoological studies, but the starting-point of his ambitions as a polar explorer was the attempt of the Swedish Baron Nordenskjöld to cross the Greenland ice-cap at the narrow, southern end. Nordenskjöld, who had won great fame by his navigation of the

---

* 1861–1930. His doctoral dissertation concerned the nerve structure in lower forms of animal life, but his main scientific interest came to be the development of oceanography. Nansen's physical prowess was combined with considerable artistic gifts, shown both in the illustrations to his books and in some of his non-technical writings. His services to Norway in 1905, as minister in London (1906–8), and as negotiator in the U.S.A. (1917–18), prepared the way for his services to mankind in the aftermath of the First World War.

North-East Passage, gave influential support to Nansen's plan for the crossing, but the patriotic desire to vie with the Swedes was always one of Nansen's motives. At twenty-eight he put his plan into operation, though it took his party twenty-four days to make their way in two small boats through the drift-ice to his intended starting-point high up on the desolate east coast—from which there was no chance of rescue in the event of failure. The six skiers, four Norwegians and two Lapps, then hauled their sledges to a height of nearly 9,000 feet, travelled 400 miles across the unknown plateau in temperatures as low as —49°F,[56] and made their way back to civilization along the west coast in a boat which they improvised from their sledge equipment. Nansen's *First Crossing of Greenland* interested the general public far beyond the confines of Scandinavia, and the scientific results were recorded in a special number of *Petermanns geographische Mitteilungen*.

In his scientific work Nansen favoured the bold hypothesis—his doctoral dissertation, for example, took many years to win full acceptance among his fellow zoologists—and the success of his first venture meant that he could now hope to obtain support for a bigger one. A hypothesis lay ready to hand. Wreckage from an American expedition having been carried from the New Siberian Islands to south-west Greenland on an ice-floe,★ the Norwegian meteorologist Henrik Mohn had deduced that no land-mass existed to bar the way to a drift of ice-covered water right across the polar basin, flowing out eventually down the east coast of Greenland. The Storting agreed to bear about half the cost, and King Oscar a considerable share of the remainder, for the building of a special ship, which might enable Nansen to crown the work done during a century of scientific exploration in the north.

With thirteen men on board, the *Fram* left Norway at mid-summer 1893, and before the end of September lay fast in the ice to the north of the New Siberian Islands. The special construction of the 307-ton vessel enabled the rudder to be hauled up and the engine dismantled; the pressure of the ice lifted but could not break the hull, which was shaped and reinforced for the purpose; and the

★ In 1881 the *Jeannette* sank in 77° 15′ N., 155° E.; in 1884 materials from the wreck were found near Julianehaab (60° 45′ N., 46° W.).

crew settled down to an indefinite period of complete isolation from the rest of humanity. Scientific observation of the polar ocean in all its aspects proceeded according to plan, but after one and a half years Nansen concluded that the direction of the current would eventually bring them out into open water without coming as near to the Pole itself as he had hoped. He then set out for the second time on a journey where he could not retrace his steps, skiing northwards with dog sledges which carried two kayaks and provisions for 100 days. His sole companion was a young army lieutenant, F. H. Johansen, who had joined the *Fram* as a stoker.

They came much closer to the Pole than any men before them, but after twenty-three days they were defeated by a 'veritable chaos of ice-blocks, stretching as far as the horizon'.[57] Killing the sledge dogs one by one as they became exhausted, they hauled and paddled what was left of their belongings across the wilderness of ice and icy water to Franz Josef Land. There they built a hut of ice-blocks, survived the winter on what they were able to shoot, and in May 1895 made a chance contact with members of an English expedition. This brought them back to North Norway one week before the arrival of the long-lost *Fram*, which had emerged unscathed from the drifting ice north-west of Spitsbergen—the result on which Nansen had pinned his faith and reputation.

His memorable venture was a triumph of meticulous organization, with which no earlier polar expedition bore comparison, and was the source of great advances both in oceanography and in polar studies. *The Voyage of the Fram* was published in many languages and widely read, while the scientific results filled the six volumes of *The Norwegian North Polar Expedition 1893–96*. By the time the last volume appeared in 1906, Nansen's scientific work had to compete for his attention with politics. But the impulse had been given to three other spectacular Norwegian achievements.

Otto Sverdrup was a ship's mate with experience of the Arctic and many other waters, who had skied with Nansen across Greenland and become his second-in-command on the *Fram*. The enthusiasm aroused by the success of the voyage induced some Norwegian businessmen to offer further support for a new expedition with scientific objectives, of which he was to take charge, and the state defrayed the cost of improvements to the *Fram* for this purpose, increasing its displacement by 100 tons. Sverdrup had no scientific qualifications, but his fifteen companions included various specialists; in any case, no Norwegian would take it amiss if he should act on his observation: 'On the map there was a good deal of white there in the north, which I should quite like to put Norwegian colour on.'[58] Sverdrup set out in 1898, provisioned for five years, in the hope of circumnavigating Greenland. Unusually bad weather conditions stopped him from penetrating through Smith Sound; they also stopped Peary, whom the Norwegians encountered, and there is some reason to think that a scrupulous reluctance to appear to be rivalling the American's thrust towards the Pole contributed to Sverdrup's decision not to persevere northwards. Instead, he spent four years in the vicinity chiefly of Ellesmere Land, finding many new islands and exploring large areas by sledge. The results were published in thirty-nine dissertations belonging to seven sciences; in cartography the gains of 58,000 sq. m. were the most extensive made by any polar expedition. Sverdrup intended to annex his discoveries to the Norwegian crown, but the authorities were negligent and when the sector principle was introduced after the First World War the Sverdrup Islands became Canadian territory. In the last year of his life their discoverer was awarded 67,000 dollars as a kind of compensation.

Roald Amundsen's choice of career* is said to have been determined by Nansen's crossing of Greenland, but even earlier the story of Franklin had fired him with enthusiasm for the three-centuries-old contest to make the North-West Passage. His experience with the Belgian Antarctic expedition of 1898–9 added a further ambition —to follow up the determination of the southern magnetic pole by a similar effort in the north; he therefore studied terrestrial magnetism in Germany. Having secured a modest amount of public and private support in his native Norway, he set off with a crew of seven in the 47-ton seal-hunter *Gjöa*, which was equipped with a small petrol engine, to try to penetrate the channels of the Passage

---

* 1872–1928. In addition to his conquest of the North-West Passage and the South Pole, his was the third expedition to navigate the North-East Passage (1920) and in 1926 he made the first flight over the North Pole.

where larger vessels had always failed to slip through. He spent nearly two years in a sheltered bay on the south side of King William Island, close to the scene of the disaster to Franklin, from where he made accurate observations in the vicinity of the magnetic pole, and explored much new territory by sledge. Then in August 1905 he seized his chance to move on west, and in eight days squeezed his way through the straits into open water, in that arm of the Beaufort Sea which now bears his name. The expedition was held up for a third winter near the mouth of the Mackenzie river, but next summer Amundsen took his ship safely into the Pacific, succeeding where so many renowned sailors had failed.

Besides some valuable scientific results, Amundsen brought back a special expertise in sledging and the handling of huskies, acquired by his study of the Eskimoes. Returning to a newly independent sovereign state, what was more natural than that he should hope to achieve a further national triumph? In 1907 an address by Nansen to the Royal Geographical Society in London led Amundsen to plan an improved version of *Fram*'s drift, which was backed by Nansen and the Norwegian government. But while money was being collected, the news of Peary's arrival at the North Pole damped the public enthusiasm, so that it was only through mortgaging his own resources that Amundsen was able to take the *Fram* to sea. Secretly, however, he had decided 'to get to the North Pole via the South Pole',[59] and from Madeira he announced his change of plan to the members of the expedition (all of whom agreed to continue), his home public—and Captain Robert Scott.

Until Amundsen's cable reached Scott at Melbourne on his way south, the British naval officer had every reason to assume that the field was clear for the expedition, well equipped for scientific work, in which he hoped to complete the conquest of the Antarctic which he had begun in 1901–4. As it was, two rival expeditions camped for the winter near the edge of the Ice Shelf, the Norwegians facing a 60-mile shorter route to the Pole but one which would involve a rougher ascent to the plateau along the line taken by their compatriot, Borchgrevink, a dozen years before. In the sequel, the tragic deaths of Scott and his four companions struck the imagination of the pre-1914 world so forcibly that Amundsen's success suffered much disparagement. It was true that he had dispensed with any scientific activities in his single-minded determination to be first at the Pole, and that—like Nansen, but unlike Scott—he had no scruples over working his huskies to death and using their carcases to replenish the larder. The Norwegians actually rode part of the way on their sledges, whereas Scott claimed that the labour of sledge-pulling was a 'fine conception' and allowed his party to trudge along with only four pairs of skis among five men. Nevertheless, when Amundsen and his three companions reached the Pole on 14 December 1911, more than a month ahead of Scott, and returned to base after ninety-nine days absence with adequate food and eleven dogs in hand, they executed what in all fairness must be acknowledged as 'the most successful polar journey on record'.[60] The Norwegian flag which he left flying at the heart of the great *Terra Incognita* marked a very great achievement by representatives of a very small people.

8. Norwegian Influences Abroad—The Arts

IN NORWAY, AS IN MANY OTHER RESURGENT NATIONS, the growth of the arts contributed greatly to the development of an independent identity and full self-confidence. When the nineteenth century began, the Norwegians had few distinctive cultural achievements on which to feed their national pride except their Norse saga literature and the treasures of folk art, such as the hand-carved and rose-painted furnishings of the larger farms. Since the middle ages their nation had produced only one major figure in the history of the arts, namely Ludvig Holberg of Bergen, whose soubriquet of 'The Danish Molière' is a reminder that all his work as playwright, historian and man of letters was accomplished in Copenhagen without his ever revisiting his native shores. An isolated narrative poem of considerable charm, Petter Dass's 'Trumpet of Nordland', was not printed until 1739, more than thirty years after its author's death. The renaissance of the arts which began in the 1830s and reached its climax in the last quarter of the century, the heyday of four major writers (Ibsen, Björnson, Jonas Lie, and Kielland) and of Edvard Grieg's music, seemed all the more remarkable against such a background; the cultural development therefore looms large in the general history of nineteenth-century Norway.

The evaluation of works of art is, however, primarily a task for experts, not least in the case of a small country on the periphery of a great cultural region, which must always derive much of its artistic inspiration and techniques from outside: every one of the classic writers referred to above spent many of his most fruitful years in France, Italy, or Germany. This chapter will attempt only the less ambitious task of estimating the Norwegian influence abroad. As regards literature, Björnson described it for the American public in 1896 in terms of a fleet which had sailed the Atlantic:

It came from one of the smallest nations of the world, but one from whose people sprung Europe's oldest aristocracies and whose marvellously beautiful country has become a permanent world's exhibition for travelers. It was the Norwegian fleet, and it came with a rush. Something firm and compact about every vessel, as if each had an

errand of its own. Not a single pleasure craft in the whole fleet. . . .
Each ship looked a realm in itself.[1]

Björnson expressed himself with his customary grandiloquence, but
if we include the treasures of music and painting as well, it was
indeed a fleet of argosies, which made port in countries near and far.
The result was that Norway became generally known to the educated public through media which gave a greater insight than tourism. In addition, three or four leading figures—Ibsen and the painter
Edvard Munch certainly, Grieg probably, and possibly Björnson
himself—did more than create new interest in a nation which was
politically and numerically almost insignificant: their individual
contributions to the common stock of European culture rendered
Norway *pro tanto* a great power, an object of respect as well as interest.

THE FORERUNNERS

The literary revival of the 1830s and 1840s, in which Wergeland and
Welhaven figured as protagonists and rivals (see p. 74), had a very
slight impact on the world outside Scandinavia: the use of a minor
language, which impedes the diffusion of all Norwegian literature,
deprived their lyrics—to say nothing of Wergeland's Miltonic epic
—of any chance of full appreciation except by an occasional scholar.
The revived interest in the national history, on the other hand, contributed notably to Europe's knowledge of its past, above all through
painstaking research in Norwegian documents which had long been
buried in foreign archives. But the work of Keyser and P. A. Munch,
including the latter's contributions to the proceedings of learned
societies in many lands, reached the general public mainly through
the writings of other historians, who allowed it to associate the
activities of the Norse Vikings and even the medieval kingdom of
Norway with a vaguely conceived, largely undifferentiated 'Scandinavia'. Only two minor works of Keyser were published in English,
one of them posthumously; from Munch's *chef-d'œuvre*, the 8-volume
History of the Norwegian People, which he carried to 1397, less than one
volume was translated into German and no more than two chapters
into English.[2]

Norway made its impact more easily in an art which did not depend on words: hence the importance of the appointment of J. C. Dahl* in 1824 as a professor at the well-known Dresden Academy of painting. In 1820–1 he had studied in Italy at the expense of Norway's ex-king, Christian Frederick, but his interests were romantic, not classical, and while strongly influenced by his German colleague, Caspar Friedrich, Dahl found in the scenery of his native land subjects ideally suited to this style of painting (Plate 1). Between 1826 and 1850 he revisited it five times to make preliminary studies for his dramatic canvases with their acute observation of Nature, which made the grandeur of the Norwegian scene widely known for the first time in Germany. His most accomplished Norwegian pupil, Thomas Fearnley, who was likewise a painter of Norway's wildernesses and majestic waterfalls, was English by descent and carried Norwegian art to some extent to London, where he painted his most famous pictures, *Labrofossen, Kongsberg* (Plate 2).

The career of Adolph Tidemand, the best-known painter of the next generation, bears a significant resemblance to that of Dahl. He too went to Germany in his youth, attracted by the school of historical painters at Düsseldorf, where he became a professor and (with two short intervals) spent the rest of his life, returning to Norway only to make studies for the romantic scenes of peasant life in which he specialized (Plates 3 and 4). Works such as 'The Haugeans' won a European renown, partly because of a genuinely felt pathos and partly because of the interest of the interiors—the primitive farm living-room, lit only by the smokehole in the roof, or the massive timbers of a stave church. Sales in Germany, Britain, and France as well as Scandinavia were so great that at Tidemand's death 886 items were catalogued, of which nearly one-half were pictures or copies of his own making. H. F. Gude, who followed Tidemand to Düsseldorf and was later a professor at Karlsruhe and Berlin, painted many idyllic Norwegian landscapes of the type of *Bridal Journey in Hardanger* (1847, Plate 5). Tidemand supplied the figures for this once celebrated work, which in all its four versions appears theatrical

---

* 1788–1857. The 'Father of Norwegian Painting' was a native of Bergen, where he worked as an artisan painter of decorations until 1811, when he entered the academy at Copenhagen.

and contrived to modern eyes; yet when Gude in 1852 painted a companion to it, *Funeral Cortège on Sognefiord*, this found a ready market in England. Until about 1870 Norwegian landscape artists continued to flock to Düsseldorf, including at least two pupils of Gude, Lars Hertervig and H. A. Cappelen, whose work conveys more feeling than their master's.

But Norwegian landscape painting, much of it of rather moderate quality, made a less dramatic entry upon the stage of European culture than did the music of Ole Bull,★ of whom Björnson wrote: 'He gave us self-confidence, which was what we needed most'.[3] Born in Bergen and a violinist from the age of five, he did less than justice to his early teachers when he assured the king of Denmark in a striking phrase that it was his native mountains that taught him to play. Bull modelled himself upon Paganini, whom he heard once in Paris, but in Norwegian eyes he was as much of a national symbol as Verdi became for the Italians. His first concert success was at Bologna in 1834; then followed tours in France, Britain (where he performed at 274 concerts in sixteen months), Germany, and Russia, from which he returned to Norway in 1839 a public hero. But Bull's first visit to America in 1843–5 marked another stage in his long career, for in 1853 he became an American citizen, though this did not lessen his devotion to Norwegian national causes, such as the theatre which he founded in Bergen (see p. 243) and Oleana, the settlement he designed for his fellow countrymen in Pennsylvania.

Ole Bull developed a marvellous technique, using a specially tensed bow and a flattened bridge so as to play chords on all four strings. He had a striking appearance and an impressive personality, and when in the mood he could make the violin 'sing' with effects which seemed magical. Many of his own compositions were sketchy; indeed, only two of those which survive, namely the quartet 'In Lonely Hours' and 'A Visit to the Seter' (which includes the famous 'Seter Girl's Song'), are still highly regarded. His greatest achievement, however, was to spread abroad for the first time the treasures of Norwegian folk music.

★ 1810–80. He was fond of describing himself to foreign audiences as a 'Norwegian Norseman from Norway', and many legends surround his rather theatrical presentation of his art.

But already in Ole Bull's day it had been learnt that the mountains of Norway were a storehouse of tales more marvellous than their tunes. In 1833 Andreas Faye, a clergyman and local historian, published summaries of such tales, which had been a subject of occasional public interest since the beginning of the century. Three years later, P. C. Asbjörnsen* and Jörgen Moe,† with whom their rescue from oblivion was already a kind of hobby, had their ideas clarified through reading *Kinder-und Hausmärchen*, the book with which the brothers Grimm had founded the study of folk-lore in Germany. In 1841 they began to produce their own collection of 'Folk Tales', *Norske Folkeeventyr*, from the woodland districts north of Oslo; these were publicized in Germany through an anonymous review by P. A. Munch in a Leipzig newspaper and were declared by the Grimms to be the most colourful so far discovered. Thus encouraged, they completed a much fuller collection in 1851, for which they searched a wide area of southern Norway. Moe's energies then became absorbed in his work as a parish priest and later as bishop, but Asbjörnsen, who was a trained zoologist and became a forestry adviser, added further stories for a third edition in 1871. In 1845–8 he had already published independently two volumes of 'Tales of the Hidden People and Folk Legends' *Norske Huldreeventyr og Folkesagn*, using T. C. Croker's *Irish Fairy Legends* (read in a German translation) as his model. These volumes are still the leading source material for Norwegian folklore, but the primary importance of Asbjörnsen and Moe's work for the Norwegian people was not scientific. They introduced the upper classes and the town population in general to a fascinating achievement of the peasant mind, imaginative and mysterious, yet impregnated with common sense and humour, and above all national. As if this were not enough, the tales had the further attraction of a novel Norwegian style, less

---

* 1812–85. The son of an Oslo glazier, he developed his life interest from his wanderings through the countryside, but he also made original discoveries in marine zoology and wrote a 6-volume *Natural History for the Young*.

† 1813–82. The son of a substantial farmer in the rural district where Asbjörnsen and he met and began their collection of folk tales; he also wrote poetry of some distinction. He was the father of Moltke Moe, who became Norway's first professor of folk language and traditions.

heavy than the conventional Danish and using many turns of expression and vocabulary derived from their sources among the
peasantry.

Since Germany already had its folk tales, the impact on the outside world came chiefly[4] through Britain, where G. W. Dasent, a
talented journalist who was formerly on the staff of the Stockholm
legation, had been inspired by Jacob Grimm with a lifelong interest
in Scandinavian literature and mythology. In 1851 he translated a
single story, 'The Master Thief', for *Blackwood's Magazine*; in 1859
he published in Edinburgh *Popular Tales from the Norse*, which was
reprinted after only three months, with thirteen tales added to
complete the reproduction of the Norwegian original. In 1874 a
selection of Asbjörnsen's legends appeared as *Tales from the Fjeld*, and
a third edition of Dasent's main work in 1888. His introduction,
which occupies one-fifth of the entire book, shows how important
he thought the Norwegian precedent was for the development of
'popular mythology', as he calls it, in England: 'The example of this
very Norway, which was at one time thought, even by her own sons,
to have few tales of her own, and now has been found to have them
so fresh and full, may serve as a warning not to abandon a search
. . . scarcely . . . begun.'[5] But Dasent was also alive to the 'sharp-
cut national forms' of the stories cherished by the Norwegian peasantry, 'an honest manly race . . . of the dales and fells, free and
unsubdued, holding its own in a country where there are neither
lords nor ladies, but simple men and women'.[6] Such words from the
pen of an assistant editor of *The Times* helped to fix a basically favourable image of Norway upon the English Victorian mind. Children,
however, for whom Dasent produced a special selection as early as
1862, have always provided the main public for the *Tales*. In the
1890s a new translation by an enterprising Norwegian journalist in
London, H. L. Brækstad, included illustrations made by Werenskiold
(see p. 261) and other leading Norwegian artists. In the twentieth
century too, new editions and anthologies containing 'fairy tales from
Norway' have continued to feed youthful imaginations in all parts
of the world with the adventures of Askeladden, the antics of the
trolls, and the Nature of a country where the North Wind blows
strong.

IBSEN AND BJÖRNSON: THE CONTRIBUTION TO ROMANTIC
LITERATURE

The two literary giants of nineteenth-century Norway, men who towered above their contemporaries in originality, productivity, and personal force alike, arrived in Oslo in 1850 to cram for matriculation at the same 'student factory'; Björnstjerne Björnson* from his father's parsonage in Romsdal, Henrik Ibsen†—who was nearly five years older—from a dead-end job as an apothecary's assistant in the tiny port of Grimstad, to which he had been driven by his father's failure as a merchant in Skien. Both of them preferred journalism and politics to academic pursuits, but quickly found a congenial field for ambition in the theatre. In spite of Wergeland's efforts, Norway still had virtually no plays of its own and only one playhouse, the *Christiania Theater*, which employed Danish performers and Danish diction in a repertoire taken from the Royal Theatre, Copenhagen. The rising tide of nationalist feeling now demanded Norwegian plays acted in a Norwegian style, for which the labours of P. A. Munch and other scholars provided ample historical materials. Both Ibsen and Björnson wrote plays to meet this demand and made their living partly from stage management and other supervisory activities in the theatre, which helped to form their technique. Thus Ibsen was engaged for five years at the first theatre to be run on national lines, which Ole Bull had founded in Bergen in 1850: and when he moved in September 1857 to a better-paid post at a similar 'national' playhouse in Oslo, where he would be artistic director instead of author-instructor, Björnson was his

* 1832–1910. Much inspired by the beauty of Romsdal, to which his father moved from a less attractive parish when he was four, and throughout life a driving force in Norwegian nationalism; but his European interests played a large part in his correspondence, which totalled *c.* 30,000 private letters. The first Scandinavian author to receive the Nobel Prize for Literature (1903).

† 1828–1906. His first play, *Catiline*, was written under the combined influence of the Latin course for matriculation and the European revolutions of 1848, and he was for a time a follower of Thrane; in later life his political sympathies were largely conservative, in spite of his radical influence on culture. After his long residence in Italy and Germany, 1864–91, he returned to Oslo, where he wrote his last four plays and suffered the stroke which ended his active life in 1901.

successor. By 1863 both these national ventures had gone bankrupt, but by this time the Christiania Theatre was going over to Norwegian actors and actresses and a proportion of Norwegian plays: it therefore offered scope for the two playwrights, and in 1865-7 it had Björnson as director.

Ibsen produced four historical plays of his own writing during his years in Bergen, counting as hort piece, *The Warrior's Barrow*, which had been shown at the Christiania Theatre in the autumn of 1850; Björnson began a little later, with two dramas of intrigue in a historical setting (*Between The Battles*, 1857; *Lame Hulda*, 1858). Both reached their climax of achievement in this field in the early 1860s, when Björnson followed *King Sverre* with his great trilogy on *Sigurd Slembe*, and Ibsen capped his saga drama, *The Vikings at Helgeland* (1857), with *The Pretenders*, where the characters of King Haakon and Earl Skule are explored in depth. But plays built round themes from medieval Norwegian history made little appeal abroad, even in the other Scandinavian countries, where the language was no serious obstacle. *The Pretenders*, for example, which a modern English critic acclaims as 'the last great historical play in the rich Shakespeare-inspired line going back to the days of Goethe's youth',[7] in spite of a highly successful production at the Christiania Theatre, took seven years to reach the Copenhagen stage and about the same period of time to sell out an edition of 1,000 copies. It was played in Berlin in 1876 by Duke Georg of Saxe-Meiningen's famous company and three years later in Stockholm; in Britain its importance was assessed in the *Spectator* in 1872 by Edmund Gosse,[8] but no English translation existed until the 1890s. Björnson's *Sigurd Slembe* was more widely read, to judge from its appearance in a second edition within twelve months; in 1869 it reached one German theatre (the ducal stage at Meiningen), where *Between The Battles* had led the way two years before, and an epitomized translation was published in London in 1873, headed 'Björnson's Masterpiece'.

Björnson, however, had made his name known independently through his stories of contemporary peasant life, which he alternated with his historical dramas as having a cognate theme, since they were to present the Norwegian peasant as a lineal descendent of his medieval heroes. *Synnöve Solbakken*, *Arne*, and *A Happy Boy*, published in 1857–60, portrayed characters and a rural setting which were authentically Norwegian. Too idealized for modern taste, their combination· of deeply felt pathetic incident with the conventional happy ending suited the reading public of the mid-Victorian period perfectly. These stories made Björnson the best-known writer in any of the Scandinavian countries, a position which he consolidated in 1860 by arranging to publish through the Copenhagen firm of Gyldendal, whose resources greatly exceeded those of any Norwegian house; with characteristic generosity, he secured the same advantages for Ibsen and other Norwegian writers. The stories also won him a general international renown: by 1870 one or more of them had been translated into German, French, Spanish, Dutch, Finnish, and Russian, and the English translations were being separately published in the United States. Two more tales closed the series, namely *The Fisher Lass* (1868), which took its heroine to the town and its problems, and *The Bridal Veil* (1872), on a more purely romantic theme supplied by the painter Tidemand.

By 1864 Björnson was a successful man with many irons in the fire, including his activities as a speech-maker and lecturer in the service of radical politics: on his return from two years of foreign travel, the Storting made him the first recipient of a regular literary stipend. Ibsen, whose post in the theatre had collapsed, was discouraged by his failure to achieve any major success, and his public reputation was so small that without Björnson's help he could not have raised the money for the foreign travel to which he too looked for further inspiration. But the two men were still alike in their sincere attachment to Scandinavianism, which suffered at this time its greatest disaster, when Norway to their bitter disappointment failed to support Denmark against the German attack (see p. 90).

Björnson was quick to recover his equanimity. He wrote some bitter verses at the time, but before the year was out, he had reconciled himself to the Danish defeat, and in 1868, when he added another 'Fatherland Song' to the National Anthem he had completed in 1863, he could sing:

> We still shall fare forth,
> For the three-cloven North
> Shall once more unite, shall become its true self.

Ibsen's occasional verse (of which the only collection was published in 1870) showed a more lasting commitment, however, whether in the flaming appeal for 'A Brother In Need' or in the lines on 'The Death of Abraham Lincoln', where he expresses ironic surprise at the consternation felt on that occasion in the Europe which had already witnessed 'the works of the Prussians and what they did at Dybböl'.[9] Moreover, this profound disillusionment over the collective character of his fellow countrymen helped to produce a great change in Ibsen's drama, which became in a sense detached from the Norway he left in early April 1864; he did not return as a visitor for ten years or re-establish his home there for twenty-seven years.

Ibsen became for a time interested in a broader view of history, which showed itself in his last partly historical play, *Emperor and Galilean* (1873), where the clash between Christianity and paganism under Julian the Apostate was handled on the basis of painstaking research by the author and, as he later observed, under the 'transforming power' of German intellectual life:[10] though planned in Rome, the play was written mainly in Dresden. Gyldendal sold 4,000 copies in two months; it was the first of Ibsen's works to be translated into English; and although the ten-act drama was clearly more suitable for reading than for acting, a shortened version eventually reached the stage for the first time in Germany (Leipzig, 1896). If its success may be attributed partly to the interest aroused by the contemporary conflict between the church and the new paganism sponsored by science; Ibsen himself often referred to it as his masterpiece,[11] and it marked his final and momentous abandonment of verse for the natural prose dialogue to which his later plays owe much of their impact. But this is to anticipate, for *Emperor and Galilean* had been preceded by the two epic verse dramas in which the exile from Norway forsook themes from the past to examine Norwegian characters of his own day—himself not least—against a Norwegian background that is all the more effective because seen from a distance.

In *Brand* (1866) the heroically uncompromising clergyman who perishes in an avalanche on the snowy heights is an intensely realized figure whose sublime struggle with fate has raised endless controversy. The satire seems to echo the teachings of the Danish philosopher Kierkegaard, but Ibsen here adopts for the first time his own profoundly disturbing standpoint—that the function of his art is to ask, but not to answer, questions. One result of his effort to teach the Norwegian people 'to think big'[12] was the grant of a literary stipend,* which gave him a new and long coveted sense of social status; but the grandeur of the drama attracted attention far outside Norway. It was reprinted three times in the first year; by 1872 it had been translated into German as well as Swedish, and two more German translations appeared in the same decade. Although *Brand* was not designed as a stage-play, the enterprising Swedish–Jewish director, Ludvig Josephson, who had directed the Christiania Theatre in 1872–7, produced it successfully in Stockholm in 1885. It was printed in its original language in Chicago in 1880, but was not translated in England or America until the close of the century; nor was it played in England until 1912. But the most remarkable evidence of its universal character was supplied by Russia, where it was taken on tour by the Moscow Arts Theatre in 1907 and was found to 'complement our times . . . completely'.[13]

Peer Gynt (1867) likewise had a Norwegian background, though this time the mountains loom up with less severity, and it made a pointed criticism of the national character in the person of its 'hero' —a legendary figure from the writings of Asbjörnsen and Moe, blown up to show the fate of one who 'goes around' every obstacle, prefers dreams to reality, and prides himself on a self-sufficiency which is often ignoble. Much of this very loosely structured work— which according to the author 'came of itself'—is more or less good-natured satire on particular features of Norwegian life, such as the *landsmål* movement and Ole Bull's American Utopia, which had no obvious appeal for the foreigner; it took fourteen, twenty-five, and

---

* The sum was 400 dollars (£80) a year for life. Ibsen later appealed unsuccessfully for an increase, on the ground that delays in making international copyright agreements, by which the government benefitted the general public in Norway, impoverished Björnson and himself; in Germany, for instance, their works had no protection until 1896. Even in the 1890s Ibsen's earnings as the world's most discussed playwright averaged no more than £1,630; on the other hand, pirated translations and performances for which no proper fee was paid had done much to spread his fame abroad.

twenty-nine years to reach the German, English,* and French languages respectively. Yet the drama has many passages of pure poetry, such as the death of Åse or Solveig's Song, which in the long run have made it a means of giving new depth to the foreigner's appreciation of Norway. It is a difficult play to present in the theatre, even with modern technical facilities, which makes it all the more fortunate that the acting version of *Peer Gynt*, when staged for the first time (by Josephson) at the Christiania Theatre in 1876, was accompanied by the music of the last of Norway's great national romanticists, Edvard Grieg.

THE MUSIC OF GRIEG

There is something paradoxical yet very characteristic of nineteenth-century Norway in the fact that its chief contribution to the most international of the arts was so essentially national: for the whole life and art of Edvard Grieg† were linked up with the national romantic movement. He was the great-grandson of a Greig who came to Bergen from Fraserburgh in Scotland: but the interest in music was aroused in early childhood by his mother, a member of the well-known Norwegian family of Hagerup, and at fifteen he was sent to the Leipzig Conservatoire at the instigation of Bergen's most nationally minded citizen, Ole Bull. Its classical training, however, did not suit his talent, and he first found himself during a further course of musical study at Copenhagen, where he met Rikard Nordråk, a fellow musician and a cousin of Björnson.

Nordråk, who died at twenty-four, is remembered by Norwegians

---

* Gosse rendered two specimen passages into English verse for his *Studies in the Literature of Northern Europe* (1879), including the lines about 'the people's right to scream', which he supposed rather prematurely to have had a great effect in 'stopping' the *landsmål* movement.[14]

† 1843–1907. Norwegian accounts of Grieg's life emphasize the generous encouragement he gave to aspiring musicians among his fellow countrymen. Mention may also be made of Frederick Delius, whose career was vitally influenced by Grieg's ability to persuade his father, a hard-headed German woollen merchant in Bradford, that his son's musical talents deserved his full support.[15] Both Delius and the Australian composer, Percy Grainger, were among Grieg's few intimate friends.

for the tune he composed for his cousin's verses, which became their National Anthem. He also had a wider importance through his influence on the diffident, half-invalid dreamer, Edvard Grieg, whom he converted into an artist with a national mission: 'The scales fell from my eyes. He first taught me to understand the Norwegian folk melodies and my own nature.'[16] In 1866–74 Grieg became the central figure in the musical life of Oslo, where his opening concert was the first to consist exclusively of works by Norwegian composers. But in the long run the appeal to national feeling could not provide him with an adequate orchestra or the sustained public interest that was needed. He returned from time to time to his native Bergen, where for two seasons (1880–1) he conducted for Harmonien, the local music society which dates from the mid-eighteenth century; but a modest government stipend and, later, a fixed annual payment from a Leipzig music publisher enabled him to concentrate on composing. From 1877 onwards much of his best work was done at a secluded chalet which he built for the purpose, overlooking the exquisite scenery of the Hardangerfiord.

As a composer Grieg has been called a lesser Chopin. He received notable encouragement from Liszt, whom he visited in Rome, but his success was greatest in the less ambitious forms of his art. His only symphony, completed and heard more than once during his years in Copenhagen, bears his autograph note, 'Not to be performed'.[17] Of his four sonatas—a form into which he did not hesitate to introduce elements from Norwegian folk dances—two had been completed by 1868, together with one string quartet and the famous piano concerto in A minor, opus 16. During the next decade he added the other two sonatas, while during the last twenty years of his life Grieg's contribution to chamber music was a second string quartet which he left unfinished. His work for the stage, indeed, was not limited to the twenty-three items of the music for *Peer Gynt*, albeit this includes much more than the two familiar suites. In 1872 Grieg provided incidental music for Björnson's last historical play, *Sigurd the Crusader*, and in the following year he began to compose the music for an opera of which Olav Trygvesson was to be the central figure; but Björnson, with whom he was collaborating, never carried the text beyond the first three scenes. Although the delays

were partly attributable to Grieg himself, who was for a time absorbed in the work on *Peer Gynt*, his disappointment was no doubt
one reason for his negative response twenty years later, when Ibsen
approached him with the first act of *The Vikings at Helgeland* already
turned into the libretto for an opera.

Nevertheless, Grieg became one of the most influential musicians
of an age in which, as his recent English biographer remarks, the
racial characteristics of such music as his were 'symptomatic of a
tendency—arising probably from complex political, social and
artistic causes—to draw fresh energy from the primitive but richly
varied song and dance of peasant communities'.[18] In 1869 he came to
know F. C. Lindeman's great collection, *Norwegian Mountain Tunes
Old and New*,[19] from which he made a long series of arrangements
and, above all, derived inspiration for a wealth of original compositions 'coloured by characteristic features of folk melody'. The
national aspect of his work is seen likewise in the songs. Including
the German and the Danish, where one of his favourite authors was
Hans Christian Andersen (who provided the words of *Jeg elsker dig*),
Grieg set more than a hundred songs to music. Although Solveig's
Song in *Peer Gynt* is the only case where he used a folk tune as a
direct model, the spirit of the music is unmistakably Norwegian and
reaches its greatest heights in interpreting Norwegian lyrics—
several of Björnson's, ten from Ibsen, more than a dozen from Vinje,
and a final series from another *landsmål* writer, Arne Garborg (see
p. 259). In spite of some barbarous translations, provided by his
German publishers and other well-meaning persons, these songs
served to spread a limited appreciation of the otherwise virtually
unknown lyrical poetry of his native land all across the globe.

Grieg's work was widely advertised by his appearance on concert
platforms as conductor or as solo pianist for his own compositions,
and the songs were rendered by his wife Nina, a cousin on his
mother's side, whom he had met during his studies in Denmark.
Together they became celebrities in the fashionable world of
concert-goers in the leading cities of Europe from Paris to Warsaw,
and Grieg performed in Kiel in the year of his death. Their first
appearances in London were in 1888, when they also visited the
Birmingham Festival; nine years later Grieg was received by Queen

Victoria with the words, 'I am a great admirer of your compositions'.[20] And although his fame was a personal achievement, he
never forgot the obligations of his position as a national leader: in
1898 he organized the first big music festival in Bergen, where he
gave other Norwegian composers a chance to have their work performed in a series of six concerts which attracted attendances of
3,000.

In estimating his own place among musicians for a German inter-
viewer, Grieg declared: 'My aim is what Ibsen expresses in his
drama, namely to build homes for the people, in which they can be
happy and contented'.[21] Ibsen's words in *The Master Builder* meant
more than appeared on the surface, but in applying them to himself
Grieg showed his awareness of the fact that the emotional and intellectual range of his work did not demand audiences with a very
highly developed capacity for musical appreciation. Moreover, in
the pre-broadcasting era a musician's influence was much enhanced
if his compositions were capable of performance by ordinary ama-
teurs, so that they became literally a part of the home. This was
the case with many of Grieg's works for the piano, such as the sixty-
six 'lyrical pieces', and with some of his loveliest songs. Two generations after his death in 1907 Grieg, like Ibsen but for very different
reasons, still had a following throughout the civilized world.

IBSEN AND BJÖRNSON: THE FOUNDATION OF MODERN DRAMA

Modern drama—the realist play, with its dialogue in contemporary
prose style and its authentically contemporary setting; the play of
social problems and discussion of revolutionary ideas; the play of
increased psychological depth and revealing symbols—owes more to
the genius of Ibsen than any other dramatist. But Björnson's much
smaller contribution must for historical reasons be considered first.
It was in November 1871 that the leading literary critic of Scandinavia, Georg Brandes, in his inaugural lecture at Copenhagen
University, called for 'a break-through to modernity,[22] and urged
that literature in order to preserve its vitality must 'submit problems to debate'. Brandes was in frequent friendly contact with Ibsen

both before and after he made this declaration, but Björnson—whose moral fervour always kept Brandes at a distance—was the first to take up this challenge. Indeed, he had to some extent anticipated the new trend, which had made its appearance a little earlier outside northern Europe, both in *The Newlyweds*, a drawing-room play of 1865 about the excessive influence of parents-in-law, placed in the home of a county governor of the day, and in his latest novel, *The Fisher Lass*.

In 1875, accordingly, he led the way with two realistic social dramas. *The Editor*, though translated immediately into German, achieved mainly a local celebrity, when all true Norwegian liberals identified the editor of the conservative Oslo paper, *Morgenbladet*, as the villain of the piece.[23] *A Bankrupt*, too laid its scene in some Norwegian town, but the history of a speculator and his conversion to strict financial probity was of general interest on account of the trade collapse which had spread outwards from Central Europe in the previous year. It was performed during the first few years in Berlin, Vienna, Budapest, and as far afield as New York, and remained the most popular of all Björnson's plays. He followed this up two years later with *The King*, which attacked the monarchy so directly that it was not performed in Norway until 1902; its author's growing interest in his foreign readers is illustrated by the fact that for a time he entertained the idea of having it published first in English.

Eleven more plays followed, most of which dealt with the private problems that beset the individual in his social relationships. *A Gauntlet*, for example, which raised the question of the different standards of sexual morality expected of men and women, was not acceptable on its publication in 1883 for the stage of any Scandinavian country: the first known performance was of a German translation in Hamburg, and one of the first press notices outside northern Europe appeared in the Chicago periodical *Scandinavia* only two months after the play was published in Copenhagen. Björnson proceeded to stump the Scandinavian countries with an outspoken lecture, 'Polygamy or Monogamy', but he handled woman's place in society with more circumspection in *Geography and Love*, a comedy about a self-centred professor which lost none of its popularity through the resemblance between the professor and the author. His most arresting dramas, however, examine the fate of the individual in relation to the great forces of religion and politics. *Beyond Our Powers* (1883) arose partly out of the heart-searching which had recently led Björnson to reject the Christian faith, preached with fervour in many of his earlier writings. The hero of the play is a devout clergyman who is reputed to work miracles by his prayers— and who dies on making the tragic discovery that the cure of his paralysed wife, to whom he is deeply devoted, is 'beyond our powers'. In *Paul Lange and Tora Parsberg* (1898) the theme is the downfall of the politician Richter (see p. 142), a case in which Björnson himself, as he said, had shared the experience and the suffering. The play shows how a man may be destroyed by the ruthless vendettas of party politics, which prompts the heroine to pose the question: 'Why must good men become martyrs? Shall we never allow them to become leaders?'[24]

These wide themes aroused wide interest: before Björnson's death in 1910 both plays had been translated into English, French, German, and Italian, while *Beyond Our Powers* was also available in Spanish, Polish, Czech, Finnish, Lettish, and Bulgarian. But the great humanitarian and optimist, wrestling with contemporary problems for the entertainment and still more the edification of a contemporary public, belonged essentially to the pre-1914 era. As early as 1893 a young French dramatist, in presenting a synopsis of *Beyond Our Powers*, which had then attracted attention at the Oeuvre Theatre in Paris, made a comparison with Ibsen which still rings true.

Björnson is an apostle and a preacher. For him art is the means, the end is an idea. He intervenes himself with the conclusion. Ibsen is first of all a poet. He gives full rein to his dreams, awaiting our comments with a sardonic smile . . . Yet they have one thing in common, which above all surprises our amiable men of letters: they take life seriously.[25]

Ibsen took longer to respond to the challenge expressed by Brandes, and he had seen *A Bankrupt* performed in Munich, where he was then living, before he started work on the first of his four social plays, which was completed in 1877. The theme of *Pillars of*

Society was the 'coffin ship', recently made notorious by Samuel Plimsoll's agitation in England but a standing temptation to Norwegian shipowners too, with their many obsolete sailing vessels which they would be glad to lose. The scene was laid in Grimstad, which Ibsen had known so well in his youth, but the tension was relieved by a happy ending (involving a link with America) which helped to give the play immediate popularity. An edition of 6,000 copies was sold within a few weeks; it was welcomed by producers throughout Scandinavia; and in its second year was seen in twenty-seven German and Austrian theatres.

But it was the other three plays in this series—*A Doll's House*, *Ghosts*, and *An Enemy of the People*—dating from 1879 to 1882—which more plainly established Ibsen's mastery in this genre. The scene is in each case laid in small-town Norwegian society where a problem of general significance is worked out—the obligations of a woman to husband and home *versus* the claims of individual liberty; the hidden ramifications of an immoral code of sexual morality; and the difficulty of exposing the built-in falsehood even when the matter at issue is nothing in appearance more complex than a tainted water supply. In each case the playwright employs the technique which he has now perfected of displaying his characters in their relationship to a series of events, many of them far beyond the time span of the drama, of which the consequences pursue them with all the remorselessness of a Greek tragedy.

A Doll's House achieved a worldwide celebrity for two reasons, neither of which represented the deepest intention of the dramatist, whose claim was always and only 'to have created human beings and human destinies'.[26] Because the play almost incidentally furthered the cause of feminine emancipation it provoked much heated discussion as far afield as Chicago, where one section of Norwegian immigrant opinion denounced the 'Godless life' portrayed. At the same time the role of Nora made an irresistible appeal to the best dramatic talent of the day: thus two distinguished English actresses on tour, and then a young American, used the part to introduce Ibsen effectively to the New York stage, and in 1891 Eleonora Duse appeared as Nora in Milan, while the greatest of Norwegian actresses, Johanna Dybwad, presented two contrasting interpretations of the part in 1890 and 1906. The action in *Ghosts*, on the other hand, involved the taboo subjects of venereal disease and incest. While this did not impede its publication in many foreign languages—five, including Russian, in the first ten years and at least seven others before 1914—public performances outside the Scandinavian countries were comparatively few. It was played once in Norwegian in Chicago in May 1882 (more than a year before the first performance in Scandinavia) and once in English in the same city in 1886. At that date it was still under a police ban in Germany, and the first performance in Paris was not until May 1900, whereupon 'Ibsen had come alive in France and the struggle began.'[27]

Although the Lord Chamberlain did not license *Ghosts* for public production in a regular theatre before July 1914, each of these three plays contributed to the impact of Ibsen on English culture, which had begun very slowly through the efforts of Edmund Gosse. These were notably reinforced by William Archer,[28] who was a nephew of a leading Norwegian boat builder and acquainted from early boyhood with Norway and its literature; in 1880 he arranged a single public performance of his own translation of *Pillars of Society*, and he subsequently used his position as a major theatre critic to make Ibsen known. *A Doll's House* was already available in England and was played in London in 1884 under the title, 'Breaking a Butterfly', but it was the publication in 1888 of *Pillars of Society*, *Ghosts*, and *An Enemy of the People*, with Archer as the main translator, which marks the break-through of Ibsen in Britain.* Distinguished productions quickly followed, and while the first performance of *Ghosts* in March 1891 provoked many bizarre denunciations—the *Daily Telegraph*, for example, compared the play to 'a loathsome sore unbandaged, a dirty act done publicly'—it gave a good advertisement to *The Quintessence of Ibsenism* by Bernard Shaw, who owed his interest in

---

* *An Enemy of the People* was translated by Karl Marx's daughter, while Archer's translation of *Ghosts* is stated in Havelock Ellis's preface to be 'to some extent founded' upon a version by Henrietta Frances Lord, which had been published in 1882 in the short-lived socialist periodical, *Today*. The unpretentious shilling volume had an unprecedented success for a work of contemporary drama, 14,000 copies being sold in five years, and in 1890 fuller collections of Ibsen's prose plays were launched under the respective editorships of Gosse and Archer.

Ibsen originally to his friendship with Archer. Based on lectures given to the Fabian Summer School in the previous year, Shaw's book was concerned with the ideas of Shaw rather than Ibsen; but the performance of Shaw's first play, *Widowers' Houses* (1892), introduced to the English stage a type of problem drama in which the influence of Ibsen was felt for many years.

Meanwhile, however, Ibsen himself had moved on from the plays that study man in society, where a moral judgement is at least implied, to the final flowering of his genius in plays that explore the psychology of the individual as isolated by his experience. The transition is not easy to trace or to define, but a leading English authority on Ibsen attaches special significance to his redefinition of his own position, as stated in a letter written to a young Norwegian poet in June 1884: 'I do not believe any of us can do anything other or anything better than realise ourselves in truth and in spirit. In my opinion this is the only true liberalism'.[29] Little need be said here about these eight masterpieces, beginning with the symbolism of *The Wild Duck* and of *Rosmersholm*, haunted by the falling water that echoed in Ibsen's mind from his childhood home among the watermills of Skien. Each new play was now a major event in the world of the theatre and of literature. In Germany, where Ibsen still made his greatest impact, his influence was almost too overwhelming, to judge from some verses published in Berlin in 1891.

> Ibsen, Ibsen überall!
> Da geht nichts mehr drüber!
> Auf dem ganzen Erdenball
> Herrscht das Ibsen-Fieber![30]

In Britain the interest was still strongest among a literary élite: Henry James, for example, reviewed at least four of these later plays, and the youthful James Joyce taught himself Norwegian in order to study Ibsen. In discussing the last play of all, *When We Dead Awaken* (1899), he urged that drama of this quality should be seen, not read: 'In a flash long reaches of life are opened up in vista . . . To prevent excessive pondering . . . Ibsen requires to be acted.'[31]

The final word, however, may rest with another young and ambitious writer, a compatriot of Ibsen, who declared on the contrary that the master had not advanced far enough beyond the consideration of external problems to the exploration of the hidden internal workings of the human mind. Delivered in a lecture which was attended by Ibsen himself, such a pontification was obviously mannerless; yet Hamsun (for he was the lecturer) showed in some measure the ability of each new generation, even in the arts and even in a small country, to stand on the shoulders of its predecessors.[32]

SOME CONTRIBUTIONS TO THE MODERN NOVEL

In the later nineteenth century Norway, in relation to its size, was rich in novelists who followed the new trend to realism with considerable success, as measured by their appeal to educated readers who understood both the language and the milieu familiar to the author. Their small effect in the world at large, however, is strikingly illustrated by the fate of the very earliest venture in this field, *The County Governor's Daughters*, in which Wergeland's sister, Camilla Collett, pleaded the cause of every middle-class Victorian woman whom social conventions taught to marry, as she had done, for reasons other than love. Her pioneer work, dating from 1855, became a classic throughout the Scandinavian countries, but after making an isolated appearance in German in 1864, has never been published in English and very rarely in any other non-Scandinavian language.

Each of the three writers whom the Norwegian public grouped with Ibsen as their four classical authors wrote realist novels. Björnson, who published them when his realistic plays were already well known, found many foreign readers for his story of a girls' school, *The Heritage of the Kurts* (1884);[33] whether in spite of, or because of, the melodramatic ending, when the illegitimate baby of one 'old girl' is introduced to spoil the wedding of another, must remain uncertain. Five years later, he wrote *In God's Paths* round the then familiar contrast between a narrowly pious cleric and a freethinker, in this case a doctor and his brother-in-law; and in his old age a much shorter story, *Mary*, whose Norwegian-American heroine has narrow escapes from a forced marriage and from suicide. Sales in English were sufficient to justify Edmund Gosse in collecting them for an edition of all Björnson's novels in nine volumes, completed in 1909.

Jonas Lie and Alexander Kielland have had contrasting fortunes, so far as the English-speaking world is concerned. Lie* makes a threefold appeal, with his vivid descriptions of life in northern Norway, where he spent his early childhood; his ability to create an atmosphere of mystery, as in the two volumes of *Trold*, which the historian Nisbet Bain translated as *Weird Tales from the Northern Seas*; and the qualities which caused Norwegians to call him 'the author of the home'. He imitated Camilla Collett with success in *The Commodore's Daughters*, provided one of the earliest pictures of an Oslo working-class milieu in *Servitude for Life*, and described the bureaucratic rural society, to which he had himself belonged, in *The Family at Gilje, An Interior from the 'Forties*. With the remarkable exception of the last, all Lie's principal works were translated into English before 1914; they were also well known in Germany, France, and the Netherlands.

Whereas much of Lie's writing now seems to the foreign reader flat and almost monotonous, Kielland† attacks the vices of the established system of society as he saw it—from Puritanism to civil-service 'red tape', from classical education to the power of money—with an ironical skill which has not lost its appeal. Yet only three of his six novels and a number of long 'short stories' or *noveller*, a genre in which he particularly excelled, were ever published in English. It may be that the rapid decline of his talent—twelve fecund years followed by fifteen of complete unproductivity, so far as imaginative literature is concerned—prevented the interest in Britain and America from gathering sufficient momentum. Notwithstanding, Kielland's work had a considerable vogue in Germany.

---

* 1833–1908. He was a lawyer's son and became a lawyer, but made his career as a novelist after he had gone bankrupt through unfortunate speculations in timber. He achieved immediate popularity in Norway with his first story (1870), and in 1882 took up permanent residence in Paris.

† 1849–1906. He came from one of the leading merchant families in Stavanger, where he was proprietor of a brickworks, 1872–81; his novels were published in 1880–91, after which he became mayor of Stavanger and, in 1902, a county governor. Translations of *Garman and Worsé* and *Skipper Worsé* appeared in London in 1885, of *Else* in Chicago in 1894.

1. Johan Christian Dahl *Stalheim, West Norway*

2. Thomas Fearnley *Labrofossen, Kongsberg*

3. Adolph Tidemand *Departure of the Emigrants*
4. Adolph Tidemand *The Haugeans*

5. Hans Gude and
Tidemand *Bridal
Journey in Hardanger*

6. Christian Krohg *Albertine in the Police Surgeon's Waiting Room*

7. Oscar Wergeland *The National Assembly at Eidsvoll, 1814*

8. Erik Werenskiold *A Peasant Burial*
9. Edvard Munch *The Sick Child*

10. Edvard Munch *Ashes*

11. Edvard Munch *The Cry*

12. Edvard Munch *Ibsen and the Lighthouse*

13. Edvard Munch *History*

14. Gustav Vigeland *Statue of Henrik Wergeland*

Garman and Worsé, the first and best of his novels, is said to have
provided Thomas Mann with 'the almost too obvious model' for
Buddenbrooks,[34] where Lübeck is described by much the same techniques as Kielland had used in bringing to life the Stavanger of his
youth.

Arne Garborg,* the first important *landsmål* writer since the
death of Vinje, made his name in 1883 with *Peasant Students*, a story
which brought out the physical miseries and mental frustration they
often experienced in adapting themselves to the life of a university
in urban surroundings. Two other novels, *Menfolk* (1886) and *Tired
Men* (1891), are chiefly of interest because they reflect the somewhat
sordid discussions about free love that were then raging in artistic
and student circles in Oslo; the central figure in the movement was a
sexually obsessed writer and anarchist philosopher, Hans Jæger, who
first raised the subject in a lecture to the Association for Workers in
1882 and four years later served 60 days' imprisonment for his
scandalous novel, *From the Christiania Bohème*, which had been confiscated immediately on publication. Garborg's later novels, however,
together with his poems and plays, are concerned primarily with the
peasant society that he had known in western Norway in his youth
and with the pietist faith which occupied so much of its thoughts.
But although his outlook was deeply rooted in the general culture
of Europe—he devoted much time in later years to *landsmål* render-
ings of Homer, Shakespeare, and other classic authors—his influence was small outside the Scandinavian countries and Germany,
where one of his weakest stories gained a literary prize as early as
1890; down to the First World War none of his works had been
translated into English.

The name of Knut Hamsun† stands out from the rest as that of a

---

* 1851–1924. Born on a farm in the monotonous coastal district of Jæren,
south of Stavanger, and influenced throughout his life by his pietist father's
suicide in 1870. He became a champion of neo-Norwegian by 1877; *Tired Men*,
which is in the form of a middle-class townsman's diary, is however written
in *riksmål*.

† 1859–1952. He was brought up at Hamarøy in Nordland, where his father
acquired a small farm, but was in America in 1882–4 and 1886–8, after which
he wrote critically on *The Cultural Life of Modern America*. After achieving success with plays and poems as well as novels he returned to Hamarøy, 1911–17,

Norwegian who was the peer of the leading modern novelists in
countries where this literary form has had a much longer history
than in Norway. Like Jonas Lie, he had spent his early youth in the
north, which provided the setting for many of his finest stories.
But he had suffered hardship as a casual labourer on the American
prairies as well as in Oslo before he wrote *Hunger*, in which his
special combination of realism and lyricism and his impressionist
technique made a seemingly formless story unforgettable. This
phenomenal work was translated into English in 1899, and his
relatively insignificant realist novel of Oslo life, *New Ground*, in
1914. But *Pan*, the partly symbolist novel which he wrote in Paris
in 1894; *Victoria* (1898), where love is portrayed as 'an unbreakable
seal that lasts through life, lasts unto death';[35] the series of tales in
which the Wanderer figures; and *Children of the Age* (1913), the
first volume of his great social study of North Norway, all made
their impact on the outer world through German. Together with
Dostoevski and Strindberg, Nietzsche was the master whose influence Hamsun specially acknowledged—an influence which confirmed him in his early belief that the civilization of Britain and
America was hopelessly decadent. This was unfortunate, if only
because it militated against the prompt recognition of his genius.

MODERN PAINTING: EDVARD MUNCH

In the early 1880s the art, no less than the literature, of Norway
entered a new phase. The long dependence upon Düsseldorf had
been followed by an association with Münich, where by 1877 no
fewer than thirty-one Norwegian artists were seeking inspiration
from the famous collections, but this quickly gave way to a new influence from Paris and the Impressionists. At the same time the
increasing wealth and sophistication of the Norwegian middle class
made it more possible for artists to establish themselves at home,
where they became numerous enough to wrest control of the Autumn

---

but in 1918 established himself as a gentleman farmer near Grimstad, where
he resided at the time of the German occupation. He was fined kr. 325,000 for
his active co-operation with Quisling's N.S., for which his final work, *On Overgrown Paths* (1949), was a kind of apologia.

Exhibition in Oslo out of the hands of laymen. A Board of Visual Artists (*Bildende Kunstneres Styre*) was set up in 1888 to represent the views of the profession whenever public money was spent on art, so that they eventually came to 'exercise direct influence on artistic life to an extent unparalleled in most other countries'.[36]

The new impressionist techniques gave heightened values to the colouring in the snowbound or twilit landscapes which are so large a part of the Norwegian scene; this was shown for instance by the earlier work of Frits Thaulow, albeit his wider reputation as a river painter was made after 1894, when he settled down in France. In general, the naturalism that was then in vogue was expected to lead to a truly national art. Erik Werenskiold depicted the peasant for the first time in his (and her) natural dignity (Plate 8), shorn of all romantic trappings; historical scenes, too, such as a session of the Eidsvoll Assembly which was painted for the Storting in 1887 (Plate 7), were reproduced with attempted verisimilitude. But Werenskiold's contemporary, Gerhard Munthe, developed a highly stylized decorative art, inspired by old Norse models: when used for imaginative illustration of the sagas, it provided his own wife and other weavers with designs for modern tapestries which the jury at the Paris Exhibition of 1900 described as 'a veritable revelation to the whole world'.[37] In the new century Norwegian handicrafts became widely known for work of this kind, based on carefully preserved national traditions.

The most consistent of the Naturalists was Christian Krohg,* who was a writer of the school of Zola as well as a painter of carefully composed scenes of urban life—scenes chosen with the eye of an ardent radical. When Oslo's bohemian artists sprang to the defence of Jæger, Krohg took the lead in justifying his attack on the bourgeois attitude to prostitution as an organized hypocrisy. *Albertine*, his story of a 'fallen woman', whom society causes to fall and then persecutes for falling, was confiscated by the police, whereupon he showed in private his most powerful painting, *Albertine in the Police Surgeon's Waiting Room* (Plate 6). The licensing

---

* 1852–1925. His father had been a prominent opponent of King Charles John's proposals in the Stortings of 1821–8; his son, who was a pupil of Matisse, became a leading fresco painter in the inter-war period.

and compulsory medical examination of prostitutes was abolished in Norway soon afterwards—as it had been in English ports and garrison towns in 1883-6—and Krohg's picture now has a place of honour in the Norwegian National Gallery. But the episode also sheds light upon the social background for the early work of an altogether greater artist, Edvard Munch,* who at nineteen had shared a studio and informal supervision by Krohg with several other radical painters or 'bohemians'. Jæger hung one of Munch's early paintings on the wall of his prison cell, and Munch returned the compliment by making him the subject of a tragically faithful portrait.

His father, who was a younger brother of the historian P. A. Munch, made a precarious livelihood as a doctor in the poorer districts of Oslo, which tended to free his family from bourgeois complacency regarding the human condition. In any case, the experience in their own midst that affected his son most deeply was of death—his mother's when he was barely five and that of a much-loved elder sister when he was fourteen. It was in 1886 that Munch painted the first version of *The Sick Child* (Plate 9), which he looked back upon as 'the cardinal event in my artistic development, expressionist in conception, cubist in construction'.[38] But although this was accompanied by two other masterpieces (*Puberty* and *The Morning After*)—now lost in their original form—conservative critics admired neither his choice of subject nor his novel and in their eyes perfunctory treatment of it. Three years later Krohg and other friends had great difficulty in obtaining him a public grant for nine months' study in France, where he acquired the pointillist and other techniques from the impressionists. However, in November 1892 he was invited by the *Verein Berliner Künstler* (which had a Norwegian among its members) to exhibit in the German capital the fifty

---

* 1863-1944. Munch never married, and after settling down at Ekely, Oslo, in 1916 lived only for his work: in addition to his paintings, which often included several versions of the same theme, he executed about 200 etchings, 140 woodcuts, and 360 lithographs. In later life he was under no financial pressure to sell his work—'I must have some friends on my own wall' was one of his sayings: hence the extraordinary richness of his collection, which he bequeathed in its entirety to the municipality of Oslo.

or more paintings that he had shown in Norway during the previous summer. These exemplified what was later called Expressionism, the natural shapes and colours of their subjects being modified so as to maximize the expression of the artist's emotion: this might well be painful and ugly, as in *The Cry* (Plate 11) and Munch's various presentations of woman as a madonna turned vampire, preying upon man.

Berlin society was outraged, but when the Artists' Association voted by 120 to 105 to close the exhibition in consequence, the minority left to found the *Berliner Sezession*, in which the young Norwegian became an important figure. The industrial magnate, Walther Rathenau, provided his first German client; the first book about his work appeared in Germany in 1894; and its author, the Polish critic Stanislas Przyszewski, together with his Norwegian wife and Strindberg, who was then living in Berlin, formed the nucleus of a circle of intimates. Although Munch was in Paris again in 1896–7, when he developed his lifelong interest in woodcuts and lithography and helped to promote two Ibsen productions (Plate 12), for fifteen years Germany became his spiritual home; summer visits to Norway were made mainly in order to use the Oslofiord scenery, which was always a favourite subject for his brush. Thus *The Frieze of Life* (Plate 10) the symphony on love and death, as he himself called it, in which Munch arranged (and rearranged) many of his works so as to give them their fullest significance, was exhibited with twenty-two items by *Sezessionen* in 1902; he executed a mural on the theme of Youth for a patron in Lübeck and made a notable entry into the realm of theatre décor for Max Reinhardt's new Berlin theatre, which opened with *Ghosts*; and in 1905 a visit to Saxony for portrait painting, from which Munch still derived much of his livelihood, led to a fruitful relationship with a group of German artists in Dresden. They founded the *Brücke* ('bridge') school of figurative expressionists, which until 1913 led the movement to bring German art back into the main current of European development.

The German debt to Munch has been compared with that of French art to Cézanne. The English critic, Herbert Read, while observing that Munch's influence did not reach Britain until after his death, nevertheless describes him as 'an exponent of the *Zeitgeist*, comparable to Ibsen or Dostoevsky in literature'.[39] The Germans in any case soon recognized how much they owed him: at the great 'Sonderbund' Exhibition at Cologne in 1912, where a small cabinet for Picasso was the only other special room allotted to any living painter, the works of Munch monopolized an entire salon.

Meanwhile, in 1908 Munch had a severe mental breakdown, said to have been brought on by excessive drinking in combination with a persecution complex which had involved him in frequent brawls;[40] one of his many self-portraits, indeed, shows a significantly bandaged hand. He spent eight months in a Danish psychiatric clinic, from which he emerged completely cured, to spend the rest of a long life as a rather retiring figure in his native land; there his genius had a second flowering, with the use of brighter colours more boldly applied and a new inclination to look outward rather than inward in the exploration of his subjects. His most ambitious achievement in this later style was a set of huge murals for the new Great Hall or Aula of Oslo University, though the execution of his designs was held up until 1914 by opposition in university circles, even when there was a prospect that they might be bought up by Jena instead. The central panel, showing the sun as it rises over a glowing Norwegian scene, is flanked by *Alma Mater* and *History* (Plate 13). The latter theme is conveyed, as the painter has explained, through the medium of 'a distant and historically impressive landscape, before which an old man from the fiords is seated, one who has worked his passage through the years, enthralling a little boy with his memories'.[41] The subject had a natural attraction for the nephew of Norway's most revered historian, and the result provides a fine setting at the present day for the annual award of the Nobel Peace Prize, when representative Norwegians pass judgement on the history of our own times.

Nineteenth-century Norway had been too poor to foster the art of monumental sculpture for public or private objects, but Munch's early contacts in Berlin included her first sculptor of outstanding talent, Gustav Vigeland (see note, p. 364), who was engrossed by ideas very similar to those expressed by Munch in his 'Frieze of Life'. Although his tremendous Fountain existed as a fully worked out design by 1908, he was still engaged chiefly on portrait busts and commemorative statuary of eminent Norwegians, which aroused little interest abroad. An exception must, however, be made for his finely imaginative bronze statue of Wergeland (Plate 14), cast in 1908, of which a duplicate was erected at Fargo, North Dakota, by the pious enterprise of a Norwegian-American. It was a felicitous thought to perpetuate on another continent the memory of the national poet who, when all these artistic developments were still in their infancy, had urged his fellow countrymen to be 'Norwegian in their inmost character, and yet . . . looking free and far out into the world'.[42]

9. Hazards of a Neutral: Gains and Losses in the First World War

THE WAR YEARS FROM 1914 TO 1918 IMPOSED A SPECIALLY severe strain upon Norway, which was perhaps the weakest of the European neutrals and certainly the one whose existence was most dependent upon foreign trade and the freedom of the seas. One prominent feature of the period was the resourcefulness and determination with which the government handled its relations with the great powers, although its previous diplomatic experience was so slight, taking advantage of the fact that both sides calculated that more was to be gained from Norway as a neutral than as a belligerent. Weak as she was, her economic resources were important for the conduct of the war, so the second main aspect of the period was a trade boom, the first two war years being the most prosperous the country had ever experienced. From August 1916 onwards, indeed, both sides (as we shall see) employed more ruthless measures to bend Norway to their will: the Allies withheld coal and other necessities, the Germans destroyed the shipping which was the chief Norwegian asset. But even in 1918 fortunes were still being made by holders of shipping shares and owners of export commodities, so that a Labour leader could claim with some justification that 'the upper class is enjoying a golden age without parallel in the nation's history.'[1]

The third main aspect of the war years, even in neutral Norway, was the rapid growth in the activities of the state. Under a government of the Left Party, which had been in some respects less addicted to state intervention than were the Liberals of pre-war Britain, economic and social life was subjected to innumerable emergency regulations—and these set a pattern for the future. In October 1918 Gunnar Knudsen and the Left Party lost their majority, and although they lingered in office for another two years it was clear that in Norway as elsewhere the liberalism that had so long embodied the idea of progress was now a waning force. The present chapter will therefore end with the peace settlement, which brought Norway into the League of Nations, that last embodiment of liberal hopes.

THE OUTBREAK OF WAR IN EUROPE

At the beginning of August 1914 the first declarations of war took the Norwegian people completely by surprise. The result was a long-remembered week of panic, during which the shops were emptied of food supplies at rapidly rising prices and the instinct to hoard even created a run on such inessentials as clothes-hangers and shoe polish. Most Norwegians were well aware of their country's dependence upon oversea supplies, and the 'hunger years' of the Napoleonic Wars constituted one of their most vivid folk memories. The same historical experience also made them immediately distrustful of paper money. The Bank of Norway, besieged by customers desiring to change its notes into gold, was relieved of this obligation on 4 August, whereupon a distrustful public bought up kroner for the sake of their silver content. A more reasonable basis for the popular anxieties was the expectation of a great North Sea battle or battles between the main fleets of Britain and Germany, which might for the time being cut off all Norway's sea-borne communications. And would territorial waters necessarily be respected? On 26 July a German squadron had lain off Bergen when the Kaiser made a hurried return from the last of his many Norwegian holidays, and it was easy to surmise that British regard for neutral rights was not proof against all temptation, even under a Liberal government. We now know that a year before the war Grey as foreign secretary envisaged the possibility of launching 'an attack upon an enemy's ships actually in Norwegian waters . . . German ships of war found in Norwegian waters on the outbreak of war would presumably have been put there for strategic reasons.'[2]

Two lines of action, which were pursued from the very outset, did much to safeguard neutrality. On 30 and 31 July, garrisons were mobilized for the coastal fortresses protecting Oslo, Bergen, Trondheim, and Kristiansand, and on 2 August the electrically fired mine defences were made operational. The navy, whose strength lay in torpedo boats and other small units, was likewise mobilized, and the recent extension of the period of service to twelve months gave it adequate manpower for its task as a neutrality guard along an intricate and extensive coastline. The five army districts were also placed in a state of readiness, with sufficient men under arms to facilitate the effective deployment of the total force of 197,000 which would be available in the event of Norway's involvement in the war. A comparatively young and very energetic officer from the coastal artillery, Major-General C. T. Holtfodt, who had first made his name as a supporter of Georg Stang, was appointed minister of defence at this juncture. Throughout the war he was backed up by the prime minister in enforcing his demands for increased military expenditure and more stringent conditions of call-up for training and garrison duties upon an often reluctant Storting; the infantry, for example, served for nearly twice the pre-war period.

The other important safeguard was an improved relationship with Sweden. The first approach came from the Swedish foreign minister, who on 29 July invited his Norwegian colleague to agree to the proposition that their two nations should 'in all circumstances dispose themselves in such a way that they did not fire at one another'. The Swedes would have liked to carry the agreement further—to the possibly dangerous commitment to fire only in the same direction, but the arrangement that was finally approved (8 August) added to the pledge of mutual amity only an announcement of the firm intention 'to maintain the neutrality of the respective kingdoms in relation to all the belligerent powers'.[3] Although the agreement could do nothing to change the facts of geography and other influences inclining the two states to look for friends in opposite directions, it allayed the fear that the quarrel of 1905 might now be deliberately reopened. In November 1914 the Swedes again took the lead, in calling a conference at which the three Scandinavian states (and initially the Netherlands) agreed to protest against the interference of the belligerents with maritime trade. This was followed a month later by a meeting of the three kings and their foreign ministers, held at Malmö rather than Stockholm so that the Swedes as hosts might not be open to the accusation of stealing the limelight. This had no concrete results, but the willingness of the Swedish to fraternize with the Norwegian monarchy was reassuring to the many newspaper readers who still saw politics in terms of persons. In addition, all three nations gained a little confidence from the fact that good relations with one another helped them from time to time to make a common stand in denouncing the recurrent infringements of international law by both sides in the war; this was a matter in which the Swedish prime minister, Hjalmar Hammarskjöld, was an acknowledged expert.

When the Storting met for a brief emergency session on 8 August, the panic was already subsiding. Although pounds sterling and dollars continued for a time to be in great demand, by November 1915 the krone had an exchange value above its gold parity which it retained until the end of the war. Unfortunately, when the normal obligation to buy foreign gold was suspended in 1916,[4] the regulations governing the issue of notes by the Bank of Norway were relaxed, so a profusion of paper money created eventually a serious problem of inflation. But in 1914 a start had been made on a financial policy which proved still more disastrous. Since the cost of military precautions and emergency supplies could not then be specified, the Storting voted a sum of kr. 15 million for 'such extraordinary measures as the present situation might demand'. The government seems to have treated this as a blanket authority; at all events it continued year by year to make no provision for meeting the cost of special expenditure, which was airily described as 'conveyed to direct expenditure on Treasury assets'.[5] Thus the accounts for 1914–15 showed a fictitious surplus of kr. 11 million instead of a real deficit of almost kr. 38 million, and although large sums were raised by taxation (including a tax on war profits) these were microscopic in comparison with the undisclosed annual increase in the national debt.

Bratlie, like the Conservative leaders in Britain, considered that a Liberal prime minister was unsuited to a war situation, and in particular doubted Knudsen's ability to co-operate satisfactorily with the Swedes. But the head of the Consolidated Left had no intention of sharing the authority he had worked so hard to win. To some extent, indeed, he widened the basis of support by the use of special committees. Thus the Provisioning Commission (which had local counterparts) included a Labour representative, Christopher Hornsrud, and the difficult problem of mutual war-risk insurance for shipping was settled by a non-political committee of experts, headed by the Bergen shipowner and rising politician of the Left Party, J. L.

Mowinckel (see note, p. 304). In the main, however, Gunnar Knudsen's position remained unshaken until the very last months of the war, because he and his foreign minister, N. C. Ihlen,★ represented an interpretation of Norwegian neutrality that commanded general support. Knudsen had been described by a Danish newspaper as 'the Bismarck of Norway',[6] a soubriquet which was to some extent justified by his strength and self-confidence and by a certain ruthlessness in his dealings with individuals. But this humane, if paternalistic, protagonist of social reform had his roots in European liberalism, and however much he might be provoked by British infringements of the rights of a small neutral power he never seriously doubted the desirability of a British victory in the war. While his control of the cabinet, Storting, party, and people kept the nation on a steady course, the diplomatic burden fell most heavily upon his foreign minister, the only one of his colleagures who retained office throughout the seven years of the Knudsen administration. The two men had no ties of personal friendship, and although Ihlen had been minister of labour in Knudsen's first cabinet, he was not his original choice for the foreign office in 1913: but once chosen he provided an admirable counterfoil to the premier. By training he was a fellow engineer, but whereas Knudsen's business developed shipping activities, which turned his attention westwards, Ihlen, who was a graduate of the Zürich Polytechnic, retained a continental outlook. He had imbibed his liberal principles in Switzerland, and his sympathies with the Entente powers were inspired by an admiration for France rather than Britain. In any case, they were not strong enough to distract his attention from an unwearying defence of purely Norwegian interests, to which he brought enormous powers of application and—what was perhaps even more important—the ability of a talented business negotiator to wait upon events and postpone final commitments until the moment was ripe. It was however a misfortune that, while he conversed with German representatives in their own language, Ihlen and the British minister,

---

★ 1855–1925. He was the owner of an iron foundry and engineering works with foreign connections. Castberg described him in December 1916 as 'a man for the day, without great lines or principles . . . so agile that he is in danger of the fate that nobody will believe his word'.[7]

Findlay, had to conduct their very frequent conversations in French.

Many Norwegians believed, once the initial shock was over, that the war might prove economically advantageous to them and their country; most hoped that the Allies would win, though the aggrandizement of the Russian Tsardom would be unwelcome; all wished to avoid the involvement of Norway in active hostilities. In circumstances of growing complexity, the government tried to carry out the nation's will.

THE BOOM YEARS

After the initial panic had subsided, the Norwegian people enjoyed two years of fairly widespread prosperity. Even during the month of August 1914, when British shipping was temporarily withdrawn, the total tonnage that sailed between Norwegian ports and those of the United Kingdom was not much below normal, and right down to 1916 Norway continued to receive the peacetime quantity of its key industrial import, namely coal. The Provisioning Commission was likewise able to get what it needed from abroad, though the government had to support its purchases by raising loans in sterling and dollars, for which they paid a higher rate of interest ($6\frac{1}{2}$ per cent) than would have been demanded before the outbreak of hostilities.

A dark shadow was, however, already cast by the naval policies of the rival maritime powers, which substituted a war on shipping for the expected trial of strength between their battle-lines of dreadnoughts. From the first day of the war the Germans sowed mines extensively in the approaches to Allied harbours, the first Norwegian victim being a vessel mined off the Scheldt on 7 August. The British reply was to declare the whole of the North Sea to be a war area, so that the risk of mines might force neutral trade into easily controlled routes. At first it was demanded that Norwegian ships should proceed through the English Channel and cross the North Sea between the Farne Islands and Lindesnes, but they were eventually authorized to pass north of Scotland, subject to an intermittently enforced liability to be taken into Kirkwall for inspection of cargo for possible contraband. In February 1915 the Germans retaliated by announcing a counter-blockade by submarine; this was expressly justified by the allegedly frequent British practice of hoisting a neutral flag to avoid capture, so Norwegian ships were now painted in the national colours and illuminated at night. When the first Norwegian vessel was torpedoed off Folkestone on the 19th, the German government agreed to indemnify the owners and soon afterwards abandoned the campaign, so far as neutral shipping was concerned, except when submarine commanders ascertained the presence of contraband and sank the carrier after due warning. In 1915 forty-nine ships were sunk by direct attack, and another twelve by means that were not ascertained; next year the rate of loss was growing, but at the second anniversary of the outbreak of war new building and purchases from abroad still enabled Norway to deploy an increased total tonnage.[8]

The Norwegian mercantile marine found itself in a very fortunate position at this time. Of the three fleets that outnumbered it, that of Britain was fully absorbed in serving her own war needs and those of her allies; the Germans were pent up in their own coastal waters and the restricted area of the Baltic; and United States shipping was concentrated mainly on the far side of the Atlantic. Norwegian shipowners were adaptable, accustomed to run risks, and familiar with all the main international trade routes. Moreover, the control that the maritime supremacy of the British enabled them to exercise over the cargoes they carried, while increasingly rigorous in its attempt to make the Allied blockade of the Central Powers effective, did not interfere with profits. The final results speak for themselves. In 1915 freight charges averaged three times the pre-war rates; by 1918 there were some hazardous trades where they had risen to twenty times. In the second half of the war more ships were sunk, but in the whole period the mercantile marine contributed kr. 2,560 million to the balance of payments—an amount which was one-quarter larger than the entire excess of import over export costs.

But the export trades were also highly profitable, for Norwegian fish, wood, wood products, and ores, together with the nitrates and other new hydro-electrical manufactures, all had an enhanced value to the warring powers. In 1913 Britain had taken 24 per cent of the whole and Germany 21 per cent; each was now anxious to obtain a larger share at the expense of the other. In the case of wood pulp and timber, Norway derived extra benefit from the fact that Germany cut off the Baltic supply: the British demand for pit-props, for instance, was virtually inexhaustible. Pyrites, on the other hand, were in special demand in Germany because, in addition to their yield of copper, the sulphur content was indispensable for the manufacture of ammunition. In May 1915 Ihlen informed a secret session of the Storting that the export to Germany, which had averaged 3,000 tons a month before the war, had risen to 25,000 tons in February and 28,000 tons in April.[9]

Fish was a commodity that in 1914 provided more than 50,000 Norwegians with their main employment, but of which less than one-tenth was absorbed by the home market. In 1915 the Germans, who normally consumed a large part of the herring catch, sent their own vessels up through the Leads and bought direct from the fishermen. The latter enjoyed an unprecedented prosperity, partly because the native wholesalers were cut out, but chiefly because for the Germans cost was a minor consideration when they were given a chance like this to circumvent the British food blockade. Next year, however, the prospects were less rosy, since the British threatened to withhold supplies of petrol, salt, and equipment from a fishing fleet that worked in German interests, while Norwegian fish had now priced itself out of markets in southern Europe, for which it was in any case difficult to arrange transport. The director of fisheries, Johan Hjort,[*] a scientific colleague of Nansen who was well known in Britain, then contrived a truly remarkable arrangement to provide for the main spring catch: about three-quarters was bought up by a Bergen agent for a secret British account, regardless of cost. £11 million was spent; the accumulating stocks could be smelt all over Bergen; and as demand in Britain was small, much of the fish was eventually sent to the Russians. The main

[*] 1869–1948. Joint author with the Canadian Sir John Murray of *The Depths of the Sea* (1912), which grew out of their North Atlantic expedition in the *Michael Sars*; professor of marine biology at Oslo, 1920–39; president of the international council for maritime research, 1939–48.

object of depriving the Germans of food was duly achieved, but total sales recovered only one-half of the money spent—and the profiteering of the Norwegians was shown up when their Provisioning Commission refused to offer more than kr. 50 for the barrel of fat herring sold to Britain's agent for kr. 89 earlier in the same season.

As regards exports in general, the Germans in their dealings with Norway had the advantage that in peacetime they supplied a larger proportion of her imports than did Britain—30 per cent as compared with 25 per cent—and the German share included much of the equipment for the new hydro-electric industries. In wartime the supplies came north in smaller quantities, the Germans claiming that their railways were monopolized by military needs, but even in the first half of 1916, when they were only equivalent to three-fifths of what was sent to Germany, they were of key significance for industry. Although Ihlen did not at this stage attempt to make a trade treaty, he was able to assure the German minister that exports to his country in the above mentioned six months were twice as valuable as those for the whole of 1914.

It is perhaps more remarkable that Ihlen did not press for a trade treaty with Britain, on which Norway was directly dependent for its essential supply of coal and indirectly for overseas imports of all kinds, which might be intercepted by the British navy as being destined in some way to serve the interests of the Central Powers. He showed much less enthusiasm, indeed, than the Swedes did for challenging the actions of the British on grounds of international law: as a businessman he knew that protracted legal arguments were often unprofitable. But he thought that 'Business as usual' would pay Norway best, even as late as the autumn of 1915, when with a little more effort he could probably have secured a general agreement on imports, such as was made by the Netherlands and Denmark. Negotiations were abandoned by the British at the end of the year, to the relief of Findlay,* the man on the spot,

---

* Mansfeld de Cardonnel Findlay (K.C.M.G. 1916, G.B.E. 1924) had served at Stockholm in 1885-6, worked under Cromer in Egypt, and was minister in Oslo from 1911 to 1923. He was a Scotsman of prodigious height, whom his friends described as 'resolute to the point of rigidity'; a circumstantial story claimed that in the autumn of 1914 he planned to kidnap Sir Roger Casement,

who feared that the Norwegian government might not readily be brought to book under such an agreement, 'if policy demanded that they should be easy with the Germans'.[10]

In default of any general arrangement, the British at first brought pressure to bear on individual firms. Thus in January 1915 the Norwegian-America Line saved its vessels from costly diversions for inspection in a British port by secretly submitting cargo lists for prior approval. In April the principal whale-oil manufacturer, De Nordiske Fabriker (D.N.F.), agreed to sell its entire output at a low price to Lever Brothers; otherwise Norway was threatened with the loss of its whaling concessions in British antarctic territory and of the vessels which operated there. The main instrument, however, was the Branch Agreements, of which the first was signed in August 1915 by the Cotton Mills Association.

Such an agreement allowed the organized members of a trade to import through the blockade a quantity of materials equivalent to the pre-war domestic consumption, on condition that whatever was imported remained within the country or was re-exported to approved destinations only or was used in manufacturing exports for such destinations. The British legation became a commercial intelligence agency to control fulfilment, and many of the agreements provided it with the right of access to business records. The government too, though not a party directly involved, was expected by the British authorities to refuse export licences which broke the terms, Findlay's importunacy being limited only by the fear that Norway might become less amenable if she was driven into closer co-operation with Sweden. In less than three years there were fifty-five of these agreements—including twenty for oil and margarine alone—operating under the shadow of a Black List of about 1,100 firms;[11] these were deprived of supplies because they were suspected of exercising their right as neutrals of trading with the enemies of Britain.

Pride might suffer, but prosperity increased. In some cases the Norwegians were dexterous enough to make the best of both worlds,

---

when the Irish nationalist travelled through Oslo with a false American passport on his way to Germany.[12]

as when Norsk Hydro contrived to get the German machinery for doubling the output of their works at Rjukan, three-quarters of which went to the Allies, including the French armaments industry, under *le grand contrat* of 1915. The rigours of the British system of rationing Norwegian imports were mitigated, too, by the need to placate American opinion, which was very sensitive about the rights of neutrals, and by the desire to keep up the level of British exports to neutral territory so as to support sterling, even at the risk of occasional seepage across the borders to the Central Powers: although the restricted capacity of Norwegian ports made them easy to watch, the value of exports to Germany did in fact increase. Moreover, wartime Europe was so starved of goods that firms which were forced to abandon their German connections had little difficulty in finding new markets.

THE DOMESTIC SCENE

The domestic scene reflected Norway's favoured position, as in other wars. Shipping shares, as we night expect, led the market, rising by as much as 500 per cent. Shipbuilding likewise had golden opportunities, and this in turn encouraged expansion in other industries. It was the period when a man like Christoffer Hannevig, who put motors into sailing ships and made kr. 150 million in three years, had a name to conjure with; when the 'Prospect Company' could raise money on the strength of the freights to be earned with its five German ships, of which possession was guaranteed—after the war; and when a certain Mr. Angus paid a rewarding visit to Oslo to collect capital for his 'Fool-proof Railway'.[13] In 1916 a mounting scarcity of raw materials made manufacture less attractive, but the rise in freights brought even forty-year-old sailing ships into the market: by October wartime investment in shipping was believed to amount to nearly kr. 500 million—more than four times the pre-war national Budget. Although food prices were controlled and the importation of corn became a government activity, farmers profited, especially if they had timber to sell. Neither the ministry nor the Bank of Norway made any serious effort to check inflation, which made the prosperity look greater than it was. In any case it was natural to feel confidence in a rising currency: by the close of 1917 it required less than kr. 13 to buy the English pound, and less than three to buy the gold-based United States dollar.[14]

The class of *nouveaux riches* which these conditions created was even more conspicuous than the war profiteers of other countries, both because Norwegian society was on such a small scale that the individual was more conspicuous, and because the sudden advance from rags to riches was hitherto an almost unknown phenomenon. The long-term effect on class relations was very serious. By 1916 wage rates had risen only 29 per cent to meet a 50-per-cent increase in prices, and although full employment—which continued throughout the war period—meant that a good deal of extra pay was obtainable by working overtime, discontent was already spreading. Industrial workers saw that wage-earners in agriculture and forestry were beginning to catch up with them, while state employees at all levels found their relatively secure position suddenly unattractive in comparison with those persons (including many farmers) who could raise money for speculation.

The struggle over compulsory arbitration in labour conflicts was resumed in 1915, when a new bill proposed to confine it to the case of enterprises whose continuous functioning was 'essential for the community'.[15] The employers' organization sympathized with the objections of the trade union federation, which gave notice of a general strike. The government thereupon substituted a broadly acceptable measure to require resort to mediation in advance of any strike or lock-out; at the same time a Labour Court was set up to determine all disputes about the legal interpretation of agreements between employers and employees. But in the summer of 1916, when a strike of miners and iron workers threatened to set off a chain reaction of lock-outs and sympathetic strikes affecting ever larger numbers, Gunnar Knudsen enacted compulsory arbitration for the duration of the war. Lack of funds compelled the trade union federation to abandon its protest strike: the first award of the arbitrators satisfied the iron-workers, though the second left the miners dissatisfied.

These two years were also marked by the enactment of the second instalment of the great social reforms long planned by Castberg (see p. 178). Opponents deprecated 'the pushing on of reforms at this motorcar speed',[16] but there was something impressive about the ability of the Norwegian Storting to legislate on behalf of such a defenceless class as illegitimate children amidst the distractions of a world at war. Since the election of that autumn left the government with an undiminished majority, it must be assumed that public opinion welcomed its social reforms as well as its successful handling of the international emergency. The premier again rejected suggestions for a coalition, but strengthened his position in his own party by giving the Church and Education Department to Lövland, who still carried great weight with the ardently nationalist farmers because of the leading part he had played in 1905.

As 1916 wore on, however, it became evident that the war would be prolonged and embittered to an extent that made 'Business as usual' and even 'Social reform as usual' inadequate maxims on which to base the national policy. Shortly after the election state intervention had to be introduced in the very sensitive area of house rents: so many people had flocked into Oslo and other towns for employment that the local authorities were given powers to stop profiteering in the charges made for small flats and apartments. One unanticipated result was that houses ceased to be built, except for the wealthiest type of purchaser. In 1916, too, the state advanced from the purchase of one or two coal boats and other small vessels to the more significant step of buying up the largest and best-equipped flour mill in Norway: apart from the effect on the cost of bread, the position of the mill near Bergen was held to guarantee its immunity from eventual air attack. Most important of all, the Provisioning Commission was replaced in August 1916 by a Ministry of Provisions (or Food), which led on to the establishment of a Ministry of Industrial Supply and a Price Board; this Board gave scope to an energetic young economist, Wilhelm Thagaard, whose activities as a kind of regulator-in-chief for the Norwegian economy continued down to the 1950s.

The increasingly direct involvement of the state in economic life is well illustrated by the fact that it was the treatment accorded to ships belonging to, and chartered by, the Norwegian government that drove Gunnar Knudsen to expostulate with Asquith about the

Admiralty's high-handedness. In a letter of September 1916, which closes with a reference to his long-standing sympathy with the international and social policies of British Liberalism, he nevertheless warns his fellow premier: 'Since the British blockade has become more severe, people are coming to fear a British as well as a German hegemony.'[17]

NEUTRALITY UNDER STRAIN: A SIX MONTHS' CRISIS

In August 1916, when the invincibility of the German land defences, as newly demonstrated in the Battle of the Somme, emphasized to the Allies the paramount importance of their naval blockade, Britain drove two hard bargains, which she was prepared to enforce upon Norway by remorseless economic pressure. The Germans in their turn resented and strove to prevent the fulfilment of these bargains, while at the same time they became involved in a sharp dispute about regulations for controlling the use of Norwegian waters by foreign submarines. By the end of October the position of the Norwegians was so critical that the British cabinet and its advisers were studying the situation that would arise if they were forced into the war.

Since Norwegian pyrites provided copper for manufacturing shells, its exportation to Germany seemed to Findlay to justify a direct remonstrance to Ihlen:

The inflated price of Norwegian copper is, in fact, the price of blood—the blood of the friendly people to whom Norway would necessarily look for assistance in time of need, and on whom she depends, not only for the continuance of her present prosperity and independence, but for her existence as one of the foremost sea-faring nations of the world.[18] *

Ihlen was prompt to rebut this rather undiplomatic argument, but the letter of April 1916 was followed four months later by the striking

---

* When this letter was later on disclosed to the Foreign Affairs Committee of the Storting, Castberg—who was a strong supporter of the Allied cause—told Ihlen that the insult to the national dignity should have been met by demanding Findlay's recall.[19]

of a bargain, based on the ability of the British navy to stop the importation to Norway of the wire and other forms of manufactured copper, urgently needed for electrification schemes and domestic uses. Thus Britain was granted first claim on the pyrites from which copper was extracted in return for an equivalent in manufactured copper, including 3,000 tons to be sent from Britain in advance in order to meet the existing acute shortage.

So far, so good: but the English-language version of the agreement, perhaps inadvertently, employed the imprecise term 'pyrites containing copper,'[20] which would cover a grade of pyrites containing too little copper to warrant its extraction but a great deal of the sulphur so urgently needed by the Germans for ammunition making. Ihlen, who promised the German minister as much consideration in this matter as might prove feasible, tried at first to exclude from an export embargo all pyrites containing less than 0·5 per cent of copper, which was well below the commercially accepted standard for cupriferous pyrites; and when British pressure obliged him to extend the embargo to all pyrites, he still authorized export to Germany from a low-grade pyrites mine on Stord which was in German ownership. The dispute was embittered by British delays in supplying Norway with the promised quantity of manufactured copper and by the low price offered for all surplus Norwegian pyrites by the British-controlled Rio Tinto company. In February 1917 Ihlen had to surrender on all points to British *force majeure* (see p. 284), but its exercise was excused to some extent by 'ambiguities which the Norwegian Foreign Ministry in a disastrous act of negligence failed to dispel in advance'.[21]

The Fisheries Agreement, signed earlier in the same August, likewise resulted in British accusations of bad faith. In return for providing the necessary equipment of every kind, Britain was to be permitted to buy up the Norwegian fish supply at prices that would remain valid until the end of the war, but reserved the right to cease purchases at only four weeks notice. The Norwegians, besides retaining what they needed for the home market, were still entitled to export 15 per cent of the catch to other destinations (including Germany), provided the fish in question had not been caught or processed with the help of Allied materials of any kind.

Since the size of the catch could not be calculated in advance, it was eventually agreed to base the excepted amount upon the average of the past five seasons' fishing—a method which proved beneficial to the Germans. Much more serious from the British point of view was the use made of a clause that exempted old stocks from the new arrangement: in early August the director of fisheries had assured the British that these were very small, but for two and a half months large amounts of herring continued to be sent to Germany. There had been some unexpectedly large catches just before the stock-taking, and it was certainly difficult to make an accurate count at each of the many minor fishing centres. But the Norwegian authorities eventually admitted to irregularities in North Norway, for which the offenders were to be prosecuted, and after the war it was ascertained from German sources that trickery went on down to the end of the year—as the British suspected.

What the British were inclined to regard as recalcitrance was in fact justified in Ihlen's eyes by a dangerous deterioration in relations with Germany. Even if they were imperfectly carried out, the two Agreements were plainly detrimental to German interests, so when September brought news of ten Norwegian steamers torpedoed in five days on the route round the North Cape to Archangel it was natural to suppose that this was an act of reprisal. In fact, the main German object had been to interrupt traffic to and from Russia at a point where Allied warships were unlikely to offer any protection; and the crews were given time to take to their boats, though nine men died before they reached the shore. But Norwegian public opinion was naturally incensed against the Germans, while influential shipowners were glad to distract attention from their share of responsibility for the grave risks incurred on dangerous routes, to which they had directed their vessels in search of maximum profits.

On the likely hypothesis that the German submarines had reached the Artic through the Leads, would it not be an appropriate measure for Norway to forbid the use of territorial waters? The government of Sweden had issued such a ban against the belligerents in November 1915, thus impeding the activities of Allied submarines in the Baltic, and in the following July threatened to open fire on any submarine found in Swedish waters which was not surfaced and flying its flag. Moreover, the Allies were now urging the propriety of some change in regulations, so as to make neutral territorial waters less available to submarines than to other vessels belonging to belligerents; an English newspaper article,* published just before the incidents in the Arctic, seemed to imply that Norway might be the first neutral state to adopt such a course. In October the Norwegian press took up the cry, and after much hesitation the government on the 13th issued a decree, which closed the Leads to the submarines of the belligerent powers unless entering on the surface 'because of bad weather or damage in order to save human life'.[22]

The Germans replied one week later by a Note which resembled an ultimatum except for the absence of any time-limit—a fact of which Ihlen took full advantage. The situation was extremely difficult. Altogether the Norwegians lost 143 ships in four autumn months, as compared with twenty in the same period of the preceding year, a high proportion of the losses being sustained on the Arctic route, from which they therefore withdrew their vessels. The Allies accordingly feared that they might surrender completely to the German demands, yet they would have been hard put to it to implement the promises they gave of 'full support'[23] in the event of a German declaration of war. There were no troops available for an expeditionary force to meet a German advance into Norway via Jutland, and the gaining of a forward base at Kristiansand was not considered to justify the diversion of even light naval forces to hold it; a handful of aircraft and ten A.A. guns to protect them against Zeppelins was all that was actually offered to the Norwegians. However, the Germans preferred to let Norway remain neutral as long as reasonable concessions were in view, and may also have been influenced in some degree by the backing that Norway received from the other Scandinavian kingdoms. Ihlen was therefore able to prolong the war of nerves until January, while making as much play as possible with his concessions to Germany over the interpretation of the fishery and copper agreements. The October decree was then amended by an extension of the conditions on which submarines might enter territorial waters, so as to read 'bad weather or damage

* *Morning Post*, 23 Sept.: the Norwegian minister in London reported that it had been planted by the Foreign office.

or in order to save human life';[24] the restrictions were also waived entirely for the category of merchant submarines, used very sporadically to run strategic materials through the Allied blockade. Two further solaces for the Germans were a temporary trade agreement and a loan from the Bank of Norway.

But this coolly considered policy, which placed Norway for some months on bad terms with both groups of belligerents, exposed the nation to severe pressure on the part of the Allies which, though not designed to force it into the war, might easily have produced that result. In early November there was a scare, for which the French minister in Oslo apparently shared the responsibility with his British colleague, that Norwegian merchant shipping was being called home at German request; thereupon the British government authorized a London broker★ to issue a circular to the Norwegian shipping firms, which combined promises of help over reinsurance if their ships remained at sea, with the bluntest of threats: 'The worst mistake you can make is to count on English softheartedness.'[25] The ships continued to sail, but when the dispute over the interpretation of the fish and copper agreements dragged on into December, Findlay's reports came before a new cabinet under Lloyd George, pledged to a more energetic prosecution of the war. His minister of blockade, Lord Robert Cecil, accordingly informed the Norwegian legation in London, 'Here are two Agreements, which must be fulfilled'; and when four days passed without any overture from their side, the decision was finally taken to freeze out the people of Norway. This was announced by the indefatigable Findlay in person, on a Christmas Eve visit to Ihlen at his home 'after the lights had been lit on the Christmas tree'.[26]

An embargo on the export of coal to Norway would have been a drastic step at any time,† but at the turn of the year 1916–17 the towns—which had no alternative fuel supply—were overcrowded because of plentiful employment and the temperature in Oslo happened to fall to −24°C. Restrictions on coal had to be imposed im-

---

★ H. Clarkson & Co., which regularly acted as an intermediary in questions of chartering.

† The British Official Historian describes it as 'perhaps the severest treatment of a friendly power that had been ordered.'[27]

mediately: the school holidays were prolonged, shops shut early, and the winter evenings at home became a misery; even so, three months was the limit to which stocks could be stretched. On 17 February Ihlen capitulated. In doing so he was helped by the completion of his difficult negotiations with the Germans (including the trade agreement already mentioned), while the British showed their eagerness to let bygones be bygones, once they got their way, by sending off ten coal ships immediately. But German policy was in any case now driving the Norwegians into the arms of the British.

THE QUALIFIED NEUTRALITY OF 1917–1918

The German decision to enforce their blockade of the British and French coasts by sinking all ships, including unarmed and clearly marked neutral vessels, without any warning, which took effect on 1 February 1917, for the first time placed Norwegian lives in jeopardy deliberately and on a large scale. It also meant that the tonnage lost now greatly exceeded the possibility of replacement by new building and foreign purchase: indeed, many Norwegians believed that commercial jealousy caused the Germans to treat their marine as a preferential target. Be that as it may, in March 1917 the Norwegian losses amounted to more than one-sixth of the tonnage lost from war causes throughout the world, and in April to more than one-ninth of a much larger total.[28] On May 17th a poet emphasized the defencelessness of all who sailed under the flag of a small neutral which dare not attempt any reprisal:

> Though fired on daily, we never fire back;
> For the sum of our power and the height of our daring
> Is to sink and to die with a true man's bearing.[29]

Norway's monthly losses, then running at more than 100,000 tons, soon fell off, but by the end of the war the total amounted to 820 vessels of 1,235,846 gross tonnage, to which must be added 69 of 60,380 tons disappeared and 22 of 17,747 tons condemned. This was equivalent to 49·3 per cent of the pre-war fleet, a greater percentage loss than was suffered by any of the Allies. As for the crews, 1,162 sailors were known to have perished as a result of German actions, and a further 943 on board the ships that disappeared presumably suffered the same fate.[30]

In June 1917 such disappearances were placed in a lurid light by the discovery of several hundred small bombs in the sealed baggage of a diplomatic courier arriving in Oslo from Germany; these included explosive lumps of coal and other incendiary material for placing in the engine-rooms of ships. The courier, a renegade Finnish Baron von Rautenfels, enjoyed diplomatic immunity, but half a dozen accomplices in different parts of Norway were imprisoned on charges arising out of the scheme; its moving spirit was a legation German official who had a naval training, and it seems to have been aimed at other merchant fleets besides the Norwegian.[31] The result was to intensify the feeling of the average newspaper reader that, though legally committed to the painful pursuit of neutrality, spiritually his country was committed to the cause of the Allies as that of humanity.

Whilst the refusal of the Norwegian shipping firms and their employees to be intimidated by the German submarine campaign had obvious roots in rates of profit, in the sailor's need to earn his livelihood, and in the dependence of the whole nation upon imports, a courage and determination which altogether transcended the economic motive won the gratitude of the British and other Allied peoples, both at the time and long after the war. Less than a month after the termination of the embargo on coal for Norway, the fact that more than fifty Norwegian ships had already sailed for Britain in defiance of the German campaign was rewarded by exemption from the restrictions on clearance from British ports, by which the ships of other neutrals were held back until it was certain that another ship under the same flag was coming in its place. The convoy system too, which for geographical reasons was introduced in the trade to and from Scandinavia as early as April 1917, created a kind of tacit partnership, since British naval units provided the escort across the North Sea—and twice suffered heavy losses from German surface raiders on the crossing—while the Norwegian navy escorted the convoys through territorial waters between Bergen and Utsire lighthouse or other points for arrival and departure. But the most important arrangement for mitigating Norwegian losses was the Tonnage Agreement, approved by the Storting in April and settled in detail by the Shipowners' Association in July 1917. As ships became available, they were chartered to the Allies for the duration of the war. In return Allied ships, which had some means of defence against submarines, replaced the Norwegians in the specially precarious North Sea traffic, and deliveries of coal were guaranteed. The Germans were never able to prove that the Norwegian authorities had connived at this un-neutral arrangement, which was passed off as high-handed requisitioning on the part of the British.[32]

When the unrestricted submarine campaign brought the United States into the war as an associate of the Allies, Norwegian support for the Allied cause was naturally strengthened by the backing of the great democracy, whose citizens and prospective fighting men included so many of their own kith and kin. Moreover, the fall of the Russian Tsardom had removed the reproach that the cause had important backers who were no more democratic than their German opponents. Nevertheless, the impact of the German submarine campaign and the collapse of resistance to German arms on the eastern front, which overshadowed all other military events in 1917, gave Ihlen grounds of prudence as well as equity for struggling to keep open what was left of the Norwegian trade with Germany. This clashed with the views of the British and French, to whom the German submarine outrages appeared to warrant the conclusion succinctly stated by Lloyd George in a letter to Gunnar Knudsen: 'We believe that our interests and those of Norway now coincide'.[33] They were in any case less disposed to respect neutral rights now that the most powerful neutral was joining them, while the Americans themselves once they were in the war were temperamentally disposed to prosecute it by the most direct and efficient methods, so as to get it over quickly. A British mission in Washington pressed for strong action to stop neutrals from trading with Germany, and although President Wilson repeatedly expressed his desire to treat Norway with special liberality, from July 1917 onwards she suffered the effects of a general embargo which was laid on American exports to any European neutral.

Early in that month a Norwegian mission was sent to Washington under Nansen to negotiate a general trade agreement, but this was not signed until the end of the following April. The unconscionable delays were partly due to a clash of temperaments: Nansen, a political opponent of Ihlen whose name had been suggested by the French minister in Oslo, undoubtedly commanded more respect in Washington than any other Norwegian, but his straightforward, rather imperious nature did not fit in with Ihlen's propensity to improvise and procrastinate as a tactical expedient. Delays were also caused by the American Exports Administrative Board, which maintained until mid-November its determination to stop any supplies from reaching Norway until the Norwegians had abandoned all exports to Germany except a small amount of fish. Wilson himself then intervened with three cables to his representative in London, saying finally: 'Inasmuch as we are fighting a war of principle I do not feel that I can consent to demand of Norway what we would not in similar circumstances allow any government to demand of us.'[34] Even then the negotiations encountered many obstacles. The British, who had suspended all their Branch Agreements and were no longer supplying Norway with anything but coal, intervened with warnings that 'Norwegians are past masters in the art of bargaining'.[35] The Americans, after issuing licences for a limited quantity of grain, were encouraged to question the urgency of Norwegian demands because it was not until January 1918 that a reluctant start was made with rationing. But the delays were due above all to Ihlen's desire to placate the Germans, which caused him to continue to haggle until Nansen eventually signed the agreement without his approval. In the end, however, Norway was supplied on an annual basis with her minimum needs in grain, iron and steel, fodder, petroleum, sugar and many other products, ranging from coffee to cottons. In return, the bulk of every Norwegian export was assigned to Allied needs, but Ihlen had retained the right to supply the Germans with 48,000 tons of fish, 8,000 tons of calcium nitrate, and very small annual amounts of five metals.

In terms of trade the Germans accepted a very modest *quid pro quo*, but they attached most importance to the issuing (on 9 March 1918) of a declaration, in which the Norwegian government undertook to maintain its neutrality and 'prevent the use of Norwegian territory as a base by any power whatever.'[36] This seems to imply that Ihlen's fear of some German action that would force Norway into the war, though shared by many Americans, was exaggerated. It also suggests that the Germans had deduced the fact that the Allies now had contingent plans for an advanced base at Kristiansand. In September 1917 the First Sea Lord had informed the British War Cabinet 'that the time might come, but had not yet arrived',[37] and his advisers listed four advantages that might accrue from the stationing of an advanced squadron of the Grand Fleet in such a position. Three months later, the arrival of American capital ships to form an additional fast squadron meant that Kristiansand might have been used for ships whose nationality would have ensured their welcome: as early as 1 March Findlay had reported a remark to this effect by the commander-in-chief of the Norwegian navy.[38]

In the event, the final threat to Norwegian neutrality arose from a different enterprise—the largely American project for closing the route north-about the British Isles to enemy submarines by stretching a 240-mile line of mines from the Orkneys to the Utsire lighthouse, south west of Haugesund. Work was started in March 1918, but although 56,000 American and 15,000 British mines were in position when the war ended, technical difficulties made the effects uncertain. What was certain, however, was that the barrage could never be rendered effective if U-boats still passed safely along the Leads. Accordingly, the British Admiralty would have welcomed a chance of using Stavanger as a base for patrolling the east end of the minefield: but it was laid down that that this must await the occurrence of some German action against Norway that might prepare the way for a friendly occupation. An alternative plan, under consideration in August, was that a British force should lay the mines in territorial waters and risk the chance of Norwegian resistance. But Admiral Beatty, who disliked the whole idea of the barrage on other grounds, took a high moral line against 'the insult to Norway's independence', which fitted in well with the sweeping objection expressed by President Wilson at this juncture against 'any unneutral action towards Norway of any kind'.[39]

Ihlen was therefore able to end the war with a final diplomatic success. On 7 August the British demanded that the Norwegians should either complete the mine barrage themselves or allow the Allies to do so. Ihlen replied by asking for evidence that German violations of the Leads existed to justify this grave step, while King Haakon appealed to his royal brother-in-law not to allow his subjects to commit a crime comparable with the German invasion of Belgium.[40] The foreign minister then circulated an inquiry to belligerent powers, which elicited one admission of an infringement of territorial waters by their submarines from the British, but none (as he expected) from the Germans. This put him in a position to justify the mining of the Leads as a precaution against further British infringements. But when the mining was eventually carried out in early October,* the concessions won from the Americans earlier in the year had just been embodied in a new trade agreement, which made relations with Germany less precarious—even if she was still capable of any effective action against Norway in what proved to be the last month of the war.

THE DOMESTIC SCENE IN THE LATER YEARS OF THE WAR

While the name of Ihlen naturally figures most prominently in the diplomatic exchanges that we have been recounting, Gunnar Knudsen was the strong man who steered the national course and kept the nation sufficiently united. His control of the Storting was helped by the ruthlessness with which he dropped unpopular colleagues. Thus in 1917 he let his minister of justice go, when a storm of opposition was aroused by a bill which would have imposed heavy penalties on publications aimed at 'inciting to hatred against a foreign power or its representative in this realm';[41] the measure was supposed to have been inspired by the British, who certainly did not relish the newspaper polemics directed against their legation by C. J. Hambro (see note, p. 296) at the time of the coal embargo. At the end of the year, too, the premier virtually dismissed his minister

* The Norwegian minefield was laid on 9–13 October between Utsire and Karmöy, but an entry in an official Norwegian publication on their neutrality guard indicates that a submarine might still pass through Karmsund, the passage through the Inner Leads east of Karmöy, on which the port of Haugesund is situated.[42]

of food, who had resisted the introduction of rationing, which was now becoming inevitable; the Labour Party suspected the minister of protecting hoarders, but the ground he stated for preferring 'rationing by price' was that the poorer fishermen and other elements of the population would not be able to buy the ration. Yet Mowinckel had the support of only ten members of the Left Party when he proposed to strengthen the hands of the government by converting it into a coalition. Instead, the Storting was conciliated by the institution of an inter-party committee on foreign affairs, which the government undertook to inform and consult. Unlike other parliamentary committees, this did not make formal reports to the Storting; but it provided a forum for the discussion of major issues of foreign policy, often on the basis of secret information supplied by the government, which took account of its subsequent recommendations.

State control of the economy was still on the increase. In December 1917 a new Concession Law, which excluded all foreign participation except 'under special circumstances',[43] gave the state the right to take over the power stations, which had continued to proliferate, at the end of thirty-five years; meanwhile, it made a preliminary foray into this field by buying up shares in a northern power station and mines. The establishment of a Directorate of Prices did not, indeed, prevent them from rising higher than in Britain or in the other Scandinavian countries. But a state-run whale fishery off the coast of North Norway was set up to eke out the supply of fats; a temporary corn monopoly was introduced; and an attempt was made to compel farmers to devote more of their land to corn-growing with the help of conscripted labour, of which the sole result was alleged to be the substitution of low-quality grain for high-quality hay. Large sums were also expended on food subsidies to restrain the rise in the cost of living, which by 1918 was two and one-third times as high as in 1914 and still moving upwards fast, and on a price guarantee to fishermen. This last was an extremely expensive item which the government could not avoid, when the British in 1917 opted out of the branch agreement which they had taken such pains to exact.

The position of the private citizen still showed many contrasts.

In shipping the high freights corresponded to the risks that were being run, but industrial production declined wherever it depended upon imported raw materials. Nevertheless, the wealth accumulated in the earlier war years continued to seek an outlet, often in unsound developments: share values did not reach their peak until May 1918, and by 1919 the commercial banks had nominal resources five times as great as before the war. In the absence of imports the krone continued to enhance its value in relation to the pound and dollar, so Norwegian interests were encouraged to buy out foreign shareholders, whose part in the ownership of industrial corporations shrank by more than one-half during the wartime boom. Particular significance was attached to the purchase of the huge paper and pulp concern run by the Manchester firm of Kellner–Partington: under its new name of Borregård this became the largest purely Norwegian business, with many small shareholders.

Wage-earners were less fortunate than investors, but as there was full employment throughout the war, workers in agriculture and forestry were able to raise themselves from a shockingly low level. In industry, however, 1918 was the first year in which the rise in wage rates exceeded the rise in the cost of living. In January the introduction of rationing at the rate of about half a pound of bread-flour per day, of sugar per week, and of coffee per month pressed very hardly upon those working-class families that had no rural connections, whereas the moneyed classes could secure butter and other farm produce by paying heavily on the black market. Many workers were also deprived of a customary solace when the sale of spirits was forbidden as a wartime measure at Christmas 1916; this was later extended to the stronger wines and beers, with the edifying result that champagne became for a time the characteristic tipple of the profiteer. But all classes alike suffered the ravages of the worldwide epidemic of Spanish influenza, which reached Norway in April 1918—and resented the long delay before the government allowed the purchase of one half-bottle of brandy per household as being allegedly a sovereign specific.

However, the Labour election programme in 1918 resembled that of the Left Party in advocating Prohibition on a permanent basis, so clearly the primary reasons for the growing unpopularity of the government's supporters must be sought elsewhere. Time and energy had been devoted to nationalist projects which were dear to the heart of the Left Party though remote from the problems of the war, such as the renaming of five dioceses, fifteen counties and 189 districts, whose existing names had been in use for several centuries but bore the taint of Danish origins.[44] Though these changes in nomenclature proved to be generally acceptable, bitter opposition had been aroused by the main language reform of 1917, which aimed at bringing its two forms closer together by prescribed alterations of spelling and inflection in both of them: these affected chiefly the *riksmål*, to the intense indignation of the Conservative Party, who were its sworn champions. Lövland pushed the regulations through the Storting by deliberately curtailing the opportunity for discussion, and although in twenty years' time these usages were no longer contested except by the hard-core philologists of either faction, in 1919 this measure was only saved from repeal by a single vote. The Left Party was also open to graver criticism for the things it had left undone—the failure to tackle war profiteering, for instance, or to curb inflation. But such explanations are scarcely needed to account for the widespread desire for a change, when the same party had ruled for two electoral periods, including four years of unparalleled emergencies and improvisations.

The election results of October 1918 certainly registered such a desire. The Left Party lost one-third of its seats, including all but one of those in town constituencies; with fifty-one members, it was barely ahead of the Conservatives (fifty, of whom ten were nominally of the Liberal Left—see p. 174) and was also opposed by eighteen Labour representatives. The total of 126 seats in the new Storting was made up by three Labour Democrats—which reduced Castberg's personal following by half—three agrarians put forward by *Landmandsforbundet*, and one independent. When it met at New Year, Gunnar Knudsen tendered the resignation of his government, and in the absence of any majority an attempt was made to form an inter-party ministry under Christian Michelsen. This failed, so Knudsen continued in office for a further one and a half years, which nevertheless marked the beginning of a new era in Norwegian politics; for the Left Party, which had established parliamentarism, never again enjoyed a majority in any Norwegian parliament. Its place as the party of the 'little man' was taken over eventually by Labour, whose growth forms a central theme of the next chapter. But the story of the war years may be rounded off now, by a brief reference to the peace settlement, made while Norwegian interests were still in the hands of Knudsen and Ihlen.

NORWAY AND THE PEACE SETTLEMENT

Having preserved her neutral status to the bitter end, Norway had of course no claim to a seat at the conference table, when the victors met to impose a settlement on the defeated powers. In spite of its huge losses, the Norwegian mercantile marine received no share in the confiscated German shipping, and ten years passed before the families of the drowned seamen and the injured survivors received a sum of 6·6 million gold marks as a voluntary compensation payment from the German republican government. But Wedel Jarlsberg, watching the situation from his post in Paris, judged that a territorial reward might be obtainable, if Norway was quick enough in filing some suitable claim, and he is alleged to have received some encouragement from Gunnar Knudsen.[45] With the Russian Empire in a state of dissolution, it might be tempting to reassert a very ancient but nebulous claim to the Murman coast or at least to ask for some minor rectification of the Russo-Norwegian frontier. But this temptation was fortunately resisted, even in the chaotic years before Russia ceded its border with Norway to the new sovereign state of Finland. A less chimerical project was for compensation along the lines suggested by the cession of German colonial territory in east Africa to the Belgians: and if a colony was too much, might not Norway be allowed a trading company there, which would supply raw materials for Norwegian industry, and perhaps preferential treatment for Norwegian settlers, under the protection of the British flag? This idea was acceptable to Ihlen and, apparently, to Lord Balfour; but shortly after he had relinquished the foreign secretaryship to Lord Curzon, the British foreign office decided that it must be dropped.* There remained, however, the third possibility of claiming Spitsbergen (including Bear Island), where Norway already had an established position and where the risk of incurring the hostility of a great power seemed smaller: this had the firm support of the government and the approval of the Storting, expressed in secret session.

The Spitsbergen archipelago has no indigenous population and lies closer to Norway than to any other European country. It was perhaps the 'Svalbard' discovered by the Icelanders in 1194, and in the seventeenth century its ownership was certainly claimed by the Dano-Norwegian Crown, though the claim was disputed by the English and the Dutch, who used it for whaling. But after the decline of that fishery the islands were left to the casual visits of arctic hunters, chiefly Russian or Norwegian, and were still regarded as *terra nullius* as late as 1906, when the exploitation of the coal deposits by J. M. Longyear, the American minerals prospector, and others created a new interest in the question of sovereignty. The result was the holding of three international conferences in Oslo, the third of which had been terminated immediately before the outbreak of the war; it left a commission of three members, who were respectively Norwegian, Swedish, and Russian, to act as a provisional administration. In 1918 Russian wishes could safely be disregarded, as could those of Germany, which had staked a claim to a share in the administration at the treaty of Brest-Litovsk; a Norwegian coal company, formed in December 1916, had bought out the Longyear interests; and British firms on the spot, which clamoured for annexation to the Empire, were of small reputation. Accordingly, Wedel Jarlsberg was able to enlist the support of both Clemenceau and Balfour, and after the signature of peace with Germany the Allied Supreme Council referred the matter to a special sub-commission.

The result was the treaty of 9 February 1920, which awarded Norway the sovereignty over the archipelago, as urged by the American, French, and Danish members of the sub-commission

* Curzon's letter of rejection shows that possible openings in Kenya and Tanganyika had been discussed by Wedel with Lord Milner, who was then colonial secretary.[46]

against the wishes of the Swedes, who proposed that Norway should have only a League of Nations mandate. Certain limitations, including the obligation not to fortify the territory, were imposed, and in economic matters the citizens of all contracting powers were to stand on an equal footing with Norwegians.[47] But the all-important fact for the people of Norway was the extension of the frontiers of the kingdom, after five long centuries during which they had experienced only a series of contractions.

In the long run the change in Norway's general international relationships and obligations, which resulted from the decision to join the League of Nations, was much more momentous. Although the record shows that Norwegians were fully alive to the weaknesses and dangers of the League project, which they tried in some ways to amend, their close relations with Britain and France in the immediate power-war era would have made it difficult for them to abstain from membership for any length of time. Furthermore, their long-standing devotion to the cause of international peace organization had given them an early interest in the discussions from which the League idea in due course emerged.

One of the few concrete results of the second wartime meeting of the three Scandinavian kings, held in November 1917 at Oslo, had been the appointment of a committee in each country to consider the position of the neutral states when the war was over. The Norwegian committee included Hagerup, the former prime minister and a delegate to the Hague Conference of 1907, C. L. Lange the peace expert, and Mowinckel; after discussing President Wilson's proposals, it reported in December 1918 in favour of a system of courts and conferences to preserve the peace of the world, but fought shy of discussing the role of force in the maintenance of such a system. Meanwhile, the growth of public interest had led to the formation in October of an Association for the League of Nations (*Den norske Forening for Nationernes Liga*), which had Nansen as chairman and was supported by Michelsen, Castberg, and other prominent figures. This body formulated a set of principles for the proposed League, which Nansen presented to the public at meetings in London and Paris. Emphasis was laid on protection for minorities, on disarmament, and on international economic regulations, including a code of conditions for seamen. But the main demand was for a League in which all civilized peoples should be entitled to membership, having as its supreme authority a World Congress, in which representation was to be weighted 'according to population and international importance, but in such a way that no nation might have more than, for example, one-twelfth of the total'.[48]

The great powers, however, were not disposed to allow the neutrals any serious influence upon the making of the League Covenant, which was to form an integral part of a peace settlement imposed by the sword. Thirteen neutral states were given a perfunctory two-day hearing in Paris—at such short notice that Wedel Jarlsberg had to deputize for Castberg and the other intended Norwegian representatives—where only two important modifications were achieved, namely, provision for a possible increase in the number of non-permanent members of the League Council and an understanding that instructions from the Council to take part in military sanctions would not be mandatory. The neutral states were subsequently allowed two months from the date of the coming into force of the peace treaty, during which they could apply for foundation membership of the League of Nations.[49]

Opinion in Norway was seriously divided, as we might indeed expect. Gunnar Knudsen and Ihlen, who knew better than any one else how little its traditional adherence to a punctilious neutrality had availed their country from 1914 onwards, wished to accept the League as the best choice available: since Sweden and Denmark were going to join, the alternative for Norway was complete isolation. Nansen carried many idealists with him in a much more optimistic view of the League as presenting great opportunities, so that 'even the smallest state can become a great power'. But there were also idealists on the other side, such as the austere radical publicist, Dr. Scharffenberg, who observed that 'the small states will play the same part in the League as poodles in a den of lions'. The rising young Conservative, C. J. Hambro,* who was destined

---

* 1885–1964. Editor of *Morgenbladet*, 1913–20; member of Storting, 1919–57, and president in 1936–45; Conservative Party chairman, 1928–34 and 1945–54; chairman of the Storting's foreign and constitutional affairs committee, 1925–45. He was president of the League Assembly in 1939 and until the

to be the last president of the League Assembly, was influenced by the refusal of the United States Senate to accept the League, and quoted Henry Cabot Lodge: 'Our first ideal is the fatherland.'[50]

On 4 March 1920 the Storting finally voted by a 100:20 majority in favour of entering the League of Nations, in spite of its obvious shortcomings, as potentially beneficial to Norway and the world. The minority, however, included sixteen votes from the Labour Party, which viewed the world and its future in a very different light. For them the Russian Revolution and not the defeat of Imperial Germany was the central event of the crowded period through which mankind had just passed.

League became defunct in 1946–7. Having paid previous visits to America in 1913 and 1925, he conducted propaganda there in 1940–4 (*I Saw It Happen in Norway*, 1940).

10. Towards a Democratic Society: The Politics of the Inter-War Period

IN THE 1920S AND EARLY 1930S THE NORWEGIAN people came closer perhaps than ever before to that sinister division into 'two nations', which Disraeli had seen to be characteristic of England in the throes of the industrial revolution. While this situation arose partly from causes that affected the rest of western Europe to much the same extent, Norway in the 1920s had three special problems. One was the Prohibition movement, whose workings overthrew three cabinets besides seriously diminishing respect for law. The second was a financial crisis more prolonged than the post-war currency difficulties of Norway's neighbours. The third was the revolutionary spirit that for a time captured the Norwegian Labour movement and rendered it a conspicuous adherent of the Third International. Broadly speaking, these three phenomena developed simultaneously and they reacted upon each other—a fact to be borne in mind in relation to accounts that for the sake of clarity must here be kept separate. In 1928–33 Norway experienced a further crisis, caused mainly by the collapse of world trade, at the end of which the Labour Party—after a long period of divided counsels—returned wholeheartedly to parliamentary evolutionary methods. These they practised in office during the last years before the Second World War, and from the standpoint of 1939 it is possible to review substantial achievements emerging from two decades of restless political changes.

TABLE V[1]

Representation of Parties in the Storting, 1918–1940

	Conservatives (including Moderate Liberals)	Left	Agrarians	Christian People's Party	Social Democrats	Labour	Communists
1918[1]	50	54	3			18	
1921	57	39	17		8	29	
1924	54	36	22		8	24	6
1927	31	31	26			59	3
1930	44	34	25			47	
1933[2]	31	25	23	1		69	
1936[2]	36	23	18	2		70	

1 One independent seat.　　　2 One seat to Social Party (*Samfunnspartiet*).

The election of October 1918 emphasized the disadvantages that had been seen to be inherent in the system of single-member constituencies ever since its introduction twelve years before. Labour had received approximately the same number of votes as the Left Party, but only eighteen seats as compared with the fifty-one of their opponents, whose strength was concentrated in the rural areas. Accordingly, in 1921 a return was made to large constituencies, returning an average of seven members apiece on a basis of proportional representation. At the same time the total number of seats was increased to 150, an arrangement which was maintained for half a century, and the voting age was reduced from twenty-five to twenty-three; moreover, since 1919 receipt of poor relief had ceased to disqualify. A further refinement was introduced to the system in 1930, when parties were allowed to set up common lists of candidates, so as to maximize their chance of securing representation in a constituency where only their united votes were likely to qualify for a seat. But although the new system was much more equitable, it encouraged the distribution of electoral support amongst a multiplicity of parties, so that the parliamentary situation of 1918 was repeated at every election until 1945. No single party ever received an over-all majority; no government could carry out the programme of its party without making concessions to win the support of some other party; each government's tenure of office was more or less precarious.

If the Moderate Liberals (*Frisinnede Venstre*) are regarded as part and parcel of the Right Party, with which they eventually merged, then the Conservative element of the Storting never fell below second place at any election, and in 1936 still stood out as the main rival to the Labour Party. The changes in the middle of the political spectrum were much more significant. Counting the Labour Democrats (renamed in 1921 the Radical People's Party) as Castberg's contribution to the Left Party, the Left was still a declining force, whose representation in the Storting fell at six out of seven consecutive elections. In 1918 it had lost its hold on the towns; from 1921 onwards its hold on the countryside was challenged by a new Agrarian Party, which cared more about farm profits than rural culture and championed especially the interests of the larger farmers, whose organization (*Landmandsforbundet*) had begun to win seats in 1918. Attempts to establish a coalition always broke down because the Left Party feared to lose its identity, which still rested mainly on cultural and national attitudes. As for the Labour movement, its divisions were for a time even deeper than those which drove its opponents apart, and differences of outlook persisted far into the 1930s.

Thus it came about that in fifteen years (1920–35) Norway experienced twelve changes of government: two were occasioned by the death of a premier in office, each of the other ten by some modification of party attitudes in the Storting towards a minority ministry.

1918–27: THE IMPACT OF PROHIBITION

It is arguable that the combination of a severe climate and a monotonous diet made inebriety a problem of special dimensions among the descendants of the Vikings. It is certain that, since the days of Schweigaard, Eilert Sundt, and Marcus Thrane, temperance reform had for long periods been a major object of Norwegian social reform policy. In the Storting its best-known champions were men of the Left Party, which in many districts had close links with the influential Home Mission movement, but the cause was also embraced by the socialist group and by Castberg's Labour Democrats. Strike organizers in 1907, for instance, closed all liquor shops in the vicinity of a labour conflict and posted guards to prevent the strikers from bringing in supplies from outside, and Tranmæl, who was an ardent total abstainer, introduced his principles into the trade union 'opposition programme' of 1912. But what brought matters to a head was the experience of the war years—an increase in drunkenness, the successful adoption of temporary Prohibition measures, and the acceptance of state intervention in many other spheres of life.

In 1918 Sven Aarrestad,* who had been chairman of the Total Abstainers' Society for thirty years and was a prominent figure in

---

* 1850–1942. Elected to the Storting for the third time in 1916; for the previous eight years he had been a county governor, but resigned office after a lawsuit in which a newspaper established his misrepresentation of statistics in temperance propaganda.

the Storting, and L. K. Abrahamsen (see p. 176), who was now minister for social affairs, put through a revised law on local option; this included a questionable provision—it had indeed been questioned and rejected in the 1890s—by which a popular vote against liquor sales was mandatory, but a similar vote in favour reversible at the discretion of the local council. After the election had put his government in a minority, Gunnar Knudsen dropped Abrahamsen as a political liability, and hesitated to base a permanent Prohibition law upon a Storting vote in which he would require the support of Labour. On the other hand, the moment was opportune for action, since the two years of temporary Prohibition had prevented the accumulation of liquor stocks. He therefore resorted to the democratic device of a referendum, which recalled the appeal to the people in 1905 and which had the approval of the Conservatives, who believed that public opinion would support their stand on behalf of public liberties—and private profits.

In October 1919 about two-thirds of the electorate went to the polls and the result was nearly 5 to 3 in favour of a permanent ban on spirits and strong wines; the Prohibitionists had an over-all majority in every main region except East Norway, but their strength lay in the rural districts rather than the towns[2] and they had no hold on Oslo. However, in the following May Gunnar Knudsen's long reign was brought to an end over a proposal to increase expenditure on roads by the modest sum of kr. 1 million. His refusal to defer to the wishes of a Storting committee was motivated in part at least by his conviction that the time had come to economize in anticipation of a trade slump; but he had been accustomed to rule in much easier circumstances, when his position could not be shaken by a tactical combination of the Right with Labour. Thus it fell to his successor, Otto Halvorsen,* a respected Conservative of moderate abilities, to face the repercussions of the plebiscite upon foreign trade. The French had threatened reprisals on a previous occasion in 1909, and Abrahamsen's successor in office, Paal

---

* 1872–1923. A prominent Oslo lawyer and, in the last year of his life, vice-chairman of a bank in grave difficulties. As leader of his party from 1919, he strengthened its position in the Storting; prime minister, June 1920–June 1921 and March–May 1923.

Berg (see note, p. 383) had warned the public before it made its decision that concessions to foreign demands might be unavoidable.

In April 1921 a delegation headed by Wedel Jarlsberg could only secure a new trade treaty with France by agreeing to a yearly importation of 400,000 litres of French brandy; whatever could not be used for medicinal or technical purposes would be a dead loss. In addition, the minimum alcoholic content required for 'strong wine' (*hetvin*) to be denied admission was raised from 12 to 14 per cent. Next there was a bitter contest with the authorities in Spain, who imposed a penal tariff on Norwegian klipfish, which had already lost much of its market during the war. At this stage the Conservative government, whose members had never wanted Prohibition, was turned out by the Left Party as being insufficiently interested in the negotiations.

The new premier, Otto Blehr (see note, p. 153) was a veteran politician of seventy-four. His government induced the Storting to make Prohibition permanent by a law which required the president's casting vote. But Blehr had no success with the Spaniards: in order to sell their fish, the Norwegians must agree to admit 450,000 litres of strong wines, which the Spaniards subsequently raised to 500,000 litres. Thereupon the Portuguese, who were accustomed to a larger share of the Norwegian wine market than the Spanish, demanded the annual admission of 850,000 litres. At this juncture the Blehr ministry was defeated by a big majority, and the returning Conservatives settled the matter by exempting strong wines entirely from the Prohibition. Halvorsen's second government was terminated after a few weeks by his death; his successor was his finance minister, Abraham Berge (see note, p. 307), whose candidature had been strongly backed by Christian Michelsen. Berge decided to entrust the sale and distribution of all classes of wine to a State Wine Monopoly, with high prices, a restricted choice of wares, and no advertisements; all the same, the ban on alcoholic liquor—which had never applied to the weaker Norwegian beers—was now obviously compromised.

The internal problems, however, gave Prohibition its *coup de grâce*. Following the precedent of the Spanish influenza epidemic of 1918, doctors and veterinary surgeons became involved in a considerable traffic in kr. 5 prescriptions for a restorative to man or beast; one physician issued them at the rate of 160 per working day, and it was not until 1923 that the medical profession agreed to their being brought under effective legal control. It was of course much harder to control smugglers, who from 1921 onwards organized a big trade in brandy and a special 90-per-cent alcohol, mainly from Baltic ports. The Oslofiord was the chief centre of distribution, but the coastline provided innumerable vantage points, where converted fishing smacks and eventually sea-going motor boats with powerful engines could operate with impunity. In 1923 the quantity confiscated amounted to 600,000 litres and smuggling cases totalled about 1,000. How much alcohol and how many smugglers escaped detection it is impossible to say, but the authorities had to arm the customs launches, which had many skirmishes with smuggling gangs. But yet a third way of circumventing the law was cheaper and on the whole less readily detected, namely the illicit distillation of spirits for home use or for the benefit of a restricted circle. In 1926 2,298 cases were recorded, nearly ten times as many as there had been only three years previously.

The situation deteriorated fast. The sale of beer, of table wine, and (from 1923) of strong wine increased to such an extent that, when the illegal consumption is included, the amount of alcohol consumed per head may well have been greater than before Prohibition was introduced.[3] From the angle of public health, the effects of injurious substitute ingredients had to be weighed against the apparent decrease of drunkenness. But, in Norway as elsewhere, the most serious adverse effect of Prohibition upon the community was through the conversion of normally law-abiding citizens to the view that a law that interfered with their private liberties was a bad law, and that a bad law need not be obeyed. It was therefore unfortunate that in 1924 Berge's Conservative government based its proposals for repeal upon the morally less adequate grounds that duties on spirits were needed to help to balance the Budget. When he proposed to take action accordingly without further reference to the electorate, he was defeated in the Storting, and the next government of the Left Party allowed two more years to elapse before deciding to hold a second referendum. A considerably larger vote than before gave a majority—about 5 : 4—against Prohibition, which was ended by law in April 1927.

Although the reversal of opinion was not overwhelming, the temperance advocates never tried again and their organized membership, which in 1919 was about 10 per cent of the entire population, dwindled to 5 per cent. The abuse of strong drink remained a serious social problem in many parts of Norway, but compulsory puritanism made a diminishing appeal.

1918–27: THE IMPACT OF CREDIT PROBLEMS

When the Left Party returned to office in 1924, its undisputed leader was J. L. Mowinckel,* who headed three governments during the next eleven years. On each occasion he was also foreign minister, and in comparison with the other Norwegian premiers of this period, he was very active on the international scene. In domestic affairs he was concerned above all with problems of credit and public finance, which had become increasingly grave every year since the collapse of trade in the autumn of 1920.

The First World War had made Norway, perhaps for the first time in its history, a creditor nation; this was no doubt one reason why the Prohibitionists had been prepared to risk the displeasure of some important trading partners. Between 1913 and 1919 a debt to foreign countries of kr. 800–850 million had been converted to a credit balance of kr. 1,360 million.[4] But the new-found wealth was quickly used to obtain the imports that had so long been unobtainable, and although Norwegian exports and especially shipping services were in strong demand, it took only two years to tip the balance once more in the opposite direction. By that time world trade was entering upon a depression, the delayed effect of a war which had greatly damaged the multilateral trade network; in Norway the fall in prices began a few months later than elsewhere, but the woodworking industries were soon in grave difficulties,

---

* 1870–1943. Founded a successful shipping firm in Bergen after two years in London (1891–3) and a spell in Michelsen's office; in 1905, a republican mayor. Foreign minister in 1922–3 and in each of his own cabinets; in 1940–2, minister without portfolio, attached to the Stockholm legation. An excellent speaker and debater.

freight rates fell catastrophically, and by the end of 1921 one-third of the mercantile marine was laid up. By 1924 the adverse balance of payments amounted to kr. 1,600 million, while in relation to population of working age the gross national product declined in 1920–6 by 0·6 per cent per annum.[5]

The Norwegian currency, which in 1919 had stood well above par, had now lost ground in relation both to the gold dollar and to the pound sterling; if it had been stabilized quickly at some lower value, the ensuing crisis of confidence might have been sharp but mercifully short. A quite different course was recommended to Mowinckel by Nicolai Rygg, director of the Bank of Norway since 1920, who exercised great authority over successive short-lived minority governments and initially had the backing of his fellow economic experts. Rygg was a moralist, who believed implicitly that debts should be paid in terms of the financial conditions stated on the face of the contract: a krone was a krone, with a gold equivalent fixed in 1875. He was also a patriot, to whom the status of the currency was an object of national pride—an attitude which he made perhaps imprudently clear in November 1923, when the distinguished Swedish economist, Gustaf Cassel, advised an Oslo audience that devaluation might well be appropriate to the case of Norway, though not to that of Sweden.[6] For a time Rygg allowed the krone to swing: in 1921, for instance, it ranged between 19·55 and 31·75 to the £. Even in 1926, when Britain (like Sweden) had returned to gold, he refused to listen to the advice of a currency commission under Gunnar Jahn,* which was endorsed by all the university economists;[7] this would have fixed the krone at the then prevailing rate of 24 to the £. Rygg still aimed at an eventual return to pre-war parity, although he must have been aware that his intentions were arousing the interest of currency speculators, in New York and later in Amsterdam.

The currency commission drew attention to another factor which

* 1883–1971. Succeeded Rygg as head of the Central Statistical Office, 1920–45; finance minister under Mowinckel, 1934–5. He was a member of the Administrative Council in 1940 and a leading figure in the resistance movement until his arrest in 1944; finance minister in the coalition government, 1945; Director of the Bank of Norway, 1946–54.

increased the precariousness of Norway's position, namely the unsatisfactory state of the public finances. Many wartime expenses had been concealed from the Storting (see p. 269), which had therefore felt no need to raise heavy taxes during the prosperous years, when they would have served also to curb inflation. Scrutiny of the records from 1913/14 to 1924/5 revealed that an over-all credit balance of kr. 150 million should be corrected to a deficit of kr. 830 million—a revelation which goes far to justify the verdict of a Norwegian economist, who wrote in 1938: 'The shortcomings in public finances in the years of the World War provide the darkest pages in the history of Norwegian democracy.'[8]

One result was to encourage strict economy in national expenditure, a policy which for many years found favour with the Storting and which had far-reaching effects—for instance on defence. In 1926 both the Conservatives and the Agrarians demanded reductions in the Budget of the Mowinckel government: their proposals were defeated separately, but together they provided a 'negative majority', which caused the government to resign. The Conservatives took office again under a Trondheim merchant, Ivar Lykke,* whose stringent economies at the expense of the needy rendered the 1927 election a signal failure for his party and correspondingly successful for Labour.

But Mowinckel and Lykke alike were faced by a long series of financial disasters, which the policy of deflation continued to intensify. Local authorities, for instance, had increased their debts since 1913/14 from kr. 209 million to kr. 1,500 million, about half of which represented expenditure on electricity undertakings. So many of them were unable to meet their obligations that in 1923 a law was passed under which thirty-nine such authorities, including several towns, were placed under direct government supervision.[9] Their troubles shook the credit of the local savings banks from which they had borrowed: in eight years thirty-two asked for public help, of which only five remained solvent.

---

* 1872–1949. Became premier after the breakdown of negotiations for a coalition government under Nansen; chairman of trade treaty delegation to the United Kingdom, 1932; Conservative member of the Storting Presidency during negotiations with the Germans in the summer of 1940.

The commercial banks fared even worse. Their numbers had expanded in 1913–19 from 116 to 198, mostly based on a capital which was wholly incommensurate with their appetite for speculative enterprises, not a few of which were headed by their own directors. But if they were allowed to fail, innocent investors suffered, employment diminished, and one bankruptcy precipitated another. In 1921 thirty-eight tottering banks were shored up by Rygg; in 1922 kr. 100 million was advanced to two of the largest concerns, the state providing two-thirds and the Bank of Norway most of the rest; and in 1923 any bank in trouble was empowered to postpone liquidation by placing itself under the administration of the Bank of Norway. But the climax was reached when the newest of the major Oslo banks, *Handelsbanken*, which had been kept going for a time by loans from the Storting and other sources, obtained a further unauthorized loan through the Conservative ministry of Abraham Berge* under threat of closure within 48 hours. This came to light soon after he had left office, whereupon the Left and Labour parties launched an impeachment against Berge and six of his colleagues, on the ground that only the Storting was constitutionally entitled to raise any loan 'on the credit of the realm'.[10] In 1927 a protracted investigation ended in an acquittal, but the court was by no means unanimous in its rather complicated findings, and on one charge of concealment Berge only escaped conviction because of the length of time that had elapsed.

One-half of the commercial banks existing in 1919 finally disappeared; the total bank loss was computed at not less than kr. 2,075 million (including about one-eighth in savings banks); and the state lost about kr. 100 million out of the kr. 123 million which it had devoted to their support. The losses incurred by shareholders and depositors in commercial banks amounted to about kr. 80 million, but the disclosures in the impeachment strengthened the view that the government had tried hard to protect the interests of the rentier class.

The position of the rural population, especially in the big valleys

---

* 1851–1936. Finance minister under Michelsen, 1906–7, and in 1909 a founder of the Moderate Liberal Party; finance minister again in 1910–12, and during his premiership, 1923–4. The loan, though approved by his fellow ministers,

of eastern Norway, was extremely difficult, for the prices of what they had to sell, including their timber, fell farther than that of the goods which the farm household required to buy. Mowinckel's minister of agriculture preached the gospel of self-help: in his view the efficient farmer ought to be able to compete with falling prices. The Conservatives, on the other hand, were induced by the Agrarian Party in 1926 to pass a corn law: this required importers of corn also to buy home-grown corn at an enhanced price, which included a 'premium for eating' in the shape of a payment to producers on the quantity consumed by their own households. But Norwegian farmers depended to a greater extent on the sale of dairy produce, not only for what they were accustomed to buy from the towns, but also for their mortgage payments, much money having been borrowed in the good times of the war for the purchase of additional land and equipment and even for stocks and shares. Thus the corn law was only a palliative for a rapidly worsening situation. When farmers failed to keep up their payments, the farms were auctioned over their heads—in 1923 2,000, four years later almost 3,000. The most unfortunate group of all were the small-holders, who had borrowed money to buy their holdings on the strength of by-employment in forestry or labour on the larger farms; in eastern Norway half of them had a debt amounting to 75 per cent of the total value of their property, as compared with the national average of 45 per cent. Forest and farm wages were forced down remorselessly by employers who themselves had little to spare: it was significant that a trade union, established in 1927 for forest and farm workers, grew quickly into the largest union in Norway.

As for the industrial workers, Rygg might be justified in proclaiming the need for deflation 'in order that our economy may be fully competitive',[11] and the fall in prices more than compensated the fall in cash earnings for fully employed workers in most major industries. But it is human nature to resent, and if possible resist, any apparent diminution in the reward of labour, and even the most prosperous worker was alive to the growth of unemployment—some of it due to rationalization, especially in the big export trades, and

lacked the formal approval of the Cabinet Council (attended by the king) as well as that of the Storting.

TABLE VI[12]

Conditions in Agriculture, 1919–1939

	total number of forced auctions of rural landed property	net income in kroner per acre, based on select farms of 25–50 acres under cultivation	smallholdings (less than 12½ acres under cultivation)	total number of farms
1917		141·84	201,501	246,634
1918		213·44		
1919		230·08		
1920	471	106·80		
1921	1,125	87·16		
1922	1,740	17·24		
1923	2,073	17·52		
1924	2,176	66·52		
1925	1,987	87·12		
1926	2,631	18·88		
1927	2,940	0·76		
1928	3,265	26·44		
1929	3,987	28·92	240,462	298,360
1930		30·12		
1931	5,862	19·92		
1932	6,568	5·28		
1933	6,090	12·56		
1934	4,468	12·64		
1935	3,757	34·20		
1936	4,306	48·80		
1937	2,630	47·84		
1938	1,349	56·88		
1939	1,228	38·88	258,562	328,181

much to the big annual influx of young people to the labour market, for whom emigration no longer supplied a ready alternative. By 1927 one trade unionist in four was out of work, and the proportion was almost certainly higher among the unorganized. Moreover, chronic discontent among industrial workers was stimulated by major changes on the political side of the Norwegian Labour movement.

1918-27: THE IMPACT OF REVOLUTIONARY LABOUR

In 1914–18 the Labour movement in neutral Norway had not been exposed to the same urgent appeals for national unity as had for a time at least stifled the voice of class war among the peoples of the belligerent powers. In 1915 the party conference criticized its Storting representatives because they had denied the anti-militarist principle by supporting the neutrality guard, and the youth movement authorized the Swedish delegates to act on its behalf at the Zimmerwald conference against 'imperialist war'. The Labour vote increased by 6·5 per cent in the election of that autumn, and as prices continued to rise faster than wages, in June 1917 the trade union federation organized a one-day general strike to demand state control both of production and of prices. The latter were then controlled to some extent through subsidies amounting to just over one-half of the sums proposed by the unions. The families that were hardest hit were already receiving some special public relief, especially where the local government was in Labour hands, as in Oslo; but in April 1918 the Statistical Office still reported a ratio between wages and prices which 'implies a miserable existence for many of the most unfavourably situated workers and employees, and for the great majority of our population constant economic worries and restrictions on every side'.[13]

Meanwhile, the revolutions in Russia had stimulated more far-reaching demands. At New Year 1918 Councils of Workers, modelled on the soviets, began to appear both in separate workplaces and on a district basis. Councils of Soldiers followed, both in Trondheim and Oslo, and in March a conference of delegates, which was addressed by Tranmæl, resolved 'That the entire social and administrative authority shall be placed in the hands of the Councils.'[14] Their concern, however, was with equitable distribution rather than problems of production, so interest declined as soon as the agreement negotiated by Nansen in America made shortages less acute.

Disappointment over the limited effectiveness of the trade-union action in June and excitement over the example now set by the Russians combined to give Tranmæl and his friends a much bigger opportunity at the Labour Party Conference, held a little later in the eventful month of March 1918. They had long taught that political democracy was an illusion; now at last the conference endorsed their views, by a majority of 159 to 126.

As a revolutionary class-war party, social democracy cannot recognize the right of the propertied classes to the economic exploitation and oppression of the working class, even if that exploitation and oppression are based upon a majority among the representatives of the people. The Norwegian Labour Party must therefore reserve for itself the right to resort to revolutionary mass action in the struggle for the economic emancipation of the working class.[15]

The conference had already voted an invitation to the Soviet minister in Stockholm and representatives of the Zimmerwald movement of 1915, to which it declared its adherence; and a further bridge-burning measure, which was passed by a large majority, demanded that the Christian religion should be deleted from the school curriculum.

Holtermann Knudsen thereupon resigned the chairmanship, which he had first held in 1889, and the trade-union leader Ole Lian the vice-chairmanship; their places were taken by Kyrre Grepp and Emil Stang, a brilliant lawyer whose father and grandfather had been Conservative premiers. Tranmæl, who always shunned the limelight, became party secretary and in 1921 editor of *Social-Demokraten*, which under its new name of *Arbeiderbladet* (1923) remained his mouthpiece—except during the German occupation—for a quarter of a century. But although the 'tranmælites' henceforth predominated, there was no immediate breach with the veterans of the movement; thus O. Lian, who had been chairman of the trade union federation since 1907, gradually brought his members to accept the new line, so that in 1923 Norway withdrew from the International Federation of Trade Unions, which had been revived in 1919 and was in opposition to the labour unions on the Russian model.

In the relaxed atmosphere at the close of the war, both the government and the employers chose the path of conciliation. Real wages, which in 1918 had for the first time risen above the level of 1914, rose more rapidly during the next two years, and the enactment of an eight-hour day was followed by the concession of the right to twelve days' annual paid holiday. But as soon as the trade boom collapsed in 1920, the inevitable friction between employer and employee was made much worse by the belief that each industrial dispute had a partly political basis, as being fomented by workers who looked to direct action for the eventual overthrow of the capitalist state.

TABLE VII[16]

Labour in Industry, 1919–1939

	number of stoppages of work	workers involved (in thousands)	days lost (in thousands)	membership of trade union federation	percentage of trade unionists unemployed	real wages in industry (1900 = 1·00)
1919				143,926	1·6	1·44
1920				142,642	2·3	1·58
1921	89	154	3,584	95,965	17·6	1·76
1922	26	2	91	83,640	17·1	1·71
1923	57	25	796	85,599	10·6	1·58
1924	61	63	5,152	92,764	8·5*	1·55
1925	84	14	667	95,931	13·2	1·65
1926	113	51	2,204	93,134	24·3	1·72
1927	96	22	1,374	94,154	25·4	1·67
1928	63	8	364	106,182	19·1	1·69
1929	73	5	197	127,017	15·4	1·78
1930	94	5	240	139,591	16·6	1·84
1931	82	60	7,586	144,595	22·3	1·85
1932	91	6	394	153,374	30·8	1·93
1933	93	6	364	157,524	33·4	1·93
1934	85	6	235	172,513	30·7	1·93
1935	103	4	168	224,340	25·3	1·89
1936	175	15	396	276,992	18·8	1·90
1937	195	29	1,014	323,156	20·0	1·90
1938	248	24	567	344,795	22·0	2·03
1939	81	16	860	356,796	18·3	2·03

* Disturbed industrial conditions made the figure very uncertain.

Between 1919 and 1939 a million days' work was the average yearly loss through industrial stoppages, with effects which were intensified by its concentration into a few short periods: this is ten times as much as in 1945–65, when the scale of Norwegian industry was considerably greater.

In December 1920 a sixteen-day railway strike marked the fact that unionism had now spread to state concerns; the railwaymen's case was that a wage rise granted only twelve months before had been more than swallowed up by rising prices, but the government retorted that the railways were running at a loss and the men gained nothing. Next spring the trade union federation called a major strike of its members to support the seamen's resistance to a one-third cut in their wages. Trotsky hopefully termed it a general strike,[17] and some participants certainly cherished revolutionary expectations. Since the funds could not supply strike pay for large numbers, the crisis lasted only a fortnight, during which troops were called in and the police had some ugly clashes with crowds of workers molesting strike-breakers on the water front. A strike-breaking organization, modelled on the German *Technische Nothilfe*, the Community Help (*Samfunnshjelpen*), came into prominence, one of its avowed objects being to take action 'when a political object is sought by means of a general cessation of work'.[18] The strike ended in a compromise for the seamen, whose pay was reduced by one-sixth instead of one-third, but the workers were bitterly disappointed: one in three quitted the federation, which did not recover for a decade.

Meanwhile, the class struggle was emphasized by the adherence of the Norwegian Labour Party to the Communist Third International or Comintern, an action separating it from the Swedish and Danish Parties, to which it had owed so much of its inspiration, and from all the pre-war socialist parties outside the Russian empire. Stang was present as an observer at the initiating congress in Moscow in March 1919, and from 1921 O. A. Scheflo,* who was second only to Tranmæl in the arts of revolutionary journalism, doubled the roles of labour leader in the Storting and member of the executive committee of the Comintern. At the very outset the post-war situation in Germany and the Russian border states was so revolutionary that the Norwegians could envisage themselves helping to direct a world movement of rapidly growing dimensions. But by July 1920 the Russian leaders had to issue directives to nearly forty delegations for keeping the revolutionary spirit alive in much less favourable circumstances. Such was the origin of the twenty-one 'Moscow Theses'. In the Norwegian view they laid a somewhat unwelcome emphasis on the techniques of deception and direct preparations for the use of violence, while the doctrine of the superior value of the élite party of dedicated individuals jarred upon the leaders of a

---

* 1883–1943. A carter's son who had been to sea; an early associate of Tranmæl in Trondheim; editor of *Social-Demokraten*, 1918–21; the main leader of the Norwegian Communist Party, 1921–8.

movement which made its appeal to the masses of the Norwegian electorate and enjoyed the collective support of trade unions. The biggest stumbling-block, however, was the demand in the Theses for a centralized regime to be directed from Moscow, with the Comintern providing a General Staff to issue orders for party members in each country to execute without question.

The nationalist and individualist feelings that characterized even socialist Norwegians were immediately offended, and in March 1921 a small group of moderates, headed by the influential Oslo politician, Magnus Nilssen,* seceded to form their own Social Democratic Party. But for another two years the main body allowed its admiration for Soviet Russia, as the one state in which socialism had triumphed, to outweigh its resentment against instructions from the Comintern which often revealed complete ignorance of Norwegian conditions. The Comintern on its part was acutely aware that the Norwegians were a solid band amidst its many phantom armies, and therefore tried hard to find a way of compromise. At the outset a whole series of special reservations were allowed by Zinoviev at a meeting in Halle with Grepp, Tranmæl, and Scheflo. Later on, when Tranmæl refused to manoeuvre to the right in accordance with the exigencies of Lenin's New Economic Plan, Radek was sent to Norway and obtained unanimous support from the national committee in January 1923 for the proposal that the party should remain in the Comintern 'as an independent section'. But tireless controversialists, including Tranmæl, pursued the matter further by drawing up a document, the 'Kristiania Proposal', which drew a clear distinction between the authority of the Comintern in international actions and that of the national party and trade union movement in local actions. Even then Bukharin in person attended the party congress in Norway in February with a view to offering further tactical concessions, which Scheflo advised him were unnecessary. Scheflo was very nearly right, for the Proposal only passed by the narrow margin of 94 to 92. However, when most of the year 1923 had been spent in mutual recriminations and unsuccessful appeals for obedience, a

---

* 1871–1947. A journeyman goldsmith, who started his own business in 1897; Labour Party secretary, 1901; member of Storting, 1906–21 and 1927–45; minister of labour, 1928; Storting vice-president, 1935–40.

special congress in November rejected a Comintern ultimatum by a decisive majority—169:103. Scheflo, Stang, and a body of members, in which the youth movement was strongly represented, then withdrew to the strains of the Red Flag and formed a separate Communist Party.

An unedifying dispute followed over the ownership of party funds and premises, with Labour in the ascendancy in the capital and the Communists in Bergen and Trondheim; in 1925 the trade union federation advised unions to abandon collective party membership, in order to avoid disputes about the party to be supported. The theoretical arguments arising out of the Moscow Theses had appealed chiefly to dialecticians, such as Tranmæl or the Marxist historian, Edvard Bull, who now became the Labour Party's vice-chairman, and to a coterie of university students and younger graduates which centred round the periodical *Mot Dag* ('Towards Daybreak').* One practical result, however, was clear: the Labour movement had, for the time being at any rate, sacrificed its effectiveness in the Storting. In 1921 its percentage of the votes cast at the election had been 30·5, which under proportional representation gave thirty-seven seats, but these were divided between the Labour and Social Democratic parties. Three years later, the percentage rose to 33·3, which gave thirty-eight seats: the Social Democrats had eight, as before, but since six seats went to the Communists, the main Labour Party was reduced by five.

Confronted by declining trade and mounting unemployment, the weakened Labour Party in the Storting supported compulsory arbitration, and some protection was gained for the workers through arbitral awards which provided for wage rates to be adjusted to the cost of living. At the close of 1923, however, an embittered dispute arose from this very cause in the iron industry, where the workers struck illegally against a valid wage agreement: they claimed that a

* Edited from 1922 onwards by Erling Falk (1887–1940), who had earlier combined a career as a cost accountant in Chicago with the maintenance of close contacts in the I.W.W. He aroused extraordinary devotion in many able students, who later became prominent in Norwegian public life. The future German Chancellor, Willy Brandt, as a youthful refugee from the Nazis, had some temporary association with the movement, which he later numbered among 'ivory towers where intellectual cliques practise spiritual inbreeding'.[19]

fall in the cost of living, which had affected their wages adversely, should have been disregarded because it was occasioned by changes in taxation and not in prices. This became entangled with a strike of harbour workers and sympathetic actions on both sides, involving a total of about 75,000 men—or about half as many as in the big strike of 1921. The contest lasted more than six months, and in the end rising prices came to the rescue of the iron-workers, who received considerably higher cash wages under their next periodical agreement. But the strike committee in Oslo had been under the control of Communists, who made a determined attempt to give the stamp of revolution to their clashes with strike-breakers and other minor disorders.

During the period of deflation that followed, employers resorted readily to lock-outs and workers felt themselves to be victimized when they submitted to wage reductions, in spite of an increase in purchasing power. At the same time, the use of troops to protect strike-breakers strengthened the long-standing objection to compulsory military service, which they claimed existed for the defence, not of the nation but of the capitalist system. In 1924–5 an attempt was made to organize resistance against training, which resulted in prison sentences for Tranmæl and other leaders; about fifty recruits obeyed the strike call, which the party decided for tactical reasons to abandon. But the use of the law courts to suppress this and other illegalities, such as incitement to acts of violence during trade disputes, encouraged the workers to view the courts as mere instruments of class justice. They were also inclined to see the Storting in the same light, when Michelsen and Nansen promoted the 'League of the Fatherland' (*Fedrelandslaget*), which from 1925 onwards tried to rally the 'national' elements in the electorate against the 'international' socialist menace. In 1927 this dangerous state of feeling was exacerbated by the enactment of the 'Penal Laws' (*tukthuslovene*), one of which tried to protect strike-breakers against social pressure by making it an offence, punishable by up to three years imprisonment, even to publish their names; the other placed the funds of a union in jeopardy, unless it could prove that it had done its best to prevent any illegal stoppage occurring in the industry with which it was concerned.

In these circumstances Labour clearly needed to act more effectively on the political plane, so in January 1927 its two parties
sought strength in nominal unity. The terms of settlement provided
for the abandonment both of the Comintern and of the rival Socialist
International (L.S.I.), to which the Norwegian Social Democrats had
adhered in 1923; the use of force was renounced except in self-
defence; and the ultimate goal was defined with studious vagueness
as 'To found upon the basis of labour the constitution and organs
that correspond to the new era'.[20] The compromise suited both sides,
since each believed that its views would ultimately prevail. Nilssen
became vice-chairman of the reunited Labour Party, but its chairman, the youthful Oscar Torp (see note, p. 389), and its leading
publicist, Tranmæl, kept it sufficiently far to the left for a good many
Communists also to be induced to join. The intellectuals of *Mot
Dag*, for example, forsook Communism in 1928, though it took
another eight years for them to dissolve their separate organization
and rejoin the Labour Party—without their leader—as individuals.
Scheflo rejoined in 1928 but continued to campaign for the dictatorship of the proletariat, while Stang abandoned politics altogether:
from 1930 to 1945 Communism was unrepresented in the Storting.

1927–1933: CRISIS CONTINUED

The election held in the autumn of 1927, in which the Communist
Party still retained 4 per cent of votes and three seats, already
marked the re-emergence of Labour as a strong parliamentary force.
While the bigger farmers demonstrated their hostility to the credit
and currency policy of the other middle-class parties by increased
support for the Agrarians, the smaller farmers and farm labourers
voted heavily for Labour. With fifty-nine seats Labour became the
largest party in the Storting, a position which it retained in 1972,
still, but one which was then a novelty creating immediate alarm
among the bourgeoisie. The defeated Conservative premier, Lykke,
advised the king that his most appropriate successor would be the
Agrarian leader,* but the efforts of the latter to form a coalition and

* J. E. Mellbye (1866–1954), a gentleman farmer who had long been chairman
of *Landmandsforbundet* and was minister of agriculture in 1904–5.

keep Labour out broke down through the opposition of Mowinckel, who feared that the Left Party might be swallowed up. King Haakon then made his first decisive intervention in the play of party politics which he had watched for so long, by observing that 'the Communists were also his subjects' and in effect inviting Labour to take office.

Although the majority in the Storting was plainly hostile, it seemed important to the Labour Party not to risk disappointing a multitude of new supporters by refusing any opportunity to influence events. A government was formed under Christopher Hornsrud (see note, p. 157), who had made his mark a quarter of a century before, when he indicated the party to renounce the Marxist principle of collective ownership of the land in favour of its expropriation for the rural population. The other members of the cabinet represented both wings of the party, but the intellectual driving force was the foreign minister, Professor Edvard Bull, who drew up the policy declaration for the government; this challenged the middle-class parties by announcing its intention 'to be guided in all its actions by regard for the interests of the working class and all labouring people'.[21]

A financial crisis loomed up immediately, although the party had announced after the election that it did not intend to devalue the krone, which had by this time climbed to parity. Nevertheless, the foreign speculators already mentioned and many nervous native investors began a flight into other currencies, which brought two of the three biggest banks (*Creditbanken* and *Bergens Privatbank*) into imminent danger of collapse. Since the Bank of Norway had only kr. 20 million left in hand, Rygg proposed a new scheme to collect supporting funds from other banks. This required a government guarantee, which was refused on general socialist principles; whereupon, instead of working for a compromise with the government, Rygg turned to Mowinckel, who agreed to restore public confidence by organizing an adverse vote in the Storting. Thus Norway's first Labour ministry was overthrown after only eighteen days (28 January–15 February 1928); its positive achievements amounted to little more than the release from prison of a few alleged victims of class injustice, including a certain Einar Gerhardsen.

Mowinckel's new government saved the threatened banks with the help of an English credit of £3 million, and in May the krone was restored by law to pre-war gold value. A month later a state Corn Monopoly was set up, which permanently solved one vexed economic problem by a system which recouped the native corn-grower partly from the tax on imports; the Monopoly was also made responsible for maintaining emergency stocks, so that Norway could survive at least a year of blockade. An important land law was also passed by the Left Party, which provided funds and powers of expropriation for the establishment of new small-holdings and the enlargement of existing ones so as to make them more viable. When the election came round in 1930, the bourgeois parties employed the new device of common lists (see p. 299) in a concerted effort against the Labour Party. It is not unlikely that they received unintended assistance—particularly in securing record support from women voters who did not usually go to the polls—from the Labour Party's apparent return to the class war. Its election manifesto now omitted a significant phrase (here italicized) from the previously proclaimed ambition 'To capture the entire working people *and therewith the majority of the people* for its socialistic principles'.[22] Labour lost twelve of its fifty-nine seats, and the Communists all their remaining three.

Norway was now experiencing the effects of the world crisis, which had begun in some parts of western Europe even before the American stock exchange crash in October 1929 and which in another year's time was to cause the abandonment of the newly restored gold standard by Britain and other countries, Norway included. The steady contraction of world trade reduced shipping freights as well as exports; unemployment mounted, so that in December 1932 42 per cent of trade unionists were without work and the average for the whole of the following year was 33 per cent; and the fall in agricultural prices brought the total of compulsory farm auctions in 1932 to 6,568. The government of a small country could do little to relieve a situation which depended on world economic conditions, as was apparent even in such a limited case as that of a concession to Unilever, affecting the Norwegian oil, soap, and margarine industries, which was heavily criticized by the recently established Trust Control. Mowinckel's second government was overthrown on this issue in May 1931, by a combination in which the nationalism of the Agrarians was reinforced by the anti-capitalism of the Labour Party: yet Unilever had its way on most points in the end (see p. 330).

The sequel was the formation of an Agrarian ministry, whose position was exceptionally vulnerable. The party mustered only one-sixth of the members of the Storting, and a majority of the cabinet which depended on their support had no previous political experience. Its first prime minister, P. L. Kolstad,* who died in office after ten months, earned more respect than his successor, Jens Hundseid,† but both men represented a new type of less substantial Agrarian politician, somewhat disparagingly identified by some as 'the agriculture teachers' (*landbrukslærarane*).²³ Foreign affairs were entrusted to an army officer who was quickly forgotten; defence to another army officer, who was not. Vidkun Quisling‡ had attracted attention when Nansen died in May 1930 by an article in the Moderate Liberal newspaper, *Tidens Tegn*, announcing himself as the political heir who shared Nansen's awareness of the dangers of Communist doctrines promoted by the Russians. He had followed this up by founding a small-scale anti-communist organization as nebulous as its name, 'The Nordic People's Resurgence in Norway' (*Den nordiske Folkereisning i Norge*); the promoters included a few scientists, such as Johan Hjort, a few leading industrialists, and a handful of retired army officers.²⁴ As a minister Quisling did very little for

---

* 1878–1932. Principal of an agricultural school, 1912; member of the Storting, 1922–31; premier and finance minister, 1931–2.

† 1883–1965. Farmer and agricultural school principal; from 1931 leader of Agrarians in the Storting, of which he was a member from 1924 to 1945; premier and minister of agriculture, March 1932–March 1933; county governor, 1935. Though his personal relations with Quisling had been very bitter, he joined N.S. during the German occupation and was subsequently sentenced to 10 years' imprisonment.

‡ 1887–1945. A clergyman's son and brilliant examinee; appointed to the general staff in 1911, he served as military attaché in Petrograd, 1918, and Helsinki, 1920–1; he was engaged in international relief work as an assistant to Nansen (see p. 340), 1922–5; and he had business employment in Russia, 1926–9, where he also earned the C.B.E. for looking after British interests while diplomatic relations were broken off. His book *Russia and Ourselves* was translated into English in 1931.

defence—except indeed to promote *Leidangen* (see p. 356), a force which might be used against an internal enemy[25]—but a great deal to antagonize the Labour opposition in the Storting by unsubstantiated charges of treason: these were all the more bitterly resented because in 1924–5 he had offered his services to Tranmæl and others as a potential organizer of 'Red Guards'. The Agrarian government's remedies for rural discontent comprised loans on rather stringent conditions and some collective marketing schemes on the pattern then becoming popular in Britain. For the industrial community it provided a new force of State Police and stricter administration of poor relief: 'The duty of the local authority,' said one circular, 'is confined to preventing a person from starving.'[26]

The result was an intensification of class war. An industrial conflict of record dimensions occurred in 1931, when the employers' organization resorted to a lock-out to enforce wage reductions, which the trade union federation would have accepted as unavoidable in the general crisis but which extremist influences, some of them Communist, got the workers to reject. In the end they submitted to the reduction, but not before the enactment of an ugly scene at Menstad quay, belonging to one of Norsk Hydro's workplaces in Telemark, where a body of 120 State Police protecting alleged strike-breakers was completely routed, so that troops and naval vessels had to be sent to the area to overawe the workers. Another bitter dispute, concerning the right of forest workers and loggers to organize and demand a collective agreement, dragged on in one area for five years, and this was typical of the determination with which farmer employers struggled to keep their employees isolated from each other and therefore powerless. In 1932 a day's work in the forest earned one-third of the average wage in industry: strikers were often in bitter conflict with strike-breakers and the police, and their trade union was not unnaturally receptive to Communist influences. Yet the most serious threat to public order came from an organization of property holders, 'Rural Crisis Support' (*Bygdefolkets Krisehjelp*), which provided strong-arm men to deter bidders at farm auctions where the bank or some other creditor had foreclosed. From small beginnings in October 1931 it expanded in a couple of years to a membership of 8,000–12,000, chiefly in Telemark, which was indoctrinated with the revolutionary teaching, 'We are being made *slaves of other classes* now and for all time to come.'[27]

In March 1933 the refusal of the Agrarians to meet the crisis by increasing public expenditure resulted in their replacement by a third Mowinckel ministry, which created some employment through public works and was in other ways more conciliatory to its Labour opponents. Yet the pressure of the world economic crisis was still felt as a disaster to the community with which the parliamentary system failed to grapple: was there an alternative to the fruitless inter-party struggle? This seemed to be Quisling's opportunity, for since October 1932—when Hundseid had tried in vain to rid himself of his troublesome colleague—he had received tentative approaches from industrial magnates, dissatisfied Agrarians, and anti-communists of all sorts, who shared the widespread though erroneous belief that he had been the 'strong man' in the Menstad episode and readily mistook his cloudy rhetoric for constructive political thinking.[28] Quisling for his part was encouraged by his personal religious philosophy of Universalism to feel a call to be the saviour of the nation. On the practical side, his unhappy experiences at the hands of the Labour Party in the Storting disposed him to favour measures for strengthening the executive against the legislative power, which might prevent a socialist majority in a future Storting from making revolutionary social changes. One month after Hitler had come into power in Germany, Quisling for the first time proposed a dictatorship, in an article in the Agrarian paper *Nationen* urging the Agrarian Party to take the lead in forming a national bloc for this purpose.

On 16 May 1933 'National Unification' (*Nasjonal Samling*, commonly abbreviated to N.S.) was launched by Quisling in an article in *Tidens Tegn* and a speech at Eidsvoll: apart from patriotic sentiments, he based his appeal on vague promises to end the economic crisis, denunciation of party divisions, disquisitions on race, and projection of himself as a leader. The League of the Fatherland, though well disposed towards Quisling and dictatorship—its press organ, *ABC*, opined at this time that both Hitler and Mussolini were obvious candidates for the Nobel Peace Prize[29]—did not think that a new party was worth backing when the election was only five months distant. Apart from an electoral alliance with Rural Crisis

Support, N.S. depended upon what could be improvised in the constituencies by supporters from *Folkereisning*, such as a German-orientated professor of jurisprudence, H. H. Aall, and Quisling's business partner in Russia, Captain F. Prytz, and by a group of much younger men, headed by an able lawyer, J. B. Hjort (a son of the scientist), and including some Trondheim students with one of their professors, Ragnar Skancke (see note, p. 393). In October their share of the poll was 2·2 per cent, which was not enough to win any seat but was more than the total polled by the Communists or any other of seven minor parties.[30] N.S. could still hope to achieve substantial results in three years time, if the prospect of class war in Norway, on which Quisling had based his propaganda, should for any reason cease to recede.

However, the Labour Party had been influenced towards what proved to be its final return to parliamentarism by the events in Germany, which suggested that it was wiser to rely upon the ballot box than risk the result of some eventual showdown involving the threat of violence. This viewpoint corresponded with a gradual change in the outlook of many trade unions, where those members who remained in steady employment from 1920 to 1933, a period in which the cost of living fell by fully one-half, were no longer true proletarians and had much more to lose than their chains. But the most important factor was the existence of definite Labour plans for using the resources of the State to create work. In 1932 the Party and the trade union federation had joined in formulating 'the working people's crisis demands' for large-scale public works and the opening up of land for smallholders, the ideas being derived mainly from Keynes (as in Sweden),* though the Russian model was also represented in an unofficial publication entitled *A Norwegian Three-Year Plan*.† When the election came, the Labour Party restored the democratic pledge to its programme and campaigned under the slogan of 'Work for All' (*Hele folket i arbeid*). With 41 per cent of the total vote, they did not gain a majority, but the possession of sixty-nine out of 150 seats in the new Storting gave them the key position.

---

* Cf. *New Cambridge Modern History* (Vol. xii, 2nd ed. 1968), pp. 64–5.
† One of the authors, O. Colbjörnsen, had held a commercial post in Russia in the years immediately preceding the first Five-Year Plan.

1933–1939: CRISIS SURMOUNTED

Mowinckel's third ministry lingered on for two more years. The Left Party and many Conservatives had too much regard for the interests of consumers to go all the way with the measures for making agriculture more profitable, which were necessary for a firm alliance with the Agrarians. Moreover, in spite of the example set by both Sweden and Denmark at this time, they assumed that the bitter animosity that the Agrarians had shown to rural trade unions and other Labour activities, not to mention their past public association with Quisling, made a Labour–Agrarian alliance unthinkable. But Johan Nygaardsvold,* a cautious socialist leader with long experience in the Storting, thought otherwise. Highly confidential and at first tentative negotiations with Hundseid resulted in a bargain, by which the Agrarians gave up their policy of keeping down the Budget and agreed to put Labour into office on the basis of a crisis expenditure of kr. 30 million, which was half the amount that Labour asked for. In return, Labour agreed to raise the money by introducing a new turnover tax and increasing direct taxation instead of by borrowing, and to assist agriculture by a system of subsidies and import controls, which would benefit first and foremost the larger producers who had always hitherto been their avowed enemies. The result was an *ad hoc* political arrangement and no more, but it provided the Labour leaders with twenty-three votes in the Storting and the opportunity to put into practice some part of their programme. They would also show whether they could govern: Mowinckel did not expect to be out of office for long.

Nygaardsvold had just completed five years as premier when the German invasion of 1940 interrupted the course of Norwegian political development. The only one of his colleagues well known abroad

---

* 1879–1952. A *husmann's* son employed in a sawmill at twelve, and as a forest and railway-construction worker in Canada and the U.S.A., 1902–7; member of Storting, 1916–49; refused party's offer of premiership and served as minister of agriculture, 1928; prime minister, 1935–45; until October 1939 (when the premier was relieved of departmental duties) he had direct charge of public works for creating employment. The post-war inquiry held him partly to blame for inadequate defence preparations.

was the Marxist historian, Halvdan Koht,[*] though the young trade-union lawyer who became minister of justice, Trygve Lie,[†] was destined to become the foremost international official of the immediate post-war period. How much longer the government would have lasted under normal conditions is a matter for guess-work. At the 1936 election Labour's share of the vote rose by 2·4 per cent, though this gave only one more seat. Their Agrarian allies lost five seats, but in order to safeguard its position the government had only to 'shop around for votes,'[31] which were readily obtainable from the Left Party. Moreover, Labour no longer had anything to fear from N.S. In the summer of 1934 Hjort had failed to put through a scheme for linking the Agrarian Party with the Moderate Liberals and the League of the Fatherland (now operating as a separate political group) in a national bloc which would capture power under Quisling's leadership. In the following year Quisling's 'universalism' had caused him to accept a post as propaganda director of the fascist international, proffered to him at Montreux, without reflecting on the extreme unpopularity in Norway of the Italian aggression against Ethiopia. Accordingly, in 1936 the N.S. vote sank to 1·8 per cent, and after bitter recriminations Hjort, who was deputy leader of the party and head of Quisling's bodyguard of about 100 *hirdmenn*,[‡] seceded with at least 330 of the Oslo membership. One consequence was a further resounding failure in the local elections of 1937, when the total representation of N.S. on local councils was reduced from twenty-eight to seven. Quisling, who had concentrated his attention

[*] 1873–1965. Professor of History at Oslo, 1910–35, and a prolific writer on historical and literary themes, some work appearing in German, French, or English; joined Labour Party, 1911. His demand to be impeached after the war was refused, but he defended his foreign policy vigorously in several autobiographical volumes.

[†] 1896–1968. Legal adviser to the trade union federation, 1922–35, and an active chairman of the workers' sports association, 1931–5; minister of justice, 1935–9, trade and supply, 1939–40, and foreign affairs, November 1940–February 1946. General secretary of U.N., 1946–53; county governor of Oslo, 1955–63; minister of industry, 1963, and of trade, 1963–5.

[‡] In the middle ages the *hird* were the retainers at the court of the Norwegian kings. Quisling planned to set up an *ordensvern* on the lines of the German S.A. soon after the 1933 election, and characteristically gave it medieval trappings.

upon the capital, made the comment: 'Oslo has chosen Marx and Mammon.'[32] The electorate had certainly not chosen Quisling: N.S. membership fell to about 1,500, and the lack of means to maintain even the single surviving party newspaper, *Fritt Folk*, caused Quisling in 1938 to appeal for financial support to the German Nazi Party, with which he had had intermittent contact since 1930.[33]

Since a constitutional change, which—much to Quisling's disgust—was made applicable to the Storting then in session, had extended the electoral period to four years, the next election was not due until the autumn of 1940, when N.S. might have disappeared together with the bogy of class war. Nygaardsvold, who was no extremist in matter of party policy, had become something of a father figure to the community at large, so that it no longer seemed wildly inappropriate when Torp, as 1939 drew to its troubled close, appealed to the party congress for national solidarity 'to bring our country safely out of the troubles'.[34]

Although a hard core of 18 per cent unemployed among trade unionists remained in 1939, the real value of a day's wage in industry had risen by 15 per cent during the decade on top of a 4-per-cent rise in the decade before. European rearmament helped to stimulate a widespread recovery of trade: the value of Norwegian exports rose by one-third, of shipping freights by more than two-thirds. Farm prices rose sufficiently for the number of compulsory auctions to dwindle, while heavy expenditure on roads, railways, and other public works, especially land development, generated fresh activity in the countryside. In five years the Budget rose from kr. 400 million to kr. 635 million, imposing a considerable burden of taxation upon business enterprise and all middle-class incomes. At the same time, however, industrial relations became much more harmonious, to the general profit of all concerned; for the trade union federation desired to promote the success of the crisis plans for which it had been partly responsible. In 1935 it had signed a general agreement with the employers' organization which set out in detail the functions of the unions in industry, with particular reference to the way in which the periodic wage settlements were to be carried out. For the time being, heavy pressure on employers was deliberately restricted to those trades where there was an obvious case for levelling up a very low wage-rate; illegal strikes were frowned upon; and the unions took a direct interest in increasing productivity. In 1939 the uncertain world outlook even led the unions to continue existing general wage settlement for a further year, although they were in a position to extract some advance from the employers. The membership of the unions rose by one-third during this short period, but their new 'policy of the undivided community' (*solidarisk samfunnspolitikk*) made them for the first time a part of the Establishment.

In addition to its crisis measures, the Labour government extended the powers of producers' organizations in agriculture and the fisheries, which had recently advanced from district to national status. The corn guarantee was maintained, the prices of animal products were enhanced to the disadvantage of the urban consumer, and in 1938 the sale of unprocessed fish was placed under the control of a fishermen's monopoly (*Norges Råfisklag*). In primary production and manufacturing industry alike, the organization of the economy rather than the elimination of the profit motive was accepted as the need of the hour, both by socialists like Koht, who acclaimed it as 'a preliminary condition for socialism',[35] and by efficiency experts, such as Thagaard.

At the same time, Labour tried to bring Norway abreast of the most advanced countries in social policy, a field in which discussions continuing since the time of Castberg had achieved little progress for fifteen years. Sickness insurance was extended to new categories —fishermen, seamen serving in foreign waters, the blind and disabled, and finally to all persons earning less than the equivalent of £300 a year. A Workers' Protection Law extended the eight-hour day to farm workers and other additional groups, guaranteed the holiday period (which had been much eroded). and restricted the employer's powers of dismissal over his staff. A small old-age pension was instituted at long last, though recipients were to bear three-eighths of the cost. Finally, in 1938 a system of unemployment insurance, available for fifteen weeks a year, was set up as a palliative for the failure to carry out their election promise of five years before. This was to take effect with the Budget for 1939/40: social expenditure had already doubled since the change of government.

Nearly all these measures had been accepted in principle, if criticized in detail, by all parties in the Storting, a circumstance which helped to destroy the notion that a large body of right-wing extremists was prepared to fight for its privileges. Under the impact of Labour's success at home and the extremities practised by Stalin abroad, Communism had shrunk to 0·3 per cent of the electorate. Meanwhile the Labour movement had resumed its former close relations with the Social Democratic parties of Sweden and Denmark, and attached itself to the Socialist Labour International; the trade union federation, too, rejoined I.F.T.U. and became for the first time directly represented in the International Labour Organization at Geneva. Only the small rise in Norway's insignificant total expenditure on armaments implied a reluctant admission of the possibility that the advance towards a democratic society might still be checked or even reversed.

THE GAINS OF TWO DECADES

Bankruptcies, unemployment, and class conflict play such a large role in the history of the inter-war period in Norway that it is easy to treat the whole subject as amounting at best to a tale of woe for which the last four or five years unexpectedly provide a happy ending. But this would be a one-sided presentation. In 1920–39 the industrial setbacks of the early 1920s and early 1930s did not prevent an over-all rise in the gross national product almost as rapid as in the years from 1900 to 1916, which included a whole decade of golden expansion. The rise was in great measure the result of the continued application of modern technologies to the latent resources of a once poor country. Since new machines and processes nearly always reduced the labour requirements, such a rise was fully consistent with the phenomenon of widespread unemployment and with the fact that two decades of industrialization did not increase the proportion of the people engaged in industrial occupations: measured per head of adult population, the rise was nevertheless outstanding large.[36]

The spread of new and more efficient electric power plants, which continued at a moderate tempo throughout the period, provided the essential basis for new industrial units, including many small concerns serving mainly a regional market. Norway's advantage in cheap power costs was no longer sufficient to make her a major world-producer of aluminium, where her share sank to 5 per cent, or of zinc and copper, where it sank to 3 per cent. But in 1939 metals nevertheless constituted the largest export, stimulated to some extent by three important Norwegian inventions—the Söderberg self-burning electrode, the Pedersen process for aluminium oxide, and the Tysland-Hole electric furnace, which in 1929 placed an Oslo ironworks in the forefront of the race to produce electric steel. But this was also the period in which the adoption of American methods of 'scientific management'* and automatic production was becoming essential if Norway was to compete in world markets; so was the introduction of new capital from foreign sources, encouraged by successive governments as a countermeasure to stagnation and unemployment.

TABLE VIII[37]

Foreign Investment, 1919–1939
(at face value, in millions of kroner)

	total corporate capital stock	percentage foreign-held	amount foreign-held	distribution by main countries						
				France	U.K.	U.S.	Sweden	Switzerland	Canada	Germany
1919	3,726	6·7	250							
1924			250							
1929	3,059	10·9	332	57·9	57·7	48·1	69·0	11·7	5·0	36·7
1934			347	100·7	57·6	50·0	60·7	31·5	17·5	10·3
1936/7	2,023	15·7	317·5	94·6	49·7	42·0	47·1	32·3	20·7	9·7
1939			317·9	96·5	59·7	43·9	34·2	32·6	23·1	5·5

Norsk Hydro trebled its output of nitrates after adopting the German Haber–Bosch process in 1927, but this was at the cost of passing more largely into foreign ownership: in 1939 this giant among Norwegian enterprises had only 2·6 per cent of its capital stock in native hands. Other new developments undertaken by foreign interests were the smelting of Canadian nickel matte at Kristiansand, the exploitation by Swedes of the Orkla electro-smelting process for separating pyrites into sulphur and copper

* F. W. Taylor's *Principles of Scientific Management* became available in Swedish and German translations (1916, 1917).

concentrate, and the use of an American electrolytic process for zinc. A big electrotechnical concern, which became the second-largest foreign employer of Norwegian labour, was likewise established under American auspices, while the Swiss Brown Boveri firm also increased its interest in this field. Since mining was in difficulties at this period, the Storting agreed that the working of ilmenite should be transferred to the National Lead Company, U.S.A., on whose paint-making process it was already dependent, and the only molybdenum mine in Europe was sold to Sweden, whose ironworks were the chief customer.

As there was only a single instance—a British-owned carbide and cyanide manufacture—in which a foreign subsidiary was allowed to go bankrupt, the general benefit to the economy in a period of great stringency was obvious. Nevertheless, the Storting sometimes imposed restrictions, as in the case of portland cement, where the Danish promoters were allowed only a 45 per cent participation, and in 1931–2 (as already noticed) a considerable stir was created by the activities of Unilever, the great international fats combine. The principal soap firm, Lilleborg, had come to terms with them through another Norwegian concern, De Nordiske Fabriker, in which Unilever's English component had bought a half-share from the Germans nearly ten years earlier. The concession was eventually confirmed, with the significant exception of a clause which would have eliminated competition in the manufacture of margarine—of which the Norwegian people were *per capita* the second-largest consumers in the world. 'Local economic patriotism was exceptionally aggressive' is the explanation of an English historian,[38] but the Norwegians had long experience of Unilever (alias Lever Brothers) in connection with antarctic whaling.

Technical improvements affecting the mercantile marine and the whaling fleet will be discussed in the context of Norway's contribution to world affairs (see p. 349), but mention must be made here of the modernization of the fishing fleet, where the number of open motor boats was trebled during the twenty years and the decked motor boats increased by one-half. Although the size of catch was affected by many factors, the growth of the annual average from 600,000 tons before the war to 1,000,000 tons in the 1930s was obviously related to improved boats and gear and the special Norwegian studies in marine biology and meteorology. By 1939 the farms, where conditions were in many respects unfavourable to progress, employed 3,000 tractors as compared with 1,000 ten years before; were putting down 30,000 tons of factory-produced artificial manure in a season, which was ten times as much as before the war; and possessed what was by foreign standards the more remarkable total of 25,000 machines driven by electric power. The development of one of the first systematic fur-farming trades, which small producers based on herring offal as a means of combating the depression, shows another aspect of Norwegian technical resourcefulness.

World developments in means of communication during this period were of special importance to Norway's scattered population. The home market was not big enough to justify an automobile industry, but road improvement was one of the main objects of public works expenditure both locally and on a national basis. The ubiquitous rock and the deep penetration of the frost add enormously to the cost of road making, but by 1930 the country had been opened up to some extent by 20,000 miles of bus routes, which was increased by a further 50 per cent in the next ten years. However, the fact that roads through the high mountain passes remained shut during the winter months helped rail transport to retain its position as the preferred alternative to the coastal steamers for the movement of men or goods. In 1923 two new main lines were decided upon, to link Oslo with Kristiansand and eventually Stavanger, and to link Trondheim with the far north, possibly as far as Bodö, which lies well within the Arctic Circle. Though neither of these was completed within this period, the work done on them and other smaller railway projects did much to open up districts whose tiny population desperately needed a connection with outside markets. To the casual visitor from Britain the Norwegian railways looked rather insignificant; yet they represented a great national effort, for by 1935 the route mileage per head of population was twice that of the British.

This was approximately the date at which two private companies, one of them backed by shipping interests, introduced internal air transport, which was eventually to solve many of Norway's special problems, at any rate for passenger traffic. In 1927, when the German Lufthansa started the first external flights from Oslo, it was said to be the only European country which had no regular international air communications. This is at first sight surprising, since the first flight across the North Sea had been made by a Norwegian, Tryggve Gran, as far back as the first fateful week-end of August, 1914. Moreover, the short runways of the pre-jet age were comparatively cheap to construct, and Norway offered almost ideal conditions for the seaplane services which were then at the height of their popularity. But private capital was scarce, and the typical member of the Storting very loath at this time to risk public money in pursuit of any novelty.

The existence of a well-developed public telephone system and the widespread interest in electrical apparatus may help to account for the fact that Norway was relatively quick to adopt the other great improvement in communications during this period, namely the public broadcasting service. The first radio programme to be heard in any Scandinavian country was sent out from Oslo in February 1923, just three years after the Marconi Company began work in Britain; in 1925 the first of four private regional stations was authorized, with 16 per cent advertising time; and in 1933 the existing state monopoly was set up on the model of the B.B.C. There were about 400,000 licence-holders before the German Occupation, and in 1938 an economic historian could claim that broadcasting had 'right away caused the remotest country districts of Norway to experience the same rhythm of contemporary events as the storm centres of world politics'.[39]

Radio was one of the many influences which combined to give the Norwegian culture of the day a less narrow and more genuinely liberal basis than that of past generations. It did not indeed oust the little local newspapers which for geographical reasons took the place of the 'national dailies' of many other countries; on the contrary, it stimulated discussion of district politics. Nor did broadcasting produce uniformity of speech, for *landsmål* interests insisted on having a full share in news bulletins and other programmes emanating from Oslo, where the minority language was little used. But radio brought into innumerable homes an unwonted familiarity with both sides—in politics, in social questions, in artistic controversies, and even in matters of religion.

This widening of the culture, which at the same time became more democratic in outlook, was greatly stimulated by changes in the educational system. Discussion began with a School Commission in the 1920s, and the bill for reforming secondary education was framed by the third Mowinckel ministry, though the schools legislation was passed (with general agreement) by the Labour ministry in 1935–40, when money was more readily available. In the elementary schools an attempt was made to bring the rural districts closer to the standards of the towns, though the latter still averaged 50-percent longer hours of instruction, which enabled them to introduce a foreign language, namely English. Seven years of compulsory elementary education could be followed by a course of five years: two in the *realskole*—which also offered a third year on more practical subjects—and three in the *gymnas* which prepared for metriculation. Both these courses were rendered more attractive to rural families by an alternative system which confined attendance to the winter months, and many other variations were introduced to suit 'the individual and local requirements of a widespread and highly differentiated country'.[40] In higher education, too, there were some new institutions provided, including a Commercial High School in Bergen and a Teachers' High School in Trondheim. But the most significant development, achieved in spite of very low Budgets, was the increase in the total number of students in the university and parallel institutions from less than 3,000 in 1920 to nearly 6,000 in 1938—a growth which implies recruitment from classes for which higher education had hitherto been inaccessible.

Many types of voluntary organization could doubtless be cited to illustrate the broadening influences at work in society. The Labour movement, for example, started a Workers' Sports Association in 1924, mainly to prevent such clubs being used to recruit strike-breakers. By 1939 the Association had 100,000 members, who regarded a purely social activity as appropriate to a movement which was no longer concerned solely with a class struggle. The same trend can be seen in the possibly more serious case of the workers' Educational Association, founded as late as 1931 'as a part of the workers' socialist class war': in 1939 it sponsored the erection of a Folk High School from trade-union funds, where the emphasis would be laid on the unprejudiced study of 'the life of society today and the forces that have been . . . and are at work upon it'.[41]

But the most striking illustration is provided by the church, which in Norway as in many other countries had become more truly a voluntary association by the relaxing of so many conventional ties during the war: in 1919 a new law even made it possible for a non-member, such as Mowinckel, to hold the office of prime minister. In 1920 Professor Ole Hallesby of the Congregational Faculty, a divine whose evangelical tracts sold a quarter of a million copies, was able to assemble nearly 1,000 delegates from a score of religious organizations for a conference in Oslo, which declared war on all liberal clergy. Three years later the strength of the boycott imposed by the Home Mission and like-minded societies was shown when only a single bishop dare take part in the ordination of a new bishop of Trondheim, denounced by Hallesby for conniving at the views of the unfortunate Professor Ording (see p. 176); in which he had detected sixteen heresies. But times were changing: new influences such as the Oxford Groups softened the asperities of theological controversy, and in 1937 Hallesby proved unable to mobilize any significant body of opinion when he proclaimed his inability to co-operate with Eivind Berggrav, a bishop with some leanings towards liberal theology, whose promotion to the see of Oslo constituted him in effect the primate of the Norwegian church.

Since Berggrav was for many years the editor of *Kirke og Kultur*, a periodical in which developments in the arts were often examined from the angle of their religious impact, one might well include here the liberalizing influence upon society of the newer work in literature, music, painting, and sculpture. This will, however, be considered in the next chapter, as part of Norway's contribution to the outside world. But the new phase in the language dispute must be mentioned here because the broadening of the culture at this period played a part in it. The Labour foreign minister Koht, who was deeply interested in philology as well as history, built up support in the Labour Party for a 'national language'. In 1937 he explained: 'It is the great goal of all labour movements . . . to build up a

national folk culture, and it is therefore natural that the working
class now joins with the farmers' movement in support of the language programme which will lead to complete national unification.'[42] In 1938 the Labour government, with support from the
Agrarian and Left Parties, enacted a second major language reform,
which aimed at a *rapprochement* between 'book-language' and 'neo-
Norwegian' with a view to the creation eventually of a common
Norwegian language (*samnorsk*). The Labour majority on the Oslo
City Council marked its approval by altering nearly 300 street
names in one day and by voting the money for new schoolbooks,
which were to employ those forms 'which are closest to the speech
of the children and are alike'[43] in the two versions of the language.
But in general the idea of moving towards *samnorsk* was already lost
in angry discussion between the two well-established factions, both
of which were aggrieved by the new legislation, when—as the
historian of this complex subject puts it—the German invasion of
1940 'gave most Norwegians other things to think of than language
planning'.[44]

11. Norway and the World Between the Wars

THE EVENTS OF 1914–18 HAD FORCED NORWAY OUT OF a seclusion to which a majority of her people would probably have been glad to return, if it had been possible; an active membership of the League of Nations was accepted as the most satisfactory alternative which was open to them. In Nansen they possessed a statesman who was well qualified to mobilize the forces of idealism which were one element in the composition of the League, and this helped to give Norway rather more influence in world affairs than her wealth, population, or unstable domestic politics might justify. But there were also one or two economic activities in which Norway was important, and in one remote region (East Greenland) she even showed imperialist tendencies, though the readiness with which she submitted her territorial claims for decision by an impartial tribunal set an example which larger empires, alas! disdained to follow. In the 1930s, however, Norway was one of the many countries which found their honest efforts to promote world peace were ineffectual. The trade group known as the Oslo Powers (see p. 358) failed in an attempt to lower trade barriers; nothing was achieved by belated gestures towards rearmament as a safeguard for neutrality; and Norway's final retreat from League obligations at the end of May 1938 was almost a measure of despair. In the fateful autumn of 1939 Norway was in many respects a country whose image in the world was more impressive than it had been a quarter of a century before, but this did not mean that she had as good a chance as in 1914 of escaping direct involvement in the tragic fate of the continent to which she belonged and whose destiny she must ultimately share.

NANSEN, THE REPRESENTATIVE NORWEGIAN

In the early 1920s Norway for the first time produced a leading actor on the stage of world politics. In comparison with the statesmen of the great powers, Nansen's impact upon events might strike the contemporary newspaper reader as rather modest: but later history shows that his aims embodied the best aspirations that arose out of 'the war to end war', that his achievements shaped the course of important events, and that his example influenced the mind of the following generation. Fridtjof Nansen, as we have already seen him, was representative of his race by virtue of his astonishing physical endurance, blunt directness of speech and action, versatility, and a closeness to primitive Nature which recalls the Vikings. As rector of St. Andrews University he exhorts the students in language appropriate to the groves of Academe: 'The first great thing is to find yourself, and for that you need solitude and contemplation, at least sometimes. I tell you deliverance . . . will come from the lonely places! The great reformers in history have come from the wilderness.'[1] But it takes a fellow hunter to show him as the wild man in that wilderness: 'When Nansen had rolled the elk over, he cut off a huge slab of the meat and started lapping it up so the blood ran all over him. Then he took a whole leg, threw it over his shoulder, and walked off with the blood dripping down the back of his neck.'[2]

But he was also representative in the more important sense of embodying Norwegian aims and policies. It was through his presidency of their Association for the League of Nations that he was able in some degree to influence the shape of the eventual structure of the League organization, and it was in the capacity of member (and later, head) of their delegation to the League Assembly that he so often took the lead in its annual deliberations. Successive governments and many private firms and individuals in Norway helped him to launch his financial appeals for the relief of suffering; and he regarded the award of the Nobel Peace Prize by a committee of his fellow countrymen as the greatest encouragement his work received. Above all, the emphasis constantly laid by Nansen upon the beneficial effect that humanitarian successes might have upon the general prestige of the League was directly in line with Norwegian foreign policy, which hoped against hope that an increase in its prestige might increase respect for the rule of law.

Nansen's earliest venture into the field of international relief work was made, however, in the spring of 1919—some nine months before the League of Nations was formally inaugurated. His mission to the United States in 1917–18 had given him excellent American contacts, while in 1913 he had paid a prolonged visit to Siberia, which meant that he had some insight into the problems of the Russian economy. He was therefore proposed by Herbert Hoover as joint leader with the Swedish social democrat, Branting, of a scheme to extend to Russia the food relief that had been administered by Hoover for the Belgians during the war. It was characteristic, however, of the difficulties that were to beset each of Nansen's international ventures that the Big Four at the Paris Peace Conference would agree to nothing that might diminish the chances of success for the counter-revolutionary forces in Russia. Nansen had to content himself with making detailed arrangements to rush supplies of food, including several tons of cod-liver oil for the children, into starving Petrograd the moment it was captured by the counter-revolution—a moment that never came. It was also characteristic of Nansen's self-confidence, which was to carry him through many disappointments, that in approving Hoover's proposals he struck out all reference to Branting as suited to share his responsibilities.

This episode, however, had a natural sequel in the approach made to Nansen by the League Council, 'as they could find no one with such great experience and authority to carry out the negotiations required',[3] when it decided in April 1920 to appoint a High Commissioner to organize the long-delayed repatriation of prisoners of war. The negotiations of the previous year, though abortive, had given him a unique status with the Communist Russian government, by whom the largest number of prisoners were held, but the motive which chiefly induced him to accept an infinitely tedious and exhausting task—placating intransigent governments, raising credits, providing ships, and fixing routes—was its value to the League of Nations. As he wrote to Lord Robert Cecil, 'If the action of the League is successful in bringing the prisoners to their homes at an early date it will do more than almost anything else could to establish the authority and prestige of the League in all the countries concerned.[4] It did succeed: by three main routes, across the Baltic and Black Seas and over the ocean from Vladivostok, a total of 447,604 prisoners belonging to twenty-six states were brought home at an average cost of about £1 a head.[5]

This success led on to four other tasks, all of them concerned with urgently needed humanitarian relief but varying in their results according to the political interests of the great powers. In the autumn of 1921, when Nansen had resumed his scientific work in Norway, he answered an appeal from the International Red Cross to accept appointment as the League's High Commissioner for the Russian refugees, whom revolution and civil war had left stranded in many parts of Europe and Asia. Since the numbers involved were about 1,500,000 and the money for their resettlement had to come chiefly from private charity—including Nansen's own donation of the Nobel prize money—this task was far from complete at the time of his death in 1930. It was continued until the Second World War, and one of its most striking features, namely the device of the Nansen Passport, which makes it easier for stateless persons to gain admission to new countries through possession of an identification document, is still in use for the benefit of the much larger body of refugees created by the political upheavals of a later generation.

Since Constantinople (Istanbul) was the most important centre of the work on behalf of displaced Russians, it was natural that Nansen should also be appealed to on behalf of the Greeks, whom furious Turkish armies evicted in the autumn of 1922 from their recent annexations in Asia Minor. The League of Nations Assembly being in session, Nansen secured money and full powers at 24 hours' notice; moreover in this case, where the acceptance of the frontier changes demanded by the Turks was not complicated by fear of helping Communism, he was able to raise an international loan to facilitate the exchange of populations. By 1930 1,250,000 Greek refugees had been found new homes in the reduced national territory, while half a million Turks had likewise been peacefully transferred from Greece to live under the White Crescent.

In organizing repatriation of war prisoners from all parts of the Soviet Russian territories Nansen had acquired an insight into their economic deterioration, which the Communist authorities for political reasons sought to conceal. Thus, when the failure of the 1921 harvest brought actual famine to an area stretching from the upper Volga to the Ukraine, he was uniquely qualified to take charge of relief operations as the emissary of forty-eight Red Cross and other charitable organizations. Within a fortnight he was in Moscow, where he made certain that whatever relief was sent would be distributed under his authority and as he directed. He deployed a staff of enthusiasts from many countries: in the Ukraine the key figure was a Norwegian army captain, Vidkun Quisling, on whom his experiences and responsibilities made a deep impression—for better and worse. In two years (September 1921–August 1923) the Nansen mission is believed to have saved the lives of 6,400,000 children and 400,000 adults; how many perished in the stricken area will never be known—perhaps 3,000,000 from direct starvation and several times that number from typhus and other epidemics. Nansen himself reported on the Samara region as a scene of 'misery worse than darkest imaginings',[6] which was corroborated by statistics from a district where the work was in the hands of the Quakers. But neither his speeches in League committees and at the annual Assembly in Geneva, nor his private appeals to Lloyd George and other leaders of the great powers, could obtain the large-scale governmental support that the situation in his view demanded. Nansen received loyal backing from his own government, but representatives of other powers reasoned, either openly at Geneva or more frequently in private, that humane scruples must not be allowed to prevent the Soviet system from collapsing.

In 1925 a similar conflict of interest arose in the case of the Armenian refugees, to whom the reviving power of Turkey refused the land which the Allies had awarded them six years before. Nansen sent Quisling to reconnoitre the position for this hapless people, long threatened with genocide, and then negotiated personally with the Russian Communist republic of Erivan, where a national home was offered for the Armenians. But its establishment required a League of Nations loan of £900,000, which was refused at the instigation of Winston Churchill (at that time British chancellor of the exchequer); the amount to be asked for was then reduced by two-thirds, but although the Norwegian and three other governments offered to contribute, the great powers again intervened to secure a refusal. By 1929 Nansen had nevertheless obtained private support which enabled him to resettle 19,000 refugees, but in September—during what proved to be his last attendance at the League Assembly—the continued indifference of the great powers led him to advise the League to drop the project. Communist Armenia is now one of the constituent republics of the U.S.S.R., but a quarter of a century after Nansen's death the memory of the 'friend of the Armenians' was honoured at Geneva by representatives of that people, many of whom were still scattered all over the world.

A LEAGUE OF NATIONS FOREIGN POLICY

Looking back on Nansen's career in the dark days of the Second World War, the great English protagonist of the League of Nations, Viscount Cecil, wrote as follows: 'He was almost the only man I have ever met who deserved to be called heroic . . . He was in a class by himself. It was a bad day for Peace, Humanity, and the League when he died at a comparatively early age. He has left no successor.'[7] But although no representative of Norway (or for that matter of any other small state) could speak with the same authority, it would be wrong to suggest that Norway's work for peace and humanity was frustrated in the League for want of other effective spokesmen. Since this was the institution through which the nation first came to play a regular part in international affairs, it was a natural consequence that her best men figured in its counsels: in 1922 the Storting endorsed the principle that the choice of delegates should not be treated purely as a party question. Thus an ex-premier, Hagerup, headed the delegation to the first Assembly, which also included Nansen and the well-known internationalist, Christian Lange. Mowinckel attended the Assembly from 1925 onwards and was its President in 1933. The most vigorous of the Conservative politicians, C. J. Hambro, realizing that there was no future in his original contention that Norway should group itself with the United States outside the League, made a mark in the Assembly from 1926 onwards and was its last President. As for the Labour Party, its ideological objections to the League could hardly survive after the entry of Soviet Russia in 1934: in the very next year Koht vigorously supported economic sanctions against the Italian aggression in Ethiopia.

Yet inasmuch as the fifty smaller members of the League of Nations could achieve virtually nothing against the wishes of the great-power members, we need do no more than indicate some of the Norwegian (or joint Scandinavian) policies by which its eventual failure might have been mitigated or conceivably averted. At the outset, for example, Norway urged the adoption of the principle of universality of membership, for the benefit of defeated Germany and also for Bulgaria; in the latter case the arguments put forward in 1920 by Nansen (and Branting) helped to secure immediate admission. Norway also championed universality in the internal organization of the League, pleading that the members of the Council should be selected so as to represent 'the whole world, politically, intellectually, geographically';[8] that three of the six vice-presidents of the Assembly should be chosen from the non-European states; and that the Secretariat should include nationals of every League country. This last was one of Hambro's favourite contentions, and the result was a gradual approximation to the principle of wide national recruitment which has been established for the staff of the United Nations.

The Norwegians, for whom responsible government was the essence of democracy, would have wished the League Council to evolve into a sort of cabinet acting on behalf of the League Assembly. Thus Hagerup at once urged that the reports and minutes of Council meetings should be distributed for study in advance of the Assembly's annual session. Then in 1925 the Norwegians secured the insertion of a special clause in the elaborate arrangements for the appointment of the nine non-permanent members (who together with the great powers constituted the Council), entitling a two-thirds majority in the Assembly to require a new election for all nine places. *The Times* commented, 'This should go far to retain for the Assembly the influence which, as an organization representative of international opinion, it should exercise over the Council.'[9] No such 'general election' was ever held, however, so Norway tried to reach the same goal by other methods. In 1928 its delegation was instructed by the Storting 'To work for the election of at least two representatives in the General Committee of the Assembly that come from states quite independent of leading great powers and who, because of their personality, will be able to take care of the interests of the smaller states'.[10] Finally, Hambro was instrumental in transferring financial control from the Council to the Assembly, the League Budget being placed under a supervisory commission, whose members were appointed by one of its democratically elected committees. But by 1931, when Hambro took his seat in the new commission, the Japanese invasion of Manchuria had shown that the League suffered from a more fundamental defect—its inability to protect a member state from aggression by a great power.

The Norwegians and the other Scandinavian members of the League had worked hard to embody the Rule of Law in universally accepted practices. In the initial discussions at Paris in March 1919, the Norwegians had urged that the League Covenant should make arbitration obligatory in all categories of international dispute. The suggestion was then brushed aside, but in 1923 Lange proposed that the right to receive assistance under the Covenant should be conditional upon acceptance of such an obligation. After the collapse of the Geneva Protocol, in which the principle was adopted by the great powers, it was nevertheless incorporated in a whole series of inter-Scandinavian treaties (see p. 346). In September 1927, accordingly, Nansen had a strong moral basis for his revival of the original project, which a year later was approved by the League Assembly as the General Act for the Peaceful Settlement of International Disputes. This Act was adopted in its entirety by the governments of Norway, Denmark, and Finland—but by no major power before 1931, when it had lost much of its value.

During the more hopeful decade of the 1920s, the Norwegians also used such influence as they possessed at Geneva in favour of disarmament, a subject in which Lange was an acknowledged expert. In 1920 he worked for the appointment of a commission of civilian advisers, to overcome the dependence of the Council for advice about disarmament measures upon officers from the armed forces of the powers, whose thinking was inevitably influenced by their professional interests. When the League Council continued to lean upon its military advisers, Lange's words were prophetic:

'Mr. Balfour says that to disarm is difficult except in a world where troubles have ceased. I tell you that states that still possess great armaments produce distrust in their neighbours and cause international crises. The fate of the League is in the hands of the Council.'[11] Four more years were allowed to pass before the Council set up a preparatory committee (December 1925), and the Disarmament Conference itself did not meet until February 1932. Meanwhile the Scandinavian states followed the example of Britain in reducing their own arms, a one-sided action which was not necessarily conducive to the maintenance of world peace.

INTER-SCANDINAVIAN RELATIONS

The events of 1914–18 had created a strong sense of the common interests uniting the Scandinavian kingdoms, such as had seemed very remote in the aftermath of 1905. This found expression in the foundation of the Nordic Association (*Foreningen Norden*), a private organization with many local branches in each country and a study centre in Denmark, which since 1919 has striven with increasing success to promote cultural and economic co-operation in the North. The Nordic or Scandinavian group of States was strengthened by the inclusion of Iceland, which in 1918 became fully self-governing except for its foreign policy, and Finland, a sovereign State with frontiers redrawn in 1920 by the treaty of Dorpat; the former had ancient cultural ties with Norway, the latter was a newly independent neighbour in the far north. In political matters, however, the sense of common Scandinavian attitudes and interests was most evident in the League of Nations, where the four countries formed a kind of entente, to which one of the elective seats on the Council was customarily allotted.

This unity was demonstrated in 1923, when Branting, the Swedish member of the Council, firmly contested Mussolini's contention that the Italian bombardment of the Greek island of Corfu was no concern of the League: both Norwegians and Danes joined him in condemning the Council's action when it diverted the adjudication of the dispute to the Council of Ambassadors in Paris, representing only the chief Allies of the war period. Nansen pleaded urgently: 'It is only by the loyal application of the solemn Covenant which we have undertaken that we can safeguard the vital interests of each of our nations and of humanity as a whole'.[12] The justification for his warning came when the League failed to grapple wholeheartedly with the Manchurian and Ethiopian problems in the following decade. Two other fields may be cited here, in which the Scandinavians showed a more enlightened attitude than the great powers of the League.

The League mandates, which authorized Britain, France, and some other states to administer the former colonial or imperial territories of the Germans and the Ottoman Turks, had been made formally subject to the authority of the Council and the Permanent Mandates Commission which it appointed. Nansen took the lead in claiming the right of the Assembly to examine the working of a system that was supposed to 'form a sacred trust of civilization',[13] and he championed, even against his friend Viscount Cecil, the right of the Mandates Commission to criticize, rather than merely to co-operate with the mandatory powers. Scandinavian educational experts obtained nomination to the Commission, and in so far as Lord Lugard was justified in claiming that its 'annual report formed an effective means of inviting a popular verdict on the fulfilment of the trust',[14] some credit rested with Scandinavian humanitarian vigilance. The Scandinavians showed a similar concern for the rights of racial and other minorities, which were placed under the guarantee of the League Council by the minorities treaties of 1919, and for the population consigned to fifteen years of French administration in the Saar, where Nansen called upon the Council to 'pay due attention to the interests of the inhabitants'.[15] In 1933 both Lange and the Swedish foreign minister wished to carry the protection of minorities beyond the terms of the 1919 treaties, claiming that the League had an overriding duty to take account of such evils as anti-semitism, which ought not to be regarded as the purely internal concern of member states.

The high moral tone adopted by the Norwegian and other Scandinavian representatives at Geneva was founded, not only on a genuine idealism of outlook, but also on what they believed to be a realistic assessment of their own ability to judge international issues without prejudice, because they belonged to a region where problems of mutual security had been satisfactorily solved. Its internal frontiers were secured by six Arbitration Conventions, of which the first was signed by Norway and Sweden at Oslo in November 1925 and the rest were completed within ten weeks. These covered every type of dispute, no exception being made for lapse of time or the exclusively domestic character of a dispute or for matters touching the national honour, independence, or other vital interests. As for its external frontiers, the peoples of Scandinavia in the 1920s felt almost carefree: neither Germany nor Russia looked dangerous for the nonce, and in the case of Norway there was no longer a Russian border to worry about, while the long border to seaward seemed safer than ever because the British navy no longer had any rival in European waters. Whereas other nations might need to look to the League to increase their security, the Scandinavians could regard themselves as producers rather than consumers of that elusive commodity. Thus Hambro described himself to the Assembly of 1926 as 'the delegate of a nation which is in the happy position of living in friendship with every neighbouring nation, and never having any claim upon the League'.[16]

Their geographical position, small size, and past record of neutrality encouraged the three Scandinavian kingdoms to assume that in the event of a major crisis their share in the 'production of security' would be achieved by taking part in economic sanctions against an aggressor; indeed, they claimed from the outset that they had never accepted military sanctions as obligatory.[17] Unlike Finland, which had had recent sharp experience of both civil and foreign war, they wished to disarm—and felt free to do so. The Social Democratic government in Sweden adopted a reduced system of defence in 1925. By that time the Danes contemplated cutting their armed forces to a 'watch' of 800 men, and although this proposal was deemed too drastic, the provision finally made in 1932 assumed that Denmark would not resist an attack. Norwegian disarmament went farther than the Swedish, less far than the Danish measures, as was perhaps to be expected: Sweden had the memory of greater military glories, Denmark of more poignant military defeats, than modern Norway had experienced.

In the final year of Gunnar Knudsen's long ministry (1913–20) the Left Party set up a royal commission to plan the future organization of the defences which had been built up during the war years. Its first report pronounced in favour of every reduction consistent with the national safety. In 1922 even the General Staff, while conceding the possibility that League of Nations obligations might make it necessary 'to take part in operations of war which we otherwise could have kept out of',[18] saw no immediate dangers—except a rather fanciful threat by Finnish activists to North Norway. Accordingly, the military system dating from 1909 was continued on a reduced scale, with shorter training periods and less renewal of equipment, until 1926, when it was decided that kr. 40 million a year was the most that could be afforded. Next year a new system of military service was planned accordingly: the annual intake of recruits was to be lowered by 30 per cent through drawing of lots, the cadre of officers and n.c.o.s approximately halved, and the standard training period for the infantry cut from 144 to 108 days.

Though the law was passed under a Conservative government, it followed the general lines laid down by the Left Party under Mowinckel. Nevertheless, in the course of the three years which elapsed before it was due to come into force, the matter was again thrown into the melting-pot by the leading member of the tiny group of Moderate Liberals in the Storting, who suggested that defence expenditure could be further reduced to kr. 30 million by allotting two-thirds to the navy and retaining only the nucleus of an army, to be expanded if and when the need arose. On his return to office in 1929, Mowinckel decided to meet the clamour for economies by dividing a total of kr. 32 million equally between the two services, both of which protested in vain. The new system on a reduced financial basis, which the Agrarian government eventually fixed at kr. 35 million, became law in 1933: it must be considered further (see p. 357) in relation to the changed world situation of that year—and of 1940, when its practical value was put to the test. In the present context it is sufficient to note that Mowinckel, who was the main driving force behind the policy, regarded the state of inter-Scandinavian relations as a strong reason for supposing

Norway to be safe from attack. In November 1929 he assured a public audience in Bergen:

Our defence must now constitute a definite guard for our neutrality. Nothing more. . . . As regards land strategy, the situation is quite clear when we reflect upon the arbitration treaties which bind together the whole of the North. As regards sea strategy, we must remember that it is Britain which rules the northern seas, and that this will presumably be the case for a long time to come.

Later in the same month, his confidential instructions for a Foreign Ministry evaluation of the situation took the same line, starting with 'a totally changed position'[19] since 1914 in Norway's relationship with its land neighbours.

MARITIME ACTIVITIES

The organization of herring export associations in 1927–8 marked an increasing awareness of the importance to the economy of Norway's position as the principal European exporter of fish. Mention has already been made of the acute difficulties that had arisen (see p. 302) when Prohibition provoked the wine-producing countries to retaliate by closing the market to Norwegian stockfish and klipfish, which were in any case less in demand because of a rising standard of living in southern Europe. Norwegian exporters therefore diverted much of their trade to the more distant markets of Africa, South America, and Cuba, where they also suffered less from the Icelandic competition which had grown up during the war years. Another change was in the extension of the fishing area, both to the vicinity of Norway's new possessions, Spitsbergen and Bear Island, and out into the Atlantic as far as the coast of West Greenland, where rising sea-temperatures were improving the quality of the catch. The State Bank for Fisheries, established in 1922, encouraged whole-time fishermen employing larger vessels and better equipment in such ventures. However, in the later 1930s the catch in more distant waters did not exceed 30,000 tons a year, as compared with a total catch of about 1,000,000 tons, so Norway's strongest interest continued to be the control of her inshore waters. In 1926 the

Foreign Affairs Committee of the Storting complained because Norway did not secure representation in the League of Nations sub-committee on the subject.

Except for particular coastal districts, lying mainly in the far north, the fisheries were of course far less significant than the carrying trade as a source both of wealth and international influence. In view of the heavy loss of ships during the war years, the prolonged internal economic troubles, and the world catastrophe of the early 1930s, when world trade shrank to one-third of its former dimensions in three years, the efforts of Norwegian shipowners may be accounted the biggest single achievement in their country's external relations. A fleet, which had suffered a net reduction of 30 per cent during the years of the war and had consequently fallen to the eighth place among the world's mercantile marines, was fourth again in 1939; its tonnage had been restored to pre-war level as early as 1922, and was subsequently doubled.

These results were not achieved without a ruthless taking of risks, in which the weakest went to the wall. The case of Hannevig, the shipowning millionaire *par excellence* of the First World War, whose interests in the United States suffered through requisitioning in 1917, is a striking example: his suit for 80 million dollars (including interest), though sponsored by the Norwegian government, did not reach the American Court of Claims until 1959, nine years after his death, and was then totally rejected. Many smaller shipping businesses faded out less sensationally, for want of the means to finance new purchases in a rapidly changing market; after 1933 there was special pressure upon the owners of older tank-ships, who were squeezed out by an international tanker pool, which made a levy on the newer ships to subsidise the laying up of others. Crews were also exposed to the full blast of competition: larger vessels, and especially tankers, provided less employment in proportion to their size, so it was difficult to resist wage cuts designed to bring Norwegian costs down to the level of other European countries, where seamen's wages had fallen more heavily since the end of the world war.

Far-sighted shipowners went in for technological improvements, in spite of the difficulty of financing the purchase of newer types of ship, which had to be obtained mainly from foreign yards. Unemployment in Britain helped to keep prices down, and from about 1926 the creditworthiness of the Norwegians enabled them to build extensively with foreign capital, repayable out of the ship's first earnings. Skill was also shown in placing the contracts most advantageously in such years as 1935, immediately before a rise in the freight market. The result was that the small steamer followed the sailing ship into almost complete oblivion: between 1920 and 1939 the proportion of motor ships increased from 5 per cent to 60 per cent of total tonnage, and the average size of all Norwegian ships engaged in foreign trade from 1,575 to 3,755 gross tons.[20]

One of the two developments that mattered most from an international standpoint was that the tonnage assigned to tramp work remained stationary, which meant that the proportion of Norwegian ships so employed in foreign waters sank in twenty years from a little over 80 per cent to a little over 30 per cent. Regular lines took their place, though this often involved owners in the risk of building vessels for one particular trade—with fast engines for the fruit trade, chillrooms for meat storage, or cranes and winches designed to lift locomotives and other heavy machinery. As the shipping lines spread their activities farther afield, they ceased in many cases to have a Norwegian port as one of their terminals: by 1939 two-fifths of a liner fleet of about 1,000,000 tons was based on North American ports, and replacements of crew travelled out as far as the Pacific to join Norwegian ships which never came nearer home.

The other development, which proved still more profitable, arose out of the rapid growth of world requirements in oil, which trebled during the inter-war years and by 1939 accounted for one-fifth of all maritime trade. Norwegians seized their chance. In 1922 they owned thirty small tankers of 144,000 tons. By 1927 the tonnage was 400,000, which was doubled in the next two years, rose to 1,250,000 in 1932, and reached 2,117,000 in 1939. Thus, at the moment when the tanker and its contents acquired exceptional value as the veritable sinews of modern war, Norway's share was one-fifth of the world's tanker fleet. Moreover, an early phase in which the Norwegians operated steam-driven tankships of an older pattern—cheap purchases bought to earn the money for later re-placements—had been followed by an intense concentration upon motor-driven vessels; in 1939 these constituted three-quarters of their tanker fleet, which in this vital respect led the world.

In the Antarctic whaling developments of the inter-war period Norwegian shipowners showed much the same readiness to exploit technical advances regardless of risk as they did in the carrying trade, and the results were for a time even more spectacular. The special type of slip for hauling the carcass of the world's largest mammal on to the deck of a factory ship, where it could be flensed and prepared for the boiler, was patented by a Norwegian whale-gunner in 1924 and was brought into use the next season. The profits were so good that, instead of adapting older vessels, capital was found for purpose-built floating factories of as much as 24,000 tons; with the help of improvements in processing, these were capable of a daily output of 2,500 barrels of whale oil and could store the re-sults of forty days' full activity for conveyance from the Antarctic to the eventual place of sale. In addition, a special kind of tank boat was devised, which could carry back the oil while the factory ship remained at work throughout the season. In 1927–8 the Antarctic produced 750,000 barrels of oil from half a dozen land stations and seventeen ships; three seasons later there were forty-one ships at work, and the product was nearly 3,500,000 barrels. The Norwe-gian proportion was almost two-thirds of the whole: the yield on whaling shares rose to 40 per cent, and the best gunners in the fleet of small whalers which served each factory ship might return home with kr. 100,000 as a season's earnings.

The situation was too good to last. In spite of its use as an in-gredient in margarine, whale oil had a strong competitor in vege-table oils; in 1931 the world economic crisis affected Unilever, who were the biggest purchasers; the price fell from £30 to £9 a ton. In the season of 1931/2 the Norwegians accordingly cancelled their expeditions, but to their disappointment the British, though de-pendent upon Norway for much of their skilled personnel and special equipment, did not do the same. From 1932/3 to 1939/40 whale hunting flourished again, and the Norwegians succeeded in making a quota agreement with British interests to avoid a disastrous further depletion of what was evidently a limited total stock of whales in the antarctic fishing grounds; one good result was a more efficient use of the carcass. But the Germans and Japanese now entered the field, and although Germany agreed with some reluctance to a regulation of catches, Japan refused. The Norwegian share—of a total which never quite regained the height of 1930/1—fell to less than 30 per cent and was slightly below the British.[21]

The adoption of pelagic whaling had been stimulated by the fear on the part of Norwegian firms that shore concessions might be terminated by the British, as had been threatened during the First World War. The success of the new method caused the shore stations in South Georgia and on Deception Island in the South Shetlands to fall into disuse, but interest in other Antarctic territory was strengthened by the search for additional hunting grounds. From 1927 onwards a series of expeditions was organized mainly by Lars Christensen, a wealthy owner of shipping and whaling companies, who took part himself and published accounts of the scientific and other discoveries;* much use was made of reconnaissance by aircraft, which were even flown from the deck of a whaling factory. The practical results included the annexation by Norway of Bouvet Island and the rather larger Peter I Island, on which landings were made in 1927 and 1929 respectively. Much of the coastline of the Antarctic continent was also examined, partly from the air, and in 1938–9 Norway established its claim to a large sector, defined by an Anglo-Norwegian agreement after the Second World War as stretching from 20°W. to 45°E. It was given the name of Dronning (i.e. Queen) Maud Land, and one or two English designations for parts of the coast were officially abolished.

THE EAST GREENLAND DISPUTE

Norway's Antarctic interests had developed out of a much older interest in the Arctic, where in 1929 she annexed Jan Mayen Island and the labours of her hunters provided some excuse for the aggression now to be described. But this Norwegian attempt to claim terri-

---

* *Such is the Antarctic* (1935); *My last expedition to the Antarctic, 1936–7. With a review of the research work . . . 1927–1937* (1938).

tory in East Greenland through a private *coup de main*, which provided a sensational news item for the world press in the summer of 1931, was so out of keeping with the general course of national policy that its causes must lie far deeper. The memory of the vanished medieval Norwegian colony in West Greenland appealed to the romantic imagination. The validity of the tacit surrender of the resulting rights of sovereignty to Denmark by the treaty of Kiel (see p. 4) was open to elaborate legal arguments such as Norwegians like to deploy. The acquisition of Spitsbergen showed that it was no longer impossible for Norway to re-expand, and in a time of widespread economic disappointment and bitter social controversy it was tempting for politicians to seek to rally the nation by an exciting programme of foreign adventure. In the words of a historian of Norwegian foreign policy: 'In some circles the nationalistic tendencies in Norway entirely got the upper hand and developed into chauvinism, directed especially against Denmark. One may even speak with some justification of a Norwegian "Arctic ocean imperialism".'[22]

In 1917 the Danish government took the opportunity of the sale of their three Virgin Islands to the United States to secure American recognition of Danish sovereignty over the whole of Greenland, although settlement was confined entirely to the west coast, except for the presence of a small group of native Greenlanders or Eskimoes at Angmagssalik. Other powers followed the American lead, but after discussion in the Foreign Affairs Committee of the Storting in July 1919 Ihlen gave the Danes no more than a cautious verbal assurance 'that the Norwegian government will not make difficulties in the arrangement of this matter'.[23] Two years later Ihlen's successor as foreign minister refused to put this in writing, because it had been belatedly realized that the exercise of Danish sovereignty might mean the extension from West to East Greenland of the Danish trade monopoly and the consequent exclusion of Norwegian hunters and fishermen. When the monopoly was thus extended, it triggered off an acrimonious legal dispute. On the one hand, the Norwegians claimed that, in spite of the debt settlement of 1819–21 (see p. 65), their country had never accepted the treaty of Kiel, on which Danish rights over any part of Greenland must be founded;

on the other, that East Greenland's existing status was that of a *terra nullius*, which ought to be allocated to the Norwegians as its established users, on the understanding that they would practise an Open Door policy. Since no settlement could be reached on the matter of principle, the two states made a twenty-year agreement in 1924 on the practical issue: except for Angmagssalik, the whole of the east coast was to be equally available for hunting and fishing to citizens of both countries, who might appropriate land and set up stations for scientific or humanitarian purposes.

By this time, however, too much suspicion had been aroused on both sides for the question of sovereignty to be allowed to rest. In 1925 a new Danish law was specifically made applicable to all Greenland, and the Danes conceded most-favoured-nation treatment in East Greenland to British and French subjects. Next year the leader of Danish activities in East Greenland was declared to have police powers over Norwegian residents, and in 1930 he was charged with the execution of a three-year plan for setting up Eskimo colonies and Danish stations in the region between 70° and 75°, where the Norwegians had previously been left in sole possession. The Norwegian government protested, and with a view to the further development of scientific interests in the disputed area the Storting in 1928 established a Council for Svalbard and the Arctic Ocean; three members of a scientific expedition were also given police powers in East Greenland, though over Norwegians only. Shortly before the fall of Mowinckel's second ministry in May 1931, the activists who dominated the Arctic Council brought matters to a head by formally demanding that the disputed region should be placed under Norwegian occupation.

Mowinckel could ride the storm; the Agrarian prime ministers who followed him could not. Their political experience was minimal, and they were handicapped by the strong nationalist sentiments of many of their followers: the founder of their party was a nephew of the national historian, P. A. Munch, and since 1927 the wrongs of East Greenland had figured in the official programme. Before the end of the Storting session in June, it was agreed that no precipitate step should be taken. But only two days later, a tiny group of hunters was incited by the chairman of the Arctic Council[24] and other activists to raise the Norwegian flag over a district stretching from 71° 30′ to 75° 40′, to which they gave the name of Eric the Red's Land. The reasonable sequel was the acceptance of an immediate Danish proposal to refer the question of sovereignty to the Hague Tribunal; what was less reasonable was the decision of the government to try to better Norway's position, in case the court made East Greenland a *terra nullius*, by turning a contested private venture into an official act of state. The Agrarian cabinet did this in July 1931, against the better judgement of the prime minister, Kolstad, and the minister for foreign affairs; a year later Kolstad's successor, Hundseid, proclaimed a second annexation of territory farther south, down to Cape Farewell.

The Hague case ended in a complete rejection of the Norwegian claims; these were not helped by Hundseid's attempt to use the indefatigable Wedel Jarlsberg to effect a compromise, which he kept secret even from his own foreign minister but could not prevent from leaking out through Danish channels. Out of the twelve international judges only the Norwegian (Vogt) found in Norway's favour; nine considered that Danish sovereignty over all Greenland had been established since 1814 and had been bindingly acknowledged by Ihlen in 1919. The judgement, announced in April 1933, was complied with immediately by the new Mowinckel government, while the Storting, by a majority of 114 to 29, recorded its regret that 'Norway's chances had been ruined' by a policy at variance with what had been approved. The practical agreement which protected Norwegian economic interests in East Greenland continued in operation for half a century. Much more important, failure over a juridical issue which, in the words of a Storting document, 'awakened in the Norwegian people the memory of ancient wrong',[25] did not prevent Norway from continuing to associate itself with Denmark in a world situation where small neighbours could ill afford to quarrel.

THE DARKENING SCENE

In the opening year of the disastrous 1930s the death of Nansen had deprived Norway of its most influential spokesman in world affairs, but the nation still pinned its faith in the League. Even the entry into power in 1935 of the Labour Party, which had always demanded withdrawal from League membership, meant only that an increased emphasis was laid upon Norway's right to opt out of any participation in military sanctions: Koht was as eager as any of his predecessors to play an active part at Geneva. Nevertheless, the failure of the League to check Japanese aggression in Manchuria, the breakdown of the World Disarmament Conference, the inadequacy of economic sanctions to prevent the Italian conquest of Ethiopia, and the long series of successes enjoyed by Nazi Germany —all these were regarded by thoughtful Norwegians as the writing on the wall. It was no longer possible to rely implicitly on defence by or through the League as a sufficient protection for Norway, while at the same time it began to appear that the fulfilment of her obligations to the League might create the very situation in which protection was suddenly needed.

In these circumstances one logical alternative was to build up the Norwegian defences as a deterrent to any potential aggressor. A very determined government might possibly have done enough to render invasion too hazardous to be resorted to at all readily by any of Norway's neighbours. But in Norway, as in the United Kingdom, France, and other western democracies, the 1930s was an era of morally weak governments, taking their cue from electorates to which economic problems were of paramount importance. Only the Conservatives believed in principle in adequate national defences. Mowinckel was an ardent believer in compulsory arbitration as a panacea, and his outlook was strongly coloured by the pacifism that had many supporters in the Left Party. As for Labour, its dread of the strike-breaking potentialities of the armed forces had given it the traditional slogan of the 'broken rifle', and as late as 1932 it bitterly opposed a scheme for establishing a kind of militia (*Leidangen*) as a voluntary reserve under the control of regular officers. At that date it nominally supported complete unilateral disarmament, though it also contemplated the institution of a civilian defence force, to be armed if necessary—but not officered by the bourgeoisie. When they came into power in 1935, the Labour government did not disarm and after cancelling *Leidangen* it discussed democratization of the army: but Nygaardsvold was impatient when the Cabinet had to give time to defence questions, while Koht believed that a more skilful foreign policy might provide the answers.

The Defence Law of 1933 (see p. 347) provided the general framework within which Mowinckel's government operated for two years and Nygaardsvold's for five. The cadre of officers was greatly reduced and only a minute 'neutrality guard' would be capable of rapid mobilization; but larger forces could be mobilized more gradually to prevent serious infringements of Norwegian neutrality or to take action, if required, in support of the League of Nations. The period of training for the annual intake of recruits was to be increased in two stages—from sixty to seventy-two days in 1935 and to eighty days in 1936—but no provision was made for regimental exercises; the navy was to depend in the same way upon short-term service, while the transfer of the coastal artillery to its charge emphasized the fact that its duties lay in coastal waters, where small, lightly armed vessels might suffice. The obvious deficiencies of the whole scheme were glossed over by means of a hypothesis that 'a far-sighted foreign-policy leadership'[26] would give warning of the approach of any danger period making further measures necessary.

Since the danger period had already arrived in 1933, the story of additions made to the defences during the following years is that of too little done too late. When economic sanctions against Italy, in which Norway participated loyally at some cost to her fish exports, were abandoned as futile in 1936, Koht deprecated 'using the present political situation in the world to scare us and get us to agree to bigger military expenditure than we would have agreed to otherwise'.[27] However, from that year onwards the full annual intake of recruits was called up for training, and in the late autumn a modest sum of kr. 4 million was voted for defence preparations in North Norway—an exception which we may perhaps relate to the concern expressed by Tranmæl, the inveterate anti-militarist of the Labour Party, for closing any route by which the western powers might attack the Soviet Union. In 1937 the Storting decided on extra military expenditure totalling kr. 17 million, to be spread over three years, but Nygaardsvold was still ready to resign office sooner than put into effect the eighty days of training prescribed by the Defence

Law. Next year, however, he gave way on this, and also approved a loan of kr. 50 million, one-half for military objects and one-half for civil air defence and emergency supplies. In April 1939, when the government proposed to spend an extra kr. 20 million on defence, only four diehards contested the grant, and some of the younger Labour members of the Storting would have liked to break their party bonds and support the Conservatives and Agrarians in voting a much larger appropriation.[28] But in any case the outbreak of war in Europe was now too close for a small power to have any chance of making up lost time.

The upshot was that in September 1939 the Norwegian armed forces were in a very much worse position than in August 1914 as regards training, quality and quantity of equipment, and definition of purpose. As to this last, a senior officer observes in retrospect: 'It was not defined. Was the defence to be a "token defence" [*etikette-forsvar*], a neutrality guard which should take action only against chance breaches of neutrality, and confine itself to observing, reporting, and protesting against serious and deliberate breaches; or was it to be a defence for life or death [*eksistensforsvar*]?'[29] In the light of after-events this uncertainty has often been condemned as showing a singular indecisiveness of purpose, though the reluctance to face disagreeable facts and rearm accordingly was shared by all the western democracies. In Norway's case it was by no means certain that, if five times as much had been spent on defence—which is approximately what the military and naval experts asked for—the result would have been a permanently effective insurance policy; the cost of buying modern arms abroad would in any event have had serious repercussions on the balance of trade and the programme of social reform, making it very difficult to execute such a project. It was therefore a natural, though in the long run disastrous, temptation to a Norwegian government to shelve intractable problems of defence, while reconsidering its foreign policy with a view to securing a neutral status which might not need to be defended.

In December 1930 Mowinckel was the prime mover in the Convention of Oslo, an attempt to counterwork the growth of protectionism, which was increasing the political tension in Europe. Where more ambitious efforts under League auspices had failed, he used his contacts made at the Assembly in Geneva to secure agreement to a very modest measure: this provided for a cooling-off period of thirty days before a tariff increase was imposed, so that states affected could present the case against it. The original signatories to the Convention were Norway, Sweden, Denmark, and the Netherlands, followed by Belgium and Luxemburg and (in 1933) by Finland. The economic results were trifling, but the formation of what was often called the 'Oslo group' of states provided a political basis for the effort to reassert a neutral status, which was the central feature in Norwegian foreign policy from 1934 onwards. In that year Mowinckel put forward the need to break away from compulsory participation in League sanctions at a meeting of Scandinavian foreign ministers in Stockholm. Next year the policy passed into the hands of Koht, but Mowinckel supported the new government, both in its inattention to defence and in its close attention to neutrality. 'Unconditional neutrality ought to be Norway's line', he declared in 1938. '. . . Every deviation from this increases the risk of being involved in a war among the great powers.'[30]

The danger that economic sanctions under Section 16 of the League Covenant, which (unlike military sanctions) were clearly obligatory for all members of the League, might result in a small country being manoeuvred into a war between rival great powers became fully evident for the first time during the Ethiopian crisis in 1935–6. Koht thereupon sought to rouse opinion in favour of more conciliatory methods of action than compulsory sanctions in all the lesser European states, even visiting Poland for this purpose, but he soon realized that his most hopeful sphere of operation was the Oslo Group or a slightly larger body made up of the seven ex-neutrals of 1914–18. In July 1936 Koht laid a strong resolution before this body, but it preferred a more tentative Danish wording, of which Koht in private observed scornfully, 'Denmark merely inquires what England wishes.'[31] After nearly two more years of great-power manoeuvrings, in which the League might at any time have been embroiled, the Storting resolved unanimously that Norway was entitled to remain neutral 'in any war that it does not itself recognize as a League of Nations action'.[32] When its members met at Copenhagen in July, the Oslo Group was still fearful of losing the benefits of League membership along with the obligations, but a resolution was passed in favour of making sanctions 'facultative', which was accepted by twenty-seven states at Geneva in September. It had taken exactly four years to vindicate the right to neutrality as proposed by Mowinckel to his fellow Scandinavians.

Even in peacetime it was not easy for a small state to steer a neutral course. In 1935 Trotsky was given asylum in Norway, but Soviet pressure made it impossible to retain him; in 1936 the Nobel prize was awarded to the German pacifist writer, Carl von Ossietzky, but it was deemed expedient for Koht to withdraw from the awarding committee in order to blunt the wrath of Hitler, who forbade the acceptance of the prize by any German. In the event of war both Nygaardsvold and Mowinckel, whose rival party ideologies scarcely affected their views on defence, intended that Norway should practise a completely impartial neutrality; Koht however was disposed to modify this to the extent of conceding trade and other non-military benefits to an approved victim of aggression. Yet when the British reaction to Hitler's seizure of the rump of Czechoslovakia convinced the Norwegian foreign minister that a major European war impended, probably within six months, the government (as we have seen) still did very little to improve the defences so that Norwegian neutrality might be more readily respected. At home, the officers of the army and navy continued to be deeply distrusted by most Labour politicians, for class reasons; abroad, Koht rejected all suggestions for a Scandinavian defence agreement, even after Norway had aligned herself with Sweden by refusing Hitler's offer of a non-aggression pact.

The Labour government had the full support of the Storting, except for the Conservative members, and of the great bulk of the electors and the organs of opinion. Heavier taxes would be unwelcome, and it was natural to cherish the belief that a neutrality which had been preserved in face of many difficulties throughout one world war could somehow be preserved again. Koht as a professional historian was doubtless more sceptical about history repeating itself. But he believed (as did Mowinckel) that no building up of its defences could enable Norway to preserve its rights of neutrality against the ruthless action of a great power. Koht held, for ideological reasons chiefly, that Russia would not attack his country, and for strategic reasons that Germany could not. This left only Britain, and although Koht was no Anglophile, he appreciated that the British navy was much more likely to be employed in an extremity to enforce an alliance than an occupation: he concluded that in the meantime 'What we may be compelled to do against our will is better left undiscussed'.[33]

THE IMAGE OF NORWAY ABROAD

Whereas the 1920s offered uniquely favourable conditions for the independent development of the smaller European peoples, the darkening scene of the 1930s had disappointed most of their hopes. But the Norwegians were fortunate in that, right down to the catastrophe of 1940, their image was becoming clearer and their special place in the community of nations more assured.

Since a small nation makes its mark chiefly through its culture—using that term in its widest sense—the Norwegian achievement was all the more remarkable because the direct cultural impact in North America was now declining. In 1916–20 Norwegian emigration sank to the level of the far-off days before the American Civil War. In the next decade it rose to about one third of the rate that had prevailed in the boom years of the transatlantic movement at the beginning of the century. But in the 1930s in spite of heavy unemployment at home the Great Depression helped to make the new industrialized America less attractive to Norwegians. The annual total of emigrants (including those who went to Canada and other destinations) was below 1,000—much smaller than the quota for Norway of 2,377 admissions to the United States, authorized by the National Origins Act of 1929.[34] Accordingly, in 1940 the Norwegian-born population of the United States was smaller than at any census since 1880: except in remote rural enclaves, the second and later generations of American–Norwegians were linked with the old country by ties of sentiment rather than cultural appreciation.

In the field of humanitarian endeavour the work of Nansen, as we have seen, eclipsed all others, though persons of insight might see a similar motive in the widely supported work of Norwegian foreign missions. In spite of the pressure of Norway's economic troubles upon the multitude of small givers who supplied the financial support, none of the main evangelizing efforts was curtailed and a new one was begun in 1925 in the French mandated territory of Cameroon. But for the newspaper readers of the world the only Norwegian who hit the headlines as Nansen had so often done was his successor in the field of Arctic exploration, Roald Amundsen. Norway's prosperity during the First World War enabled him to raise funds—including kr. 200,000 from the Storting and kr. 100,000 from Hannevig—for building a new ship, the *Maud*, in which he set out at midsummer, 1918, to repeat the voyage of the *Fram* (see p. 232), though on a more northerly course through the ice. Adverse weather conditions prevented him from carrying out his plan, for which the *Maud* was kept in operation until 1925. But he began by making the North-East Passage, and up-to-date equipment enabled H. U. Sverdrup (a distant relation of Nansen's earlier associate) to achieve important scientific results, while Amundsen busied himself with an alternative plan for reaching the North Pole by aeroplane. This, too, failed, but Amundsen subsequently enlisted the support of the wealthy American explorer, Lincoln Ellsworth, for two joint ventures—an attempt to reach the Pole by seaplane from Svalbard, which nearly cost them their lives, and a voyage across the Pole to Alaska by airship in 1926, which triumphantly fulfilled Amundsen's ambition to be the first man to reach both Poles. Two years later he disappeared on an attempt to rescue the crew of an Italian airship, which had been wrecked north of Svalbard.

In the general advance of science, which was increasingly an international achievement, Norway was perhaps best known in two branches to which polar studies were particularly relevant. In oceanography Nansen's pioneer work was continued by Johan Hjort (see p. 273) and by H. U. Sverdrup, who later became the first director of a Norwegian polar institute. The name of Norway was, however, most specifically associated with the Bergen School of meteorology, that is to say, the modern methods of weather forecasting which were first developed at an institute in Bergen by the physicist, V. F. K. Bjerknes,[*] his son, and other Norwegians. The value of

[*] 1862–1951. The son of a well-known physicist, C. A. Bjerknes, whose work

their basic discovery of the 'polar front' was triumphantly demonstrated by the storm warnings for fishermen, first issued in the
winter of 1919–20. In the humane studies a minor language imposes
a serious handicap, but philology and archaeology were fields of
special interest to Norwegian scholars, while Halvdan Koht, who
lived to be 'the dean of living historians',* was the first president
(1926–33) of the International Committee of the Historical Sciences.

What of the arts? By 1914 the world of culture, as we have seen,
had accustomed itself to the idea that the mountains of Norway
fostered a remarkable proportion of creative talent; a quarter of a
century later Norwegian prestige in the arts was still considerable.
From about the year 1920, when the Nobel Prize was awarded to
Hamsun for *The Growth of the Soil*, his reputation as one of the foremost European novelists spread from Germany to the English-
speaking countries. A comparable psychological depth, together
with a wonderful ability to re-create to her readers' satisfaction the
supposed social atmosphere of medieval life, won a tremendous
vogue for the long historical novels of Sigrid Undset, another recipient of the Nobel Prize for literature. Olav Duun's six-volume
masterpiece *The People of Juvik* and the wide-ranging novels of
Tarjei Vesaas gave great distinction to neo-Norwegian. Together
with Johan Bojer, author of *The Last of the Vikings*, and Johan Falkberget, a historical novelist whose milieu was the Röros copper
mines, these writers helped to create what Norwegians regarded as
a second golden age in their literature, though their impact abroad
was reduced to some extent by the regional character of much of
their work: Bojer alone was extensively available in English. The
drama and lyric poetry also flourished in the hands of authors who
were often politically 'engaged'; Arnulf Överland, for example, expounded the views of *Mot Dag*, and Nordahl Grieg (a connection of

---

he continued; published *Dynamic Meteorology and Hydrology*, 1910–11; professor
of physics at Leipzig, 1913–17. In applying theory to practice at Bergen in
1918, he was helped by his son, J. A. Bjerknes, who in 1940 became a professor
at the University of California, L.A., and played a leading part in weather
forecasts for military purposes.

* So described by William L. Langer in the year of his ninetieth birthday, 1964,
when a Koht bibliography enumerated 3,104 published items, including 184
books.

the musician) was for a time one of the most uncritical admirers of Stalin's Russia. Neither their plays nor their lyrics lent themselves to translation, but the Norwegian theatre was known to have high standards, and some of its leading actors and actresses appeared on foreign stages.

A recent writer observes that in Norway 'musical life has always had poor conditions'.[35] Grieg had no true successor: the work of Harald Sæverud, who derived a rather similar inspiration from the native folk music, was well received abroad, but the highly original atonal compositions of Fartein Valen first gained international recognition at a festival of contemporary music held in Copenhagen in 1947. In painting and sculpture, however, Norway's position was greatly enhanced during the inter-war years. Edvard Munch continued, almost until his death in 1944, to produce the richly coloured landscapes and profound human studies that made him one of the most influential of modern painters. The revival of the art of fresco-painting, which was brought to Oslo from Copenhagen by Emanuel Vigeland, also produced some works of merit—chiefly by Norwegian pupils of Matisse—to engage the attention of foreign visitors. Norway owed much more, however, to Emanuel's sculptor brother, Gustav Vigeland.*

The quality of his work varied from brilliant portraiture and ethereal fancy to a Teutonic heaviness and sheer repetition, but at his not infrequent best Vigeland might bear comparison with Rodin, the French master whose influence he would not acknowledge. It is, however, the overwhelming quantity that makes most impact, whether in the Fountain elaborated over half a century or in the hundred life-size figures on his Tree of Life or in innumerable separate studies of childhood, manhood and womanhood, and old age. For better and worse, this had a social origin in the unique generosity of the Oslo municipality, which from 1921 until his death in 1943

---

* 1869–1943. He was the son of a puritanical carpenter in the little south-coast town of Mandal, and was apprenticed to wood-carving in Oslo, 1884. He showed his first sculptures at the Oslo Autumn Exhibition, 1889; sought inspiration in Paris, Berlin, and other foreign art centres, 1892–6; and won the competition for the university's memorial to Abel, 1902. The proliferating Sculpture Park was incomplete at his death.

provided Vigeland with his livelihood, studio, and team of crafts-men, leaving him free to develop his art in whatever way he chose as the city's eventual inheritance. The fact that Oslo could act in this way as a collective Maecenas during a period of almost continu-ous economic stress gives the reflective visitor a striking impression of the extent to which the arts in Norway have been promoted as a national possession.

An increase in foreign visitors of all kinds resulted from the general growth of communications and leisure. At first the expan-sion was chiefly through the vogue for cruises to the fiords, but in the 1930s the tourist season began to be profitably lengthened by the rising interest in winter sports. The prowess of Norwegian skiers and skaters (especially Sonja Henie, who had a second career as a film star) helped Norway to establish itself as a possible alternative to Switzerland in this field, and capital was made available, partly in support of the campaign to reduce unemployment, for a much-needed modernization of hotels: in five years the supply of bath-rooms, for instance, was doubled. In 1931 the number of tourists was 72,000, about 50 per cent more than in the best pre-war years, but by 1937 it rose to nearly a quarter of a million. For the present pur-pose it is of interest to see what were the main countries to which they carried back their impressions. not only of scenery but also of society. The Swedes, having only a land frontier to cross, were in-evitably the most numerous visitors, but the British came second, followed by the Danes; then the Germans, the Americans, and the Dutch. The fact that Americans stand so high on the list is signific-ant, for after the Wall Street crash in 1929 the long journey was a serious expense for most members of the middle-income group. A majority were probably drawn to visit Norway by ties of Norwegian ancestry, sedulously cultivated by organizations such as *Nordmanns-forbundet*, which in 1922–45 had C. J. Hambro as its very active chairman; but Norway was also attractive to Americans as a peace-ful democracy, agreeable to visit and even to study at a time when these were beginning to be in short supply.

For the image of Norway was increasingly affected by the pro-ficiency that its people showed in a different kind of art from those that have been briefly touched upon here. In a book which reached its second edition in 1939, an Englishman reported that from ten years' residence among them he had 'discovered that this people had learned the extremely difficult art of living—not merely existing'.[36] To some extent it was a matter of a slower tempo of life, but the writer, who was an enthusiast for the co-operative movement, found that 'the co-operative spirit' which had made economic relationships more harmonious in Norway was also responsible for the development of a sensitive social conscience. As we saw in an earlier chapter, the social services made little progress during the years of endemic crisis after the First World War: indeed, as late as 1933 an official inquiry showed that Norwegian expenditure *per capita* on social welfare was less than two-thirds of the provision made in Sweden or Denmark.[37] But the measures of the Labour government from 1935 onwards aroused considerable interest abroad, both for their own sake and because they might help to explain the calm and contentment which appeared as a contrast to the ominous developments elsewhere on the European continent.

An American survey, published in April 1939, summed up Norway's position as follows:

The days of Communist agitators seem to be over and the ship of state is sailing forward on a remarkably even keel . . . In a world increasingly totalitarian, Norway governs by reason. With a record which has its failures and a system which has its faults, she is, nevertheless, true to her conviction that governmental democracy can exist only in conjunction with economic democracy, and she progresses steadfastly towards those two allied objectives. Such a point of view rests not only upon the national instinct for equality and passion for democracy, but also upon education.[38]

Only twelve months before the German onslaught, the American authoress rounded off her picture by noting with approval that in the preceding year the Storting had made a larger appropriation for education than for defence.

12. War and Recovery, 1939–1949

IN THE GENERAL HISTORIES OF THE SECOND WORLD War, Norway figures chiefly as the victim of a skilfully planned and callously executed German stroke, which Britain and France proved quite unable to parry. The fact that one element in the population subsequently collaborated with the German occupation is also remembered almost fortuitously from the name of its leader, Vidkun Quisling, while the vital service that the Norwegian mercantile marine rendered to the Allied cause is known, perhaps, as a matter of bare statistics. But there are other aspects of the wartime events which deserve consideration, because they contributed much to the Norway of today.

After the declared policy of strict neutrality had failed to preserve their country from the menace of intervention by either set of belligerent powers, the two-months campaign of April–June 1940 showed the Norwegian people that lack of arms, training, and psychological preparation for war could not be compensated either by their own improvisations or by hastily planned assistance from outside. Accordingly, the summer of 1940 was a time of profound disillusionment, accentuated by the failure of Allied arms in France and the long-uncertain issue of the Battle of Britain. However, from the last months of 1940 onwards civil and, later, military resistance to the 'new order' imposed by the Germans was organized with increasing skill and success by resolute leaders who emerged from many walks of life; their appeal was directed above all to national pride as outraged by the usurpations of the quislings. Close relations were gradually established between this 'home front' with its expanding military organization (*Milorg*) and the government in exile in London, which engaged the merchant fleet and whatever other forces it could muster in Allied service. Norwegians both at home and overseas prepared themselves to take part in a second Allied campaign in Norway, which during the middle period of the war was believed to be imminent; even after the attention of the Allies was concentrated upon other threatres, it still seemed unlikely that their native soil would be liberated without a costly struggle. The peaceful surrender of the huge German garrison was therefore an unexpected denouement which enabled the nation to concentrate upon the rapid rehabilitation of the economy, for which plans had also been prepared during the last years of the war. The resistance movement produced its heroes and its martyrs, whose record the Norwegian people rightly treasure, but the total loss of life from the war was smaller in proportion to population than that of most other belligerents, and insignificant when compared with the holocausts in eastern Europe.

THE GATHERING STORM

From the standpoint of a small, would-be neutral power such as Norway, the general situation in September 1939 was considerably more perilous than in August 1914. It was true that on the earlier occasion Belgium had been almost completely overrun in the first phase of the campaign, but in 1939 Poland was the third country to be overwhelmed by the Germans in less than two years—and Britain and France had done nothing practical for its defence, even before the Russians joined Hitler in the partition. Yet the Western Allies claimed with greater vehemence than in 1914 that they had a moral right to preferential treatment, because they were fighting the battle of all small nations. This did not indeed prevent a satisfactory settlement of the questions of the distribution of Norwegian exports and the employment of the mercantile marine, which had caused so much trouble in 1914–18. An arrangement was made in November, by which Britain secured the use of 1,500,000 tons of tankers and 700,000 tons of other shipping—almost one-half of the total Norwegian fleet.[1] The British then tacitly conceded that trade with Germany might continue on the basis of pre-war quantities, so in March 1940 Norway was able to sign trade agreements with both sides. Meanwhile, however, the Allies had raised three more intractable issues.

One was the abuse of territorial waters in the Leads for German military purposes. As in the previous war, it was difficult to establish the exact position in which an Allied merchantman was sunk and that the cause was a torpedo, not a mine; the Norwegians not unnaturally gave the Germans the benefit of the doubt. They also treated the Germans considerately in the case of a naval supply ship, the ex-tanker *Altmark*, which committed several breaches of neutrality regulations while exercising an alleged right of 'mere passage' through 400 miles of Norwegian territorial waters in order to dodge the British navy. As the vessel was believed to be carrying prisoners taken by a German battleship in the Atlantic, Captain Philip Vian was instructed to ignore Norwegian protests, and a boarding party rescued 303 sailors from the holds at the cost of seven German lives. Many Norwegians took grave exception to what they regarded as a clear breach of international law,* but the most important result of the episode was the strengthening of the German belief that they could not afford to leave Norway alone.

The second issue was the use of territorial waters for German trade. About one-tenth of their annual import of high-grade Swedish iron ore was shipped via Narvik: because the Soviet–German Pact made their blockade so much less effective than in 1914–18, the Allies were disposed at all costs to stop up such holes as might be within their reach. From the first month of the war Churchill urged that the Leads should be mined, or alternatively patrolled by the British navy, so as to drive the ore ships out to sea. In early January the threat to do so, based on the allegations of German submarine sinkings already mentioned, became so serious that King Haakon appealed to King George VI to prevent action 'which will inevitably drag Norway into the war and place its existence as a sovereign state in the utmost danger'.[2]

This issue, however, was not pressed for the time being, because the Allies were busy with a larger project. On 30 November the Russians had invaded Finland; their action had been certified as aggression by the moribund League of Nations; and the Allies were therefore entitled on League principles to request free passage across

---

* Although an interchange of Notes on the legal aspects of the matter was interrupted by the German invasion of Norway, ten years later the Norwegian authorities still showed their displeasure by refusing permission for Vian, whose brilliant services in the Norwegian and later campaigns had brought him the command of the British Home Fleet, to take a destroyer into Jössingfiord in order to revisit the scene of the action.[3]

northern Norway and Sweden for forces designed to rescue the Finns. In passing through, these forces would automatically gain control of Narvik and of the Swedish ore-fields, thus cutting off the entire German supply from this source and thereby—according to the wildly over-optimistic reports then current—reducing their munitions supply to one year's campaign requirements. The preposterousness of a scheme which would almost certainly have brought the Allies, ill prepared as they were to face Germany, face to face with the Soviet armies as well, caused the British to hesitate; but the French favoured any strategy that might divert the main campaign of 1940 away from their own frontiers. The Swedish and Norwegian governments were firm in their refusal of passage; but there was much wishful thinking in Allied circles about the unlikelihood of serious armed resistance in any case by Norwegians or Swedes and the certainty of their co-operation if the Finns, whose cause they warmly supported, directly asked for Allied help. By the end of February a first echelon of 15,500 combatant troops was made ready to seize Narvik and advance up the railway to the mines; other bases would be occupied farther south in Norway, so that the second echelon of 42,000 men might move inland from Trondheim to stem any attempt to retrieve the situation on the part of the presumably dumbfounded Germans. It was indeed fortunate that on 12 March the Finns made peace with Moscow, thus destroying any pretext for the expedition, which had been due to start that day.

The situation in the seventh month of the war gave Norwegians good reason to be apprehensive about the intentions of the Allies, which the French took little trouble to conceal. The continuing discussion of the *Altmark* affair in Norway showed, indeed, that one large section of opinion was more concerned about the final outcome of the conflict between democracy and Fascism than about the niceties of international law and a violation of their neutrality which after all had humanitarian objects. But Koht felt justified in describing Churchill to Braüer, the German minister in Oslo, as 'a demagogue and a windbag' and Chamberlain as a 'bungler' for placing him at the head of the Admiralty.[4] The Germans, on the other hand, had so far created little apprehension, partly because their strategy originally preferred a neutral Norway, a policy which could perhaps be inferred from their not unconciliatory dealings over questions of trade. But the main factor was of course the secrecy in which an absolutist government can conduct its deliberations.

From October onwards Grand-Admiral Raeder had urged upon Hitler that the failure of the Imperial German navy to seize the Norwegian coastline as a means of egress to the Atlantic was a strategic blunder of the First World War which ought not to be repeated. But his master's gaze was fixed on France, whose Atlantic coast offered some of the same advantages; and he would have preferred to leave the future of Scandinavia for settlement at a later stage, if the many signs of Allied pressure in that direction had not aroused the fear that he might be forestalled. By this time Raeder as well as Rosenberg had his own contact man in Oslo—Schreiber as assistant naval attaché, Scheidt, as representative of the Scandinavian section of the German Nazi Party[5]—and it was decided to present Quisling to the Führer. At two interviews on 14 and 18 December, at which a Norwegian intermediary, A. V. Hagelin (see note, p. 392) and Scheidt were also present, Quisling confirmed Hitler's suspicion that the existing Norwegian government was hand-in-glove with the British; and while he remained sceptical about Quisling's ability to engineer a *coup*, he judged that he and his followers might prove useful tools, like the Nazi parties which provided a Fifth Column almost everywhere in Europe. Before the end of the month an operation against Norway was being studied; in January it was planned; in February troops were earmarked and—after the *Altmark* episode —General Falkenhorst was appointed commander; and, after a short lull when the Finnish armistice temporarily allayed Hitler's fears that the Allies might anticipate him, he finally decided that the seizure of Norway and Denmark should precede the campaign in the west, giving his general order on 26 March but delaying until 2 April to fix the most convenient day.

While the Germans awaited only the unfreezing of the Great Belt and the period of the new moon, which would facilitate a concealed approach to the Norwegian coast by night, the Allies again drew attention upon themselves by launching a project whose fulfilment was to some extent conditional. On 28 March they decided to revert to the mining of the Leads and to embark part of the military forces originally destined for Finland, so as to forestall the Germans by landing at Narvik, Trondheim, Bergen, and (temporarily) Stavanger, if the German reaction to the mining pointed to a forthcoming enemy invasion of Norway. A further implied 'if' was: if the Norwegians shared the Allied view of the German intentions, at any rate to the extent of admitting the Allied garrisons—for the troops were not organized to land against military opposition. The first report that something of this kind was in the wind reached Oslo through a British associate of Nansen, Philip Noel-Baker, on 3 April; two days later an Allied Note asserted the general right to take counter-measures against assistance given by Norway and Sweden to the German war effort in spite of their own obvious interest in the success of the Allies. Warning of the mines—allegedly laid at three points in the Leads but in fact only in the Vestfiord, which has Narvik at its head—was given in the early morning of the 8th, and provided the chief subject of discussion at the meeting of the Storting that evening, after which the cabinet decided to contest the action of the British navy by sweeping.

By a truly remarkable coincidence, however, the German navy was already at sea in full force for an operation which had the same primary object of forestalling the other side, but which depended for its success upon an altogether higher degree of organization and of unscrupulousness: if the Norwegians did not choose to receive them as friends, they were prepared from the first moment to enter the country as enemies. Before the Allied plans pass out of the picture, which from midnight on 8–9 April is completely filled by the German operation and reactions to it, two final points may be noticed. The concentration of attention and righteous indignation upon what the British had just done helps to explain the inability of Koht (to whom Nygaarsdvold was only too happy to relinquish responsibility in these matters) to base any precautionary action upon warnings, received from the Berlin legation and other sources, that a German expedition was moving northwards with Norway as its possible objective; these had been dramatically confirmed in the course of the 8th, when German soldiers from a torpedoed transport told their Norwegian rescuers that they had been bound for Bergen, and a special message from the British Admiralty directed attention to

Narvik. But Koht's 'failure to put two and two together', as he calls it,[6] had also a deeper reason. Though he found the British mine-laying outrageous, he shared the general belief of his compatriots that, although Britain might misuse its naval power, in the North Sea at least that power was unchallengeable. And British plans were based broadly speaking upon the same belief—until weather conditions and poor intelligence work favoured an audacious challenge, to which the still novel use of air power over coastal waters restricted the navy's reply.

In September 1939 Norway had mobilized its naval forces, including two pre-dreadnought ironclads, and about 7,000 soldiers; and four months later an additional brigade of troops under General C. J. Fleischer* had been placed in the far north on account of the Russo-Finnish War. The days of mounting tension might have been used for further mobilization, as was vainly urged by the General Staff on 5, 6, and 8 April. This would not of course have made up for the lack of training and equipment, but it would have permitted the orderly deployment of such military resources as Norway had immediately available, including the coastal fortresses which, when fully manned and with their minefields operational, secured the sea approaches to the main ports pending attack from the air. In view of the general disparity between German and Allied resources at this stage in the war, the Allies might not have enabled Norway to hold out for long, even if the German surprise attack had been repelled initially, but national pride was deeply wounded by the ease with which their country was overrun. The short-term result was to blacken the reputation of the government of 1940 as inept blunderers, if not worse; the long-term result was to make the Norwegians defence-minded. The historian will be reluctant to blame the government of a very small power, which had enjoyed 125 years of peace, for hoping against hope and sedulously avoiding any step that might be

---

* 1883–1942. He shared with Béthouart the distinction of inflicting upon the German army its first defeat in the Second World War. In June 1940 he accompanied the government to Britain as military adviser and army commander, but had great difficulty in co-operating harmoniously with the British and was passed over in 1942 for the appointment of defence commander; committed suicide shortly after he had been posted to Ottawa.

construed as provocative by a watchful but not yet fully committed aggressor.

THE GERMANS OVERRUN SOUTHERN AND CENTRAL NORWAY

Shortly before midnight of 8–9 April the German attack began at the entrance to the long Oslofiord, where the captain of a tiny Norwegian watch-boat lost his life in challenging the entry of the line of warships. Other ports, from Kristiansand to Narvik, were likewise approached in the darkness, with a view to a synchronized landing by 15,000 soldiers, commencing at 4.15 a.m. The coastal defences failed to keep them out, because their armament was meagre, their garrisoning incomplete, and the personnel as a whole psychologically unprepared for a brutally abrupt transition from peace to war. The forts protecting Bergen inflicted some damage as the German ships passed, those at the mouth of the Trondheimsfiord none: the second and third towns in Norway were occupied before breakfast. At Narvik the defences depended upon the two 4,000-ton ironclads, which dated from 1900 but were armed with six-inch guns. One was torpedoed as it attempted to close the enemy in the very heavy weather before opening fire; the other, stationed at the harbour, fired some ineffective salvoes as the first two German destroyers approached the quay, but was likewise torpedoed. Both ships sank within a minute; 276 lives were lost.[7] At Kristiansand the fort repelled the enemy twice, but let them pass at the third attempt shortly before noon, when a misread signal was taken to mean that the approaching ships were French—a clumsy mistake but understandable in the light of expected Allied intervention.

The Germans suffered only one serious setback. The fortress of Oscarsborg, which had been established to guard the narrows a few miles below Oslo at the time of the Crimean War, was resolutely commanded and received due warning of an enemy's advance up the long fiord. Its guns and torpedoes took full effect upon Germany's newest cruiser, which led the line; the advance was halted, the vessel eventually sank, and about 1,000 men were drowned, including Gestapo and other specialist troops for the occupation of Oslo.* The city was captured by airborne forces instead—the method adopted at the outset for securing Stavanger, with the only large Norwegian airfield—and within 24 hours the air bombing of Oscarsborg also reopened the sea route to the Norwegian capital. But the delay was politically decisive, for it enabled the royal family, the government, the members of the Storting, the general staff, and a handful of civilian officials, plus the gold reserve of the Bank of Norway, to be withdrawn into the interior, where the possibility of continued resistance could at least be examined.

The government had belatedly ordered a general and immediate mobilization,† and it firmly rejected the ultimatum presented by Braüer at the appointed hour of 4.20 a.m. But the outlook in the following afternoon, when the Storting met at Hamar (about 80 miles north of Oslo), was very black. The Allies had promised to send help 'as soon as possible',[8] but it would obviously be a harder task for them to dislodge the Germans than it would have been to keep them out in the first place. The commander-in-chief and many of his staff were resentful over the failure to mobilize in time, and were not inclined to underestimate the difficulty of organizing any effective resistance when many of the mobilization centres, which contained the equipment for the army, and all the main ports with their more readily deployed manpower were in enemy hands. It was known, too, that Denmark, engulfed in the same attack, had surrendered to avoid useless bloodshed. Moreover, at 7.32 p.m. Oslo Radio announced the formation of a rival government of N.S. members under Quisling. He had been in touch with German Intelligence at Copenhagen on 3 April, but learnt of the invasion

---

* A German vessel, *D. Widar*, had been placed in the harbour area beforehand to expedite the landings and maintain wireless communication with parties sent ashore. A gap of precisely five minutes was provided between the landing time and the diplomatic action to be taken by the German minister.[9]

† The order was misinterpreted by the General Staff, and first became known through an interview with Koht, which was broadcast about 8 a.m. Post-war inquiries divided the blame: the ministers had no copy of the mobilization scheme, and recorded no resolution; the commander-in-chief did not think it necessary to go to the ministers for further instructions; the defence minister though a professional officer, was new to his job.

early on the morning of the 9th from Scheidt and Schreiber, whose adroit management made possible a *coup* which was contemplated neither by Braüer nor by Falkenhorst.[10] Quisling used his usurped authority to cancel mobilization and order full co-operation with the Germans. Unpopular as he was, his intervention obviously added to the confusion and encouraged people to wait and see rather than take any action against the invaders.

Shortly afterwards, the legal rulers of the country had to move hurriedly to Elverum, 20 miles farther east and in the direction of the Swedish frontier, because four busloads of German paratroops were on their way to Hamar. At Elverum, however, the resourceful president of the Storting, C. J. Hambro, obtained the adoption by the silent assent of all members present[11] of a resolution investing the government with plenary powers until the legislature was reconvened by agreement between the government and its own presidential body. Nygaardsvold, who had intended to resign the premiership in despair, agreed at the same meeting that the cabinet should continue in office, reinforced by three consultative ministers from the opposition parties. His sense of democratic principle had been outraged by Quisling's usurpation, and this was likewise the point on which King Haakon took his stand next day, when Braüer arrived to negotiate with him and a delegation consisting of Koht and three members of the Storting. In the meantime, however, Hitler, incensed by the unexpected escape and defiance of the Norwegian government, had given a direct order to make Quisling premier, which made it impossible for Braüer to effect a compromise. While leaving it to the cabinet as his constitutional advisers to decide the fate of the nation, the king told its members in a moving scene that he would abdicate for himself and his house sooner than call to office a man who had no support 'either among our people as a whole or its representative organ, the Storting'.[12] The ministers followed the royal lead and determined to fight: the ignominy of a forced submission to Quisling steeled them to face a desperately difficult alternative.

On the morning of 11 April a new commander-in-chief, Otto Ruge,* who had fought in person to check the enemy sortie outside

* 1882–1961: A very active staff officer, who had been considered for the post

Elverum two evenings before, issued his first orders to a number of small and scattered units, his purpose being to hold the maximum of ground at the minimum of cost until the Allies came to the rescue. On the east side of the Oslofiord the Norwegian Army possessed a few small forts and its supplies were intact, but both in that area and at Kongsvinger on the Glomma, a little farther north, its men were quickly overrun by German forces fanning out from Oslo. In the south-west of Norway a considerable body of troops which fell back into the hinterland of Kristiansand surrendered on the 15th without a blow struck, and eight days later another isolated body, after inflicting some casualties from well-chosen positions east of Stavanger, likewise decided that further resistance would be pointless. On the Oslo–Trondheim axis, however, the delaying operations had a more obvious strategic value, and there the commander-in-chief was in a better position to assert his will. Volunteers made their way out of Oslo to fight the first small skirmishes in the nearby woods on 11 and 12 April, and ten days later the German advance north towards Trondheim was still being held by delaying actions south of the mountain massif—at points in the Glomma valley above Elverum; on both sides of Lake Mjösa above Hamar; and farther west at the head of the Randsfiord, to which a brigade had been transferred from the west of Norway by the Bergen railway. As some Norwegian troops had been mobilized both north and south of the 1,700 Germans in Trondheim, it was reasonable for Ruge at that stage to suppose that Allied aid might enable the city to be retaken. The civil and military authorities would then have a base for operations astride the rail and road routes back to the south.

But for reasons which are as familiar as they are painful, Allied aid proved to be a broken reed. From the Norwegian angle it must suffice to record the intense disappointment of the discovery that,

---

of defence minister in 1931 and helped to organize the reduced system of defence in 1933. He was promoted in April 1940 from general inspector of infantry to general in command, and in May to (supreme) defence commander; a prisoner of war in Poland and Germany, 1940–5; defence commander again in 1945, but retired the same year on account of disagreements with the defence minister, J. C. Hauge.

instead of fully equipped professional fighting men to match the oncoming Germans, the first arrivals were half-trained, half-armed territorial battalions, and that even the Regulars, who gave a good account of themselves, lacked the tanks and artillery for stemming an advance for which the Germans were now bringing in reinforcements. Meanwhile a second Allied force, which was intended to co-operate with the Norwegians in an advance against Trondheim from the north side, was likewise driven back, as the result of an engagement in which the enemy had unexpected artillery support from a destroyer in the fiord. The decisive factor, however, for both expeditions was German air supremacy. The Norwegians had lost most of their few aircraft on April 9th; an attempt to base British fighters on a frozen mountain lake collapsed within 24 hours; and the systematic bombing of the bases at Åndalsnes and Namsos made it impossible to build up larger forces or even to maintain those already committed. After considering and eventually rejecting the alternative of a direct assault on Trondheim from the sea, in which battleships would be exposed to air attack in the 30-mile-long fiord, the British decided to evacuate their forces and the French under British command (who had not been engaged). Although Ruge was notified in advance, the secrecy necessary for an evacuation added to the bitter disappointment of the Norwegians.

When the last Allied ships left the Norwegian coast under heavy air attack on 3 May, the Germans had already cleared the whole route from Oslo to Trondheim, so that further resistance in southern Norway served no strategic purpose. Yet in two places the Norwegians still demonstrated their skill in improvising a local defence on their own against heavy odds. At Hegra, north of Trondheim, an obsolete fort equipped with four 4-inch guns repulsed attacks by infantry, artillery, and aircraft, and its garrison of 200 men and one woman nurse held out until their food was completely exhausted. Another force of about the same size put up an even longer resistance under a junior officer in the mountains north of Kristiansand, causing the diversion of two German battalions to attack it and contriving to demobilize its members before the final surrender on 6 May, when the party comprised one officer, seven or eight men, six women auxiliaries—and twenty-nine enemy prisoners.[13]

NORWEGIAN AND ALLIED OPERATIONS IN THE NORTH

Concurrently with the Allied evacuations, the king and cabinet and General Ruge with his staff were transferred by sea past the long coastal strip, very sparsely inhabited and with no through route as yet by road or rail, separating southern from northern Norway. Although the whole of the three northern counties contained only one-ninth of the population, they could provide a temporary seat of government at Tromsö, and the military prospects centring on the siege of Narvik were still hopeful. It was here that the British had made full use of their naval power in the two battles of 10 and 13 April, which had eliminated all the ten German destroyers carrying the 2,000 mountain troops for the occupation of the town and the railway, which climbs steeply up the mountains to the Swedish frontier. Three battalions of British regular soldiers, which arrived on the day after the second naval engagement, had not risked an immediate assault, thus giving the enemy time to organize the destroyer crews as reinforcements for their garrison; but by the end of April five French and four Polish battalions were arriving on the scene under a French general, M.-E. Béthouart, who was trained in mountain and winter warfare. The Norwegians were encouraged even more by the situation of their own troops. In the early morning of April 9th, when the local commander had surrendered the town of Narvik without a fight, a part of the small garrison had escaped to join the brigade already under arms farther north, and by the end of the month a second brigade had been able to mobilize undisturbed. General Fleischer had begun operations immediately so as to contain the Germans in the wilderness of mountains north of Narvik. In spite of their meagre equipment, his two brigades could cope more effectively with the elements than could any of their allies,[14] and they made skilful progress through the icy wastes.

The first important Allied advance was carried out by Béthouart with two battalions of the Foreign Legion on 13 May, when the provision of landing craft and a few small tanks made it feasible for them to force their way ashore in face of German opposition at Bjerkvik, a point on the fiord directly opposite the little peninsula on which Narvik lies. This was synchronized with an advance by a

Norwegian brigade, which worked its way through snow deeper than a man's height, so as to press the enemy back from the mountains overlooking the fiord. Meanwhile the other Norwegian brigade was making its way inland with a view to cutting off an eventual retreat across the frontier—where some German reinforcements were arriving on the high plateau from the air and supplies at least by train through Sweden. Otherwise, the Germans in Narvik were now completely isolated: the British navy had full control of the fiord; British troops moving along its south shore had gained positions at the end of April which overlooked the Narvik peninsula on that side; and the presence of an aircraft carrier and, later, of British fighters gave local control of the air.

But immediately after the occupation of Namsos on 4 May, the Germans began a most resolute march northwards to remedy the situation. Their resolution unfortunately was not matched by that of the Norwegian battalion withdrawing from that area, which was too disheartened by the Allied evacuation to fight the delaying actions prescribed in their orders. Moreover, they received only ineffective support from five Independent Companies of British volunteers: these forerunners of the famous commandos had been set up by Churchill in a great hurry for guerrilla warfare to be conducted with supplies and other help from the local population—which was too small to signify. A further, more acute disappointment followed when the three British battalions in the Narvik area were diverted to the task of stemming the enemy advance from the south. Serious delays were caused by the bombing of a transport and the grounding of a light cruiser used for the same purpose, while in each of three actions fought at battalion strength the British were driven back, having been outmanoeuvred and, to a less extent, handicapped by German air support. The enemy still had a long way to go to reach Narvik, but to the disgust of the Norwegians by 29 May the British troops were falling back on Bodö, leaving the Germans free to continue northwards unmolested through a roadless district of high mountains.

However, on the previous day Narvik had been captured by a combined effort, to which the British contributed the sea and air support, the French their two battalions of Foreign Legionaries, and the Norwegians one battalion. The Norwegians played a resolute part in the fighting on the rough hillside where they were put ashore, and were invited to head the entry into the town itself—an inspiring occasion, since this was the very first time that Hitler's predatory hand had been forced to relax its grip. In spite of the handicap now imposed by the thaw, the Norwegian brigade in the mountains worked hard to cut off the Germans withdrawing along the railway to the frontier. In four days they breached the line of defence posts, and on the evening of 7 June they were ready to launch the final attack. But it was too late.

Since the commencement of the blitzkrieg on the western front on 10 May, Norway had inevitably become a sideshow for the Allies, and after the disasters of the first fortnight in France and the Low Countries it was plainly a liability from which they must contract out. Evacuation orders were received three days before the capture of Narvik, but were not disclosed to the king or his ministers until 1 June—when the first stage, namely the re-embarkation of troops from Bodö, had already been carried out. For the Allies secrecy was of paramount importance: France and Britain now needed every man, ship, and aircraft for their own defence, and the loss of the carrier *Glorious* on the homeward voyage with 1,515 men and twenty fighter planes was soon to emphasize how vulnerable an undertaking a large-scale evacuation is. When the Norwegians were at last informed, their first thought was to gain time to complete their operations on the frontier, and to make fresh inquiries about the feasibility of the 'Mowinckel Plan', a scheme for neutralizing the Narvik area under Swedish supervision with which the ex-premier had been busy in Stockholm.[15] The Allies provided some air support for the operations, which could not be completed at such short notice, and conceded a 24-hour delay for inquiries about the plan, in which the Germans were reported from Stockholm to have lost any interest.

Faced with the disappointment of all their hopes, the king and government might well have thrown in their hand: a surrender would at least rid them of the reproach that they did not remain to share with their fellow countrymen in the disaster to which the government's policy had led. Instead, they resolved to continue the war from such resources as could be mustered in exile, embarking with heavy hearts for a beleaguered Britain. General Ruge, who stayed behind to organize demobilization and terminate the existing hostilities on Norwegian soil, gave what comfort he could to his listeners on Tromsö Radio: 'The first chapter in our struggle for freedom is over, and we have a dark time to face now in a conquered land. But the war continues on other fronts—Norwegians are joining in the struggle there. The day will come when you can raise your heads again.'[16]

PROBLEMS OF A DISILLUSIONED PEOPLE

Although the events of the two-months campaign impinged upon the thoughts and imaginations of all Norwegians, it had been fought in areas remote from the main centres of population by a small number of partly mobilized units and hastily assembled groups of volunteers.* The number of casualties—about 1,700 members of the armed forces killed or wounded and brought to hospital, plus about 300 civilians killed by enemy action—shows clearly that the nation as a whole played no active part. But non-participants had all the more time and energy to spare for blaming the government, which had made self-help impossible by its long-continued neglect of the defences and then placed its faith in the Allies, whose help had produced one fiasco after another. As for its professed intention of continuing the struggle from overseas, throughout the summer of the blitzkrieg the news from the seat of war was likely to induce the man in the street—still more, perhaps, the man in the isolated Norwegian farmstead—to harbour the thought that this was only prolonging the agony: soon the armies of Hitler might cross the English Channel, extinguish the resistance of the islanders, and bring all western Europe under the aegis of the Nazi 'New Order'. Moreover, that 'new order' had a positive side. In the summer of 1940 German plans for expanding the electro-metallurgical,† min-

---

* The army mustered altogether about 50,000 men, which was one-half of its mobilization strength, but the maximum force available at any one time did not much exceed 25,000.[17]
† In the case of aluminium, which was urgently needed for military purposes, the first German negotiator arrived in Norway on the fifth day of the invasion;

ing, woodworking, fishing, and shipbuilding industries of Norway were not so obviously chimerical as they seem in retrospect.[18]

While the campaign was still in progress, the legal authorities had been to a considerable extent thrust aside through the pressure of events. Quisling's initial *coup d'état* on April 9th had completely failed to provide the Germans with smooth co-operation in a return to normalcy, which was what they wanted to receive from the population of the occupied regions, especially the capital. His so-called 'national government' was therefore replaced within a week by an Administrative Council of officials, headed by Oslo's county governor, I. E. Christensen. This had been proposed to the Germans by the highly respected chief justice, Paal Berg,* as a non-political arrangement to prevent sporadic disorders and unemployment; and although the Germans used the news of its formation to weaken resistance in the unoccupied regions,[19] the king and government accepted it as a limited interim arrangement. But Hitler, to whom it had been represented as a means of forcing them to reopen negotiations for the sake of their own future, on finding that this did not occur, regretted the ousting of Quisling and dismissed Braüer from his post. Instead, the management of Norwegian affairs was entrusted to a Reichskommissar in the person of Josef Terboven, the ruthless and resourceful Nazi Gauleiter of Essen and Oberpräsident of the Rhine Province. From the time of his arrival in Norway at the end of April until his suicide followed that of his master in May 1945, he was answerable only to Hitler, who had made him 'lord over life and death'.[20]

Terboven's original instructions directed him to win over the Norwegians, a task which his cool intelligence quickly convinced him could best be accomplished with other tools than Quisling. He created a counterpoise to N.S. by encouraging the pro-German League of the Fatherland, in which Hjort and other former sympathizers

---

by October 1940 he was planning to secure materials from France and south-eastern Europe for an eventual output of 243,900 tons a year.

* 1873–1968. He had been minister of social affairs, 1919–20, and minister of justice, 1924–6, and was appointed chief justice in 1929. In the later war years he became the secret leader of the Home Front, and was the first person commissioned to form a government in 1945.

with N.S. were now active: he also required the ministry of justice to find a place for Jonas Lie,★ who had refused an invitation to join Quisling's cabinet on April 9th. But he made his most important moves through a senior German civil servant on his staff named Dellbrügge, who could talk in conciliatory terms with such men as Bishop Berggrav and Chief Justice Berg. On 30 May a delegation of the four main political parties agreed to support the Administrative Council, whose limited authority was soon afterwards extended to the whole country as there was no longer any unoccupied region. But on 13 June Dellbrügge presented the council with the agenda for a meeting of the Storting at Eidsvoll, which was to dismiss the Nygaardsvold government, dethrone the royal house, and give plenary powers to a new government pending an election to be held within three months of the return of peace. Discussion centred upon the dethronement, which the Supreme Court certified to be unconstitutional and which—unlike the dismissal of the ministry—could not be justified by claiming that king Haakon had any responsibility for the now bitterly regretted neglect of defence measures. But it was difficult to reject outright an accommodation in return for which they were promised the withdrawal of the Reichskommissariat, so the Norwegians made a counter-proposal that a Council of the Realm (*Riksråd*) should exercise the royal authority on a provisional basis. The Germans rejected the proviso: at most they might allow an appeal to Hitler's magnanimity on behalf of the child Prince Harald—which might be expected to prove as ineffective as was the appeal on Haakon's behalf made at this juncture by the king of Sweden.

Under the impact of the French capitulation on 17 June, when even Berg judged the situation to be hopeless, the presidential body of the Storting—headed by the moderate Labour leader, Nilssen, and including the former Conservative premier, Lykke, in place of

---

★ 1899–1945. A grandson of the writer, who had entered service in the State Police in 1930, and had presided as League of Nations representative over the plebiscite in Saarbrücken, 1935, and Alexandretta, 1938. His later career as a ruthless police minister culminated in the enforcement of the German orders for the evacuation of Finnmark in the winter of 1944–5, but he died when his arrest impended, May 1945.

Hambro—agreed to demand that the king should abdicate for himself and his house and, if he refused, to request the Storting to depose him. After the king had broadcast his refusal from London, the Storting was scheduled to meet on 15 July, but instead there was a long interval, during which Terboven's plans were challenged in Berlin. Both Raeder and Rosenberg wanted Quisling to have a position that gave them influence in Norway; the parallel situation in the Netherlands suggested that it was advantageous to use the native Nazi leader; and Quisling himself, who spent August in Germany, played his cards well enough for Hitler to say that 'he could rely on him'.[21] When Terboven resumed negotiations in September, the prospect of a long war meant that he could no longer promise the abolition of the Reichskommissariat, and he was also ordered to give Quisling's supporters recognition in forming the proposed Council of the Realm.

With quite other hopes of a return to self-government, the members of the Storting assembled on 10 September to vote in party groups on the suspension of the royal house. The votes added up to 92:53 in favour of so doing: this was five short of the two-thirds majority required for a constitutional change, but the fact that every party except the Left and the numerically insignificant Christian People's Party was in favour would have given the change at least a veneer of legality.[22] The reward for disavowing their king was to be the right to influence the composition of the new council, of which Christensen was to be chairman: an optimistic member of the Labour Party named Trygve Bratteli even proposed that 'There shall be no representative of N.S. on the council'.[23] On the contrary, their names were already there, though in a minority, and pressure from Hitler finally induced the disappointed *Stortingsmenn* to agree by a vote of 76 to 55 that membership of the council would be replenished by a kind of cooption, without any control by their own presidential body. But when a name already approved was suddenly replaced by that of an additional N.S. man, the politicians began to realize that they had been duped and ceased to be compliant: it now seems clear that Hitler, in a two-and-a-half-hour interview on 11 September, had promised Quisling that the entire council would be nazified in due course.[24]

The political parties having ceased to co-operate with him, Terboven on 25 September announced the dissolution of all except N.S. and the replacement of the Administrative Council by 'commissary ministers' (*kommissariske statsråder*) at the head of the departments, including Jonas Lie in charge of an ominous new department of police. Trade affairs, where German interests required that everything should run smoothly, were entrusted to four well-meaning business experts, who soon regretted their position; the other nine were members of N.S. It was only a question of time until Quisling himself, now doubly detested, should return to office (see p. 394); power, however, was firmly in the hands of Terboven and an administrative apparatus of several hundred German officials, which there was no longer any thought of dissolving.

In spite of repeated disappointments in the later years of the war, the national morale never again sank so low. It is gratifying to reflect that the anxiously awaited result of the Battle of Britain contributed to its recovery. But even during the darkest part of what Norwegian historians call 'a dark chapter in our recent history',[25] those who still cherished the thought of resistance found their first rallying point in the defence of the constitutional rights of King Haakon. His dignified and cogent reply to the demand for his abdication was circu-historians call 'a dark chapter in our recent history',[25] those who still loyalty. But before considering the further growth of this nascent Home Front, it will be convenient to notice the achievements of 'Norway in exile', which had so narrowly escaped a formal severance from the rest of the nation.

EVENTS ON THE OUTER FRONT, 1940–1944

When the Norwegian government arrived in London, its assets were in many respects small. Two destroyers and a few smaller craft accompanied it, with their crews; a few small planes were flown over; and the army was represented by General Fleischer and other senior officers, but they had no troops to command. The ministers lacked archives, expert assistance, familiarity with their new surroundings, and almost everything except a burden of grievances against the British, who were now their hosts. Moreover, invasion appeared so imminent that one tangible asset, namely the Bank of Norway's gold, was immediately redirected from England to Ottawa and New York.

One asset of tremendous value, however, was already safeguarded. While retreating with the army through Central Norway, the government had issued an ordinance to requisition the merchant fleet and provide for its administration from London by a Shipping and Trade Mission under two leading shipowners. In July 1940 its activities were extended to New York, so that it could manage shipping services based on American ports and keep up some of the pre-war liner trades, while still deploying the main body of the fourth-largest mercantile marine in an ever-expanding war. In 1940 it served the British in the Mediterranean, in 1942 it took part in the Murmansk convoys, and it contributed to all the later Allied landing operations as far afield as the Pacific. But its most signal achievement was in the Battle of the Atlantic, especially in the critical year 1941, when 40 per cent of foreign tonnage entering the ports of the United Kingdom was Norwegian, including almost two-fifths of the tankers bearing the oil without which the island would have been forced to capitulate. The Norwegian mercantile marine was acclaimed at the time as being worth more than a million extra soldiers:[26] and many of its crews suffered a soldier's death. By 1945 a fleet of 4·8 million tons had been reduced to 2·7 millions, with a loss of one in every ten of the men who sailed in it.

The armed forces were always short of manpower. Conscription was applied to the few Norwegians resident on Allied soil, and the whalers returning from their seasonal expedition to the Antarctic provided an initial windfall; but recruits came mainly from Norway, escaping either across the North Sea or into Sweden, whence the journey to an isolated Britain was long and precarious. Though small in numbers, this personnel was high in quality, while the earnings of the mercantile marine enabled the government to buy whatever material it could employ.

By the end of 1941 the Royal Norwegian navy was manning fifty-five vessels, but except on small-scale incursions into the Leads they operated with larger British forces. Thus in December 1943 the destroyer *Stord* played a part in the sinking of the German battle cruiser *Scharnhorst* off the coast of North Norway, where it had latterly been based. For air operations the establishment of a training centre in September 1940 at 'Little Norway' in Ontario marked a new start, and before the war ended the old army and navy air detachments were united to form a Norwegian air force. Meanwhile, two fighter squadrons had shown the natural aptitude of the Norwegian for a form of conflict in which the nerve and self-reliance of the individual count for most. Both squadrons inflicted heavy losses on the Luftwaffe in the Dieppe Raid of August 1942, and in the following year they occupied first and third place among all the fighter squadrons in Britain in the toll they took of the enemy.

The army had more restricted scope, because its one brigade of about 1,500 men was kept in Scotland after training, in readiness to land and fight in Norway; as the idea of a new landing there made a strong appeal to Churchill's imagination,[*] it was for a long time a possibility, though the veto of the chiefs of staff was never finally overruled. A small Norwegian detachment helped to garrison Iceland; another was sent, chiefly for meteorological work, to Svalbard, where it survived a raid by German battleships; and the brigade included a very active Independent Company, generally known by the name of its first leader, Martin Linge. Although it was not formed as a separate unit until July 1941, in March fifty-two of its men took part in the first British commando raid on the Lofoten Islands; in the following December seventy-seven of them were in the second Lofoten raid and sixteen in the more ambitious attack on a fortified position at Målöy in the Inner Leads, when Linge was killed. These commando operations were carried out chiefly by British forces for what seemed to be adequate strategic reasons. But the destruction on the coast of Norway of ships and installations believed to be in enemy service and the bringing back of some hundreds of volunteers and a handful of N.S. prisoners closely concerned the Norwegian government in London, which had not been consulted. The severity of German reprisals against the local population—which on the

---

[*] 'We should attempt the liberation of Norway at the earliest possible moment' and 'We ought, of course, to have liberated Norway in the campaign of 1943' are representative Churchillian pronouncements, dating from September 1941 and February 1944 respectively.[27]

occasion of the second Lofoten raid was encouraged to believe that the raiders intended to remain in the islands—damaged its reputation at home, and it protested strongly to the British authorities to prevent any repetition.

In general, however, the successful employment of their small forces, to which Allied propaganda gave ready publicity, helped to strengthen the position of the government. That of the king, indeed, was always strong. His frequent appearances on public occasions and his affability and unaffectedness made him almost as popular a figure in British eyes as in those of his fellow countrymen, for whom he embodied the national cause, while behind the scenes he was the sage and unself-seeking counsellor of his ministers as they faced new problems. Though Nygaardsvold was often overwhelmed by their complexity, it seemed impolitic to make a change of premier without reference to some outside body of opinion, and proposals to set up a representative council in London (as was done by some other exiled governments) were unacceptable to the resistance movement at home. But relations with the British authorities were rendered more cordial by a series of changes. Koht was replaced as foreign minister by Trygve Lie; Mowinckel, who in his capacity as a consultative minister in Stockholm was judged to have taken a defeatist line, eventually joined Koht in America; and with the resolute Torp* as defence minister a unified command of the armed forces was established, to which the British were willing to entrust military secrets relating to Norwegian affairs.

In May 1941 an Anglo–Norwegian agreement defined the use to be made of the Norwegian forces, which remained operationally under British control for the duration of the war, and specifically included 'the complete liberation of Norway from German rule'[28] among the war aims. When Hitler invaded Russia, the Norwegian government refused to declare war on Finland in spite of the assistance given to the German invasion; but in every other way it was

---

* 1893–1958. An electrician by trade and in his youth a noted footballer, he had been a popular Labour Party chairman, 1923–40, and actively promoted the reunion of 1927; temporary minister of defence, 1935–6, minister for social affairs, 1936–9, minister of defence, 1942–5; prime minister, 1951–5; president of the Storting, 1955–8.

encouraged by its Labour orientation to welcome the new Russian ally, not only as a war-winning force but also as a leading influence in the 'community of nations' which was to follow the war. But it was easier to build upon the long-standing friendship with the American people, who had been fervent in their moral condemnation of the German attack upon Norway, dramatized by sensational newspaper accounts of Oslo's inability to grasp the reality of the situation on April 9th.[29] President Roosevelt gave practical help by inviting crown princess Märtha and her children to take refuge in America, to which they removed from Sweden in August 1940; this placed them out of reach of dangerous proposals for bringing the child Prince Harald back to Norway with German connivance as a puppet king. When the Americans in their turn were taken by surprise at Pearl Harbor, Lie had already become the spokesman for an association with the great Atlantic powers as the most appropriate for the future of 'a seafaring people, an ancient Atlantic Ocean people';[30] and in the later war years Norwegian foreign policy looked more towards this than to a link with European powers alone.

A strong argument in favour of such a reorientation was provided by the unhappy position *vis-à-vis* Sweden, which both during the campaign and afterwards stretched international law in many ways to suit the German forces in Norway and their occupation policy. After the death of the Norwegian minister in Stockholm in October 1940, difficulties were raised about the status of the legation; refugees from across the frontier were subjected to many vexatious restrictions by the Swedish police; and in March 1942, when sixty-two lives were lost in an attempted break-out by Norwegian ships from Gothenburg harbour, it seemed clear that the Swedish authorities had done nothing to prevent them from falling into a German trap. The policy of appeasement was perhaps inevitable, and it was certainly abandoned as soon as the Swedish government and even the pro-German king were convinced that Germany would lose the war. But in Norwegian eyes Sweden had sacrificed much of its prestige, and would henceforth be recognized less readily as *primus inter pares* among the Scandinavian states: in words attributed to King Haakon, 'There could be no more talk about the big brother.'

GROWTH OF THE HOME FRONT

Norway was a country with no recent tradition of illegal political activity on which to base a resistance movement. To start such a venture was in any case a forlorn hope, since Terboven's control of the administrative machine appeared to be a model of German efficiency—and ruthlessness. Even if more had been known about the intrigues conducted against the Reichskommissar behind the scenes by his compatriots, the enemy garrison of all arms was always overwhelming: in 1942 it was increased in accordance with Hitler's prognostication, 'Norway is the zone of destiny in this war',[31] and eventually rose to one soldier for every ten inhabitants. In addition to all this, the Norwegian economy was firmly tied to Germany by its need for supplies of breadstuffs, fats, fodder, petroleum, and other essentials, of which a minimum was obtainable in return for a maximum of exports. By 1944 German demands absorbed four-fifths of these, the only other available markets of any importance being Sweden and Denmark. In the fisheries and metal industries, for example, masters and men worked hard and profitably for German account, and for a long time any proposals for sabotage would fall on deaf ears. An even more direct service to the German war effort was provided by the building industry, which helped to construct huge gun emplacements, submarine pens, and military accommodation of all kinds; although there was much reviling of a class of profiteers known as 'barrack barons', the numbers in building employment doubled. Watchwords such as *Vivere non est necesse* and 'No Norwegian for sale' were treasured by the few, even in the disastrous summer of 1940;[32] but the mass of the population might have settled down to a passive acquiescence in the occupation, such as prevailed for at least two years in Denmark.

The Home Front, however, developed rapidly as a movement against Nazism in the shape of Quisling' (*Nasjonal Samling* (N.S.) — the only political party that the Germans tolerated and the source from which most of the commissarial ministers were drawn. In a little over twelve months the party membership grew, indeed, from 7,000 to nearly 37,000 and it eventually reached 43,000, which was equivalent to about 5 per cent of the electorate. But the new recruits were time-servers or worse, and Quisling himself lacked the political realism and skill to act as an intermediary between German and Norwegian interests, even if he had succeeded in his efforts to regularize relations by obtaining a peace treaty. The loyalists who had espoused the king's cause during the summer vehemently denounced all N.S. activities as treasonable, which did much to keep the major part of the population uncommitted during the darkest period. Profiting by the clumsiness as well as the brutality of their opponents, a nucleus of independent-minded individuals, drawn initially from the ranks of the urban middle class and the professions rather than the regular politicians, linked every interest in turn to the national cause until morale was finally built up to the stage at which N.S. members were very widely ostracized and resistance actions very widely supported.

The last vestiges of the old constitutional order disappeared before the end of 1940. Local self-government passed from popular control when A. V. Hagelin,★ the commissarial minister of the interior, transferred the powers of the district councils to nominated local 'leaders'. The members of the Supreme Court laid down their office at the Christmas vacation, in protest against a series of measures which infringed the independence of the law courts. But the struggle was already being transferred to other, more or less voluntary, organizations, over which it was more difficult for N.S. to assert its authority. One of the earliest actions was that of the sports clubs, which united to boycott sports meetings arranged by the new N.S. Department for Sports and Labour Service; when the dispute caused the clubs to shut down, many young people became interested for the first time in politics—and these provided some of the first recruits for secret military training. Another very important lead was given by the bishops, who in October 1940 had founded a Joint Christian Council (*Kristent Samråd*) for the Norwegian church,

---

★ 1882–1946. A Norwegian citizen long resident in Germany, where he had made money and influential political contacts, both of which were useful to Quisling, with whom he became associated in 1936; he played a leading part in the *coup* of April 9th and in 1942 claimed to be Quisling's deputy, but was dismissed by him from his post as minister of the interior in November 1944; executed, 1946.

which had the backing of Berggrav and Hallesby and Hope. The bishops demanded to know whether the state still accepted its obligation truly and indifferently to administer justice, with particular reference to the violence practised by the N.S. Hird. On receiving an unsatisfactory answer from Professor Skancke,* the commissarial minister for ecclesiastical affairs and education, they published the correspondence as a pastoral letter, of which 30,000 copies were distributed. This informal mobilization of public opinion culminated in May 1941, when forty-three mainly professional organizations presented Terboven himself with a protest, which again deprecated the activities of the Hird and more particularly demanded that N.S. should be forbidden to interfere with appointments in the civil service and other professional bodies. Terboven replied by dissolving some of the organizations concerned and placing the majority in the hands of Hagelin, with the result that they soon had no members except such as belonged to N.S. But the protest of the forty-three and the pastoral letter had given a stimulus to the spirit of resistance, not only in Norway but also in other occupied territories, to which the B.B.C. spread the news of even the smallest crack in what then looked to be a monolithic New Order for a Nazi Europe.

Although the protest of the forty-three organizations had been signed by the vice-chairman of the trade union federation and on behalf of a few of the unions, the attitude of the trade-union movement as a whole was still uncertain. During the period of disillusionment the Communist element gained a ready hearing for its attacks on the government in exile and its 'treacherous lackey-service to the money matadors of London City',[33] and opposition to the New Order seemed to be confined to a minority, including the young Labour Party secretary, Einar Gerhardsen, and the legal adviser to the federation, Viggo Hansteen, who had been a *Mot Dag* enthusiast and until very recently a Communist. The Germans, for whom the smooth working of the industrial machine was of paramount importance, kept N.S. out of wage negotiations. But by the autumn of

---

* 1890–1948. Studied at Karlsruhe, and became professor of electrical engineering at Trondheim in 1923; joined N.S., 1933; an active persecutor of clergy and teachers; executed after protracted legal arguments, June 1948.

1941 the situation was changing. The German invasion of Russia converted the Communists overnight into the most whole-hearted advocates of resistance, and the workers in general were coming to realize that, although the Germans provided plenty of employment for Norwegian industry, their system of exploitation meant that wages would not be allowed to rise with the price level. Accordingly, about 25,000 discontented Oslo workers, drawn mainly from the metal industries, engaged in a protest strike against the denial of a milk supply at their place of work, which Terboven seized upon to proclaim a state of emergency; Hansteen and a young shop steward from the metal workers, both of whom were known to have opposed the rash protest, were shot and many other Labour leaders such as Gerhardsen imprisoned. N.S. nominees were subsequently put in charge of the unions, but the main result was that the Home Front became more fully national in its composition at the same time as it was driven underground by the menace of the Gestapo inquisition, the concentration camp, and the firing squad.

Both on the civil and on the military side (which will be considered separately) the leadership was to begin with very loose and informal; but in 1942 a co-ordination committee (K.K.) of about a dozen members was successfully established, which had the confidence of the many suppressed organizations and was able to guide opinion and conduct through its formulation of brief directives (*paroler*). These figured prominently in the illegal newspapers, whose growth had been stimulated in the previous autumn, when the Germans tacitly acknowledged the ascendancy of the B.B.C. over their own propaganda in Norway by a general confiscation of radio sets. At a higher level there was the Circle (*Kretsen*), a small group of leading personalities in public life, headed by Paal Berg, which gave general guidance to the national effort inside Norway and linked it with the government in London, where one of its members, the municipal treasurer of Oslo, joined the cabinet. Since it was now engaged against the Germans as much as N.S., the leadership at all levels was liable to frequent changes in consequence of arrests and flights to avoid arrest.

In February 1942 the installation of Quisling as minister-president over a cabinet of N.S. ministers brought the internal struggle to a head. In March the bishops and nine-tenths of the clergy gave a lead to public opinion by refusing to function under the auspices of the N.S. government, so the churches stood empty. The school teachers boycotted a proposed N.S. Youth Service, with the result that 1,100 of them were arrested and nearly half that number sent for a period of hard labour in the far north: but the end-product was 200,000 objections recorded by parents to the inclusion of their children in the new service, which ended in a fiasco. Quisling's biggest failure, however, was in his attempt to set up his long-planned Chamber of Corporations (*Riksting*)[34] on the model of Fascist Italy, which might have given an appearance of popular support for his position. He was defeated by mass resignations from the organizations on which the chamber was to be based; at least 80,000 trade unionists were among those who took the decisive step of resigning, and although they were driven back into the unions by dire German threats, Quisling's project had by then collapsed. Further evidence of high morale at this period is provided by the devotion with which the escape to Sweden of more than one-half of the 1,800 defenceless Norwegian Jews was arranged by the resistance movement before the Germans and N.S. could lay hands on them for deportation to the death camps.

But the mood of exhilaration gave place to war weariness and depression, affecting the minds of all but the most resolute. When the N.S. Party saw that it could not win the support of the people, its members more readily acted as tools of the Germans: the activities of informers became a nightmare, and in 1943 the death sentence was pronounced for the first time by a N.S. court. The Germans were less inclined than before to regard the Norwegians as erring 'Nordic brethren' and took more comprehensive measures of repression: in the summer of 1943 they deported 1,300 army officers, 271 'unreliable' policemen, and about 700 university students to concentration camps. Meanwhile, N.S. followed up its anti-communist propaganda, which had produced 5,000 volunteers for the eastern front, by agreeing to help to meet the German labour shortage. The nominal object of their first scheme, which broke down through administrative muddles, was to increase the home-grown food supply, but in April 1943 3,000 men were supplied for German

construction works in North Norway. It was significant that the
only strong counteraction was taken by the Communists, who blew
up one of the Oslo labour offices. They had long since proclaimed the
desire 'to wake people up', but their plans for local Freedom Councils on the Danish model were opposed by the central Home Front
authorities, who at this time leant rather heavily to the side of
caution.

In 1944, however, the Home Front finally defeated N.S., in a
struggle which began with the interception of a letter from the N.S.
minister of justice, urging a call up of the 18–23 age groups for labour
service and their immediate transfer, as recruits for the eastern
front, to military units incorporating an equal number of 'reliable'
German soldiers. All sides of the resistance movement were by
this time united and firmly linked with the government in London,
so the necessary instructions were openly broadcast from the
B.B.C. on behalf of 'the Home Front leadership'. The first action
was directed against the order issued to the two youngest age
groups to register for the existing Labour Corps (*Arbeids Tjenesten*),
which had originally been a non-party provision against unemployment: its offices were systematically sabotaged, and about 30 per
cent of those affected refused registration. The second action was
against the labour mobilization proper, which concerned the other
three age groups. The injunction, 'Refuse registration—cost what
it may', diffused five days in advance, created a mass exodus into
the forests and mountains. Out of a possible 70,000 only 300 were
actually in service, when Terboven wound up the N.S. enterprise as
a complete failure. Many young men crossed the frontier to join
the Norwegian 'police troops' now under training in Sweden (see
p. 400), while a few hundred remained in hiding in Norway as
special recruits for Milorg, the 'military organization' which had
grown up step by step alongside the civil activities of the Home Front.

THE HOME FRONT MILITANT

The collection of secret military intelligence in Norway dates from
the period of the Allied campaign, when information was assembled
from districts already overrun by the enemy. On a much larger

scale, news of German military and naval dispositions was sent by secret radio transmitters and other methods throughout the war years; in 1942 some sixteen stations reported the movements of enemy warships to the British Admiralty from all along the coast. But this highly dangerous work, in which many lives were sacrificed, was directly controlled by the Norwegian and Allied military authorities in London. Secret military resistance planning, on the other hand, began with some burying of arms on demobilization in June 1940 and discussion among little groups of veterans, whom the sports clubs (as already mentioned) provided with the first body of new recruits. By May 1941 at least 20,000 men had been enlisted, under a commander nominated by General Ruge and a small committee of officers and middle-class civilians which had some contact with the government; at the end of the year this 'Milorg' was placed directly under the High Command in London as an additional branch of the armed forces, and soon afterwards a representative of the Labour element in its membership was belatedly added to the committee. The rank and file were grouped in very small districts spreading over the entire country, with 8–10 marksmen (*jegere*) forming a section. Numbers rose to 32,000 in June 1944 and eventually to 47,000; about 10,000 auxiliaries were recruited in the later stages among engineers and other industrial employees (including railwaymen) to slow down work done for the Germans and to facilitate acts of sabotage. Growth may also be measured by the communications network, whose operation cost sixteen lives: in 1941 only two stations were on the air, in the summer of 1944, about thirty-five, and at the end of the war, sixty-nine.

Milorg suffered, however, from several severe handicaps. Its training was at first directed towards providing infantry units to act in direct support of a substantial Allied landing: for knowledge of the more profitable guerrilla techniques practised in other occupied territories spread rather slowly. Equipment and arms were in any case in very short supply, as long as the Allies had little to spare and lacked the aircraft for sending it over. Moreover, whatever was available was under the control of the British S.O.E., the Special Operations Executive which had been set up by Churchill in July 1940 to harass the enemy in occupied Europe. S.O.E. at first operated independently of Milorg, using members of the Linge Company and other Norwegians who had been trained in Britain; some justification was provided by the need for stringent security precautions, which Milorg learnt only from bitter experience, but the consequence was unhappy misunderstandings and some avoidable losses. However, in February 1942 a newly formed separate Norwegian Section* of S.O.E. was successfully linked up with the Norwegian High Command in London, and by the end of that year full co-operation was at last established also in the field.[35] A contributory factor was the emergence of a young lawyer, J. C. Hauge, who became by stages the 'general manager' or leader of Milorg's operations.†

In 1942 the Home Front militant suffered a series of disasters. In April, when two recently landed S.O.E. agents shot two Gestapo men who were sent to arrest them at Tælavåg near Bergen, the Germans took a horrifying revenge: they obliterated the hamlet and interned every inhabitant, so that thirty-one of the men died later in Sachsenhausen, besides executing eighteen persons arrested two months before while attempting to cross to Britain from another point on the west coast. Nevertheless, the local population continued to give full support to an S.O.E. venture in a lonely part of Nordland, where munitions were being landed for operations that would cut communications when a promised British expedition arrived. There was also co-operation with S.O.E. in other districts of western, eastern, and south Norway, especially in the south, where it was likewise believed that an expedition would arrive before the year ended. In every one of these districts the Germans, with some help from N.S. informers, uncovered and crushed the conspiracy; by the end of the year they had executed 105 of their victims, killed about as many out of hand, and held about 10,000 prisoners. In the Trondheim area a state of emergency in October had been touched off

---

* Headed by Colonel J. S. Wilson, formerly deputy commissioner of police in Calcutta, and latterly a leading figure in the international boy scout movement; this had made him sensitive to national susceptibilities.

† Hauge (b. 1915) was an official in the price control department who joined Milorg at Christmas 1941, became its 'Inspector for East Norway' in August 1942, then 'General Inspector' of all units, and in September 1943 a member of the Committee, whose members regarded him as their *administrerende direktör*.[36]

by S.O.E.'s first successful sabotage operations, directed against a power station and an iron mine, both of which served important German interests. Otherwise the only gains were imponderable—the long-term effects which acts of overt resistance had upon the morale of a small people, who needed to obliterate from their consciousness bitter memories of the shortcomings of their defence effort in April 1940. The 'Linge Company' was already beginning to create a saga of folk heroes of the type of 'Shetland Larsen', who made thirty-eight hazardous crossings to and from Norway in a single year; such tales spread fast by word of mouth, and lost nothing in the telling.

In 1943 Milorg's position was still precarious. In March the Circle protested in London against plans for promoting guerrilla warfare if the Allies landed, on the ground that the civil population would be exposed to mass terrorism against which it was not yet 'vaccinated.'[37] Seven months later, when an attack on a German military train led to five executions by way of reprisal, Milorg had still to reckon with a public protest by what a historian of the resistance describes as 'several thousand well-meaning and peace-loving citizens'.[38] It was therefore fortunate that in this year better joint planning and a more restricted choice of objectives brought the toll of executions down by one-quarter, while Norwegians notwithstanding carried out triumphantly the only act of military sabotage which might influence the whole outcome of the world war. Norsk Hydro's plant at Rjukan, in the heart of the mountains between Oslo and the west coast, was the sole source of heavy water for the German attempts to produce the atomic bomb. Placed under six layers of concrete at the head of a very narrow valley, the storage premises could not be bombed effectively from the air and might seem equally impregnable from the ground, especially as the Germans were alerted by the wrecking through bad weather of two gliders carrying a party of thirty Royal Engineers, whom it had been intended to land on the desolate plateau behind the little town. But a Norwegian with local knowledge* managed to survive

---

* He had escaped to Britain nearly a year before, and was flown back eleven day later, after a quick training course which included one parachute jump. 'Only two or three people in London knew the real reason.'[39]

the winter alone in that freezing wilderness until February 1943, when a party of his fellow countrymen were parachuted to join him. Nine of them crept down from the mountains unobserved, climbed a 300-foot precipice to an unguarded entrance, and planted explosives which destroyed the heavy-water stock and damaged the plant. A year later, when the plant and other stock were being removed to Germany, three of them also sank a lake ferry conveying the irreplaceable cargo.

The destruction of Norwegian industry working for German account had been one of the prime objects of the Allied commando raids, which ended in January 1943 with a successful attack on the pyrites mines on the west-coast island of Stord; it was then rumoured that any repetition would cause all the islands to be compulsorily evacuated. But in the later war years the plenitude of Allied bombers provided a tempting alternative, albeit air raids were liable to kill more Norwegians than Germans and might hit targets which rendered no substantial service to enemy interests. To avoid the possibility of haphazard destruction from the air, Milorg now co-operated more closely with the sabotage agents sent from Britain. In a few cases the output from mines and factories was seriously affected and railway service interrupted, but the most recent Norwegian survey concludes, 'Germany's economic exploitation of Norway was not seriously hampered.'[40] On the other hand, very persistent attacks were directed against enemy shipping up and down the coast, which compelled the Germans to expend much manpower in its protection.

In 1943 the termination of the war by direct military action, in which Milorg might have a part to play, seemed to be coming nearer. In that summer the Swedish government allowed 8,700 Norwegian exiles to be assembled in so-called 'health camps', where by the end of the year a force of police troops was being trained in readiness for the liberation of their native soil. Meanwhile, in Norway itself close collaboration between S.O.E. and the American Office of Strategic Services achieved a regular flow of military supplies and qualified instructors through air transport and the boat service run from the Shetlands. This culminated during the last year of hostilities, in which weapons were brought in by air alone for 35,000 men and 211 members of the Linge Company were sent to work in Norway. A considerable proportion of the nation's youth became inured to the risks attendant upon serious military training undertaken under the nose of the enemy, for instance in the forest just outside the capital; and from October 1944 onwards an élite force was even held in readiness in several remote mountain fastnesses.

The expected confrontation in arms never came. In June 1944 sixty Norwegian ships took part in the Allied landings in Normandy, together with the fighter squadrons and naval units; about fifty officers served with a Scottish division, to which they had been originally attached for service in Norway; and a commando company helped later on in the clearance of Walcheren. But Milorg was assigned a waiting role, parallel with that of the Norwegian brigade in Scotland and the police troops in Sweden: 'No steps must be taken to encourage the Resistance Movement as such to overt action since no outside support can be forthcoming.'[41] Current operations against shipping and other agreed targets were, however, to continue; during the autumn oil tankers, a stock of aircraft engines, and an A.A.-gun factory were blown up, a new destroyer was sunk at its berth, and about 50,000 tons of shipping was heavily damaged in Oslo harbour by a Communist action group. With these exceptions the prescribed task at this stage was to prepare protective action for the likely eventuality that a German surrender on other fronts would lead to a 'confused situation' in Norway—in other words, the possibility of a holocaust before large-scale Allied help was available.

Geographical factors prevented Milorg from playing any considerable part in Finnmark—the northernmost, largest, and least populous county—whose liberation began in late October 1944, when the Russians crossed the border from north Finland in pursuit of the retreating German army. The latter proceeded to destroy every building that could offer shelter, thus interposing a broad belt of 'scorched earth' between themselves and the Russians, who did not advance beyond Kirkenes. They allowed the Norwegian government to send in a military mission of 300 men from Britain and two companies of the police troops from Sweden; but these could do little for a part of the local population which remained in hiding from the Germans near its ravaged homes, and Allied shipping for their evacuation was not available until near the end of the arctic winter. Proposals for a Norwegian expedition to cut the Germans off at Bodö were likewise found irreconcilable with the needs of the main campaign on the continent. By April, however, transportation from Sweden by American planes (under the command of the Norwegian-American pilot and polar explorer, Bernt Balchen) and local recruitment increased the Norwegian force in Finnmark to about 3,200 men, with whom Major-General A. D Dahl completed the clearance of the county before the war ended. [42]

Meanwhile the big German counter-offensive in the Ardennes had caused the issue of new instructions in December 1944: Milorg was now to do all it could to prevent the German garrison, swollen by the withdrawal from Finland, from being used to reinforce the western front By the end of the following month nearly thirty sabotage attacks had been made, in one of which a major bridge was blown up, blocking the railway north of Trondheim for a fortnight. Finally, on the night of 14/15 March a thousand Milorg men broke the north–south rail route at 750 places, while a special group of saboteurs in Oslo destroyed the railway administration building: three-quarters of the German troop movement was stopped.

When Dönitz signed the armistice with Eisenhower at Rheims in the early morning of 7 May, the situation in Norway was still uncertain: it is now known that Terboven wished to continue the fight with the huge forces available. The German army, however, chose to obey Dönitz as Hitler's lawful successor, so the task for which Milorg was at last brought into the open was to preserve order during a short period of transition and help a small Allied force, which began to arrive on the 9th, to disarm the well-disciplined Germans. Terboven and his chief of police committed suicide, but members of the Gestapo were carefully identified: a dozen Germans were eventually executed as war criminals, having committed atrocities against members of the Resistance. Adherents of N.S. and other alleged collaborators with the enemy were quickly rounded up for trial; even in the case of informers, Milorg helped the Norwegian love of due legal process to stand the strain.

New county governors, advisers in government departments, and local heads of police took office at once, in accordance with arrangements previously made between the Home Front leaders and the government in London; on 15 July Milorg was formally disbanded. Although liberation came about in this unexpected way without any direct sacrifice, it is worth noticing that the resistance movement was second only to the mercantile marine in the lives given for the common cause. Its dead numbered 2,091, including 266 women, which is approximately equal to the military losses incurred in the two months' campaign and on the outer front.[43]

THE RESTORATION

King Haakon returned to his capital amid scenes of unparalleled enthusiasm on 7 June 1945, exactly five years after his departure into exile. He had been preceded by the crown prince and a delegation of the Nygaardsvold cabinet, to which the Home Front leaders surrendered their authority, pending the formation of a new government which bore no responsibility for the débâcle in 1940. Paal Berg felt that he lacked support in the Storting, which had been summoned within a week of the king's return, so Gerhardsen,* now chairman of the largest party, was invited to head the new government instead. His fourteen colleagues included only two members of the London cabinet (Lie and Torp) and consisted mainly of persons who—like himself—had distinguished themselves in the Resistance; the key post of finance minister went to Gunnar Jahn, but the majority was socialist and included two Communists. Interparty plans were smoothly carried out for replenishing food supplies, maintaining employment, and evacuating not only the Wehrmacht but also the 40,000 prisoners of forty nationalities who had been forced to work for it. By October the Scottish general, who had

---

* b. 1897. The son of an Oslo road-worker who for a time followed his father's occupation, he was removed by the Germans from the chairmanship of the Oslo City Council; before the war he had been a strong supporter of Tranmæl, but resistance work and imprisonment brought him into friendly relations with men of all parties, which continued during his premierships (1945–51 and 1955–65).

supervised the military side with an Allied force which the Germans outnumbered by ten to one, declared with pardonable exaggeration that he had nothing left to evacuate but himself. Conditions in the far north were still far from normal, but on 8 October it proved possible to hold elections for a new Storting, the first for nine years.

The results followed the general European trend to the left. The Labour Party gained its first majority of seats, 76 out of 150. Its percentage of votes showed a slight fall from 42·5 to 41, but this was attributable to the quadrupling of the Communist vote at a moment when the war efforts both of the Russian armies and of the native Communist saboteurs made their maximum appeal: the eleven Communists might be expected generally to side with Labour against the non-socialist parties in the Storting. Among the latter the most noteworthy change was the growth of the Christian People's Party from two to eight, which was believed to be due to the association of the church with the resistance. Two-thirds of all members had never sat in the Storting before, and more than one-half could count among their credentials the fact that they had suffered personally in the conflict with the enemy occupation. When local elections had been held a few weeks later, the country was clearly ready to embark on a new era on the old democratic basis; an inter-party programme, which had been drawn up before liberation as a framework into which all party programmes must be fitted, accordingly yielded place by degrees to the detailed election programme of the victorious Labour Party.

The inter-party programme had provided for a commission of inquiry into the responsibility of the government and the civil and military officials for the shortcomings of the campaign in Norway, the actions of the Administrative Council and all persons concerned with the Storting's negotiations in the summer of 1940, and the work done by the authorities in exile. Much dirty linen was washed in public, though the Storting eventually decided against an impeachment of the much-criticized Nygaardsvold cabinet. But a far graver problem was that of the collaborators, who were to be tried under certain provisions of the penal code which the government in London had modified in agreement with the resistance leaders.[44] As a result the death penalty was no longer applicable only to military personnel or restricted to the period of hostilities, and while the penalties for acts of treachery were in some respects softened, a remarkably severe provision made members of N.S. jointly and severally liable for damage attributable to the party.

The Norwegian passion for litigation probably helped to swell the total of cases to be investigated to about 90,000—one to every forty inhabitants. Three political leaders—Quisling, Hagelin, and Skancke—suffered the extreme penalty, as did twenty-two other Norwegian citizens who had practised systematic torture, murdered prisoners, or murdered indirectly by informing against persons who were subsequently done to death. About 18,000 prison sentences were passed, but in 1948 those of less than eight years were cut by one-half and in 1957 an amnesty was given, even in cases where a death sentence had been commuted to imprisonment for life. Another 28,000 convictions resulted in fines or deprivation of civil rights. The fines ranged up to kr. 2 million, but bore some proportion to the financial position of the individual offender; it is possible that the loss of civil rights, which was liable to affect business activity and employment as well as the franchise and public office, inflicted more widespread hardship. Broadly speaking, justice was done and was seen to be done; but in a small country, where everyone knows about everyone else, it is very hard to let bygones be bygones. Hence perhaps the long-continued exculpatory activities of 'a relatively small but intellectually well-equipped group, who have made it their prime purpose in life to find the weak points in the settlement with the collaborators'.[45]

The enhanced feeling of national unity, which the years of occupation and/or exile had fostered among all other sections of the population, was further strengthened by the unexpected speed of recovery. There had been many dark forebodings: the national capital had in fact been reduced by 18 or 19 per cent, and to the ordinary man, before whose eyes one-third of current production had been for four years diverted to German use, the loss might seem much more. Accordingly, the inter-party programme had stipulated for a united effort by capital and labour; this found expression in joint production committees and branch councils, in a ban on strikes and lock-outs, and in a tacit agreement for the time being to steer a middle course between free competition and the fully planned economy of socialist aspirations. As for the government, wide powers of control had been placed in its hands by the 'Lex Thagaard', a law promulgated immediately before the move back from London, which took its name from the expert on price control but its underlying principles from the theories of Professor Ragnar Frisch.* In 1947 a yearly National Budget was introduced, correlating the proposed activities of the public and private sectors of the economy.

The results were unquestionably gratifying. In 1947 the gross national product was as great as before the war, and by the end of that year the standard of living had likewise been restored. In spite of shipyard costs which soon outstripped the proceeds from wartime insurance, in the course of 1949 the mercantile marine reached its pre-war tonnage. Even the bogy of inflation was for a time held at bay, thanks to the control of economic activities of all kinds and a high level of taxation, which included a creaming of all wartime profits. With the help of Marshall Aid the krone, which had been in such jeopardy in the years immediately following the First World War, was kept from devaluation until September 1949.

Yet foreign relations was the sphere in which Norway seemed most easily to find her place in the post-war world. Whereas her entry into the League of Nations had been rather hesitant, the government in exile had the backing of the Home Front leaders for a full participation in the San Francisco Conference which launched the United Nations Organization. When Trygve Lie became its first secretary-general in February 1946, his successor as foreign minister was Halvard Lange, the son of the well-known internationalist; he believed equally in Norway's mission, envisaged since 1941, to keep her closest friends, the great Atlantic powers, in harmony with her mighty Russian neighbour in the north. The national defences were, indeed, reconstructed on the basis of a three-year plan, which used the experience gained in the war to

---

* b. 1895. An early exponent of Keynesian economics, who was later a consultant in planning for the U.N. and in India and Egypt. In 1969 he received a half-share in the new Nobel economics prize for his pioneer contribution to econometrics.

rectify the most obvious inadequacies of the system set up in 1933, so as 'to hold out alone until we get effective help from our allies, whoever they may be.'[46] The formula chosen by Hauge as defence minister accorded with an active policy of 'bridge-building' and support for a strong United Nations Organization under the joint control of America, Britain, and Soviet Russia, as the surest way of promoting and preserving world peace.

The assumption, however, did not last for long. On the one hand, her trade needs exposed Norway to a diplomatic humiliation by Franco, when she joined with five other small states to promote action by the U.N. against the Fascist regime in Spain, which the United States and Britain would not support. On the other hand, both the government and the Storting were alarmed by the revival of Russian suggestions, dating from the war period, for a bipartite agreement for the future defence of Svalbard, though these were dropped when the Norwegians claimed that they would have to be submitted to all signatories of the Svalbard treaty. Then in 1947 Marshall Aid, from which the Norwegian economy eventually benefited directly and indirectly to the extent of nearly kr. 2,000 million, had the effect in Norway, as in the other countries concerned, of strengthening its ties with the great transatlantic power. By the autumn of the same year the onset of the Cold War in Europe, against which Marshall Aid was in part prophylactic, caused both Lange and Hauge to suggest in their speeches that 'bridge-building' might have no future relevance.

In the short view, the agonizing reappraisal of foreign policy that was soon to follow marked the close of a dramatic period in Norwegian history, which began with the European convulsions of September 1939. In a longer view, however, the events of the campaign, the occupation, and the restoration might be seen also as episodes in a continuing process—in internal affairs, towards an integrated social structure; in external affairs, towards integration in western Europe.

13. The Latest Age

A NORWEGIAN HISTORIAN, SUMMING UP AT THE CON-clusion of a three-volume survey of his country's achievements since 1814, warns his readers that

The period after the Second World War is not yet the subject of historical research, except for some small and scattered sections. But it has perhaps brought greater changes in the land than the whole period from 1814 to 1945. The first task was to restore what had been destroyed during the war . . . This was followed by a tremendous expansion, with over-employment and large-scale investment, with increased national income and increased consumption, with the Wel-fare State, with rising figures in every Budget and with development programmes in every social sector . . . A growth and progress which —to borrow a phrase from the liberal optimists of the last century— would have appeared unthinkable only a generation ago.[1]

In spite of this warning to beware of a subject where most of the pioneering work has still to be done, its inherent interest tempts us to look for factors whose significance may be confirmed by later studies. A start might be made from the statistics of population. Although the birth rate rose to 23 per thousand in the first year after the war, it soon declined to a level that was only slightly above that of the 1930s: in 1935 it was 14, and in 1960 17·5 per thousand. A low death rate, on the other hand, gave an expectation of life (71·3 years for men, 75·6 for women) that was claimed to be 'the most favourable mortality rate in the world'.[2] Since the labour force therefore constituted a dwindling proportion of a total population which climbed slowly towards four millions, prime importance must be attached to the shift of emphasis from work on the land and in the fisheries to advanced forms of industrial production; this change raised the standard of living to one of the highest in Europe.* But the socialist government which presided over the two

* In 1969 Norway occupied sixth place among twenty European countries for which O. E. C. D. collected over-all statistics of private consumption per head of population. As regards six items selected for detailed comparison (educa-

decades of transformation also used prosperity as an opportunity to strengthen the egalitarian trends which had long been characteristic of Norwegian politics and society. At the same time Norway's adherence to NATO earned a new prominence, even in foreign eyes, for the external relationships of a small people which struggled hard to preserve its identity against many pressures.

POLITICS UNDER LABOUR RULE

After the election of October 1945 the common programme drawn up during the war gave place gradually, as we have already noticed, to the programme of the Labour Party which had triumphed at the polls. But in the sequel Norwegian politics differed from those of most west European countries in two important respects: the socialists remained in office for a much longer period, and they derived continuing help from the informal concordat with their political opponents that had developed before and during the liberation. The laws that built up the Welfare State, for example, though criticized in detail, were passed by the Storting with virtual unanimity; likewise the historic decision that carried Norway into NATO. Not only did Labour cabinets succeed one another, apart from a single month's interruption, for a period of twenty years, but in all that time only one minister was driven out of office by the disfavour of the Storting. The exception was significant, for the former leader of Milorg, J. C. Hauge, as defence minister from 1945 to 1952, had often been at odds with the army leaders, whose smooth co-operation with the government was now considered essential; he disappeared from politics in 1955 after a brief return to office as minister of justice.

The general stability of the parties may be shown by the number of seats and percentage of votes that they obtained respectively at successive elections.

---

tional expenditure, dwellings completed in the year, and the number of doctors, telephones, cars, and TV sets) Norway's position averaged seventh. The United Kingdom was ahead of Norway in cars and TV sets.[3]

TABLE IX[4]

Representation of Parties in the Storting

	Labour	Communist	Socialist People's Party	Conservative	Left	Centre	Christian People's Party
1945	76	11		25	20	10	8
	(41·03)	(11·8)		(17·01)	(13·79)	(8·04)	(7·93)
1949	85	0		23	21	12	9
	(45·69)	(5·84)		(15·91)	(12·45)	(4·86)	(8·36)
1953	77	3		27	15	14	14
	(46·66)	(5·03)		(18·42)	(9·98)	(8·82)	(10·49)
1957	78	1		29	15	15	12
	(48·33)	(3·35)		(16·83)	(9·57)	(8·64)	(10·23)
1961	74	0	2	29	14	16	15
	(46·76)	(2·91)	(2·39)	(19·26)	(7·20)	(6·83)	(9·32)

In terms of percentages, the Labour, Communist, and (in 1961) the new Socialist People's Parties taken together received the support at each election of a majority of the voters; in terms of seats, however, Labour—in spite of proportional representation—received slightly more, and the smaller socialist party or parties slightly less, than their due. The latter were nevertheless called into existence by one of the two big changes in the general character of the parties: the Labour Party having shed much of its Marxian ideology directed its appeal in some measure to members of all social groups, in the name of social welfare and social justice for all. The second big change was a similar move to make the Conservative Party more comprehensive by ceasing to challenge the state control of the economy in principle, while still seeking to modify its practice. But this did not result in any tendency for the non-socialist parties to coalesce: at every election the three smaller ones together outnumbered the supporters of Conservatism.

The standpoint of these middle parties may be illustrated by the replies to a questionnaire, asking political leaders in a fairly typical area of western Norway, the town of Stavanger, what their party stood for. For Labour the answer preferred by the majority was 'social welfare, social justice', for Conservatism 'freedom from government regulations, private initiative'. The Left Party, however, preferred the more nebulous concept of 'democracy: protection of the rights of the individual'; the Agrarians put first 'the interests of rural districts'; and the Christian People's Party professed few interests beside 'protecting and strengthening Christianity'.[5] Thus a Labour policy which inclined towards the middle had what might almost be termed a built-in advantage.

The tranquil development of the nation was assisted by its figurehead. In the last twelve years of his long reign Haakon VII, the doyen of Europe's few remaining crowned heads, was regarded almost universally as the father of his people, to be greeted on his public appearances with a warmth that had not hitherto been characteristic of the modern Norwegian. When his son succeeded him in 1957 as Olav V, his adoption of his father's motto, 'All for Norway', symbolized the intention to follow a similar course. He has never succumbed to any temptation to play an active role in politics, though his experience as Defence Commander in the last year of the war gave him a strong interest in the efficiency of the armed forces. He was known to the general public as an Olympic yachtsman and formerly a keen skier, and made a dignified figure on State occasions at home and abroad. His consort, the Swedish princess Märtha, had unfortunately died some years before her husband's accession, but in 1968 the democratic basis of the modern Norwegian monarchy was strikingly reaffirmed through the general approval shown by the younger generation for the marriage of the sole heir to the throne, Crown Prince Harald, to the daughter of an Oslo draper of humble origins, endowed with intelligence and poise.

Among the four main leaders of the Labour Party, Gerhardsen stood out as a personality who was completely trusted by the workers and at the same time commanded general respect for his level-headedness and transparent honesty of purpose. In 1951–5 he stepped down from the premiership on the plea of ill health and acted as Labour leader in the Storting for four years, during which his place was taken by Torp, who had been defence minister in exile and, later, minister of justice. Otherwise, Gerhardsen's principal party lieutenant was a younger man, Trygve Bratteli,* who like him had been mayor of Oslo and party secretary; he was minister

---

* b. 1910. Worked as an errand boy, whaler, and builder; Labour Party journalist, 1934–41; imprisoned by the Germans, 1942–5; minister of finance, 1951–5 and 1956–60, and of transport, 1960–4; succeeded Gerhardsen as party chairman, 1965; prime minister, 1971.

of finance and, later, of transport. All three had left school young to earn their living as manual workers and entered politics through the trade unions. The foreign minister, Halvard Lange, had first made his name as a teacher and writer, but like Gerhardsen and Bratteli he had been imprisoned as a dangerous antagonist by the Germans—a circumstance which created important links of sympathy for them all, both in the party and beyond.

The changes in foreign relations, in the economy, and in the social scene during these two decades require separate treatment. But it may be useful to mention first some of the accompanying developments in political institutions and attitudes. The most revolutionary change was the abolition in 1952 of the constitutional provision that required that two-thirds of the members of the Storting should always be returned by specifically rural constituencies. This recognition of the fact that the farmers were no longer the predominant element in the nation caused the Agrarian or Farmers' Party to search for a new name to suggest a broader basis for its politics, and it became eventually the Centre Party. The seats in the Storting were rearranged in county blocs, varying from thirteen to four in rough accordance with population, though this still left the purely urban county of Oslo greatly under-represented.[6] A rather similar work of streamlining was carried out gradually in local government; by 1964 boundary changes had reduced 744 units to about 475, with the same type of council structure for both rural and urban communities and all councils directly represented on the county council. In elections the more refined Sainte-Laguë method of proportional representation was now adopted, though its elaborate provisions for sharing out seats by a whole series of calculations was modified to the disadvantage of small parties: as Table IX shows, a party might still manage to secure nearly 3 per cent of the total vote without winning a seat in any county. In 1946 the age qualification for voters had been lowered to twenty-one; legal disfranchisement, for instance of collaborators with the wartime enemy, was reduced to a maximum period of ten years; and the freedom of choice of the electors was widened, at least in theory, by the abolition of the residence qualification for Storting candidates.

Other measures have been needed to protect and extend democratic liberties. In 1956 difficulties arising out of the Council of Europe's Convention on the Rights of Man brought about the admission of Jesuits to the realm, but it took another eight years to establish the principle of complete freedom for adherents of all religions and none. In the secular sphere, we may note that, while the Labour Court was still the only administrative court, the chief justice remarked in the early 1950s that one-third of all civil cases reaching the Supreme Court concerned the actions of public institutions, and ten years later this proportion was still rising. In 1949 the Storting introduced a weekly period of ministerial answers to questions.[7] In 1952 an official was appointed to hear the complaints of citizens during military service, which provided a precedent for the appointment a decade later of a civil Ombudsmann. His painstaking investigations, the results of which are embodied in annual reports to the Storting, have done much to protect the rights of the individual against official neglect or incompetence. He was soon handling about 1,000 complaints a year, of which a quarter resulted in some action on his part; one in three now concern local authorities, to which the Ombudsmann's jurisdiction was extended in 1968.

For reasons already indicated, the strife between parties was rather muted, as compared with the bitterness of the inter-war period, but from 1947 onwards the rise of prices on the world market brought strong criticism of the Lex Thagaard. This finally came to a head in the summer of 1953, when the price-control powers of the government were made permanent. But the Labour Party had to abandon a bill for rationalization, which would have empowered the government to reorganize private industry on the basis of 'social considerations', so that its steering of the economy continued to operate chiefly through financial and administrative measures. In a long period of almost continuous full employment the Right to Work, which had been named in the wartime joint programme, was readily incorporated in the constitution as a fully acceptable public obligation. For a long time domestic political controversy centred mainly on the housing shortage, the acuteness of which was due less to the war than to the steady rise in social expectations.

The political calm was disturbed eventually by the formation of the Socialist People's Party (*Sosialistisk Folkeparti* or S.F.), which won two seats at the 1961 election with a demand for a new foreign policy and an unequivocal denunciation of atomic warfare. It held the balance of power, but since its domestic views placed it well to the left of the Labour Party, the latter for two years enjoyed its grudging support. Dissatisfaction with the running of state undertakings, which was a recurrent theme with the non-socialist parties, then culminated in a vote of censure which had wide public support, after twenty-one lives had been lost in an explosion at the state-owned King's Bay colliery in Spitsbergen.[8] The new party helped to bring down the government, which was replaced by a coalition of the four bourgeois parties under a Conservative premier, John Lyng. After one month (August–September 1963) the same two S.F. votes were used to restore the Labour government, but the conviction became widespread that Gerhardsen and his colleagues were now tired men. Taxes continued to rise, while public attention was called to the cost of the state steel works in the far north (see p. 426), which greatly exceeded the estimate, to the ever-popular theme of an extravagant concession to foreign interests (in this case, for a much-needed expansion of the aluminium industry), and other alleged administrative scandals. At the 1965 election the pendulum swung definitely against Labour.

THE RE-ORIENTATION OF DEFENCE POLICY

In the light of what we now know about the post-war policies of Stalin, the ambition of Lie and Lange to 'build bridges' appears almost absurdly optimistic. But it fitted in well with the widespread Norwegian hope that the United Nations might become a forum where the smaller powers could exercise a proper influence on the decisions of the greater, and with their wish to justify the postponement of a thorough reconstruction of the national defences—a popular theme during the occupation—until the economy had first been put in order. The establishment of a Communist government in Czechoslovakia in February 1948 therefore gave a great shock to Norwegians in general, when they saw a genuinely democratic people, which practised a 'bridge-building' policy not unlike their own, pulled suddenly behind the Iron Curtain.

One important consequence was to direct attention to possible dangers from the Communist Party in Norway, which was represented in the Foreign Affairs Committee of the Storting: a special committee was set up with no Communist members, to consider 'in particular foreign questions and matters arising'.[9] But expert opinion did not consider that the change of regime in Czechoslovakia made any substantial change in Norway's strategic position and prospects. The treaty of mutual assistance, on the other hand, for which the Russians were pressing the Finns in this same February (though it was not signed until April), was much more directly alarming for Norway. In the first week of March there was a hastily denied newspaper story from Washington about 'some ugly presumptions that Czechoslovakia and Scandinavia were probably lost to western Europe',[10] while circumstantial private reports reached the Norwegian foreign office from Helsinki, Warsaw, and Moscow itself, all to the effect that Norway stood next on the list for a similar Russian demand. The government was determined to resist inclusion in the Russian sphere of influence, and all parties in the Storting except the Communists united to vote an extra kr. 100 million for defence. But vivid memories of April 9th, 1940, gave an extreme urgency to the negotiations of the next twelve months, during which the politicians worked to achieve a defence alliance of adequate external strength without creating the internal divisions which might also spell disaster.

In March a confidential talk with Bevin in Paris opened up for Lange a rather uncertain prospect of participation in an eventual Atlantic agreement; but in May, when the Swedish foreign minister came to Oslo with definite proposals for a Scandinavian defence union, the latter alternative still had much to recommend it to Norwegian sympathies. All three kingdoms aimed primarily and wholeheartedly at the preservation of their neutrality; their attitude to international affairs, as shown for instance in the U.N. Assembly, was broadly similar; the war years had left the Norwegians with an increased sympathy for the Danish people; and as for the Swedes, if their attitude during the war had been at first unco-operative, they had even then been canvassing the idea of a post-war union for mutual defence.[11] Imponderable factors also argued in favour of such a union, as the Norwegian historian of this diplomatic crisis suggests:

Nordic fellow feeling, established over long periods of time, would be a psychological factor of the first order of importance. The practical co-operation of the North was so intimate that Nordic co-ordination was a regular mode of thought and pattern of action, both in political speculation and official practice. It would seem unusual and to many people indefensible if an important choice was made without a Nordic alternative being examined with all possible imaginativeness, determination and good will.[12]

Accordingly, by the end of the year a joint committee of three civilians and one services member from each country had a joint defence scheme in readiness, subject to political agreement. Sweden postulated that the other two should bring their military organizations to the Swedish level of preparedness, which would have imposed a severe economic strain on Norway (and doubtless on Denmark), even if the Swedes—who themselves were not wholly self-supplying—had proved right in their contention that arms would be readily obtainable from American sources. But the eventual breach came from the basic Swedish concept of neutrality—which led them, for instance, to opt out of any obligation to assist the other two states in the unlikely event of hostilities arising out of their token participation in the military occupation of West Germany, then still in force. In January 1949 a meeting was held in Copenhagen, at which the political parties of the three countries (Communists excepted) were represented as well as the cabinets, but no deployment of statecraft could contrive a satisfactory compromise between Swedish insistence on a self-contained pact for the maintenance of strict neutrality without outside entanglements of any kind and the Norwegian proviso, that it must be a pact that could eventually be strengthened by some link with the security arrangements of the greater western powers.

The situation in early February, when Lange and Torp set off to explore possibilities in Washington, was rather tense, for the Russians were not satisfied by the assurance that had just been given them in answer to a direct inquiry that, although the Norwegian government was examining an Atlantic regional security system, it undertook to 'make no agreement with other states which lays obligations upon Norway to open bases on Norwegian territory to the armed forces of foreign powers, so long as Norway is not attacked or exposed to threats of attack'. The Soviet ambassador received orders to press for fuller assurances and the signature of a non-aggression treaty, which was eventually refused. The instructions for use in Washington nevertheless required the emissaries first to sound out the American attitude to the alternative of a relationship between the Americans and Scandinavia as a whole, which the Norwegians still preferred to a separate relationship for themselves alone, if arms would be obtainable on equally favourable conditions of quick delivery and low cost. Dean Acheson, who had just succeeded General Marshall as secretary of state, avoided the appearance of using any pressure, but admitted that 'it would seem difficult to correlate things if you had a barrier between two groups' —which was what the Swedish project in fact imposed. The upshot was that, after a secret debate in the Storting, the decision to adhere to the North Atlantic Treaty Organization was adopted against the votes of the eleven Communists and only two of the Labour members. On 4 April the Danes, who at the Copenhagen meeting had inclined to the Swedish view, signed the treaty of Washington along with the Norwegians. For the internal well-being of Norway it was particularly significant that the Communist vote at the elections in the autumn fell by one-half: the government's appraisal of the situation for the mission to Washington in February was that a 20 per cent support for Communism would create 'a serious threat to political safety'.[13]

Adherence to NATO involved a change of outlook in defence questions. In 1950 five Defence of the Realm Acts (*Beredskapslover*), which were the subject of heated discussions in the Storting, equipped the government with very wide powers in the event of any future international conflict involving Norway. The armed forces were expanded by building on to the provisional arrangements made directly after the war, and their organization was gradually adapted to NATO requirements. The navy, for instance, completed the transfer of its headquarters from the Oslofiord to a large new

base adjoining Bergen; the air force took up its station preponder-
antly in the far north; and the training of army recruits was organized in such a way that each district always had a nucleus of men in
readiness. The bulk of the national service manpower was still
drafted into the army, where the men of the line regiments (aged
20–34) and militia (aged 35–44) would be supported in time of war
by the Home Guard (H.V.), embodying all able-bodied men up to
the age of fifty-five not required for other service. The Norwegian
navy could make only a small contribution to the defence of Atlantic waters, but obsolescent vessels were now quickly replaced and
one-half of a later eight-year building plan was covered by weapon aid
from the United States Treasury. Norway's main contribution to
the Alliance was its air force, with eight fighter squadrons fully
manned at all times; new airfields were provided, especially within
the Arctic Circle, under the infrastructure programme, and jet planes
were supplied from American stocks, as were Nike missiles for the
defence of the capital. Norway's own contribution to total costs was
heavy, for in the course of a decade defence expenditure rose to
about one-fifth of the total Budget, which was three or four times as
high a proportion as in the 1920s and 1930s. Yet there was no gain-
saying the conclusion of a military expert: 'Our participation in
NATO and the American programme of assistance have permitted
us to build up defence after the war at a much faster tempo and on a
larger scale than we could have managed by ourselves.'[14]

In the full NATO membership of fifteen states Norway ranked
twelfth in population but fifth in territorial extent, and only one
other member, namely Turkey, had any territory which was con-
tiguous with the expanded Russian domain. Soviet intentions remained inscrutable, but NATO gave Norway a sense of security at a
time when they seemed very threatening. The experience of belonging to a large group of nations united for a common purpose was
also valuable. Although the ban on placing foreign bases on Norwegian soil was strictly maintained, the Oslo area was selected for
the NATO headquarters in northern Europe, with responsibilities
stretching from the Arctic down to the Schleswig–Holstein province of West Germany; senior officers of many nationalities were
always stationed there, under a British commander-in-chief; and

Norway became the scene of multi-national exercises, especially winter manoeuvres. Moreover, while accepting the paramount importance of the military purposes of the alliance, the Norwegian government made full use of the meetings of the North Atlantic Council to try to influence fellow members on civil questions, such as colonialism, and took a keen interest in programmes of scientific and cultural co-operation.

Inevitably, a price had to be paid in an uneasy relationship with the mighty Russian neighbour, who not only watched the frontier in East Finnmark very closely but was believed from time to time to conduct clandestine investigations in the fiords by means of her huge fleet of submarines. In May 1960, after the rivalry between the superpowers in nuclear armaments had become fully established, Norway was exposed to risk through the shooting down of an American plane which was crossing Russian territory on a secret mission of photographic reconnaissance, its intended destination being Bodö airfield. The Norwegian government disavowed any prior knowledge of the intended misuse of its air base, and placated the Russians by promising that it should not recur. Next year it supplemented its promise regarding foreign bases by an undertaking that no nuclear weapons would be stationed anywhere on its territory (Spitsbergen included) except under immediate threat or actual conditions of war.

This was not enough for the supporters of nuclear disarmament, who had been active for several years, particularly in the Labour movement and in the Left Party. In 1960 they collected 223,000 signatures for their petition on the subject, and the upshot was the formation of the previously mentioned Socialist People's Party, which demanded that Norway should leave NATO and renounce the use of nuclear arms, even if she were attacked. The new party won two seats in the Storting at the elections of 1961 and 1965; counting the Communists, the results on these two occasions showed a small but increasing percentage of voters (5·30, 7·36) in support of parties that were definitely hostile to NATO.

EXTERNAL RELATIONS IN GENERAL

While the defence interests of the Norwegian people became concentrated upon NATO, they continued to regard the U.N. as an
institution whose authority should be supported: in 1970 a representative of the foreign ministry could claim that 'Activities in
the U.N. are of central importance for Norwegian foreign policy.'[15]
But an idealistic championship of the claims of small nations to
political freedom and economic advancement was tempered by a
realistic awareness that only the great powers could give any
effective lead. As a member of the Security Council in 1950, Norway
supported the resolution that declared the Communist invasion of
South Korea to be a breach of the peace and contributed transport
ships and a field hospital for the war that followed. From 1957 onwards Norwegian troops took part in the U.N. control of the Israeli–
Egyptian frontier, and they also served under U.N. command in the
Congo. Eventually, a small force was permanently earmarked for
such purposes: this comprised a battalion of infantry, a frigate, four
transport aircraft, and four helicopters, plus fifty officers available for
staff and observation duties.

Their economic being much more considerable than their military
resources, the Norwegian people played a noteworthy part in world
humanitarian activities. A Help for Europe organization (later styled
the Council for Refugees) was set up shortly after the war—when
North Norway itself was still in dire need—which in eighteen years
collected kr. 50 million. When a World Refugee Year was arranged
by the U. N., the Norwegian contribution of kr. 15 million was much
the largest per head of population, and over a four-year period the
rate of giving was more than twice that of the by no means ungener-
ous Swedes or Danes. The U.N. Commissioner for Refugees,
through whose hands the money passed, was moved to pay a grace-
ful tribute: 'By its generosity, its elasticity, and the imaginative
sympathy which has suggested many pioneer projects the Norwegian Council for Refugees has continued the tradition which
Fridtjof Nansen founded with his work in the service of humanity.'[16]
As regards the underdeveloped countries, in 1952 Norway launched
a special project for developing the fisheries in Kerala (Travancore-

Cochin), the most densely populated area in the whole of India. In 1963 the Storting authorized the formation of a Peace Corps, and other specific undertakings included assistance with the Ghana fisheries and participation in Scandinavian projects in Tanzania and Korea. When the U.N. Assembly in 1962 urged the richer countries to set aside 1 per cent of national income for the development of the poorer countries of the world, the Norwegian government responded by appointing a directorate under Trygve Lie to supervise its contribution; this was to be doubled immediately so as to bring it to ·25 per cent of income, and then quadrupled again by slower stages. As far as possible, these larger sums were to be channelled through the U.N., with a view to benefiting its prestige as well as the interests of the eventual recipients.

Officials and institutions of the United Nations figured six times in twenty-one post-war awards of the Nobel Peace Prize. Other recipients who might be identified with the cause of the United Nations included a Belgian Dominican, honoured for his services to refugees; Martin Luther King; and another, less famous victim of race hatred, the interned South African chieftain, Luthuli. But perhaps the most imaginative choice was that of the seed expert, Norman Borlaug, whose citation declares: 'Through his improvement of wheat and rice strains he has made a technical break-through which renders the abolition of hunger possible in the developing countries.'[17] His work was based to some degree upon Norwegian as well as American experience, for Borlaug's parents had come to Iowa from a farm in Norway, where the harvest yield is often extremely problematic.

Emigration having fallen to 2,400 souls a year, the Norwegians made no new mark as settlers in distant places. But the pioneering spirit was shown in Thor Heyerdahl's expeditions on his famous rafts, *Kon-Tiki* and *Ra*, whose safe arrival demonstrated the possibility of unrecorded intercontinental migrations across both the Pacific and Atlantic Oceans. Norwegians also helped to explore Antarctica. In 1947 the whaling interest financed an expedition, which found no new whaling grounds but set up numerous stations for oceanographical observations; the veteran H. U. Sverdrup was chairman of the committee that sent out a combined party of Britons, Swedes, and Norwegians—the first of its kind; and in 1957–8 another antarctic expedition constituted the Norwegian contribution to the first International Geophysical Year. Moreover, in spite of the discouragements imposed by the world wide influence of Communism, secularism, and fanatical forms of nationalism, the Norwegian people retained their devotion to foreign missions. When China became a forbidden land, new churches were established in Japan, Hong Kong, and Taiwan; and although Madagascar was still the main field, expansion continued in other regions of Africa, such as Cameroon. In 1970 1,134 Norwegian missionaries and wives of missionaries were spread over thirty-eight states all across the world, and their religious labours were supplemented by schools for about 115,000 pupils and hospitals handling more than 500,000 patients every year.

In foreign missionary work, as indeed in most of the external activities so far mentioned, the Norwegians associated closely with the other Scandinavian or Nordic peoples. In 1940 the nations of the North had been driven apart, but in the later war years the Norwegians had admired the courage shown by the Danish Resistance and had collaborated with its Freedom Council in London. They were also grateful to the Swedes, both for the work organized by Count Bernadotte, which had secured the evacuation of Norwegian prisoners from Germany just before its final collapse, and for financial and other aid in reconstruction. Norwegian sympathy for the Finns had been strong ever since the Winter War, while the new Republic of Iceland, proclaimed in 1944, was welcomed as a fourth full partner. Furthermore, in March 1952 the foreign ministers of the five countries approved a scheme drawn up by the Nordic Interparliamentary Association for establishing a Nordic Council, to act as a forum for the discussion of all matters of mutual concern to the northern peoples. Its annual sessions came to be attended by ministers as well as by the accredited delegates of the five parliaments, and although only the latter had voting powers, about one-half of the recommendations adopted by the Council resulted in some action being taken by the states concerned. Matters of foreign policy and defence were in practice excluded from the discussions, but their total effect was to promote a general spirit of cooperation. Thus an official of the Norwegian foreign ministry recorded that it had become 'a daily routine for the authorities in the separate countries to consult each other on a long series of questions'.[18]

The improvement of communications was an obvious common interest. A Scandinavian Airlines System was formed in the first year after the war, with three-sevenths Swedish, two-sevenths Danish, and two-sevenths Norwegian capital; it took over in succession the intercontinental, the European, and the main internal networks of the three countries, and became one of the major air companies of the world. The Nordic Council concerned itself with humbler matters, such as the improvement of the road-links between Norway and Sweden and the common interests in tourism; but it also focused the attention of the three countries concerned on the possibility of developing their neglected territory in the Arctic, where the provision of roads, air routes, and power stations might encourage, not only the tourist and other industries but also the long-neglected culture of the Lapps. Yet the most significant development was not in the communications themselves but in the facilities for their use. In 1952 the Scandinavian governments agreed to waive passport requirement for visits of up to three months' duration from one country to another, and from this modest start they advanced to a complete abolition of passports and labour permits and to interchangeability of social insurance rights, so that even the traveller in search of employment scarcely noticed the frontier. Norwegians living in border areas have been heard to complain because it costs more to telephone into Sweden than over the same distance inside Norway.

Practical convenience provided the chief motive for efforts to harmonize the various legal systems, which produced regular meetings of ministers of justice and numerous legislative modifications. The work that the Nordic Association had been doing since 1919 in the schools received a new impetus, especially in the Folk High Schools which were a common Scandinavian inheritance. A Scandinavian Council for Applied Research was set up in 1947; special facilities were made available for students and teachers to move freely from country to country; and in 1962 and 1963 Nordic Prizes for literature and music were introduced, which quickly achieved a five-country celebrity. Since there was hardly any limit to the possible fields of co-operation among nations for which language differences (except in the Finnish case) were not an insurmountable barrier, a variety of other more or less successful projects were launched, which might be mentioned: but it is more important for the present purpose to note that Norwegian participation was never quite wholehearted.

Their historical tradition rendered the Norwegian people very sensitive to any suggestion that an obviously desirable co-operation among closely related but politically independent units might somehow impair the independence which they cherished above all things. This fear was voiced by C. J. Hambro and other opposition leaders when membership of the Nordic Council was discussed in the Storting; it was approved by the rather small majority of 74 to 39. Ten years later the supposed lukewarmness of the Norwegians was one of the main reasons why the Swedes and Finns pressed for a formal treaty to strengthen the informal resolutions of parliaments which had sufficed to set up the Nordic Council: but the resulting Convention of Helsinki in June 1962 did little more than confirm the general fact that all five powers 'desire to continue the valuable co-operation in the Nordic Council and other organs of co-operation'.[19] Besides their sensitiveness about points of sovereignty, the Norwegians were reluctant to countenance any move towards the economic unification of Scandinavia except for matters of practical convenience—such as the interchange of electric power with Swedish stations. A Nordic customs union had been under discussion during and after the war, but after the failure of 'Uniscan'—an agreement signed in January 1950 to promote trade between the United Kingdom and the Scandinavian countries by the removal of financial and other obstacles—Norway followed the British lead in working towards something larger than a Nordic common market where Swedish industry and finance would be predominant. The establishment of the European Free Trade Association in 1960 by the treaty of Stockholm was a step in this direction, but its results must be considered in relation to the general development of the Norwegian economy.

ECONOMIC POLICY

The economic policy of the Norwegian Labour government subjected private enterprise to public control in a manner which was
effective but not strikingly original; its interest for the foreigner lies
chiefly in the fact that it held the field for a continuous period of
twenty years. Its long duration may be attributable in part to the
trend of events during the first post-war years, which has already
been described. The inter-party programme had declared: 'The task
for our industry and the whole economic activity of the country is
to create work for everybody and an increase of production, so that
a just distribution of the proceeds may provide good conditions for
all.'[20] But very few people expected reconstruction of the damaged
economy to be achieved as smoothly and rapidly as it was, with no
trade slump following: in 1947 the government had been busy
establishing local labour exchanges, to be co-ordinated by a Labour
Directorate with plans for public works to absorb the prospective
unemployment. Since work continued to be plentiful and the use of
subsidies kept prices stable, the first results of Labour planning were
widely approved. The rationing of consumer goods came to an end
in 1952, and although the housing shortage in the larger towns remained so acute that King Haakon called public attention to it that
year in a speech on his eightieth birthday, it was thought that
the new Housing Bank would soon be able to finance sufficient
building.

However, the devaluation of 1949—when the krone followed the
pound for reasons which in retrospect were judged inadequate—and
the rise of prices on the world market during the three years of the
Korean War (1950–3) made a 30-per-cent price increase inside Norway virtually inevitable. It was at this time that the government, in
the face of strong opposition from the non-socialist parties in the
Storting, secured a permanent Price Law but failed (as has already
been noticed) to get direct powers of control over private industry.
Although some price subsidies were continued, by 1956 the cost of
living had risen about 50 per cent above the level maintained during
the first four years after the war. A slow inflation might be accepted
as a necessary accompaniment of economic growth, but it com-

plicated the working of the financial and other pressures that Labour employed for its largely indirect control of the economy.

Apart from a few exceptions of special and limited scope, such as monopolies of medical supplies and fishing equipment, the Norwegian state indulged in no new measures of nationalization; but it became an important participant in industry through its retention of many of the German holdings, all of which had passed into its hands as reparations. In this way the state became the largest shareholder in Norsk Hydro, was able to build up from small German beginnings one of the biggest aluminium companies in Europe,[21] and controlled most of the mining. In addition, it made the largest single capital investment of the two decades in a steel works at Mo i Rana, just outside the Arctic Circle, as part of a development programme for the long-neglected northern counties, to whose plight the wartime devastation had called attention. This plant took half the power available from a state-owned hydro-electric development, and also stimulated the provision of a state coke-works in the same area, using coal from state-owned mines in Svalbard.

Nevertheless, the method most widely employed was the use of general administrative controls to direct private enterprise into approved channels. The operations of banks and other credit institutions were subject to many official sanctions: it was significant that in 1954 a former Labour finance minister, Erik Brofoss, became director of the Bank of Norway. A plethora of regulations governing foreign exchange, imports and exports, building permits, price levels, and so forth was always at hand for help or hindrance. There were some conspicuous failures, such as the dearth of housing mentioned above; in this case supply never came near to meeting the demand, in spite of cheap money from public sources, large-scale expropriation of land by municipal authorities, and facilities for co-operative organizations to work through private builders. And as in other countries, grandiose schemes for regional development could not prevent people from moving where they wished—in Norway the south-east attracted, the far north was still a deterrent—although transport, power, and housing requirements all received preferential treatment in those districts where the government wished to attract or retain population.

Labour cabinets, whose personnel was recruited to a very considerable extent from the trade union movement, encouraged 'democracy in the factories'—a concept which grew out of the joint committees of 1945—and the participation of the trade union federation in national affairs. Membership of affiliated unions, which was 350,000 in 1939, rose to 575,000; real wages increased fairly steadily —between 1954 and 1960, for instance, by as much as one-fifth— while hours of work were reduced; and leaders of the federation encouraged their members to 'look upon open conflict as a completed phase in development'.[22] In 1952 the system of compulsory arbitration which had been reintroduced at the end of the war was replaced by a Wage Board, whose decisions in any dispute were binding on both sides; this too was discontinued after eight years, but strikes and lock-outs continued to be extremely rare. The emphasis was increasingly laid upon carefully negotiated wage settlements involving very large groups of workers and their employers; apart from adjustment for changes in the cost-of-living index, these were legally binding, usually for a period of two years, and once accepted, were seldom challenged.

Trade unionists were encouraged to accept their allotted share of the national product without undue cavilling by the pains that the government took to keep the shares of other groups in the community on approximately the same level. The standard of living of the farming and fishing population as a whole was being raised by price agreements regarding their products, and these were taken into consideration at each biennial renewal of the industrial wage agreements. At the same time the standard of living of the entrepreneurial, rentier, and most professional groups was deliberately reduced by steeply progressive rates of taxation on both income and capital. A budget which by 1963 reached a figure twenty times as high as before the war necessarily imposed a heavier burden on all taxpayers, but the considerable proportion allotted to the social services (see p. 436) benefited the workers to a greater extent than these typical middle-class groups. In addition, the dividends of limited companies were held down for the sake of the 'cheap money' policy, and share issues were carefully controlled.

Yet the Labour government never lost sight of its responsibility for the growth of exports and shipping services, in the absence of which no measures for controlling the economy would produce a higher standard of living for the mass of the Norwegian people. For two years during the period of national reconstruction, financial anxieties caused ministers to lay a much-resented embargo on the placing of shipbuilding contracts in foreign yards; otherwise the shipowners suffered little direct interference, and a steady reduction in the manning requirements of the newer types of vessel enabled them to cope easily with rising wage costs. A high proportion of capital investment was directed by the government to the export industries and the hydro-electric developments on which they so largely depended. Seeing that this temporary advantage would need to be replaced eventually by a lead in some of the newly developing branches of technology, the government interested itself in scientific research, which besides direct subventions was allotted part of the profits of the state-run football pools; in addition, the industrialists themselves contributed a sum which by 1962 averaged 1·16 per cent of the value created by manufacture. As the possibilities of domestic accumulation from the ploughing back of profits were very limited, American and other foreign capital was welcomed. This policy resulted by 1966 in a situation in which foreign-owned industry was responsible for 8·4 per cent of value from manufacture and 6·2 per cent of employment.[23] Table X illustrates the increase in foreign holdings of all kinds, which had declined by kr. 40 million in 1939–46.

TABLE X[24]

Foreign Investment, 1947–1962

	total of corporate capital stock (at face value in million kroner)	percentage foreign-held	amount foreign-held	France	U.K.	U.S.	Sweden	Switzerland	Canada	West Germany
							distribution by main countries			
1947			287·8	64·7	52·5	48·8	34·7	15·9	20·2	—
1952	3,047·6	9·6	292·4	72·4	39·4	50·4	33·4	11·4	26·0	—
1956			353	101	46	68	39	12	28	1
1962	5,002	14·5	599	131·6	98·6	185·5	54·2	33·8	62·0	6·4

Finally, the government did what it could to promote free conditions in international trade, both for the benefit of the mercantile marine and because a big external market was necessary to justify the industrialization of so small a country. Although Norway like Britain was chary of making any sacrifice of sovereignty to the Council of Europe or other outside bodies, in 1958 she strongly supported the British effort to bring the rest of the members of O.E.E.C. into a free-trade union with the newly formed European Economic Community. When this failed, Norway again followed a British lead in the formation of the European Free Trade Association, believing that the existence of EFTA would help negotiations with E.E.C. The Storting now came round to the view that some diminution of sovereignty might eventually be necessary as the price of access to the Common Market, and a bill was passed by 115 to 35 votes, permitting a three-quarters majority of the Storting to transfer powers other than constitution-making powers from national to international authorities. Two months later, in May 1962, Norway followed the example of Britain (and Denmark) in applying for full membership of E.E.C., but negotiations were suspended indefinitely after De Gaulle had caused the British application to fail.

Meanwhile, however, the policy which brought Norway into EFTA had begun to produce significant results. Norwegian industry proved more adaptable in the face of competition than had been expected, exports to EFTA countries growing in the first six years at a yearly rate of 11·9 per cent. Even more striking was their growth in the Nordic sector of the EFTA market considered separately, where they increased during the same period by a total figure of 154 per cent; this was more than twice the rate of increase for Norwegian exports as a whole, and greater than the increase in exports to the United Kingdom, though this was still Norway's biggest single market. In Norway, as in other member countries, the temporary import duties imposed by the Wilson government in November 1964 were widely regarded as a breach of the spirit, if not of the letter, of the EFTA treaty, with the result that Norwegian trade policy was henceforth a little less readily orientated towards Britain.

ECONOMIC PROGRESS

The growth or non-growth of an economy is seldom, if ever, attributable solely to policy. Full employment, for example, was one of the aims that the Norwegian Labour government pursued most sedulously, but the comment of their own Central Statistical Office divides the credit for its achievement.

The explanation lies partly in the economic policy which has been adopted . . . the maintenance of a high and generally stable level of investment . . . and the ability to keep the rise in the internal level of wages and prices within such limits that Norwegian goods have always been able to compete with foreign. Nevertheless, there is no doubt that success must also be attributed to the course of international trade.[25]

At all events, twenty years of empirical socialist administration were accompanied by general economic results which the Statistical Office appraised as very much better than Norway had obtained during the 1920s and 1930s and fully comparable with the contemporary results achieved in other western countries, though the latter comparison 'leaves less room for superlatives'.

In the course of this period the proportion of the labour force engaged in agriculture, fisheries, and forestry sank to 13 per cent—about half as many as were employed in industrial production, by which the economy made faster growth. The prospect of earning more money and earning it more easily in more or less urbanized surroundings was a magnet which withdrew from the farms not only their supply of hired labour but also the farmer's own children, with the possible exception of the *odelsgutt* who would inherit the property. In the 1950s small holdings vanished at the rate of 1,500 a year, in the 1960s twice as rapidly; in terms of man-years of work on the land, the drop between 1946 and 1962 was 36 per cent. Many a remote *seter* or inaccessible farmstead fell into decay—or was turned into summer chalets for townsfolk—but agriculture benefited from a long-overdue doubling in the productivity of labour, thanks to the introduction of many more tractors and combine harvesters, a great increase in the use of artificial manure and concentrated feedingstuffs, and improvements in the quality of seed and breeds of cattle. In forestry too, a big drop in the labour force (21 per cent, 1946–62) was accompanied by a resort to more efficient methods, especially through a 10-per-cent levy on timber sales to provide better equipment, such as motor saws, additional haulage roads, and up-to-date accommodation for forest workers. But the over-all result in both cases was an increased dependence upon foreign supplies: the agriculture of Norway produced less than one-half of the calorie requirements for its population, and the yield of its forests had to be supplemented by an annual importation of about 1,000,000 cubic metres of timber to keep its woodworking industries supplied.

Their special advantages and long-standing traditions as a fishing nation made the Norwegians in this case less disposed to forsake primary production for the gains of advanced industry. When the Antarctic whale fishery was restarted in 1945–6, six Norwegian vessels took part; Norway also provided the first chairman for the International Whaling Commission, which tried to prevent the total stock of whales from being reduced to unprofitable dimensions. However, by the time national quotas were belatedly introduced in 1962, the Norwegians—who had made a vain attempt to prevent their crews from serving in foreign expeditions—were preparing to follow the British and Dutch example by resigning what was left of the trade to their Russian and Japanese competitors. The Russians had the advantage of unlimited state capital, the Japanese of an unlimited domestic market for whale meat, which made them less dependent upon the variable profits from the oil; both these countries had invested in highly efficient, diesel-powered whale-catchers. In 1967–8 Norway sent a factory ship to the Antarctic for the last time.[26] But small whales were still hunted to some extent off North Norway, and after two years an experiment was made with a new kind of whale ship of only 800 tons; this did its own catching, froze the meat for sale to the Japanese, and could operate in the North Atlantic when the season in the Antarctic was finished.

As regards the fisheries in general, the Norwegian government strongly defended the inshore monopoly of its nationals, as prescribed by a decree of 1935, which was increasingly contested by British trawler-owners as waters nearer home became over-fished.

A 4-mile limit, to be measured from base-lines drawn between outer points of the Norwegian coast and its islands, was successfully claimed before the Hague Court in 1951, and ten years later this was extended by unilateral action to 12 miles; in the outer 6 miles a temporary concession was reluctantly made for Britain and other states whose vessels already frequented these waters. Although the teeming stock of fish to be harvested so near the coast in the far north was the chief factor that made the Norwegians the sixth-largest fishing nation of the world and Europe's principal exporter, technical advances now played a big part in producing a catch that never fell below the pre-war maximum of 1,000,000 tons and in 1956 reached a peak of 2,000,000. The use of echo-sounding devices to locate the shoals of fish and powered equipment to haul the nets reduced the drudgery of the fisherman's task; by 1958 twenty-seven big trawlers were in use, as well as more than 400 of less than 300 tons; and the frozen-fish industry was developed to add to the profitable ways of disposing of the catch. But just as in agriculture, manpower was declining. Between 1946 and 1962 it fell by 14 per cent, while the proportion of regular inshore fishermen who were over fifty years of age rose to one-third. Many of the small-boat fishers lived in deep poverty in remote regions of the coast, from which they could not easily move, even if they wished. The Storting therefore introduced subsidies, to be made available whenever the shifting conditions of their occupation failed to provide earnings 'in reasonable proportion to the income from other trades'.[27]

A big drive for further electrification had figured in the inter-party programme of 1945, not only for the sake of the economy but to meet the domestic needs of the so-called 'dark districts', which then contained one-fifth of the population.[28] In the hydro-electric developments which followed, the state and local government authorities increased their share at the expense of private enterprise; indeed, in 1962 it aroused little controversy when Gerhardsen claimed that the central and local government ought to have a monopoly under the control of the former. As for the technical side, new methods led to the construction of larger power stations, many of which were built underground, as were also the transformers, and were based on dams which would resist bombing. By tunnelling from one valley to another the water from a wide catchment area was often concentrated in a single reservoir, which made the operation of the turbines more economical; in 1956 it was decided to form a nationwide network for distribution, such as was already to be found in countries with a more convenient topography. The results were impressive. With 7 per cent of gross investment earmarked for this purpose, the equivalent of the entire pre-war development of electricity was achieved in four years; in seventeen years machine installation was more than trebled; and it was calculated that by 1970 Norway would have developed one-half of its enormous hydro-electric potential.

By the end of 1962 only three per thousand of the Norwegian population were without electricity, of which they were—on a *per capita* basis—by far the largest consumers in the world. The simplest Norwegian home employed electricity profusely for lighting, heating, and the running of domestic appliances: but these uses, together with the needs of agriculture, communications, and business life, accounted for only one-third of the total consumption. In 1960, for example, the share of general industry was 17 per cent, some of which served new undertakings in out-of-the-way places where the development of manufactures would otherwise have been impossible. But the economy gained most from the 45 per cent (13,000 million kWh.) consumed by the special group of industries for which cheap power was the basis of their profitability. Norsk Hydro, whose various enterprises used more electricity than the whole of Denmark, was still much the largest producer of electro-chemicals: the growth in its fertilizer output after 1945 was from 90,000 to 300,000 tons, measured in terms of pure nitrogen. The production of carbides in Norway was likewise trebled, with a firm at Arendal on the south coast ranking as the largest supplier of carborundum in Europe. Electro-metallurgy showed even bigger advances. In aluminium, a combination of public and private enterprise succeeded in maintaining Norway's share at 5 per cent in a period when the world output was mounting very fast. Norwegian mining was now concentrated chiefly upon iron ore, pyrites, and ilmenite (the source of titanium), and Norsk Hydro became the world's second-largest producer of magnesium, from the dolomite of the far north. Electric furnaces enabled Norway to make seven times as much steel in 1960 as before the war, and the output of ferro-alloys was more than doubled.

The cement industry being located mainly on the seaboard, Norway became the chief European exporter of a bulky material, which was supplied to markets both in Africa and in the United States. Plastics became important, and the development of a trade in materials for isolation and other light building requirements did something to compensate for the general stagnation of the wood-working industries. A growing trade in advanced types of machinery, including electronic equipment, harmonized well with the official policy already mentioned, of encouraging technological research with a view to competing effectively under changing world conditions. Thus in 1951 the Norwegian Institute for Atomic Energy completed the first heavy-water nuclear reactor, which was followed by experiments with nuclear power for ships. Although these had no immediate practical results, Norwegian shipbuilding enjoyed a considerable renaissance at this period. Before the war the yards were limited to an output of about 50,000 tons a year; in 1965 they built 375,000 tons of shipping (besides executing much repair work), and they possessed slips in the form of dry docks, which provided for vessels up to 130,000 tons deadweight. Home-built ships still covered no more than about one-quarter of Norway's enormous requirements, but the exports included vessels of very advanced design. Norway rose to the sixth place among shipbuilding nations, and her shipyards now employed the largest force of any branch of the metal industries.

As already noticed, the mercantile marine had made good its wartime losses by 1949, but it has been justly claimed that 'the gigantic expansion which has taken place since then constitutes the third romance in a century and a half for Norwegian shipping'.[29] In fifteen years tonnage trebled, a rate of growth which did not quite keep pace with the expansion of the world's sea-borne trade but was considerably faster than that of its total shipping resources. Norway suffered two serious handicaps—the resort to Liberian and other flags of convenience, whose users were believed to pay about one-seventieth of the rate of taxation levied upon Norwegian shipwners; and the subsidies and discriminatory regulations by which the United States and many other governments protected their mercantile marines from free competition. Nevertheless, in 1965 the Norwegian fleet of 15,641,498 tons was exceeded only by those of the United Kingdom (21,530,264), the United States (21,527,349), and Liberia (17,539,462); since the American total included the Reserve Fleet, laid up in readiness for a major war, and the Liberian —except in the eyes of the law—was international, the United Kingdom was the only power that actually took a larger part than Norway in world trade. In spite of the inroads of air transport upon the profits of passenger traffic, the liner trade was further developed on a transoceanic basis. Time and man-power were saved by the introduction of bulk-carriers and container ships of many types: some even carried fully loaded lighters, or had folding decks to accommodate alternate loads of motor vehicles and coal. But Norwegian shipowners showed their expertise above all in the competition for oil freights, where their share of an enormously increased and highly lucrative world trade declined by no more than 5 per cent. Tankers of unprecedented dimensions were built for letting on long-term contracts to the major oil companies; forward planning was adapted with great promptitude to the new situation created in 1956 by the closure of the Suez Canal; a modern version of the old tramp steamer even made its appearance in the OBO-ship, which was equipped to carry oil to one port, bulk cargo to a second, and iron ore to a third. To sum up a story that had many interesting ramifications: while these ventures involved the provision of a higher proportion of new vessels than ever before, in 1946–62 net freight earnings averaged kr. 2,400 million, as compared with a balance of imports over exports averaging kr. 3,200 million, and in 1962–5 the gap closed to kr. 315 million.[30]

The unfavourable balance of trade did not in any case weigh heavily upon the community. Since Norway's borrowings from abroad had been used to increase fixed capital in the shape of new factories, ships, and industrial equipment, interest payments were easily met and the total balance of payments showed a net increase in reserves of foreign exchange, which in 1965 amounted to more than kr. 1,000 million. As for the internal situation, capital equipment per worker was twice what it had been in 1938; almost every

trade activity had been speeded up by the construction of local airfields, the improvement of road surfaces, and the electrification of
the principal rail routes; and a big transfer of labour into the service
industries likewise marked an economy on the up-grade. Above all,
the economic basis was available for a new society.

THE NEW SOCIETY

There is a sense in which each generation in every country forms a
new society, but in Norway the effects of two decades of socialist
government, after the established order had been in many ways
shaken up during the war years, were unusually far-reaching. The
steady growth of national prosperity meant that there was much
more levelling up than levelling down, but the results of an egalitar-
ianism which aimed at a classless society were nevertheless very
striking. Income tax rose so steeply that, above a figure roughly
equivalent to £4,000 a year, the proportion payable to central and
local authorities reached 70 per cent, while the additional tax on
capital discouraged the accumulation of savings. Post-war Norway
was therefore a country which was noticeably deficient in Rolls
Royce cars (except at embassies) and chauffeurs to drive them, in
large residences and servants to staff them. On the other hand, the
combination of subsidies to agriculture and fisheries, in which the
poorest strata of the population were to be found, with high wage
rates and comprehensive social services reduced poverty to a very
limited phenomenon of backward and remote areas, feckless and
very unfortunate families, and especially of friendless old age.

For a number of years after the war the development of the social
services followed the same general pattern as in Britain: family
allowances were begun in 1946, and the existing sickness and unemployment insurance schemes were in various ways improved. But
in the 1960s Norway made a special feature of 'help to self-help': the
rehabilitation of disabled persons was carefully fostered by the provision of State Rehabilitation Institutes in the three main towns, of
working premises adapted to the needs of the handicapped, and of
qualified counsellors attached to Labour Exchanges. The same principle was applied to the case of widows and unmarried mothers, who

were to be supported whilst being trained or educated to qualify for paid employment. Then in 1964 the Labour government laid the coping-stone upon its edifice of services covering the whole community by its proposals for the 'People's Pension', of which 'the basic philosophy is that each citizen shall be able to maintain the standard of living that he has attained during his working life'.[31] This was to be achieved by combining a basic pension for old age with a sliding-scale pension derived from the best twenty of the working years on which the individual paid contributions; the result would be equivalent to two-thirds of the income before retirement, and was made subject to regulation in accordance with the cost of living and the general level of incomes. The Storting gave its unanimous approval in June 1966, by which time the majority was non-socialist.

The inter-party programme of 1945 had demanded that 'the whole school system be co-ordinated, so that all stages from the elementary school to the highest level of instruction form a natural succession in the case of both practical and literary types of schooling'.[32] In 1948–52 a Royal Commission made nineteen recommendations for implementing this, but the decisive reform did not come until 1959, by which date the maximum hours of instruction in the rural schools had been raised almost to the minimum hours in the town schools, of which the standards had always hitherto been much higher. All local authorities were now authorized to make attendance from 7 to 16 compulsory, with the result that large 'youth schools' were built to accommodate the last three years of the general course. Meanwhile, mounting prosperity and declining social prejudice brought larger numbers of pupils into the *gymnasier*, whose courses qualified them for admission to the university. As in so many other countries, the demand for education at this highest level was insatiable. At Oslo University, where the student body in 1938 had totalled 4,229, the main expansion came after 1960, when a total of 5,584 was doubled in five years, so that a succession of new buildings on a post-war campus were no sooner opened than they were overcrowded. In 1946 the Storting gave final approval to a pre-war proposal for a second university at Bergen, which by 1965 had nearly 2,000 students, and rather more than this number were then in attendance at the Technical High School in Trondheim, which had had only 1,060 students as recently as the session of 1946–7. Plans were already on foot to make a third university at Trondheim and a fourth, with a special view to the needs of the far north, at Tromsö. In the early 1960s there were still about 3,000 students following courses in engineering, medicine, and other technical subjects at foreign institutions.

Since most students were dependent upon interest-free loans from the State, many of the ablest chose vocational subjects, whether at home or abroad, which would make eventual repayment relatively easy. But the mass demand for such subjects as sociology, psychology, and political science, where the teaching and the textbooks were least authoritarian, showed the egalitarian trend of the new society. This was even more evident in the administration of education. The work of local education authorities, for instance, was supplemented by school management committees (*tilsynsnemnd*) of five members, of whom three were elected by parents of pupils, and the pupils themselves became legally entitled to some degree of self-government, even in the upper forms of the primary schools. At university level junior staff and students wrested some rights of control over curricula and discipline from the formerly all-powerful professors, and student co-operatives played a dominant role in the provision of much-needed residential and catering facilities.

The number of newspapers published in Norway fell from 260 in 1939 to 160 in 1964, but circulation had doubled since the war. Although an editor reviewing their progress since 1814 claimed no more than a lessening of the gap 'between the best that we can offer and the journalism of the countries that lead in this field',[33] the one and a half papers read daily by the average Norwegian household provided a coverage of news and party politics which was comprehensive, even if the presentation was often pedestrian, and it was enviably free from sensationalism and snob appeal. Allowing for the difference in the medium, much the same might be said of the state broadcasting and of the television services which began only in 1960. Politics on the local as well as the national level received an extensive treatment, in which edification was always preferred to entertainment: in the summer of 1963, for instance, the long-drawn-out debate that led to the temporary fall of the government was shown on TV at full length. Since no proposals for a commercial alternative programme were acceptable to the authorities—including an advisory council to which slightly more members were appointed by the Storting than by the government—the pattern of cultural and educational programmes often resembled those of the B.B.C. in the days of its monopoly, except that the insistent claims of neo-Norwegian provided a bone of contention.

The institution of a Cultural Council in 1965 showed that the arts were taken seriously in the new society. In this sphere Norway's reputation abroad was not, indeed, notably enhanced, though from 1953 onwards the Bergen Festival attracted some attention to Norwegian music and an attempt to establish a Norwegian opera was presided over by a native singer of world reputation, Kirsten Flagstad. The work of the successors to Hamsun and Sigrid Undset in the art of the novel did not make sufficient appeal in a translated form, and out of the thirty-two lyricists who figured in an anthology of 1939–54 Nordahl Grieg was almost the only one whose name was known outside Scandinavia. Nevertheless, Norway still had its powerful novelists, such as Johan Borgen, author of the first substantial study of the stresses of the occupation,[34] who was known internationally as a short-story writer, and poets with a wide national appeal, including Wildenvey and Överland, whose war poems sold 50,000 copies. Vesaas, who remained active as novelist, poet, and playwright almost until his death in 1970, received the Nordic Council's literary prize in 1964, the year in which his work, already translated into many other languages, first reached the English-speaking public. In the graphic arts the most significant figure was Rolf Nesch, who became a Norwegian citizen in 1946: inspired during his youth in Germany by the work of Munch, he achieved a wide reputation for his experiments with metals and other new materials. A state-financed travelling theatre (*Riksteater*) and theatre school were also characteristic of an era in which the growth of education and leisure had brought appreciation of the arts within the reach of the many.

Since the standard working week was reduced to 42½ hours and the annual period of paid holiday extended to four weeks, leisure was especially a feature of the new society. Nevertheless, promoters of the arts were only one of several groups which were in some measure disappointed by the results. The church, for example, which had proved a rallying point for many troubled souls during the war, found that the pre-war drift away from its ministrations was resumed. As the great majority of the population were still nominally members, popular controversy could be aroused on such issues as disestablishment, religious instruction in the schools, the admission of women to the priesthood (which was approved in 1961), or even the indefatigable Professor Hallesby's protests against any mitigation of the Lutheran concept of hell. But information collected in 1956 showed that the state church enjoyed the regular support, Sunday by Sunday, of no more than 3·6 per cent of its nominal supporters. The increase of leisure was also accompanied by positive abuses: temperance workers deplored the fact that convictions for drunkenness continued at the rate of one to every hundred citizens every year, youth workers the extent to which a noticeable element among the young rejected the constructive use of leisure and succumbed to the temptations of petty thieving, vandalism, and violence.

Tourism was no longer one of Norway's main sources of foreign exchange, for her own people now spent in the south of Europe and even farther afield very nearly as much money as foreign visitors left behind them in the north[35]—another striking illustration of the growth of prosperity and leisure. Nevertheless, many of the 468,000 non-Scandinavians, who came to Norway in 1965 from the world outside, would agree that the country was not merely ideal for a healthy use of leisure but was being developed as such by its inhabitants. This was perhaps most evident in the proliferation of the *hytte* or chalet, the unpretentious second home in the mountains or by the fiords, made readily accessible by Volkswagen along the new asphalted roads; there the typical Norwegian family could be seen to practise the simple life as often as its members could escape from town. They were encouraged by new laws which gave democratic rights of access almost everywhere for fishing and hunting, for exploration by sailing boats and motor boats, or for the mere hiker with his tent. As for athletic sports in the narrower sense, in 1952 Oslo was the first capital to provide for the winter Olympic Games, which the *New York Times* correspondent described appreciatively as 'the Olympics of the common man'.

A new society of the common man was, indeed, what Gerhardsen and his colleagues were aiming at, with a degree of success which one of their most experienced supporters, who had been a very youthful mayor of Narvik in the hard times before the war, appraised as follows.

Our country has certainly had the best period in its history in these years when it came to its senses after the war. Yet it has been a sober time without emotional or artistic peaks. We have not even been completely satisfied with the results achieved, whether economic, social, or political. Very many of us live a hectic, rushed existence. But we have become expert in the use of leisure.[36]

Epilogue, 1965–1972

THE ELECTION OF 1965 WAS DESCRIBED BY A NORWEGIAN political observer of long experience as 'an epoch-making event: perhaps it will prove to mark a historic turning-point'.[37] The experience of the next half-dozen years showed, indeed, that this was not after all the opening of a period of continuous non-socialist administration comparable to the long preceding era of Labour rule. But in matters of more moment than the interplay of political parties decisive changes did appear to be approaching, so that Norway might soon be developing upon lines not foreseen even by the leaders of the 1950s and 1960s, busy with their 'new society'. This may justify a very brief summary of some recent events which may prove to have been significant.

The history of the parties is indicated by Table 11.

TABLE XI[38]

	Labour	Communist	Socialist People's	Conservative	Left	Centre	Christian People's
1965	68 (43·14)	0 (1·37)	2 (5·99)	30+1* (20·30)	18 (10·15)	17+1* (9·37)	12+1* (7·83)
1969	84 (46·7)	0 (1·0)	0 (3·50)	29 (19·4)	13 (9·3)	20 (10·6)	14 (9·4)

Although the controversy regarding the record of the Labour government must have stimulated the record turnout of 85·4 per cent of the electorate in 1965, the non-socialist parties received slightly less than half the votes, so that they owed their majority in the Storting to the fact that the two smaller socialist parties were unrepresented. In these circumstances it seemed advisable for the members of the new coalition to choose a premier from one of the three middle parties and to content themselves with a gentle slowing down of the socializing trends of the past two decades. The People's Pension, as we have already noticed, was approved unanim-

* These seats were gained on inter-party lists, which received 5·17 per cent of the total vote: their effect on the party percentages cannot be shown precisely.

ously. But before the next election the government rashly decided to meet rapidly rising Budget costs by imposing a Value Added Tax at a higher rate than that advocated by their Labour opponents, who fought under a vigorous new leader, Trygve Bratteli. The result was almost a tie, so the coalition became dependent for survival upon a close harmony both of purpose and personalities—neither of which was forthcoming. In February 1971 the prime minister, Per Borten of the Centre Party, was guilty of a serious indiscretion in his handling of a confidential paper regarding Common Market discussions then in progress in Brussels. His resignation was probably inevitable, but the coalition could have continued under another leader, if Borten's party had not been privately anxious for the Common Market negotiations to stall—a fact which had much bearing on his conduct as head of the government. Bratteli then took office with a minority administration, whose provisional character was emphasized by the local elections in the following autumn, when the non-socialists recovered some lost ground.

In these circumstances social policy in the broadest sense of the term followed an even course. The nine-year school system became obligatory, and some of the demand for more advanced education was met by the establishment of the two new universities of Trondheim and Tromsö and by the introduction of district high schools. Local democracy was still cherished in Norway. Great emphasis was laid upon support for economically backward, outlying districts; extensive powers were given to protect local amenities against pollution and other damage to the environment, not only from industry but also from new causes such as the proliferation of holiday chalets; and debate on local affairs was stimulated by the subsidizing of small newspapers on a basis that favoured such as were neither the biggest nor the sole organ of opinion in their area. But although expenditure on social services of all kinds continued to grow rapidly,[39] Norway in common with many other lands was confronted by social problems—crimes of violence, drug addiction, drunkenness, and other forms of anti-social behaviour—which show that a section of the population, including a part of the nation's youth, found insufficient motivation in the life offered by the Welfare State. Mention must be made, however, of two older, cultural problems which seemed to be in course of settlement. The institution of a nationwide Church Council with two-thirds lay membership gave effect to a proposal first made in 1908, though it was based on existing diocesan councils; and the establishment of a Language Council (*Språkråd*) to protect both forms of the Norwegian language was designed to substitute mutual respect and toleration for their long-standing rivalry.

In 1965–9 the gross national product grew at the rate of 4·4 per cent per annum, real wages continued to rise, and an inflow of foreign workers began to be noticeable. New hydro-electric installations added 6·3 per cent per annum to the use of electricity for industrial and other purposes; by 1970 45 per cent of the Norwegian potential had been developed. By the same date the mercantile marine had been outstripped by the Japanese, but its latest additions included seven super-tankers of more than 100,000 tons, and in four successive years its net earnings outweighed the excess of imports over exports. But the Achilles Heel of a very prosperous economy was the alarming increase in inflation, which at the close of 1970 led to the imposition of a price stop: this was maintained for nearly twelve months, but could only serve as a palliative in a country so dependent upon imports, not only for its food but also for the raw materials of its industries. Yet it was possible that Norway's situation in this last respect was due for a transformation as extraordinary as a happening in one of their own folk tales. From borings begun in 1963, soon after the continental shelf of north-west Europe first became of interest to others besides fishermen, it was established that oil (and natural gas) in commercial quantities awaited exploitation, at any rate in the area where Norwegian and British rights converge. But since the Norwegian share of the shelf is larger than the whole of Norway and has a generally favourable geological structure, it was not altogether fanciful to envisage a future in which Norway might become the main European source of a commodity at present brought at great expense from other continents to satisfy one-half of our total energy requirements.

In its international relationships, Norway stood more definitely upon the verge of changes which might prove very far-reaching. Defence policy, indeed, had so far remained stable: only six members of the Storting opposed Norway's continuing in NATO after the mistreatment of Czechoslovakia by the rest of the eastern bloc in 1966. The idealistic trends in foreign policy also continued as before, both in the United Nations (where a son of C. J. Hambro was president of the Assembly in 1970) and in individual dealings with oppressed peoples—Greek democrats and those who struggled for freedom in Africa or Bangladesh—while in 1970 the tax to benefit the under-developed nations duly rose to 1 per cent. But the great issue of the day concerned the attitude the Norwegian people should adopt towards inclusion in a larger politico-economic unit, where the ingrained love of independence and self-sufficiency in the fellow-countrymen of Peer Gynt was perhaps at war with a more enlightened self-interest.

When Britain made its second application to join the Common Market in 1967, Norway followed suit with a little more alacrity than on the first occasion. But after the collapse of that venture, attention was diverted to proposals for a Nordic Economic Union, to be based on a full customs union; these were sponsored by the Nordic Council and accepted in principle by all five Nordic governments, on the unreal assumption that the terms were compatible with an eventual adhesion to E.E.C. on the part of some of their number. The feasibility of this alternative grouping was never put to the test, as the Finns withdrew at the last moment (March 1970), but when the Storting in the following June endorsed the coalition government's decision to apply again for membership of E.E.C. by a majority of 132 to 17, it quickly became apparent that the vote did not represent the balance of opinion in the country.

The farmers feared competition in an industry where Norway is naturally weak, the fishermen in an industry where its natural resources are the richest in Europe. Many of the older generation dreaded the loss of sovereign independence through accepting the treaty of Rome, while the youth organizations of every political party except the Conservative agitated against the prospective surrender to 'monopoly capitalism', a term which was often loosely employed to cover competition in hard work and industrial inventiveness. The fall of the coalition government, as already indicated, was largely due to the desire of the Centre Party to exploit the situation for the benefit of the agrarian interest which it represented. The new Labour government, on the other hand, under the leadership of a convinced supporter of the Common Market, was fully alive to the fact that the entire nation depended in the long run upon the continued prosperity of its manufactured exports and of the carrying trade.

After protracted bargaining at Brussels, the government secured what it regarded as tolerable terms for Norwegian agriculture and fisheries; though bitterly denounced by opponents as inadequate, deceptive, and impermanent, they could be seen to represent a strong desire on the part of the Community to remove the impediments to Norway's inclusion. On a basis of party ties Bratteli might reasonably expect to carry the day: at least two-thirds of active Labour politicians at all levels were on his side in the matter, as were virtually all Conservatives and at least a strong minority in the Left and Christian People's Parties. But as early as 1969 the farmers' organizations took the initiative in establishing a 'People's Movement Against E.E.C.', which built up a powerful propaganda machine in preparation for the advisory referendum promised by successive governments. A free-trade treaty was declared to be preferable to any closer association with E.E.C., and the Danes (who were to vote later) were pictured as certain to join the Norwegians in a kind of Scandinavian bloc. Making free use of the national flag and such question-begging slogans as 'Norway is not for sale', the Movement appealed strongly to the latent suspicion of foreign influences; these would allegedly expose the nation, not only to the spread of big capital and neo-imperialism, but also to increased environmental pollution and even to a spiritual atmosphere in which Lutheranism might wilt. It also played skilfully upon the dislike felt by the 'little man', especially in the smaller and remoter communities, for the entire apparatus of the modern centralized State, as represented by the government, the majority in the Storting, and the leadership of the largest political parties and the trade union federation—against which he now had a chance to assert himself. The counter-propaganda of those in power was much slower to get under way and less uninhibited in its mode of appeal; in addition, it lost some of its effect through the action of Norway's only elder statesman, Gerhardsen, who insisted that, although he personally would vote Yes, any member of the Labour Party could be equally justified in voting No.

On September 23-4, 1972, four-fifths of the electorate recorded its vote, which revealed a majority of 53·5 to 46·5 per cent against entering an enlarged European Community. Oslo and three neighbouring counties supported the government; but fifteen counties were ranged on the other side, and in what might loosely be described as 'village Norway'—the local government areas with a population below 2,500—Noes averaged no less than 73 per cent. Bratteli and his colleagues resigned office, as they had said they would do if their proposals were rejected by the people, and were replaced by a government under Lars Korvald, representing the agricultural and allied interests. In the Storting it was supported only by the Centre Party, the Christian People's Party (from which the prime minister was drawn), and a section of the Left Party, but was promised the backing of the hostile majority, amounting to nearly three-quarters of the whole, in its efforts to negotiate a free-trade treaty on the most favourable terms available from the Europe whose overtures had been so abruptly rejected. As for internal politics, the full effects of the populist intervention would not be evident until the next election in September 1973. By the end of 1972, however, the Left Party had split in two, as at other times of political ferment, and the Socialist People's Party—whose outspokenly bitter antagonism to E.E.C., based partly on hostility to NATO, had attracted much sympathy in the Youth Movements of the other parties (except the Conservative)—seemed at last to present a serious threat to the once monolithic structure of the Labour Party.

According to *The Times*, the nation was being led by the heart rather than the head; it might perhaps be more fairly described in this period of stress as the involuntary prisoner of its history. As a people of the far north, the Norwegians have acquired from the physical conditions of their existence a special respect for the qualities of individual self-reliance and stubborn loyalty to ties of neighbourhood and calling, which were developed as the labours of many generations built up 'the thousand homes' of their national anthem. As a very small people, they have learnt to consider national independence to be the *summum bonum*: and who will blame them for this, remembering that, in the one and a half centuries spanned by this book, they emerged from Danish tutelage only to spend ninety years in shaking off what they felt to be the yoke of Sweden, and for five more were subjected to the more real yoke of Nazi Germany? As a highly civilized people, which believes that through a long and painful process of trial and error it has achieved a special, small-scale harmony in the relationship between man and man, and man and Nature, they hesitate to submerge themselves in a larger whole, where faster economic growth and perhaps a wider influence in the world might cost too much in terms of values that they cherish. And as a peace-loving people, who were among the first and sincerest advocates of an international society based on law instead of arms, their attitude to NATO is loyally acquiescent rather than deeply committed, whilst their Scandinavian sympathies tempt them to overlook the dangers of a closer association with neutralist Sweden and precariously balanced Finland.

Yet the history of modern Norway has another side to it, which in normal times is readily if tacitly acknowledged by every thoughtful Norwegian. In the nature of things their society and way of life on the outskirts of western Europe are indissolubly linked with events at its centre. This is equally true of the seminal political years 1814 and 1905, or of the phenomenal growth and resilience of the mercantile marine, or of the flowering of the genius of an Ibsen or an Edvard Munch. If it were the business of the historian to prophesy, this underlying factor might suggest the tentative conclusion that the events of 1972 will not bar the way for very long against a further stage in the integration of Norway in Europe—to their mutual advantage.

Reference Notes

The full reference for each book is given at the first mention, and is repeated after any considerable gap.

The place of publication is not stated for books in Scandinavian languages published in Oslo or for English-language books published in London.

The following Norwegian collective works are referred to by initials:

AK   *Aschehougs Konversasjonsleksikon*, 5th edition, Vols. i–xix, 1968–72.
DEN   *Dette er Norge 1814–1964*, 3 vols., 1963–4.
DNS   *Det norske Storting gjennom 150 år*, 4 vols., 1964.
GSK   *Gyldendals Store Konversasjonsleksikon*, 3rd edition, 5 vols., 1972.
HT   *Historisk Tidsskrift utgitt av den norske historiske forening*, 1871– .
NBL   *Norsk Biografisk Leksikon*, Vols. i–xvi, 1923–69.
NFLH *Det norske folks liv og historie gjennom tidene*, 11 vols., 1930–8.
NOS   *Norges Offisielle Statistikk*, 12 Rækker (series), 1828– .
SS   *Samfunnsökonomiske Studier*, published by Statistisk Sentralbyrå (Central Office of Statistics), Numbers 1–21, 1954–71.
VFH   *Vårt Folks Historie*, 9 vols., 1961–4.

Chapter 1

1 Sverre Steen, *Det frie Norge* (Vols. i–vi 1951–72), I. 34.
2 T. T. Höjer, *Karl XIV Johan*, Vol. ii (Stockholm, 1943), p. 229.
3 Steen, I. 51; cf. 27 and 31.
4 Introductory paragraph in his addresses to the Tsar, the emperor of Austria, and the king of Prussia (Axel Lindvald, *Kong Christian VIII*, Vol iii (Copenhagen, 1965), p. 362).
5 Instructions from Christian Frederick, 1 Mar. 1814, Section 5. See also letter of 21 Apr. (C. J. Anker, *Christian Frederik og Carsten Ankers brevveksling 1814* (1901), pp. 10 and 30).
6 Steen i. 186.
7 The successive references in this and the following paragraphs are to *Constitution for Kongeriget Norge*: A, Section 1; B, Section 28; C; and E, Section 110. The text is reprinted in G. C. Wasberg, *Historien om 1814* (1964), pp. 156–70.
8 *på allerhögste befallning*, an ambiguous phrase devised by General M. F. F. Björnstjerna, who negotiated under Charles John's instructions at Moss (Höjer ii. 315).
9 Letter of 12 July 1814 (Höjer ii. 312).
10 Höjer ii. 317.

11 Letter to Carsten Anker, written on board ship, 11 Oct. (C. J. Anker, *Brevveksling*, p. 83).
12 Steen i. 247.
13 Steen i. 267.
14 Steen i. 270.
15 Steen i. 273.

Chapter 2

1 Samuel Laing, *Journal of a Residence in Norway* (1836), p. vi.
2 Riksakten, Preamble (reprinted in Wasberg, p. 150).
3 *Mina Memoarer*, 3 vols. (Stockholm, 1960–2).
4 *HT* xlvii. 35, and xxxvii. 3 and 7.
5 Law of 8 Feb. 1816 (*DNS* i. 72).
6 *DNS* i. 127 and 129.
7 The figure ranges between 52·27 and 41·82 per cent (*DNS* i. 113). This seems all the more remarkable because the total numbers are so small: at the 1838 election, for example, *c.* 100,000 persons were entitled to register for voting, *c.* 70,000 registered, and *c.* 35,000 voted (Steen vi. 300).
8 *VFH* vi. 98.
9 Laing, *Journal*, pp. 44 and 394.
10 The figures were 30 and 51 (*Storthings-Forhandlinger 1830*, iv. 259).
11 In full, 'Thoughts of a udal landholder on Norway's present constitution together with a conversation containing guidance for peasants as to a more correct mode of procedure in the choice of electors and representatives' (Steen v. 251).
12 *Norges historie fremstillet for det norske folk*, ed. A. Bugge *et al.*, vi, Pt. I (1913), 2nd section, p. 333—material first published in 1904 in the Oslo Liberal newspaper, *Verdens Gang*.
13 Steen vi. 246.
14 *NFLH* ix. 72. A later medical pioneer was A. Hansen, who fought leprosy.
15 *NFLH* ix. 248.
16 E. Pontoppidan, *Sandhed til gudfrygtighed* (1737; republished in a shorter version, 1771).
17 E. Molland, *Church Life in Norway 1800–1950* (Minneapolis, 1957), p. 32.
18 Molland, 52.
19 Thorvald Klaveness, a young clergyman who later adopted liberal views (Molland, p. 67).
20 O. Björklund, *Marcus Thrane* (rev. ed. 1970), pp. 24–5. The first edition (1950), p. 24, suggested on rather slender evidence that Thrane may also have visited England at this time.
21 Björklund, p. 171.
22 S. Skappel, *Om husmandsvæsenet i Norge* (1922), p. 170.

23 Besides the hatter, who was from the sawmill town of Hönefoss, this episode involved a neighbouring rural schoolmaster and about eighty supporters (Björklund, pp. 248–9; *NFLH* ix. 192).

24 According to an agricultural adviser writing in *Morgenbladet*, 1867 (Skappel, p. 174).

25 H. O. Christophersen, *Eilert Sundt. En dikter i kjensgjerninger* (1962), p. 128; M. Drake, *Population and society in Norway 1735–1865* (Cambridge, 1969), pp. 43–5.

26 *Om ædruelgheds-tilstanden i Norge* (1859), p. 1.

27 An account by H. Refsum in *NBL* xv (1966), 276–93, mentions Sundt's influence on Thorstein Veblen and lists twenty-three books and articles since 1945, including Martin S. Allwood, *Eilert Sundt, a pioneer in sociology and social anthropology* (Oslo, 1957) and A. Hillman, *Eilert Sundt, social surveyor extraordinary* (*Sociological Review*, xliii, Section 3, Keele, 1951).

28 *NFLH*, ix. 265.

29 The educational reformer Hartvig Nissen also succeeded in establishing a non-classical grammar school for matriculation through the *real-gymnas*; this is said to have been 'something entirely new in European school organization' (E. Höigård and H. Ruge, *Den norske skoles historie* (2nd ed. 1963), p. 136).

30 *HT* xl. 160.

31 *Morgenbladet*, June 1863 (*NFLH* ix. 427).

32 *DNS* ii. 204.

33 *NBL* i. 281.

34 Although the electorate could have been enlarged indefinitely by this means, either the cost of it, or public indifference, or 'reverence for the constitution' (the reason preferred by the government) kept the proportion of *myrmenn* down to one in fifty (*DNS* ii. 33–4).

35 *NFLH* x. 117.

36 *Memoarer* ii. 41—a section apparently composed in Oslo in February 1883.

37 Broch was reluctant to turn to the liberal clergy, because he did not want the political situation to be complicated by the issue of church reform, which he perhaps took too seriously as a result of his experience of religious politics in France (J. A. Seip, *Ole Jacob Broch og hans samtid* (1971), p. 616).

38 *HT* xxxviii, 539; Oscar II, *Memoarer*, ii. 75.

Chapter 3

1 A. G. Silverstolpe's expectations were reported in *Nationalbladet*, Oslo, 17 July 1815 (T. Jorgenson, *Norway's Relations to Scandinavian Unionism 1815–1871* (Northfield, Minn., 1935), p. 25).

2 Steen, ii. 15.

3   Steen iii. 10.

4   Steen v. 114 (report dated 14 Mar.).

5   *VFH* vi. 196–9. A visit to Bergen by an agent named Rosensvärd is mentioned by Steen, ii. 113.

6   Steen v. 158.

7   Pierre Flor, 29 May 1821 (Steen iii. 189).

8   *DNS* i. 242.

9   Memorial to Lord Castlereagh, 1 June 1819 (G. M. Gathorne-Hardy, *Bodö-saken* (Oslo, 1926), p. 26).

10 Dispatch from Stockholm legation to Lord Castlereagh, 2 Feb. 1821 (Gathorne-Hardy, p. 70).

11 Reply recorded in cabinet (*diktert til protokols*) on 7 Aug. 1827, when a unanimous address from the Storting had demanded increased Norwegian influence in foreign affairs (Steen v. 54).

12 Steen v. 126.

13 *Storthings-Efterretninger 1836–1854*, i. 257.

14 *For menigmand*, no. 4 (17 Oct. 1836).

15 *NFLH* ix. 156.

16 He said on his death-bed, ' *Jeg var intet andet end Digter.*'

17 *GSK* v. 3343 (Professor Hans Midboe).

18 Article for *Forum*, April 1896 (*Artikler og taler*, ed. C. Collin and H. Eitrem, 1912–13, ii. 309).

19 'The art of Gustav Vigeland is the first to have shown us the inspired poet: the soul "stepping forth from the veil of the countenance." ' (P. Svendsen, *Norsk litteraturhistorie*, ed. F. Bull *et al.*, Vol. iii (rev. ed. 1959), p. 137).

20 Jacob Aall, *Nutid og fortid. Et hæfteskrift*, Vol. i (Arendal, 1833), Pt. III, p. 58. Many such writings, which express strong cultural sympathies with Denmark, are mustered and reviewed by K. Nygaard, *Nordmenns syn på Danmark og danskene i 1814 og de förste selvstendighetsår* (1960).

21 Student petition for constitutional reform in Denmark (Jorgenson, p. 84).

22 Published in *Hertha* (Swedish), *Fædrelandet* (Danish), and finally *Den Constitutionelle* (Norwegian); the original is quoted by Jorgenson, pp. 122–3.

23 Presidential address of welcome, Copenhagen, 3 July 1840.

24 *Danmarks historie*, ed. J. Danstrup and H. Koch (Copenhagen, 1963–6), xi. 205.

25 Article and reply published 1 and 13 May (Jorgenson, pp. 153, 168).

26 *Storthingets Forhandlinger 1848*, viii. 50.

27 George Stephens, the runic archaeologist, who had recently moved from Stockholm to a university post in Copenhagen and was a devotee of Scandinavianism (Jorgenson, p. 193).

28 *VFH* vii. 87–8.

29 Diary entry for 20 Aug. (*NFLH* ix. 208).

30 Carl Ploug (Jorgenson, p. 224).
31 Jorgenson, p. 225.
32 *Lilla och stora krigskreditivar*, provided by the constitution of 1809 and retained until 1941.
33 H. Koht, *Johan Sverdrup* (3 vols., 1918–25), i. 262, 391.
34 Letter from Sibbern to Birch-Reichenwald, 27 Feb. 1868 (*DNS* i. 417).
35 *Aftenbladet*, Oslo, 9 Dec. 1859 (*NFLH* ix. 224).
36 *Memoarer*, ii. 8.
37 *Storthingets Forhandlinger 1859–60*, ix. 76–7.
38 Report of 31 Dec. 1856 (*HT* xlvi. 154).
39 Including two years in *krigsforsterkningen*, a special part of the reserve into which troops were drafted on completion of their normal line service.
40 Jorgenson, pp. 350–1.
41 Per Fuglum (*HT* xlvi. 87).
42 *Storthingstidende 1862–1863*, p. 684.
43 Letter to Frederik Stang, 9 Feb. 1863 (*NBL* xiii. 276).
44 *Storthings-Efterretninger*, 1871, p. 203.
45 H. R. Astrup (*NBL* i. 303).
46 *Stockholms Dagblad* (*VFH* vii. 233).
47 Wilhelm Bergstrand, editor of *Nya Dagligt Allehanda* (*Svenskt Biografiskt Lexicon*, iii. 170; *NFLH* x. 129).
48 'Germany would readily have intervened at this juncture, given a different state of opinion in—Sweden!' (note made by King Oscar on the results of soundings in May 1884). Baron Holstein in a much later record suggests that the king employed a Swede, Baron von Mecklenburg, as his secret intermediary in Germany. See F. Lindberg, *Kunglig utrikespolitik* (Stockholm, 1966), pp. 90–1, and *Den svenska utrikespolitikens historie*, Vol. iii, Pt. IV (Stockholm, 1958), pp. 67 and 70–1.

Chapter 4

1 Gunnar Jahn (*DEN* i. 143).
2 *NOS* x. 178, Table 7.
3 G. Jahn *et al.*: *Norges Bank gjennom 150 år*, 1966, p. 167.
4 *DEN* ii. 199.
5 *NOS* x. 178, Table 48. The figures are examined by Steen, iv. 27–8, using the 4-bushel *tönne* instead of tons.
6 Redemption had been promised at about one-quarter of the face value but was carried out at one-tenth; the sum involved, estimated by the Storting at 25 million, was 27·3 million paper dollars (*NFLH* viii. 194, 197).
7 *NOS*, x. 178, Tables 117 and 114; Steen iv, 189–90.
8 K. Amundsen, *Norsk sosialökonomisk historie 1814–1890* (1963), p. 52.
9 Steen iv, 202.

10 *Norges Bank*, 53; *NOS*, x. 178, Table 223. The first expansive Budget was presented in 1836–7, when the Storting agreed to increases of 16–17 per cent (Steen vi. 179–80).

11 A. Bergsgård, *Norsk historie 1814–1880* (new ed. 1964), p. 144.

12 *DEN* ii. 358 (chapter by H. Stigum on handicrafts between the age of the gilds and that of the machine).

13 *HT* xlv. 98.

14 At the 1875 census 45,657 industrial workers were returned (see Table, p. 126) out of a total of 199,786 workers employed in trades of all kinds (*NOS, Ældre Raekke C*, i, 3rd Hæfte, Table 20).

15 'The Swedes had adopted the Norwegian system because they found that the Norwegians were farsighted in this instance' (speech of 7 Nov. 1868: *Stortings-Tidende, 1868–9*, Storting, 45).

16 *NFLH* ix. 117.

17 As related by J. A. Seip (*HT* xxxix. 34). Robert Stephenson, on the other hand, died regretting 'the inadequate manner in which his services had been recognized by the Norwegian government and people' (J. A. Seip, *Ole Jacob Broch og hans samtid* (1971), p. 221, quoting a letter from Stephenson's son to the minister of the interior).

18 Figures in the rest of this section are cited from *DEN* ii. 416–21 and *NFLH* ix. 372–81.

19 Based on 159 returns made to the Statistical Office (*NFLH* ix. 377).

20 S. Grieg, *Norsk Tekstil*, Vol. i (1948), pp. 238–9.

21 E. B. Schieldrop, *Christiania Spigerverk* (1961), p. 83.

22 F. Valen-Sendstad, *Norske landbruksredkap 1800–1850–årene* (Lillehammer 1964), describes their introduction in detail, and is also the source for the next paragraph: see pp. 139, 141, and 142, together with the Tables, pp. 297–302.

23 *NFLH* ix. 389. Official supervision of the fisheries was achieved mainly by K. J. M. Motzfeldt, a brother-in-law and political ally of Birch-Reichenwald.

24 Made by an apothecary, Peter Möller; exports rose from an annual average of 10,000,000 litres in 1866–70 to 133,000,000 in 1875 (*DEN* ii. 376).

25 *NOS* x. 178, Table 113.

26 *NOS* iii. 102: examples in (6) *Fabrik-og Industrianlæg*.

27 Pyrites (*svovelkis*) was first mined at Ytteröya in order to produce sulphuric acid for chrome-making at Trondheim in 1841 (*DEN* ii. 334).

28 *Beretning om Kongeriget Norges Oeconomiske Tilstand* (1843), p. 47, reprinted in G. C. Wasberg and A. S. Svendsen, *Industriens historie i Norge* (1969), pp. 88–9.

29 *NOS* x. 178, Table 89.

30 Introductory Information, p. (9) (7th ed. 1880).

31 Öyeren, Mjösa, Randsfiord, Sperillen, Kröderen (J. Broch, *Norges första statsbaner* (1935), p. 151).

32 *NFLH* ix. 404–8.
33 1*s.* 1½*d.* In 1873–5 Norway had held out against a Scandinavian unit; Broch entertained hopes of a 'world coin' (Seip, p. 556).
34 *NFLH* x. 347.
35 Shown by a graph in *NFLH* x. 339.
36 *HT* xlv. 111.
37 *Om Piperviken og Ruselökbakken*, published as a supplement to *Folkevennen*; a full account of the book is given by H. O. Christophersen, *Eilert Sundt. En dikter i kjens gjerninger* (1962), pp. 182–205.
38 Four persons per room was still very common *c.* 1895 (*DEN*, i. 276).
39 The Church Department raised the issue on this ground; statistical evidence was collected in the 1875 census for draft proposals made in 1878–9, which became law in 1892 (*NFLH* x. 395–6).
40 *AK* xi. 336 (Edvard Bull).

Chapter 5

1   *VFH* vii. 257.
2   *DNS* ii. 38.
3   In place of *almueskole*, 'school for the common people'—a deliberate renaming (H. Koht, *Sverdrup*, iii. 509).
4   *det norske folkemålet* (*NFLH* x. 201).
5   *Stortingsforhandlinger 1887*, Vol. iii: Od. Prop. no. 20, sect. 2.
6   Military developments throughout the century are summarized by J. Schiötz in *Den norske hær og flåte*, ed. F. Abel (1915), pp. 18–22.
7   *Memoarer*, ii. 132 (dated February 1888).
8   *NFLH* x. 207.
9   *NFLH* x. 211 (J. G. Lövland).
10 *DNS* ii. 289.
11 This complicated *cause célèbre* in Norwegian political life is fully examined by Per Fuglum, *Ole Richter*, Vol. ii. (1964), pp. 314–40, and H. Koht, *NBL* xi. 431–3; xv. 422–6. An ex-colleague of Sverdrup and ex-friend of Björnson (Ludvig Daae) said, 'Sverdrup loaded the pistol and Björnson pulled the trigger' (Fuglum, p. 325).
12 *DNS* ii. 83, Table showing 'persons in superior government service'.
13 *DNS* iii. 31.
14 Letter to Christopher Bruun, May 1891 (*VFH* vii. 275).
15 *AK* viii. 675.
16 *HT* xlviii. 49.
17 *DNS* ii. 366; *NOS* x. 178, Table 223.
18 *VFH* vii. 310.
19 *AK* xvii. 299.
20 Count Lewenhaupt (*VFH* vii. 322).
21 *knyttnevepolitikken* (*VFH* vii. 325).

22 NBL xiv. 424.

23 HT xxxix. 150.

24 83, 165 to 81, 462 (NFLH x. 389).

25 In a memorandum dated 5 May 1886, he had cited the way in which 'foreign policy is managed between Sweden and Norway' as having a possible bearing on the discussion of his first Home Rule Bill (J. L. Hammond, Gladstone and the Irish nation (1938), p. 509). His general attitude towards Norway is examined in P. Knaplund, British views on Norwegian-Swedish problems 1880–1895 (Oslo, 1952).

26 F. Lindberg, Kunglig utrikespolitik (Stockholm, 1966), pp. 116–21.

27 Hemliga utskottet, a committee of the Riksdag set up under the 1809 constitution to deliberate with the crown on matters that must be kept secret. The military preparations are referred to in Den Svenska Historien (Bonniers, Stockholm, 1966–8), ix. 180.

28 The Storting would have eliminated Classics entirely, but Jakob Sverdrup managed to insert a clause allowing Latin to be taught in any particular gymnas as a permitted exception (E. Höigård and H. Ruge, Den norske skoles historie (2nd ed. 1963), p. 195).

29 His observations there convinced him of the merits of high-lying land batteries protected by earthworks (NBL xiv. 340).

30 The number of registered electors rose from 195,956 to 426,593 and that of votes cast from 167,207 to 238,617 (NOS x. 178, Table 226). Ignoring the old distinction between qualified and registered voters (see p. 26) which was removed by the new electoral law, we find that the percentage of the electorate that voted sank from 70 to 54 (DNS ii. 65).

31 DEN i. 450 and 392–3.

32 A majority of career consuls was Norwegian, as a result of increased postings in 1895–1902 (R. E. Lindgren, Norway–Sweden, union, disunion, and Scandinavian integration (Princeton, 1959), p. 74).

33 NFLH x. 430.

34 J. Broch, Av Norges Statsbanshistorie, Vol. iv (1937), pp. 16–20.

35 NFLH x. 434.

36 Forhandling, bare forhandling (DNS ii. 376).

37 In many other constituencies, votes transferred from the Left Party to Labour contributed heavily to Blehr's defeat (HT li. 57).

38 Lydrikepunkter, 'vassal-state clauses', was the term first employed by Sigurd Ibsen, who defended this interpretation in Samtiden, 1906, (pp. 197–236, 'When the Union broke up'). J. Weibull, Inför Unionsupplösningen 1905 (Stockholm, 1962), Ch. 6, shows in the light of documents not available to contemporary historians that these clauses had been adumbrated in earlier discussions between the two governments.

39 The views of the crown prince are further examined by E. Vedung, Unionsdebatten 1905 (Stockholm, 1971), pp. 23–5.

40 The historic meeting is described in *NFLH* x. 452, and the official protocol is in *Unionens Oplösning 1905* (ed. J. V. Heiberg, 1906), p. 195. The king's observation about 'good Norwegians' is not mentioned, however, in the Norwegian ministers' detailed report of the meeting for Michelsen (*U.O. 1905*, pp. 192–4).

41 The omission cannot have been accidental, for the king is correctly quoted in the statement by Michelsen which immediately preceded the resolution (*U.O. 1905*, pp. 205–6).

42 S. C. Hammer, *Det merkelige år* (1930), pp. 150–1.

43 *U.O. 1905*, pp. 207–8.

44 *Norge og foreningen med Sverige*, which was also published in English (*Norway and the Union with Sweden*), German, and French.

45 Fridtjof Nansen, *Dagbok fra 1905* (ed. J. S. Worm-Müller, 1955), pp. xl–xli.

46 *NFLH* x. 465.

47 *VFH* vii. 381; *Den Svenska Historien*, ix. 180.

48 From Michelsen's telegram to his Cabinet colleagues at midday on 14 Sept. (*VFH*, vii. 380).

49 Preamble to convention on neutral zone, etc. (*NFLH* x. 469).

50 Articles 1 and 2 of arbitration convention (*U.O. 1905*, p. 651).

51 *NFLH* x. 469.

Chapter 6

1 The resolution of 11 June 1913 modified Section 112 of the constitution by providing that constitutional changes should be sent by the Storting to the king 'for publication as valid decisions' (*DNS* iii. 201).

2 The principle of the *negativt flertall*, used again in 1926 and 1963, is applied at the prime minister's discretion (*GSK* iv. 1164).

3 J. S. Worm-Müller, A. Bergsgård, and B. A. Nissen, *Venstre i Norge* (1933), p. 272.

4 Speech in Storting, 7 Mar. 1913 (*DNS* iii. 212).

5 H. Koht, *Syn og Segn*, xvii. 376–7.

6 *NFLH* xi. 183.

7 *DEN* i. 450.

8 *DEN* i. 136; *Dödeligheten og dens årsaker i Norge 1856–1955* (*S.S.* 10, 1961), pp. 124–7, 242.

9 Law of 10 Sept. 1909, Section 21: children were restricted to 'lighter tasks', must have a medical certificate of fitness, and if still attending school were limited to a total day of seven hours.

10 *VFH* vii. 390.

11 F. Lindberg, *Scandinavia in Great Power Politics* (Stockholm, 1958), pp. 11, 45–6.

12 *NFLH* x. 497–8; Lindberg, pp. 64–5.

13   *NFLH* x. 498–9: Lindberg, p. 285.

14   R. Omang, *Norsk Utenrikstjeneste*, Vol. ii (1959), p. 27.

15   R. E. Lindgren, *Norway–Sweden*, p. 237.

16   *NFLH* x. 501; F. Wedel Jarlsberg, *Reisen gjennom livet* (1932), p. 286.

17   *DEN* ii. 152, 154 (article by Lt.-General Ole Berg); N. Örvik, *Sikkerhets-Politikken 1920–1939*, Vol. i. (1960), pp. 59–60.

18   O. Gjerlow, *Norges politiske historie: Höires innsats fra 1814 til idag*, Vol. iii (1936), p. 68.

19   O. N. Eng (*NFLH* xi. 19).

20   *NOS*, xii. 245, Table 13.

21   J. L. Hirsch, lecture to the Norway Welfare Society, 20 Apr. 1896 (*NFLH* xi. 46).

22   G. Jahn *et al.*: *Norges Bank*, p. 154 (Fig. 7), shows the relationship from 1860 to 1913.

23   *NFLH* xi. 231.

24   Article by B. Kolltveit in *Sjöfartshistorisk Årbok* (1968), p. 90.

25   Article by J. N. Tönnessen in *Polar Record*, xv. 283.

26   A Stonehill, *Foreign ownership in Norwegian enterprises* (*S.S.* 14, Oslo, 1965), pp. 40–1.

27   *NFLH* xi. 89 (propostion dated 15 Feb. 1892).

28   *DEN* ii. 225. In 1897 Norway had used 106,000 h.p. of water power and 40,500 h.p. of steam power (*NFLH* xi. 88).

29   *DEN* ii. 382.

30   Stonehill, pp. 38–9.

31   Kykkelsrudfossene, four falls of 61 feet (*NFLH* xi. 97–9).

32   *NFLH* xi. 130.

33   Stonehill, pp. 33–5.

34   Wasberg and Svendsen, *Industriens historie*, p. 115.

35   *NFLH* xi. 121.

36   Edvard Bull, *Arbeiderklassen i norsk historie* (1954), p. 174.

37   *DNS* iv. 274.

38   *NFLH* xi. 205.

39   *NOS* v. 147: pp. xvii, xxi.

40   *NFLH* xi. 199.

Chapter 7

1   T. C. Blegen, *Norwegian Migration to America*, 2 vols. (Northfield, 1931, 1940), i. 351–2.

2   Table from C. C. Qualey, *Norwegian Settlement in the United States* (Northfield, 1938), p. 251; *Ökonomisk utsyn 1900–1950* (*S.S.* 3, 1955), p. 22. American census figures in S. E. Morison and H. S. Commager, *The Growth of the American Republic*, 4th ed. (New York, 1951), ii. 908.

3   Qualey, p. 43.

4   Blegen i. 65.

5   *Varselsord til de udvandringslystne Bönder i Bergens Stift. Et Hyrdebrev fra Stiftens Biskop* (Bergen, 1837) (I. Semmingsen, *Veien mot vest*, 2 vols. (1941, 1950), i. 188). Jacob Neumann, who had held the see since 1822, was keenly interested in the welfare of the peasantry and had befriended Ivar Aasen.

6   *Fjeldstuen*, in which a *bulder* compares the activities of an emigration agent to the ravages of the Black Death.

7   Ole Rynning, *Sandfærdig Beretning om Amerika, til Oplysning og Nytte for Bonde og Menigmand*. The first edition was published in Oslo in 1838, a slightly enlarged second edition posthumously in 1839 (Semmingsen i. 84, 486).

8   Johan Reinert Reiersen, *Veiviser for de Norske Emigranter til de forenede nordamerikanske Stater og Texas* (1844), (Blegen i. 244).

9   O. E. Dreutzer (Blegen ii. 411).

10   Blegen ii. 462; Semmingsen ii. 400.

11   Semmingsen ii. 456–7.

12   *Selskabet til Emigrationens Indskrænkning*, which in 1916 became *Ny Jord*— a society to promote 'internal colonization'.

13   In 1814 four seamen released from wartime imprisonment in the hulks at Chatham returned as Quakers to Stavanger, where their co-religionists were much haressed by the local clergy. In October 1822, for example, one of them was ordered by the Supreme Court under a penalty of 5 dollars a day to exhume the corpses of his twin daughters, which had been buried in unconsecrated ground to avoid church rites; English Quakers eventually obtained a pardon (Semmingsen i. 13; Blegen i. 45).

14   Published in *Krydseren*, 5 Mar. 1853—'a folk song which is still remembered' (Blegen i. 303).

15   *The Homes of the New World* (English translation, 2 vols., New York 1854), ii. 56–7.

16   Blegen ii. 387.

17   Semmingsen ii. 448.

18   Semmingsen ii. 225.

19   K. O. Bjork, *West of the Great Divide* (Northfield, 1958), p. 17.

20   Blegen i. 332.

21   Blegen ii. 376.

22   Semmingsen ii. 396, 389.

23   Semmingsen ii. 404.

24   O. M. Norlie, *History of the Norwegian People in America* (Minneapolis, 1925), pp. 324–6.

25   Semmingsen ii. 293, 514.

26   *Thirteenth Census of the United States*, v. 179 (K. Gjerset, *History of the Norwegian People* (New York, 1915), ii. 604).

27   Semmingsen ii. 280; Blegen ii. 336–7.

28   'One of the two greatest Norwegians in America', according to M. Ulve-
     stad, *Nordmændene i Amerika*, Vol. i (Minneapolis 1907), pp. 219–22,
     the other being Knute Nelson (see below, p. 218).

29   K. O. Bjork, *Saga in Steel and Concrete* (Northfield, 1947), p. 132.

30   N. A. Grevstad in *Norwegian Immigrant Contributions*, edited by H.
     Sundby-Hansen (New-York, 1921), p. 122.

31   Blegen ii. 391–2.

32   The *forlikskommisjon* was introduced in Norway in 1795, and under the
     name of *forliksråd* still functions as a locally elected board to which
     reference must be made at the first stage in all civil disputes.

33   N. A. Grevstad, ibid.

34   K. O. Bjork, *West of the Great Divide* (Northfield, 1958), p. 4.

35   T. Jorgenson and N. O. Solum, *Rölvaag: A Biography* (New York, 1939),
     pp. 295–6.

36   Norlie, pp. 269–70, 379–80.

37   A. M. Norlie (editor), *Norsk Lutherske Prester i Amerika 1843–1915* (2nd
     ed. Minneapolis, 1915), pp. 628, 630.

38   *Nordlyset*, 29 July 1847; published from Norway Post Office, Racine
     County, Wisconsin, and edited by J. D. Reymert, an immigrant from
     Farsund whose mother was Scottish (Blegen ii. 286, 290, 292).

39   Norlie, p. 234.

40   Norlie, p. 357.

41   *Norwegian–American Studies and Records* (Minneapolis, 1926–   ), xvii. 30.

42   B. J. Hovde (L. N. Bergmann, *Americans from Norway* (Philadelphia, 1950),
     p. 159).

43   G. Ristad, first president of the Association (*Studies and Records*, i. 148).

44   K. C. Babcock, *The Scandinavian Element in the United States* (Urbana,
     1914), p. 49.

45   Semmingsen ii. 305, 320.

46   Semmingsen ii. 333.

47   Jonas W. Cröger (Semmingsen ii. 294). Neither his emigration plan nor
     his book, *En reise til Brasilien og Uruguay* (1856), is mentioned in the
     article on Cröger in *NBL* iii. 153–4.

48   Marburg at the mouth of R. Umzimkulu, *c.* 100 miles from Durban; its
     success was partly due to earnings at the gold diggings in the Trans-
     vaal (Semmingsen ii. 347–8.)

49   1,603 in 1911; in 1921 it had shrunk to 1,353, of whom one-third re-
     sided in Durban (Semmingsen ii. 354).

50   Professor E. Molland claims that 'Church life in Norway is marked by a
     Christianity of associations and meetings to a greater extent than in
     any other country' (*DEN* i. 489).

51   *NBL* xii. 541 prefers the appellation,' 'Apostle of Zululand'. The article
     in *Norsk Misjons Leksikon*, 3 vols. (Stavanger, 1965–7), which has been

followed here, also mentions Schreuder's activities as an intermediary between Cetewayo and the British during the way of 1879 (iii. 724).

52 *NBL* iii (1926), 245, says that the Malagasi Bible translation is 'regarded as one of the best in the world'.

53 *Misjons Leksikon* i. 354.

54 Skrefsrud's life is traced in *Misjons Leksikon* iii. 776–89; his impact on Söderblom is mentioned in *NBL* xiv. 14.

55 L. P. Kirwan, *The White Road* (1959), p. 221.

56 F. Nansen, *The First Crossing of Greenland* (1890), ii. 480.

57 F. Nansen, *Farthest North*, Vol. ii, chapter 5—diary entry for 8 Apr. 1895.

58 *NBL* xv. 433; for the meeting with Peary, see pp. 434–5.

59 *NBL* i. (1923), 126. Nansen is mentioned as one of the few persons with prior knowledge of Amundsen's change of plan.

60 Kirwan, p. 190.

Chapter 8

1 Article for *Forum*, New York, also published in *Die Zukunft*, Berlin, and in *Kringsjaa*, Oslo, 30 Apr. 1896 (*Artikler og Taler*, Vol. ii (1913), p. 305).

2 Vol. i, Chs. 1–4, published at Lübeck, 1853–4; Vol. iv, Pt. I, Chs. 46 and 47, *The Norwegian Invasion of Scotland in 1263*, published at Glasgow, 1862. Munch also provided an introduction and notes in English for the *Chronica Manniae et Insularum* (Oslo, 1860), which he edited from a British Museum manuscript. The information on translations and dramatic performances throughout this chapter is based primarily on J. B. Halvorsen, *Norsk Forfatter-Lexikon 1814–1880*, 6 vols. (1885–1908).

3 *NBL*, ii. 416.

4 A German translation in two volumes was published, however, in 1847, and by 1874 a selection of the Tales had reached as far as Russia.

5 G. W. Dasent: Introductory Essay (reprinted with *Popular Tales*, 1969), p. 367.

6 Ibid. pp. 369, 368.

7 B. W. Downs: *Modern Norwegian Literature 1860–1918*, Cambridge 1966, p. 46.

8 Sir Edmund Gosse (1849–1928) took up Scandinavian literature in 1871 to advance his career as a man of letters, after hearing about Ibsen from Brækstad (see p. 242), whom he had contacted by chance as a bookseller in Trondheim. He studied Norwegian in order to review Ibsen's work, established strong connections with Denmark, and published 330 items in all on Scandinavian subjects. Although Gosse in later life found other literary fields more profitable, the use of his name as an editor did much to promote translations of Ibsen, Björnson, and other Scandinavian authors. See *Sir Edmund Gosse's correspondence with Scandinavian writers*, edited by E. Bredsdorff, Copenhagen 1960, pp. 1–3, 21, 316–38.

9 The 81-line poem was sent from Rome on 30 April 1865 and was printed in *Fædrelandet* (Copenhagen) on 15 May.

10 H. Koht: *Life of Ibsen* (revised edition of 1954, translated by E. Haugen and A. E. Santaniello, New York 1971), p. 278.

11 M. Meyer: *Henrik Ibsen* (3 vols, 1967–71), ii, 182, iii, 265; Downs, 52, 228.

12 Ibsen described it as his calling *at vække Folket og bringe det til at tænke stort* in a letter to King Charles XV applying for a literary stipend (*diktergasje*), 15 April 1866 (Koht, 213; *Samlede Verker*, centenary edition, Vol. v, 1928, p. 164). The details in the footnote are taken from Meyer, ii, 288, 306.

13 Maria Germanova, who played Agnes (Koht, 211).

14 *Studies*, pp. 55 and 56: *Folkets Rett til Skriget.*

15 Sir Thomas Beecham: *Frederick Delius* (1959) modifies the earlier, more dramatic versions of this story.

16 *NBL*, iv. 602.

17 J. Horton: *Grieg* (1950), p. 21.

18 Horton, p. 101.

19 This comprises 636 items, including dance tunes, ballads, and hymns, and was published in 3 volumes, 1853–67 (revised edition, 1874; supplement, 1907). The quotation is from D. Winding-Sörensen's contribution to *One Hundred Norwegians*, p. 98.

20 G. Schelderup in *Grieg A Symposium* (1948), p. 13.

21 The interview with *Signale* is recorded by D. Monrad-Johansen: *Edvard Grieg* (English translation, Princeton 1938), p. 269.

22 *Det moderne gjennombrud* is discussed in T. Jorgenson: *History of Norwegian Literature*, New York 1933, pp. 291–6.

23 Christian Friele, editor 1857–93, when '*Morgenbladet* was the flagship of conservatism and Friele its pilot' (*NFLH*, x. 78).

24 Act III, Scene 4—the last lines of the play.

25 Gabriel Travieux, son of a Dreyfusard senator, in *Pages Libres*, Paris, no. 106 (10 January 1903).

26 Koht, p. 322.

27 Koht, p. 411.

28 His uncle, Colin Archer, who designed the *Fram* for Nansen, was the son of a Scottish immigrant and kept open house at Larvik for his British relations.

29 J. W. McFarlane, *The Oxford Ibsen* (Oxford, 1960–   ) vi. 17; Koht, p. 346.

30 Koht, p. 418.

31 J. W. McFarlane, *Ibsen and the temper of Norwegian literature* (1960), p. 72.

32 McFarlane, *Oxford Ibsen*, vii. 573–5, examines the episode in the light of Hamsun's lecture notes, which were published by Tore Hamsun in *Paa Turné* (1960). Ibsen commented: 'If we had been living in a civilized country, the students would have knocked the man's brains out this evening.'

33 Det flager i byen og paa havnen.
34 NFLH x. 167.
35 H. Beyer, History of Norwegian Literature, translated by E. Haugen (New York, 1956), p. 274.
36 J. Askeland, Norwegian painting: a survey (Oslo, 1971), pp. 24-5.
37 NFLH x. 288.
38 N. Stang, Edvard Munch (Oslo, 1971), p. 52.
39 Edvard Munch 100 år (published by Oslo Kommunes Kunstsamlinger, 1963), p. 129.
40 R. Stenersen, Edvard Munch—a close-up of a genius (Oslo, 1969), p. 30.
41 Stang, p. 224.
42 Speech on 17 May 1833, when a pillar was unveiled in Oslo in memory of the elder Christian Krohg (Samlede Skrifter, Vol. iv, Pt. I (1923), p. 336).

Chapter 9

1   O. A. Scheflo (see note, p. 313), Samtiden, xxix. 517.
2   British Documents on the Origins of the War 1898-1914, x, Pt. II, 695.
3   Olav Riste, The Neutral Ally (1965), p. 37.
4   Law of 15 Apr. 1916 (W. Keilhau et al., Sweden, Norway, Denmark and Iceland in the World War (Newhaven, Conn., 1930), p. 394).
5   NFLH, xi. 334, 335.
6   Riste, p. 43.
7   J. Castberg, Dagböker 1900-1917 (1953), ii. 146.
8   NFLH, xi. 266; J. Schreiner, Norsk Skipsfart 1914-1920 (1963), p. 305.
9   Riste, p. 109, quoting the Storting's secret archives for 14 May.
10 A. C. Bell, The Blockade of the Central Empires 1914-1918 (Official History of the War) (1937), p. 317.
11 Figures supplied to the American War Trade Board in 1918 (Riste, p. 93).
12 C. J. Hambro, Under den förste verdens-krig (1958), p. 91, has a facsimile of the minister's supposed offer to the prospective kidnapper, written on Legation notepaper. The German allegations were printed only in Morgenbladet (see note, p. 296).
13 Per Vogt, Jerntid og Jobbetid (1938), pp. 83, 142-3.
14 On 3 November the pound stood at kr. 12·90 and the U.S. dollar at kr. 2·79 (NFLH, xi. 321).
15 NFLH, xi. 208.
16 Wollert Konow (H.): DNS iii. 239.
17 B. A. Nissen, Gunnar Knudsen (1957), p. 261.
18 Letter of 7 Apr. 1916 (Riste, p. 111).
19 Castberg, Dagböker, ii. 159 (20 Feb. 1917).
20 All Norwegian pyrites contains some trace of copper: the English phrase was therefore tautological unless it referred to cupriferous pyrites (svovelholdig kopperkis), defined by trade practice as containing not less

than 1 per cent of copper. Bell (p. 497), skirts the difficulty by stating the arrangement for buying the copper and then adding: 'Similar stipulations were made in regard to pyrites, a substance used for making sulphuric acid.'

21 Riste, p. 118. The same Norwegian source illustrates one aspect of the 'disastrousness' from the claim by Norwegian exporters, in a letter to Ihlen on 2 Dec. 1916, that Rio Tinto bought pyrites at kr. 41, and sold to Denmark at kr. 103 per ton (Riste, p. 264).

22 Riste, p. 139. But *havari* (*avarie* in the official French translation) has a wider meaning than 'shipwreck'.

23 Report of the War Committee (Bell, p. 499).

24 Decree issued on 30 Jan. 1917 (Riste, pp. 156–7). Italics added.

25 Schreiner, p. 138.

26 Riste, p. 162; K. Fasting, *Nils Claus Ihlen* (1925), p. 237.

27 Bell, p. 501.

28 In March 106,111 out of 590,545 tons; in April 102,312 out of 866,610 tons (*NFLH* x. 513).

29 Nils Collett Vogt (*NFLH* xi. 297).

30 Ships: Schreiner, p. 307; Riste, p. 238. Men: *NFLH* xi. 301.

31 Rautenfels, alias von Gerich, had fled to Germany in 1916 after his dismissal from a post in the Finnish civil service (*VHF* viii. 84; Hambro, pp. 183–5). According to Bell, p. 630, 'The common people and the press were so roused that Mr. Findlay wondered whether the Norwegian government would not, in the end, be forced to declare war.'

32 'Norway's best-kept war secret' (Riste, p. 178).

33 Letter of 24 Mar. 1917 (Nissen, *Knudsen*, p. 276).

34 Department of State, *Papers Relating to the Foreign Relations of the United States, 1917* (Washington, D.C.), Suppl. 2, ii. 986.

35 Lord Robert Cecil (Riste, pp. 208, 272).

36 Department of State, op. cit., 1918, Suppl. 1, ii, 1150; Bell, p. 647.

37 A. J. Marder, *From the Dreadnought to Scapa Flow*, Vol. iv (1969), p. 252.

38 Cited by Riste, p. 180, from the Milner Papers at New College, Oxford.

39 Marder, Vol. v (1970), p. 71; letter from Wilson to the Secretary of State, 23 Aug. 1918 (State Department 763.72111 N 83/61, cited by Riste, p. 221).

40 *VFH* viii. 110.

41 Lex Urbye, from the name of the minister, A. T. Urbye (*VFH* viii. 107).

42 *Nöytralitetsvernet 1914–1918* (1940), p. 33. Both Bell (p. 647, footnote) and Marder (v. 71) suggest mistakenly that the Norwegians were never induced to lay any mines.

43 Law of 14 Dec. 1917, Section 4 (*NFLH* xi. 145).

44 In addition, *fylke* replaced *amt* for 'county', and *bispedomme* replaced *stift* for 'diocese' (*NFLH* ix. 450).

45 *NFLH* xi. 351.

46   *Documents on British Foreign Policy 1919–1939*, 1st Series, v. 563–4.

47   A. Hoel, *Svalbard*, i (1966), pp. 73–7; *VFH* viii. 316–20.

48   *NFLH*, xi. 348.

49   S. S. Jones, *The Scandinavian States and the League of Nations* (Princeton, 1939), pp. 50–2, 60–3.

50   R. Omang, *Norsk Utenrikstjeneste*, Vol. ii (1959), pp. 343, 345, 346.

Chapter 10

1   *DNS* iii. 11; B. Furre, *Norsk Historie 1905–1940* (1971), Tables 19 and 20.

2   489,660 to 305,241, the rural vote being 70 per cent for, the urban 55·5 per cent against, Prohibition (*NFLH* xi. 378; *DEN* i. 452).

3   *DEN* i. 455.

4   Estimated figure for 1 May 1919 (*NFLH* xi. 396).

5   Balance of payments in G. Jahn *et al.*, *Norges Bank g jennom 150 år* (1966), p. 266; G.N.P. measured in fixed prices in *Ökonomisk Utsyn 1900–1950* (*SS* 3) (1966), Table 29.

6   Lecture to Industriforbundet, 23 Nov. 1923 (*NFLH* xi. 420).

7   Report, 23 Jan.; economists' recommendation, 25 Mar. (*NFLH* xi. 423, 426).

8   Professor Wilhelm Keilhau (*NFLH* xi (1938), 336).

9   More than one-quarter of all local authorities had part of their debt written off (*NFLH* xi. 433).

10   Loan made, 26 May 1923, and disclosed to the Storting, January 1925; the relevant clause of the constitution is Section 75b (*NFLH* xi. 413).

11   Annual Report of Norges Bank for 1920 (*Norges Bank*, p. 218).

12   *NOS* x. 178, Table 204; xii, 245, Tables 74 and 100; Furre, Tables 14 and 15.

13   Edvard Bull, *Arbeiderklassen i norsk historie* (1954), p. 244. The author is a son of the politician named on pp. 315, 318.

14   Bull, p. 261.

15   Bull, pp. 258, 260.

16   Furre, Tables 10–13.

17   H. F. Dahl, *Norge mellom krigene* (1971), p. 54.

18   *VFH* viii. 264. A corresponding paramilitary organization, *Samfunnsvernet*, was set up in 1923, which in 1928–35 was officially recognized as a reserve police force.

19   W. Brandt, *Min vei til Berlin* (Norwegian translation by L. and H. Holmboe, 1960), p. 50.

20   Bull, p. 305.

21   *VFH* viii. 304.

22   Bull, pp. 315–16.

23   Furre, p. 215.

24   H. D. Loock, *Quisling, Rosenberg og Terboven* (Norwegian translation by A. and E. Lorenz, 1972), p. 53. This book gives a detailed objective

account of the various small, anti-democratic, Right-wing movements in Norway from 1930 to September 1940.

25 *Norsk Militært Tidsskrift* (1969), p. 203.
26 Dahl, *Norge mellom krigene*, p. 41.
27 K. Fröland, *Krise og kamp. Bygdefolkets Krisehjelp* (1962), p. 80.
28 A. Lindboe, *Fra de urolige tredve årene* (1965), pp. 187–8 gives an account at third hand of a dinner on 25 Oct. 1932, at which leading Conservatives, including an ex-premier (Bratlie), were addressed by Quisling, and the vice-chairman of the Agrarians talked of rallying round him ('*Norges bönder slår ring om Quisling*'). Lindboe, who was then minister of justice, also records in his diary (p. 36) that Quisling played no active part in the cabinet decision to send troops to Menstad.
29 22 June 1933; the editor was Victor Mogens.
30 N.S. obtained votes chiefly in Oslo, Telemark, and Opland, but contested seats throughout the country; the two small parties which won a seat (see Table V, p. 298) concentrated their efforts on a small area. See P. M. Hayes, *Quisling* (Newton Abbot, 1971), pp. 99 and 103–4.
31 *HT* xxxix. 139.
32 Hayes, p. 118.
33 These early contacts may have been important, but as late as April 1939 Quisling was not invited to the celebrations of Hitler's fiftieth birthday, as were two of his associates, Hagelin (see note, p. 392) and H. H. Aall. Although Quisling may have visited Rosenberg as head of German Nazi Party activities abroad in Berlin in 1936, June 1939 was the date of the conversations in which he offered support against British machinations in Norway in return for financial assistance through Rosenberg for N.S.: 'Quisling had crossed the Rubicon' (Loock, p. 152).
34 Bull, p. 338.
35 Furre, p. 272.
36 In 1920–39 G.N.P., measured in prices of 1938, increased from kr. 3,597 million to kr. 6,141 million; measured in relation to population aged 18–64 years with the figure of 100 for 1905 as basis it increased from 149·7 to 228·1 (*Ökonomisk Utsyn 1900–1950*, Tables 27 and 28).
37 A. Stonehill, *Foreign ownership in Norwegian enterprises* (*SS* 14, Oslo, 1965), pp. 44, 46–7.
38 C. Wilson, *History of Unilever* (1954), ii. 216.
39 *NFLH* xi. 463.
40 E. Höigård and H. Ruge, *Det norske skozes historie* (2nd ed. 1963), p. 298.
41 E. Bull, *The Norwegian Trade Union Movement* (Brussels, 1956), pp. 114, 116.
42 E. Haugen, *Language Conflict and Language Planning* (New York, 1966), p. 139.
43 Ibid., pp. 144–5, the two versions being *bokmål* and *nynorsk*.
44 Ibid., p. 157.

Chapter 11

1   Address of 3 Nov. 1926 in, Per Vogt (editor), *Fridtjof Nansen: Explorer—Scientist—Humanitarian* (Oslo, 1961), p. 174.

2   Ibid., p. 186, recollections of E. Buviken.

3   Telegram from Sir Eric Drummond, 14 Apr. 1919 (S. Kjærheim, editor, *Fridtjof Nansens Brev*, Vol. iv (1966), p. 323).

4   Letter of 18 June 1920 (Kjærheim iv. 26).

5   *NBL* ix. 639.

6   Telegram to International Red Cross, on his return to Moscow from Samara, 9 Dec. 1921 (Kjærheim iv. 76).

7   *A Great Experiment* (1941), pp. 131–2.

8   Benjamin Vogt, arguing in favour of proportional representation in the election of non-permanent members, 1926 (S. S. Jones, *The Scandinavian States and the League of Nations* (Princeton, 1939), p. 130).

9   *The Times*, London, 15 Sept. 1926.

10   *Stortingets-forhandlinger 1929*, Vol. ii, St. med. no. 3 (*Utenriksdepartementet*), p. 8.

11   Jones, p. 223.

12   Jones, p. 255.

13   Article 22, Paragraph 1, of the League Covenant.

14   *Encyclopedia Britannica* (1968 edition), xiv. 770: Lugard's article on Mandates, revised by Quincy Wright.

15   Jones, p. 156.

16   Jones, p. 137.

17   F. Castberg, *Folkenes Forbund* (1925), p. 13, explains to Norwegian schools that economic sanctions under Article 16 are obligatory, but military sanctions voluntary. Jones, p. 61, points to the alteration made in the draft covenant, substituting *racommander* for *indiquer* as the action to be taken by the Council in calling upon member states for the application of military sanctions. D. H. Miller, *The Drafting of the Covenant* (New York, 1928), ii. 629–30, and i. 308, confirms the Norwegian view that their wishes had been met from the outset, but G. M. Gathorne-Hardy, *A Short History of International Affairs* (3rd ed. 1942), p. 57, shows that the legal as distinct from the practical position was unclear.

18   N. Örvik, *Sikkerhets Politikken 1920—1939*, Vol. i (1960), p. 141.

19   Örvik i. 161, 163.

20   *DEN* ii. 436, 438.

21   *DEN* ii. 308; *Polar Record*, xv. 286–7 (article by J. N. Tönnessen).

22   *DNS* iv. 130 (R. Omang).

23   *VFH* viii. 324.

24   G. C. H. Smedal. He was versed in international law, had built up a propaganda organization, *Norges Grönlandslag*, and believed that a weak government would not venture to disavow the *coup* that he set in motion by cabling instructions from Gothenburg.

25 *VFH* viii. 325.
26 *VFH* ix. 106–7; Örvik i. 176, 185.
27 *VFH*, ix. 111.
28 Örvik, Vol. ii (1961), p. 307.
29 *DEN* ii. 165 (Lt.-General Ole Berg).
30 T. Öksnevad, *Joh. Ludw. Mowinckel* (Bergen, 1963), p. 147.
31 Telephone conversation with Trygve Lie (Örvik i. 297).
32 31 May 1938 (*Stortingstidende 1938*, pp. 1365, 1373; Örvik i. 344).
33 Örvik ii. 339.
34 *NOS* xii. 245, Table 33.
35 *VFH* viii. 434.
36 O. B. Grimley, *The New Norway* (2nd ed. 1939), p. 122.
37 *Social Handbook for Norway* (Oslo, 1937), p. 63.
38 Agnes Rothery, *Norway Changing and Changeless* (New York, 1939), pp. 133, 141.

Chapter 12

1 *VFH* ix. 122 (figures include *c*. 500,000 tons already in British service).
2 *VFH* ix. 134.
3 The British case is argued at length by Professor C. H. M. Waldock in *The Year Book of International Law 1947*, pp. 216–381; the Norwegian documents were published in 1950, the British in 1953. Admiral of the Fleet Sir Philip Vian comments, 'Norwegians have long memories' (*Action This Day* (1960), p. 31).
4 *Documents on German Foreign Policy 1918–1945*, Series D, Vols. 8–9, pp. 695–6 (cited by D. Clark, *Three Days to Catastrophe* (1961), p. 102).
5 H. W. Scheidt was given special responsibility for 'Nordic questions' by Rosenberg early in 1939, and first visited Quisling in January; Lt.-Commander R. Schreiber was posted to Oslo in October as assistant to the naval attaché, who was based on Stockholm. The details of German political activities in relation to Norway as far as 25 Sept. 1940 are available in H. D. Loock, *Quisling, Rosenberg og Terboven*, Norwegian translation by A. and E. Lorenz (1972).
6 *kombinasjonsevna som svikta* (*VFH* ix. 146).
7 Commander E. A. Steen, *Norges Sjökrig 1940–1945*, Vol. iv (1958), pp. 69–72.
8 *VFH* ix. 170. Nygaardsvold was unimpressed by the promise (Trygve Lie, *Leve eller dö* (1955), p. 120).
9 Loock, pp. 216, 211.
10 Scheidt and Schreiber had acted without authority, but Rosenberg's diary suggests that they correctly anticipated Hitler's reaction to the news that the Nygaardsvold government had defied him and escaped to Hamar: 'He smiles over his entire face. Now, Quisling can form his

government.' They reported their action to Hitler's headquarters through military channels (Loock, pp. 217–19).

11 'The proposal was approved without a formal vote' (*DNS* iii. 380).

12 *VFH* ix. 178. Trygve Lie was certain that the official record is wrong in stating that the king abdicated only for himself (Lie, p. 136).

13 Major-General O. Lindbäck-Larsen, *Krigen i Norge 1940* (1965), p. 139.

14 Even the three battalions of Chasseurs Alpins proved to be 'neither trained nor equipped for the winter conditions in North Norway' (Lindbäck-Larsen, p. 156).

15 Trygve Lie suggests that Mowinckel's proposal, which first reached the Norwegian government on 14 May, was prompted by the Swedish authorities.

16 Broadcast of 9 June (Lie, p. 252).

17 Lindbäck-Larsen, p. 48.

18 A. S. Milward, *The Fascist Economy in Norway* (Oxford, 1972), p. 94, observes: 'It is almost the case that Norway was nearer to her future role in the New Order in the summer of 1940 than at any other time.' The aluminium project is shown in Table 38 (p. 178).

19 The Germans printed 500,000 leaflets with the news, and dropped them over areas where fighting was still in progress (Loock, p. 247).

20 *VFH* ix. 219.

21 Interview of 16 Aug.; Quisling was in Germany from 5 July to 20 Aug. (Loock, pp. 386, 387, 390).

22 The vote was made up as follows: Labour, 44 to 22; Conservatives, 18 to 15; Agrarians, 18 to 0; Left Party, 10 to 14; Christian People's Party, 0 to 2. Two members not included in any party group were believed to side with the majority in favour of the king being deposed (*VFH* ix. 236).

23 *DNS* iv. 268–9.

24 Loock, pp. 406–9.

25 *VFH* ix. 234, echoing *Norges Krig*, edited by S. Steen (1948), ii .566.

26 This famous comparison seems to have originated in *The Motor Ship*, December 1940, cited by *Norsk Tidend*, London, 7 Jan. 1941.

27 W. S. Churchill, *The Second World War*, Vol. iii (1950), p. 732; Vol. v (1952), p. 608– . Minutes for Chiefs of Staff, 12 Sept. 1941 and 19 Feb. 1944. The British Official History (*Grand Strategy*, Vol. iv (1972), by M. Howard, p. 551) describes this operation as his *'idée fixe* in Europe'.

28 Agreement signed on 28 May 1941 (*Norges Krig* ii. 214).

29 Chiefly the work of the American correspondent Leland Stowe, who reported from Oslo on 9–13 April to the *Chicago Daily News*. His material also appeared in *Life* and the London *Daily Telegraph*.

30 Broadcast of 15 Dec. 1940 (*Norges Krig* ii. 212).

31 *das Schicksalsgebiet in diesem Kriege* (Führer Conference of 22 Jan. 1942, *Brassey's Naval Annual 1948*, p. 260).

32   The Latin title was given by Dr. Scharffenberg to an influential article he
     wrote in *Arbeiderbladet*; the nationalist slogan appeared in a Stavanger
     newspaper, *Første mai*, which was immediately suppressed.

33   *Arbeideren*, 11 June 1940 (*VFH* ix. 281).

34   The *Riksting* had figured in the plans for *Nordisk Folkereisning* in May 1931
     and more vaguely in Quisling's article on the death of Nansen a year
     earlier (Loock, pp. 49, 36).

35   S.O.E. adopted a new 'Long-Term Policy in Norway' on 21 Sept. 1942,
     and friction was finally eliminated in the course of the following year
     (S. Kjelstadli, *Hjemmestyrkene I* (1959), pp. 184, 190–1, 409).

36   Kjelstadli, pp. 233–4, 425.

37   *VFH* ix. 387.

38   O. Riste and B. Nökleby, *Norway 1940–45. The Resistance Movement*,
     (Oslo, 1970), p. 70.

39   Einar Skinnarland knew the installations at Rjukan, was familiar with the
     surrounding district, and had had recent contact with engineers work-
     ing on the spot, thus providing S.O.E. with an unexpected 'godsend'
     (Kjelstadli, p. 405, n. 99, and p. 218).

40   Riste and Nökleby, p. 62.

41   Section 1 of June Directive, which remained in force until 5 Dec. (Kjel-
     stadli, pp. 324–5, 443).

42   *Norges Krig* iii. 608.

43   *VFH* ix. 476–7, where total loss of life from the war is given from official
     sources as 10,262 persons, of whom 883 were women.

44   Reintroduction of the death penalty, hitherto restricted to military
     offences and the duration of hostilities (ordinances of 3 Oct. 1941 and
     22 Jan. 1942); new penalties for treason (*landsvikanordningen*, 15 Dec.
     1944).

45   J. Andenes, O. Riste, and M. Skodvin, *Norway and the Second World War*
     (Oslo, 1966), p. 154.

46   M. Skodvin, *Norden eller NATO?* (1971), pp. 29, 347.

Chapter 13 and Epilogue

1   *DEN* iii. 512 (M. Skodvin).

2   *Norway Year Book 1967* (Oslo, 1966), p. 217.

3   *O.E.C.D. Economic Surveys: Norway* (January 1972)—Basic Statistics:
    International Comparisons.

4   *DNS* iii. 389–90, 394, 405.

5   H. Valen and D. Katz, *Political Parties in Norway* (Oslo, 1964), p. 35.

6   Cf. Gerhardsen's speech of 24 Nov. 1952; 'All the parties are in agreement
    that the votes in Finnmark, for example, shall weigh more than the
    votes in Oslo' (*Stortingsforhandlinger 1952*, Vol. 7b, p. 2871).

7   Including more formal interpellations for which provision had been made

earlier, the average in 1950–63 was 270 questions a year, of which the prime and foreign ministers answered only half a dozen apiece.

8 An inquiry disclosed six weaknesses in the organization and management of the mine, where fifty-nine other lives had been lost since work was resumed under state ownership after the Second World War (A. Hoel, *Svalbard*, Vol. iii (1967), pp. 1276, 1262).

9 M. Skodvin, *Norden eller NATO?* (1971), pp. 92, 348.

10 Original text of Alistair Cooke's article in the *Manchester Guardian*, 3 Mar. 1949 (Skodvin, p. 93).

11 See, for example, article by Colonel W. Kleen in *Nordens Förenta Stater* (Stockholm, 1942), pp. 51–66.

12 Skodvin, p. 264.

13 All three citations in this paragraph are from Skodvin, pp. 335, 319–20, and 295.

14 Lt.-General Ole Berg (*DEN* ii. 173).

15 Ekspedisjonssjef T. Greve (*AK* xiv. 611).

16 *Aschehougs Leksikonservis*, 1962-3, p. 149.

17 Citation, 10 Dec. 1970.

18 Greve (*AK* xiv. 609).

19 O. Wallmen, *Nordiska Rådet och Nordiskt Samarbete* (Stockholm, 1966), p. 113.

20 *Fellesprogrammet* ii. 1 (*Grunnloven vår med andre dokumenter av nasjonal viktighet*, ed. T. Andenæs (6th printing 1960), p. 107). A precis of the programme is given by one of its authors in *VFH* ix. 488.

21 A/S Årdal og Sunndal Verk (A. Stonehill, *Foreign Ownership in Norwegian Enterprises* (*SS* 14, Oslo, 1965), p. 62.

22 L.O. Council meeting in the summer of 1945 (E. Bull, *The Norwegian Trade Union Movement* (Brussels, 1956), p. 101).

23 G. C. Wasberg and A. S. Svendsen, *Industriens historie i Norge* (1969), pp. 305, 290.

24 Stonehill, pp. 59, 60.

25 *Norges Ökonomi etter Krigen* (*SS* 12, 1965), pp. 406, 418.

26 *Kosmos IV*, surrendered by Germany as reparations after the war (*Polar Record*, XV. 289).

27 Agreement between the Fisheries Department and Norges Fiskarlag, 1964 (K. Midttun and S. Thon, *Norges Næringsliv* (1966), p. 90).

28 *DEN* ii. 234. *NOS* xii. 245, Table 149 shows that the household and agricultural consumption of electricity increased from *c*. 3,300 GWh. in 1946 to 9,529 GWh. in 1962.

29 *DEN* ii. 442 (J. N. Tönnessen).

30 The balance on all current transactions ranged between a credit of kr. 571 million (1951) and a deficit of kr. 1,315 million (1961). Full details are given in *NOS* XII. 245, Table 68.

31 *Norway Year Book 1967*, p. 252.

32 *DEN* iii. 44.

33 *DEN* iii. 396 (C. A. R. Christensen).

34 *Ingen Sommar*, first published in Swedish, 1944. Several of Borgen's books have been translated into German and Russian.

35 In 1963–5 Norwegians spent kr. 1,553 million abroad, while foreigners spent kr. 1,674 million in Norway (*Norway Year Book 1967*, p. 445).

36 *DEN* i. 526 (Theodor Broch, author of *The Mountain Wait*, 1943).

37 C. A. R. Christensen (*Nordisk Tidskrift*, Stockholm, xlii. 262).

38 *Keesing's Contemporary Archives*, 20986A, 23567A; *Nordisk Tidskrift*, xlii. 265–8, and xlvi. 137–8.

39 *NOS* xii. 269, Table 270 shows that social insurance expenditure increased in 1968–70 by 60 per cent: allowing for inflation, a steep rise.

A Short Survey of Books Available in English

Preference is given to newer works, and no reference has been made to articles in periodicals or to pamphlet literature.

Biographies, which could in many cases be placed under more than one heading, are listed separately at the end.

All books have been published in Britain or the United States unless they are marked with an asterisk, which indicates Oslo, or a place of publication is stated. 'Tr.' marks a translation from the Norwegian unless another language is named.

BIBLIOGRAPHICAL GUIDES AND PRINTED DOCUMENTARY SOURCES

Norway in English by Erling Grönland (1961*) gives a systematic coverage of 'books on Norway and by Norwegians in English 1936–1959'; its author had a continuation under active preparation in 1972 at the University Library, Oslo. Earlier books can be traced with some difficulty in the *Bibliotheca Norvegica* of H. M. Pettersen (7 vols., 1899–1924*) and in the alphabetical lists of *Norwegian Literature and Books on Norway Printed Abroad*, compiled by G. E. Raabe for 1926–30 and 1931–5 (1935*, 1941*). A short list was produced for the National Book Council by A. Sommerfelt in 1944 (list no. 199). Recent subject bibliographies include *Itineraria Norvegica* by E. H. Schiötz (1970*), which lists *c.* 650 British and American travel books issued before 1920; *Norwegian Foreign Policy* by N. Örvik (1968*), which covers 1905–65 and may be supplemented from *The Scandinavian Countries in International Affairs, 1800–1952* by F. Lindberg and J. I. Kolehmainen (1953); *Norwegian Legal Publications in English, French, and German* by K. Haukaas (1966*); an *Ibsen Bibliography 1928–1957* by I. Tedford (1961*); and a *Sigrid Undset Bibliografi* by I. Packness (1963*). Books in English on industrial subjects are separately indexed in *Industriens historie i Norge* by T. A. Höeg and G. C. Wasberg (1972*). Norwegian–American historical publications since 1928-9 are listed in *Norwegian–American Studies*, Vol. v– .

Humaniora Norvegica (5 vols., 1954–61*) has provided a survey in English of Norwegian research for 1950–8; *Excerpta Historica Nordica* (Stockholm, 1955–) gives biennial summaries of important historical research published in Scandinavia since 1950; and the catalogue of *Norwegian Scholarly Books 1825–1970* (1970*) includes a list of periodicals written partly in English, to which should be added *Historisk Tidsskrift*, where in recent years some major articles have had English summaries.

The Constitution of Norway, edited by T. Andenæs (3rd edition, 1962*), also includes the original English translation made in 1814 and documents from 17 May 1814 and 7 June 1905. *The German Aggression in Norway* gives an official translation of a Norwegian White Book (1940); much legislation can be located in *Norwegian laws, etc., selected for the Foreign Service* (1963*); and all treaties that originated in English are in *The Treaties of Norway, 1661–1967* (3 vols. and index to 1968, 1970*). English material for the Bodö dispute was collected by Gathorne-Hardy (p. 459, n. 9), and dispatches from the Stockholm legation on Norway's relations with Sweden in 1880–95 were quoted extensively by Knaplund (p. 456, n. 25). *Norway and the War September 1939–December 1940*, edited by Monica Curtis for the R.I.I.A. (1941), with contents dating from May 1938 to February 1941, is to a small extent supplemented by *Correspondence respecting the German steamer Altmark* (1950).

DESCRIPTIONS OF LAND AND PEOPLE

The nineteenth century is well covered by travel books: Samuel Laing's *Journal of a Residence in Norway* (1836) and R. G. Latham's *Norway and the Norwegians* (2 vols., 1840) are especially valuable, but other useful suggestions may be obtained from B. A. Butenschön's anthology, *Travellers discovering Norway in the last century* (1968*), or *Norwegian Life and Literature* by C. B. Burchardt (1920). The introductory sections in the older editions of such guide books as Baedeker's *Norway, Sweden, and Denmark* and Murray's *Handbook for Travellers in Norway* likewise help to recreate the picture of the past. An authoritative survey of the national development was given in *Norway— Official Publication for the Paris Exhibition* (1900*), while the first half-century under the new monarchy was briefly but skilfully reviewed by C. A. R. Christensen in *Norway. A Democratic Kingdom* (1955*).

A Handbook of Norway and Sweden was produced by the N.I.D. for the British Admiralty in 1918, but its two-volume *Norway* (1942, 1943) is a much more comprehensive geographical study. *Norway. A Brief Presentation* by J. Vidnes (tr., 1935*) is a careful survey by a journalist, which may usefully be compared with the impressions of O. B. Grimley (p. 468, n. 36) and Agnes Rothery (p. 468, n. 38). Among the many individual accounts of post-war Norway mention may be made of *The World of the Norseman* by O. Hölaas (1950), *The Norwegian Way of Life* by the well-known jurist, F. Castberg (1954), *Norwegian Life and Landscape* by A. Martin (1952), and an American investigation, *The Norwegians. A Study in National Culture*, by D. Rodnick (1955). W. A. Warbey and others presented a Fabian Society standpoint in *Modern Norway. A Study in Social Democracy* (1950), and a factual introductory account appeared in *The Scandinavian States and Finland*, prepared for the R.I.I.A. in 1951 by G. M. Gathorne-Hardy and other experts.

Present-day surveys with a strong geographical and/or economic flavour include the indispensable *Norway Year Book* (7th edition, 1967*); *Norway Today*, edited by Per Vogt (9th edition, 1970*); *New Norway*, edited by B. Jerman and F. P. Nyquist (1970*); and the concise *Norway—Land, People, Industries* by M. Helvig and V. Johannessen (3rd edition, 1970*). North Norway is examined in unusual detail in *Norway North of 65*, edited by Ö. Vorren (1960*). S. Pivot's *Norway* (tr. from French, 1963) also breaks new ground with its imaginative observations. Norway in relation to its Nordic neighbours is effectively presented in *Scandinavian Lands* by R. Millward (1964) and *A Geography of Norden*, edited by A. Sömme (new edition, 1968*); the human side is emphasized in *The Scandinavians* by D. S. Connery (1966).

GENERAL HISTORIES

Knut Gjerset's two-volume *History of the Norwegian People* (1915) dealt rather summarily with the period after 1814, but G. M. Gathorne-Hardy's *Norway* (1925) is still a valuable introduction to many aspects of the national development. W. Keilhau's *Norway in World History* (1944) was a slighter production than any of the four volumes that he contributed to *Det norske folks liv og historie gjennom tidene*. This fundamental work was fully used, however, in *A History of Norway* (1948) by Karen Larsen, professor of history at St. Olaf College, Minnesota. In 1952–6 F. N. Stagg introduced a wealth of local history into his five regional studies: *North Norway*, *The Heart of Norway*, *South Norway*, *West Norway and its Fjords*, and *East Norway and its Frontier*. *A Short History of Norway* by T. K. Derry (2nd edition, 1967) has been followed by *A Brief History of Norway* by J. Midgaard (3rd edition, 1970*), while 'The Span of History' provides one of the four parts of *Norway* by R. G. Popperwell (1972); this comprehensive survey is particularly valuable for its account of the language and literature, based on many years' teaching of the subject in Cambridge.

General Histories of Scandinavia should also be consulted. *The Scandinavian Countries 1720–1865* by B. J. Hovde (2 vols., reissued 1948) deals illuminatingly with the rise of the middle classes and has full references to Scandinavian and some other sources. *The Northern Tangle* by R. Kenney (1946) gains weight from the author's experience with the Norwegian government in London during the war. *The United States and Scandinavia* by F. D. Scott (1950) examines the common history from an American standpoint, while *Scandinavia Past and Present*, edited by J. Bukdahl and others (3 vols., Odense, 1959) deserves to be known as a carefully illustrated work which deals separately with the cultural and general development of each country. Other titles for the period 1945–67 are listed by H. A. Barton in an article in *Scandinavian Studies*, xl (1968), 286–93.

INTERNAL POLITICAL DEVELOPMENT AND EXTERNAL RELATIONS

Norwegian Democracy by J. A. Storing (1963) surveys contemporary institutions in detail and briefly describes their history. A much shorter account, which is also serviceable, is given in *Government and Politics in the Nordic Countries* by N. Andrén (Stockholm, 1964), while the legislature is separately examined in *Norway's Parliament—the Storting* by P. Öisang (1962*). Apart from the pioneer work of Valen and Katz (p. 470, n. 5) and what may be gathered incidentally from the books on Quisling, the strong Norwegian interest in the history of political parties is reflected chiefly in *Division and Cohesion in Democracy. A Study of Norway* by H. Eckstein (1961), who writes of 'cleavages balanced by a strong sense of community'. Other specialized work is contained or surveyed in *Scandinavian Political Studies. A Year Book* (Stockholm, 1961–).

External relations have attracted much more attention outside Norway. The history of the union with Sweden has been traced to 1871 by Jorgenson (p. 451, n. 1) and, with reference chiefly to the later years, by R. E. Lindgren (p. 456, n. 32); several contemporary publications, of which Nansen's (p. 457, n. 44) is representative, state the Norwegian case against Sweden in 1905; and the separation with its immediate diplomatic consequences for both countries has been recently reviewed by a Swedish scholar, F. Lindberg (p. 457, n. 11). The period since 1905 is traced very briefly in *Trends in Norwegian Foreign Policy* by N. Örvik (1962*), while one uniquely Norwegian contact with international affairs is examined in *Norway and the Nobel Peace Prize* by O. J. Falnes (1938) and *The Nobel Peace Prize* by A. Schou (1950).

O. Riste's *Neutral Ally* (p. 463, n. 3) has largely superseded both *The Neutrality of Norway in the World War* by P. G. Vigness (1932) and the work by Keilhau (p. 463, n. 4). Norway's relations with the League of Nations were traced to 1938 by S. S. Jones (p. 467, n. 8); Norway's acquisition of Spitsbergen and its consequences were treated by T. Mathiesen (1954) in *Svalbard in International Politics 1871–1925* and its sequel, *Svalbard in the Changing Arctic*; and the main controversy of the inter-war period in *The Eastern Greenland Case in Historical Perspective* by O. Svarlien (1964). The last-named work may be compared with Jon Skeie's *Greenland. The Dispute between Norway and Denmark* (tr., 1932), where the Norwegian claims are stated by a legal expert.

No major Norwegian study of the Second World War period has yet been translated, but two short complementary accounts by Norwegians are *Norway and the Second World War* (p. 470, n. 45) and *Norway 1940–1945. The Resistance Movement* (p. 470, n. 38). The fighting in Norway has been examined recently in *The Norwegian Campaign of 1940* by Major-General J. L. Moulton (1966), *Norway 1940* by B. Ash (1964), *The German Northern Theater of Operations* by E. F. Ziemke (1960), and *Narvik* by Captain D. F. W. Macintyre (1959). The British official military history, *The Campaign in Norway* by T. K. Derry, was published in 1952, and a vigorous account based on British War Office papers, *Norway, The Commandos, Dieppe* by C. Buckley (1951), covers the raids on the Norwegian coast as well. Non-military contemporary accounts were given by H. Koht in *Norway Neutral and Invaded* (1941), T. Broch (p. 472, n. 36), and the American minister, Florence J. Harriman, whose *Mission to the North*

(1941) also covers in lighter vein the years before the war. The start of the resistance movement is traced in *Norway Revolts against the Nazis* by J. Worm-Müller (1941), and the following may be singled out among the many stories of individual achievements: D. Howarth's careful accounts, *The Shetland Bus* (1951) and *We Die Alone* (1955); *Day After Day* by Odd Nansen, son of Fridtjof Nansen (tr., 1949); *Two Eggs on my Plate* by O. R. Olsen (tr., 1952); and *Skis against the Atom* (tr., 1954) by K. Haukelid, a leader of the heavy-water raiders. Contemporary accounts of feats of endurance by Norwegian seamen are collected in *Norway's New Saga of the Sea* by L. E. Lindbæk (tr., 1969). The biographies of Quisling deal exhaustively with one aspect of the German occupation, which is also treated by two of his apologists in *Vidkun Quisling—the Norwegian Enigma* by L. L. Unstad (1959, reprinted 1964) and *I Was Quisling's Secretary* by F. Knudsen (tr., 1967). On the economic side *The Fascist Economy in Norway* (p. 469, n. 18) shows the gap between German intentions and achievements.

The course pursued since the war is traced in *Norway in the United Nations* by B. Jensen (3rd ed., 1971*); *Norway in European and Atlantic Co-operation* by E. Löchen (1964*), which discusses the effects of membership of the Council of Europe, E.E.C., and NATO; *Norway and NATO* (1968*) by T. Greve, a senior Foreign Ministry official; and *The Foreign Policy of Norway*, a short appraisal by B. A. Böstrup (1968*). A scientific approach to the phenomena of policy making is offered in *Élite images and foreign policy outcomes. A study of Norway* by P. M. Burgess (1968), which examines the years 1940-9, and in *International relations and world images. A study of Norwegian foreign policy élites* by H. Hveem (1972*), based on information collected in 1967. The workings of the new instrument of Scandinavian co-operation established in 1952 are usefully shown in *The Nordic Council* by S. V. Anderson (1967), and the conflict of Norwegian attitudes to the European Community was studied on the eve of decision in *Fears and Expectations* by N. Örvik (1972).

ECONOMIC AND SOCIAL HISTORY

Since the only general economic history in any language is *Norwegische Wirtschaftsgeschichte* by O. A. Johnsen (Jena, 1939), the reader must start with the rather small proportion of Norwegian articles in *The Scandinavian Economic History Review* (Stockholm, 1953–), *The Industrial Revolution in Scandinavia 1850-1914* by L. Jörberg (Fontana Economic History of Europe, iii, Ch. 8, 1970)—which includes agriculture—or the rather slight *Industrialization of Norway 1800-1930* by Sima Lieberman (1970*). *Main Aspects of Economic Policy since the War* by P. Kleppe (1968*) is a short study by a leading Labour Party politician, while the post-war experiments in state planning and control are fully covered in *Norway, The Planned Revival* by Alice Bourneuf (1958), *Planning in Norway, 1947-56* by the director of the central statistical office, B. J. Bjerve (Amsterdam, 1959), and a chapter by J. Faaland in *Economic*

Policy in Our Time, Vol. ii (Amsterdam, 1964). The latest achievements in many branches of the economy are briefly reviewed in *Norway At Work* by Ole Knudsen (1972*).

The labour aspect is dealt with by Edvard Bull (p. 466, n. 41), in *Labor in Norway* by a former U.S. Labor Attaché, W. Galenson (1949), and in *Labor Relations in Norway* by an experienced journalist, H. Dorfman (rev. ed., 1966*); all sides of the co-operative movement are described in *Co-operatives in Norway* by O. B. Grimley (1950) and *Co-operative Organization in Norway*, published in 1960* by the co-operation committee of the Norway Welfare Society, *Norges Vel*. The influence of foreign ownership in industry has been carefully examined by A. Stonehill (p. 458, n. 26), and accounts of its various branches are given in *Industries of Norway*, edited by O. J. Adamson (1952*), and more briefly in Norway's Industries (published by Industriforbundet, 1958*). *Norwegian Agriculture* by O. T. Bjarnes (2nd ed., 1932) was an authoritative short description: some idea of modern developments may be gained from the captions in *Norwegian Agriculture in Pictures* by J. Kringlebotten (1959) and one special socio-economic problem is studied in *Norway's Internal Migration to New Farms since 1920* by K. H. Stone (The Hague, 1971). Useful information may also be gleaned from *The Fishing Industry in Norway* by H. Angerman (1971), a short survey with statistics; *The Saga of Norwegian Shipping* by K. Petersen (1955*), which includes the post-war reconstruction; *An Outline of Norwegian Forestry* by K. Skinnemoen (2nd ed., 1964*), with a section on the forest industries; and a short account of *Norsk Hydro* (tr., 1957*).

Michael Drake's *Population and Society* (p. 451, n. 25) makes an interesting combination with the present-day study of *Norway's Families* by T. D. Eliot, A. Hillman and others (1960). Yet a third book which owes some of its inspiration to Eilert Sundt is *Brewing and Beer Traditions in Norway* by O. Nordland (1969*), but the student of modern society will find more of value in *A Social Handbook for Norway* (1937*), *Social Service in Oslo* (1963*), and the series of volumes produced for the Norwegian Joint Committee on International Social Policy. These include *The Care of the Aged in Norway* by F. Danielsen (rev., ed., 1959), *Social Insurance in Norway* by D. B. Scårdal (4th ed., 1960), *Social Defence in Norway* by A. Evensen (1965), and *Health Services in Norway* by their veteran director, Karl Evang (tr., 3rd ed., 1970). A large-scale comparative study is available in *Freedom and Welfare. Social Patterns in the Northern Countries of Europe*, edited by G. R. Nelson (Copenhagen, 1953). The most recent account of developments in schools and universities is O. Hove's short *System of Education in Norway* (1968); reference may also be made to his *Outline of Norwegian Education* (2nd ed., 1958), to *The Education of Children and Youth in Norway* by H. Huus (1960), and to *The Organization and Administration of the Educational System of Norway* by G. M. Wiley (1955). *Facts about the University of Oslo* is recompiled almost annually by its Office for Foreign Students.

Church Life in Norway 1808–1950 by E. Molland (p. 450, n. 17) gives a brief authoritative introduction; a present-day picture is in *The Scandinavian Churches*, edited by L. S. Hunter (1965); H. Holloway has translated and traced the history of *The Norwegian Rite* (1935); and light is shed upon the work of the church in North Norway by E. Berggrav, who had been its bishop, in *Land of Suspense* (tr., 1943). *Women in Norway* by Betty Selid (1970) briefly records the early history of the feminist movement. Norway's racial minority problem is treated in *Changing Lapps* by G. Gjessing (1954) and mentioned in *Introducing the Lapps* by the professor of Lappish studies at Oslo, A. Nesheim (1964*); *The Lapps* by B. Collinder (1949) is a fascinating general account by a Swedish language-expert. Another special aspect of social life is emphasized in *Norway the Northern Playground*, the classic account by the rock-climbing pioneer, W. C. Slingsby (1903; reissued 1941), with which may be coupled two lavishly illustrated modern works, *Shooting and Fishing in Norway* by P. Hohle (1959*) and *The Rivers of Norway* by T. Slyte (1966*), though the latter also examines industrial uses. *Skiing, a Way of Life in Norway* by E. Bergsland (tr., 1952*) has smaller historical pretensions than Olav Bö's *Skiing Traditions in Norway* (tr., 1968*); many types of Norwegian sailing vessel down to the time of Colin Archer are presented in *Boats of the North* by A. E. Christensen (tr., 1968*).

For the transatlantic emigration the publications of the Norwegian-American Historical Association (*Studies and Records*, 1926– ; *Travel and Description* series, 1926– ; unnumbered series, 1928–) illustrate and amplify the named works of Blegen, Qualey, Bjork, and Norlie (pp. 458-9, n. 1, 2, 19, 24). *Immigration and American History*, edited by H. S. Commager (1962), has noteworthy contributions by Blegen (in whose honour the volume was produced), Qualey, Ingrid Semmingsen, and F. D. Scott. *The Scandinavians in Australia, New Zealand, and the Western Pacific* have been recorded by J. S. Lyng (1939). The explorations of Nansen, Otto Sverdrup, and Amundsen were described by them in ample volumes, which were translated before 1914; an interesting modern study, which includes some recent ventures, is *Great Norwegian Expeditions* by T. Heyerdahl, S. Richter, and H. Riiser-Larsen (1954*).

LITERATURE AND THE ARTS; LITERATURE IN TRANSLATION

The standard histories of Norwegian literature by Downs, Jorgenson, McFarlane, and Beyer (pp. 461-3, n. 7, 22, 31, 35) are supplemented by *The Norseman* (Vols. i–xvi, 1943–58; *Index*, 1959*), which was launched in wartime London as 'a medium through which the cultural heritage of Norway could be presented to the free world'. *National Romanticism in Norway* by O. J. Falnes (1933) includes a section on the beginnings of the language movement, which is discussed in *The Written and the Spoken Word in Norway* by A. Sommerfelt

(Taylorian Lecture, 1942) and exhaustively examined in *Language Conflict and Language Planning* by E. Haugen (1966). The most recent short introductory study is *Milestones of Norwegian Literature* by T. Stöverud (1967*). There are sections on Norwegian authors in *Six Scandinavian Novelists*, edited by A. Gustafson (2nd ed., 1966); *An Introduction to Scandinavian Literature* by E. Bredsdorff, Brita Mortensen, and R. Popperwell (1951); and the W.E.A. lectures of W. J. Allen, *Renaissance in the North* (1946). Specialists may be referred to the *Ibsen Yearbook* with annual bibliography (1952*–) and to the disclosures of *Gosse's Correspondence* (p. 461, n. 8).

Askeland's *Norwegian Painting* (p. 463, n. 36) gives a serviceable introduction; magnificently illustrated studies are provided in *Painting from Norway* by A. Durban (3 vols., 1951–3*) for the nineteenth century and *Modern Norwegian Painting* by L. Östby (tr., 1949) for 1919 onwards. The work of Edvard Munch is the subject of studies by S. S. Madsen (*The Aula Pictures*, 1959*), O. Benesch (tr. from German, 1960), J. H. Langaard and R. Revold (1960*), and W. Timm (tr. from German, 1969); a total of 472 items in all languages was recorded in the *Munch Bibliography* by H. B. Muller (1951*; supplement in Norwegian, 1959*). *The Graphic Art of Rolf Nesch* was edited by Ellen Sharp in 1969. *Norwegian Sculpture* by Ö. Parmann, with copiously illustrated English and German texts (tr., 1969), is supplemented by N. C. Hale's *Embrace of Life: The Sculpture of Gustav Vigeland* (1969). *Norwegian Music*, a brief general survey by K. Lange (1971*), is amplified in different respects in *Grieg: A Symposium*, edited by A. Abrahamsen (1948), with chronological list of compositions; D. Schjelderup Ebbe's *Edvard Grieg* (1964), a study of his harmonic style; A. Östvedt's *Music and Musicians in Norway Today* (1961*); and J. Krogsæter's *Folk Dancing in Norway* (tr., 1968).

The principal art galleries and museums and a few buildings of special interest, such as Oslo Town Hall and Grieg's home at Trollhaugen, Bergen, publish English translations of guide books and other relevant literature.

Norwegian Architecture through the Ages (1950*), a compilation with five authors, includes a historical survey by G. Eliassen; *Building in Norway* by G. Abrahamsen (1959) is also historical, while the period since 1814 occupies one-third of the fully illustrated work, *Norwegian Architecture Past and Present*, by G. Kavli (1958*). Norway also has a very modest place in *Scandinavian Architecture* by T. Paulsson (1958). *Norwegian Industrial Design* by A. Böe (1963) is concerned with the present, but the inspiration of past achievement in wood carving, rose painting, art weaving, and folk costume is suggested by the many beautiful designs shown in *Native Art of Norway*, edited by R. Hauglid (1965*); see also *Folk Arts of Norway* by J. S. Stewart (1953).

Erling Grönland's *Norway in English* (1961*) has an appendix of Norwegian literature in English translation, 1742–1959; this gives details of eighteen anthologies and 257 separate publications by eighty Norwegian authors. Select lists for some leading writers are also available in Beyer (p. 463, n. 35) and McFarlane (p. 462, n. 31).

The following publications subsequent to these lists may be useful for the study of authors mentioned in the text:

Anthology of Scandinavian Literature, edited by H. Hallmundsson (1965).

O. *Duun: Floodtide of Fate*, tr. by R. Popperwell (1960).

J. Falkberget: *The Fourth Night Watch*, tr. by R. Popperwell (1968).

K. Hamsun: *Hunger*, tr. by R. Bly (1967).

  Victoria, tr. by O. Stallybrass (1969).

  The Cultural Life of Modern America, tr. by B. G. Morgridge (1969).

H. Ibsen: *Brand*, tr. by G. M. Gathorne-Hardy (1966).

  The Oxford Ibsen, tr. by J. W. McFarlane (the editor) and others (Vols i, ii, iv–vii, 1960–70).

T. Vesaas: *The Birds*, tr. by T. Stöverud (1968).

  The Bridges, tr. by E. Rokkan (1969).

  The Great Cycle, tr. by E. Rokkan (1967).

  The Ice Palace, tr. by E. Rokkan (1966).

  The Seed. Spring Night, tr. by K. G. Chapman (1964).

  Thirty Poems, tr. by K. G. Chapman (1971).

BIOGRAPHIES

A. Collective, *they were from:*

One Hundred Norwegians, with full-page photographs, edited by S. Mortensen and P. Vogt (1955★).

They were From Norway. Portraits of ten men who made history, edited by L. Eckhoff (1956★).

B. Individual (listed by subject, with autobiographies first; titles of books are not given if they include the subject's name):

ABEL, NILS HENRIK: Ö. Ore (1957).

AMUNDSEN, ROALD: *My Life as an Explorer* (1927).

  C. de Leeuw (1967); J. A. Kugelmass (1955); B. Partridge (1953); H. Hanssen (who served in *Gjöa* and *Maud*) (1936).

ARCHER, COLIN: J. Archer (1949).

BALCHEN, BERNT: *Come North With Me* (1958).

BERNADOTTE: see CHARLES JOHN

BJÖRNSON, BJÖRNSTJERNE: H. Larsen (1945); G. Brandes (1883)— essay, translated by W. Archer; reprinted in *Ibsen and Björnson*, (1969).

BOYESEN, HJALMAR HJORTH: *Boyhood in Norway* (1927).

BULL, OLE: M. Smith (1947); Inez Bull (1961).

CHARLES JOHN, KING: D. P. Barton, *Bernadotte, Vol. iii 1810–1844* (1925); *The Amazing Career of Bernadotte* (1929).

DYBWAD, JOHANNE: C. R. Waal (1967★).

FLAGSTAD, KIRSTEN: *The Flagstad Manuscript* (edited by L. Biancolli, 1952). E. McArthur (1965).

FURUSETH, ANDREW: H. Weintraub (1959).

GRIEG, EDVARD: J. Horton (1950); D. Monrad-Johansen (tr., 1938); H. T. Finck (1929).

HAAKON VII, KING: M. Michael (1958); W. Keilhau (1942).

HAMSUN, KNUT: *On Overgrown Paths* (tr., 1967; written in internment, 1946–8). J. Wiehr (1922).

HAUGE, HANS NIELSEN: *Autobiographical Writings* (1816; tr. by J. M. Njus, 1954). M. Nodtvedt, *Rebirth of Norway's Peasantry* (1965*); J. M. Shaw, *Pulpit under the Sky* (1955); A. M. Arntzen, *The Apostle of Norway* (1933); W. Pettersen, *The Light in the Prison Window* (enlarged ed., 1926).

HENIE, SONJA: *Wings on my Feet* (1940).

HEYERDAHL, THOR: J. Arnold, *Señor Kon-Tiki* (1968).

IBSEN, HENRIK: Koht, H. (p. 462, n. 10); M. Meyer (p. 462, n. 11)—a vivid and unprejudiced study of the life, designed for the general reader; H. Heiberg (tr., 1969); *Letters and Speeches* (including fifty previously unpublished letters), edited by E. Sprinchorn (1965).

IBSEN, SIGURD: Bergliot Ibsen, *The Three Ibsens* (tr., 1951).

KNAPLUND, PAUL: *Moorings Old and New* (1963).

KOHT, HALVDAN: *The Education of an Historian* (tr., 1957).

LARSEN, L. A. ('Shetlands-Larsen'): F. Sælen, *None But The Brave* (tr., 1955).

MUNCH, EDVARD: N. Stang (tr., 1972); R. Stenersen (p. 463, n. 40).

NANSEN, FRIDTJOF: Per Vogt, editor (p. 467, n. 1); P. Noel Baker, *Nansen's Place in History* (1962); L. N. Höyer (a family portrait by his daughter, tr., 1957); W. Hutchinson (1969); E. Berry (1969); J. F. Denzel (1968); E. Shackleton (1959).

QUISLING, VIDKUN: P. M. Hayes (p. 466, n. 30); R. Hewins (1965), a journalist's account, marred by much special pleading.

RÖLVAAG, OLE EDVART: Jorgenson and Solum (p. 460, n. 35).

SKREFSRUD, LARS OLSEN: O. Hodne—1867–81 covered in detail (1966*); J. Nyhagen, *From Prison Cell to Mission Station* (tr., 1964).

SUNDT, EILERT: M. S. Allwood (p. 451, n. 27).

SVERDRUP, OTTO: *Sverdrup's Arctic Adventures*, edited by T. C. Fairley (1959).

UNDSET, SIGRID: *Return to the Future* (1942); *Happy Times in Norway* (1942); *Men, Women, and Places* (tr., 1939). Lives by C. F. Bayerschmidt (1970) and A. H. Winsnes (approved shortly before her death, tr., 1953).

VALEN, FARTEN: B. Kortsen (1965), Vol. i of *Life and Music*.

VIGELAND, GUSTAV: Ragna Stang, *Gustav Vigeland 1869–1969* (tr., 1969); an outline sketch by the same author (tr., 1965*).

Index

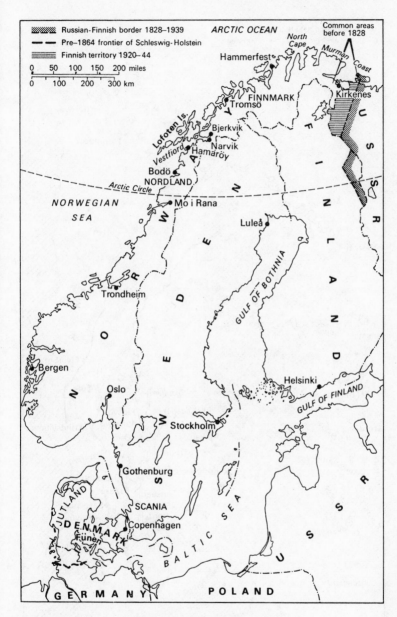

MAP I NORWAY AND ITS NEIGHBOURS

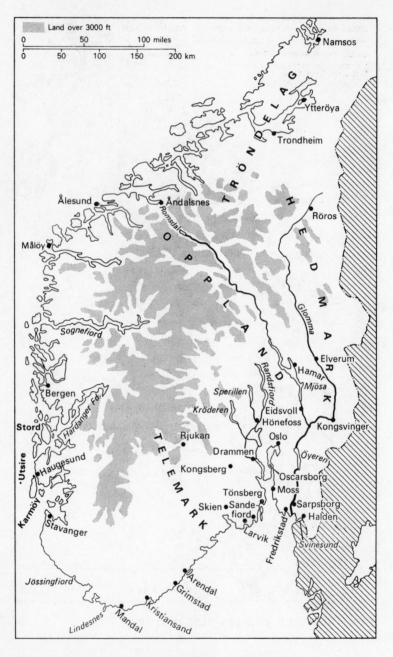

MAP 2 CENTRAL AND SOUTHERN NORWAY
(showing places named in text)